# INTELLIGENCE
# SCIENCE

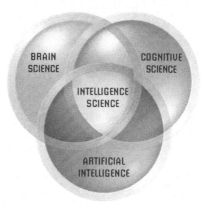

# Series on Intelligence Science

**Series Editor:** Zhongzhi Shi *(Chinese Academy of Sciences, China)*

Series on Intelligence Science  Vol. 2

# INTELLIGENCE SCIENCE

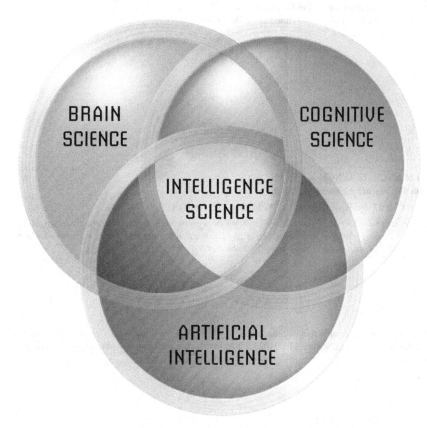

BRAIN SCIENCE

COGNITIVE SCIENCE

INTELLIGENCE SCIENCE

ARTIFICIAL INTELLIGENCE

## Zhongzhi SHI

**World Scientific**

NEW JERSEY · LONDON · SINGAPORE · BEIJING · SHANGHAI · HONG KONG · TAIPEI · CHENNAI

*Published by*

World Scientific Publishing Co. Pte. Ltd.

5 Toh Tuck Link, Singapore 596224

*USA office:* 27 Warren Street, Suite 401-402, Hackensack, NJ 07601

*UK office:* 57 Shelton Street, Covent Garden, London WC2H 9HE

**British Library Cataloguing-in-Publication Data**
A catalogue record for this book is available from the British Library.

**INTELLIGENCE SCIENCE**
**Series on Intelligence Science — Vol. 2**

ISBN-13 978-981-4360-77-7
ISBN-10 981-4360-77-5

Desk Editor: Tjan Kwang Wei

Printed in Singapore.

# Preface

Intelligence science is an interdisciplinary subject which is jointly studied by brain science, cognitive science, artificial intelligence and others. Brain science explores the essence of brain, research on the principle and model of natural intelligence in molecular, cell and behavior level. Cognitive science studies human mental activity, such as perception, learning, memory, thinking, consciousness etc. In order to implement machine intelligence, artificial intelligence attempts simulation, extension and expansion of human intelligence using artificial methodology and technology. Intelligence science not only to conduct functional simulation, but also from the mechanism to study and explore new concepts, new theories, new methods of intelligence. The study not only to the use of intelligent reasoning, since the top-down, but also through learning from the bottom-up, both at once. Intelligent nature and behavior of the open systems are studied by intelligence science through comprehensive and integrated approach.

Intelligence science is the essence of life science, the core of information science and technology, front and high ground of modern science and technology, involving the deep mysteries of the natural sciences, reaching the basic propositions of philosophy. Therefore, when a breakthrough progress on study of intelligence science will have a profound, massive impact to the national economy, social progress, national security. At present, intelligence science is in the period of methodology changes, the height of theoretical innovation and large-scale applications with full opportunities for originality.

The rise and development of intelligence science marks the research on human-centered cognition and intelligence has entered a new stage. Intelligence science research will make the human self-understanding and self-control, so that the person's knowledge and intelligence to an unprecedented height. Complex biological phenomena, many questions have not been well illustrated, but also from it learning the large and multifaceted contents. How to get to extract the most important, critical issues and the corresponding technology, which many scientists have long been pursued. To solve mankind in the 21st century facing many difficulties, such as high energy demand, environmental pollution, resources depletion, population expansion and so on, rely on the existing scientific achievement is not enough. We should learn from biology and look for new development road of science and technology. Intelligence science research will establish the theoretical basis for intelligence revolution, provide new concepts, new ideas, new ways for the development of intelligent systems.

The book is a systematic introduction to science concepts and methods of intelligence, absorbing brain science, cognitive science, artificial intelligence, mathematical logic, social thinking, systems theory, scientific methodology, philosophy and other aspects of research achievments in an integrated manner to explore the principles and laws of human intelligence and machine intelligence. Whole book is consists of 17 chapters. The first chapter introduction, pointing out that the rise and contents of intelligence science. The second chapter describes the physiological basis of Intelligence Science. Chapter 3 discusses the progress of neural computation. The fourth chapter deals with an important mind models. Chapter 5 discusses perception theory. Visual information processing will be discussed in Chapter 6, focusing on the latest modern vision theory. Chapter 7 is the auditory information processing. The development of human language has a significant impact on the evolution of human brain, which will be discussed in Chapter 8. Chapter 9 focuses on important learning theory. Chapter 10 explores memory mechanism which is the basis of thinking. Chapter 11 focus on the form and type of thought. Chapter 12 studies intellectual development. Discussion of the emotion and affection theory in Chapter 13. The immune system is to protect the body's own and gives us the inspiration, the fourteenth chapter is on the immune system. The origin and nature of consciousness is one of the most important scientific problems. In intelligence science, consciousness issue is particularly challenging. Chapter 15 is the preliminary study of consciousness. Formalization is an important basis for Machine Intelligence. Chapter 16 illustrates symbolic logic. The final chapter prospects the future of intelligence science.

The book can serve as a textbook for senior and graduate students in the area of intelligent science, cognitive science, cognitive informatics, artificial intelligence in university. The book also has important reference value for scientists and researchers engaged in intelligence science, brain science, cognitive science, neuroscience, artificial intelligence, psychology, philosophy, and others.

Intelligence science is at the forefront of research and development in the disciplines, many of the concepts and theories are waiting to be explored. Combined with author limited knowledge, so the book may be a lot of errors, I am looking forward reader to giving correction.

Zhongzhi Shi

27/12/2009

# Acknowledgement

I would like to take this opportunity to thank my family, particular my wife, Zhihua Yu and my children, Jing Shi and Jun Shi, for their support in the course of the book. I would also like to thank my organization, Institute of Computing Technology, Chinese Academy of Sciences, for providing good condition to do research on intelligence science.

I should thank Intelligence Science Laboratory for my colleagues and students valuable works. During the book has been translated into English version, Xiujun Gong, Guoliang He, Daoshan Chen, Shiwei Ye, Zhiping Peng, Zhixin Li, Xi Liu, Zhiping Shi, Yufang Yang, Xiaohong Yang, Jiye Liang, Zuqiang Meng, Jing Luo, Gaoxia Wei, Quansheng Dou, Jinghua Zheng, Zhiliang Wang, Xuejing Gu, Jie He, Ningjuan Shi, Hongwei Mo, Liang Chang, Limin Chen, Chuan Shi made contribution, I am very grateful to their help.

The book contains our research efforts granted by National Basic Research Priorities Programme (No. 2007CB311004, No. 2003CB317004), National Science Foundation of China (No. 60435010, 60775035, 60933004), 863 National High-Tech Program (No. 2007AA01Z132), National Science and Technology Support Plan (No. 2006BAC08B06), the Knowledge Innovation Program of Chinese Academy of Sciences and other funding. The book is not possible without these financial supports.

My special thanks to Tsinghua University Press for their publishing the book in Chinese in 2006. I am most grateful to the editorial staff and artist from World Scientific Publishing who provided all the support and help in the course of my writing this book.

# Contents

# Chapter 1

# Introduction

Intelligence Science is an interdisciplinary subject which dedicates to joint research on basic theory and technology of intelligence by brain science, cognitive science, artificial intelligence and others.

## 1.1 The Dream of Mankind

There are three revolutions with impact in the human history, the tool-making revolution, agricultural revolution and industrial revolution. Accompanying these revolutions, the situation of society, economy and civilization have transformed from one to another. What is the next revolution? The answer is the intelligence revolution with the goal of replacing work performed by human brain work with machine brain which is the dream of mankind.

The Industrial Revolution was a period from the 18th to the 19th century where major changes in agriculture, manufacturing, mining, and transport had a profound effect on the socioeconomic and cultural conditions in the United Kingdom. The changes subsequently spread throughout Europe, North America, and eventually the world. The industrial revolution was one of the most important events in history which extends human's hand to achieve physical power enlargement.

In the history of human development, it is a never-ending pursuit to free people from both manual and mental labor with machines. The industrial revolutions enable machines to perform heavy manual labor instead of people, and thus lead to a considerable economic and social progress. To make machines help relieve mental labor, a long cherished aspiration is to create and make use of intelligent machines like human beings.

Aristotle (384-322, BC) proposed the first formal deductive reasoning system, syllogistic logic, in the Organon. Francis Bacon (1561-1626) established the inductive method in the Novum Organun (or "New Organon"). Gottfried Leibniz (1646-1716) constructed the first mechanical calculator capable of multiplication and division. He also enunciated the concepts of "characteristica universalis" and "calculus ratiocinator" to treat the operations of formal logic in a symbolic or algebraic way, which can be viewed as the sprout of the "thinking machine".

Since the 19th century, advancement of sciences and technologies such as Mathematical Logic, Automata Theory, Cybernetics, Information Theory, Computer Science and Psychology laid the ideological, theoretical and material foundation for the development of AI research. In the book "An Investigation of the Laws of Thought", George Boole (1815-1864) developed the Boolean algebra, a form of symbolic logic to represent some basic rules for reasoning in the thinking activities. Kurt Gödel (1906-1978) proved the incompleteness theorems. Alan Turing (1912-1954) introduced the Turing Machine, a model of the ideal intelligent computer, and initiated the automata theory. In 1943, Warren McCulloch (1899-1969) and Walter Pitts (1923-1969) developed the MP neuron, a pioneer work of Artificial Neural Networks research. In 1946, John Mauchly (1907-1980) and John Eckert (1919-1995) invented the ENIAC (Electronic Numerical Integrator And Computer), the first electronic computer. In 1948, Norbert Wiener (1894-1964) published a popular book of "Cybernetics", and Claude Shannon (1916-2001) proposed the Information Theory.

In 1956, the term "Artificial Intelligence" was coined, and the Dartmouth Summer Research Project on Artificial Intelligence (AI), proposed by John McCarthy, Marvin Minsky, etc., was carried on at Dartmouth College with several American scientists of psychology, mathematics, computer science and information theory. This well-known Dartmouth conference marked the beginning of the real sense of AI as a research field. In 1958, A. Newell and H. A. Simon made the following forecasts of AI boldly:

(1) Within ten years, a computer would become the world chess champion.

(2) Within ten years, a computer would discover or prove meaningful mathematical theorems.

(3) Within ten years, a computer would be able to compose a beautiful music.

(4) Within ten years, a computer would be able to implement most of psychology theories.

These optimistic forecasts made by artificial intelligence pioneers motivated people to do research continuously and leaded many encouraging progresses. But along the way, the traditional artificial intelligence researchers still faced considerable confusions.

During the past more than 50 years, great progress has been made of AI research. Theories of heuristic searching strategies, non-monotonic reasoning, machine learning, etc. have been proposed. Applications of AI, especially expert systems, intelligent decision making, intelligent robots, natural language understandings, etc. also promoted the research of AI. Presently, knowledge engineering based on knowledge and information processing is a remarkable characteristic of AI.

## 1.2 The Rise of Intelligence Science

The goal of AI research is to make computer have human like behaviors, such as listening, talking, reading, writing, thinking, learning and adopting to ever-changing environments etc. In 1977, E. Feigenbaum, a young scholar of Stanford University and graduate student of Simon put forward the concept of knowledge engineering in the 5th International Joint Conference on Artificial Intelligence (IJCAI'1977), which marked the transition from the traditional reasoning to the knowledge-centered research in artificial intelligence research.

Knowledge is the national wealth and information industry is vital for a country's development. The fifth generation computer - intelligent computer symposium was held in Tokyo Japan in October of 1981. Professor Moto-Oka Tohru from Tokyo University proposed "the fifth generation computer system: FGCS". After that Japan made an ambitious plan to develop the fifth generation computers in 10 years. In the summer of 1982, Japan established "the new generation of computer technology institute" (ICOT) headed by Fuchi Kazuhiro. Japan Ministry of International Trade and Industry fully supported the plan and the total investment budget reaches to $430 million. Eight large enterprise including Fujitsu, NEC, Hitachi, Toshiba, Panasonic and sharp were invited to this project.

It took almost ten years on the project for ICOT colleagues, who even had no time for normal lives and spent all times between the lab and their apartments. However the outcome of the FGCS was somehow tragic. Its failure in 1992 might come from the bottleneck of key technologies such as human-machine dialogue and program automatic proving. After that, Professor Fuchi Kazuhiro had to return to his university. Also somebody thought that the FGCS is not a totally failure, in that it achieved some expected goals in the first two phases. In

June 1992, ICOT demonstrated the prototype of FGCS with 64 processors for parallel processing, which had similar functions of human left brain, and could perform advanced precision analysis on proteins.

The failure of FGCS pushed people to find a new way for researches on intelligence. Intelligence requires not only function simulation, but also mechanism simulation. Intelligence requires not only top-down reasoning also bottom-up learning as well, which may be finally combined to achieve human level Intelligence. The perceive components of brains including various feelings such as vision and auditory, movements and language cortex regions play not only the role of input/output channel, but also contribute to thinking activities directly.

In 1991, a special issue on the foundation of AI was published in *Journal of Artificial Intelligence* (Vol. 47) to point out some trends of AI research. D. Kirsh proposed five foundational problems in AI (Kirsh, 1991):

(1) Pre-eminence of knowledge and conceptualization: Intelligence that transcends insect-level intelligence requires declarative knowledge and some form of reasoning-like computation-call this cognition. Core Al is the study of the conceptualizations of the world presupposed and used by intelligent systems during cognition.

(2) Disembodiment: Cognition and the knowledge it presupposes can be studied largely in abstraction from the details of perception and motor control.

(3) Kinematics of cognition are language-like: It is possible to describe the trajectory of knowledge states or informational states created during cognition using a vocabulary very much like English or some regimented logic-mathematical version of English.

(4) Learning can be added later: The kinematics of cognition and the domain knowledge needed for cognition can be studied separately from the study of concept learning, psychological development, and evolutionary change.

(5) Uniform architecture: There is a single architecture underlying virtually all cognition.

All these questions are cognitive problems critical to AI research, which should be discussed from the perspective of fundamental theories of Cognitive Science. These questions have become the watershed for different academic schools of AI research, as different academic schools usually have different answers to them.

In 2003, the author published the paper entitled "Perspectives on cognitive informatics" (Shi et al., 2003). This article points out that intelligent science is the study of fundamental theory and technology of intelligence and the interdisciplinary subject of brain science, cognitive science and artificial intelligence. Brain science studies the intelligence mechanism of the brain, establishes the model of the brain and reveals the essence of human's brain from molecular level, cell level and behavior level. Cognitive science studies perception, learning, memory, thinking and awareness of human. Artificial intelligence studies simulations, extensions and expansions of human intelligence using artificial methods and techniques to realize machine intelligence. The three disciplines work together to study and explore the new conceptions, new methods and new theories of intelligence science, and will create a brilliant future in the $21^{st}$ century.

In 2004, J. Hawkins published a book entitled "On Intelligence" (Hawkins, 2004). He started carefully the study at the interrelation of intelligent and intelligent behavior, and analyzed the famous Turing test. Intelligence cannot make intelligent agent think they are intelligent in any case. Turing offered a profound insight. But as time goes by, J. Hawkins gradually realize this is mediocre and useless: it is more of an escape, rather than a useful definition of intelligence (Colwell, 2005).

J. Hawkins described John Searle's "Chinese house" test. In this test, an intelligent agent is put in a room. The agent followed physical instructions without pausing in any place of the room. By this way, the agent would answer a series of questions correctly (these questions are written in Chinese which can not be understood by the agent) and eventually walked out of the room.

John Searle pointed out that the recipients with Chinese output presumed the agent in the room must understand Chinese, might even show thought-provoking insights. But the agent itself did nothing intelligently at all, neither a machine. It only simply followed instructions which are written by some people.

John Searle said that he did not know what intelligence is, but this test showed that computers do not have intelligence. John Searle's experiment clearly showed that the Turing test can be easily fooled. We must do more on intelligence, not just some subjective judgments.

Some people think the agent, instructions and room all reflect the intelligence- try our best to avoid the fact that we know little about intelligence, although we have done plenty of long-term works in many branches of science.

The human brain is the most complicated system in the known universe. It is formed by the huge quantity of neurons and synapses. The neurons and synapses both are highly complicated, highly multifarious and highly complete electronic-chemical apparatus. The beauty of thinking may just contain in the complexity of the brain. The research in neural science has revealed that a simple nervous may have the amazing complexity, which reflects that its function, evolution history, structure and encoding scheme will work on any future disciplines of the brain complexity.

Brain science is a big science system consisting of various brain-researching disciplines. It studies the structure and functions of the brain, the relations between the brain and human behavior and thinking. Brain science also explores brain evolution, its biological components, neural networks and its corresponding mechanisms. Human's recognition on brains takes a long time from the superficial to the deep. This history can be divided into three phases according to the research levels.

The first phase may be called precursor period. In this period, humans gradually realize that the brain is the organ for thinking, and have a superficial understanding of its structures. During the 5th to 7th century BC, people in China had realized the association between brain and thinking.

Brain has been deeply studied in Ancient Greece. Pythagoras and Plato both hold that the brain produces senses and wisdom. Democritus thought that the brain produces atoms, which in turn produces soul activities. Hippocrates affirmed that the brain was the thinking organ with an anatomy approach. Erasistratus from the Alexander school studied structures of brains using the same approach. Herophilus distinguished cerebellums and cortexes. Galen, an ancient Greek doctor, further discovered internal structures of brains, such as corpus callosum, pineal gland, and put forward the theory that the left brain is responsible for feeling and the right brain for movement.

The second phase is the mechanical period. The major progresses were the establishments of reflexology and positioning theories. Middle Age witnessed little progress in researches on anatomical brain. With the development of modern sciences, researches on brain developed rapidly. In the 18th century, Hubble, a Swiss physiologist, found that brains transmit stimulates using nerve. René Descartes put forward the brain's reflexology theory and the dualism theory in which spirit and brains interacted with each other. Russian scholar N. M. СечНОВ perfected the brain's reflexology theory. In the 19th century, Austrian physician F. J. Gall established the positioning theory initially, which later formed as cranioscopy science. French doctor Paul Broca discovered the Broca's area by dissecting the brains of aphasia patients, which marked as the science foundation of positioning theory. The study of brain in this period has some traits of Mechanism.

The third phase is the modern period. In this period, the brain was studied from multi-levels, multi-layers and multi-views, including not only global study but also partial study, not only systematical study but also study on the Neurons, cell and molecular level, not only the study on physical, chemical, psychological but also comprehensive research. At present, there are many methods for brain-investigating. Some of them are listed as follows:

(1) Black-box methods. Due to the complexity of brains, researchers can not study brain's thinking mechanisms from outside, so the only remainder method is to presume its work mechanism from the processed results after information is sent to brains.

(2) Electrical science methods. These methods explore the mechanism of brains' activities by investigating brain waves. In 1848, German scholar DuBois Reymond firstly recorded the current activities of nerve tissue. In 1929, H. Berger from German firstly recorded electroencephalograms in his son's scalp. He recorded rhythmical slow-wave at about 10 times/sec. Now, the brain electrical methods have been used for many purposes and researches.

(3) Brain damage methods. The relations between the degree of injured brains with their influences on intelligence and behavior are used to reveal brains' function. These methods have been widely used in the theories about brains positioning and unitary.

(4) Neuron methods. Neurons are used to understand brains.

(5) Chemical methods. In brains, there are not only electrical activities, but also chemical movements. It relies on chemicals for information transferring, memory, thinking, and controlling mood. The chemical method investigates activities in brains by studying brains chemical substance and its functions.

Computational neuroscience is the stimulation and study of nervous systems using mathematical analysis and computer simulation methods from different levels ranging from the real creature physical models of neurons, their dynamic interactions and structure learning of neural networks, to quantitative calculation theory of brain tissue and nervous tissue, from studying the non-program, adaptive and brain-style nature and potentials of information processing to explore new mechanisms of information processing mechanism, to finally create artificial brains.

It takes a long period for the study of computational neuroscience. In 1875, Italian anatomists C. Golgi firstly identified individual nerve cells using a dyeing method. In 1889 R. Cajal founded the neuron theory, in which nervous systems are built with independent nerve cells. Based on this theory, in 1906 C. S. Sherrington put forward the notion of synapses between neurons (Sherrington, 1906). In the 1920s, E. D. Adrian proposed the nerve action potentials. In 1943 W.S. McCulloch and W. Pitts put forward the M-P neural network model (McCulloch & Pitts 1943). In 1949, D. O. Hebb put forward the rules for neural network learning (Hebb, 1949). In the 1950s, F. Rosenblatt proposed perception machine model (Rosenblatt, 1962). The neural computation has made great progress since 1980s. J. J. Hopfield introduced the "Lyapunov" function (also called calculated energy function) and proposed the criterion of network stability for associative memory and optimization calculation (Hopfield, 1982). Amari did various works on the mathematical theory of neurons network including statistical neural dynamics, dynamics theory of neuron field, associative memory, and particularly fundamental works in information geometry (Amari, 1985). The research on computational neuroscience tries to reflect the following characteristics of the brain: ① Cerebral cortex is a grand and complex system with extensive connections. ② The computation in the brain bases on large-scale parallel simulation processing. ③ The brain is strongly "error-tolerate" and is skilled in association, generalization, and analogy. The function of the brain was restricted not only by innate factor, but by the other acquired dispositions as well, such as experience, learning and training. This shows that the brain is self-organized and adaptive to environments. Many human intelligence activities are not controlled by logical reasoning, but by training.

Cognitive psychology explains human's complex behaviors in terms of information processing. It absorbs the outcomes of Gestalt psychology and behaviorism. It also holds that complex phenomena can be study when they are decomposed into simpler primary parts. When a person is stimulated, he relies on his experience to decide how to response. Experiences include the state of his body and the context of his memory. Therefore, stimulation and current psychological states both decide the reactions.

Cognitive science is the interdisciplinary study of mind and intelligence, embracing philosophy, psychology, artificial intelligence, neuroscience, linguistics, and anthropology. In recent years, the development of cognitive science to be the international scientific community, especially developed countries, the government attached great importance and large-scale support. With perceptual expression, learning and memory in the process of information processing, thinking, language model, and based on environmental awareness as a breakthrough point, the calculation of cognitive theory and scientific experimental methods and strategies to achieve the direction of original innovation; explore innovative learning mechanism, the establishment of functional brain imaging database, put forward a new machine learning theory and methods.

Since firstly proposed in 1956, Artificial Intelligence had made great progress and success, especially in the aspect of using knowledge to solve problems, and promoted knowledge science. Since knowledge plays more and more important roles in the civilization of mankind, humans has entered the society of informationism, and walked towards the knowledge society. People aim at the general rules and characteristics of the knowledge. In 1977, E. Feigenbaum proposed the concept of knowledge engineering, which made the knowledge information processing into an engineering phase.

We can see that 1980's is knowledge engineering, 1990's is intelligent information processing. The rise of intelligence science quietly when enter the 21st century. In 2002 a dedicated Website entitled Intelligence Science and Artificial Intelligence has appeared on Internet, which is constructed by author and his colleagues. A special book entitled Intelligence Science written by author was published by Tsinghua University Press in 2006 (Shi, 2006). The first International Conference on Advanced Intelligence was held in 2008 in Beijing. World Scientific Publishing has decided to publish the Series on Intelligence Science in 2008.

## 1.3 Research Contents

Intelligence science is an interdisciplinary subject mainly including brain science, cognitive science, artificial intelligence and others. Brain science explores the essence of brain, research on the principle and model of natural intelligence in molecular, cell and behavior level. Cognitive science studies human mental activity, such as perception, learning, memory, thinking, consciousness etc. In order to implement machine intelligence, Artificial intelligence attempts simulation, extension and expansion of human intelligence using artificial methodology and technology (Intelligence Science Website). Following Ten big issues of intelligence science will be viewed as main research contents.

### 1.3.1 Basic process of neural activity

The brain is a collection of about 10 billion interconnected neurons. Neurons are electrically excitable cells in the nervous system that process and transmit information. A neuron's dendritic tree is connected to a thousand neighboring neurons[15]. When one of those neurons fire, a positive or negative charge is received by one of the dendrites. The strengths of all the received charges are added together through the processes of spatial and temporal summation. The aggregate input is then passed to the soma (cell body). The soma and the enclosed nucleus don't play a significant role in the processing of incoming and outgoing data. Their primary function is to perform the continuous maintenance required to keep the neuron functional. The output strength is unaffected by the many divisions in the axon; it reaches each terminal button with the same intensity it had at the axon hillock.

Each terminal button is connected to other neurons across a small gap called a synapse. The physical and neurochemical characteristics of each synapse determines the strength and polarity of the new input signal. This is where the brain is the most flexible, and the most vulnerable. In molecular level neuron signal generation, transmission and neurotransmitters are basic problems attracted research scientists to engage investigation in brain science.

### 1.3.2 Synaptic plasticity

One of the greatest challenges in neuroscience is to determine how synaptic plasticity and learning and memory are linked. Two broad classes of models of synaptic plasticity can be described by Phenomenological models and Biophysical models (Shouval, 2007).

Phenomenological models are characterized by treating the process governing synaptic plasticity as a black box. The black box takes in as input a set of variables, and produces as output a change in synaptic efficacy. No explicit modeling of the biochemistry and physiology leading to synaptic plasticity is implemented. Two different classes of phenomenological models, rate based and spike based, have been proposed.

Biophysical models, in contrast to phenomenological models, concentrate on modeling the biochemical and physiological processes that lead to the induction and expression of synaptic plasticity. However, since it is not possible to implement precisely every portion of the physiological and biochemical networks leading to synaptic plasticity, even the biophysical models rely on many simplifications and abstractions. Different cortical regions, such as Hippocampus and Visual cortex have somewhat different forms of synaptic plasticity.

### 1.3.3  Perceptual representation and feature binding

The perceptual systems are primarily visual, auditory and kinesthetic, that is, pictures, sounds and feelings. There is also olfactory and gustatory, i.e. smell and taste. The perceptual representation is a modeling approach that highlights the constructive, or generative function of perception, or how perceptual processes construct a complete volumetric spatial world, complete with a copy of our own body at the center of that world. The representational strategy used by the brain is an analogical one; that is, objects and surfaces are represented in the brain not by an abstract symbolic code, or in the activation of individual cells or groups of cells representing particular features detected in the visual field. Instead, objects are represented in the brain by constructing full spatial effigies of them that appear to us for all the world like the objects themselves or at least so it seems to us only because we have never seen those objects in their raw form, but only through our perceptual representations of them.

### 1.3.4  Coding and retrieval of memory

A brain has distributed memory system, that is, each part of brain has several types of memories that work in somewhat different ways, to suit particular purposes. According to the stored time of contents memory can be divided into long term memory, short term memory and working memory. Research topics in memory exist coding, extract and retrieval of information. Current working memory attracts more researchers to involve.

Working memory will provides temporal space and enough information for complex tasks, such as understanding speech, learning, reasoning and attention. There are memory and reasoning functions in the working memory. It consists of three components: that is, central nervous performance system, video space primary processing and phonetic circuit (Dehn, 2008).

Memory phenomena have also been categorized as explicit or implicit. Explicit memories involve the hippocampus-medial temporal lobe system. The most common current view of the memorial functions of the hippocampal system is the declarative memory. There are a lot of research issues that are waiting for us to resolve. What is the readout system from the hippocampal system to behavioral expression of learning in declarative memory? Where are the long-term declarative memories stored after the hippocampal system? What are the mechanisms of time-limited memory storage in hippocampus and storage of permanent memories in extra-hippocampal structures?

Implicit memory involves the cerebellum, amygdala, and other systems (Tarsia, 2003). The cerebellum is necessary for classical conditioning of discrete behavioral responses under all condition. It is learning to make specific behavioral responses. The amygdalar system is learning fear and associated autonomic responses to deal with the situation.

### 1.3.5 Linguistic cognition

Language is fundamentally a means for social communication. Language is also often held to be the mirror of the mind. Chomsky developed transformational grammar that cognitivism replaced behaviorism in linguistics (Chomsky, 1957).

Through language we organize our sensory experience and express our thoughts, feelings, and expectations. Language is particular interesting from cognitive informatics point of view because its specific and localized organization can explore the functional architecture of the dominant hemisphere of the brain.

Recent studies of human brain show that the written word is transferred from the retina to the lateral geniculate nucleus, and from there to the primary visual cortex. The information then travels to a higher-order center, where it is conveyed first to the angular gyrus of the parietal-temporal-occipital association cortex, and then to Wernicke's area, where the visual information is transformed into a phonetic representation of the word. For spoken word the auditory information is processed by primary auditory cortex. Then the information input to higher-order auditory cortex, before it is conveyed to a specific region of the parietal-temporal-occipital association cortex, the angular gyrus, which is concerned with the association of incoming auditory, visual, and tactile information. From here the information is projected to Wernicke's area and Broca's area. In Broca's area the perception of language is translated into the grammatical structure of a phrase and the memory for word articulation is stored (Mayeux etc., 1991).

### 1.3.6 Learning

Learning is the basic cognitive activity and accumulation procedure of experience and knowledge. Through learning the system performance will be improved. Perceptual learning, cognitive learning, implicit learning are active research topics in the learning area.

Perceptual learning should be considered as an active process that embeds particular abstraction, reformulation and approximation within the Abstraction framework. The active process refers to the fact that the search for a correct data representation is performed through several steps. A key point is that perceptual learning focuses on low-level abstraction mechanism instead of trying to rely on more complex algorithm. In fact, from the machine learning point off view, perceptual learning can be seen as a particular abstraction that may help to simplify complex problem thanks to a computable representation. Indeed, the baseline of Abstraction, i.e. choosing the relevant data to ease the learning task, is that many problems in machine learning cannot be solve because of the complexity of the representation and is not related to the learning algorithm, which is referred to as the phase transition problem. Within the abstraction framework, we use the term perceptual learning to refer to specific learning task that rely on iterative representation changes and that deals with real-world data which human can perceive.

In contrast with perceptual learning cognitive leaning is a leap in the process of cognition and generate knowledge through clustering, classification, conceptualization and so on. In general, there are inductive learning, analogical learning, case-based learning, explanation learning, evolutional learning connectionist learning.

The core issue of cognitive learning is self-organizing principles. Kohonen has proposed a self-organizing maps which is a famous neural network model. Babloyantz applied chaotic dynamics to study brain activity. Haken has proposed a synergetic approach to brain activity, behavior and cognition. Introspective learning is an inside learning of brain, which means without input information from outside environment.

In the Machine Learning Department within Carnegie Mellon University's School of Computer Science researchers receive $1.1 million from Keck

Foundation to pursue new breakthroughs in learning how the brain works. Cognitive neuroscience professor Marcel Just and computer science professor Tom Mitchell have received a three-year grant from the W. M. Keck foundation to pursue new breakthroughs in the science of brain imaging (Machine learning Website).

### 1.3.7 Thought

Thought is a reflection of essential attributes and internal laws of objective reality in conscious, indirect and generalization by human brain with consciousness (Shi, 2008). In recent years, there has been a noteworthy shift of interest in cognitive science. Cognitive process rises man's sense perceptions and impressions to logical knowledge. According to abstraction degree of cognitive process, human thought can be divided into three levels: perception thought, image thought and abstraction thought. A hierarchical model of thought which illustrates the characteristics and correlations of thought levels has been proposed (Shi, 1990).

### 1.3.8 Emotion

The mental perception of some fact excites the mental affection called the emotion, and that this latter state of mind gives rise to the bodily expression. Emotion is a complex psychophysical process that arises spontaneously, rather than through conscious effort, and evokes either a positive or negative psychological response and physical expressions. Research on emotion at varying levels of abstraction, using different computational methods, addressing different emotional phenomena, and basing their models on different theories of affect.

Since the early 1990s emotional intelligence is systematically studied (Norman, 2002). Scientific articles suggested that there existed an unrecognized but important human mental ability to reason about emotions and to use emotions to enhance thought. Emotional intelligence refers to an ability to recognize the meanings of emotion and their relationships, and to reason and problem solve on the basis of them. Emotional intelligence is involved in the capacity to perceive emotions, assimilate emotion-related feelings, understand the information of those emotions, and manage them.

### 1.3.9 Nature of consciousness

The most important scientific discovery of the present era will come to answer how exactly do neurobiological processes in the brain cause consciousness? The question "What is the biological basis of consciousness?" is selected as one of 125 questions, a fitting number for Science's 125th anniversary. Recent scientifically oriented accounts of consciousness emerging from the properties and organization of neurons in the brain. Consciousness is the notions of mind and soul.

The physical basis of consciousness appears to be the most singular challenge to the scientific, reductionist world view. Francis Crick's book 'The astonishing Hypothesis' is an effort to chart the way forward in the investigation of consciousness (Crick, 1994). Crick has proposed the basic ideas of researching consciousness:

a) It seems probable, however, that at any one moment some active neuronal processes in your head correlate with consciousness, while others do not. What are the differences between them?

b) All the different aspect of consciousness, for example pain and visual awareness, employ a basic common mechanism or perhaps a few such mechanisms. If we could understand the mechanisms for one aspect, then we hope we will have gone most of the way to understanding them all.

Chalmers suggests the problem of consciousness can be broken down into several separate questions. The major question is the neuronal correlate of consciousness (NCC) which focuses on specific processes that correlate with the current content of consciousness[29]. The NCC is the minimal set of neurons, most likely distributed throughout certain cortical and subcortical areas, whose firing directly correlates with the perception of the subject at the time. Discovering the NCC and its properties will mark a major milestone in any scientific theory of consciousness. Several other questions need to be answered about the NCC. What type of activity corresponds to the NCC? What causes the NCC to occur? And, finally, what effect does the NCC have on postsynaptic structures, including motor output.

### 1.3.10 Mind modeling

Mind is a very important issue in intelligence science, and also it is a tuff problem. Mind could be defined as: "That which thinks, reasons, perceives, wills, and feels. The mind now appears in no way separate from the brain. In neuroscience, there is no duality between the mind and body. They are one." in Medical Dictionary (Medical dictionary Website). A mind model is intended to be an explanation of how some aspect of cognition is accomplished by a set of primitive computational processes. A model performs a specific cognitive task or class of tasks and produces behavior that constitutes a set of predictions that can be compared to data from human performance. Task domains that have received considerable attention include problem solving, language comprehension, memory tasks, and human-device interaction.

Researchers try to construct mind model to illustrate how brains do. Anderson and colleagues have demonstrated that a production rule analysis of cognitive skill, along with the learning mechanisms posited in the ACT model, provide detailed and explanatory accounts of a range of regularities in cognitive skill acquisition in complex domains such as learning to program Lisp (Anderson, 1993). ACT also provides accounts of many phenomena surrounding the recognition and recall of verbal material, and regularities in problem solving strategies.

In the early 1980's, SOAR was developed to be a system that could support multiple problem solving methods for many different problems (Newell, 1990). In the mid 1980's, Newell and many of his students began working on SOAR as a candidate of unified theories of cognition. SOAR is a learning architecture that has been applied to domains ranging from rapid, immediate tasks such as typing and video game interaction to long stretches of problem solving behavior. SOAR has also served as the foundation for a detailed theory of sentence processing, which models both the rapid on-line effects of semantics and context, as well as subtle effects of syntactic structure on processing difficulty across several typologically distinct languages.

## 1.4 Research Methods

Many different methodologies are used to study intelligence science. As the field is highly interdisciplinary, research often cuts across multiple areas of study, drawing on research methods from psychology, neuroscience, cognitive science, artificial intelligence and systems theory.

### *1.4.1 Behavioral experiments*

In order to have a description of what constitutes intelligent behavior, one must study behavior itself. This type of research is closely tied to that in cognitive psychology and psychophysics. By measuring behavioral responses to different stimuli, one can understand something about how those stimuli are processed.

(1) *Reaction time.* The time between the presentation of a stimulus and an appropriate response can indicate differences between two cognitive processes, and can indicate some things about their nature. For example, if in a search task the reaction times vary proportionally with the number of elements, then it is evident that this cognitive process of searching involves serial instead of parallel processing.

(2) *Psychophysical responses.* Psychophysical experiments are an old psychological technique, which has been adopted by cognitive psychology. They typically involve making judgments of some physical property, e.g. the loudness of a sound. Correlation of subjective scales between individuals can show cognitive or sensory biases as compared to actual physical measurements.

### *1.4.2 Brain imaging*

Brain imaging involves analyzing activity within the brain while performing various cognitive tasks. This allows us to link behavior and brain function to help understand how information is processed. Different types of imaging techniques vary in their temporal (time-based) and spatial (location-based) resolution. Brain imaging is often used in cognitive neuroscience.

(1) Single photon emission computed tomography (SPECT) and *Positron emission tomography* (PET). SPECT and PET use radioactive isotopes, which are injected into the subject's bloodstream and taken up by the brain. By observing which areas of the brain take up the radioactive isotope, we can see which areas of the brain are more active than other areas. PET has similar spatial resolution to fMRI, but it has extremely poor temporal resolution.

(2) *Electroencephalography (EEG).* EEG measures the electrical fields generated by large populations of neurons in the cortex by placing a series of electrodes on the scalp of the subject. This technique has an extremely high temporal resolution, but a relatively poor spatial resolution.

(3) *Functional magnetic resonance imaging* (fMRI). fMRI measures the relative amount of oxygenated blood flowing to different parts of the brain. More oxygenated blood in a particular region is assumed to correlate with an increase in neural activity in that part of the brain. This allows us to localize particular functions within different brain regions. fMRI has moderate spatial and temporal resolution.

(4) *Optical imaging.* This technique uses infrared transmitters and receivers to measure the amount of light reflectance by blood near different areas of the brain. Since oxygenated and deoxygenated blood reflects light by different amounts, we can study which areas are more active (i.e., those that have more oxygenated blood). Optical imaging has moderate temporal resolution, but poor spatial resolution. It also has the advantage that it is extremely safe and can be used to study infants' brains.

(5) *Magnetoencephalography (MEG).* MEG measures magnetic fields resulting from cortical activity. It is similar to EEG, except that it has improved spatial resolution since the magnetic fields it measures are not as blurred or attenuated by the scalp, meninges and so forth as the electrical activity measured in EEG is. MEG uses SQUID sensors to detect tiny magnetic fields.

### 1.4.3 Computational modeling

Computational models require a mathematically and logically formal representation of a problem. Computer models are used in the simulation and experimental verification of different specific and general properties of intelligence. Computational modeling can help us to understand the functional organization of a particular cognitive phenomenon.

There are two basic approaches to cognitive modeling. The first is focused on abstract mental functions of an intelligent mind and operates using symbols, and the second, which follows the neural and associative properties of the human brain, and is called subsymbolic.

(1) *Symbolic modeling* evolved from the computer science paradigms using the technologies of Knowledge-based systems, as well as a philosophical perspective. They are developed by the first cognitive researchers and later used in knowledge engineering for expert systems. Since the early 1990s it was generalized in systemics for the investigation of functional human-like intelligence models, such as personoids, and, in parallel, developed as the SOAR environment.

Recently, especially in the context of cognitive decision making, symbolic cognitive modeling is extended to socio-cognitive approach including social and organization cognition interrelated with a sub-symbolic not conscious layer.

(2) Subsymbolic modeling includes *Connectionist/neural network models*. Connectionism relies on the idea that the mind/brain is composed of simple nodes and that the power of the system comes primarily from the existence and manner of connections between the simple nodes.

### 1.4.4 Neurobiological methods

Research methods borrowed directly from neuroscience and neuropsychology can also help us to understand aspects of intelligence. These methods allow us to understand how intelligent behavior is implemented in a physical system. There are several approaches, such as Single-cell recording, Direct brain stimulation, Animal models, Postmortem studies and so on.

### 1.4.5 Simulation

Simulation is an artificial testing means, which establishes on the basis describes the system structure or course of conduct, and has a certain amount of logical relations or relations between simulation model, accordingly test or quantitative analysis, in order to obtain the correct all kinds of information in terms of analyzing the nature of the system elements and their mutual relations and in accordance with the purpose of system analysis. The difference with experimental or practical systems is that simulation is not based on actual environment, but as the actual system image of the system model and the corresponding "artificial" environment carried out under. Simulation can truly describe system operation, evolution and the development process.

## 1.5 Research Roadmap of Intelligence Science

Human's scientific undertaking is facing the challenges from the following four big problems: the nature of matter, the origin of universe, the essence of life and the generation of intelligence. Intelligent science aims at the last one, maybe the most difficult and important one - how is the intelligence generated from materials?

Intelligence is the essence of life science and technology, the core of information science and technology, and the frontier and commanding height of modern science and technology. Its research involves deeper mysteries of science and touches the fundamental topics in philosophy. Therefore, once the researches in intelligence make a breakthrough, deep influence will be made on the national economy, the progress of society development, and the security of nation. At present, intelligent science is in the transition period of methodology, the high tide of theoretical innovations and the start period of large-scale applications. So it is full of original opportunities.

Research on intelligence science just started. It is difficult to give the precise roadmap. Following the development trends will be outlined.

## 1. Short-term goal (2010-2020)

Research on the representation of perceptual information, including the visual, auditory information processing, explore perceptual feature binding mechanisms and objects. Develop computer has human like behaviors such as listening, talking, reading, writing.

Learning is the accumulation process of experience and knowledge, as well as performance improvement of system's behaviors by understanding and mastering temporal associations towards outsides, a basic kind of cognitive activities. The neural biology foundation of learning is the synaptic plasticity for associative structures between nerve cells, which has became a very active research field. The emergence from perceptual cognition to rational knowledge is also an interesting problem.

During the human evolution, language's utilization makes the brain's two hemispheres develop with different functions. The language is the most complex, systemized and widely used symbol system. Language symbols represent not only specific things, status and actions but also abstract concepts. The Chinese possesses the unique characters coupling sounds, shapes and contents tightly and is significantly different from Indian and European languages because of its unique morphology and syntax system, text system, and voice tone system. It is a best opportunity for us to open the door of wisdom by studying Chinese from the nerve, cognition and computation levels.

## 2. Medium-term goal (2020-2035)

Explore the central location of human memory, hippocampus, and other human-related learning and memory center of the working principle, clarify the initial memory information storage and retrieval mechanisms, particular working memory.

Working memory system can store and process information simultaneously, which is different from short-term memory which emphasizes only the storage function. Working memory is divided into three components: central executive system, visual-spatial preliminary processing system and the articulatory loop. A large number of behavior researches and neuropsychological evidences show the existence of the three components. Knowledge on the structures and functions of working memory are constantly enriched and perfected. People found that working memory is tightly related to language comprehension, attention and inference, and may contain mystery of intelligence.

## 3. Long-term goal (2035-2050)

Explore the neural basis of human consciousness and its biological mechanism, as well as joint consciousness and so on. Consciousness is perhaps one of the biggest mysteries and the current research results may be one of the highest achievements. The study on consciousness can start with awareness and unawareness, and finally discover the difference between nerves related materials in brain's activities. The final goal will develop brain-like computer, or machine brain with human-level intelligence and reach the football team composed of intelligent robots defeat the professional football team in the 2050 World Cup.

## Chapter 2

# Foundation of Neurophysiology

Life activities are the most advanced movements in the nature. Human brain is the most complicated material in the world, which is the physiological foundation of human intelligence and advanced spiritual activities. The brain is the organ for human knowledge about the outside world, so it's necessary to know the physiological mechanism of the brain, the highly complicated and orderly material, for studying human cognitive process and intelligent mechanism. Brain science and neural science promote enormously the development of intelligent science through studying natural intelligent mechanism at molecular, cellular and behavioral levels, setting up brain model and revealing human brain's nature. Neurophysiology and neuroanatomy are the two keystones of neural science. The former introduces functions of nervous systems while the latter introduces its structures. This chapter mainly introduces the neurophysiological foundation of the intelligence science.

## 2.1 Brain

A human brain is composed of three parts: a forebrain (prosencephalon), a midbrain (mesencephalon) and a hind brain (epencephalon). Each part of the brain undertakes different functions, and has connection with the cerebral cortex such that information from all over the body is assembled and processed in the cerebral cortex. Forebrain includes cerebral hemispheres and diencephalons.

(1) *Cerebrum* comprises of a right and a left cerebral hemispheres. There is a longitudinal crack between them, at the bottom of which some laterigrade fibres (called the corpus callosum) connect with the two hemispheres. There are spaces (called lateral ventricles) inside the hemispheres, which locate symmetrically on both sides. Each cerebral hemisphere is covered by the grey matter, the cortex. Many sulci and gyri on the surface increase the surface area. Medulla is beneath

cerebral cortex and some grey nucleus groups including basal ganglia, hippocampus and amygdale are hidden in the medulla. Cerebral cortex can be divided into frontal, temporal, parietal and occipital lobes.

(2) *Diencephalon* is the encephalic region surrounding the third ventricle. The very thin superior wall of the ventricle is composed of choroids plexus. Gray matter within the superior of both lateral walls is called thalamus. Its dorsal is covered by the stratum zonale, a thin layer of fibres. Internal medullary lamina is consecutive to the stratum zonale, which splits the thalamus into anterior, medial and lateral nuclear groups in a Y-shaped manner. Epithalamus locates in the superior wall of the third ventricle while hypothalamus locates in the anterior-inferior of the thalamus which includes some nuclear groups within the inferior part of the lateral walls of the third ventricles. Thalamus extends backward to form metathalamus, which consists of lateral geniculate body (related with vision) and medial geniculate body (related with audition). In addition, subthalamus is a transitional zone between diencephalons and caudal mesencenphalon. Thalamus is responsible for encoding and transferring information to the cerebral cortex and coordinating functions of vegetality, endocrine and internal organs.

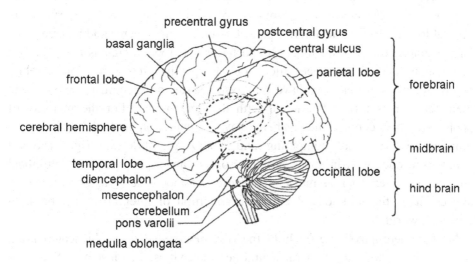

Fig. 2.1 The structure of a brain

(3) *Mesencephalon* comprises of cerebral peduncle and corpora quadrigemina. It takes charge of coordinating the functions of sensation and movement.

(4) *Metencephalon* is composed of pons varolii, cerebellum and medulla oblongata. Cerebellum has two cerebellar hemispheres joined by a sagittal, transversely narrow median vermis. It coordinates the functions of movement. Pons varolii is so named in that it likes a bridge connecting bilateral cerebellar hemispheres, which mainly transfers information from cerebral hemispheres to cerebellar hemispheres. Medulla oblongata locates between pons varolii and spinal cord, which is the autonomic nervous center controlling heart beat, respiration and digestion. The pavimentum ventriculi of the fourth ventricle (fossa rhomboidea) is formed by the dorsal of pons varolii and medulla oblongata, while its cupula is covered by cerebellum. It communicates upward with the third ventricle through cerebral aqueduct, and downward with spinal canal.

Human brain is a system of complicated structure with complete functions. As a whole, two cerebral hemispheres can be divided into several regions with different functions. Among them, occipital lobe in the posterior part of cerebral hemisphere is visual area for analyzing and synthesizing visual stimulation. Parietal lobe is anterior to occipital lobe. Its anterior part is in charge of analysis and synthesis of tactile stimulations and stimulations from muscles and joints. Temporal lobe is inferior-anterior to occipital lobe. Its superior part takes responsibility of analysis and synthesis of stimulations from auditory organ. Frontal lobe locates in the anterior part of cerebral hemispheres and its area is the largest among those of all lobes. Its posterior part reports signals about body's movements and their space allocation. Respective researches on cerebral hemispheres show that they have two systems for information processing and their neural nets reflect the world with different modes. For the majority of people, the left cerebral hemisphere plays a main role in languages, logical thinking, mathematical computing and analyzing, while the right cerebral hemisphere does well in space problem-solving and is in charge of intuitional creative activities, such as music, art. These two modes serve as good partners, and co-shape the unified and complete cognition of integral human brain to objective world.

Modern neurophysiologists hold that the emergence of sophisticated brain functions is linked closely with neural-net's activities. For instance, Sperry, a famous American neurophysiologist and the laureate of Nobel Prize said very clearly in his view that the subjective consciousness and thinking depending on neural network and relevant physiological characteristics was one component of the brain course and the result of the high-level activities of the brain. Sanger, a French neurophysiologist also said that all kinds of behaviors, thinking, emotion and so on, are stemmed from physical and chemical phenomena produced in that brain and they are resulted from the assemblage of concerned neurons.

The real neuroscience is originated in the end of the last century. C. Golgi, an Italian anatomist discerned the single nerve cell at first by staining in 1875. R. Cajal founded neuron doctrine in 1889, which thought the whole nervous system was formed by relatively independent nerve cells on the structure. In recent decades the researches in neuroscience and brain function make progress extremely fast. It is estimated that the quantity of the whole human brain neurons is about $10^{11}$. Each neuron comprises of two parts: neural cell body and processes (dendrites and axons). The size of cell body ranges from the diameter of 5 to 100 microns. The quantity of processes arising from each nerve cell and their length and branches are all different. Some processes are above one meter long while others are not longer than 1/1000 of the long process. Neurons communicate with each other by synapses. Quantity of synapses is tremendous. According to measurement, synapse quantity of one neuron in the cerebral cortex is above 30 thousand while synapse quantity of the whole brain ranges from $10^{14}$ to $10^{15}$. There are various communication models among the synapses. The most common type of synapses occurs between the terminal of an axonal branch of a neuron and the dendrite or the soma of another. Besides it, there are other types such as axo-axonal synapses, soma-somatic synapses. Different types of synapses have different physiological functions.

Combinations among neurons are also of diverse types. One neuron can form synapses with many neurons by its fiber branches, which makes the information from the neuron transfer to other neurons. Whereas the nervous fiber terminals from those neurons locating in different regions can also aggregate in one neuron, which makes information with different sources centralize together in the same area. In addition, there are ring-shaped and catenuliform combinations. Therefore, communications among the neurons are very reticular.

The complexity and diversity of neural net not only lies in the great quantity of neurons and synapses, complicated combining types and extensive communications, but also in the complicated mechanisms of synaptic transmission. The elucidated mechanisms of synaptic transmission at present include postsynaptic excitation, postsynaptic inhibition, presynaptic inhibition, presynaptic excitation and long term depression and so on. Among them, releasing of neurotransmitters is the central step of realizing synaptic transmission and different neurotransmitters have different effects and characteristics.

The human brain was a product of the long evolution of living being. It took the animal kingdom about one billion years to evolve. Unicellular organism had nothing with nervous system. The neurons began to concentrate on the head to form the ganglia until living being evolved to flatworms. The primary differentiation of animal cerebrum was related with smell, the amphibian animals and the animals inferior to fish only had olfactory lobe related with smell. Vertebrates began to have central nervous system. A fish's brain had five parts including telencephalon, diencephalons, mesencephalon, metencephalon and medulla oblongata. Cerebral neocortex began to occur in reptiles while real brain-the neocortex was seen in mammals. Primates' cerebral cortex with sufficient development took charge of overall and subtle regulations on various functions of body. At the end of the evolving process, the extremely complicated neural net formed, which constituted the thinking organ of huge system---human brain.

The research of the human brain has already become the advanced front of scientific research. Some experts estimate brain science will be the next tide following the tide of molecular biological research in biology set up by J. D. Watson and F. Crick, the winner of Nobel's physiology -- medicine rewards, because they proposed double coiled spiral structure of DNA in 1950s and explained the questions about hereditary knowledge successfully. Many first class western scientists engaging in biological or physical research shift their research field to human brain research one after another after they have obtained the Nobel Prize.

## 2.2 Nervous Tissues

The nervous system is composed of two principal cellular constituents, the nerve cells (or neurons), and neuroglial cells (or glia). The characteristics exhibited by the nervous systems include excitation, conduction and integration and so on, all of which are the functions of neurons. Although glia account for more than half volume of brain and their quantity exceeds largely over that of neurons, they just play an assistance role.

## 2.2.1 Basal composition of neuron

Nerve cell is the most elemental unit constituting nervous system, so it is usually called neuron. Each neuron has tree specialized regions: cell body (soma), axon and dendrites. General structure of neuron is shown in Figure 2.2.

*Soma or cell body.* The cell bodies are main part of neurons, which locate in gray matter of the brain and spinal cord and ganglia. They are of different shape, and star-shaped, pyramid-shaped, pear-shaped and ball-shaped neurons are observed commonly. The sizes of cell bodies are not uniform and their diameters range from 5 to 150μm. The cell body is the metabolic and nutrient center of the neuron. Its structure is similar to that of common cell, including nucleolus, cell membrane, cytoplasm and nucleus. The cytoplasm of the living neuron takes a granular shape, and appropriate staining shows it contains neurofibrils, chromophil substance (Nissl bodies), Golgi apparatus, endoplasmic reticulum and mitochondria and so on. Neurofibrils are the unique character of neurons.

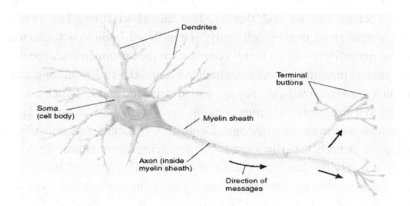

Fig. 2.2 Appearance of neuron

*Cell membrane.* The cell membrane covering the cell body and the processes is continuous and intact. Except for the membrane of process with specialized structure, the majority of cell membrane is a unit membrane. The cell membrane of neuron has sensitive and excitable characters. There are various receptors and ionic channels in the cell membrane, which are composed of distinct membrane proteins. The membrane of process thickens. The receptors in the membrane can bind with relative neurotransmitters. When the receptors bind with acetylcholine or γ-aminobutyric acid (GABA), the ion permeability of the membrane and the potential difference between two sides of membrane will change, causing related physiological activity of membrane: excitation or inhibition.

*Nucleus*. The nucleus locates usually in the center of cell body of neuron, big and round. It has few heterochromatin usually locating inside of nuclear membrane while many euchromatin dispersing in the center of the nucleus. Therefore the nucleus has superficial staining. It has 1or 2 big and obvious nucleoli. The nucleus migrates usually to the periphery when cell degenerates.

*Cytoplasm*. The cytoplasm surrounds the nucleus, so it is called perikaryon. It contains developed Golgi bodies, smooth endoplasmic reticulum (SER), abundant mitochondria, Nissl bodies, neurofibrils, lysosomes and lipofuscin, and etc. For the neuron with secretion function, its cytoplasm has secretory granules, such as the neurons located in the hypothalamus.

*Process*. Process is the extension of the cell body of neuron. It can be divided into dendrite and axon according to its structure and functions.

*Dendrite*. One cell body can arise one to multiple dendrites, arranged in radiated-shape. Their proximal trunks near the cell body are thick and their branches become thinner and thinner, like an arborization. The structure of dendrite is similar to that of cell body. It has Nissl bodies, mitochondria and paralleling neurofibrils but no Golgi complex. In the specimen with special silver staining, many spine-like processes which are about 0.5 to 1.0μm long and 0.5 to 2.0μm thick are visualized and they are called dendritic spines which are the sites of forming synapse. dendritic spine contains several flat uesicae (spine apparatus) under general electronic microscope. Dendrite's branches and dendritic spines can increase neuron's surface area for receiving stimulation. Dendrite has functions of receiving stimulation and transferring impulse to cell body.

*Axon*. Each neuron has only one axon. The initial segment of axon is cone-shaped, called the axon hillock, which contains mainly neurofibrils but no Nissl bodies. The initial segment of the axon is about 15 to 25μm long and is thinner than the dendrite, with the adqulis thickness. Its smooth surface has few branches, no myelin sheath surrounding it. The portion of axon far from the cell body is wrapped by myelin sheath, and that is the myelinated nerve fiver. Fine branches at the end of axon are called as axon terminals, which can touch with other neurons or effector cells. The membrane covering the axon is axolemma while the plasma in the axon is axoplasm, in which there are many neurofibils paralleling with long axis of the axon and slender mitochondria, but no Nissle bodies and Glogi complex. Thus there is no protein synthesis in the axon. Metabolic turnover of axon's components and the synthesis of neurotransmitters in the synaptic vesicles are undergoing in the cell body and then they flow to axon terminal through the microtubules and neurofilaments in axon. The main role of axon is conducting nerve impulse from cell body to other neurons or effector cells. Impulse conduction begins at the axon's initial segment and then continues along the axolemma. Axon terminals formed by continuous branching constitute synapses with other neurons or effector cells together.

During the long evolving process, neurons form their own specialized functions and morphous. The neurons associated directly with receptors and conducting information to the centre are called sensory neurons or afferent neurons. While the neurons associated directly with effector and conducting impulse from the centre to the effector are called motor neurons or efferent neurons. Besides above neurons, the rest of neurons are interneurons forming neural networks.

The total number of efferent neurons in the human nervous system is several hundreds of thousands. The number of afferent neurons is more 1 to 3 times than that of efferent neurons. The number of interneurons is the biggest. The number of interneurons just in the cerebral cortex is known as 14 to 15 billion.

### 2.2.2 Classification of neurons

There are many kind of classifications about neurons. It is classified usually according to the number and function of neural processes.

1) Neurons can be divided into three classes according to the number of neural processes:

*Pseudounipolar neuron*: One process arises from the cell body and then splits in T-type into two branches at the site not far from the cell body. Thus it is called as pseudounipolar neuron. One branch with the structure similar to the axon is long and thin and extends to the periphery, which is called peripheral process, and its function is same to that of the dendrite. Peripheral process senses stimulation and conducts impulse to the cell body. The other branch called central process extends to the center and its function is equal to that of the axon, conducting impulse to another neuron, like the sensory neuron in the spinal ganglia.

*Bipolar neuron*. Bipolar neuron erupts two processes. One is the dendrite and the other is the axon, for example, the sensory neurons in the cochlear ganglion.

During the long evolving process, neurons form their own specialized function and morphous. The neurons associated directly with receptors and conducting information to the centre are called sensory.

*Multipolar neuron.* Multipolar neuron has one axon and multiple dendrites. Multipolar neurons are such kinds of neurons with the most quantity, such as the motor neurons in cornu anterius medullae spinalis and the pyramidal cells in the cerebral cortex and so on. Based on the length of axons, multipolar neurons are also classified into two types: *Golgi type I neuron* and *Golgi type II neuron.* Golgi type I neurons have big cell bodies and long axons, which can extend collateral branches on their way, such as the motor neurons in cornu anterius medullae spinalis; Golgi type II neurons have small cell bodies and short axons, which extend collateral branches nearby the cell bodies, for example, small neurons in the cornu posterius medullae spinalis and association neurons in the cerebrum and cerebellum.

2) Based on their functions, neurons fall into three types

*Sensory neurons* (afferent neurons) receive stimuli and transmit afferent impulse to the central nervous system, and their cell bodies locate in the cerebrum and spinal ganglia. Most of them are pseudounipolar neurons and their processes constitute the afferent nerves of peripheral nerves. The terminals of nerve fibers form sensors (receptors) in the skin or muscles.

*Motor neurons* (efferent neurons) transmit efferent impulse. Most of them are multipolar neurons and their cell bodies locate in gray matter of the central nervous system or vegetative ganglia and their processes constitute efferent nerve fibers. The terminals of nerve fibers locate in the muscle tissues and glands to form effectors.

*Interneurons* (association neurons) play a role of communication between the neurons. They are multipolar neurons and their quantity is the greatest in the human nervous system. Interneurons construct the complicated network of the central nervous system. Their cell bodies locate in gray matter of the central nervous system and their processes locate generally in gray matter too.

### 2.2.3 Neuroglial cells

Neuroglial cells (abbreviated as glial cells) are distributed extensively in the central and peripheral nervous systems and their quantity is largely more than that of neurons, and the ratio of glial cell to neuron is about 10:1 to 50:1. Similar to the neurons, glial cells have also processes, but the processes have no difference as the neurons' dendrites and axons and they can't transmit impulse. Glial cells can be divided into several types and each of them has different shape characteristics.

1. *Astrocyte.* Astrocyte is one kind of glial cells with biggest volume. Astrocytes and oligodendrocytes are also called macroglia. Cell appears star-shaped and its comparatively large nucleus is round or oval and has light staining (Figure 2.3):

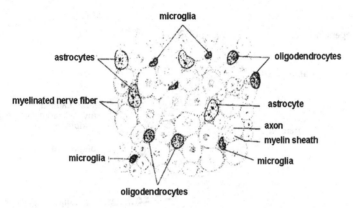

Fig. 2.3 Transection of the nucleus of glial cells and nerve fibers (substantia alba medullae spinalis, Nissl staining)

Astrocytes can be divided into two kinds: a) Fibrous astrocyte is distributed mainly in white matter. It has thin and long processes with fewer branches and cytoplasm containing a mass of glial filaments. Glial filaments are composed of glial fibrillary acidic protein (GFAP). This kind of astrocytes can be observed by immunocytochemical staining. b) Protoplasmic astrocyte is distributed mainly in gray matter. It has short and thick processes with many branches and cytoplasm containing fewer glial filaments. The processes of astrocytes extend and fill between the cell bodies and processes of neurons, which play their roles of supporting and separating neurons. The terminals of some processes form end feet attaching to the capillary wall or the surfaces of brain and spinal cord to form the glial limiting membrane.

Intracellular spaces between astrocytes are narrow and tortuous, about 15 to 20nm wide, and they contain tissue fluid, by which neurons carry out substance exchanging (Figure 2.4). Astrocyte can absorb K+ from intracellular spaces to maintain stable K+ concentration of the circumstance of neurons. It can also uptake and metabolize some neurotransmitters, such as γ-aminobutyric acid and so on, to regulate the concentration of neurotransmitters, which is in favor of the activities of the neurons. During the developing period of the nerve system, some astrocytes can introduce neurons migrating to presumptive area and make neurons set up synaptic linkage with other neurons. When the central nervous system is damaged, astrocytes will proliferate, become hypertrophy to fill defective space and form glial scar.

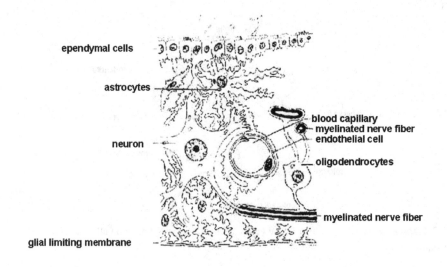

Fig. 2.4 Relationship among glial cells and neurons and blood capillary

2. *Oligodendrocyte*. Oligodendrocyte has few processes in specimen with silver staining. But it is not so in specimen with specific immunocytochemical staining and many branches can be observed. Oligodendrocyte has smaller cell body compared with astrocyte. Its nucleus is round, with dark staining (Figure 2.3). Its cytoplasm has seldom glial filaments but many microtubules and other organelles. Oligodendrocyte is distributed nearby the cell bodies of neurons or around nerve fiber, and its process terminals extend to form flat and thin pellicle, which wraps neuron's axon to form myelin sheath. Thus it is the cell of myelination in the central nervous system. Recent researches believe that oligodendrocyte also has the function inhibiting the growth of regenerated neurite.

3. *Microglia*. Microglia is the smallest glial cell. It has slim and long or oval cell body, flat or triangle small nucleus, dark staining (Figure 2.3). Its process is long and slim and has branches. Its surface has many small spinous processes. Microglias account for only 5% of the total glial cells. When the central nervous

system is damaged, microglia can convert to macrophages which swallow cell debris and degenerated myelin sheath. And circulating monocytes also intrude into damage zone and convert to microphages to take part in phagocytosis. Some one think microglia originates from monocyte in blood and belongs to mononuclear phagocyte system due to its phagocytosis.

4. *Ependymal cell.* Cube or cylinder-shaped ependymal cells are distributed in the cavosurfaces of cerebral ventricles and spinal canal to form simple epithelium, called ependyma. The surfaces of ependyma cells have many microvilli (Figure 2.4). The ependyna cells in some regions are called tanycytes for that their basal surfaces have slender processes extending to the deep part.

## 2.3 Synaptic Transmission

A special kind of cell junction between neurons or between neuron and non-neural cell (muscle cell, glandular cell) is called synapse, which are connections of neurons and the critical structure of undertaking physiological activities. Intercellular communication is realized through its transmission. The most common type of synapses occur between a terminal of an axonal branch of one neuron and a dendrite or dendritic spine or a soma of another neuron to form axon-dendritic synapses, axon-dendritic spinal synapses, or axosomatic synapses. In addition, there are axoaxonal synapses and dendrodendritic synapses and so on. Synapses can be classified into two major types: the chemical synapses and the electronic synapses. The former takes chemical substance (neurotransmitter) as communicating media while the latter, also named gap junctions, transfers information by electric current (electronic signal). For the mammal nervous system, chemical synapses account for the majority, so the synapses mentioned usually refer to the chemical synapses.

Synaptic structure can be divided into presynaptic element, synaptic space and postsynaptic element. Cell membranes in presynaptic element and postsynaptic element are called presynaptic membrane and postsynaptic membrane respectively, between which is a 15-30nm narrow gap, called synaptic cleft, containing glycoproteins and some filament. Presynaptic element is usually an axonal terminal of a neuron, appearing globular intumescentia and attaching to the soma or the dendrite of another neuron, called synaptic button.

### 2.3.1 Chemical synapse

Under electronic microscope, synaptic button contains many synaptic vesicles and small amounts of mitochondria, smooth endoplasmic reticulum, microtubules and microfilaments and so on (Figure 2.5). Synaptic vesicles have different size and shape, mainly round, and their diameters are 40 to 60nm, some vesicles are thin and flat. Some synaptic vesicles are clear and bright, and some contain pyknotic nuclei (granular vesicles). The diameter of the big granular vesicle is about 200nm. Synaptic vesicles contain neurotransmitters or neuromodulators. Both of presynaptic membrane and postsynaptic membrane are thicker than the common cell membrane, which is caused by some densic materials attaching to the membrane (Figure 2.5). The presynaptic membrane has electron-dense coned dense projections which intrude to the cytoplasm and the spaces between dense projections hold synaptic vesicles. Synaptic vesicle related protein attaching to the surface of synaptic vesicle is called synapsin I, which makes synaptic vesicles gather and attach to the cytoskeleton. The presynaptic membrane contains abundant voltage-gated channels while the postsynaptic membrane contains rich receptors and chemically-gated channels. When nerve impulse is transferred along the axolemma to the synaptic terminal, voltage-gated channels in presynaptic membrane are triggered and open, which cause extracellular $Ca^{2+}$ flow into the presynaptic element and make synapsin I phosphorylate with ATP, and trigger synaptic vesicles moving and attaching to the presynaptic membrane, and then the neurotransmitters in the synaptic vesicles are released into the synaptic cleft by exocytosis. One part of neurotransmitters combine concerned receptors in the postsynaptic membrane and induce receptor-coupled chemically-gated channels open, which makes related ions go in or out to change the distribution of ions at both sides of postsynaptic membrane, showing excited or inhibited effects, and then affect the activities of postsynaptic neuron and/or non-nervous cells. The synapse exciting postsynaptic membrane is excitatory synapse while the synapse inhibiting postsynaptic membrane is inhibitory synapse.

1. *Presynaptic element.* Axon terminal of a neuron oncoides like globularity and axolemma thickens to form the presynaptic membrame, about 6 to 7nm thick. Within the cytoplasm of the presynaptic part, there are many synaptic vesicles, some microfilaments, microtubules, mitochondria and smooth endoplasmic reticulum and so on. The synaptic vesicle is characteristic structure of presynaptic element and contains chemical substances called neurotransmitters. The shape and size of the synaptic vesicle in various synapses is very different

because it contains different neurotransmitters. The common types of synaptic vesicles include: a) globose vesicle with a diameter of 20 to 60nm is clear and bright, and contains excitatory neurotransmitters like acetylcholine. b) granulated vesicle with electron-dense granules can be divided into two subtypes according to its size: the small granulated vesicle with a diameter of 30 to 60nm contains usually amines-neurotransmitters like epinephrine and norepinephrine and so on; big granulated vesicle with diameter of 80 to 200nm contains some peptides-neurotransmitters such as 5-hydroxytryptamine or enkephalin and so on. c) flat synaptic vesicles with long diameter of 50nm or so is flat and round and contains the inhibitory neurotransmitters like γ-aminobutyric acid and so on.

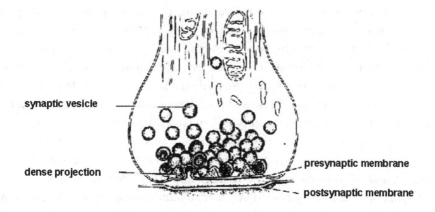

synaptic vesicle

dense projection

presynaptic membrane

postsynaptic membrane

Fig. 2.5 Ultrastructure pattern of chemical synapse

Various kinds of neurotransmitters are synthesized in the soma and transported rapidly toward axon terminal by forming vesicles. New research discovers that two or above neurotransmitters coexist in one neuron of central and peripheral nervous system, thus there are two or above synaptic vesicles in the synaptosome. For instance, acetylcholine and vasoactive intestinal peptide coexist in the sympathetic ganglia. The former takes charge of secretion of sweat glands while the latter acts on vessel smooth muscles around glands to relax them, which can increase regional blood flow. Coexistence of neurotransmitters can coordinate neurophysiological activities and make nervous regulation more precise and concordant. At present, many facts indicate that coexistence is not an individual phenomenon but a universal law, and many novel coexisted transmitters and their location have been confirmed. The majority of them are coexistence of non-peptide (choline, monoamine and amine) and peptide transmitters.

It is known that synaptophysin, synapsin and vesicle associated membrane protein are associated with package and storage of synaptic vesicles, and releasing of transmitter. Synaptophysin is a $Ca^{2+}$ binding protein in synaptic vesicle. When excitation arrives at synapse, $Ca^{2+}$ entry increases abruptly, as is probably important to the exocytosis of synaptic vesicles. Synapsin is phosphorylated protein with the function of regulating release of neurotransmitters. Vesicle associated membrane protein is a structural protein of the membrane of synaptic vesicles, which is probably important to the metabolism of synaptic vesicles.

2. *Postsynaptic element*. Postsynaptic element is usually the membrane of soma or dendrite of postsynaptic neuron. The portion opposite presynaptic membrane thickens to form postsynaptic membrane. It is thicker than presynaptic membrane, about 20 to 50nm. There are receptors and chemically gated ion channels in postsynaptic membrane. According the thickness of dense materials in cytoplasm surface of presynaptic and postsynaptic membrane, synapses can be divided into type I and type II: i) In type I synapse, dense materials in cytoplasm surface of postsynaptic membrane is thicker than that of presynaptic membrane. It is called asymmetrical synapse due to its asymmetrical thickness of the membrane, and it has round synaptic vesicles and 20 to 50nm wide synaptic cleft. Type I synapses are usually considered as excitatory synapses which are mainly axon-dendritic synapses distributed in the trunk of dendrite. ii) In type II synapse has few dense materials in cytoplasm surface of presynaptic and postsynaptic membrane and their thickness in presynaptic and postsynaptic membrane is similar, so it is called symmetrical synapse. Symmetrical synapse has flat synaptic vesicles and narrow 10 to 20nm synaptic cleft. Type II synapses are usually considered as inhibitory synapses which are mainly axon-somatic synapse distributed in the soma.

3. *Synaptic cleft*. About 20 to 30nm wide synaptic cleft is an extracellular space between presynaptic and postsynaptic membranes which contains glycosaminoglycan such as sialic acid and glucoprotein and so on. These chemical components can bind to neurotransmitters and promote transmitters moving from presynaptic membrane toward postsynaptic membrane, which limits external diffusion of transmitters or eliminates redundant transmitters.

When nerve impulses propagate along the axolemma to the presynaptic membrane, voltage gated $Ca^{2+}$ channels are triggered to open and extracellular

$Ca^{2+}$ enter the presynaptic element. Inflow $Ca^{2+}$ cooperates with ATP, microfilaments and microtubules to make synaptic vesicles move toward presynaptic membrane and release neurotransmitters into synaptic cleft by exocytosis. One part of neurotransmitters bind to related receptors on the postsynaptic membrane and cause receptor-coupled chemically gated channels open which makes corresponding ions enter the postsynaptic element and changes bilateral ion distribution of membrane, showing excitatory (the depolarization of the membrane) or inhibitory (the hyperpolarization of the membrane) alteration, thereby affecting the activity of the postsynaptic neuron (or effector cell). The synapse exciting or inhibiting postsynaptic membrane is called excitatory or inhibitory synapse respectively. Synaptic excitation or inhibition is decided by species of neurotransmitters and their receptors. It is a series of physiological activities of the organells of the neurons including the synthesis, transportation, storage, release and effects of neurotransmitters and their inactivation by action of related enzyme. A neuron usually has many synapses, among which some are excitatory and others are inhibitory. If the summation of the excitatory synaptic activities surpasses that of the inhibitory synaptic activities, which makes the initial segment of the axon of the neuron produce action potentials and nerve impulses occur, the neuron appears excitatory, conversely, it appears inhibitory.

The characters of the chemical synapse include two species: the neuron of its one side releases neurotransmitters of vesicles by exocytosis to the synaptic cleft and the postsynaptic membrane of the neuron (or effector cell) of its other side has related receptors. The cell with related receptor is called the effector cell or target cell of the neurotransmitter. Its characters ensure the unilateral of chemical synaptic transmission. The two specialized neurolemma portions-the presynaptic and postsynaptic membranes maintain the structures and functions of two neurons and realize unification and balance of the organism. Therefore, the synapse is very sensitive to the changes of the internal and external environments. For instance, anoxia, acidosis, fatigue and anesthesia and so on all decrease its excitability, whereas theophylline and alkalosis and so on all increase its excitability.

### 2.3.2 Electrical synapse

Electrical synapse, the simplest style of information transmission between the neurons, locates in the touching site of two neurons, in which there is a gap junction and the diameter of the touching point is above 0.1 to 10μm. Electrical synapse has also the presynaptic and postsynaptic membranes and synaptic cleft with only 1 to 1.5nm width. Membrane protein particles of the presynaptic and postsynaptic membranes span over the full-thickness of the membranes and show hexagonal structural unit. Their top exposes to the surface of the membrane and their center forms micro-passage with about 2.5nm diameter which is vertical to the surface of the membrane and permits the substance with diameter of smaller than 1nm pass through, like amino acid. Bilateral membranes of the gap junction are symmetric. The tops of membrane protein particles of neighboring two synaptolemmas get in touch with each other and the central tubules communicate with each other. The axonal terminal has no synaptic vesicles and conduction needn't neurotransmitters. Electrical synapse conducts information by electric current and the transmission of nerve impulse is usually bidirectional. Local current passes easily through it due to intercellular small electric resistance and high permeability of the neurons. The bidirectional transmission of the electric synapse decreases the space of the transmission, which makes the transmission more effective. Under electronic microscope, synaptic button contains many synaptic vesicles and small amounts of mitochon.

It has been identified now that electric synapses are dispersed in mammal corticocerebral astrocytes, basket cells and astrocytes of cerebellar cortex, horizontal cells and bipolar cells of the retina and some nuclei like the motor nuclei of oculomotor nerve, vestibular nuclei and spinal nuclei of trigeminal nerve. Electric synapse has various styles such as dendrodendritic synapse, axoaxonal synapse, soma-somatic synapse, axosomatic synapse, axon-dendritic synapse and so on.

Electric synapse is very sensitive to the changes of the internal and external environments. Its excitability decreases under the conditions of fatigue, anoxia, anesthesia or acidosis, whereas its excitability increases under the condition of alkalosis.

### 2.3.3 Mechanism of synaptic transmission

During the synaptic transmission, where action potential conducts to the axonal terminal and causes depolarization of the soma portion and increases $Ca^{2+}$ permeability of the membrane, extracellular $Ca^{2+}$ influx promotes synaptic vesicles move forward and fuse with presynaptic membrane, and then laceration occurs in the fusion site and transmitters are released into the synaptic cleft and bind to special receptors in the postsynaptic membrane by diffusion. Then chemically gated channels open which increases the permeability of some ions of postsynaptic membrane. The postsynaptic membrane potential changes (depolarization or hyperpolarization of postsynaptic potential) produce summation effect which makes postsynaptic neuron excitatory or inhibitory. Figure 2.6 shows the basic process of the synaptic transmission

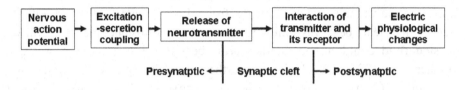

Fig. 2.6 The basic process of synaptic transmission

Effects of $Ca^{2+}$ in the process of synaptic transmission are as follows:

(1) to lower the viscosity of axoplasm, which is in favor of migration of synaptic vesicles by reducing combination of actin binding protein on the uesicae with actin.

(2) to eliminate interior negative potential of the presynaptic membrane, which promotes synaptic vesicles contact and fuse with presynaptic membrane and then membrane splits and releases neurotransmitters.

The presynaptic electric activity of the nervous system of higher animal never causes directly the activity of postsynaptic component, and no electric coupling exists. Synaptic transmission acts uniformly by the medium with special chemical substance called neuromediator or neurotransmitter. Synaptic transmission is carried out only from presynaptic membrane toward postsynaptic membrane and it is unidirectional. It takes 0.5 to 1ms to finish the excitation-secretion coupling from releasing of mediator and diffusing of mediator in the cleft until depolarization of postsynaptic membrane, as a synaptic delay. Synaptic transmission has the following characters: a) Unidirectional transmission; b) Synaptic delay; c) Summation, including temporal summation and spatial summation; d) Sensitive to internal environment and fatiguability; e) Excitatory rhythmicity modification: impulse frequency firing from afferent nerve and efferent nerve is inconsistent in the same reflex; f) After-discharge: efferent nerve still fires impulse some time even after stimulant stops.

## 2.4 Neurotransmitter

In 1904, Elliott, a student of medical school of British Cambridge University had pointed out prudently in presenting his thesis in a physiological society meeting that impulse conducted to sympathetic nerve terminal, from which epinephrine was released and then affected effector cell. It was the earliest record about chemical transmission indicated definitely. In 1921, O. Loewi, an Austria physiologist manifested firstly chemical transmission through experiments. Stimulating the vagus nerve of perfusion frog's heart in vitro with electricity, he observed that heart beat was inhibited, meanwhile a substance occurring in the perfusion fluid could inhibit another heart beat and it was named as vagus substance. In 1926, he elucidated further that the vagus substance was acetylcholine (Ach), the first transmitter discovered. H.H. Dale, a British physiologist and pharmacologist and his colleagues had manifested throught experiments that Ach was a transmitter in the neuromuscular junction of skeletal muscles. He introduced the term, cholinergic to physiology, which was used to express the neuron utilizing Ach as transmitter. O. Loewi and H. Dale was endowed with Nobel Prize in 1936 due to their research in this field. The consideration that sympathetic nerve terminal released epinephrine was proposed at first and in 1921 Cannon named the substance released from the liver by stimulating sympathetic nerve as sympathin and believed that it was very similar to epinehrine. But von Euler identified it as norepinephrine (NE) until 1949 and he was endowed with Nobel Prize in 1970 for it. After this, about 10 small-molecule types of transmitters and more than 50 types of neuro-activation polypeptides involving in synaptic transmission are discovered one after another. Recently, nitric oxide (NO) was discovered as a gas messenger.

There are five standards to identify whether endogenous nervous active material is a transmitter or not:

(1) *Existence*. It should exist specially in the neurons and the terminals of the neurons have enzymatic system used to synthesize the transmitter.

(2) *Location*. After the transmitter is synthesized in the terminals of the neurons, it is usually stored in the vesicles, which can prevent it from being destroyed by other enzymes.

(3) *Release*. Presynaptic terminal can release enough substance to cause a certain response of postsynaptic cell or effector cell.

(4) *Effect*. Transmitter passes through the synaptic cleft to act on the special site of the postsynaptic membrane called receptor to cause the changes of ion permeability and potential of the postsynaptic membrane.

(5) *Mechanism of inactivation*. Transmitter's function must end rapidly once it has produced the above effects to ensure synaptic transmission active highly. There are several pathways for ending effect of transmitter: i) being hydrolyzed by enzyme and losing its activity; ii) being uptaken by presynaptic membrane or partly by postsynaptic membrane; iii) one part of transmitters enter the blood circulation and others are degraded by enzyme.

Many neurotransmitters have been discovered so far. Some of the best known are Ach, catecholamines (NE and dopamine), 5-hydroxytryptamine, gamma-aminobutyric acid (GABA), some amino acids and oligopeptides and so on.

## 2.4.1 Acetylcholine

Acetylcholine (Ach) is an excitatory neurotransmitter secreted by neurons in many areas of the brain but specially by the terminals of the large pyramidal cells of the motor cortex, by the motor neurons that innervate the skeletal muscles, by preganglionic neurons of the autonomic nervous system, by the postganglionic neurons of the parasympathetic nervous system.

Ach is synthesized in the presynaptic terminal from choline and acetyl coenzyme A in the presence of the enzyme *choline acetylase*:

$$(CH_3)_3N^+\!-\!CH_2\!-\!CH_2\!-\!OH \ + \ CH_3\!-\!CO \sim CoA \xrightarrow{\text{Choline acetylase}}$$

$$\text{Choline} \qquad\qquad\qquad \text{Acetyl CoA}$$

$$(CH_3)_3N^+\!-\!CH_2\!-\!CH_2\!-\!O\!-\!CO\!-\!CH_3 \ + \ CoA$$

$$\text{Acetyl choline}$$

Choline acetylase locates in the cytoplasm, so it is conceived that Ach is firstly synthesized in the cytoplasm and then it is transported into its specific vesicles. In normal time Ach in vesicles and Ach in cytoplasm account for half of total quantity respectively and they are probably in a balance. Ach stored in the vesicles binds with proteins while it becomes free when it is released.

When nerve impulse conducts to the terminals along the axon, vesicles move toward synaptic membrane, fuse with it and then break. At this time, binding Ach converts to free Ach and they are released into the synaptic cleft. At the same time, some freshly synthesized Ach in cytoplasm are also released to join the response.

Ach makes a physiological effect by acting on the receptor on the surface of the postsynaptic membrane. It has been identified that Ach receptor is a lipoprotein present in the membrane, with a weight of 42,000 molecular.

Ach separates from its receptor after transferring information and dissociates in the synaptic cleft. Very few Ach is uptaken to the presynaptic neuron by its carrier system. Majority of Ach is hydrolyzed into choline and acetic acid in the presence of acetylcholine esterase and loses its activity. One part of Ach departs from the synaptic cleft by diffusion.

### 2.4.2 Catecholamines

Catecholamines are the amines containing basal structure of catechol. Catecholamines with biological activity in vivo include dopamine (DA), NE and E. Their structures are as follows:

Dopamine (DA)

Noradrenaline (NE)

Adrenalin (E)

NE and E are both the hormones secreted by adrenal medulla and the neurotransmitters secreted by noradrenergic fibers of the sympathetic nerve and the central nervous system. NE is dispersed extensively in the center with a big content. E has little content. Thus here we mainly introduce the metabolism of NE. DA is also a kind of neurotransmitter mainly present in the extrapyramidal system.

1. Biological synthesis of catecholamines.

Raw material used to synthesize catecholamines in the nervous tissues comes from tyrosine in blood.

During the above process, tyrosine hydroxylase, tetrahydrobiopterin, $O_2$ and $Fe^{2+}$ are involved in the first step. Among them, tyrosine hydroxylase locates in the cytoplasm of the noradrenergic fibers and it is a rate-limiting enzyme of NE synthesis due to its few content and low activity while tetrahydrobiopterin is its coenzyme, and $O_2$ and $Fe^{2+}$ are also the indispensable factors for NE synthesis. The reaction in the second step is catalyzed by the aromatic amino acid decarboxylase with not high specifity in the cytoplasm. Similar to the general amino acid decarboxylase, the aromatic amino acid decarboxylase requires pyridoxal phosphate as coenzyme. The oxidizing reaction in the third step is catalyzed by dopamine hydroxylase, with oxidation site being in $\beta$ carbon atom. Dopamine hydroxylase is not in the cytoplasm but attaching to the inner wall of vesicles, and it belongs to the protein family containing $Cu^{2+}$ and needs vitamine C as its cofactor.

In the view of the subcellular level distribution of the above enzymes, the last step of NE synthesis is only undertaken within the vesicles and synthetic quantity of NE is not regulated by tyrosine hydroxylase. Furthermore, free NE with high concentration in nerve terminal may inhibit activity of tyrosine hydroxylase by negative feedback to fall down the synthesis of NE.

Phenylethanolamine-N-methyltransferase is mainly in the adrenal medullary cells and it can methylate NE to produce E. This enzyme in the brain is few, thus it is believed that normal mammal brain contains very few E. Some people consider that if the content of phenylethanolamine-N-methyltransferase is too high, it can convert dopamine to N-methydopamin directly and cause metabolic disorder of these neurotransmitters, which is probably the reason of schizophrenia.

2. Norepinephrine (NE).

(1) *Storage and release.* NE is stored inside its specific vesicles after its synthesis. It binds loosely with ATP and chromogranin, which makes NE not easily penetrate into the cytoplasm and avoid being destroyed by monoamine oxidase. When nerve impulse is conducted to the terminals, the vesicles nearby the presynaptic membrane fuse with it and break into pores. At this time, NE inside the vesicles is released into the synaptic cleft together with chromogranin.

(2) *NE's removal in the synaptic cleft.* NE released into the synaptic cleft can bind with NE receptor in the postsynaptic membrane to produce physiological effects. Then, about 3/4 of NE is reuptaken by the presynaptic membrane and transported into the vesicles again. Reuptaking is a process with energy comsuption, which is related with $Na^+$, $K^+$-ATPase in presynaptic membrane

and $Mg^{2+}$-ATP ase in vesicle membrane. One part of NE can be uptaken by the postsynaptic membrane and degraded and loses its activation there. Others are either destroyed in the synaptic cleft or diffused into blood. Except that NE reuptaken by the presynaptic membrane can be reused, the rest is suffering generally from enzymatic degradation and loses its activation. Monoamine oxidase (MAO) and Catechol-O-Transmethylase (COMT) are two main enzymes catalyzing catecholamine to degrade, which are not only in the nervous tissues but also distributed widely in non-nervous tissues and in the mitochondrial membrane of neurons. In the presence of MAO, NE is oxidated firstly to aldehyde by oxidative deamination, and then the latter is converted into ethanol or acid. 3-methoxy-4-hydroxyphenylglycol (MHPG) is the main degradation product of NE in the center while vanillylmandelic acid (VMA) is the main degradation product of NE in the peripheral. In the presence of COMT, circulating NE (mainly as hormone) is converted into methoxyl metabolic products in livers and kidneys to be excreted. Nowadays, VMA content in urine has been a clinical index to know the function of sympathetic nerves. For the patient suffering pheochromocytoma or neuroblastoma, VMA, metabolic product of NE or E increases accordingly because tissue of tumor also produces NE or E. Therefore, it is very significant to measure VMA content in urine for diagnosis.

The somas of adrenergic neurons in the central nervous system concentrate upon medulla oblongata and pons varolii, and their pathways have been identified. However, it is not sure that NE in the center is inhibitory or excitatory neurotransmitter, which may be related with position. It is difficult to express the physiological effect of NE with the simple terms like excite or inhibit. Some animal experiments show that NE can cause animal drowsiness, hypothermy and feeding behavior. Some people believe that a fall of NE in the brain can induce ademosyne, conversely, overdose of NE can induce mania. In short, NE in the brain is probably associated closely with body temperature, feeding behavior, analgesia, regulation of cardiovascular system and mental status

3. Dopamine (DA).

In the process of the biological synthesis of catecholamines transmitters, dopamine is the precursor of NE. Dopamine exists in any tissue of the body where NE exists. Because there is high concentration of dopamine in some portions of the center and its distribution is not parallel to that of NE, it is also considered as an independent neurotransmitter generally.

Dopamine in the brain has various functions including enhancing body movement, enhancing the endocrine of pituitary gland and regulating psycho-activity.

$$CH_3O-\langle\bigcirc\rangle-CH_2-COOH$$
$$HO-$$

**3-methoxyl-4-hydroxyphenylacetic acid**

The vesicles of the dopaminergic nerve terminal are the storage sites of dopamine and they are different from those vesicles storing NE. The former have no dopamine-β-hydroxylase, therefore, it can't convert dopamine to NE. In addition, only if the substance has the β-hydroxyl structure, can it store in vesicles of the noradrenergic fibers, but no β-hydroxyl exists in the structure of dopamine. Storage, release and degradation of dopamine are all very similar to those of NE, but its renewal velocity is faster than that of NE. 3-methoxyl-4-hydroxyphenylacetic acid (homovanillic acid, HVA) is the main metabolic product of dopamine in the brain.

### 2.4.3 5-hydroxytryptamine

5-hydroxytryptamine (5-HT) is also referred to as serotonin which was discovered initially in serum. There are 5-hydroxytryptaminergic neurons in the central nervous system. However, no 5-hydroxytryptaminergic neuron is discovered in the peripheral nervous system up to now.

5-HT can't permeate blood-brain barrier, so 5-HT in the center is synthesized in the brain and it has different source from peripheral 5-hydroxytryptamine. It is identified by histochemical method that 5-hydroxytryptaminergic neural somas are mainly distributed in rapheal nuclei group of midbrain stem and their terminals are distributed widely in the brain and spinal cord. The precursor of 5-HT is tryptophane which is converted to 5-HT by two enzymatic reactions: hydroxylation and decarboxylation. The process is similar to that of synthesis of catecholamines to some degree.

Similar to tyrosine hydroxylase, tryptophan hydroxylase also need $O_2$, $Fe^{2+}$ and tetrahydrobiopterin as coenzyme. But it has less concentration in brain and lower activity, so it is a rate-limiting enzyme for biological synthesis of 5-HT. In addition, the concentration of 5-HT in brain may affect the activity of tryptophan hydorxylase and plays its self-regulation by feedback. Free tryptophane concentration in serum can also affect the synthesis of 5-HT in brain. When free tryptophane in serum increases (for example, inject tryptophame into rat's abdominal cavity), tryptophane entering the brain increases, which can accelerate the synthesis of 5-HT.

Similar to catecholamines, 5-HT released into synaptic cleft is reuptaken premodinantly by presynaptic nerve terminal, and then one part is restored in the vesicles and one part is oxidized by monoamine oxidase (MAO) in mitochondrial membrane.

5-hydroxytryptamine                    5-hydroxyindolacetic acid

This is the main mode of degradation of 5-HT. 5-hydroxyindolacetic acid is inactive.

By detecting the functions of 5-HT to various neurons, it is discovered that 5-HT can excite the majority of sympathetic preganglionic neurons while it can inhibit parasympathetic preganglionic neurons. 5-HT content in brain decreases apparently when animal rapheal nuclei are destroyed and the synthesis of 5-HT is blocked with drugs, which can make animal suffer sleep disorders and its pain threshold fall down, at the same time the analgesic effect of morphine decreases or disappears. Stimulating rat's rapheal nuclei with electricity can cause its temperature to rise and then accelerate renewal of 5-HT. These phenomena reveal that sleeping, analgesia and temperature regulation are all related with 5-HT in brain. Furthermore, it is reported that 5-HT can alter hypophyseal endocrine function. In addition, someone suggests that hallucinations of the patient suffering psychiosis results from destruction of 5-hydroxytraminergic neuron. It is thus clear that psychoactivity is also related with 5-HT in some degree.

### 2.4.4 Amine acid and oligopeptide

Amine acids are present everywhere in the brain. It is considered previously that they were only the materials of synthesis of proteins or the metabolic products of proteins. For the past few years, people notice that some amine acids play a role of transmitter in synaptic transmission of the center. Furthermore, neutral amine acids such as γ-aminobutyric acid, glycine, β-alamine and so on, all appear inhibitory to the central neurons while acidic amino acids like glutamic acid and aspartic acid appear excitatory.

Some micromolecular peptides also have the functions of neurotransmitter. Enkephalin discovered in 1975 is an oligopeptide composed of 5 amino acid residues. Enkephalin separated from pig brain can be divided into 2 types: i) Met-enkephalin: H-Tyr-Gly-Gly-Phe-Met-OH, and ii) Leu−enkephalin: H-Tyr-Gly-Gly-Phe-Leu-OH, both of which are the peptides synthesized by brain cells. They are with similar functions to morphine and hence are called enkephalin. It is well-known that morphine must be bind to morphine receptor firstly and then plays its role of analgesia and euphoria. Morphine is exogenous while enkephalin is endogenous. Besides it, there is another peptide called endorphine in brain, which can bind to morphine receptor and produce morphine-like effects. It is still not sure if these peptides are real neurotransmitters, but it is very significant for elucidating brain's function, especially algesia principle to study their effects.

### 2.4.5 Nitric oxide

There is breakthrough in the field of intracellular information transmission, which is initiated from the important experimental results obtained from rabbit aorta specimens by Furchgott etc, in 1980. They observed, with the endothelium of the specimen being moved, Ach lost its role of relaxing smooth muscle of the specimen. However, its relaxation of smooth muscle could be recovered as long as the specimen without endothelium contacted with arterial stripe specimen with endothelium. Their conclusion was that Ach played its role of relaxation by inducing vascular endothelial cells to release a substance which is called relaxing factor from vascular endothelium by them. The substance was very easy to be decomposed, thus it took several years to identify it as nitric oxide for three research teams led by Furchgott, Ignarro and Murad respectively. The three leaders were endowed with Nobel Prize in 1998 for it.

Nitric oxide is a kind of gas, only slightly soluble in water. The academic circles were shocked by the discovery of the gas messenger. Nitric oxide is converted from L-arginine in the presence of nitric oxide synthetase and affects target material not by the transduction of receptor but by diffusing directly through cell membrane. It has many target materials. Among them, guanosin monophospate cyclase is the representataive one which can foster GTP to form cGMP. Once guanosin monophospate cyclase is activated by nitric oxide, it can decrease the concentration of intracellular $Ca^{2+}$ by signal transduction to cause relaxation of smooth muscle.

As a messenger, nitric oxide produced under neurologic type of nitric oxide synthetase is involved in many functions of the central nervous system such as synaptic plasticity, memory, vision and smell and so on. It is the main messenger of non-adrenergic and non-cholinergic neurons in the peripheral nervous system.

### 2.4.6 Receptor

The concept of receptor (R) is proposed firstly in 1905 by Langley, an English pharmacologist. He observed that curare could not repress directly muscle contraction by electric stimulation but could antagonize muscle contraction caused by nicotine. Hence he imagined that both of the agents just bond to intracellular definite non-nervous and non-muscular substances. The difference between the combinations among nicotine and the definite substance produced further biological effect, muscle contraction while the combination between curare and the definite substance produced antagonism of muscle contraction. He named the definite substance as receptive substance. As a matter of fact, the concept of receptive substance (receptor) proposed by Langrey at that time is still in use now, in that he pointed out two important functions of a receptor, recognizing special substance and producing biological effect.

Nicotine and curare can affect selectively specific molecules in the body and produce biological effects. They are called bioactive substances that can be divided into two types according their sources: endogenous bioactive substances, inherent in vivo, such as transmitters, hormones, nutrition factors and so on; exogenous bioactive substances, present in vitro, for example, some drugs like nicotine, curare and poisons. Receptors are the biological macromolecules in the membrane and cytoplasm or nuclei which can recognize and bind with the special bioactive substances to produce biological effects. The bioactive substances with the character of binding selectively to receptors are called ligands. Among them, those substances which can bind to receptors to produce biological effects are called agonists while those substances which can bind to receptors to antagonize the biological effects produced by agonists are called antagonists. Those substances which have agonism and antagonism are called partial agonists. The receptors in the neuron are called neuroceptors.

Since Numa and his colleagues purified and determined successfully the primary structure of AchR in 1983 and established the first river of studying the structure and functions of receptor molecules, the primary structures of many receptors and their subunits have been identified, which makes it possible for us to classify the receptors according to their molecular structure characters and analyze their activity mechanisms.

Generally, receptor should have the following four characteristics according to biochemical identification: i) *Saturability*. The quantity of receptor molecules is limited, so the dose effect curve of binding ligand with receptor is also limited and their specific bindings appear as high affinity and low capacity. There are nonspecific bindings between cell and ligand, and they appear as low affinity and high capacity amd no saturability. ii) *Specificity*. A specified receptor only binds to specific ligand to produce biological effect. Therefore, people often study the characters of receptor by comparisons of a series of biological effects of ligands, and classify them according to their functions. iii) *Reversibility*. The combination of ligand and receptor should be reversible in the physiological activities. The dissociation constant of the ligand-receptor complex is different; however, the dissociated ligand should be not its metabolic product but primal ligand.

Receptors have two main functions: recognizing selectively transmitter and activating effector. Thus, on the one hand, according to their transmitters, receptors can be classified into Ach-receptor, Glu-receptor, GABA-receptor, Gly-receptor, 5-HT-receptor, Histamine-receptor, Ad receptor recognizing NA and A, and receptors recognizing various of neuropeptides. On the other hand, the primary structures of many receptors have been elucidated, so according to their molecular mechanisms of acting on effectors, they can be also divided into ionic channel type and metabolic regulating type, which regulate the activities of ionic channels directly or indirectly. Receptor molecules of ionic channel type have both receptor sites of recognizing transmitter and ionic channels, so their activity speed are very fast. This type of receptor includes nAch-receptor, $GABA_A$-receptor, $5-HT_3$-receptor and iGlu-receptor. Receptor molecules of metabolic regulating type contain only receptor sites of recognizing transmitter but no micropores permitting ions pass through. Their function coupling with effector is realized by guanine-nucleotide-binding protein, G-protein. This type contains two gene families: mAch-receptor, $GABA_B$-receptor, mGlu-receptor, $5-HT_{1,2,4}$-receptor, and various of receptors of neuropeptides and so on. In addition, there are some receptors with C-terminal containing kinase or not, which are activated by nutrition factors, hormones and some neuropeptides.

## 2.5 Transmembrane Signal Transduction

Briefly speaking, signal transduction is the stimulating factors of external environment or intercellular signaling molecules in vivo, the first messengers such as hormones, neurotransmitters or ligands bind to receptors on the surface of cells or intracellular receptors, and intracellular second messengers form through transmembrane signal conversion, and then information is transferred by a cascade of responses to the specified sites of effectors to produce physiological effects or induce gene expression. The classical transduction pathway is as follows briefly:

External or internal stimulators → ligands → receptors → transmembrane → the second messengers → a cascade of phosphorylation signaling transmission → functional regulation of the body.

Hydrophilic neurotransmitters can not only pass generally into cells but can bind to receptors in the membrane and transfer as well information to receptors. Ionic channel type of receptors receives signals and responses directly by the effectors themselves. While metabolic regulating type of receptors must transfer information to the inside of the cell by a series of transmission and then transfer to ionic channels or effectors of metabolic pattern. The process of information transferring from receptors to ionic channels or intracellular effectors of metabolic pattern is called signal transmembrane transduction. In recent 20 years, the researches in this field develop rapidly since the second messenger hypothesis about hormone action was proposed and G-protein was discovered. The hypothesis proposed in the research of the action mechanism of hormones and the novel discovery further push the research of the action mechanisms of neurotransmitters and other bioactive substances.

### 2.5.1 Transducin

In 1958, Sutherland discovered that glycogenolysis of the hepatocytes spurred by glucagons and adrenalin is realized by cyclic adenosine monophosphate (cAMP), a novel substance discovered by him. Both of hormones bond to their own receptors to activate adenylate cyclase (ACase), the latter catalized ATP to produce cAMP. He also discovered that cAMP was essential for the activation of cAMP-dependent protein kinase (PAK) and then activated PAK activated phosphoesterase to further catalize decomposition of liver glycogen. Sutherland proposed the second messenger theory about hormone action in 1965 based on the results, that was, not entering cell, hormones brought information to specified receptors on the membrane as the first messengers, then receptors activated ACase in the membrane to convert intracellular ATP to cAMP. Whereafter, cAMP as the second messenger transferred information to effectors to respond. The hypothesis led to the discovery of guanosine nucleotide binding protein (G protein).

In the experiment of preparation of lipocyte debris, Rodbell demonstrated that several hormones like glucagons, adrenalin and ACTH and so on all catalized ATP by ACase to produce cAMP, the common second messenger. In 1970, he also discovered that GTP was essential in the conversion of ATP to cAMP by the system of hormone, receptor and ACase. The experiment still showed that GTP neither was decomposed nor bond to receptor and ACase in the reaction. In 1987 Gilman isolated and purified successfully the transduction from membrane specimen, which could both bind to GTP and connect with receptor and ACase, called as GTP-binding protein. This is the signal transmembrane transduction pathway proposed firstly. For it, Sutherland obtained Nobel Prize in 1971 and Gilman and Rodbell obtained Nobel Prize in 1994.

G-protein is a group of soluble intramembrane proteins with molecular weight of 100 000 which are involved in signal transmembrane transduction of neuron. According to its function it can be divided into four species: Gs, Gi, Go and Gt. Gs can activate ACase and it can be activated by Cholera Toxin (CTX) directly and open some $Ca^{2+}$ channels. Gi can inhibit the activity of ACase and it is sensitive to pertussis toxin (PTX). In the presence of PTX, Gs can not be activated by a receptor. It can open some $K^+$ channels to produce inhibitory response. At the beginning Go indicated those G-proteins which didn't affect ACase, but now they only represent those G-proteins which are sensitive to PTX and can activate PKC, while those G-proteins which are not sensitive to PTX but can activate PKC are called Gpc. Go and Gpc are abundant in brain tissues. They can open some $K^+$ channels and also inhibit T-type and N-type voltage-gated $Ca^{2+}$ channels. Gt is a kind of G-protein coupling rhodophane in photoreceptor with the enzyme cGMP-PDE in primary effectors, which can close $Na^+$ channels.

At the resting statement, receptor is in activated state and has high affinity with ligand, while G-GDP is inactivated. When the ligands (A) bind to receptors (R) to form A-R complex, the latter has high affinity with G-GDP to form A-R-G-GDP complex. Following the formation of the complex, GDP is replaced by GTP in cytoplasm to form activated G-GTP. During this process, G-protein converts from inactivation to activation. Once GTP substitution is finished, the complex is decomposed into three components: A-R, α-GTP and βγ. Among them, α-GTP can hydrolyze GTP to form GDP, thus at the same time of activating effectors, α-GTP loses its phosphoric acid molecules to become α-GDP. α-GDP has high affinity with βγ subunit and they combine together to form G-GDP again, which indicates it returns to the inactivated form at the resting statement. On the other hand, the combination of A-R and G-GDP lowers the affinity of receptor with ligand, which makes R separate itself from A-R, so R also returns to the activated form at the resting statement. While effectors activated by G-protein become inactivated.

### 2.5.2 The second messenger

There are nearly 100 kinds of transmitters and endogenous bioactive substances as the first messenger while their receptors are twice or three times of them. The majority of them are the metabolic regulating receptors which depend on G-protein's coupling with effector in some fashion.

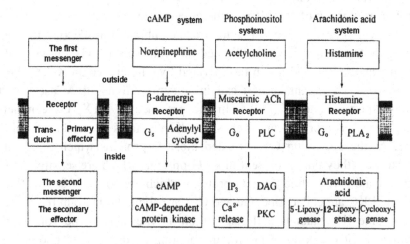

Fig. 2.7 Schematic diagram of transmembrane signal transduction pathway

The second messengers produced by hydrolysis of membrane phospholipids include inositol triphosphate (IP$_3$), diacyl glycerol (DG) and aracidonic acid and so on. Transmembrane signal transduction is divided accordingly into cAMP system, IP₃ system and aracidonic acid system. In the recent years, NO produced by the action of the enzyme nitric oxide synthetase is also discovered as a second messenger. Maybe CO is another one.

The common transduction pathway of the second messenger is shown in Figure 2.7. The activities of the three systems can be divided into 3 steps: a) the first messenger outside the cell; b) receptor in the membrane, transducin binding to the inner wall of the membrane and primary effector (enzyme) in the membrane; c) intracellular second messenger and secondary effector. Different transmitters act on their own receptors respectively to activate their own primary effectors by the transduction of some G-protein, and conduct information to the second messenger to activate the secondary effector.

Most of secondary effectors are some kinases. One kind of kinases often phosphorylates different target proteins, which can cause signal to be magnifid and cross each other, finally make ions channels open or close, or induce relevant metabolic changes. The quantity of G-proteins is far larger than that of receptors, thus one receptor binding with transmitter can activate multiple molecules of G-protein, causing signal to be magnified.

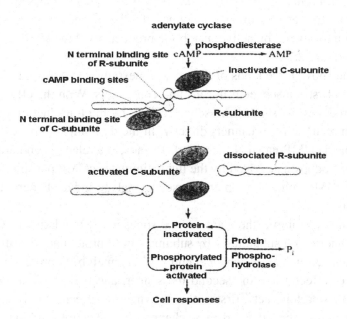

Fig 2.8 Molecular mechanism of cAMP signal transduction pathway

cAMP-dependent protein kinase that is the secondary effector in cAMP system is composed of 2 regulatory subunites (R-subunites) and 2 catalytic subunites (C-subunites). The two identical R- subunits have four regions: a) N terminal region is the binding site of companion subunites; b) the following region combining with C-subunite inhibits its enzymatic activity; c) two identical regions bind with cAMP. The molecule of PKA can be written as $R_2C_2$. ATP is converted into cAMP by the action of the enzyme ACase: $R_2C_2 + 4$ cAMP $= 2$ $(R \cdot 2cAMP) + 2$ C, and then C can further phosphorylate effector-protein (as shown in Figure 2.8).

As shown in Figure 2.7, in phosphoinositide system, phosphoinositide is firstly hydrolyzed by PLC into $IP_3$ and DG. Hydrophobic DG is kept in the membrane. PKC is inactive in the cytoplasm. When DG is produced, PKC is activated due to binding with DG in the membrane, and then activated PKC phosphorylates its substrates in the membrane or in the cytoplasm. $IP_3$ is another second messenger. Some receptors can cause $IP_3$ to be produced. It can open $Ca^{2+}$ channels in sarcoplasmic reticulum $Ca^{2+}$ store to increase intracellular $Ca^{2+}$ concentration, and then to arouse various of cell responses.

In the arachidonic acid system, arachidonic acid is released from the membrane by the action of the enzyme of $PLA_2$, and then is converted immediately into several bioactive metabolic products by three kinds of enzymes as shown in Figure 2.7.

Besides the above three kinds of the second messenger systems, there is also a cGMP system firstly discovered in rods and cones cells. With the effect of light, rhodopsin produces the second messenger cGMP by the transduction of Gt, and the latter can regulate $Na^+$ channels directly. In the dark, higher concentration of cGMP can open cGMP-gated $Na^+$ channels to cause the relative depolarization of visual cells. Rhodopsin activated by the light stimulates cGMP phosphodiesterase to lower the cGMP concentration and close channels to induce hyperpolarization of visual cells.

In the point view above, there are several styles about regulation of G-protein on ionic channels: a) $\alpha$ subunite or $\beta\gamma$ subunites in G-protein acts/act directly on the ionic channels such as, $K^+$ channel and $Ca^{2+}$ channel; b) G-protein acts firstly the enzyme of effector and the second messenger, and then the latter acts ionic channels; c) G-protein acts firstly the enzyme of effector and the second messenger, and then the latter acts ionic channels by the actions of kinases.

As indicated by some data recently, with the effects of exogenous factors such as transmitters, modulators, nutrition factors and hormones, membrane receptors and nuclear receptors of neurons transfer signals to nuclei by the transduction of G-proteins and phosphorylation of intracellular effectors to induce the changes of gene expression which are associated closely with the mechanisms of synaptic plasticity, learning and memory. Among them, there are many researches on direct early genes and delayed early genes.

Zhuan Zhou, an investigator of Shanghai institutes for biological science of Chinese Academy of Sciences discovered with and his student, Chen Zhang in the experiment of rat sense dorsal root ganglia that neurotransmitter was released to the next neuron not only by the command of $Ca^{2+}$ but also by voltage impulse (Zhang et al., 2002). The neural signal conduction mechanism induced only by the neural impulse was a unexpected novel discovery, causing a series of new projects in the neural science research are proposed.

How is the neural signal transferred from one neuron to another? It is a focus of neural science research. Currently the dominant view in academic field is: the first neuron in excitatory state produces electric impulse (action potential), then extracellular $Ca^{2+}$ flow into the cell and induce the cell to secret some bioactive molecules (neurotransmitters), the latter diffuse to the surface (membrane) of the next neuron. When membrane receptors bind with neurotransmitters, the second neuron produces electric impulse. In a similar way, neural signals pass on as a cascade until brain senior functions like learning and memory occur finally. This is the neurotransmitter releasing and neural signal transduction mechanism commanded by $Ca^{2+}$. Another neural signal transduction mediated merely by neural electric impulse not by $Ca^{2+}$, that is the discovery of Zhuan Zhou and Chen Zhang, may take an important effect on neural signal transduction and information integration. Zhuan Zhou revealed that there was only one neurotransmitter secretion pathway in some neural cells, for example the adrenal chromaffin cells. In addition, the signal transduction mechanism of non-$Ca^{2+}$ voltage-secretion coupling had also been an important project to be further solved in the neural science research.

## 2.6 Resting Membrane Potential

Bioelectricity is discovered firstly in the research of neural and muscular activities. The so-called ballony experiment undertaken in the end of 18 century by Galvani, an Italian doctor and physiologist, is the beginning of bioelectricity research. When he hanged the specimen of frog lower limb with cuprum hook to the iron baluster on the ballony to observe effects of lightening on nerves and muscles, he discovered unexpectedly that muscles contracted when frog limb touched iron baluster with the effect of winds. Galvani thought it was a proof of bioelectricity.

I. Nobeli, a physicist improved current meter in 1827 and used it to record the current flow between muscular transection and intact longitudinal surface, with negative charge in the trauma site and positive charge in intact portion. This was the first direct measurement of bioelectricity (injury potential). Du Bois Reymond, a German physiologist, on the one hand, improved and designed many equipments used to study bioelectric phenomena such as key set, non-polarizable electrode, induction coil and more sensitive current meters. On the other hand, he carried out extensive and deep-going researches on bioelectricity. For example, he found bioelectricity in cerebral cortex, gland, skin and eyeball. And especially in 1849, he recorded injury potential in nerve trunk and its negative electricity changes in activities, which were neural resting potential and action potential. Based on it, he proposed firstly hypothesis about bioelectricity generating mechanism, the polarized molecule hypothesis. He conceived that the surface of nerve or muscle was composed of magnet-like polarized molecules lining up in order. There were a positive charge zone in the center of each molecule and negative charge zones in its two sides. Positive charge assembled in the longitudinal surface of nerve and muscle while negative charge assembled in their transactions, thus a potential difference occurred between them. When nerve and muscle excited, their polarized molecules lining up in order became in disordered state and the potential difference between the surface and the inside disappeared.

With the progress of electrochemistry, Bernstein, a student of Du Bois Reymond developed bioelectric existence hypothesis which is still considered fairly correct now, and pushed the membrane theory of bioelectric research. The theory presumed that electric potential existed in the two sides of neural and muscular membrane. In resting state, cell membrane permitted $K^+$ but not multivalent cations or anions to penetrate. The resting potential occurred due to the selective permeability of membrane to $K^+$ and the $K^+$ concentration difference between the outside and inside of membrane. When nerve excited, the selective permeability of membrane to $K^+$ disappeared, causing electricity difference between two sides of membrane to disappear transiently, so action potential formed.

In 1920s, Gasser and Erlanger introduced modern electronic equipments like cathode ray oscilloscope to neuro-physiological research, which advanced bioelectric research to develop rapidly. They obtained the Nobel Prize in 1944 together because of their analysis of electric activities of nerve fibers. Young had reported that inkfish nerve trunk had giant axon with 500μm diameter. British physiologists, A.L. Hodgkin and Huxley realized intracellular record of resting potential and action potential firstly by inserting glass capillary electrode longitudinally from the cut into the giant axon. They proposed sodium theory about action potential based on exact quantitative analysis of the two kinds of potential and confirmed and developed Bernstein's membrane theory about resting potential. After that, they further utilized voltage-clamp techniques to record action current in the inkfish giant axon and confirmed the current could be divided into two components: $Na^+$ current and $K^+$ current. Based on it, they proposed double ion channels pattern again and guided people to study molecular biology of ion channels.

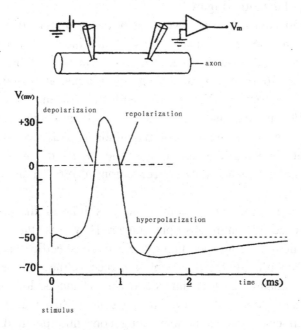

Fig. 2.9 Potential difference between two sides of the membrane

With the push of microelectrode recording techniques, neural cellular physiological research stepped into a new developing period. Eccles began his electrophysiologic study on the spinal neurons in vivo and their axons by utilizing glass microelectrodes and discovered the excitatory and inhibitory postsynaptic potentials. Because of their dedication to neural physiology, A.L. Hodgkin, Huxley and Eccles shared the physiology or medicine Nobel Prize in 1963. Meanwhile Katz began to study the neuromuscular junction synapse using microelectrode techniques and obtained the Nobel Prize in 1970 for it. Based on the explosion of nervous system researches, a comprehensive subject, the neurobiology and the neuroscience formed in 1960s.

Various of transient electric changes occurring in their activities like receptor potential, synaptic potential and action potential are all based on resting potential, so it is the most fundamental electric phenomenon in the excitable cells such as neurons and muscle cells. In order to describe conveniently, the state of potential difference between two sides of the membrane is usually referred to as polarization, the rising of absolute value of resting potential is referred to as hyperpolarization while the falling of absolute value of resting potential is referred to as depolarization (Figure 2.9).

The potential difference between two sides of the membrane of excitable cells like neurons and muscle cells is about 70mV, which indicates that negative and positive ion clouds are dispersed respectively on the inside and the outside of the membrane surface. No ion has equal concentration in neural cytoplasm to that in extracellular fluid, especially $K^+$, $Na^+$, $Cl^-$, with the concentration reaching the level of mmol/L in external or internal fluid and the transmembrane concentration difference, of one order of magnitude, called as constant ions. $Na^+$ and $Cl^-$ gather outside while $K^+$ gather inside. There are some big organic anions ($A^-$) only being in the cells and their concentrations also reach about the level of mmol/L.

Ion channels are some big protein molecules inlayed dispersedly in the membrane composed by continuous lipid bilayer. They cross the membrane and contain hydrophilic micropores permmiting selectively specific ions pass through the membrane. According to the permeable ion species, they can be classified to $K^+$ channels, $Na^+$ channels, $Cl^-$ channels and $Ca^{2+}$ channels. Ion channels have two states at least: opening state and closing state. When the channels open, specific ions will cross the membrane along concentration gradient. Resting potential forms just because specific ions pass through the so-called resting ion channels continuously open in the resting state along the concentration gradient.

Cell membrane of neuron plays a role of electric resistance on electric current. This electric resistance is called membrane resistance. Besides as electric resistance, cell membrane has also the function of capacitor, which is called membrane capacitance. Figure 2.10 shows how to detect the changes of membrane potential. Whether switching on or off the current toward cell membrane both must go firstly through the charging or discharging the capacitor respectively, and then make the electrotonic potential rise or fall exponentially. When t = 0, inject current into cell membrane, and the potential at any time is recorded as $V_t$, then:

$$V_t = V_\infty (1 - e^{-t/\tau}) \qquad (2.1)$$

$V_\infty$ in the formula is a constant value after the charging to the capacitor is finished. When $t = \tau$, the formula (2.1) can be written briefly as:

$$V_t = V_\infty (1 - \frac{1}{e}) = 0.63 V_\infty \qquad (2.2)$$

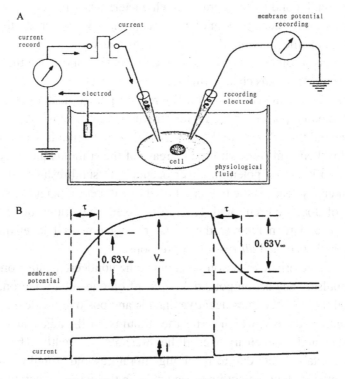

Fig. 2.10 Membrane potential of neuron

That is, $\tau$ is duration time of electrotonic voltage rising to $0.63V_\infty$. Thus, $\tau$ is the time constant value representing the changing velocity of membrane's electrotonic potential and it is equal to the product of multiplication of membrane capacitance (C) and membrane resistance (R): $\tau = RC$.

Among them, R can be figured out by electric current value in experiment dividing $V_\infty$. In this way, membrane resistance and membrane capacitance can be measured respectively. In order to compare the electric characteristics of various excitable cells, it is necessary to further figure out specific membrane resistance and specific membrane capacity per membrane unit area. Membrane capacitance originates from lipid bilayer in the membrane while membrane resistance comes from ion channels in the membrane.

## 2.7 Action Potential

Excitability and conductivity are two characteristics of neuron. When some portion of neuron receives stimulant, excitation will occur in this part and propagate along the neuron. If the conditions are right, it can transfer to the related neurons or other cells by synaptic transmission and make the activities or states of the target organs change finally.

When cell is stimulated, based on the resting potential, the potentials in two sides of membrane perform once rapid retroversion and recovery, which is called action potential (as shown in Figure 2.9). For the stimuli with subthreshold intensity, local current rises with the increase of the stimulus intensity. However, different from it, action potential never occurs with subthreshold stimulus. Once stimulus intensity reaches the threshold or above it, action potential will occur on the basis of local current and reach the fixed maximum quickly by self-regeneration, and then recover the initial resting potential level quickly. This responsive style is called *all-or-nothing* response.

Another characteristic of action potential is the nondecremental conduction. As electric impulse, once action potential is set off on one site of neuron, membrane potential on this site becomes negative outside and positive inside explosively, so the site becomes battery, which forms the stimulus for the adjacent site in resting potential state and its intensity exceed the threshold apparently. The adjacent site enters the excitable state due to receiving suprathreshold stimulus and produces action potential with all-or-nothing principles. In this way, the action potential on one site of neuron will induce the adjacent site to produce action potential orderly, and it can conduct toward the distal sites with no decrement because of its all-or-nothing response. However, the amplitude of action potential in axon terminal becomes lower because its diameter becomes thinner.

Once action potential is set off on some site of neuron's membrane, the excitability on this site will produce a series of changes. In the overshooting phase of action potential, any stimulus with any intensity can't elicit action potential on the site again. This phase is called absolute refractory period. In the following period, only suprethreshold stimulus is strong enough to elicit action potential on the site but its amplitude is lower. This phase is called relative refractory period. For example, if the duration of action potential is 1 ms, then the summation of the two phase should be shorter than 1 ms, otherwise the next action potential will overlap the former.

The main functions of action potential are as follows:

(1) conducting electric signals rapidly and in long distance;

(2) regulating release of neurotransmitters, contraction of muscles and secretion of glands and so on.

Action potentials of several excitable cells have the common characteristics, but there are differences in their amplitudes, shapes and ionic bases to a certain extent.

The discovery of the overshooting phase of action potential denied the explanation about action potential with classical membrane theory proposed by Bernstein, that is, the view of contributing occurrence of action potential to transient disappearance of selective ion permeability of the membrane is unacceptable. In the 1950s, A.L. Hodgkin, etc carried out precise experiments on the axons of inkfish, which showed that $K^+$, $Na^+$ and $Cl^-$ permeability coefficients of axolemma in rest state were: $P_K : P_{Na} : P_{Cl} = 1: 0.04 : 0.45$ while they became in the peak of action potential: $P_K : P_{Na} : P_{Cl} = 1: 20 : 0.45$. Apparently, the ratio of $P_K$ to $P_{Cl}$ didn't change, but the ratio of $P_K$ to $P_{Na}$ increased notably three orders of magnitude. According to the data of these experiments and others, they proposed the sodium ion theory, that was to say, the occurrence of action potential was up to the transient rise of $Na^+$ permeability of cell membrane, in other words, because cell membrane changes abruptly from the resting state based mainly on $K^+$ equilibrium potential to the active state based mainly on $Na^+$ equilibrium potential.

The changes of sodium conductance and potassium conductance in action potential process are shown in Figure 2.17. Increased $Na^+$ permeability causes membrane potential to approach $Na^+$ equilibrium potential, soon it falls down rapidly. Following it, $K^+$ permeability raises continuously, which makes membrane potential recover to the proximal level of $K^+$ equilibrium potential in resting state. Sodium conductance decreases by two different ways: fixing membrane potential level to -9mV sodium conductance occurs and then making membrane potential recover to the resting level in a short time (0.63 ms in this example) as shown in Figure 2.11 (left dashed line), sodium conductance disappears rapidly to follow it (as shown by the dashed line). At this time if makes membrane potential depolarize again, sodium conductance may still occur. The other way is, if membrane potential jumps to -9mV and lasts in the level, sodium conductance will become small gradually until it disappears. At this time if makes membrane potential depolarize again, no sodium conductance occurs. This phenomenon is called deactivation of sodium current. Only if membrane potential have recovered for several milliseconds, the second stimulus becomes effective. The process from the deactivation to recovery of activation is called reactivation. Different from sodium conductance, potassium conductance can still maintain the highest level after depolarization for above 6ms (Figure 2.11, right dashed line). It disappears in the curve opposite to that of emergence when membrane potential recovers the primary level. Potassium current deactivates very slowly, thus it has been considered that it has no process of deactivation.

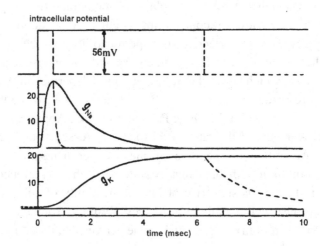

Fig. 2.11 Sodium and potassium conductance changes when depolarization of giant axon of inkfish reaches 56mV (From Hodgkin, A.L, 1965)

The action current of giant axon of inkfish is composed of $Na^+$ inward flow and delayed $K^+$ outward flow. The two ion currents are produced when two kinds of ions pass through their own voltage-gated channels to cross membrane. After progress was obtained in the research of giant axon of inkfish, the researches of action current analyzed by voltage clamp technique expanded quickly to other excitable cell membranes. Results indicated that two voltage-gated channels existed in all excitable cell membranes that had been studied. In addition, voltage-gated $Ca^{2+}$ channel was also discovered. Voltage-gated $Cl^-$ channel was discovered in some neurons. Four voltage-gated channels have different subtypes. $Na^+$ channel has two subtypes at least: neurological type discovered in neurons and muscular type discovered in muscles; $Ca^{2+}$ channel has four subtypes (T, N, L and P type); $K^+$ channel has four types (delayed rectifier $K^+$ channel, fast transient $K^+$ channel or A channel, anomalous rectification $K^+$ channel and $Ca^{2+}$ activated $K^+$ channel). Cells producing action potential are called excitable cells, but the amplitudes and duration of action potential produced by different types of excitable cells are different because the type and the quantity of ion channels involving in formation of action potential are different.

Formation mechanism of action potential in axolemma and multiple kinds of neuron membrane is simple. Its ascending phase is formed by $Na^+$ current and it is called $Na^+$ dependent action potential. This kind of action potential has relatively big amplitude and short duration and rapid conduction velocity. Whether $K^+$ current involved in the descending phase of axon action potential or not is up to the kinds of animals. For example, action potential of nodal membrane of myelinated nerve fibers in rabbits is different from that of giant axon in inkfish. The former has no component of $K^+$ current. As for the axolemma of ranvier node of frog, and especially the axolemma of excitable node of invertebral prawn, the action potential has the component of $K^+$ current, but it is not only very small and its threshold of activation is relatively high, thus it has no apparent effect on shortening duration of action potential.

Different types of neurons and even different sites of one neuron have different excitability. For example, there are difference of excitability among axon hillock, axon terminals and dendrites. Difference of excitability is determined by the kinds of voltage-gated channels in excitation membrane and their density. The action potentials of the cell body and axon terminals in some neurons are co-formed by $Na^+$ current and $Ca^{2+}$ current and their durations are relatively long. It is also discovered in some neurons' dendrites that action potential with low amplitude and long duration is formed by $Ca^{2+}$ current.

Once action potential (nerve impulse) is elicited at one point in the membrane of neuron (except in the thin dendrites), it travels over the rest portion with constant velocity and amplitude. When action potential occurs explosively, membrane potential at one point which can make local current develop to action potential is called threshold potential. Depolarization from resting membrane potential to threshold potential is usually called critical depolarization. The critical depolarization value is about 32mV. Generally speaking, threshold value is the difference of resting membrane and threshold potential, that is, the threshold value is in direct proportion to the critical depolarization and it will change with relative changes of the two potentials. Threshold potential is the membrane potential at the point where $Na^+$ permeability caused by depolarization increases to make $Na^+$ inward flow volume just equal to $K^+$ outward flow volume. Local current occurs because sodium conductance ($g_{Na}$) begins to rise, but potassium conductance ($g_K$) is still bigger than $g_{Na}$ before depolarization reaches threshold potential level. Because $g_K$ is the factor causing membrane change toward hyperpolarization, membrane potential change ends in local current. When depolarization reaches threshold potential level, $g_{Na}$ is equal to or bigger than $g_K$, so $g_{Na}$ is the factor causing depolarization. With depolarization developing, $g_{Na}$ will further rise while a rise of $g_{Na}$ will promote depolarization all the more. This self-regeneration develops until $Na^+$ equilibrium potential occurs. This process is called activation of $Na^+$ current. When $Na^+$ current reaches the peak, even though membrane potential is clamped in stable level, it becomes small rapidly until resting level. This process is called deactivation of $Na^+$ current. As Figure 2.17 shows, it seems undergoing mutation from local current to action potential, but the changes of membrane sodium conductance and potassium conductance are continuous. If $g_{Na}=g_K$ is taken as a border, one side is negative local current and the other side is self-regenerative action potential.

Local current is the weak electric change (smaller depolarization or hyperpolarization) produced between two sides of membrane when cell receives subthreshlod stimulus. That is to say, local current is potential change before depolarization reaches threshold potential when cell is stimulated. Subthreshold stimulus makes one part of membrane channels open to produce a little depolarization or hyperpolarization, so local current may be depolarization potential or hyperpolarization potential. Local currents in different cells are formed by different ion flows and ions flow along concentration gradient without energy consumption. Local current has the following characteristics:

(1) *Ranking*. The amplitude of local current is in positive correlation with stimulus intensity but is not related with ion concentration difference between

two sides. It is not *all-or-nothing* because just parts of ion channels open and the ion equilibrium potential can't occur.

(2) *Summation*. Local current has no refractory period. One subthreshold stimulus can not elicit any action potential but one local reaction, however, multiple local reactions elicited by multiple subthreshold stimuli may cause membrane depolarize to threshold potential by temporal summation or spatial summation and then action potential breaks out.

(3) *Electrotonic spread*. Local current does not propagate to distal sites as action potential does, but it can affect adjacent membrane potential in the way of electrotonic spread. It attenuates with propagation distance increasing.

Figure 2.12 shows the formation of action potential. When membrane potential surpasses threshold potential, a great quantity of $Na^+$ channels open, which makes membrane potential reach critical membrane potential level to elicit action potential. Effective stimulus itself can make membrane depolarize partly. When depolarization reaches threshold potential level, its regenerative circulation mechanism makes a great quantity of $Na^+$ channels open through positive feedback.

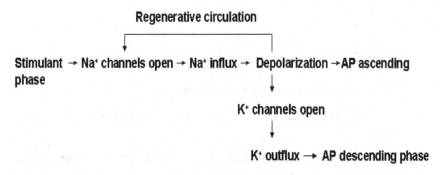

Fig. 2.12 Formation of action potential

There is potential difference between the excited area and adjacent un-excited area, so local current occurs. Local current intensity is several times of threshold intensity and it can make un-excited area depolarize, thus it is an effective stimulus which makes un-excited area depolarize to threshold potential to produce action potential and realizes conduction of action potential. Conduction of excitation in the same cell is a gradual excitation process elicited by local current in fact (Figure 2.13).

Nerve impulse is the excitation conducted along never fibers and its essence is the depolarization process of membrane propagates quickly along never fibers, that is the conduction of action potential. Conduction of receptive impulse has two kinds: *impulse conduction along nonmyelinated fiber*. When some area of nonmyelinated fiber is excited by stimulant, spike potential occurs immediately, that is to say, membrane potential at that area inverses temporarily to depolarize (positive charge inside and negative charge outside). Thus potential difference between the excited area and adjacent un-excited area occurs and causes electric charge to move, which is called local current. The local current stimulates adjacent rest portion one by one, making the spike potential conduct along the entire never fiber; *impulse conduction of myelinated never fiber*. It is salutatory conduction.

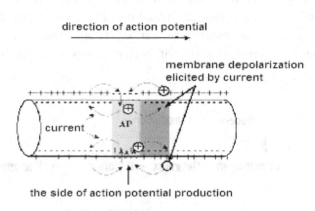

Fig. 2.13 Conduction of action potential by local current

In 1871, Ranviar discovered that myeline sheath didn't wrap continuously the axon of peripheral myelinated fiber but broke off once every 1~2mm regularly. People named the breaks as Ranviar's node after Ranviar. Its physiological function hadn't been elucidated for a long period. In 1925, Lillie had proposed the hypothesis based on the experiments of simulating nerve fiber conduction with wire: nerve excitation probably jumped down the fiber from node to node. Myelin sheath of myelinated nerve fiber has electrical insulating property, so local current can only occur between two Ranviar's nodes, which is called salutatory conduction (Figure 2.14).

Myolin sheath of myelinated nerve fiber doesn't permit ions pass effectively. However, the axon at Ranviar's node is naked and membrane permeability at the site is about 500 fold of unmyelinated nerve membrane permeability, so it is easy for ions to pass. When one Ranviar's node is excited, depolarization occurs in the area and local current only flows within axon until the next Ranviar's node. With the stimulant of local current, excitation jumps forward from node to node, thus the conduction velocity of myelinated fiber is faster than that of unmyelinated fiber. The conduction of nerve impulse has the following characteristics: *integrity*. It indicates that nerve fiber must keep integrality both in anatomy and in physiology; *insulation*. That is to say, nerve impulse can't conduct to adjacent nerve fiber in the same nerve trunk; *bidirectional conduction*. Impulse produced by stimulating any site of nerve fiber can conduct simultaneously toward two terminals; *relative indefatigability* and *nondecrement*.

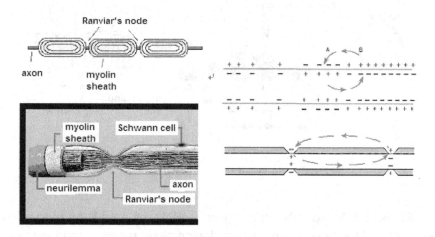

Fig. 2.14 Saltatory conduction of action potential

## 2.8 Ion Channels

On October 7th, 1991, in the conference of presenting Nobel Prize, Erwin Neher and Bert Sakman were endowed with Nobel Physiological Prize because of their important achievements - the discovery of single ion channel in the cell membrane. Cell membrane isolates cell from outside, however, there are many channels in the membrane by which cell undertakes material exchanges with outside. The channels are composed of single molecule or multiple molecules, and they permit some ions pass through. Regulation of the channels has influence on the life and function of cell. In 1976, Erwin Neher and Bert Sakman cooperated to record successfully the current of single channel in nAc subdivision by a newly-established patch clamp technique and initiated the first river of studying ion channel function directly. The results showed that a very slender current occurred when ions passed through ion channels in the membrane. Because their diameters were proximate to those of ion channels, Erwin Neher and Bert Sakman selected $Na^+$ and $Cl^-$ to do experiments and finally they got consensus in the existence of ion channels and how the ion channels exerted their functions. There are. And they even discovered the inductors in some ion channels and their location in channel molecules (as shown in Figure 2.15).

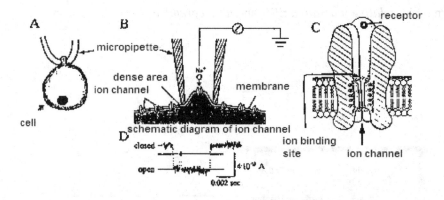

Fig. 2.15 Schematic diagram of ion channel

In 1981, British Miledi laboratory injected cRNA of nAchR by biosynthesis into egg cell of Africa clawed frog in developing phase (phase V) and succeeded in expression of the ion channel receptor in the membrane. During 1983 to 1984, Japanese Numa laboratory firstly determined the entire primary structure of nAchR and $Na^+$ channel of electric fish organ with over 200 000 molecular weight. Above three works not only confirmed directly the existence of ion channels from the function and structure but also provided efficient research methods for analysis of the function and structure of ion channels.

Above 12 basic types of ion channels have been discovered in the membrane of neurons and each of them has some similar isomers. Ion channel can convert among multiple conformations. However, from the phenomenon of permitting ions pass through or not, it has only two states: open state and close states. Conversion of ion channels between open and close states is controlled by the gate of micropore. This mechanism is called gated control. In fact, many ion channels has still a shut-off state called as inactivation besides the open and close states, for instance, $Na^+$ channel.

The gated control mechanism is still not very clear. People have imagined three styles: a) one site of the porous channel is gated (like voltage-gated $Na^+$ channel and $K^+$ channel); b) the structure change of whole porous channel envelops the porous channel (like the gap junction channel); c) specific inhibitory particles stop up the channel entrance (like voltage-gated $K^+$ channel) (Kandel et al., 1991)。 It is known three motives including voltage, mecho-stretch and chemical ligandin can regulate the activities of channel gates. The ion channels are called voltage-gated ion channel, mechanically-gated ion channel and ligand-gated ion channel respectively.

Ion channel is a kind of constitutive protein in cell membrane. They penetrate the cell membrane dispersedly. Since Numa laboratory determined firstly total amino acid sequence of nAchR and $Na^+$ channel in electric organ of electric fish by DNA cloning technology, the primary structure of multiple ion channels have been elucidated. It is possible to judge their second-level structures, functional groups in molecules, their evolution and heredity through the analysis of data from X light diffraction, electron diffraction and electron microscopy.

According the data about the primary structure of ion channels, genes coding ion channels can be divided into three families. Each member of one family has very similar amino acid sequence, so they are considered evolving from common progenitor gene: a) gene family coding voltage-gated $Na^+$ channel, $K^+$ channel and $Ca^{2+}$ channel; b) gene family coding ligand-gated ion channels, its members include the ion channels activated by Ach, GABA, glycine and glutamic acid; c) gene family coding gap junction channels.

## 2.9 The Nervous System

Nervous system is the organization of all kinds of activities in the body. It receives literally millions of bits of information from the different sensory organs and neurons and then integrates all these to determine the responses to be made by the body.

A nervous system can be divided into central nervous system (CNS) and peripheral nervous system (PNS) according its morphology and location. CNS comprises of the brain and spinal cord. The former lies in the cranial cavity while the latter locates in the vertebral canal. It can also be divided into somatic nervous system and autonomic nervous system according to its quality. The nerve centre of somatic nervous system locates in the brain and the spinal cord while its peripheral part constitutes the brain nerves and the spinal nerves. Somatic sensory nerves receive the stimulants from the skin, muscles, junctions, bones and so on via the receptors in their terminals and conduct the impulses to the nervous centre while somatic motor nerves transfer the impulses from the centre to the effectors, controlling the contraction and relaxation of skeletal muscles. The nerve centre of autonomic nervous system also locates in the brain and the spinal cord, whereas its peripheral portion has two parts: a) constituting the brain nerves and the spinal nerves; b) constituting self-governed autonomic nerve. The autonomic motor nerves include the sympathetic nerve and parasympathetic nerve, controlling the activities of cardiac muscles, the smooth muscles and glands.

### 2.9.1 The second messenger

CNS is composed of two parts, the brain and the spinal cord. The brain is the most important part of the whole central nervous system. For individual behaviors, the brain nerve is almost linked closely with all intricate activities, such as learning, thought, perception and so on. The brain includes hindbrain (epencephalon), midbrain (diencephalons) and forebrain. Each of them includes multiple kinds of nervous tissues.

Spinal cord locates in the spinal column, which connects with the brain and the 31 pairs of peripheral nerves distributing in both sides of spinal column. The functions of the spinal cord are:

(1) To conduct nerve impulse from the sensory receptors to the superior center of the brain, then transmitting nerve impulse from the brain to the motor organs via efferent nerve. Thus the spinal cord is the pathway connecting the peripheral nerve with the superior center of the brain.

(2) To accept the impulse transferred via afferent nerve and cause reflex activity directly as the reflex center.

Figure 2.16 shows the transection of the spinal cord. Butterfly-shaped internal mass of gray matter encompasses the central canal, which opens upward into the fourth ventricle. Bilateral gray matters extend anteriorly and posteriorly to the anterior horn and posterior horn respectively. The former connects anterior root and relates with movements while the latter connects posterior root and relates with sensation. Grey matter between the anterior horn and the posterial horn of thoracic and upper two or three lumbar spinal segments are referred to as lateral horns, which are preganglionic nueron of autonomic nerves.

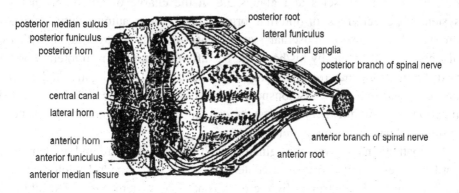

Fig. 2.16 Transection of spinal cord

White matter around gray matter has anterior, lateral and posterior funiculi, which consist largely of longitudinal nerve fibers and are the pathway connecting the brain with spinal cord. Propriospinal tracts adjacent to the gray matter are linked with each of segments.

### 2.9.2 Peripheral nervous system

PNS includes somatic nervous system and autonomic nervous system. Somatic nervous system innervates in the striated muscles spreading all over the head, face, trunk and four limbs. According to its functions, somatic nervous can be classified into two species: afferent nerve and efferent nerve. The afferent nerves connect with receptors of sense organs and take responsibility of transferring nerve impulse induced by external stimulant to the central nerve, so this species of nerves are called sensory nerves, which construct the basal unit of sensory nerves, that is, sensory neuron.

After receiving external nerve impulse, the central nerve will give response. Response is also a style of nerve impulse, which is transferred by efferent nerve to motor organs to cause muscle movements. Thus, this species of nerves are called motor nerves. Basal unit of motor nerve is motor neuron, which transfers impulse from the center to motor organ to produce related action and give determinate response.

The above somatic nervous system manages the behaviors of striated muscles while the managements of the functions of internal organs such as inner smooth muscles, cardiac muscles and glands are in the charge of autonomic nervous system. The activities of internal organs have some automaticity, which is different from somatic muscular system. Human can't control the activities of his/ her internal organs by his/her will. The afferent impulse from internal organs is different from that from skin or other specific sensory organs, and it can't produce clear sense on consciousness. According to the originated sites and their functions, autonomic nervous system can be divided into sympathetic nerve system and parasympathetic nerve system.

Sympathetic nerve system originating in thoracic spinal cord and lumbar spinal cord receives impulse from the centers of spinal cord, medulla oblongata and midbrain and it is controlled by the central nervous system. Strictly speaking, it can't be called autonomic nerves and just can't be dominated by individual will. Sympathetic nerves mainly innervate internal organs including heart, lung, liver, kidneys, spleen and gastrointestinal, and also reproduction organs and adrenal glands. Another part of them innervate the vessels of head and neck, body wall, arrector muscle and iris of eyes. The main function of sympathetic nervous system is to excite internal organs, glands and other related organs. For example, excitation of sympathetic nerves can increase heart rate, blood pressure, respiratory volume and blood glucose, expand pupil and promote secretion of E but only inhibit secretion of saliva.

Parasympathetic nervous system is composed of a set of cranial nerves (III-oculomotor nerve, VII-facial nerve, IX-pharyngeal nerve, X-vagus nerve) and pelvic nerves originated in pelvic portion of spinal cord. Parasympathetic nerves locate near or within the effectors, so their postganglionic fibers are very short and just their preganglionic fibers can be observed usually. Their main function is contrary to that of sympathetic nerve, so it produces antagonism to sympathetic nerve. For example, parasympathetic nerve inhibits the function of heart while sympathetic enhances its function. In contrast, parasympathetic nerve enhances the movement of small intestine while sympathetic nerve inhibits its movement. The functions of autonomic nerve system are as shown in Table 2.1

Table 2.1 The functions of autonomic nerve system

| Organs | Sympathetic nerve system | Parasympathetic nerve system |
|---|---|---|
| Circulating organs | Heart rate↑, relaxation of coronary vessels, contraction of visceral vessels and peripheral vessels in skin, and contraction of blood reservoir (spleen). | Heart rate↓, contraction of coronary vessels, relaxation of peripheral vessels of partial organs |
| Respiratory organs | Bronchodilatation | Bronchoconstriction |
| Digestive organs | Secrete viscous saliva, inhibit gastrointestinal movement, lower the tension of intestinal smooth muscles, inhibit gallbladder contraction. | Secrete dilute saliva, enhance gastrointestinal peristalsis, increase its tension, promote gallbladder contraction. |
| Urination and reproduction organs | Vessels of kidney contract, detrusor muscles of bladder relax, promote gravid uterus contract but non-gravid uterusrelax | Detrusor muscles of bladder contract, external genitalia relax, erection of penis. |
| Eyes | Mydriasis, orbital and palpebral muscles contract (eye balls evaginate), ciliary muscles relax. | Miosis, ciliary muscles contract, promote secretion of tear gland. |
| Skin | Hair follicle muscles contract, sweat secretes | |
| Metabolism | Promote catabolism and secretion of E. | Promote assimilation and secretion of insulin. |

## 2.10 Cerebral Cortex

In 1860, P. Broca, a French surgeon observed the following case: the patient could not speak but understand language. His larynx, tongue, lip, vocal cords and so on had no disability of routine movements. He could give off individual word and sing a tune, but he could neither speak a complete sentence nor express his thought by writing. The autopsy discovered there was a damage zone of egg size in posterior frontal lobe of the left hemisphere of the patient's cerebrum, degenerated brain tissue adhered to meninges, but the right hemisphere was normal. Afterward, P. Broca studied eight similar patients with the same damage zone in the left hemisphere of cerebrum. According to these discoveries P. Broca announced a famous principle about brain's function in 1864: "we speak in left hemisphere", which was the first direct proof about functional localization obtained of human cerebral cortex. This zone (Brodmann 44, 45 areas) is now called Broca's expressive aphasia area or Broca's area, which exists only in the cerebral cortex of left hemisphere. This is also the first proof that left hemisphere is the predominant cerebral cortex.

In 1870, G. Fritsch and E. Hitzig, two German physiologists discovered that stimulating a certain region of cerebral cortex with electric current could elicit regularly a certain movement of limbs of the opposite side, which confirmed firstly by experiments that there were different functional localization in cerebral cortex. Later, Carl Wernicke discovered another cortex area related with linguistic capacity, which is now called Carl Wernicke area and locates in the junctions among temporal posterior part, parietal lobe and occipital lobe. When this area is damaged, the patient can speak but can't understand language, that is, he can hear the sound but can't understand its meaning. This area is also well-developed in the left hemisphere.

Since the 19th century, a great deal of knowledge about the functional localization of cerebral cortex has been achieved through all-round experimental researches and clinical observation of physiologists and doctors, and the combination of clinical observation, surgical treatment and science research. In the 1930s, Wild Penfield, etc undertook a great quantity of researches about the functional localization of human cerebral cortex. In the process of neurosurgical procedures, under the condition of local anesthesia, they stimulated the patients' cerebral cortex with electric current, observed the patients' movement response and asked their subject feeling. According to cytoarchitectural difference, Brodmann divided human cerebral cortex into 52 areas (Figure 2.17). From the angle of function, cerebral cortex is composed of sensory cortex, motor cortex and associated cortex. The sensory cortex includes visual cortex (17 area), auditory cortex (41, 42 areas), somatosensory cortex (1, 2, 3 areas), gustatory cortex (43 area) and olfactory cortex (28 area); motor cortex includes primary motor cortex (4 area), premotor area and supplementary motor area (6 area); associated cortex includes parietal association cortex, temporal association cortex and prefrontal association cortex. Associated cortex is not involved in pure feeling or motor function, but accepts and integrates information from the sensory cortex, and then transfer information to the motor cortex, thereby regulates the activities of behavior. Associated cortex plays a role of association between sense input and motor output, which is the origin of its name.

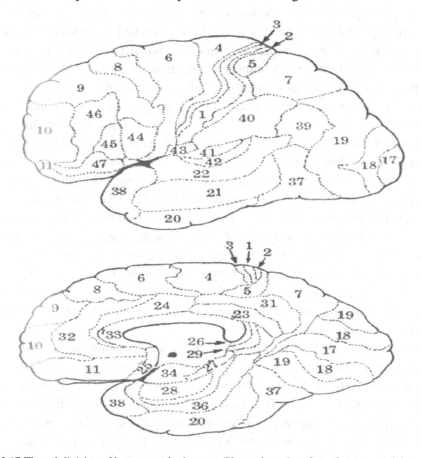

Fig. 2.17 The subdivision of human cerebral cortex (Upper: lateral surface. Lower: medial surface)

Human parietal association cortex includes Brodmann 5, 7, 39, 40 areas. 5 area mainly receives the projections from the primary somatosensory cortex (1, 2 and 3 areas) and mucleus lateralis posterior thalami while 7 area mainly receives the projections from the anterior of striate visual area, tuberculum posterior thalami, superior temporal gyrus, prefrontal lobe cortex and cingulated gyri (23, 24 areas). 5 area and 7 area have different input sources, but they have the common target areas of projections which consist of premotor area, cortex of prefrontal lobe, cortex of temporal lobe, cingulate gyri, insular gyri and basal ganglia. The more projections from 5 area are in the premotor area and motor area while the projections from 7 area are in sub-area of temporal lobe related with border structure. In addition, 7 area projects directly toward parahippocampal gyres and receives the projections from the locus ceruleus and raphe nucleus. Therefore, 5 area is mainly involved in somatosensory information and movement information processing while 7 area is probably mainly involved in visual information processing and movements, attention and regulation of emotions and so on.

Human association cortex of prefrontal lobe is composed of Brodmann's 9-14 areas and 45-47 areas. General name of 11-14 areas and 47 area is orbital gyri of prefrontal lobe. General name of 9, 10, 45 and 46 areas is the dorsolateral of prefrontal lobe, and some authors also induce 8 area and 4 area to the cortex of prefrontal lobe. Association cortex of prefrontal lobe has several notable anatomic characteristics: i) it locates in the anterior aspects of neopallium of the brain, ii) it has significantly advanced granular layer (IV layer), iii) it receives the direct projections from the mediodorsal thalamic nucleus, iv) it has wide association with afferent and efferent fibers. During the evolving process of animals from the low grade to the high grade, the area of association cortex of the prefrontal lobe becomes bigger and bigger accordingly. The primates including human have the most advanced association cortex of the prefrontal lobe. The area of human association cortex of the prefrontal lobe accounts for about 29 % that of the entire cerebral cortex.

Association cortex of the prefrontal lobe has fiber association in the cortex and beneath cortex. The interactive fiber associations exist among the cortex of prefrontal lobe, striate visual anterior area, temporal association cortex and parietal association cortex. The cortex of prefrontal lobe is the only one neopallium which has interactive fibers with mediodorsal thalamic nucleus and has also direct projection toward the hypothalamus. The cortex of prefrontal lobe has direct or indirect fiber associations with basal forebrain, cingulated gyri and gyrus hippocampi. It sends fibers out to project to the basal ganglis (caudate nucleus and putamen) and so on. Functional complexity of the cortex of prefrontal lobe is attributed to the complicated fiber associations.

Human cerebral cortex is a very subtile controlling system. The layer of gray matters covering the cerebral cortex has an average thickness of 2-3mm. There are many upfolds called gyri and downfolds referred to as sulci on the surface of the cortex, which increases the surface area of cerebral cortex, reaching 2200 centimeters square. It contains about 14 billion neurons which are mainly pyramidal cells, stellate cells and spindle cells. Complicated associations exist among the neurons, but the distribution of several of neurons in the cortex is not disordered but hierarchical strictly. The archaeocortex locating the inside of the cerebral hemisphere only has three layers: a) Molecular layer, b) Pyramidal layer, c) Polymorphic layer. The neopallium locating the outside of the cerebral hemisphere has six layers:

(1) Molecular layer contains a very small quantity of cells but has a great number of nerve fibers paralleling with its surface.

(2) External granular layer is mainly composed of many small pyramidal cells and stellate cells.

(3) Pyramidal layer consists mainly of medium-sized and mini-sized pyramidal cells.

(4) Internal granular layer is composed of dense stellate cells.

(5) Ganglionic layer consists mainly of medium-sized and big-sized pyramidal cells. Pyramidal cells in the anterior central gyrus is specially big and their dendrite tops extend to the first layer and their long and thick axons travel to the brainstem and the spinal cord, which are the main components of pyramidal tracts.

(6) Polymorphic layer mainly contains spindle cells. One part of the axons of spindle cells and the axons of the cells of the fifth layer compose together the efferent nerve fibers downwards the brainstem and the spinal cord, the other part of them running to the homolateral or contralateral hemisphere compose the association fibers associating all areas of the cortex.

In the view of the functions, the first, second, third and fourth layers of cerebral cortex mainly receive nerve impulses and associate related nerves, especially specific sensory fibers from the thalamus go into the fourth layer directly. The axons of pyramidal cells and spindle cells in the fifth layer and the sixth layer consist of efferent fibers which run downward to the brain stem and spinal cord, and then cranial nerves or spinal nerves conduct impulses to related domain in the body to regulate the activities of a variety of organs and systems. In this way cerebral cortex not only has the character of reflex path but also a complicated chain system among various neurons. The complexity and catholicity makes cortex have the abilities of analysis and synthesis, which constitutes the material basis of human conceptual work.

The study on the structure and function of cerebral somatosensory area indicates that longitudinal columnar-arranged cortical cells consist of the most fundamental functional electric potential, which is called function column. The column structure has 200-500μm diameter, running toward the brain surface through the six layers. Neurons within the same column structure all have same function, for instance, responding to the same type of stimulation of senses from the same receptive field. After receiving the same stimulation, the discharging latency of the neurons is very similar, only with difference of 2-4ms, which illustrates that only successive several neurons lie between the first activated neuron and the last activated neuron, and only successive several neurons can finish the contact loop of the neurons in the same column structure. One column structure is one integration processing unit of input-output information. The afferent impulses firstly go into the fourth layer and are propagated vertically by the cells of the fourth and second layers, finally, the cells of the third, fifth and sixth layers send out the efferent impulses departing from the cerebral cortex. The horizontal fibers of the third layer cells also have the function of inhibiting the adjacent cell column, thus once one column elicits excitation, its adjacent cell column will be inhibited, which form the excitation-inhibition mode. The shape and function of the column structure exists in the second sensory area, visual area, cortexes of auditory field and motor area still.

The neurons in cerebral cortex have the bioelectric activities. the cerebral cortex often has the sustaining rhythmic electrical potential changes called spontaneous electrical activity, which can be recorded in human scalp through the electroencephalogram technique. Under different conditions, there is distinguished difference in the frequency of brain waves, which can be classified into alpha, beta, theta, and delta waves mainly according to their frequency. Delta waves have frequencies between 0.5 and 3 per second, theta waves have frequencies between 4 and 7 per second, alpha waves have frequencies between 8 and 13 per second, and beta waves are fast waves with frequencies of above 14 per second. Generally speaking, the waves with slower frequencies usually have higher amplitudes while the waves with faster frequencies have lower amplitudes. For example, for the brain waves induced in adult scalp, delta waves have amplitudes between 20 and 200 μV, alpha waves have amplitudes between 20 and 50 μV, while beta waves only have amplitudes 5 and 10 μV.

Evoked potentials are the potential changes induced in the central nerve system when the sensory afferent system is stimulated. The sites receiving stimulation may be the sensory organs, sensory nerve or any point in the pathway of sensory conduction. Broadly speaking, the potential changes of the central nerve system induced by other stimulating methods are also called evoked potentials. For instance, by stimulating spinal anterior root directly, when impulses conduct reversely to spinal anterior horn and cause electric potential afferent system to be stimulated, potential changes in some local cortex will be induced. Since cortex is in the activities and produces spontaneous brain electricity, evoked potentials frequently occur on the background of spontaneous potentials.

Evoked cortical potential induced on the surfaces of the related sensory projection areas can be divided into two parts: one is the primary response, the other is afterdischarge. The latency of primary response is commonly between 5 and 12 milliseconds, which depends on the duration of sensory conduction and conduction velocity of impulses. The primary response of evoked cortical potentials is the potential change, firstly positive then negative. The formation of primary response is considered mainly the grouping representation of electric activities of giant pyramidal cells. The giant pyramidal cells have apical dendrites extending to the cortical surface, thus it can be conceived that impulses can be conducted from the cell body to cortical surface along the apical dendrite when giant pyramidal cells is excited by afferent impulses. In the initial stage of excitation conduction of giant pyramidal cell, the potential in its cell body becomes negative firstly and the assembling point of electric current while its dendrite terminal becomes electric source and is relatively in positive state. Many apical dendrites have the same direction, therefore, powerful electric field will be formed when they act simultaneously. On the basis of the principle of volume conductor, a big positive potential can be induce in cortical surface. When excitation reaches superior side of apical dendrite and enters superficial cortex, cortical surface becomes the assembling point of electric current and its potential becomes negative. Certainly, primary response have also other components, for example, the electric activities of thalamic projection fibers can be involved in the formation of positive potential, while the electric activities of neurons in superficial cortex can be also involved in the formation of negative potential.

After primary responses, there are a series of cyclical positive phasic electric changes called afterdischarge. Whether it occur or not and its duration depend on stimulus intensity and anesthesia statements. Generally speaking, greater stimulus intensity and less superficial anesthesia are apt to induce afterdischarge and its duration is long. Circadian rhythm of afterdischarge is generally 8 and 12 per second, thus which is apt to be mixed with alpha waves of spontaneous brain electricity. However, alpha waves are the potential changes close to sine wave while afterdischarges are positive phasic electric changes generally. Meanwhile, alpha waves are controlled by thalamic non-specific projection system, but afterdischarges as the results of the activities of the loop between the cortex and thalamic nucleus are not. In addition, alpha waves can be induced in wide areas of the cortex while afterdischarges an be induced only in a certain area of the cortex. For example, afterdischarges caused by sound stimulus can just be induced in auditory cortex.

# Chapter 3

# Neural Computation

## 3.1 Overview

Neural computation studies the nature and capacity of information processing of artificial neural networks with procedure, adaptive, and brain-style (Shi, 2009a). Artificial neural network, which is composed of a large number of processing units, is a large-scale adaptive non-linear dynamical system with learning ability, memory capacity, computing power and intelligent processing functions, and in varying degrees and levels it imitates the information processing, storage and retrieval functions of human brain. It is based on the results of modern neuroscience researches in an attempt to design a new ith the information processing capacity of human brain by simulating brain network processing, and memorizing information. At the same time, such researches for artificial neural network will further deepen the understanding of thinking and intelligence. In order to simulate the mechanism of brain information processing, artificial neural network is non-linear, non-local, unsteady, non-convex and so on. Artificial neural network unified algorithm and the structure can be seen as the mixture of hardware and software.

Modern neural computation started at pioneering work of WS McCulloch and Pitts (McCulloch et al., 1941). WS McCulloch is a neuroscientist and anatomist. He spent 20 years considering the nervous system expressing the incident. W. Pitts is a mathematics genius and in 1942 he began to study neural computation. In 1943 WS Mcculloch and W. Pitts published their papers in a neurons modeling group. The group was very active five years ago under the leadership of N. Rashevsky of the University of Chicago.

In their classic paper, WS McCulloch and W. Pitts combined study of neurophysiology and mathematical logic, described the logic analysis of a neural network. In their model neurons were assumed to follow yes-no model law. If the number of such simple neurons is enough and connection weights are appropriately set and synchronously operated, WS McCulloch and W. Pitts proved that in principle, any computable function can be calculated with such a network. This is a significant result, which marks the birth of neural network and artificial intelligence.

The 1943 paper of WS McCulloch and W. Pitts was widely read. It affected Von Neumann, who used WS McCulloch and W. Pitts neurons to derive idealized switching delay elements in his EDVAC (Electronic Discrete Variable Automatic Computer), thus improving EDVIC (Electronic Numerical Integrator and Computer). EDVIC is the first general-purpose electronic computer, which was made from 1943 to 1946 at the University of Pennsylvania Moore School of Electrical Engineering. WS Mcculloch and W. Pitts formed neural network theory, became the second report with significant characteristics in the four reports of von Neumann made in 1949 at University of Illinois.

In 1948 N. Wiener's famous "Control Theory" published which described a number of important concepts for control, communications and statistical signal processing (Wiener, 1948). In 1961 the second edition of the book published, and new materials on the learning and self-organization were added. In the second chapter of the second version, N. Wiener seemed to have grasped the physical meaning of statistics mechanism in the main context, but the fruitful results on joint statistics mechanism and learning system were left to J. J. Hopfield.

The second important development happened in 1949. In D. O. Hebb's book "Behavior Histology" (Hebb, 1949), he clearly explained the amendment to the physiological synaptic learning rules for the first time. In particular, D. O. Hebb argued that the brain's connection continuously changes with the brain learning different tasks and nerve tissue is created by this change. D. O. Hebb inherited Ramony and Cajal's early assumption introduced his now famous learning hypothesis: variable synapses between two neurons was increased by repeated activation of neurons at both ends of the synapses. D. O. Hebb's book has widely affected psychologists, but, unfortunately, has little impact on engineers.

D. O. Hebb's book is a source of inspiration for learning and development of computation model of self-adaptive system. In 1956 Rochester, Holland, Habt, and Duba's thesis might be the first attempt to use computer to simulate test of Hebb's learning hypothesis of the neural theory. Simulation results of the paper show that the inhibition must be added to work actually. In the same year, Uttley demonstrated that neural network with a modifiable synapse can learn to classify the simple binary model set. Uttley introduced the so-called quadrature leakage and fire neurons (leaky integrate and fire neuron), then Caianiello conducted a formal analysis of it. In some later work, Uttley assumed that effects of variable synapses in the nervous system depend on statistical relationship of fluctuation state of both ends of synapses, and so it was associated with Shannon's theory.

In 1952, Ashby's book "Design of the Brain: the Origin of Adaptive Behavior," published (Ashby, 1952). Today it seems as interesting as it was in the past. This book is eye-catching because of its basic view that the adaptive behavior is not innate but learned and, through learning animals (system) behavior changes for the better. The book stressed the dynamic view that living body is like a machine, and the concept of stability.

1954, Minsky at Princeton University wrote a doctoral thesis of Neural Network, which entitled "Enhanced neural systems theory and its application in modeling the brain." In 1961, Minsky published an early paper on the AI "Progress in Artificial Intelligence." This article included a large chapter on the neural network. 1967, Minsky published a book entitled "Calculation: finite and infinite machines". It is the first to expand the results of W. S. McCulloch and W. Pitts in the form of a book and put them in the context of automatic theory and computing theory.

Also in 1954, as one of the earliest pioneers of Communication Theory and the inventor of holography, Gabor put forward the idea of non-linear adaptive filter, and together with his partners they established such a machine. Samples generated by random process, as well as machine-generated objective function together completed the online learning.

In the 1950s, Taylor began to study associative memory, followed by Steinbuch introducing the learning matrix; this matrix was composed by switching the plane network which was interpolated between the "feel" receiver and "motor" effect pose. In 1969, Willshaw, Buneman and Longuet-Higgins issued an outstanding paper on the non-holographic associative memory. This article gives the network model of two types: the simple optical system of correlation matrix realization and associated neural network made by the optical memory. An important contribution to early development of associative memory includs Andelson, Kohonen and Nakano's article of 1972, in which they independently introduced idea of correlation matrix memory on the basis of learning rules.

Von Neumann was the master of science at the first half of the 20th century. To commemorate him, people named the basis for the design of digital computer Von Neumann structure. Yale University in 1956, invited him to make Silliman report. He died in 1957, and later, his unfinished Silliman report was published in

1958 as a book: "Computers and the brain." This book is very meaningful, because it prompted what Von Neumann would do. He began to realize the great differences between the brain and the computer.

A particular concern to be considered of neural network is the use of unreliable neuron component to build reliable neural network. In 1956 Von Neumann solved this important issue by using the idea of redundancy. Such thinking made Winograd and Cowan propose in 1963 to use distribution of redundancy in neural networks and this shows the individual concept of robust and parallelism of how a large number of elements is demonstrated in the collective.

W. S. McCulloch and W. Pitts's classic paper was published 15 years after Rosenblatt's works about perceptron, a new method of pattern recognition, a new method of supervised learning (Rosenblatt, 1962). Perceptron convergence theorem gave Rosenblatt's work a complete success. He raised in 1960 the first proof of perceptron convergence theorem. Proof of the theorem also appeared in Novikoff (1963) and other people's work. Widrow and Hoff introduced the least mean square (LMS) algorithm, and used it to constitute the Adaline (adaptive linear element). The difference between Adaline and perceptron lies in the training process. One of the first trainable hierarchical neural network with multiple adaptive elements was Madaline (multiple-adaline) structure put forward by B. Widrow and his students (Widrow, 1962). In 1967 Amari used statistical gradient method for pattern classification. N. Nilsson published the book in 1965 "Learning machine" (Nilsson, 1965). So far it is still the best works on the use of hyper-plane to distinct dividable linear model. In the 1960s, perceptron neural networks seemed to be able to do anything. Minsky and Papert co-wrote the book in 1969 "Perception". Mathematical theory was used to prove the nature limitations of the calculation done by the single-layer perceptron (Minsky et al., 1969). In the section about Multi-layer perceptron, they believed that there is no reason to suppose that any limitation of single-layer perceptron can be overcome in the case of multi-layer. An important issue to face in the design of Multi-layer perceptron is the issue of confidence level (that is, the confidence level issues of hidden neurons in the network). Minsky in 1961 in his book "Strengthen the issue of confidence level in the learning system" first used terminology "confidence level". In the 60s most of the ideas and basic concepts necessary for solving the problem of confidence level had been formulated, and so had been many inherent ideas of recursive (attractor) network now known as Hopfield network. However, it was not until the last century 80's that solutions to these very basic questions appeared.

In the last 70s, these factors in one way or another hindered further study of neural network. In addition to a number of psychological and neurological experts, many researchers had changed their researching field. Indeed only a handful of early pioneers continued to study neural network. From the engineering point of view, we can trace back the last 70's as the incubation period for the neural network.

In the 1970's an important activity was that self-organization theory that used competitive learning emerged. In 1973 von der Malsburg's work of computer simulation might be the first demonstration of self-organization. Inspired by topology order in the human brain mapping, in 1976, Willshaw and von der Malsburg made their first paper on the formation of self-organization mapping.

In the last 1980s a number of achievements were made in the neural network theory and design, then neural network research has entered a recovery phase. Grossberg, on the basis of his early work in competitive learning theory (Grossberg, 1972), established a new principle of self-organization, which is the now well-known adaptive resonance theory (adaptive resonance theory, ART). Basically, this theory includes a bottom-up recognition layer and a top-down production layer. If the input forms and learning feedback forms match, a state of uncertainty called "adaptive resonance" (ie, the extension and enlargement of neural activity) happened. This forward or reverse mapping originally had been rediscovered by other researchers under different conditions.

In 1982, J. Hopfield formed a new method which understands calculation with the idea of energy function implemented by the recursive network with symmetric connection. And he established isomorphism between the Ising models used in such recursive network and statistical physics. The analogy paved the way for a series of physical theories entering neural model, so the field of neural network changed. Such special neural network with feedback caused a great deal of concern in the 80's. At that time the well-known Hopfield network appeared. Although Hopfield network can not be a true model of neural biological system, they are covered by the principle, that is, the principle of storing information in a dynamic stable network, which is extremely profound. In fact, this principle can be traced back to many of the early work of other researchers:

(1) In 1954 and 1955 through observation, Gragg and Tamperley, respectively, derived that neurons could be due to "Ignition" (activated) or "non-ignition" (static), so in a grid atoms can be used in the spin pointing to "on" or "under."

(2) In 1967 Cowan introduced "sigmoid" activation characteristics and a neuron's smooth activation conditions based on Logist function.

(3) Grossberg introduced in 1967 and 1968 a combined model of neurons, involving non-linear difference/differential equations, and detection of use of a model based on short-term memory.

(4) In 1972 Amari independently introduced the additive model of neurons and used it to study the dynamic behavior of the elements of type neurons connected randomly.

(5) Wilson and Cowan derived in 1972, including exciting and inhibitory model neuron space localized group dynamics coupled nonlinear differential equations.

(6) Little and Shaw in 1975 described the neuronal activation or non activation probability model, and used it to develop a short-term memory theory.

(7) J. A. Anderson, J. W. Siverstein, S. A. Ritz and R. S. Jones in 1977 raised BSB (brain-state-in-box, BSB) model, formed by a simple association network of coupled non-linear dynamics.

Therefore, it was not surprising that in 1982 J. Hopfield's paper caused a great controversy after publication (Hopfield, 1982). However, the paper for the first time made clear the principle of storing information in the in the dynamic stability network. J. Hopfiled showed his insight in testing from the spinning glass of statistical mechanics special recursive network with symmetry connection. The symmetry design can guarantee the convergence to a stable condition. In 1983, MA Cohen and S. Grossberg, established the general principles of memory, which included continuous Hopfield network as a special case of the evaluation to find the site in accordance with the contents. A distinguishing characteristic of attractors neural network is the necessary volume of learning - the time, appeared in the network of nonlinear dynamics in a natural way. In this context, Cohen-Grossberg theorem is very important.

Another major development in 1982 was T. Kohonen's work on the use of self-organization mapping of one-dimensional or two-dimensional structure (Kohonen, 1982), which in some ways, Willshaw was different from earlier work of von der Malsburg. In the literature, T. Kohonen's work has attracted more attention than Willshaw and von der Malsburg model in the analysis and application, and has become the assessment criteria of other innovations in this area.

In 1983 S. Kirkpatrick, C. D. Gelatt and M. P. Vecchi described a new method of solving the problem of combination optimization, which was called simulated annealing (Kirkpatrick et al., 1983). Simulated Annealing, rooted in statistical mechanics was based on a simple technique which was used for the first time in computer simulation by N. Metropolis (Metropolis et al., 1953). D. H. Ackley, G. E. Hinton and T. J. Sejnowski used the idea of simulated annealing to develop a random machine called Boltzmann machine (Hinton et al., 1986), which was the first successful resolution of multi-layer neural network. Although it was proved that learning algorithm of Boltzmann (Bolzmann) machine not as computationally efficient as back-propagation algorithm was, but it proved that Minsky and Papert's suspect was not to set up, and it broke the psychological barrier; it also foreshadowed the work of subsequent sigmoid belief network by R. M. Neal (Neal, 1995). Sigmoid belief network achieved two things: a) significantly improved learning; b) Connect the neural network and belief network. Further improvement of Sigmoid belief network learning performance was made by L. K. Saul, T. Jakkolla and M. I. Jordan using mean-field theory rooted in statistical mechanics (Roy, 1999). Papers by A. G. Barto, R. S. Sutton and J. A. Anderson on reinforcement learning were published in 1983 (Barto et al., 1983). Although they were not the first to use the reinforced learning (for example, Minsky, in his doctoral thesis in 1954 considered it), this article caused great interest in reinforced learning and its application in controlling. In particular, they proved that a reinforced learning system could be useful in the absence of teachers in learning the inverted pendulum (that is, a pole stood on a vehicle) balance. Learning system only requires the failure signal at the time when the tilt pole to the vertical direction exceeding a certain angle or the vehicle to reach the endpoint of the orbit. In 1996 D. P. Bertsekas and J. N. Tsitsiklis published "Neural dynamics program". This book linked enforced learning to Bellmam's dynamic programming and put it on an appropriate mathematical basis.

In 1984 V. Braitenberg published a books "Tool: experiment of synthesis psychology." In this book, V. Braitenberg put forward a objective-oriented self-organizing behaviors principle: the use of universally recognized synthesis of a basic mechanism rather than top-down analysis is the best approach to understand a complex process. In the form of science fiction, V. Braitenberg explained this important principle by describing a variety of machines with simple internal structure. He directly or indirectly, studied the brain of animals for more than two decades and relevant facts inspired characteristics of these machines and their behaviors.

In 1986 D. E. Rumelhart, G. E. Hinton and R. J. Williams reported the development of back-propagation algorithm. The same year, the famous book "parallel distributed processing: Exploration of the Microstructure of Cognition", edited by D. E. Rumelhart, and J. L. McClelland was published (Rumelhart et al., 1986). This book caused significant impact on the use of back-propagation algorithm. It has become the most common multi-layer perceptron training algorithm. In fact, the back-propagation learning was found independently at the same time in two other places. In the mid 1980's after back-propagation algorithm was found, we found that as early as August 1974 in Harvard University P. J. Werbos in his Ph.D thesis had described it (Werbos, 1974). P. J. Werbos' doctoral thesis is the first documentation of effective back-propagation model to describe the gradient calculation, and it can be applied to the general network model, including neural networks as its special case. The basic idea of back-propagation can be further traced back to the book by A. E. Bryson and Y. C. Ho "Applied Optimal Control," a book. In 2.2 of the book entitling "multi-stage system", using Lagrange form to derive back-propagation is described. However, the final analysis concluded that a number of back-propagation algorithm honor should be given to D. E. Rumelhart, G. E. Hinton and R. J. Williams, because they made it in the machine learning application and demonstrated how it worked.

In 1988 R. Linsker described a new principle of self-organization in the cognitive networks (Linsker, 1988). The principle was designed to maintain the input activity patterns information to a maximum under synaptic connectivity and synaptic dynamic range limits. Several other visual researchers also made similar recommendations. However, it was R. Linsker who used abstract concepts rooted in information theory to constitute the formula of a great infomax principle. R. Linsker's article re-stimulated interest in applying information theory to neural networks. In particular, A. J. Bell and T. J. Sejnowski's application of information theory to the problem of Blind Source Separation (Bell et al., 1995), had led many researchers to explore other information theoretical models for solving the well-known blind deconvolution.

Also in 1988, DS Broomhead and D. Lowe described the process of using RBF (radial basis function, RBF) to design multi-layer feed-forward network. RBF provided an alternative for multi-layer network. The basic idea of radial basis function dated back at least to O. A. Bashkirov, E. M. Braverman and I. B. Muchnik, who first proposed the potential function method (Bashkirov et al., 1964), and M. A. Aizerman, E. M. Braverman and L. I. Rozonnoer, who developmented potential function theory. In 1973, R. O. Duda and P. E. Hart's classic work "Pattern classification and scene analysis" gave a description of potential function method. Nevertheless, D. S. Broomhead and D. Lowe's article link led to significant research efforts in important areas of the design of link neural network and numerical analysis, as well as the linear adaptive filter of a large number of. In 1990 T. Poggio and F. Girosi used the Tikhonov regularization theory to further enrich the RBF network theory (Poggio et al., 1990).

In 1989, C. A. Mead's book "Analog VLSI and neural system" was published. This book provided unusual hybrid concepts from neurobiology and VLSI technology. In short, it included sections wrote by Mead and his collaborators wrote on silicon retina and silicon, which were living examples of Mead's creative thinking.

In the early 1990s, V. N. Vapnik and his collaborators put forward a supervised learning network, which was strong in computing and was called SVM (support vector machines, SVM). It was used to solve pattern recognition, regression and density estimation problems (Vapnik, 1995). The new method was based on limited samples of the learning theory. A novel feature of Support Vector Machine was that the Vapnik-Chervonenkis (VC) dimension was included in the design in a natural way. VC dimension provided neural networks with a measure of capacity of learning from a sample set.

Now chaos constituting a key aspect of physical phenomena has been well established. Many people raised a question: In the study of neural network, does chaos play a critical role? W. J. Freeman in the biological sense believed that the answer to this question was yes (Freeman, 1995). According to Freeman's neural model, activity patterns were not added outside the brain, but built from the inside. Chaotic dynamics provided a basis for describing a necessary condition when self-organization mode appeared within and between groups of neurons.

Perhaps J. Hopfield's articles in 1982 and two books of D. E. Rumelhart and J. L. McClellan in 1986 were the most influential works rather than other works that revived interest in neural network in the 1980s. Of course, neural network had come a long way in the early years from McCulloch and Pitts. Indeed they had established themselves the status of cross-disciplinary as rooted in neuroscience, psychology, mathematics, physics and engineering. Needless to say, now they have established such status and will continue to deepen in the theory, design, and the application. Born in the brain there is a delicate structure and the capacity of establishing its own rules through the often referred "experience". In fact the experience accumulated by time. The most dramatic development occurred to the brain during the first two years of birth (that is, the hardware line), but the development will go beyond this stage and continue.

A "development" neuron is at the same time with the plastic brain. Plasticity allows a development nervous system to adapt to its surrounding environment. Just as plasticity seems to be the key of the function of neurons of an information processing unit in the human brain as in the key, similarly, it is also the case with neural networks composed of artificial neurons. The most common form, neural network is a machine designed to the human brain to complete specific tasks or functions of interest to model; network is generally realized by using electronic devices or simulating the digital computer through software. In this chapter, our interest is more or less locked in a class of important neural network. This network achieves useful calculation through the learning process. In order to obtain good results, neural network uses a very large internal connections between simple calculation units. These simple calculation units are known as "neurons" or "processing units." Accordingly, we will give a definition which regards neural network as an adaptive machine.

A neural network is a large-scale parallel distribution processor consisting of a simple processing unit. It's born with the characteristics of storing knowledge and experience with they can be use. Neural network simulates the brain in two ways:

(1) The knowledge neural network obtains is learned from the outside environment.

(2) The intensity of internal neuronal connection, or synaptic weights are used for the storage of knowledge acquired.

The procedure for the completion of learning process is known as the learning algorithm, and its function is to obtain the desired design objects by changing the system weight values in an orderly manner.

The modifications of synaptic weights provide traditional methods for neural network design. This method is very close to linear adaptive filter theory. Filter theory has been well established and successfully applied in many different areas. But it is also possible for the neural network to modify its topology, and this fits such circumstances as human's neurons will die and synaptic connections will be established.

Neural networks in the literature is also known as neural computers, connectivity networks, parallel distributed processors etc. Obviously the calculation capacity of neural network comes from the following points: a) large-scale parallel distributed architecture. b) neural network learning ability and thus generalization ability. Generalization refers to reasonable output of neural network to the non-training (learning) data. The two information-processing capabilities allow neural networks to solve some complex (large scale) problems which can not be dealt with today. However, in practice, neural network alone can not solve every problem. They need to be integrated in a consistent systems engineering approach. Specific, a complex problem of interest is divided into a number of relatively simple sub-problems, and the neural network distributes the sub-problems that its inherent ability matches. However, there is still a long way to go before we can build a computer structure which is able to simulate the human brain (if possible) and this is a very important point. Application of neural networks provides the following useful properties and capabilities:

(1) Nonlinearity: an artificial neuron can be linear or nonlinear. A neural network formed by connected nonlinear neurons is nonlinear, and the nonlinear is a special nature distributed in the whole network. Nonlinear is a very important nature, especially if the internal physical mechanism to generate the input signal (such as voice signals) is inherently nonlinear.

(2) Input-output mapping: supervised learning or learning with teacher is a change in the prevalence of learning involving the use of training samples or task examples with labels to modify synaptic weights of neural network. Each sample is composed of an input signal and the corresponding desired response. Randomly select a sample from a training set and give it to the network, the network will adjust its synaptic weights (free parameters) to minimize the difference between the desired response and the actual response generated by the input signal by the appropriate statistical criteria. Use many samples in the training set to repeat neural network training until the network arrives at a steady state with no big synaptic weights modifications. During the training period previous samples used may be repeated in a different order. Thus for current problem the network learns from the samples through the establishment of input-output mapping. Such an approach is reminiscent of the study of non-parametric statistical inference, which is a statistical processing branch of non-model estimating, or from the biological point of view, known as the tabula rasa learning. Here the use of "non-parametric" express the fact that there is no priori assumptions to the statistical model of the input data. For example, consider a pattern classification task here is to classify the input signal which represents

specific objects or events into a few pre-classified groups. In this issue of non-parametric method, it is requested that example subset is used to "estimate" the border ruling of the pattern classification task in the input signal space, and not to use the probability distribution model. Examples of supervised learning implied a similar view, which suggests a similar close between the input-output mapping of a neural network and the non-parametric statistical inference.

(3) Adaptation: self-adjusting connection weights are embedded in the neural network in order to adapt to changes. In particular, the neural network can be trained in a specific environment, which allows it to be easily re-trained to small changes. Furthermore, when it runs in a time-varying environment (that is, its statistical properties change with time), the network synaptic weights can be designed to change over time. Neural network used for pattern recognition, signal processing and control can couple its adaptive capacity to become an effective tool capable of adaptive pattern recognition, adaptive signal processing, and adaptive control. As a general rule, when the system remains stable, the better the self-adaptive capacity of the system is, when asked to run in a time-varying environment, the more robust its performance is. However, it needs to be emphasized that adaptation does not necessarily lead to robustness, and it is likely the opposite. For example, a transient adaptive system may be changed, so fast that it responses to peak interference, which would cause rapid deterioration of system performance. In order to maximize adaptability, system stability should be a long enough to ignore peak interference and short enough to response to the general changes in the environment. This is a stability - plasticity dilemma (Grossberg, 1988).

(4) Evidence response: in pattern recognition problems, neural networks can be designed to provide not only choice of information of a specific model, but also provides confidence information for decision-making. The latter can be used to refuse decide those patterns that appear too fuzzy. With this information, output of the network will be improved.

(5) Information of former-latter relation: the specific structure and activities of the neural network represent knowledge. Each neuron in the network is potentially subject to influence of the overall activities of all other neurons. Of course, information of the former-latter relationship is processed by one neural network.

(6) Fault tolerance: neural networks realized with the form of a hardware have the potential fault-tolerance by nature, or robust computing power, which means that its performance gradually decreases under adverse operating conditions.

For example, a neuron or a connection is damaged, the retrieved quality of memorized pattern is undermined. However, due to the distribution features of network information storage, prior to a serious deterioration of the overall response in the network this damage is spread. In principle, therefore, the performance of a neural network shows a slow degradation rather than catastrophic failure. There are some empirical evidence on the robustness of computing, but usually it is not controllable. In order to ensure the actual fault-tolerant feature of the network, it is necessary to use correct measures in the design of the algorithm to train the network (Kerlirzin et al., 1993).

(7) VLSI realization: the large-scale parallel of neural network gives it a potential capacity of quickly dealing with certain tasks. This feature makes use of neural network suitable for the realization of ultra-large-scale integration. A special advantage of VLSI is to provide a way to capture complexity in a way of high degree of hierarchy.

(8) Analysis and design consistency: Basically, the neural network as an information processor is versatile. We say this in such a sense, that is, the application of neural networks involved in all areas use the same symbols. This feature is performed in different ways: a) regardless of the form of neurons, in all the neural networks they represent the same components. b) this makes it possible that neural network in different applications share the same theories and algorithms. c) Seamless integration can be used to achieve modular network.

(9) Neural biological analogy: the design of neural networks is caused by analogy to the brain, and the brain is a living example of fault-tolerant parallel processing; the design of neural networks is not only realizable in physics but also is rapid and efficient. Neurobiologists regard (artificial) neural networks as research tools to explain neural biological phenomena. On the other hand, engineers pay attention to neurobiology and use it as a new idea to solve complex problems. These problems are more complicated than the conventional hardware-based circuit design techniques can solve the problem. The following two examples illustrate the two views.

The vestibulo-ocular linear system model was compared by T. J. Anastasio (Anastasio, 1993). VOR (vestibulo-ocular reflex, VOR) is a part of the eye movement system, whose role is to allow the eye to move in the opposite direction of head rotation in order to maintain the visual (retinal) image stability. VOR is regulated by the front-end neurons from the vestibulo nucleic acid; front-end neurons sense neurons from the vestibulo and receive head rotation information and process it, and inform eye muscle movement neurons of the results. Inputs (head rotation information) and output (eye rotation) can be precisely determined, so VOR is very suitable for modeling. In addition, it is relatively simple reflex and its neurophysiology content that constitutes neurons has been well described. In these three types of neurons model, the front-end neurons (inner reflection neurons) in the vestibulo nerve nucleic acid is the most complex and most interesting. VOR was already modeled by block linear system descriptor and control theory. These models explain some overall natures of VOR, but is of little use to understanding the nature of neurons. This situation has been greatly improved through the neural network model. VOR recursive network model can reproduce and explain the nature of regulating neurons in the VOR in many aspects when dealing with signals as being static, dynamic, nonlinear and distributed, in particular vestibule nucleic acid neurons.

The retina is a place where we start to project the external physical image onto the receiver and form a visual representation and combine with the first neural image. It is the thin nerve tissue in the rear of the eyeball, and its function is to convert the optical images into neural images and transmit them to a large number of visual centers along the optical nerve for further processing. This is a complex task, and can be proved from the complex organization of the retina. The process of optical images being changed into neural images in the retina is made up of three stages (Sterling, 1990):

(1) Induction of the image conduction from the neuron layer.

(2) Transmission of the result signal (light stimuli generated) to a second polarity unit in the form of chemical synaptic.

(3) Similarly, transmission of result signal to neurons called ganglion in the form of synaptic chemical.

In the two induction phases (that is, from the receiver to the diode unit and from the diode unit to ganglion cells), there are special connection lateral connections known as the level neurons and non-longer neuronal cells. The work of these neurons is to transmit between the sensor layers. In addition, there are cells called the distribution element of the middle mesh, whose work is to transmit the signal from the internal sensor layer to the external sensor layer. Some researchers have established electronic chip simulating the structure of retina (Boahen, 1996). Such electronic chip is called neuromorphic circuit. An image sensor with neural form is composed of rows of photosensitive devices, with each element (pixel) analog circuits. It can simulate the retina to adapt to partial changes in brightness, edge detection and movement testing. Simulation in neurobiology, such as the integrated circuits in neural has another important application: it provides a hope and faith, and to some extent a proof of existence, that is, the physical understanding of structure of neurobiology has a creative impact on electronic Science Technology and ultra large scale integrated circuit technology.

So far, according to structure of large-scale parallel distribution of bio-neural network, various artificial neural networks built have been playing an increasingly important role in the information processing, but did not show wisdom to people's expectations. To make some analyses and reflection on the researching history of artificial neural network with the purpose of simulating the brain system, and to explore the next steps that might be taken would be useful to further development of the future intelligent information science. To make artificial neural network learn from human brain better and faster, there is a need to make some consideration and adjustment for the main direction of research, methods, steps, key technologies and measures to be taken in context in the future artificial neural network study.

To sum up, in order to make artificial neural networks learn better and faster from brain network, we can proceed from the following aspects.

(1) Make clear that the main advantage of artificial neural network is its non-accuracy of information processing. In accordance with the difference of input and output characteristics, the type of information that the intelligent system most frequently deal with can be grouped into four categories. Among them, the numerical calculation and the information processing tasks corresponding to logical deduction, the existing von Neumann digital computer has a mature and great ability, artificial neural networks are neither necessary nor in these areas of advantage to compete with them. The other three categories of information contain a non-precise information processing in the input or output message, and therefore they are fields the artificial neural network can play a role. It is these three categories of information processing that the vast majority of human mental work into.

(2) Explore new artificial neural network architecture. Neuroanatomical studies show that in human brain apart from a potential pulse circuit system constituted by the nerve cell body - axon - synapses - the nerve dendrites, there is a conditioning system that releases chemical neurotransmitter (glutamate) in about 0.02 micro - second gap between former-latter synapses; this chemical transmitter is equivalent to the gate circuit of semiconductor, and plays an

essential role in the regulation, control to enlargement. Therefore, how to create a synthesized mathematical model of the coupled system by nerve impulse transmitter system and chemical systems, analyzing its work mechanism and proposing feasible simple algorithm, is a way that deserves our attention, which in modeling makes the artificial neural network closer to the human nerve network.

(3) Search for new network topology and the corresponding learning algorithm. To date, feed-forward multi-layer (especially the three-tier) neural network and the structure of artificial neural network system based on to and - the plot-type neurons matching with error back propagation (back propagation, BP) learning algorithm are the most widely used. However, it still exists in the performance a number of areas to be improved. For example, it can only adjust the weights but not the network topology and it can not realize focus on function; when learning new samples it will be a "joyous chaos," the original preserved old samples; their learning algorithm, contains a more complex process of derivation and computing of the nonlinear activation function.

## 3.2 Neuron Model

From the features and functionality of neurons, we can know that neuron is a multi-input single-output information processing unit, and its information processing is nonlinear. According to the characteristics and function of neurons, they can be abstracted as a simple mathematical model. Artificial neural model used in engineering is shown in Figure 3.1.

In Figure 3.1, $X_1$, $X_2$, ..., $X_n$ is the input of $n$ neurons, that is the information of the axons from n neurons of the former level of. $A$ is the threshold of neuron $i$; $W_1$, $W_2$ ..., $W_n$ are the neurons weights to $X_1$, $X_2$, ..., $X_n$, also known as the transmission efficiency of synaptic; $Y$ is the output of neurons; $f$ is activation function, which determines the manner of the output when neurons reach a threshold at the common stimulation by input $X_1$, $X_2$, ..., $X_n$.

From Figure 3.1 the model of neurons, neurons expressions of the mathematical model can be given:

$$f(u_i) = \begin{cases} 1 & u_i > 0 \\ 0 & u_i \leqslant 0 \end{cases}$$

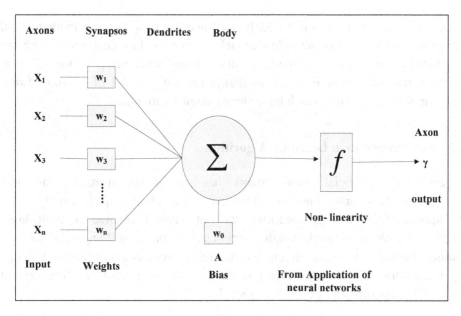

Fig. 3.1 The mathematical model of neurons

For activation function f there is a variety of forms, the most common of which include type of step, linear and S-type three forms, and the three forms are shown in Figure 3.2.

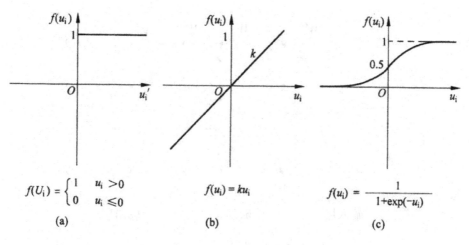

$$f(U_i) = \begin{cases} 1 & u_i > 0 \\ 0 & u_i \leq 0 \end{cases}$$

(a)

$$f(u_i) = ku_i$$

(b)

$$f(u_i) = \frac{1}{1+\exp(-u_i)}$$

(c)

Fig. 3.2 A typical activation function

Described above is the most widely used and the most familiar mathematical model of neurons and is the oldest model of neurons. In recent years, with the development of neural network theory, there have been a lot of new mathematical models of neurons, including the logic model of neurons, fuzzy neural models and so on, which have slowly come to attention.

## 3.3 Back-Propagation Learning Algorithm

In recent years, artificial neural networks has been applied in many areas, most of which use feed-forward network (feedforward) and backpropagation algorithm (backpropagation: BP). BP algorithm was put forward to solve the multi-layer feedforward neural network weights optimization and so, BP algorithm usually implies that the topological structure of neural network is a non-feedback multi-layer feedforward network. Therefore, non feedback multi-layer feedforward network is sometimes also called BP model.

### 3.2.1 Back propagation principle

Back propagation algorithm is used for feedforward multi-layer network learning algorithm, feed-forward multi-layer network structure is generally as shown in Figure 3.3.

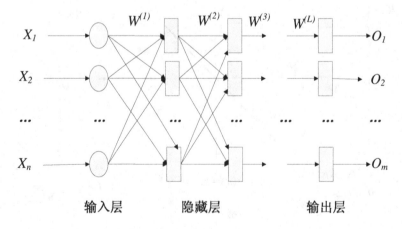

Fig. 3.3 Feedforward multi-layer network structure

It contains the input layer, output layer and the hidden layer between input and output layers. Neurons in the hidden layer are also known as hidden units. Hidden layer and the outside world is not connected. However, its state affects the relationship between input and output. That is to say changing the hidden layer weights can change the multi-layer neural network performance. Experiments show that the increase in the number of the hidden layers and hidden units does not necessarily improve network accuracy and power expression. Therefore, selection of BP network is generally the secondary network.

Back propagation algorithm is divided into two steps, namely, forward propagation and back propagation. The work of these two processes can be summarized as follows:

(1) Forward propagation. Sample input is processed layer after layer from the input layer through the hidden units after all the hidden layers, transmitted to the output layer; in the layer by layer processing, the state of neurons in each layer has an impact on the state of neurons in the next layer. In the output layer current output and expected output is compared. If the current output is not equal to the desired output, then back-propagation process is entered.

(2) Back-propagation. In back-propagation, the error signal returns reversely of forward propagation, and the coefficients of neurons in each hidden layer are modified in order to expect the smalle,t error signal. Suppose a neural network with M layers, and add in the input layer a sample X; suppose the sum of the input of neuron I in layer k is expressed as Uik, output Xik; the weight coefficient from neuron j of layer k-1 to neuron I of layer k is Wij; for each neuron, excitation function is f, then the relationship between the variables can be expressed as below:

$$X_i^k = f(U_i^k) \tag{3.1}$$

$$U_i^k = \sum_j W_{ij} X_j^{k-1} \tag{3.2}$$

### 3.2.2 *Back propagation algorithm*

In the application of back propagation algorithm to feedforward multi-layer network, when Sigmoid is used as activation function, the following steps can be used on the network for weights $W_{ij}$ recursive. Note if there are n eurons in each layer, that is, $i = 1, 2, ..., n$; $j = 1, 2, ..., n$. For neuron $i$ of layer $k$ there are $n$ weights $W_{i1}, W_{i2}, ..., W_{in\,+1}$ is taken for the threshold $\theta i$; and when inputting sample $X$, let $X = (X_1, X_2, ..., X_n, 1)$. Algorithm steps are as follows:

(1) Set the initial of weight $W_{ij}$. Set a smaller random non-zero number as coefficient $W_{ij}$ of each layer, but $W_{i,n+1} = -\theta$.

(2) Enter a sample $X = (X_1, X_2, ..., X_n, 1)$, as well as the corresponding desired output $Y = (Y_1, Y_2, ..., Y_n)$.

(3) Calculated output at all layers. For output $X_i^k$ of neuron $i$ in layer $k$ there is:

$$U_i^k = \sum_{j=1}^{n+1} W_{ij} X_j^{k-1}$$

$$X_{n+1}^{k-1} = 1, \quad W_{i,n+1} = -\theta$$

$$X_i^k = f(U_i^k)$$

(4) Find learning error $d_i^k$ for all layers. For output layer $k = m$, there is

$$d_i^m = X_i^m (1 - X_i^m)(X_i^m - Y_i)$$

For other layers, there is

$$d_i^k = X_i^k (1 - X_i^k) \cdot \sum_l W_{li} \cdot d_l^{k+l}$$

(5) To modofy weights $W_{ij}$ and threshold $\theta$:

$$\Delta W_{ij}(t+l) = \Delta W_{ij}(t) - \eta \cdot d_i^k \cdot X_j^{k-1}$$

Can get:

$$\Delta W_{ij}(t+l) = \Delta W_{ij}(t) - \eta \cdot d_i^k \cdot X_j^{k-1} + \alpha \Delta W_{ij}(t)$$

Where

$$\Delta W_{ij}(t) = -\eta \cdot d_i^k \cdot X_j^{k-1} + \alpha \Delta W_{ij}(t-l) = W_{ij}(t) - W_{ij}(t-l)$$

(6) When weights of different layers are calculated, the quality indicators can be set to determine whether the requirements are met or not. If the requirements are met, the algorithm ends; if not, return to step (3).

The learning process, for any given sample $X_p = (X_{p1}, X_{p2}, \ldots X_{pn}, 1)$ and the desired output $Y_p = (Y_{p1}, Y_{p2}, \ldots, Y_{pn})$ should be implemented, until all the input and output requirements are met.

### 3.2.4 Advantages and disadvantages of back-propagation network

Multi-layer feedforward back propagation network is currently the most widely used model of neural network, but it is not perfect, in order to better understand and apply neural network to problem solving, here its advantages and disadvantages are discussed. The advantages of multi-layer back propagation network:

(1) Network substantially realizes mapping function from input to output, and the mathematical theory has proved it has the function of realizing any complex non-linear mapping. This makes it particularly suitable for solving complex problems of internal mechanisms;

(2) The network can automatically retrieve "reasonable" rules of solution through learning from example set with correct answers, namely, self-learning ability;

(3) The network has a promotion, a generalization ability.

Disadvantages of Multi-layer back propagation network:

(1) BP learning algorithm is very slow, and its main causes are: a) as the nature of BP algorithm is the gradient descent method, and the objective function it is to optimize is very complex and, therefore, it is bound to occur "zigzag phenomenon", which decrease the efficiency of BP algorithm; b) the existence of the paralysis phenomenon, as the optimized objective function is complex, and it will result in the emergence of some flat areas when neurons output is close to 0 or 1; in these areas, change of weights error is so small that it almost halts the training process; c) in order to enable the network to implement BP algorithm, the traditional one-dimensional search for each iteration step length shouldn't be used, and the update rule must be given to the network in advance. This approach will lead to inefficient algorithm.

(2) More possibilities of network training failure, and its causes are: a) from the mathematical point of view, BP algorithm is a local search optimization method, but the problem it is to solve is the solution of overall extreme value of

the complex nonlinear function, so the algorithm is likely to fall into local extremum, and the training fails; b) network approximation and promotion capacity is closely related to typical of the learning samples, and selecting typical example problems to form a training set is very difficult.

(3) It's difficult to solve the conflict between the scale of the application and the network size. This involves the relationship of network capacity possibility and feasibility, that is, the complexity of learning.

(4) There is no unified and complete theoretical guidance for choice of network structure and generally it can only be selected by experience. To this end, there are claims that the selection of structure of neural network selected is a form of art. Network structure gives a direct impact on network approximation capacity and promotion nature. Therefore, how to choose a suitable network structure in the application is an important issue.

(5) New samples have to influence the successful network, and describe the characteristics of each input sample must with the same number.

(6) The contradictions between network ability to forecast (also known as generalization ability) and training capacity (also called approximation ability, learning ability). Under normal circumstances, poor training means poor forecasting ability and to some extent, with the improved training ability, forecasting ability is also improved. However, this trend has a limit, when this limit is reached, with the improvement of training capacity, the forecasting ability decreases, that is the so-called "over-fit" phenomenon. At this point, the network has learned an excessive number of samples details, and can not reflect the law of contained in the samples.

## 3.4 Neural Network Ensemble

In 1990, L. K. Hansen and P. Salamon put forward the neural network ensemble method (Hansen et al., 1990). They prove that simply by training a number of neural network and fitting results significantly can improve the generalization ability of the neural network. Neural network ensemble can be defined as a finite number of neural networks learning the same issue. The output integrated in a sample of input is co-decided by the output integrated in the sample which composes of the neural network. Neural network ensemble theoretical analysis and its implementation are divided into two aspects, namely, the generation of conclusions and the generation of the network individual.

### 3.4.1 Generation of conclusion

Hansen and Salamon have proved that for the neural network classifier, the adoption of the integrated approach can effectively improve the generalization ability. Assume that integration consists of $N$ independent neural network classifiers. Using absolute majority voting method, then assume that each network gives correct classification with $1-p$ probability, and the error between the network is not related, then the error probability for the neural network ensemble is $p_{err}$

$$P_{err} = \sum_{k>N/2}^{N} \binom{N}{k} p^k (1-p)^{N-k} \tag{3.3}$$

When $p < 1/2$, $p_{err}$ monotonously decreases with $N$ increasing. Therefore, if each neural network prediction accuracy is higher than 50%, and error between the network is not related, the more networks in the neural network ensemble, the higher accuracy of integration. When $N$ tends to infinity, integrated error rate tends to 0. When using relative majority voting method, the neural network ensemble error rate is much more complicated than the Equation (3.3), but Hansen and Salamon analysis showed that the relative majority voting method in most circumstances can get better results than absolute majority voting method.

In 1995, A. Krogh and J. Vedelsbygave the generalization error formula of neural network integration (Krogh et al., 1995). Assume that learning task is an integration composed of n neural networks for approximation f: $\Re' \to \Re$. The integration uses weighted average, and the networks are given weight value of $\omega_\alpha$, and satisfies Equation (3.4):

$$\omega_\alpha > 0$$

$$\sum_\alpha \omega_\alpha = 1 \tag{3.4}$$

Assume the training set is drawn randomly by distribution $p(x)$, while the output of network $\alpha$ to input $X$ is $V^\alpha(X)$, then the output of neural network ensemble is

$$\bar{V}(X) = \sum_\alpha \omega_\alpha V^\alpha(X) \tag{3.5}$$

Generalization error Ea of neural network $\alpha$ and generalization error $E$ of neural network ensemble are, respectively,

$$E^{\alpha} = \int dx p(x)(f(x) - V^{\alpha}(x))^2 \qquad (3.6)$$

$$E = \int dx p(x)(f(x) - \overline{V}(x))^2 \qquad (3.7)$$

Weighted average of generalization error of the network is

$$\overline{E} = \sum_{\alpha} \omega_{\alpha} E^{\alpha} \qquad (3.8)$$

Degree of difference $A^{\alpha}$ of the neural network and degree of difference $\overline{A}$ of neural network ensemble respectively are:

$$A^{\alpha} = \int dx p(x)(V(x) - \overline{V}(x)^2 \qquad (3.9)$$

$$\overline{A} = \sum_{\alpha} \omega_{\alpha} A^{\alpha} \qquad (3.10)$$

Generalization error of the neural network ensemble is

$$E = \overline{E} - \overline{A} \qquad (3.11)$$

$A$ in Equation (3.11) measures degree of the of relation of neurons in the neural network integration. If integration is a high degree of bias, that is, for the same input, all the networks in the integration will given the same or similar output; at this time the difference in degree of integration close to 0, and the generalization error is closer to the weighted average of the network generalization error. Conversely, if the network integration is independent of each other, then the degree of differences in the integration is much larger, and the generalization error will be far less than the weighted average of the network generalization error. Therefore, in order to enhance generalization ability of the neural network integration, error of networks in the integration should be made integrated unrelated as much as possible.

### 3.4.2 Generation of individual

In 1997, Y. Freund and R. E. Schapire as representatives, analyzed Boosting-type method (Freund et al., 1997), and proved the training error of the final prediction function $H$ generated by such methods satisfies Equation (3.12), of which $\varepsilon_t$ is the training error of function $h_t$, $\gamma_t = 1/2 - \varepsilon_t$

$$H = \prod_t [2\sqrt{\varepsilon_t(1-\varepsilon_t)}]$$

$$= \prod_t \sqrt{1-4\gamma_t^2} \le exp(-2t\sum_t \gamma_t^2) \tag{3.12}$$

From Equation (3.12) we can see, as long as the learning algorithm is slightly better than random guessing, the training error will decrease with the $t$ exponentially.

In 1996, L. Breiman made a theoretical analysis on Bagging (Breiman 1996). He pointed out that the highest attainable accuracy of classification and the accuracy rate of Bagging as shown in Equation (3.13) and Equation (3.14), in which C represents input set of correct sequence, C' for C's complementary set, and I (•) for the indicator function.

$$r^* = \int \max_j P(j \mid x) P_X(x) \tag{3.13}$$

$$r_A = \int_{x\in C} \max P(j \mid x) P_x(dx) +$$

$$\int_{x\in C'} [\sum_j I(\phi_A(x) = j) P(j \mid x)] P_X(x) \tag{3.14}$$

Obviously, Bagging can make the correct sequence set achieve optimal classification accuracy, but the predictive function alone can not do this.

## 3.5 Bayesian Linking Field Model

### 3.5.1 Related works

Evidence from neuroanatomy and neurophysiology indicates that various sensory information such as color, motion, location, and object identity is processed in separate brain regions (Damasio et al., 1985; Livingstone et al. 1988). The brain must combine inputs from several different sensory modalities and then generate a complete internal representation. How does the brain accomplish this task is called "binding problem" (Crick, 1984; Sejnowski, 1986). Yet, it is surprised and disappointed that although binding problem is so important to both the functional and mechanistic understanding of cognition, although increasing attention and enormous research resources are devoted, we still cannot achieve consensus towards binding mechanisms.

Many theories have been proposed to probe binding mechanisms, including the feature integration theory (FIT) suggested by Treisman (Treisman et al., 1980), convergent zones investigated by Damasio (von der Malsburg, 1986), and so forth. Among these theories, temporal neural synchronization theory, which comes from the Correlation Theory of Brain Function (Gray et al., 1989), is the most influential theory on binding mechanisms. According to neural synchronization theory, feature binding is achieved via neural synchronization. When external stimuli come into the brain, neurons corresponding to the features of the same object will form a dynamic neural assembly by temporal synchronous neural oscillation, and the dynamic neural assembly, as an internal representation in the brain, codes the object in the external world.

Since temporal neural synchronization theory was proposed, it has gained growing support in terms of neurobiology. In 1989, Gray et al. published their research result on the gamma oscillation in the human brain (Guo, 1997). After that, researchers found that synchronous neural oscillation exists not only in the human brain, or mammal brain, but also in the entomic brain.

In 1990, Eckhorn and coworkers proposed a Linking Field Network according to the synchronized neural oscillation in the visual cortex of cat (Johnson et al., 1999). Linking Field Network can synchronize stimuli-evoked oscillations in different regions of the visual cortex if the regions have similar local coding properties. The proposed model is composed of many interconnected neurons. Each of the neurons has two functionally distinct inputs, namely feeding inputs and linking inputs. The two parts of inputs are coupled by multiplication, not by addition like the traditional neural networks.

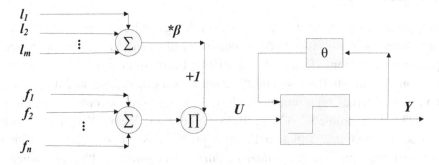

Fig. 3.4 The structure of a neuron in the Linking Field Network

Figure 3.4 illustrates the structure of a neuron, which has only one dendrite, in Linking Field Network. Let the feeding inputs of the dendrite be $f_1(t)$, $f_2(t)$, ..., $f_n(t)$, and the linking inputs be $l_1(t)$, $l_2(t)$, ..., $l_m(t)$. Then the output of the neuron is calculated with formula (3.15).

$$\begin{cases} U(t) = (\sum_{i=1}^{n} f_i(t)) \cdot (1 + \beta \sum_{j=1}^{m} l_j(t)) \\ Y(t) = \begin{cases} 1 & \text{if } U(t) > \theta(t) \\ 0 & \text{else} \end{cases} \end{cases} \tag{3.15}$$

where $U(t)$ is the membrane potential of the neuron; $\beta$ is the coupling parameter indicating the coupling strength; $Y(t)$ represents the output of the neuron; and $\theta(t)$ is an adaptive threshold, which is determined by the values of $Y$ and $t$.

Since it provided a simple, effective simulation tool for studying synchronous pulse dynamics in networks, Eckhorn's model was soon recognized as having significant applications in image processing. Later, this model and its modifications and variations became known collectively as Pulse Coupled Neural Networks (PCNN). The central new concept of Eckhorn's model was the introduction of a secondary receptive field, the linking field, whose integrated input modulated the primary feeding receptive field input by means of an internal cellular circuit. By analyzing the neuron circuit in this model (here we used the simplest neuron model, a compartmental neuron model with only one dendrite and one soma), researchers proved that the coupling relations among different inputs are not merely additive coupling. In fact, the integrated input is a combination of linear and multiplicative terms (Gerstner, et al., 2002).

Bayesian Linking Field Model is also a network model composed of Interconnected neurons. Neurons in our model contain two types of inputs, namely feeding inputs and linking inputs, and they are coupled via multiplication as well. The difference is that: we also imposed noisy neural model, Bayesian method and competition mechanism to tackle the problem we mentioned above in feature binding.

### 3.5.2 Noisy neuron firing strategy

According to the detailed neuron model, the change of neural membrane potential exhibits threshold like property. When input stimuli exceed some threshold, neuron will generate an action potential. For simplicity, many formal neuron models import the threshold concept directly. When the nonlinear transformation of inputs exceeds some predefined value, neuron will fire. Spike response model (SRM), integrate-and-fire model (I&F) and Eckhorn's model all utilize this strategy. *In vivo* recordings of neuronal activity are characterized by a high degree of irregularity, which is caused by various noises in neural system. On the one hand, the existence of noises makes the modeling of neurons more complicated; on the other hand, it improves the coding capability of neuron models, for it allows noisy models to code sub-threshold inputs. One of the popular noisy neuron models is Escape Noise Model (Perry et al., 1982). In this model, firing of neurons is not controlled by a threshold, but is described by a firing probability. Different input will change the firing probability of a neuron. In our Bayesian Linking Field Model, we adopt the noisy firing strategy from the Escape Noise Model, viz. the outputs of neurons in our model are probabilities but not pulse. As a result, in our model the coding sphere of input stimuli is largely enlarged, and the proposed model carries more neurobiological properties.

### 3.5.3 *Bayesian coupling of inputs*

As a result the coupling of inputs of a neuron needs to couple firing probabilities. In cognitive research, if we use a neuron to represent a perceptual object, its feeding pre-synaptic neurons usually denote its composing features or compartments and its linking pre-synaptic neurons indicate other objects, which have more or less relations with this neuron. Thus, if we leave linking inputs out of consideration, based on the relationship of parts and whole, we get:

$$P(X) = \sum_i w_i P(f_i) \qquad (3.16)$$

where $X$ is the neuron we concern, $f_i$ is its feeding, pre-synaptic neuron, and $w_i$ is weight for synaptic connection, which indicates the importance of $f_i$ as a part in the whole entity $X$.

In the following we examine the influence from linking inputs. Suppose that all the linking inputs are conditionally independent. Based on Bayesian theorem, we get:

$$P(l_i \mid l_1, \ldots, l_{i-1}, l_{i+1}, \ldots, l_n) = P(l_i) \quad i = 1, \ldots, n \qquad (3.17)$$

where $X$ is the neuron we concern, $lj$ is its linking pre-synaptic neuron, and $w'j = P(lj|X)/P(lj)$ is weight for synaptic connection, which represents the importance of $lj$ to $X$. $P(X)$ is the prior probability calculated from feeding information; $P(X |l_1,l_2,l_3,...)$ is the post probability after getting information from linking inputs; $P(l_j)$ is the firing probability of $l_j$. Figure 3.5 illustrates the structure of a sample neuron in our model. From formula (3.16) and (3.17) we can see that in our model, coupling among feeding inputs is additive, while coupling among integrated feeding inputs and all the linking inputs is multiplicative. These coupling rules are deduced based on the Bayesian Theorem. From the analysis of J. L. Johnson and co-workers (Johnson et al., 1999), we learn that the coupling of inputs from presynaptic neurons is quite complicated. It contains many high order multiplicative coupling factors. So our coupling strategy fits the neurobiological properties of neurons.

### 3.5.4 Competition among neurons

Sufficient biological evidence shows that there are numerous competition phenomena in the neural activities of brain. Perry and Linden's work demonstrated that there are competitive relations among the cells in retina Poldrack and Packard's research proved that, for both human beings and animals, there are broad competitive phenomena in various regions of brain cortex (Poldrack et al., 2003). Accordingly, we import competitive mechanism into our model.

Let $X_1$ and $X_2$ be two different neurons; $F_1$ and $F_2$ be the set of their feeding pre-synaptic neurons respectively. Then there exists competitive relation between $X_1$ and $X_2$ if and only if at least one of the two conditions below holds.

(1) $F_1 \cap F_2 \neq \emptyset$

(2) Exist $f_1 \in F_1$ and $f_2 \in F_2$, $f_1$ and $f_2$ are competitive.

To implement competitive relations, we normalize the firing probabilities of the neurons that are competitive each other.

Let $X_1, X_2, ..., X_n$ be $n$ neurons that are competitive each other; $P_{before}(X_i)$ is the firing probability of $X_i$ before competition. Then the firing probability of $X_i$ after competition is:

$$P_{after}(X_i) = \frac{P_{before}(X_i)}{\sum_{j=1}^{n} P_{before}(X_j)} \tag{3.18}$$

Based on the above discussion, the complete Bayesian Linking Field Model is shown in Figure 3.5.

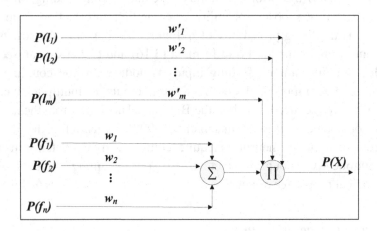

Fig. 3.5 The structure of Bayesian Linking Field Model

## 3.6  Neural Field Model

Artificial neural network is considered a learning machine with a broad non-linear relationship approximation mechanism and a non-linear data relationship classifier. It is essential in that it provides a nonlinear function relationship approximation theory. In 1985 S. Amari proposed information geometric and used in the study of the theory of neural computation (Amari, 1985). The basic idea is to regard the space consisting of all the neural network transformation as a manifold space. The manifold space is extension of general Euclidean space and Hilbert space, which enables us to establish approximation theory and topology correction theory in a more generalized non-linear space and non-Euclidean space, to better understand the neural network model transformation mechanism and learning problems through geometry and topology structural analysis. SHI Zhong-Zhi and Zhang Jian analyzed the expression of neural network architecture, system identification, the mechanism of transformation from the perspective of the micro-shape and topological transform in order to understand the organizational structure and the positioning mechanism of the neural network in more general information processing system space. We consider the overall structure of neural computation, propose the overall structure coupling of field organization transformation and field response transformation as the new method of information processing, the mechanism of transformation of artificial neural network model; introduce modular, hierarchical, scalability of models, use manifold geometry dual to explain it, raise the corresponding learning algorithm (Zhang, 1996).

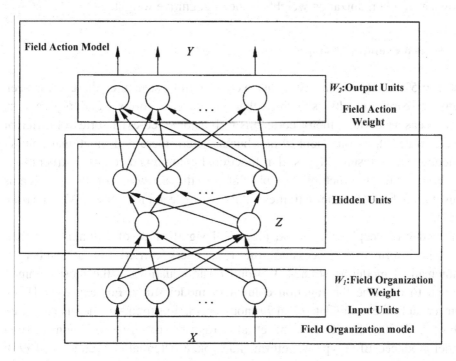

Fig. 3.6 Neural field model

Neural network includes input units, hidden units and output units. Because of the existence of hidden units, hidden units are regard as non-measurable, and are values which need to be estimated in the information processing. We understand the information processing of neural network as non-complete data information processing. We give a new form of description of neural network transformation mechanism. Transformation mechanism of neural network consists of two processes: the organization process of neural field realizes expression from the input mode through the hidden units; neural field reaction process realizes the transform from expression to the output (see Figure 3.6). Here, X is the input space; X × Z is the space, or called neural field expression; Y is the output space. Field organization transform model is expressed as T: X → X × Z, which, Z is measurable space, or space for auxiliary information. Field organization model realizes the characteristics of input patterns which may be achieved by the algorithm or mapping. Its purpose is to extract the characteristics of the structure of input mode, so that the desired output mode is much easier; in the neural network, the connection weights contained in the field organization model, known as field organization weights value or cognitive weight.

## 3.7 Nrural Column Model

Since 1957 V. B. Mountcastle discovered column structure, there have been many research results showing that in visual cortex, auditory cortex, somatosensory cortex , motor cortex, as well as other co-exist cortex of different species (rat, cat, rabbit, monkey and human, etc.), there is a functional column structure. These results suggest that functional column is a common structure, is the basic unit of structure and physiology; the activities of these columns constitute a basis for the activities of the entire cerebral cortex (Mountcastle, 1957).

In order to deeply understand biological significance of columns and their roles in information processing, the researchers carried out a number of mathematical modeling studies. Wilson-Cowan equations is the most common method to describe the function column in model study. For example: H. G. Shuster and others simulated synchronous oscillation found in the visual cortex (Shuster, 1990); B. H. Jansen, et al. proposed coupling function column model produced EEG type waveform and evoked potential (Jansen et al., 1993); T. Fukai designed a functional column network model to simulate the access of visual design and so on (Fukai, 1994). Some other feature column modes describing functional oscillation activities of the column are phase column models. Only a small number of model is based on the single neuron. For instance: E. Fransén and others replaced the single-cell in the traditional network with multi- cell functional columns to build an attractor network, to simulate the working memory; D. Hansel, etc. built a super column model under the structure of the direction column of visual cortex column, studied synchronization and chaotic characteristics, and explained mechanism of the function column with the direction selection.

Su Li used modeling neurons as the basic unit, organized function column model in accordance with cortical function structure, and explored the relationship between these models and the outside input and network structure, researched network model formed by a number of functional column link and what new characteristics it has in patterns of activity (Li et al., 2004).

Rose-Hindmarsh equations is selected to describe the single neuron:

$$\dot{x} = y + ax^3 - bx^2 - z + I_{syn} + I_{stim}$$
$$\dot{y} = c - dx^2 - y \qquad\qquad (3.19)$$
$$\dot{z} = r[s(x - x_0) - z]$$

where: $x$ represents membrane potential; $y$, the rapid return current; $z$ describes the slow change in the adjustment of current; $I_{syn}$, the synaptic current; $I_{stim}$, external input; a, b, c, d, r, s, $x_0$ are constants. Here a = 1, b = 3, c = 1, d = 5, s = 2 and $x_0$ = -1.6. The time scale in Rose-Hindmarsh model is 5 units, equivalent to 1ms.

According to the results of physiological tests, neurons cortical functional columns of in accordance with the physiological characteristics have two categories: RS cells (regular-spiking, RS) and FS cells (fast-spiking, FS). RS cells are excited, in the form of the pyramidal cells, is characterized by its clear and rapid dissemination frequency of adaptation, for continuous current stimulation over time to rapidly reduce the dissemination frequency. FS cells are suppressed in the usual form of non-pyramidal cells, with physiological characteristics of low adaptability to continuous input current frequency. We use different parameters r to represent the characteristics of these two cells: rRS=0.015, rFS=0.001.

The model takes synaptic model based on currents. Before the synaptic action potential in each cell will trigger the postsynaptic cell input $I_{syn}$ Synaptic current $I_{syn}$ is expressed as:

$$I_{syn} = g_{syn}V_{syn}(e^{-t/\tau_1} - e^{-t/\tau_2}) \qquad\qquad (3.20)$$

where, $g_{syn}$ is the membrane conductance, $\tau_1$ and $\tau_2$ are time constants, $V_{syn}$ is the postsynaptic potential. $V_{syn}$ is used to regulate the strength of synaptic coupling. Use $V_{RR}$ to express the excitement connection $V_{syn}$ between RS cells. Similarly, Vsyn projected from RS cells onto FS cells and from FS cells onto RS cells are expressed, respectively, as VRF and $V_{FR}$. Parameter is set to $g_{RR}$=4, $\tau_1$(RR)=3, $\tau_2$(RR)=2, $g_{RF}$=8, $\tau_1$(RF)=1, $\tau_2$(RF)=0.7, $g_{FR}$=4, $\tau_1$(FR)=3, $\tau_2$(FR)=2.$V_{FR}$ is always set to -1. $V_{RR}$ and $V_{RF}$ in the process of the simulation vary between 0.1 to 1.

# Chapter 4

# Mind Model

The mind means all spiritual activities of human being, including sensibility, perception, will, feeling, learning, memory, thinking and the intuition etc., in which the formation, the process and the principle of combining the non-rational psychology and the rational cognition of human being are studied through the modern scientific methods.

## 4.1 Introduction

The anthropologists believe that every living being has its mind. The development of mind has experienced four stages, that is, simple reaction, condition reaction, tool using and language symbol. Only the human being can use language symbol to communicate with the outside environment. Thus the Creation and the development of mind in human being are concerned to the language that people use. The words take the role of carrier in symbolic language. Although the appearance of words came later, it is unique to the development of mind and civilization. 250 million years ago human consciousness emerged. 300,000-100,000 years ago humans started using symbolic language. China's first writing Oracle has more than 3,000 years of history. In this long evolutionary process, the human use of symbolic language and symbolic words is a very short period of time, but the development of the human mind, human culture and civilization has achieved such a brilliant achievement which indicates how closely the relationship between language and mind.

Cognitive science research is the use of information views and information processing theory to study how care and select the information. The cognition and memory of information and the decision making through the information to direct outside action, etc, have become the major area in the development of modern science. The theory of information processing is the major direction of modern experimental psychology, which has contributed to the perception, the memory, the attention, the language, the thinking, the problem solving and so on.

Information has penetrated into all fields of human society has become important concepts in modern society. Information is neither matter and energy are not things "Properties" and "relationship", but the properties of things, contact, and the meaning of the symptoms. Scientific information largely abandoned the concept of various specific contents of the communication process, while the extraction of their quantity, the amount of information and the possibility emerged of things linked to describe very different phenomena and processes to provide a unified approach. The use of information, ideas and theories, analysis of system performance and the way the information law of motion method, which has now become an effective means of complex things. In the cognitive science research, involving a variety of sensory contact with the outside world, the nerve center and the link between the various senses, the brain's thinking and memory and so on, all of them there is information on the receipt, storage, processing and the message transformation, and thus maintain normal when purposeful movement, Figure 4.1 shows the system information transformation process.

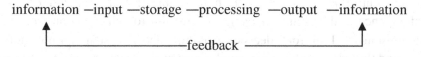

information —input —storage —processing —output —information
feedback

Fig. 4.1 the information conversion processing of system

In the year 1948, C. Shannon, the mathematician from American Bell Academe, had the paper "A mathematical theory of communication" published in Bell System Technical Journal (Shannon, 1948). Some basic problems about the communication were illustrated theoretically from the aspects of information source, information channel, coding and information host. So the information theory was born. The appearance of information theory furthered the research of cognitive theory. The cognitive processing of human being has close relationship to the information obtaining, conversing, transmitting and processing. The sensing cognition is the process of information obtaining, transforming and transferring while the rational cognition is that one of information dealing in the brain of human being.

In a word, the information theory turns the problems of communication into the science. People have begun to form their information view. Now people have known three elements of the objective world – the material, the energy and the information. The material is the first element to be known, while the importance of energy has not been known until the industry period. The World War II and the development of communication after that war led the birth of the information theory. With the fast development and extension of computer science, the ability of data processing has been improved greatly, from which people have come to know the meaning and usage of information. In the late 1970's, based on the information theory, the controlling theory, the electronic technology, the automation technology and the computer science, the information science was formed.

Information science is an interdisciplinary science primarily concerned with the analysis, collection, classification, manipulation, storage, retrieval and dissemination of information. The research of information science is not only in the field of communicating engineer, but also the whole process for people to recognize the world and change it. From the information science point of view, the system is both information source and information host; while communication is information transmission; transformation, computing and thinking, are information processing; decision-making is information on regeneration; control is the reaction from the subjective information on the object; intelligence is the ability of using information to achieve some goal in certain circumstances. Therefore, decision-making, control, system optimization, intelligence and thought are all fundamental issues of information science. As for its application is a comprehensive and pervasive in the natural and social sciences in various fields.

Information Science has developed an own unique methodology system. Information processing approach is from the information point of view to qualitative and quantitative analysis of the information process contained in the things, establishing information models which reflect the movement laws, and understanding its working mechanism, that is, information analysis methods. The other hand, in design system, but also from the information point of view, constitute a requirement to meet the user performance information model, and then the appropriate technical means to achieve this model, to meet the design goal, which is an information integrated approach. Information analysis to solve the problem for the understanding of complex systems, information integrated solutions for complex design problems. Information processing are two important criteria, namely, functional criteria and the overall criteria. Functional behavior of the criteria for functional simulation of the criteria, namely, a comprehensive analysis of the system, the grasping function of system behavior is similar to the structure is not pursuing similar. Overall optimization of the overall criteria are the criteria, namely, the use of information integrated approach to design the system, when, it is necessary to optimize the overall performance of the system, rather than the pursuit of each local optimum. Information method reveals machines, living organisms and social life of information between the movement patterns of the different linkages, reveals a deeper laws of the movement of things, and provided a scientific description to some of the difficult understand phenomena of the past.

Mind problem is a very complicated nonlinear problems, we must use modern scientific methods to study the mind world. Mind scientific research is the psychological or mind processes, but it is not a traditional psychological science, it must find neurological evidence of biology and brain science in order to provide certainty for the intellectual foundation. Mind world and the modern logic and mathematics may be described there was a marked difference in the world: logic and mathematics may be described in the world is a non-contradictory world, while the mind is everywhere in the world is full of contradictions; logic and mathematics may be the world's to understand and grasp can only be used deductive reasoning and analytical methods, while the human mind to grasp the world there are deduction, induction, analogy, analysis, synthesis, abstraction, generalization of association and intuition, and so various means. Mind world is much more complex than the possible world described with mathematics and logic. How should we enter from the finite, non-contradictory, the use of deductive method, relatively simple possible worlds into the infinite, contradictions, the use of a variety of logic and cognitive methods, more complex mind world? This is a fundamental issues should be explored by mind research.

## 4.2 The Physical Symbol System

Simon has defined that a physical symbol system is a machine that, as it moves through time, produces an evolving collection of symbol structures. Symbol structures can, and commonly do, sever as internal representations (e.g., "mental images") of the environment to which the symbol system is seeking to adapt (Simon, 1982). A symbol system possesses a number of simple processes that operate upon symbol structures - processes that create, modify, copy and destroy symbols. It must have means for acquiring information from the external environment that can be encoded into internal symbols, as well as means for producing symbols that initiate action upon the environment. Thus it must use symbols to designate objects and relations and actions in the world external to the system.

Symbol systems are called "physical" to remind the reader that they exist in real-world devices, fabricated of glass and metal (computers) or flesh and blood (brains). In the past we have been more accustomed to thinking of symbol systems of mathematics and logic as abstract and disembodied, leaving out of account the paper and pencil and human minds that were required to actually bring them to life. Computers have transported symbols systems from the platonic heaven of ideas to the empirical world of actual processes carried out by machines or brains, or by the two of them working together.

Symbol system (SS) consists of a memory, a set of operators, a control, an input, and an output. Its inputs are the objects in certain locations; its outputs are the modification or creation of the objects in certain (usually different) locations. Its external behavior, then, consists of the outputs it produces as a function of its inputs. The larger system of environment plus SS forms a closed system, since the output objects either become or affect later input objects. SS's internal state consists of the state of its memory and the state of the control; and its internal behavior consists of the variation in this internal state over time. Figure 4.2 shows you a framework of symbol system.

Two notions are central to this structure of expressions, symbols, and objects: designation and interpretation. Designation means that an expression designates an object if, given the expression, the system can either affect the object itself or behave in ways dependent on the object. Interpretation has been defined that the system can interpret an expression if the expression designates a process and if, given the expression, the system can carry out the process. Interpretation implies a special form of dependent action: given an expression the system can perform the indicated process, which is to say, it can evoke and execute its own processes from expressions that designate them.

The 1975 ACM Turing Award was presented jointly to Allen Newell and Herbert A. Simon at the ACM Annual Conference in Minneapolis, October 20. They gave Ten Turing Lecture entitled *Computer science as empirical inquiry: Symbols and search*. At this lecture they presented a general scientific hypothesis—a law of qualitative structure for symbol systems: *The Physical Symbol System Hypothesis* (Newell and Simon, 1976). A physical symbol system

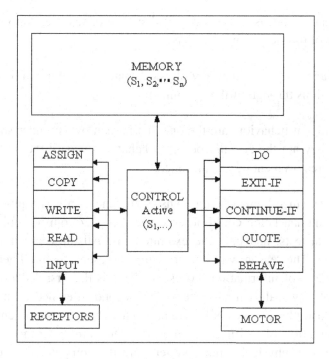

Fig. 4.2 Structure of symbol system (Newell, 1980)

has the necessary and sufficient means for general intelligent action. By "necessary" we mean that any system that exhibits general intelligence will prove upon analysis to be a physical symbol system. By "sufficient" we mean that any physical symbol system of sufficient size can be organized further to exhibit general intelligence. By "general intelligent action" we wish to indicate the same scope of intelligence as we see in human action: that in any real situation behavior appropriate to the ends of the system and adaptive to the demands of the environment can occur, within some limits of speed and complexity. The Physical Symbol System Hypothesis clearly is a law of qualitative structure. It specifies a general class of systems within which one will find those capable of intelligent action. Its main points of the hypothesis list as the following:

(1) The hypothesis of physical symbol system: the necessary and sufficient condition of representing the intelligent actions through physical system is that it is a physical symbol system.

(2) The necessary means that any physical system of representing intelligence is one example of physical symbol system.

(3) The sufficiency means that any physical symbol system could represent the intelligent actions through further organizing.

(4) The intelligent behaviors are the one that human owns: under some physical limitations, they are the actually occurred behaviors that fit the system purpose and meet the requirement of circumstance.

From above, since human being owns intelligence, so it is a physical symbol system. The human being could observe and recognize outside objects, receive the intellectual tests, and pass the examinations. All these are human being's representation. The reason why human could represent his intelligence is based on his procedure of information processing. This is the first deduction from the hypothesis of physical symbol system. The second inference is that, since the computer is one physical symbol system, it must show its intelligence, which is the basic condition of artificial intelligence. The third inference is that since human being is a physical symbol system and the computer is also a physical symbol system, we can simulate human being's actions through the computer. We can describe the procedure of human's action, or establish one theory to describe the whole activity procedure of human being.

## 4.3  ACT-R Model

**ACT-R** (Adaptive Control of Thought–Rational) is a cognitive architecture mainly developed by John Robert Anderson at Carnegie Mellon University. Like any cognitive architecture, ACT-R aims to define the basic and irreducible cognitive and perceptual operations that enable the human mind. In theory, each task that humans can perform should consist of a series of these discrete operations.

### 4.3.1  Brief history

The roots of ACT-R can be backtraced to the original HAM (Human Associative Memory) model of memory, described by John R. Anderson and Gordon Bower in 1973. The HAM model was later expanded into the first version of the ACT theory. This was the first time the procedural memory was added to the original declarative memory system, introducing a computational dichotomy that was later proved to hold in human brain. The theory was then further extended into the ACT* model of human cognition.

In the late eighties, Anderson devoted himself to exploring and outlining a mathematical approach to cognition that he named Rational Analysis. The basic assumption of Rational Analysis is that cognition is optimally adaptive, and precise estimates of cognitive functions mirror statistical properties of the environment. Later on, he came back to the development of the ACT theory, using the Rational Analysis as a unifying framework for the underlying calculations. To highlight the importance of the new approach in the shaping of the architecture, its name was modified to ACT-R, with the "R" standing for "Rational".

In 1993, Anderson met with Christian Lebiere, a researcher in connectionist models mostly famous for developing with Scott Fahlman the Cascade Correlation learning algorithm. Their joint work culminated in the release of ACT-R 4.0, which included optional perceptual and motor capabilities, mostly inspired from the EPIC architecture, which greatly expanded the possible applications of the theory.

After the release of ACT-R 4.0, John Anderson became more and more interested in the underlying neural plausibility of his life-time theory, and began to use brain imaging techniques pursuing his own goal of understanding the computational underpinnings of human mind. The necessity of accounting for brain localization pushed for a major revision of the theory. ACT-R 5.0 introduced the concept of modules, specialized sets of procedural and declarative representations that could be mapped to known brain systems. In addition, the interaction between procedural and declarative knowledge was mediated by newly introduced buffers, specialized structures for holding temporarily active information (see the section above). Buffers were thought to reflect cortical activity, and a subsequent series of studies later confirmed that activations in cortical regions could be successfully related to computational operations over buffers.

A new version of the code, completely rewritten, was presented in 2005 as ACT-R 6.0. It also included significant improvements in the ACT-R coding language.

### *4.3.2 The ACT-R architecture*

Figure 4.3 illustrates the basic architecture of ACT-R 5.0 which contains some of the modules in the system: a visual module for identifying objects in the visual field, a manual module for controlling the hands, a declarative module for retrieving information from memory, and a goal module for keeping track of current goals and intentions. Coordination in the behavior of these modules is achieved through a central production system. This central production system is not sensitive to most of the activity of these modules but rather can only respond to a limited amount of information that is deposited in the buffers of these modules. The core production system can recognize patterns in these buffers and make changes to these buffers. The information in these modules is largely encapsulated, and the modules communicate only through the information they make available in their buffers.

The architecture assumes a mixture of parallel and serial processing. Within each module, there is a great deal of parallelism. For instance, the visual system

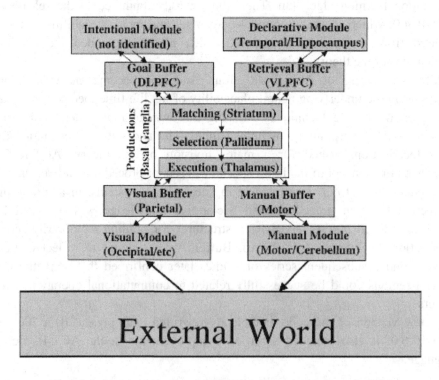

Fig. 4.3 the basic architecture of ACT-R 5.0 (From Anderson et al., 2004)

is simultaneously processing the whole visual field, and the declarative system is executing a parallel search through many memories in response to a retrieval request. Also, the processes within different modules can go on in parallel and asynchronously.

### 4.3.3 ACT-R works

ACT-R contains main components modules, buffers, and pattern matcher. The workflow of ACT-R is shown in Figure 4.4.

(1) Modules

There are two types of modules: a) perceptual-motor modules, which take care of the interface with the real world (i.e., with a simulation of the real world). The most well-developed perceptual-motor modules in ACT-R are the visual and the manual modules. b) memory modules. There are two kinds of memory modules in ACT-R: declarative memory, consisting of facts such as *Washington, D.C. is the capital of United States*, or *2+3=5;* and procedural memory, made of productions. Productions represent knowledge about how we do things: for instance, knowledge about how to type the letter "Q" on a keyboard, about how to drive, or about how to perform addition.

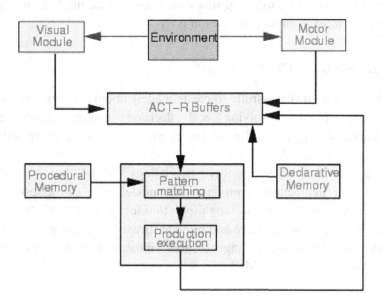

Fig. 4.4 The workflow of ACT-R (From http://act-r.psy.cmu.edu/about/)

(2) Buffers

ACT-R accesses its modules through buffers. For each module, a dedicated buffer serves as the interface with that module. The contents of the buffers at a given moment in time represents the state of ACT-R at that moment.

(3) Pattern Matcher

The pattern matcher searches for a production that matches the current state of the buffers. Only one such production can be executed at a given moment. That production, when executed, can modify the buffers and thus change the state of the system. Thus, in ACT-R cognition unfolds as a succession of production firings.

ACT-R is a hybrid cognitive architecture. Its symbolic structure is a production system; the subsymbolic structure is represented by a set of massively parallel processes that can be summarized by a number of mathematical equations. The subsymbolic equations control many of the symbolic processes. For instance, if several productions match the state of the buffers, a subsymbolic utility equation estimates the relative cost and benefit associated with each production and decides to select for execution the production with the highest utility. Similarly, whether (or how fast) a fact can be retrieved from declarative memory depends on subsymbolic retrieval equations, which take into account the context and the history of usage of that fact. Subsymbolic mechanisms are also responsible for most learning processes in ACT-R.

### 4.3.4  Applications of ACT-R

ACT-R has been used successfully to create models in domains such as: learning and memory, problem solving and decision making, language and communication, perception and attention, cognitive development, or individual differences.

Beside its applications in cognitive psychology, ACT-R has been used in human-computer interaction to produce user models that can assess different computer interfaces; education (cognitive tutoring systems) to "guess" the difficulties that students may have and provide focused help; computer-generated forces to provide cognitive agents that inhabit training environments; neuropsychology to interpret fMRI data.

## 4.4 SOAR

SOAR is the abbreviation of State, Operator And Result, which represents the state, operand and result. It means the basic principle of realizing weak method was to continuously use the operands in the state and obtain the new results. SOAR is a theoretical cognitive model. It carries out the modeling of human's cognition from the aspect of psychology and proposes a general problem solving structure.

By the end of 1950s, a model of storage structure was invented by means of using one kind of signals to mark the other signals in neuron simulation. This is the earlier concept of chunks. The chess master kept memory chunks about experiences of playing chess under different circumstances in mind. In the early of 1980s, Newell and Rosenbloom proposed that the system performance can be improved by acquiring knowledge of model problem in task environment and memory chunks can be regarded as the simulation foundation of human action. By means of observing problem solving and acquiring experience memory chunk, the complex process of each sub-goal is substituted and thus ameliorates the speed of the problem solving of the system, thereafter laid a solid foundation for empirical learning.

In 1986, J.E. Laird from the University of Michigan, Paul S. Rosenbloom from the University of Stanford and A. Newell from Carnegie Mellon University developed SOAR system (Laird et al., 1986), whose learning mechanism is to learn general control knowledge under the guidance of outside expert. The outer guidance can be direct, or an intuitionistic simple question. The system converts the high level information from outer expert into inner presentations and learns to search the memory chunk (Golding et al., 1987). Figure 4.5 presents the architecture of SOAR.

The processing configuration is composed of production memory and decision process. The production memory contains production rule, which can be used for searching control decision. The first step is detailed refinement; all the rules are referred to working memory in order to decide the priorities and which context should be changed and how to change. The second step is to decide the segment and goal that needs to be revised in the context stack.

Problem solving can be roughly described as a search through a problem space for a goal state. This is implemented by searching for the states which bring the system gradually closer to its goal. Each move consists of a decision cycle which has an elaboration phase and a decision procedure.

SOAR originally stood for State, Operator And Result, reflecting this representation of problem solving as the application of an operator to a state to get a result. According to the project FAQ, the Soar development community no longer regards SOAR as an acronym so it is no longer spelled all in caps though it is still representative of the core of the implementation.

If the decision procedure just described is not able to determine a unique course of action, Soar may use different strategies, known as *weak methods* to solve the impasse. These methods are appropriate to situations in which knowledge is not abundant. When a solution is found by one of these methods, Soar uses a learning technique called chunking to transform the course of action taken into a new rule. The new rule can then be applied whenever SOAR encounters the situation again.

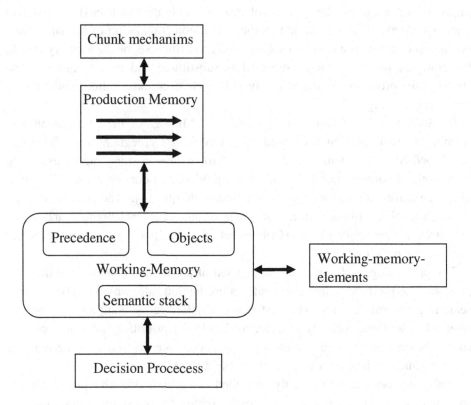

Fig. 4.5 Architecture of SOAR (Picture from Laird et al., 1986)

In the process of SOAR problem solving, it is very important in how to use the knowledge space. It is basically the trilogy about the analysis, decision and action when using the knowledge to control the action of SOAR.

1. Analyzing phrase
   Input: the object in library.
   Task: put the object into the current environment from library.
       Increase the information role of object in the current environment.
   Control: repeat this process until it is finished.

2. The phrase of decision
   Input: the object in library.
   Task: agreement, opposing or denying the objects in library. Select a
       new object to replace the congeneric objects.
   Control: agree and oppose simultaneously.

3. The phrase of execution
   Input: current state and operands
   Task: put the current operand into the current state. If a new state
       appears then put it into the library and use it to replace the original
       Current State.
   Control: this is a basic action which can not be divided.

The memory chunk, which uses working-memory-elements to collect conditions and constructs memory chunk in SOAR system, is the key for learning. When a sub-goal is created for solving a simple problem or assessing the advice from experts, the current statuses are stored into w-m-e. System gets initial statuses of sub-goal from w-m-e and deletes solution operators as the conclusion action after the sub-goal is solved. This generative production rule is memory chunk. If the sub-goal is similar to the sub-goal of the initial problem, memory chunk can be applied to initial problem and the learning strategy can apply what has already learned from one problem to another.

The formation of memory chunk depends on the explanation of sub-goal. The imparting learning is applied when converting the instructions of experts or simple problems into machine executable format. Lastly, experiences obtained from solving simple and intuitionistic problems can be applied to initial problems, which involve analogy learning. Therefore, the way of learning in SOAR system is a comprehensive combination of several learning methods.

The hypothesis behind cognitive architectures such as Soar and ACT-R (Anderson, 2007) is that there are useful abstractions and regularities above the level of neurallybased theories. This hypothesis plays out both in longer time scales of modeled behavior and in the symbolic representations of knowledge about the world. A related hypothesis is that the structures and discoveries of the symbolic architectures will be reflected in the neurally-based architectures. Probably the most interesting question is whether the extra detail of the neurally-based architectures is necessary to achieve generally intelligent agents, or whether the more abstract architectures sufficiently capture the structures and regularities required for intelligence.

## 4.5 Society of Mind

The book titled *The Society of Mind*, published in 1986, was the first comprehensive description of Minsky's society of mind theory (Minsky, 1986). In a step-by-step process, Minsky constructs a model of human intelligence which is built layer by layer from the interactions of simple parts called agents, which are themselves mindless. He describes the postulated interactions as constituting a "society of mind", hence the title.

A core tenet of Minsky's philosophy is that "minds are what brains do". The society of mind theory views the human mind and any other naturally evolved cognitive systems as a vast society of individually simple processes known as agents. These processes are the fundamental thinking entities from which minds are built, and together produce the many abilities we attribute to minds. The great power in viewing a mind as a society of agents, as opposed to the consequence of some basic principle or some simple formal system, is that different agents can be based on different types of processes with different purposes, ways of representing knowledge, and methods for producing results.

## 4.6  CAM Model

Based on the similar aspect between human brain and the computer functions Atkinson and Shiffrin in 1968 proposed a cognitive process model (Atkinson et al., 1968). In this model, input from outside stimulation, information being sent to the sensory information storage (memory) (SIS). Remained there for tens of milliseconds, through a variety of symbolic processing, sent to short-term storage (memory) (STS). STS information in a few seconds inside the forgotten, and repeated the information in order to maintain repeat is necessary. However, memory constraints, thus limiting the number of items one can be repeated. Information is again sent to the long-term storage (memory) (LTS) when Repeated, that information was organized into long-term memory within the existing information to become knowledge, which can be long term. When knowledge use, knowledge-based retrieval issues, according to a predetermined plan search and retrieval methods, from the long-term memory in the retrieved information is sent to the short-term memory, and from there the output to the outside.

In the process model based on the cognitive model, there are two development direction. One is the sensory information memory (SIS) which is not a single, every perceptual channel is independent. Another is to emphasize transmission operations of information from the sensory information memory (SIS) to the short-term memory (SIS), as well as the variety of transformations and effects in long-term memory for short-term memory. This is difference with single direction and series flow of information. The typical approach is the cognitive–information processing model proposed by Japan Koyatsu Takaaki In 1982 (Takaaki, 1982).

In 2006 Pat Langley proposed a cognitive architecture Icarus (Langley, 2006). Icarus is neither the oldest or most developed architecture, some frameworks, like ACT (Anderson, 1993) and Soar (Laird, Newell, & Rosenbloom, 1987), have undergone continual development for over two decades. Like its predecessors, it makes strong commitments to memories, representations, and cognitive processes. Another common theme is that it incorporates key ideas from theories of human problem solving, reasoning, and skill acquisition. However, Icarus is distinctive in its concern with physical agents that operate in an external environment, and the framework also differs from many previous theories by focusing on the organization, use, and acquisition of hierarchical knowledge structures. These concerns have led to different assumptions than those found in early architectures such as ACT and Soar.

For mind model should consider Consciousness. It is the awareness and controlling of human brain for the external world and impersonal object such as oneself psychological or physiological activity. Crick proposed an "astonishing hypothesis" based on the "reduction theory" (Crick, 1994). Crick argues that neuronal mechanisms of consciousness are intricately related to prefrontal cortex — cortical areas involved in higher cognitive function, affect, behavioral control, and planning. He firmly believes that consciousness, as a psychological problem, can be solved with the nerve scientific method. In 《The Astonishing Hypothesis》, he thinks the vision is the breach of the consciousness problem and the consciousness comes from the combination of "attention" and "short-term memory". Crick thinks that the brain location of consciousness may be in the cingulate gyrus.

Minsky thinks the consciousness activity includes the recognizing and purposeful behavior. We have ability to signify, control and make a plan, predict, use the language, process information, be aware of states. All these are the general functions of the consciousness, which can all be realized by an ingeniously designed computer. The so-called consciousness activity is the behavior of the complicated operation carried out by the brain. Minsky pointed out that the consciousness relates to the short-term memory and handles the recently memorized states in his report on consciousness machine in 1991(Minsky, 1991).

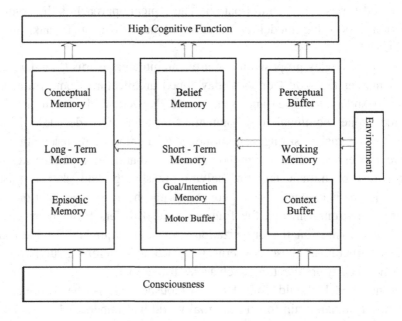

Fig. 4.6 Architecture of CAM

Author has proposed a mind model CAM (Consciousness And Memory model, for short is CAM) shown in Figure 4.6 (Shi, 2006d). It consists of three parts: consciousness, memory and high cognitive function. Dynamic Description

Logic (DDL) will be used for the representation and reasoning of CAM (Shi et al., 2005). Conceptual inference is the most basic activity. On each action cycle, the system matches concept definitions in long-term memory against perception in perceptual buffer and beliefs in short-term memory. When a concept matches, the module adds an instance of that concept to short-term belief memory.

## 4.7 Synergetics

Synergetics (Greek: "working together") is an interdisciplinary field of research originated by Hermann Haken in 1969 (Haken, 1977). Synergetics deals with material or immaterial systems, composed of, in general, many individual parts. It focuses its attention on the spontaneous, i.e. self-organized emergence of new qualities which may be structures, processes or functions. The basic question dealt with by Synergetics is: are there general principles of self-organization irrespective of the nature of the individual parts of a system? In spite of the great variety of the individual parts, which may be atoms, molecules, neurons, up to individuals in a society, this question could be answered in the positive for large classes of systems, provided attention is focused on qualitative changes on macroscopic scales. Here "macroscopic scales" means spatial and temporal scales that are large compared to those of the elements. "Working together" may take place between parts of a system, between systems or even between scientific disciplines. Characteristic of Synergetics is the strong interplay between experiment and theory.

The systems under experimental or theoretical treatment are subject to control parameters which may be fixed from the outside or may be generated by part of the system considered. An example for an internally generated control parameter is hormones in the human body or neurotransmitters in the brain. When control parameters reach specific critical values the system may become unstable and adopt a new macroscopic state. Close to such instability points, a new set of collective variables can be identified: the order parameters. They obey, at least in general, low dimensional dynamics and characterize the system macroscopically. According to the slaving principle, the order parameters determine the behavior of the individual parts which may still be subject to fluctuations. Their origin may be internal or external. Because the cooperation of the individual parts enables the existence of order parameters that in turn determine the behavior of the individual parts, one speaks of circular causality. At a critical point, a single order parameter may undergo a non-equilibrium phase transition with symmetry breaking, critical slowing down and critical fluctuations.

Haken thinks that the macro refers to the space, time, or functional structure, and these structures are considered in comparison with each of a micro- or meso-particles in nature, but merely act as a cumulative, is in the probability of the cumulative sense. For a description of nonlinear differential equations of dynamical system, the adoption of a linear stability analysis method obtained unstable results, under certain conditions may be variable or equation by changing variables and the method of equations of the month the number reduced to very few, qualitative analysis of the driving force behind the system can analyze over by the reduced equations obtained. In 1996 Haken published the book titled "Priciple of Brain Function" (Haken, 1996), which systemically outlined his study findings for brain activity and cognitive Synergetics. Brain function in the traditional experimental and theoretical studies to a single cell basis, while the synergetics focused on the cellular network activities.

Haken predicted that the long-term point of view, it is possible to create a synergetics computer which executes program with self-organization to simulate human intelligence.

Synergetics has a number of connections to other disciplines, such as complexity theory, dynamic systems theory, bifurcation theory, center manifold theory, chaos theory, catastrophe theory, the theory of stochastic processes, including non-linear Langevin equations, Fokker-Planck equations, master equations. The connection with chaos theory and catastrophe theory is in particular established by the concept of order parameters and the slaving principle, according to which close to instabilities the dynamics even of complex systems is governed by few variables only.

## 4.8 Dynamical System Theory

As the study of dynamical systems theory, dynamical systems theory of cognitive science gradually formed. For example, papers and books by G. G. Globus (Globus, 1995), S. S. Robertson (Robertson et al., 1993), E. Thelen and L. B. Simth (Thelen et al., 1994) are given a dynamic understanding of cognitive thinking. In particular, T. van Gelder and R. Port published a book on dynamics of cognition in 1995 (van Gelder, 1995), proposed the dynamics researching ideas of cognitive science, which was viewed as the declaration of the third competitive form in the cognitive science. This book attracted a lot of attentions.

For example, in 1996, C. Eliasmith at the University of Washington, published "The third contender: a critical examination of the dynamicist theory of cognition." (Eliasmith, 1996). Other people also joined in this huge discussion.

Since the 1980s symbolism and connectionism paradigm were arising the difficulties, T. van Gelder presents his dynamics hypothesis. For the cognitive science of time, architecture, computing and characterization concepts are put forward different interpretations.

The dynamical system, which describes the nature generally, includes any system that is changed with time. The scholars expect to outline a dynamical system that could describe the special and appropriate cognition. In 1995, T. van Gelder showed his dynamics hypothesis in which the natural cognitive system was some kind of dynamical system and the way of comprehending the cognitive system through the dynamics would be the best. The dynamics hypothesis describes the cognition through the mathematical dynamical system. The inside cognitive processing of cognitive agent that is concerned to the environments is explained through the mathematics concepts such the state space, the attractor, the track, the certain chaos, etc. The cognitive track of cognitive agent in the state space is represented by the differential equations. That is to say, the cognition is described as the multi dimensions constructed by all possible thoughts and actions of cognitive agent, and is especially observed through the thought track of cognitive agent under the environments and the inside pressures. The thoughts and actions of cognitive agent are decided by the differential equations. The variables inside system evolve from time to time and the system meets the non-linear differential equation, which is complicated and certain.

Motivational oscillatory theory (MOT) is the model about cyclical dynamical system which is a simplified dynamical system model recommended by T.van Gelder to be the dynamics hypothesis form. The biggest problem in this system is how to choose the system parameters. The initial values of dynamics system is sensitive and "the whole dynamics would be changed when changing only a parameter in this system" (van Gelder, 1995).

Dynamic Theory Paradigm of Cognitive compares with other important paradigm, the important difference is the different understanding of representation. Symbolism model is based on symbols. The representation of connectionism is based on the paralleling representation or local symbol. But the dynamical theory of cognitive paradigm declares that a dynamic model should be "no representation".

Dynamical system theory provides a continuity of cognitive-behavioral change over time naturalistic description. This is the other paradigm can not explain, other paradigm generally ignores the concept of time. But the human brain and the environment at any time between the exchange of information, but also in the ever-changing, transient continuous cognitive change over time.

The advantage of dynamical system theory to describe the cognitive is multi dimensions. This theory is the one in which its experience could be verified. The differential equations describing the cognitive system can be analyzed and modified. It is a quantitative analysis is to understand cognition as a deterministic point of view. Another advantage is the description of dynamical systems can show the complexity of human behavior, and chaotic features. Dynamical theory scholars argue that such a cognitive analysis of description, should have found a new alternative paradigm to replace symbolism, connectionism in the cognitive science. How to ensure that the various variables and parameters of dynamical system will be properly selected, system stability and reliability issues, understanding representation and so on, all of these issues are questionable to dynamical system theory.

# Chapter 5

# Perceptual Cognition

Perceptual cognition is an objective external direct role in the human sense organs. The development of perceptual cognition goes through three kinds of basic form: sensation, perception, representation.

## 5.1 Dialectic Process of Understanding

People's knowledge can be divided into perceptual knowledge and rational knowledge. Perceptual knowledge is people's understanding on the superficial phenomena and outside relation of objective things on the basis of practice. It is the primary stage of understanding. Perceptual knowledge generates when objective external world act on sense organ of people directly. In social practice, people can contact the phenomena of objective things through five organs: eyes, ears, nose, tongue and body. Under the stimulus of the external phenomenon, people's sense organ has produced information flow which is conveyed to the brain along the specific neural channel, forming feeling and impression to objective things, such as color, shape, sound, cold and hot, smell, pain, etc.

The development of perceptual knowledge should go through three basic forms: feeling, perception and representation. Feeling is the reflection in people's brain of the specific attribute and characteristics of objective things. The perception is the integration of various feelings. It is the reflection in people's brain of the whole objective thing and it is more complete and more complicated than feeling. Representation generates on the basis of perception. Representation, i.e. impression, is reproduced through reminiscence and impression. It is different from feeling and perception. It is formed on the basis that perceived to the same thing or similar things many times in the past. Thus it has certain indirectness and generality. But representation can only summarize the simplest form of the perceptual materials, it can't reveal essence and law of the things yet.

At the stage of perceptual knowledge, most of the judgments toward phenomenon and events observed by people are intuitive. In observations or experiments, researchers must compare things to be judged with known things and make judgments using relations between different things, so that scientific questions, such as "what is this" or "whether it has scientific meanings", can be answered. There often exist little logical necessary connections between things to be judged and known things.

With the continuance of practice, after the feeling and impression of people that caused in practice repeated many times, a qualitative leap has taken place. People's understanding leaps from perceptual knowledge to rational knowledge. Rational knowledge is the understanding in the stage of concepts, judgments and inferences. It is people's reflection of essence, unity, internal relation of objective things on the basis of practice. Rational knowledge is the advanced stage of understanding, developed by perceptual knowledge. It is represented as a series process of abstract, generation, analysis and integration. On the basis of a large number of accumulations on perceptual knowledge of objective things in practice, People produce concepts by catching the essential attribute of the things, that is, by taking essence, unity and internal relation of the things and labeling them with some physical shell word. The concept is a thinking form which reflects target's essential attribute. It is the "cells" of thinking. Its production is the leap in the process of cognition. The judgment is an unfolded concept. It is thinking form that judges positive or negative for internal relation of a thing. Inference is thinking from that infers new judgments from known judgments. Therefore, concept, judgment and inference are the three kinds of basic form of rational knowledge. The characteristic of rational knowledge is that it is the abstract, general and indirect reflection of objective things.

Perceptual knowledge and rational knowledge are two stages of understanding process, and they are united on the basis of practice. On one hand, the dialectical unity of perceptual knowledge and rational knowledge appears in their dependence on each other. Rational knowledge depends on perceptual knowledge. Otherwise it will become water without source, a tree without roots, a subjective and spontaneous thing. On the basis of abundant perceptual knowledge, rational knowledge must become rational knowledge through abstract thinking and integration and analysis of perception materials. Perceptual knowledge needs to be developed to rational knowledge, because perceptual knowledge is only the superficial, one-sided reflection of the things. Only on the basis of abundant perceptual knowledge, the rational knowledge formed through the processing of thinking may reveal the inherent contradictions and regularity of objective things, and reflect objective things more deeply, more correct and more completely. On the other hand, the dialectical unity appears in the mutual infiltration between perceptual knowledge and rational knowledge. Perceptual knowledge contains rational knowledge. The rational knowledge infiltrates in people's perceptual knowledge. Scientific knowledge is one of the people's most basic and important understanding activities. In scientific knowledge, the role of thinking in the stage of perceptual knowledge is embodied in many aspects, such as the proposition of the problem and forming of research subject, observation design or experimental design, the application of observation or laboratory apparatus, the judgment and affirmation of the experience fact, the catching of the opportunity, etc. Likewise, rational knowledge contains perceptual knowledge. Rational knowledge is based on perceptual materials and takes the language form that can be perceived in certain letter symbol or sound as one's own material shell and form of expression.

On the basis of practice, perceptual knowledge becomes rational knowledge, and rational knowledge gets back to practice again to guide practice so that the subjective things become objective things. Then, people's understanding of a certain objective course at a certain developing stage can be considered as accomplished. But as for the process of the course, people's understanding is not accomplished. With constant development of the objective course and constant continuance of practice, people produce new perceptual knowledge and rational knowledge, and start new understanding activities. Lenin says while mentioning all dialectical courses of people's understanding activities: "the orbit of people's understanding is not a straight line (that is to say, understanding is not along a straight line), but similar to a bunch of circles limitlessly, similar to the spiral curve."

## 5.2 Sensation

When objective things act on people's sense organ directly, the reflection to the specific attribute of these things is generated in the human brain. This kind of reflection is called feeling. Objective things, phenomenon act on people's sense organ, stimulate people's nerve fiber. When this kind of stimulus arrives at the hemisphere cortex of brain along the centripetal nerve, the feeling generates.

People's understanding process of the objective world is started from feeling. In this sense, feeling is the source of all people's knowledge about the world. Through it, people may progressively understand the objective world which does not depend on him. With the help of feeling, people can feel all kinds of attribute of things, such as color, shape, smell, sound, etc. Feeling also make people know the changes of their own body, such as activities and the position of the body, working state of the internal organs, etc. Without feeling, we can't know any form of the material objects and the activities.

Since feeling generates when objective things (stimulate things) act on the sense organ, so studying the sense process should start from understanding stimulate things, i.e. understanding how it acts on the sense organ, and produces feeling accordingly. Three links of studying feeling process are stimulation and stimulation course, conducting to central nerve and feeling phenomenon and law. The latter two links among them, especially the last link, are the main object of psychological research. These two links are linked with activities and results of the analyzer. The analyzer is formed by three parts:

(1) Some peripheries (receptor) which accept the stimulant things acting on it;
(2) Afferent nerve which transmit neural excitement to the central nerve;
(3) Lower cortex and the centre of cortex where the peripheral nerve impulses are analyzed and synthesized.

Things have many different attributes, which act on different analyzer of people and produce different feeling. According to the analyzer that produces feeling and specific stimulant things it reflects, feeling can be divided into different kinds. All analyzers can be divided into two classes, outside analyzer and internal analyzer. Various receptors of the outside analyzer lie in the surface of the body, accepting various external stimuli. The internal analyzer is distributed various tip receptors in internal organ and tissue of the body, accepting the signal changing within the organism. The sport analyzer is in the middle position. Its tip receptor is in muscles and the ligament. Furthermore, it can offer the movement and position of each organ in body and confirm the attributes of the external things. The feelings generate by the movements of the outside analyzer include vision, hearing, touch, taste and smell. Feelings related to the work of internal analyzer include organic sensation. Feelings related to the work of movement analyzer include kinaesthetic sense. The sense of pain can send out the signal about the injury intensity about stimulate things. It is distributed in all analyzers.

Around us, the material energy exists in a lot of forms: One that give out light, vibrant one, chemistry one, heat, machinery. Except that their kind is widely different, their intensity vary widely too. The energy forms of these materials are the directly relation between things in the material world and us. According to this, our sense organs which accept the energy have stipulated that we can whereby grasp the range of the firsthand knowledge about the external world. The feeling ability to the stimulant things is called sensitivity. It is measured by the sensory threshold. Sensory threshold is stimulant quantity that causes the feeling and lasts for a period of time.

Not all stimulant things can cause feeling. In order to produce feeling, stimulant things should reach certain quantity. The minimum amount of stimulus that can just cause feeling is called absolute sensory threshold. In order to set up a united standard, the psychologists agree that absolute sensory threshold can be defined as the minimum stimulating intensity which can be perceived more than a half times.

Absolute feeling sensitivity is the ability to feel minimum stimulus. The weaker the stimuli needed to cause feeling, that is to say, the smaller the absolute sensory threshold is, the greater the absolute feeling sensitivity is. Absolute feeling sensitivity and absolutely sensory threshold have inversely proportional relation in the quantity. If we represent absolute feeling sensitivity with letter E, absolute sensory threshold with letter R, then the relation between them can be represented as the formula (5.1):

$$E = \frac{1}{R} \qquad\qquad (5.1)$$

Table 5.1 Webber fraction K

| Type of stimulus | Webber fraction |
|---|---|
| Pitch (2,000 Hertz) | 1/333 |
| Deep pressure (400 Grams) | 1/77 |
| Visual lightness (1,000 Photons) | 1/62 |
| Weight lifting (300 Grams) | 1/53 |
| Loudness (100 decibels; 1,000 Hertz) | 1/11 |
| Rubber smell (200 Olfactory units) | 1/10 |
| Skin pressure (5 grams per square centimeter) | 1/7 |
| Saline taste (3 gram molecules per kilogram) | 1/5 |

If there are two stimuli with different intensity, appearing at the same time or in sequence, they can be distinguished by sense organs only when their difference attains a certain degree. The amount of minimum difference of stimulant things that can be aware is called differential sensory threshold. The corresponding sensitivity is called differential sensitivity. The differential sensitivity is also inversely proportional to the differential sensory threshold. The differential sensory threshold varies widely because of the difference of the stimulant property and the organism state. In 1834, German physiologist E. H. Webber finds that the differential sensory threshold is approximately a constant fraction of the stimulant intensity in certain limit, which can be expressed as following mathematics formula:

$$\frac{\Delta I}{I} = K \tag{5.2}$$

where $\Delta I$ denotes the differential sensory threshold, $I$ denotes the initial intensity of stimulant things, K is a constant. Later on this fact is called Webber laws. As for every material energy type, their values of Webber fraction K are different. Table 5.1 gives examples of providing Webber fraction.

## 5.3 Perception

Cognitive psychology regards perception as organization and explanation of sensory information, that is, the course of getting the meaning of sensory information. Objective things acted on people's sense organ directly, producing the whole reflection of each part and attribute of these things in human brain. This kind of reflection is called the perception. Both perception and feeling are the reflection of present things in the brain. Their difference lies in: feeling is reflection of specific attribute (such as color, smell, temperature) of external things, while perception is reflection of each part and attribute of things and comprehensive reflection of their interrelation. In the perception, what generated by brain is not isolate reflection of the specific attribute or part of things, but the reflection of the concrete things combined by various feeling — for instance, people, computer, house, etc.. Anything is a complex which is composed of a lot of attributes and parts. The whole thing and its specific attribute and part are inseparable. See houses, one should aware that this is institute, factory, residential block, etc. Meanwhile, knowledge must regard feeling as foundation. One must see bedroom, kitchen, etc. to aware the residential block. The more abundant the specific attributes and parts of the things, the more intact and correct of the perception to the things. All People directly reflect the things in actual life in the form of perception, that is to say, the objective reality is reflected in the brain as the concrete things. People seldom have isolated feelings.

Only when doing scientific analysis in psychology, people divide feeling to study solely.

The perception is the subjective reflection of objective reality in the human brain, therefore the perception is limited by people's various characteristics. One's knowledge, interest, mood, etc. all influence the perception course directly. People have accumulated the experience and knowledge of certain targets in practice, then he recognizes current stimulus as the definite things of the realistic world with the aid of the knowledge and experience. If current things have no relation with past experience and knowledge, one can't confirm it as certain object at once.

Experience plays an important role in the perception, because the perception is a result of the brain activities of complicated analysis and integration. It is the reflection activity of stimulating things and the relation of stimulating things. The temporary relation formed in the past will influence content and property of the perception.

In general, the perception is produced by united activities of many kinds of analyzers. The common participation of many analyzers can reflect the target's various attributes and produce the comprehensive and intact perception. For example, when people watch TV, in fact it is the result of united activities of visual analyzer and audio analyzer, but visual analyzer plays a leading role.

While compound stimulant things act, intensity and interrelation of each component are significant. The strong components of compound stimulant things cover the weak components. The weak components seem to lose their own effect. The same components in different relation become different perception unity, i.e. they have formed different relational reflex, such as different melody in the music. The overall of the perception has great meanings for life. Things and phenomena in the objective world are all constantly changeable. Due to the overall of the perception, people can adapt the changing environment. When people encounter the object in new environment, he can recognize it by various relations between objects, for example, the recognition of relative and script. The overall of the perception makes people's understanding of objective things become more and more complete, thus it guarantees the effective execution of the activities.

When the condition of the perception has changed within a certain range, the reflection of the perception has still kept relatively not changing. This is the constancy of consciousness. In visual perception, the constancy is very obvious. The reflection of objects, such as color, shape, size, etc., is not always governed by the law of physics. Whether in the daytime or night, the perception of coal is always black. This kind of perception constancy has very great effect on life. It guarantees to reflect things in terms of the real appearances of the things in different cases, thus it can adapt the environment in terms of the actual meaning of objects.

## 5.4 Combination of Perception

Single figure — there are generally few modes of the background, the typical mode is that several figures have a common background. Some single figures are inclined to different combinations which gathered by perception. Wertheim, One of the founders of Gestalt psychology, elaborated "Combination Principle" systematically. It can be sum up as follows now:

### 1. Approaching combination
Stimuli approaching to each other have greater inclination to combine than stimuli separated farther. The approaching may be in space or time. Given a series of pat sounds according to irregular time interval, pat sounds approaching to each other in time are inclined to be put together. Stimuli that combined due to approaching needn't be the same kind of feeling forms; For example, rain, lightning accompanied by peals of thunder, we think them as a whole, that is, the perception is components of the same incident.

### 2. Similar combination
Stimuli similar to each other have greater inclination to combine than dissimilar stimuli. The similarity means that things are similar on some physical attributes, such as the intensity, color, size, shape etc. There is a saying: "birds of a feather flock together, people of one mind fall into the same group", which contains this kind of principle.

### 3. Combination of the good figure
If other conditions are the same, the stimulus of forming a good figure will have inclination to combine. Its concrete forms include:

(1) A good consistency: A kind of inclination, i.e. some components and other components are linked together by such way, in order to make a straight line, a curve or a movement that keep it up along the direction that is already established.

(2) Symmetry: A kind of condition, it is beneficial to such combinations, which lead to symmetric or balanceable unity other than asymmetric unity.

(3) Fitting: Some components combine with such way so that it is helpful to form a closer and more intact figure.

(4) Common destiny: The combinations of those components moved or changed in a common direction, which is different from the components moving or changing in other directions in the visual domain. This combination principle is essentially the application of similar combination on the body in motive things. It is an important means in the choreography.

Fig. 5.1 Competition of approaching combination and fitting combination.

In every kind of stimulating mode, some components have a certain degree of approaching, approximation and some things suitable for "the good figure". Sometimes some combination inclination act in the same direction. Sometimes they conflict each other. For example, Fig. 5.1 shows that how fitting influent approaching. The left 7 lines become 3 pairs and a single line naturally due to the fitting. However, the right redrawn lines are inclined to combine with a farther line because the lines are added short horizontal line and the influence of fitting overwhelm the influence of approaching.

The basic form of the perception is decided by the mode of its components. So, so long as the mode of each component keeps unchanged, the whole can keep unchanged even if its components change prominently. When this kind of situation takes place, we call it relation transfer.

While judging the perception characteristics of things, we usually use a standard, or reference system to judge the properties of special things. When we ask how large an object is, we use size of other objects as the standard. H. Helson has proposed a kind of theory: When one makes the judgment to any quantitative respect of any stimulating attributes, such as size, weight or loudness, the carries on it by setting up a table of quantity which is judgment stimulate, subjective, or personal. He calls the midpoint of this quantitative table as adaptation level. The stimulating value higher than the adaptation level is felt as "the big one", "the heavy one", "the loud one", etc. While the stimulating value lower than the adaptation level is felt as "the small one", "the light one", "the soft one", etc.

## 5.5 Perception Theories

Our perception system gets a large amount of abundant information about the external world, and monitors one's own action (Table 5.2). In this way, we can regard the perception system as a part of the chain cable, which is stretched from the external world, pass each of us, and gets back to the environment. If the information about external world is reliable, and if the result that we take action is what ourselves want to do too, this proves that each link in this chain cable is indispensable.

Table 5.2 Perception system

| Name | Attention mode | Feel unit | Anatomy position of the organ | Activity of the organ | Stimulus | Acquired external information |
|---|---|---|---|---|---|---|
| Basic location system | General location | Mechanical feel | Vestibular organ | Body balance | Gravitation and acceleration | Orientation of gravitation when pushed |
| Hearing system | listening | Mechanical receptor | Cochlear organs including middle ear and external ear | Determination of audio orientation | Vibration of air | Property and position of vibration events |
| Skin sensation system | touching | Mechanical receptor and possible Thermo receptor | Skin (and its attachment or open mouth), joint (including ligament), muscles (including tendons) | Exploration of many kinds | Cell tissue, deformed joint, perfect muscle, stretch of fiber | Contact with ground, shape and material state of mechanical collision things |
| Taste system | Smelling | Chemical receptor | Nasal cavity (nose) | Smell flavor | Components of medium | Property of volatile |

| Smell system | Tasting | Chemical and mechanical receptor | Oral cavity (mouth) | Taste savor | Components of swallow things | Nutrient and biochemical value |
|---|---|---|---|---|---|---|
| Visual system | Looking | Photic receptor | Visual mechanism (eyes and eye muscles inside and outside it, such as the muscles connected with vestibular organ, head and the whole body) | Adapt to the pupil adjustment, pay attention to the exploration of complex | Variant in surround structure | All things that can be denoted by variant of optical structure (information about things, animals, events and address) |

(1) The chain cable starts from the environment. What feature does the environment have as the source of the last perception? What targets does it include? How are their position and distribution? What is the material attribute making us have the experience of volume, color, hardness, sport, duration, change etc.?

(2) The second link of the chain cable is an intermediary thing. Through it, external environment transmit its features to our sense organs. Some objects reflect light to our eyes. Some objects transmit the sound wave or chemical material through air. Some materials are dissolved in the mouth. Some objects give pressure to our skin. Some are strength such as gravitation. Some (such as heat energy) act on our skin through radiating hot or conducting heat.

(3) The third part of the chain cable includes various forms of energy, and interaction between other stimuli in intermediary things and feeling receptor of perception system. Note that we say "interaction" other than simple "reception". As a certain receptor (such as the eyes) is stimulated, its states may change. Then the next stimulation may cause the effects not the same. For example, a strong light will make pupil smaller, thus fewer light can enter eyes.

(4) The fourth link refers to the sensory nerve from receptor to brain. Some sensory nerve has very long transmission part, such as from toe to brain. Some are very short, such as from eyes to brain.

(5) The fifth part of the chain cable is the brain, especially the throwing area that sensory nerve stops in the brain. Some theorists assume that our feeling is mainly determined by the neural signal reaching these areas. Other theorists infer that our feeling not merely reflects the information that spreading into to the throwing area from the sensory nerve, and reflects some information that exists in other places in the brain previously, such as faith, emotion and memory.

In the perception chain, is the brain the only best place for perception? Many perception researchers have proposed the discussion with more or less difference. There are four main discussions on setting up perception theory. The Gestalt discussion prefers to emphasize the factor of the congenital theory of perception organs. The exploration of constructing theorists places an important influence on the factors of study and memory. The movement investigation concentrates on the feedback produced by his action detection in his environment. The discussion of Gibson's ecology stresses on the information of all intrinsic environment in stimulating mode.

### 5.5.1 Constructing theory

The past knowledge and experience acts in the perception mainly in the form of supposing, expecting or factor. While people perceive, he receive feeling as input, forming what present stimulus is on the basis of past experience, or forming a certain expectation of target by activating some knowledge units. The perception is carried on under the guide and plan of these assumption and expectation. Bruner (J.S. Bruner) proposed the constructing theory, thinking that all perception is influenced by people's experience and expectation (Bruner et al., 1987). Constructing theorist's view about the perception is to place an important effect on the function of memory. They think that adding the traces of the memory of experience before to the feeling induced by stimulus induce here now would construct a perception image. Moreover, constructing theorists maintain the organized perception foundation is the process to choose, analyze and add stimulate information from a man's memory, but not the natural operation function that the brain organizing law causes that Gestalt theorists maintain.

J.S. Bruner make an outstanding contribution on educational psychology. He advocates: "Any subject can be taught to any child in any developing period effectively in a certain appropriate way in intelligence". This gives rise to a gigantic and vigorous course reformation movement in USA. Bruner think that the school should make great efforts to teach the general properties or structures of subject, but not teach the details and concrete facts of subject. Education should promote the development of children's cognitive ability. He proposes that the child's early education should be paid attention to, thinking that finding method is the main learning method of children, emphasizing the importance of intuition in study. He thinks that intuition is a means to solve problem, children's immediately understanding or intuitive understanding would be much better than planned analyzing knowledge step by step.

Existing knowledge and experience influent on perception in many aspects. The most noticeable one is the effect on the context. Some present psychologists think that the past knowledge and experience mainly act on the perception in the form of supposing, expecting or factor overall. While people perceive, he receive feeling as input, forming what present stimulus is on the basis of past experience, or forming a certain expectation of target by activating some knowledge units. The perception is carried on under the guide and plan of these assumption and expectation. According to Gregory's view, perception is a constructing process including hypotheses testing. Through receiving the message, forming hypotheses testing, and receiving or searching the message again, testing hypotheses again, until verifying a certain hypothesis, then people make correct explanation to feeling and stimulating, this is called hypotheses testing theory of perception. According to the theory, physical characteristics of feeling stimulus, stimulant contexts and related concept can activate related knowledge of long-term memory and form various assumptions. Thus perception is the reconstruction of combining realistic stimulant information and memory information which regarding hypothesis as link. Under general circumstances, people cannot aware the participant of hypothesis when they perceive. But under some special circumstances, such as looking the things under the weak illumination, people can experience this kind of hypotheses testing sometimes. The hypotheses testing theory endow the perception course with initiative and intelligence. It is an influential perception theory in cognitive psychology at present.

Hypotheses testing theory of perception is a kind of perception theory based on past experience. There are other evidences to support this theory. For example, the outside stimulus does not have one-to-one relation with perception experience. Same stimuli may cause different perception, but different stimuli may cause the same perception. So, the dimension of feeling stimulus is fuzzy and has a double meaning. Feeling inputs are also fuzzy and partial, and they can't provide the true and intact description for external stimuli. The stimuli of near end, such as the retina images, only offer the clue about external stimuli. It is needed to employ these clues to infer on the basis of experience in the past, and to evaluate or explain stimuli of near end, thus the perception of external stimuli will be achieved. These views are obviously beneficial to the hypotheses testing theory and place importance on the effect of past knowledge and experience. They think, the perception is orienting, extracting feature, comparing with knowledge in memory, then orientation and extracting feature again, comparing again, iterating like this until confirming the meaning of stimuli. This has many similarities with the hypotheses testing theory.

### 5.5.2 Gestalt theory

Gestalt psychology was born in 1912 (Wertheimer, 1923). It emphasizes the globality of experience and perception, and object to popular constructing element theory and stimulus-reaction formula of behaviorism at that time. It does not think that the whole is equal to the sum of parts, perception means feeling the set of the element, and the behavior means the circulation of the reflex arc. Although the principle of Gestalt is not only a theory of perception, it leads and comes from the study on perception. Moreover, some important principles of Gestalt were mostly offered by the research institute of the perception.

Gestalt theory thinks that the perception question involves comparing and judging. As we say this kind gray is lighter than that kind of gray, this line is a bit longer than that line, and this sound is louder than that sound, what on earth are the experiences of us? This can be explained with an experiment: two gray small squares are placed together on a black surface, it is required to judge whether these two squares are identical. There are four kinds of possibilities for answer: a) See one great gray rectangle with the same color on the black surface, there is a boundary in the rectangle, divide the rectangle into two squares; b) See a pair of lightness gradient, rise from left to right, the left square is relatively dark and the right one is relatively bright; c) See a pair of lightness gradient with opposite directions, drop from left to right, the left square is relatively bright, the right one is relatively dark; d) See neither a rectangle with the same color nor gradient, there are only some fuzzy things can not be confirmed.

The judgements obtained from the experience is: a) The same judgement; b) The left square is dark grey, the right square is light gray; c) The left square is light gray, the right square is dark grey; d) Do not affirm or not sure.

According to the previous description, what can be inferred in theory? Gestalt psychology thinks that the description explains two comparative phenomena, "Comparison is not a kind of new purpose added to the particular feeling…, but finding an integral whole." With b) and c) as examples, the meaning of gradient means not only two different levels. It means rise itself too, that is, upward trend and direction. It is not a detached, mobile and transitive feeling, but the central characteristics of the whole integral experience.

Gestalt psychology believes the inherent and innate rule in the organization of brain. There exists a "simplicity" principle behind various perception factors. If a construction can be seen by more than one type of ways, "the simpler" way is known more general. Although it emphasizes the importance of the experience to the perception, the primary emphasis point is put on the inherent mechanism of the nervous system.

Gestalt scholars believe the inherent and innate rule in the organization of brain. They argue that this has explained these important phenomena: division, contrast, outline, fitting, principle of combination of the perception and other organizational facts of the figure-background. Gestalt scholars think that a piece of "simplicity" principle exists behind various perception factors they proposed. They affirm that units including greater symmetry, fitting, interweaved together closely and any pattern of similar units appear to be "simpler" for observers. If a construction can be seen by more than one way, for example, the picture formed by lines can be regarded as the flat one or a square, the "simpler" way is known more general. Gestalt scholars do not ignore the effect on the perception of experience before, but their primary emphasis point is put on the function of inherent mechanism which becomes integral part of the nervous system. So they suppose that apparent motion or Φ phenomenon is the trend or result naturally organized by brain.

### 5.5.3 *Movement theory*

In terms of the direction that I. Pavlov worked in early years, modern Russian perception research concentrated on the effect that movement behavior influences and guides the function (Pavlov Website) of the perceptual direction. They think that there exists one "movement replica", which controls the perception of some our modes. They believe that the movement replica made in exploring an object is one of the decisive factors of things can be seen.

Someone uses photograph to record the mode of the eyeball movement reflecting the new object name. Note that these modes have a kind of inclination, i.e. they are similar with those modes that observed by watching objects. This similarly seems to be temporary. It occurs only in the "middle period" of the spoken learning process. When the name has been already skillful, this similarity disappears. Certainly, its meaning is it may function as a certain middle media while eyeball movements studying the neologisms. One association is worthy of noting. This association is: there exists a very close connection between visual attention course and linguistic acquisition course.

### 5.5.4 Gibson's ecology theory

American psychologist J. J. Gibson is well-known in the academia because of his study on perception. He proposed the ecological perception theory in 1950. He thinks the perception is direct, does not have any inference step, intermediary's variable or association. Ecology theory (theory of stimuli) is in contrast with the constructing theory (Theory of hypotheses testing). It maintains that the perception has direct properties, and denies the function of past knowledge and experience. Gibson (J. J. Gibson) thinks that the stimulus of the nature is intact, and it can offer very abundant information. People can utilize the information completely, generating the perception experience corresponding to stimulus produced and acted on the sense organ directly, without the need of forming hypotheses and testing on the basis of past experience at all. According to his ecological perception theory, the perception is the course kept in touch with the external world, and the direct action of stimuli. He interprets such direct stimulant function as types and variables of physical energy to react to the sense organs. The view that perception is the result of direct action of environment is deviated from the traditional perception theory. Gibson uses formula to denote the concept of "stimulant ecology" which expresses the surroundings of a person, including relation of slope and reflected surface, and the gravitation which people all experience while walking, sitting down and lying down. He firmly believes the perception does not change, so when the environment provides continuous and stable information flow for the active organism, the organism can react to this. These views reflect in the work "the Perception of Visual World" published in 1950 and "the Senses Considered as Perceptual Systems" (Gibson, 1966) published in 1966.

Gibson's perception theory is entitled in "the ecological perception theory". The reason lies in that it puts emphasis on the environmental facts which have the relation with the living beings most. As to Gibson, feeling is the adaptation of the environment for evolution. Furthermore, there are some important phenomena in the environment, for instance gravity, diurnal circulation and comparison sky with ground, do not change in the history of evolution. The environment not changed brings stability, and offers the reference frame of individual life. So, the success of species evolution depends on the sensory system which reflects the environment correctly. From the point of view of ecology, the perception is the course that the environment appears to the perception person. The nervous system does not build the perception, but extract it. In Gibson's opinion, the abundant information of feeling stimuli had been get rid of much more under the condition of the laboratory, for example using tachystoscope to show stimuli rapidly. But people usually have enough time to observe in daily life, and people can walk around and change the angle to observe. With the change of the viewpoint, some characteristics of the light stream change, while others keep unchanged. As what was pointed out above, there exists light distribution in any point in the space. The change of the viewpoint must cause the change of light distribution, but the light distribution always contains certain structure. Gibson believes that the perception system extracts invariance from the series of flowing. His theory is called the ecology theory of the perception now, and forms a school.

Gibson refers to the superficial perception with structure as normal or ecological perception. He thinks, compared with his own view, the Gestalt theory is mainly based on the analysis of the perception in special circumstances. In this kind of circumstance, constructing is reduced or a not relevant one, just like the structure of this paper is irrelevant with the content printed above it at all.

In the constructing theory, the perception often utilizes information from memory. And Gibson thinks that the world which has structure and is highly structured has supplied with abundant and accurate information. The observer can choose from it, and needn't choose from the information that was stored in the past. Gibson believes that it is usually the perception that guides our movements. This is different with the movement theories of the perception. The movement theory assumes the signal that our muscles got has been turned into the impact on the perception. The developing athletic skill guides the developing perception skill. The ecology theory firmly believes people all treat the world by similar means. It places emphasis on the importance of overall complex of the information that can be got in the natural environment.

Gibson's ecology perception theory has certain scientific basis. He assumes that the perception reaction is an innate view and is in accordance with the deep perception of new born animal. At the same time, it conforms to the research conclusion in neural psychology that the single cells of visual cortex can react to specific visual stimuli. However, his theory emphasizes excessively that individual perception response is biological, and ignores the function in the perception reaction of factor such as individual experience, knowledge and personality characteristic, etc. Thus it is also criticized by some researchers.

## 5.6 Representation

Representation is the repeated course that the images of objective targets which are maintained in the notion appear in the notion when objective targets do not appear in front of the subject. Representation has the following characteristics:

### 1. Intuitivity

Representation generates on the basis of perception. The materials that construct representation all come from the content perceived past. So the representation is the perceptual reflection of intuition. However, representation is different from perception. It is the general repeated appearance of perception. Compared with perception, representation has the following characteristics: (1) Representation is not so intact as the perception. It cannot reflect the exhaustive characteristic of the object, and it is even a incomplete one and a partial one; (2) Representation is not so stable as the perception. It is varying and flowing; (3) Representation is not so vivid as the perception. It is fuzzier and dimmer, and it reflects only the outline and some main characteristics of the object. But under some conditions, representation can present the details of the perception. Its essential feature is intuitivity. For example, the phenomenon "eidetic image" can happen among children. Show a picture with complicated content to children, remove the picture dozens of seconds later, and make his eyesight to one gray screen, then he can "See" a same clear picture. These children could describe the detail in the picture accurately according to the image produced at that time, at the same time they do not think the picture is before eyes now.

As for the classification of representation, it reflects a certain images of concrete object, which is called specific representation or single representation. The phenomenon "eidetic image" previous described is a kind of specific representation. Representation that reflects a kind of target's common characteristic is called general representation. General representation has those characteristics that distinguish with the perception described above even more.

## 2. Generality

Generally speaking, representation is the result that summarized from perception many times. It has a prototype perceived, but not limited to a certain prototype. So representation has generality, it is the generality reflection of the perceptual image of surface to a kind of target. This kind of generality is often denoted as the target's outline instead of the details.

The generality of representation has certain limits. As for complexity and relation, the representation is difficult to include. For example, if the aforementioned pictures produced by "eidetic image" present one part of story, then, about the cause and effect of the whole story, person's ins and outs with interactive relation, can not appear in representation completely. Each representation about the story is only the illustration to express the story part. If we want express story plot and meaning, concept and proposition in language description should be used. Understanding of picture-story book depends on the language to make pages getting consistent. The deep meaning of the book is revealed by the generalization of the word too.

Therefore, representation is a transitive reflection form and intermediary phase between perception and thinking. As a reflection form, representation is not only close to the perception but also higher than the perception, because it can be produced without the concrete target; Representation has generality, and it is lower than the generalization level of the word. It offers the perceptual material for thinking of the word. From the development of individual psychology, the emergence of representation is between perception and thinking.

## 3. Representation happens on paths of many kinds of feelings

Representation can be various images of feeling, including representation of visual, hearing, smell, taste and touching, etc.. Representation will happen in the general people, but it can also vary with each individual. Because of the visual importance, most people have more vivid and visual representation that often happened. A lot of examples prove, scientist and artist can finish the creative work through visual thinking in image. It is even quite valid in mathematics, physics research.

Visual representation brings creativity to artist, writer too. It is an intact fine piece of writing appeared by visual representation that Coleridge's masterpiece poem "King Khan". The artist often has advantage of visual representation. The sound representation plays an important role on the forming of the intelligence of language hearing and music hearing. Movement representation is extremely important in forming of various movements and their skill; to the operation of some musical instruments, such as the string instruments of piano and violin, etc., the advantage of both hearing representation and visual representation is needed.

## 4. Role of representation in thinking

Representation is not only a person's image, but also a kind of operation. That is, psychological operation can go on in the form of representation. This is the thinking of image activity. In this sense, the psychological operation, image thinking and concept thinking of representation are in different interaction.

Representation thinking (image thinking) is the thinking operation which depends on the representation. Research on "The psychological rotation" is convincing evidence. In a experiment of "the psychological rotation", a letter "R" with different rotation angle is appeared each time, the letter appeared is "R" positive written sometimes and is "R" negative written instead sometimes. The task of testing is to judge whether letters are being positive written or negative written. The results indicate that the bigger the rotated angle in vertical direction, the longer the time of making judgement. The result can be explained as follows: the letter must rotate in the head at first, until it is in the vertical position, then the judgment can be made. The time difference when reflect psychological rotation and representation operation has proved the existence of image thinking and representation operation. In fact, attempt to use other methods, such as through example, to describe the position of the letter it is difficult.

In more cases, information can be encoded in the brain. It can also be encoded with the pictures. Representation and word can be double encoded in the psychological operation. Under certain condition, picture and word can be mutually translated. The concrete picture can be drawn, described and organized by the language. For example, authors of screenplay usually carries on the picture encoding, then store it through the language finally, this is a screenplay; Meanwhile, the director regenerates the pictures according to the screenplay, this is performance, that is to say, the pictures are resumed through the language.

Participation and support of necessary representation in thinking operation of the word, even whether representation operation is needed to be appeared in thinking operation, are different because thinking task is different. For example, in computation, geometry depends on the support of image operation to a great extent. Graphical operation is the essential backbone of geometric computation. However, algebra and equation make mathematical calculations according to the formula only with the symbol concept. They have totally got rid of the image to operate.

It can be seen that representation and perception are all perceptual knowledge and vivid intuition. But representation is different from sensation that things act on sense organs directly. It is formed based on perceiving many times to the same thing or same kind of things in past. It has certain indirectness and generality. Under the adjustment and control of people and word, these representations with certain generality probably grow from perceptual knowledge relying mainly on perceiving to the rational knowledge relying mainly on concept and thinking progressively, this is a qualitative leap. Therefore, representation is a necessary intermediate link of transition from perceiving directly to abstract thinking. However, representation is the most arbitrary form of general materials. It can't reveal the essence and law of the things yet.

Representation has more generality than feeling and perception. It is a key psychological question. But because the representation is an internal psychological process, it is not as apparent outside as feeling and perception. Therefore, the research of representation has been in lagging and confused state all the time. Behaviorism psychology denies the existence of perception, only acknowledges the so-called objective stimulus reaction. Thus it gets rid of representation with other perception phenomena out of psychology. Although the Gestalt psychology acknowledges the existence of representation, it uses the viewpoints with the same type of "dualistic theory" to explain. Modern cognitive psychology uses the information processing theory, emphasizes the operation order of the mental process, therefore has made certain progress in this respect, has proposed theories such as the antithesis encoding, mutual encoding, etc.

Modern cognitive psychology thinks that studying representation is studying internal courses that people process the visual information and space information without any outside stimuli. Through objective condition and effect that can be observe objectively, such as the reaction speed and success rate, we can explore the same effect generated by representation and corresponding perception under the same objective condition. At this moment, representation is regarded as the analog of the true object, but the processing of representation is similar to the information processing in feeling the real object. Through the experiment and studying, it can be proved that representation is not limited by visual passway or the other feeling passway, and it is not the primitive image without processing stored in the brain, i.e. it is not a mechanical duplication of things. This enables people to see more objectively and concretely, representation is the same as feeling, perception and other psychological phenomena too. It is the initiative reflection of objective things.

Representation can reflect both the specific characteristics and the general characteristics of things. It has both intuitivity and generality. Look it from intuitivity, it is close to the perception. From generality, it is close to thinking. The general representation is accumulated and fused by specific representation progressively. Specific representation develops to general representation in people's activity. Without the general representation that reflects objective things leaving the concrete things, people's understanding will only be confined to the perception of the present things forever, and will only confine to real, intuitive and perceptual understanding forever. Therefore, the general reaction function of representation, not limited by concrete things, makes it possible to become transition and bridge from perceiving to thinking.

From the physiological mechanism, the representation is reproduced (resumed) in human's brain because of the stimulant trace. This kind of trace is analyzed and synthesized constantly in people's reflecting course of external things, thus it has produced the general representation, and has prepared the conditions for transition to thinking. From the view of the information theory, modern cognitive psychology has proved the storage of this kind of trace, that is, the storage of information. This kind of trace of representation, not only can store, but also can process and encode various traces stored (information).

To summarize the forming of representation, it can generally be divided into two modes — combination and fusion. The combination of representation is the course that the representation is accumulated continuously, such as the representation to the same thing or the same kind of things is combined continuously and this makes it more abundant and broad. On the day that an undergraduate entered the university for the first time, his representation regarding the university is simply and poor. But in the university life afterwards, the representation about the classroom, auditorium and classmates will be accumulated and combined. This makes the perceptual knowledge have more generality. Here, association law (close, similarity, comparison) plays an important role. The combination of representation is the main characteristic of the memory representation.

The fusion of representation is a form of creative transformation of a kind of representation which is more complicated than the association. All the representations taking part in this kind of fusion change their own quality more or less, and fuse a new image. The mermaid in the mythology or typical character that the writer creates is the new representations after fused. This is the main characteristic of creative representation.

General representation is the direct foundation that the feeling and perception transit to the concept. Continuously generalizing the representation makes it continuously leave the direct perceptual foundation, thus it may transit to the concept and thinking.

Generality of representation and the transition to concept and thinking cannot be separated from the function of people's language and word. The participation of the language and word is not only the essential condition of transition from concrete representation to the abstraction, but also can cause, restrict and transform representation. Therefore, modern cognitive psychology mostly thinks that the representation is encoded by the antithesis. It can be either an image code or a language code. Image and language can be mutually translated under certain conditions, because the mutual restraints of abstract concept can lead to the concrete image: red, round, hard, ball, three, inch, diameter, what these words refer to is all abstract concepts. In the sentence of "the hard red ball of three inches in diameter", because these abstract concepts limit each other, it expresses a concrete thing. So the image can be kept in stock in the form of language through encoding; Language can be resumed to image through decoding, such as reproducing imaginary. To employ which kind of code is completely transferred by subject. However, it should be pointed out that representation is an important link that transits from perception to concept and thinking, but there exist essential differences in representation and thinking. No matter what great generality the representation has, it always has the characteristic of iconicity, and it belongs to perceptual knowledge. Therefore, representation and thinking have relations and differences. It is incorrect to see the connection only and cannot see the difference. As Lenin said, "representation can't hold the whole sport, for example, it can't hold sport of 300,000 kilometers per second, but thinking can hold and should hold."

In the transformation from the generality of representation to the concept and thinking, there are generally two routes. Although these two routes are close and integral in the understanding of average people, they have different advantages for people engaged in different work or activity. For example, scientists and philosophers are generally good at the abstract thinking, writers and engineers are mostly good at image thinking. We can't say one thinking is good and the other one is not good. In children's thinking developments, children before studying have more image thinking, and this kind of image thinking awaits to develop towards abstract thinking. In this sense, we can say that image thinking is lower one grade than abstract thinking. But in the thinking of adult developments described above, to make a certain kind of thinking take advantage because of need of the work is not an advanced or low-grade problem. No matter scientists, philosophers, or writers, engineers, they all not only need abstract thinking ability but also need the image thinking ability. None of them can be lacked, but they are required to develop a certain kind of thinking further due to their different working ranges.

Representation has various forms or kinds. This was divided according to different angles or standards. According to generality of representation, representation can be divided into specific representation and general representation (or generalization representation).

When we perceive a certain thing, the perception which reflects this specific thing is produced. For example, perception about a certain desk is not the perception of another desk. The corresponding representation is the image about a certain desk but not the image of another desk, this is specific representation. In people's understanding, they usually not only perceive a certain desk but also perceive a lot of different desks. Then it exceeds the representation of the specific thing at this moment, and reflects the representation of a kind of things briefly (such as various desks). This is general representation or generalization representation. Specific representation reflects the characteristics of the specific thing, and general representation reflects general characteristics that a lot of similar things own in common.

General representation is produced based on specific representation. It is generalized by specific representation. The characteristics of the specific representation that generalization representation reflects are not remaining untouched, stiff reflection, but change to some extent, selective reflection. What general representation reflects are often those similar (or common) and relatively fixed characteristics of specific representation. The language and word play an important role in the course of forming general representation.

Because of people's activity, generally speaking, representation is always developed along from a specific to general, and general representation is always developed to more general direction and developed more widely and deeply.

However, no matter what big generality the representation has, it always has certain intuitivity, materiality and iconicity. It is always the reflection of the intuitive characteristics of things. Compared with concept, there is an essential difference. Since the concept is formed in the abstract activity of thinking, when people forms the concept, they always leave general representation and get away the concrete characteristics that some objects have, only reflect the most general connection and regularity of things.

Certainly, during the process of studying children's thinking, we often discuss intuitive action thinking, concrete image thinking based on the source and process of concept and thinking. We absolutely do not want to confuse the boundary of perception, representation and logical thinking.

According to the function of representation, they can be divided into remembering representation mainly includes memory and imagining representation mainly includes innovation.

1. The remembering representation is the image of trace of things which is reproduced in brain based on past perceived things, when the things are not in the front. Remembering representation has the following characteristics:

(1) It is different from eidetic representation. Eidetic representation can be very distinct, confirming and complete as perception, while remembering representation is often relatively dim, unstable and partial.

(2) These characteristics of remembering representation are its shortcoming (not so good as the perception) and its advantage too. Because of these characteristics of representation, it is not restricted and constrained by present perception. Therefore, on the basis of people's continuous activities, the representation in the brain can continuously become from specific to general through perceive a kind of things repeatedly. General representation is no more the simple reproducing of the image of things. It achieves the standard more abundant and more deeply than specific representation through compound and merging. Thus it makes representation become the supreme form of perceptual knowledge. Abundant and deep general representation is the crucial link that transits from people's direct and concrete perception to the objective world to indirect and abstract thinking.

(3) The generality of remembering representation is the result that the people continuously perceive the things in the activity. It is the result that language and word take part in this reflection course too. The language and word can not only cause representation, more important, it can also strengthen the generality of

representation, make it reaches qualitative leap and achieves the level of concept and thinking.

(4) Forming and development of memory are determined by the memory law. In order to make children and teenagers have abundant and deep remembering representation, they should be trained according to the memory law.

2. Imagining representation is new image that processed and reconstructed by brain based on original representation.

(1) Imagining representation and remembering representation all have certain generality, but imagining representation is different from remembering representation. It is the new image that processed and reconstructed by brain based on original representation. For example, the infant acts mother in "playing house" game. This combines representation about mother and representation about children together in the brain. The creativity here is very low. When the writer moulds typical role, it is an extremely complicated creation course. Here exists abstract thinking and image thinking too, but imagining representation plays an important role.

(2) As remembering representation, imagining representation stems from both specific perception and the help of the language and word.

(3) Imagination can be divided into accidental imagination and intentional imagination according to different intention. Accidental imagination is without specific intention, unconscious and inferior. It is common in imagination of infant. Dream is the extreme form of accidental imagination. Intentional imagination is with some intention and conscious. Intentional imagination plays an important role in people's positive and creative thinking.

(4) Imagination can be divided into reconstituted imagination and creative imagination because of different independence, novelty and creativity. Reconstituted imagination is the image that is imagined in terms of things never perceived on the basis of present and others' description, such as images of students' thinking about the ancient slaves, geographical images far away, etc. Reconstituted imagination plays an important role in the course while student study and the thinking activity in the work of scientific and technical personnel. Creative imagination is image of new things created independently and do not depend on existing description. It plays a key role in student's creative study, in the thinking activities that people create new technology, new products and new works.

3. Remembering representation is different from imagining representation, not mainly because the representation materials that they use are different, it is because of the goal and the need of people's activity are different, therefore the processing and using mode of representation are different too. In people's activity, some need more remembering representation, while others need more imagining representation. For example, when a music player plays the particular melody, he need certain creative factor (display on his specific understanding and special attitude toward the melody played) too, but not reproducing the content of the melody briefly without emotion at all. Otherwise he is not a good player. However, it is the memory representation that occupied main position in the playing course after all. He must play following the representation, because what he plays is a melody with specific characteristic, instead of other melodies. However, in the creative work of the writers, poets, composers and design engineers, the case is different. They work mainly based on imagining representation. Certainly, abundant and deep remembering representation is also very important in their working course. In this sense, remembering representation is often a foundation of imagining representation.

To divide the representation from people's feeling passway (or the analysor), there can be representation in conformity with every kind of feeling passway, such as visual representation, hearing representation, tasting representation, smelling representation, touching representation, movement representation, etc.

This kind of representation divided by the feeling passway, just have a relative meaning. For most people (including musicians, painters), feeling representation all has the mixed properties. In people's activity, generally speaking, we do not have single visual representation and single hearing or movement representation, but often the mixing of different representation, because people should always use various sense organs when they perceive things. Only in a relative sense, we can say that some people's visual representation is a bit more developed, while others' hearing representation is a bit more developed.

The form is a mental process with particular characteristics. It is noticeable in the early development of modern psychology. But as behaviorism psychology dominated, representation had begun to become quiet in the twenties of the 20th century. After cognitive psychology rises, the research of representation is paid attention to and developed rapidly again, and the achievement is very abundant too. The research of cognitive psychology on "the psychological rotation" and "the psychological scanning" also makes attractive achievement. In the psychological consultation and psychotherapy, the function of representation also plays an important role.

## 5.7 Attention in the Perceptual Cognition

Attention is the status of psychological activity or perception at a certain moment. It is shown as direction or centralization of certain target. People can control one's own attention direction consciously most of the time. Attention has two obvious characteristics: directivity and centrality. The directivity of attention means people have chosen a certain target in psychological activity or perception in a moment, and has neglected other targets. In the boundless universe, a large amount of information act on us all the time, but we unable to make reflection to all information, and can only direct our perception to something. For example, you go shopping, you have only noticed the thing which you need, and has neglected the other goods. So, the directivity of attention is that which direction the psychological activity or perception act on. If the directivity is different, the information that people accept from the external world is different. When psychological activity or perception directs to a certain target, they are concentrated on this target, attention concentrated, excitability improved. This is centrality of attention. We can say that directivity of attention means psychological activity or perception is directed to which direction, while centrality means the activity intensity or nervous degree of psychological activity or perception in certain direction. While people highly concentrate their own attention, the range of attention is reduced; when the direction range is extensive but not centralized, the whole intensity is decreased. When people's attention is highly centralized, except the goal things, other things around oneself cannot be seen and heard.

Attention has selecting function, maintaining function, regulating function etc. A large number of stimuli are provided at any time by the environment around us, but the information has different meaning for us. Some information is important and beneficial, but some information has nothing to do with the task that we are engaged in, even some harmful interference information. The first function of attention is to select important information from a large amount of information provided and react it, exclude harmful information interference at the same time, this is the selecting function. Attention can keep people's psychological activity or perception in nervous state within a period of time. This depends on the maintaining function of attention. People can carry on deeply processing and handling the selective information only under the continuous nervous status. The maintaining function of attention is still embodied in the continuity of time. It has important meanings for the successfully carrying out the complicated activity. The regulating function of attention is not only reflected in the steady and continuous activity, but also in the change of the activity. When people switch from one activity to another activity, attention reflects important adjustment function. Only the regulating function of attention could realize the transition of the activity, and could adapt to the fast changing environment too.

The explanation of Attention mechanism in perceiving often includes filter model, decay model, response selection model, energy distribution model, etc.

### 5.7.1 Filter model

This model is initially proposed by British famous psychologist D. Broadbent in 1958 shown in Figure 5.2. It is an earlier theory model about attention. The model is called the single channel model by Welford. The filter model thinks that there exists a large number of information comes from external world, but the processing ability of people's advanced centre of nervous system is extremely limited, then the bottleneck appears. In order to prevent the system from overloading, it is needed that the filter to regulate, choose some information to enter advanced analysis stage. Other information may be stored in a certain memory temporarily, and then decline rapidly.

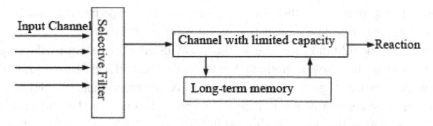

Fig. 5.2 Filter model

The function of attention just likes the filter. Through its filtration, it enables some information of the input channel to enter advanced centre through the limited passing of internal capacity, while other information is filtered. So, the work of noticing is carried on in the whole or nothing.

At cocktail party or other parties, you are talking with several people absorbedly. At this moment, you cannot discern the conversation of other people, but if someone outside mentions your name, you may notice, while other people talking with you might not notice. When we put sound on both ear through headset at the same time, the stimulant message that each ears accepts is different. We investigate the relation between tested reaction information and accepted information of both ears through the experiment, thus we can understand the characteristics of tested attention. The experimental result finds that the test can reproduce the stimulant information according to the characteristics of the material in such an experiment, such as 6, 2, 9; DEAR AUNT JANE.

As for this kind of experimental results, there are two kinds of views:

(1) The filter channel can be shifted fast;
(2) The working mechanism of attention does not work with the single channel model and in whole or nothing way, the filter model is incorrect.

### 5.7.2 Decay model

The decay model is proposed base on the revised filter model by American psychologist A. M. Treisman in 1960 (Treisman, 1982). This theory does not think the filter works in "whole or nothing" way. The channel which accepts information is not single channel, but multi-channel. This model is the result that Treisman improved the filter model based on the experimental results of processing the non-follow information in following experiment.

The decay model thinks that the working way of attention is not by the single channel way of the whole or nothing, but the multi-channel way. However, in the information processing of multi-channel, it is different that the degree of information processing of each channel, as shown in Fig. 5.3. The information processing way of follow ear is showed in filter model, while the information of non-follow ear is also probably processed through the filter. Nevertheless, the signal of non-follow ear is processed when it passes the filter, so it is denoted with the dotted line. In the course of significance analysis, it is probably filtered, or probably strengthened because of some other factors too (such as one's own name).

Decay model introduces an important concept for the information that entered advanced analysis level — threshold. It thinks that the excitement threshold with which information stored in the brain is at the advanced analysis level is different with each other, thus influencing the selection of the filter.

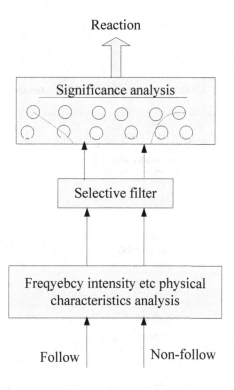

Fig. 5.3 Decay model

### 5.7.3 *Response selection model*

In 1963, J. Deutsch propose response selection model (Deutsch et al., 1963). This model (See Fig. 5.4) thinks that attention does not lie in selecting the perception stimuli, but lie in selecting the response to stimulus. This theory thinks that all the stimuli felt by sense organ should enter the senior analytic process. The centre is processed according to certain rules, thus it can react to important information, while the unimportant information may be washed out by the new content soon.

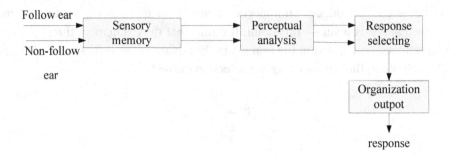

Fig. 5.4 Response selection model of attention

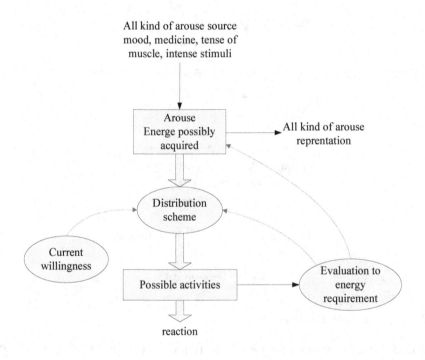

Fig. 5.5 The energy distribution model

### 5.7.4 Energy distribution model

In 1973 D. Kahneman proposed the energy distribution model (Kahneman, 1973). The energy distribution model thinks that attention is the energy or resource limited in quantity that the people can use for executing the task. The resources and arouse are linked together in people's activity, its arouse level is influenced by many factors, such as mood, medicine and tense of muscle, etc. The energy produced is assigned to different possible activities through an distribution scheme, and form various responses finally. Figure 5.5 provides the sketch map of the energy distribution model.

# Chapter 6

# Visual Information Processing

Vision is a process finding what the objects are and where they are in scenes from images, i.e. in the process symbol descriptions useful to observers are gained. Thus, vision is an information processing related with certain inputs and outputs.

## 6.1 Visual Physiological Mechanism

An eye is the outer organ for vision, which is the most complicated organ of a human body. Most external information is received through eyes. Lights from objects enter eyes, and focalize on retinas to bring images. Nerve impulses emitted by retinas are transmitted through optic nerves to optic areas of palliums, and result in vision.

Vision plays an important role in perceptive world of human. Environment information that men can react to is mostly transmitted by vision to cerebra. Vision occupies a dominative position in perceptive system. If a piece of information that is received by another organ is contradictive to a piece of vision information, human must react to vision information.

Light entered eye and reached retina pass through tree refracting surface: a) air–cornea interface; b) aqueous humor–lens interface; c) lens–vitreous humor interface. The refracting system of the eye consists of four kinds of medium with different refractive indexes, as well as several refractive surfaces with different curvatures. It is possible to exactly describe the route light refracts through eyeball but it is over complicated. The usual method is employing the simplified eye, by which the route light passes through the eye can be figured out enough exactly.

### 6.1.1 Retina

The retina is a part of the brain, which consists of several kinds of neurons processing visual information. The retina, about 0.5mm thick, clings to the back wall of the eyeball. It contains three level nerve cells: the first level is light receptors comprising countless rod cells and cone cells; the second level is bipolar cells; the third level is ganglion cells. Axons stemmed from ganglion cells form optic nerves. The three level cells comprise the direct passage through which visual information transfer in the retina. Besides, there are two kinds of middle nerve cells between the first level and the second level cells and between the second and the third cells: horizontal cells and amacrine cells. Their tubers stretch horizontally between cell layers, connecting the neighboring cells. Figure 6.1 shows the retina structure of quadrumanas.

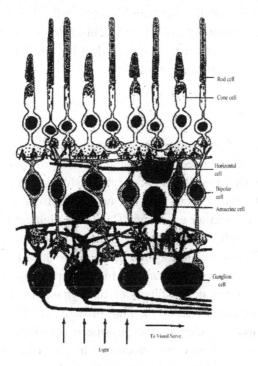

Fig. 6.1 The quadrumana's retina structure

Rod cells and cone cells are light receiving cells of eyeballs. Rod cells are thin and long whereas cone cells are thick and short. They have distinct different photosensitivity. Rod cells are able to perceive extremely faint light but they are not able to distinguish colors; cone cells are just able to response to stronger light but they can perceive different colors. There are much more rod cells than cone cells in a retina. There are about 6 – 7 millions cone cells but 110 – 130 millions rod cells in a human retina. The number of retina's efferent nerve cells – ganglion cells is only about one percent of the huge number of the receiving cells. About tens – hundreds of receiving cells connect with a ganglion cell via bipolar cells (and horizontal cells and amacrine cells). The center area of a retina is called optic macula where rod cells are the most. The center of the macula is called the fovea which is composed of cone cells. The area of the fovea is only about 1 mm$^2$, but it can produce the clearest vision because the crystal concentrates images on the fovea, and also because there are one-vs-one links between the fovea, where cone cells are most densely packed, and advanced brain nerve centre. Rod cells are less dense in the fovea while the densest in the parafovea. The ganglion cells distribute like cone cells. The distributive character determines that the visual field of the central retina has very high visual sensitivity (ability of distinguishing special details), while the visual field of the parafovea are the most sensitive to dim light.

### 6.1.2  Photoreceptor

There are four kinds of photoreceptors in human retinas: rod cells and three kinds of cone cells. Each kind of receptors contains a kind of special pigment. Such a pigment molecule triggers a series chemical transformation when it has absorbed a photon; meanwhile, it releases energy causing electrical signal generating and synaptic chemical transmitter excreting. The photo pigment of rod cells is called visual purple, of which the peak wavelength value of the spectrum absorbing curve is 500nm. The spectral absorption peaks of the three kinds of cone cells are 430, 530 and 560nm, being most sensitive to blue, green and red respectively.

The character (excited or inhibited) of the synapses between receptors and bipolar cells may be dependent on the kind of transmitters released by receptors or dependent on the character of the passage of the bipolar cell postsynaptic membranes. At present there is no evidence indicating that a receptor can release two kinds of transmitters. More evidences indicate that the two kinds of receptors have diverse receiving molecules. The central areas of the receptive fields the bipolar cells are formed by direct connection between receptors and bipolar cells, while the outer surrounding areas are formed by indirect connection between horizontal cells and receptors. Each receptor contacts with both bipolar cells and horizontal cells. Horizontal cells through their dendrite's branches contact many neighbor receptive cells in horizontal direction, and then transmit the integrated signal to bipolar cells. The information transmitting between receptors and horizontal cells is through excitatory synapses. It is not clear at present where the fan-outs of the horizontal cells of quadrumanas are since horizontal cells have not axons. Transverse contact of horizontal cells generates outer surrounding areas of receptive fields of bipolar cells and ganglion cells. The receptive fields of horizontal cells are a kind of even structures, taking homogeneous hyperpolarizative response for light stimulating any position. The larger the stimulative light spots, the stronger the hyperpolarization.

Bodys of amacrine cells locate between bipolar cells and ganglion cells, contacting with lots of neighboring ganglion cells in horizontal direction through broad dendritic branches. They have not axons, and their dendrites have both presynaptic functions and postsynaptic functions. Amacrine cells contact with one another. Because of this character, the space area of the kind of cells is greater than that of horizontal cells. Amacrine cells have diversified shapes. The kinds of nerve transmitters used are very complex.

Ganglion cells are output nerve cells of retinas. A ganglion cell is able to contact with inputs of many sensitive cells through bipolar cells and horizontal cells, and the neighboring ganglion cells contact with each other through horizontal branches of amacrine cells. The complex nerve contacts between ganglion cells and other retinal cells are reflected on the sensitive field structure. Unlike all fore-level nerve cells, conductive act potentials are produced by ganglion cells. We can research the cell's functional characters and receptive field structure by recording electrical pulses of ganglion cells or optic nerve. The receptive field of a ganglion cell is like that of a bipolar cell, including a center area and an outer surrounding area. No matter which kind of cells, the functions of the center areas of receptive fields are mutual antagonist, and light's stimulating surrounding areas will reduce the reactive intensity of stimulating center areas.

### 6.1.3 Lateral geniculate nucleus

Optic nerve intercross in a special fashion before entering the brain nerve centre. Fibres from the binocular nasal retina cross into the opposite side cerebral hemisphere; Fibers from the temporal retina, which do not cross, cast into the same side hemisphere. The result is: the fibres from the temporal retina of the left eye and the fibres from the nasal retina of the right eye pool the left optic tract getting to the left lateral geniculate nucleus; then travel to the left hemisphere responding to the right hemifield. On the contrary, the fibres from left nasal retina and that from right temporal retina pool the right optic tract, getting to the right lateral geniculate nucleus; the travel to the right hemisphere responding to the left hemifield of the brain. The visual cortexes of both the hemispheres connect with each other through the fibres of the callus. The connection mixes the information from both the hemifields. Having been processed primarily, visual information travels to thalamencephalon through optic nerves and optic tracts. There are two pathways in the thalamencephalon: 1) lateral geniculate nucleus – cortex pathway, which is the dominant visual input pathway. For primates, 90% fibres from the retinas travel through the pathway to the visual cortex. 2) prebrachium-pulvinar-cortex pathway, through which 10% fibres of the retinas of primates contact with visual cortexs. What are related with vision in pulvinar are mostly ventral lateral pulvinar and hypothalamus receiving input fibres from retinas and prebrachium respectively. The nerve contacts and function characters of the pathway need more research.

Quadrumana's lateral geniculate nucleus comprises six layers cells. Binocular input is projected to three different levels. The fibres issuing from the homolateral eye (for lateral geniculate nucleus) end at the fifth, third, second layer; the fibres issuing from the opposite side eye end at the sixth, forth, first layer. Each of the overlapped layers has point-to-point projection to retinas. So the points that are neighboring in retinas are also neighboring in each layer of lateral geniculate nucleus. Because the six layers are superposed tidily according to retina projection, if a certain point cell receives input from a certain point of the left retina, the corresponding point in the fifth layer must receive input from the corresponding point of the right eye. The anatomical corresponding relation favors constituting the two eye's mutual relation, establishing foundation for generating binocular parallax (depth and stereo sense) tune.

There is a relative big area out of the traditional receptive field of cells of retinas and lateral geniculate nucleus. The area do not directly response to visual stimulation, but it has modulating function for reaction caused by stimulation on receptive fields. For a sensitive central cell, when the size of the stimulative light spot is bigger than that of the receptive field center, as causes decrease of reaction of the optic nerve cell, which indicates that there is a inhibitory peripheral areas area out of excitatory receptive field center area. Color reciprocity between disinhibitory areas and receptive areas probably is the nerve basis of psychological phenomenon such as generating color contrast and color constancy etc. Color contrast and color constancy are two important characters of human chromatic vision. What is called color constancy refers to that vision systems keep color perceiving invariability relatively when the spectral ingredients of ambiences have changed obviously. Color contrast means that human eye's sensitivity for red color increase (or reverse) in green background. When ambience light tend to become red, nerve cells of lateral geniculate nucleus can debase sensitivity for red light and enhance sensitivity for blue light through disinhibitory area's effect, vice versa. Thereby human eyes retain color sense constancy and strengthen color contrast.

### 6.1.4 Visual cortex

Visual cortex has two main kinds of nerve cells: stellate cells and cone cells. The axons of stellated cells contact with projecting fibers. A cone cell is triangle, with the tip towards surface layer emitting upwards a long dendrites, the fundus issuing several dendrites to contact breadthwise.

Visual cortex, like other cortex areas, includes six cells layers, denoted by I-VI from surface to inner. The trunks of cortex cell's tubers (dendrites and axons) all distribute in direction vertical to cortex surface; the branches of dendrites and axons distribute breadthwise in different layers. The different cortex areas contact with one another by axons through deep white matter, while the inner of cortexes contacts through transverse branches of dendrites and axons in cortexes.

In recent years, the scope of visual cortexes has already extended to many new cortex area including parietal lobe, occipital lobe and part of frontal lobe (VanEssen 1985), amounting to 25. Besides it has seven visual association areas, which has both visual and other sense or movement function. All visual areas account for 55% area of new brain cortex. Thus it can be seen the importance of visual information processing playing in the whole brain function. It is a present edge-cutting issue of visual research to research function division, grade relationship and reciprocity of the visual areas. The evidences of confirming an independent visual cortex area are: 1) the area has independent visual field projecting map, 2) the area has the same input and output nerve connection as other cortex area, 3) the area has similar cellular structure, 4) the area has different function characters from other visual cortex area.

Wernicke and Geschwind believe that the pathway of visual recognition is as shown in Figure 6.2. According to their model, visual information is transmited from retinas to lateral geniculate body, passing from lateral geniculate body to primary visual cortex (V17), then reaching a more advanced visual nerve centre (V18), from here traveling to angular gyrus, then arrive at Wernicke area (Mayeux 91). Visual information is translated to speech (hearing) idea. After the sound patterns formed, they passe on to the Broca area.

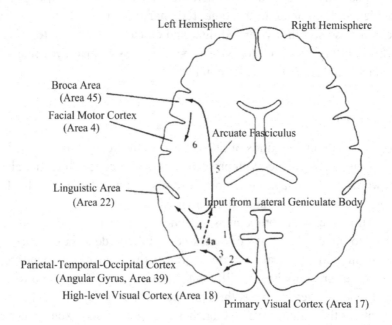

Fig. 6.2 Visual nerve pathway

The 17th area in visual cortex is called as first visual area (V1) or stripe cortex. It receives the direct input of lateral geniculate body, wherefore also known as primary visual cortex. The functional studies for visual cortex mostly are conducted on the level cortex. Except for the 17th area receiving direct projection from lateral geniculate bodys, the vision related cortex has also stripe proparea (the 18th area) and stripe outskirt (the 19th area). According to morphology and physiological research, the 17th area does not project to the lateral cortex but to 18th area, and 18th area projects forward to the 19th area, and again feedbacks to the 17th area. The 18th area includes three visual areas, called V2, V3 and V3A respectively, and their main input is from V1. Vl and V2 are the biggest visual areas. The 19th area buried deeply in the posterior paries of superior temporal sulcus includes the fourth (V4) and the fifth visual area (V5). V5 also called as the middle temporal area has entered the scope of the temporal lobe. The other vision related cortex areas in the temporal lobe are inner upper frontal area and inferior temporal area. There are the top occipital area, the ventral interparietal, the post abdominal area and the 7a area in the parietal lobe. The cerebral cortex area outside the occipital lobe possibly belongs to a higher level. Why are there so many representative areas? Do or not different representative areas detect different graphical characteristics (such as color, shape, brightness, movement, depth, etc.)? Or do the different representative areas deal with information at different levels? Is not there a higher level representative area integrate the separative graphical characteristics; thereby give the biological meaning of graphics? Is there a special representative area which is responsible for the storage of images (visual learning and memory) or in charge of visual attention? These will be the issues to be resolved in visual research in a longer period of time.

## 6.2  Visual Cortex Information Processing

### 6.2.1  Visual cortex receptive field

Visual cortical neurons' response to light spots stimulation is very weak points, and excites only when the due direct (orientation) light bars are given to stimulate the receptive field. According to different receptive field structure of cortical neurons, Hubel and Wiesel research firing modes of single neuron in visual cortex of cats and monkeys, and they found that there were four types of visual cortical neurons - simple cells, complex cells, ultra-complicated cells and extreme complex cells.

Simple cell receptive field size is relatively small, of which the light-on area and the light-off area are separated with relatively visible space integration, with linear response characteristics, and there is no (or little) the spontaneous discharge. Stimulations with a specific direction and a fixed position in the visual field can mostly inspire simple cells.

Complex cell receptive field size is relatively large, of which the light-on area and the light-off area are overlapped, with non-linear response characteristics, space integration being not obvious, with strong spontaneous discharge. Unlike simple cells, complex cell's response demands certain direct linear stimulation but regardless the position in the visual field. Another difference with the simple cells is that complex cell's linear stimulation in the appropriate direction will continue to inspire when the light had move through the visual field. Simple cells stop exciting when stimulation moves in the visual field although the direction of stimulation remains unchanged. Because complex cells be able to continue to inspire for moving proper direct linear stimulus, it can be believed that they receive a large number of input stimulus from simple cells, so these simple cells respond to certain direction stimulus, but each of simple cells has a sense of stimulation in different parts of visual field.

Ultra-complicated cells receive excitatory and inhibitory input information from several complex cells. Ultra-complex cells also respond to the special direct linear stimulation, but the stimulation cannot exceed a certain length. Response's characteristic is the same as complex cells, but with obvious terminal inhibition.

A very high degree of super-complex cell responds to edges shifting over the visual field, as long as the edges have specific width. Some very high degree of super-complex neurons the 90 angle of the two edges in particular, so that this very high degree of super-complex of neurons is also known as angle detectors.

### 6.2.2  Character selectivity

Visual cortex neurons are highly selective to visual stimulation of a variety of static and dynamic characteristics, including the orientation/direction selectivity, spatial frequency selectivity, speed selectivity, binocular parallel selectivity, and color selectivity.

The orientation/direction selectivity

Visual cortex cells show the most exciting (the best or the best direction of orientation) only when the stimulating lines or edges are in the appropriate azimuth direction and shift in certain direction. The histogram made according to cell's discharge frequency relative to the orientation and moving direction of the stimulus is able to show the location and direction tuning properties of the cell.

The spatial frequency selectivity

The grating of sine wave modulation is a common used stimulating graphic in visual experiments. The main advantage of this stimulating graphic is convenient to do quantitative mathematical analysis to the spatial-temporal characteristics of the visual response. Each of visual cortex cells has a certain spatial frequency tuning. In the same cortex area, different cells have different spatial frequency selectivity.

The speed selectivity

Visual cortex cells have much stronger response to moving graphics than to static flashing graphics. Each cortical cell has not only the selectivity of direction of movement, but also selectivity of a certain velocity. Only when the stimulating graphics move in a certain speed and the appropriate direction does the cell reach the largest response. The speed is known as the best speed of the cell. If speed is higher or lower than the best speed, the response will be reduced.

The binocular parallel selectivity

Unlike lateral geniculate body cells, the majority of visual cortex cells receive binocular inputs. Therefore, each cell has a receptive field in the left and right retina, the position difference of the pair of receptive fields in retinas (as opposed to fixation point) referred to as "parallax". If the difference of distances from the left and right receptive fields to fixation points is zero, it indicates the point is on the fixation plane. If the two receptive fields depart toward frontal sides, it is indicated that the cell's tuning distance (best distance) is farther than the fixation points; if both receptive fields deviate to nasal sides, that indicates the cell's tuning distance is nearer than the fixation points.

Color selectivity

Like retinas and latenal geniculate body cells, cortical cells have also color selectivity. Unlike subcortical single antagonism type receptive field, the visual cortex cell color receptive field has dual antagonist structure. For example, for the R-G (red - green) type receptive field, its color structure may have two forms. The receptive field center could be excited by the green cones input at the same time be inhibited by the input of red cones, or vice versa. Peripheral response character for color is contrary of the center. Therefore, the dual-antagonist-type receptive field distinguishes red and green through the center's color antagonism, enhances red-green contrast edge through the central and peripheral interaction. For the B-Y (blue - yellow)-type receptive field, the situation is the same.

### 6.2.3 Functional columns

Finding visual cortex function columns is the most eye-catching progress of research of the visual center in recent years. As a result of these column systems coincide with the various feature detecting functions, so it is considered as the strong support feature detection theory. So far a variety of features found in the cortical columns are vertical cortex surface, arranged in lamellae.

## 1. Position columns

Electrophysiological and morphological observations have been repeatedly proved that there are the structure of orientation columns in the 17th area and the 18th area of monkeys and cats. Hubel and Wiesel punctured inclinedly to the visual cortex using microelectrode, in the micro-electrode pathway, the cells' sensitive positions recorded in order always changed regularly by clockwise or counterclockwise. Position columns arrange vertically to the surface of the cortex.

## 2. The ocular dominance columns

According to the different extent of cells affected by two eyes, Hubel and Wiesel classified the visual cortex cells into right dominance cells and left dominance cells. While researching position columns they also observed that the vertical inserted microelectrodes tend to record the cell bunch with the same ocular dominance character, however, when tilt punctured, the left ocular dominance cells and the right ocular dominance cells appear alternating with certain intervals. It can be seen that cortical neurons' ocular dominance characteristics is also arranged in the form of vertical columns. The width of each column is about 500μm, the left column and right column jointly account for the scope of 1mm. Later, a variety of morphological method (axon degeneration and reinstated silver and autoradiography) have successfully demonstrated the ocular dominance column structure.

## 3. The spatial frequency columns

Thompson and Tolhurst using a similar method observed that the microelectrode puncture also made it appear that the spatial frequency characteristics change systematically. In their view, cortical cell's the best spatial frequency characteristic is also arranged regularly in the cortical surface in form of vertical columns. Tolhurst using 2DG autoradiography method proved that there is indeed the structure of spatial frequency columns in the cat cortical 17th area. This system of vertical columns is vertical to the cortical surface from the surface into the deep, the width of columns being about 0.8-1mm.

## 4. The color columns

Micheal, while researching color characteristics of monkey cortex, found that some cells are sensitive only to the color light but no response to the white light. He also noted that when the tilt microelectrode puncture visual cortex, color-specific cells and non-color-specific cells appeared by turn. According to the results of several parallel puncturing channels, they believed that the color-specific cells are also arranged in lamellae structure. Color column are about

100-200μm wide throughout the cortex thickness, and all cells in a same column have the same spectral properties.

### 6.2.4 Spherical functional structures

Li Chaoyi and his student Yao Haishan, which are with Institute of Neuroscience Shanghai Academy of Biological Sciences, found that there exists a kind of spherical functional structures relative to processing large-scale and complex graphics features in the primary visual cortex. The new found spherical structure is a novel structure of brain function, and is very important significance for understanding the neural mechanisms for brain to deal with complex image information. So far as the computer cannot quickly identify objectives from ever-changing image backgrounds, while the human brain can easily do so. The traditional research of functional columns still cannot explain how the visual system deals with large-scale complex image information. The two Chinese scientists this time using a special microelectrode recorded hundreds of nerve cells of the cat visual cortex, and described in detail the cell's large-scale integration characteristics, as well as the reaction of graphics, and confirmed there was the functional structure for processing large-scale and complex graphics features in the primary visual cortex.

## 6.3 Color Vision

Color is a subjective feeling. Color can be divided into two broad categories non-color and color. Non-color refers to black to white and the various different level gray, and they can be arranged in a series, called the black-and-white series. Color means a series of color other than black and white colors, with has three characteristics: lightness, hue and saturation. Lightness refers to the brightness of light color. Hue is the characteristics of colors to distinguish each other, depended on the human eye feeling generated by the light source spectral composition. Saturation is the purity of color. A variety of monochromatic light is the most saturated color in visible spectrum. The more white mixed into the color, the more unsaturated.

In 1854 H. Glassman established the law of color mixture:

(1) Human color vision can only distinguish three color variables: lightness, hue and saturation.

(2) In a mixture of the two color components, if an element change continuously, the appearance of mixed colors also change continuously. This law derives the other two laws:

The law of complementary color: every color has a corresponding complementary color, and they mixed in proper proportion to produce white and gray; if they mixed in other proportion, they produce a non-saturated color similar to the proportion of components. The law of middle color: mixing any two non-complementary colors, the hue of the mixed color is determined by the relative number of the two colors, its saturation is depended on the distance the hue orders of the two.

(3) The same visual colors, regardless of its spectral composition, are equivalent in color mixture. The law derives the Lieu Law: The Lieu law: mixtures of similar colors are still similar.

(4) The mixed color's brightness equal to the sum of brightness of total composition of the mixed color, that is, the law of brightness adding.

The process of color vision can be divided into several stages. The first stage, there are three different types of retinal cone cells, which have their own independent pigments to absorb selectively visible light of different wavelengths, at the same time each individual substance can generate white – blach responses, white response for strong light, black for no light stimulating. The second phase, during the nerve excitation passing from the cones to nerve center, the three responses are re-mixed, and finally generating three pairs of the neural response antagonist, red - green, yellow - blue, white - black response.

The sketch map of the process is shown in Figure 6.3. Now it is believed that the Young – Helmholtz's three-color theory and Herring's antagonist theory both acquire only one aspect of correct understanding of color vision, and we can get a more comprehensive understanding through the two theories complementing each other. In 1807, according to the color mixing rule which says the three primary colors, red, green, blue, can produce a variety of colors and gray, Young proposed an assumption that there are three kinds of retinal nerve fibers, the excitation of each kind of fibers causes the sense of the primary color, that is, red, Green, blue color sense. Since then, Helmholtz further in 1860 complemented the three color theory and proposed that the different spectral compositions arouse three different proportion exciting of three kinds of fibers, which have different exiting curves. In 1878, Herring has always observed the color phenomenon color appear always in the pairs of red - green, yellow - blue, black - white, so he assumed that there are three pairs of the retina pigments: white - black pigment, red - green, yellow – blue. Each pair pigments have inverse responses to light and darkness.

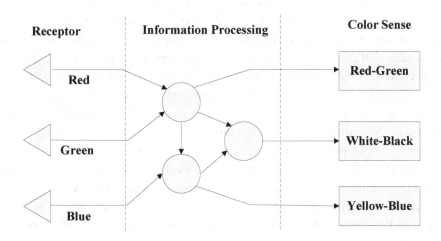

Fig. 6.3 The sketch map of color vision mechanism

## 6.4 Marr's Visual Computing Theory

Visual information processing is a process one find what objects there are in surrounding scene and where they are based on images, that is, a process that the observer acquire useful symbol description from the image. There is a huge gap between an input image to the scene description, so it is necessary to go through a series of information processing and understanding processes. Understanding the nature of this process is the key to discover the visual mystery, but we are still far from a better understanding of these.

Visual recognition of objects is to constitute correspondent relationship between image elements and the descriptions of the known landscape objects. Elements of images are point pixels; the value of a pixel is the pixel's gray value, which is point data. While the other hand, an object is described through its shape, size, geometry, color and other features. These features represent the overall character of the object. To constitute correspond relationship between the input point data and the overall character of objects have to go through a process grouping point data. This grouping process is not only in the vision, but also in the sense of hearing and others.

The issue relative to how to generate overall characters is the issue of constancy. As we all know, the gray of each point of images is the integrated result of many factors. These factors include light, the reflective properties of the object surface, the distance and position of the observer relative to the object and object's shape. Any changes in these factors will lead to changes of the gray images, also will change the images we see. However, shape, size and color of the object we feel by vision are unrelated to the situation of observers, as well as lighting conditions. More specifically, when lighting conditions and distance from the observer position relative to object change, even though the images produced in the retinal change, people always see certain the shape and size of the object. People perceive in the brain constant characteristics of the objects behind their variable appearances. Therefore, the brains not only organize point sensor information into a whole, but also through a factoring process separate these conditions affecting sensor information, that is, lighting conditions, distance and position of the observer, to acquire purely information of the objects. This information is not changed with the above-mentioned conditions, and therefore known as the constancies. In short, rather than directly imaging from the retinal projection of the outside world, the brain recognizes objects by means of the information from grouping and factoring process.

A very important issue related to analysis of these two processes is the relationship between the grouping process, which converts point information of the image into the overall description, and the factoring process, which parse a variety of factors affecting results of imaging. Can we proceed with the gathering process before finishing the decomposition process? Some scientists D. Marr led believe that before acquire pure information of objects, such as depth, surface orientation, reflectance etc., any grouping processing is vain (Marr, 1982). They called this kind of pure information as intrinsic images, so they adopted the visual information processing methods based on reconstruction, namely through the reconstruction of these intrinsic images to identify the objects. While the other scientists believed that some pre-organizing process not only provide the necessary foundation for factoring process, but also form image relationship responding to the object's spatial structure, in accordance with the relationship between these images generating the image content assumption. Therefore, they adopted the reasoning and identification based visual information processing methods. The former point of view is represented by Marr's computational theory of human vision; the latter point of view is represented by Gestalt school, and his follow-up, such as Lowe, Pentland and other Perception Organization

Theory. The two theories have reflected the basic contradictions in the visual process respectively, but both have not interpreted the visual process satisfiedly. Arguments of the two theories promote the research of vision (see Figure 6.4).

The professor of MIT Artificial Intelligence Laboratory, D. Marr, at the end of 1970's to early 1980's, created the visual computing theory, advanced visual research a major step forward. D. Marr's visual computing theory based on computer science, systematically summed up the all important results of the psychological physics, neurophysiology, clinical neuropathology, and is by far the most systematic theory of vision. The emergence of Marr's theory has had a profound impact on development of neuroscience and artificial intelligence research.

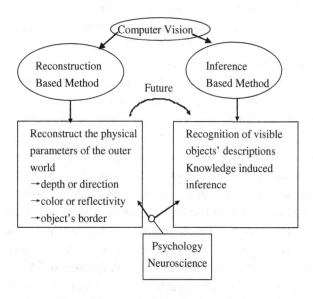

Fig. 6.4 Two methods in Computer Vision

D. Marr believed that vision is an information processing process. This process generates descriptions useful to observers in accordance with outside world images. The descriptions are composed in turn of many different but fixed representations, each of which records certain characteristics of the outside world. The reason why a new representation is improved by a step is because it expresses certain information, and this information will facilitate further explanation of information. According to this logic to think such a conclusion could be gotten: that is, before interpreting the data further, we need some information of the observed objects, the so-called intrinsic images. However, the data's entering our eyes needs light be media. Gray-scale images contain at least information of lighting situation and observer position relative to objects. Therefore, according to the method of Marr the first problem to be solved is how to decompose these factors. He believes that low-level vision (that is, the first stage of visual processing) is to distinguish which changes are caused by which various factors. Generally speaking, this process goes through two steps: The first step is to obtain representations representing changes and structures of images. This includes such processing as the detection of gray-scale changes, representation and analysis of local geometry, as well as detection of lighting effects. The results of the first step is known as the Primal Sketch appearance; the second step carry out a series of operations to the initial sketch to obtain representation which can reflect the geometric features of the surface appearance, and such representation is known as 2.5 D sketches or intrinsic images. These operations include extracting the depth information from three-dimensional visual computing, restoring the surface direction in accordance with gray shadow, texture and other information, obtaining surface shape and space relationship from movement visual computing. The results of these operations are integrated into intrinsic images, the level of intermediate representation. Because the intermediate representation is derived by remove many different meanings of the original image, representing purely the object's surface characteristics, including illumination, reflectance, direction, distance and so on. These information represented by intrinsic images can reliably divide images into clear-meaning regions (This is known as segmentation), obtaining more high-level description than lines, regions, and shapes etc. The processing level is known as the intermediate Processing. The next representative level of Marr's theory is the three-dimensional model, which applies to the object recognition. This level processing involves objects, and relies on and applies priori field knowledge to constitute a description of scenes, called high-level visual processing.

Marr's theory of visual computing is the first visual system theory, promoting research on computer vision significantly, but it is still far from resolving the issue of human visual theory, in practice has encountered serious difficulties. Many scholars have already made improvements.

Marr has first researched strategies addressing the issue of visual understanding. He believed that vision is an information processing process. It requires three levels to understand and address:

(1) Computing theory level - researching what information and why should be computed.

(2) Representation and algorithm level - the actual computation according to the computing theory, how to represent input and output? And the algorithm transforming input to output.

(3) Hardware implementation - the implementation represented by representation and algorithm, implementing and executing algorithms, researching to complete a specific algorithm and specific institutions.

For example, the Fourier transform belongs to the first level of the theory, and while the algorithms of Fourier transform, such as fast Fourier transform algorithm, belongs to the second level. As for the array processors realizing fast Fourier algorithms belongs to the hardware implementation level.

We can think that vision is a process that generates descriptions useful to observers in accordance with outside world images. The descriptions are composed in turn of many different but fixed representations, each of which records certain characteristics of the outside world. Therefore choosing the representation method is of utmost importance to visual understanding. According to the assumption made by Marr, visual information processing process includes three main levels: the primal sketch, half-and-two-dimensional and three-dimensional models. According to some evidence of psychology, human visual system representation is as shown in Figure 6.5.

## 1. The primal sketch

Gray-scale images include two important pieces of information: the gray-scale change and the local geometric characteristics in images. The primal sketch is a primitive expression method, which can fully and clearly express information.

The primal sketch is a primitive expression method, which can fully and clearly express information. The most of the information in primal sketches focus on the gray-scale rapid changes relative to actual edges and termination points of edges. Each gray-scale change arising from edges has corresponding description. The description includes: the gray-scale change rate of edges, a total change of gray-scale, the edge length, curvature and direction. Roughly speaking, the primal sketches represent changes in gray-scale image in draft form.

## 2. 2.5D sketch

Gray-scale images are influenced by many factors, which mainly include the lighting conditions, object geometry, surface reflectivity, etc., as well as the perspective of the observer. Therefore, we must distinguish the effects of these

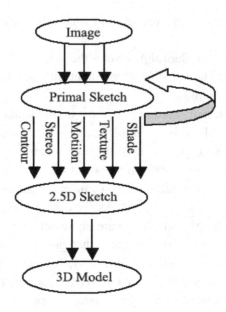

Fig. 6.5 Visual system representation levels

factors, that is, first describe more fully surfaces of objects in scene in order to proceed with the establishment of three-dimensional model of objects. So it is needed to build an intermediate representative level, 2.5D sketch. Local surface characteristics can be described by the so called intrinsic properties. Typical intrinsic characteristics include surface orientations, distances from observers to the surfaces, reflecting and incident light, surface texture and material properties. Intrinsic images comprise single intrinsic property values of image points, as well as where the intrinsic properties generate the discrete information. 2.5D sketch can be seen as a mixture of some intrinsic images. In short, 2.5D sketch represents fully and clearly the information on the object's surface.

In primal sketches and 2.5D sketches, the information are often represented referring the coordinates linked to observers, this representation is referred to as an observer-centered one.

In Table 6.1:

$\gamma$-relative depth (according to vertical projections), that is, the distance from observers to surface points $\delta\gamma$ - $\gamma$'s continuous or small changes $\Delta\gamma$ - $\gamma$'s discontinuous points S – the direction of local surface $\delta$S – S's continuous or small changes $\Delta$S – S's non-consecutive points

Table 6.1 2.5D sketch

| Information Source | Information Type |
| --- | --- |
| Stereo vision | Parallax, thus possibly can get $\delta\gamma$, $\Delta\gamma$, and $S$ |
| Direction selectivity | $\Delta\gamma$ |
| Reconstruct structure from motion | $\gamma$, $\delta\gamma$, $\Delta\gamma$ and $S$ |
| Light source | $\gamma$ and $S$ |
| Shade contour | $\Delta\gamma$ |
| Other shade clues | $\Delta\gamma$ |
| Surface direction contour | $\Delta s$ |
| Surface texture | Possible $\gamma$ |
| Surface contour | $\Delta\gamma$ and $S$ |
| Tone | $\delta s$ and $\Delta s$ |

## 3. 3D model

In three-dimensional model representations, factoring based on standard axises of a shape is the most readily available. Each of these axes conne is relative to a rough spatial relationship; this relationship provides a natural combination of main shape element axis in scope of the spatial relationship. We call the module defined in this way as the three-dimensional model. Therefore, every three-dimensional model represents (Marr, 1982):

(1) A model axis, referring to a single axis determining the scope of the spatial relationship of the model. It is an element of representation that can tell us roughly several characteristics of the overall shape described, for example, the size and direction information of the overall shape.

(2) There are the relative spatial position and size of the main element axis for choosing in the spatial relationship determined by the model axis. The number of element axes should not be too much, and they should also be roughly the same size.

(3) Once the three-dimensional model of the spatial elements associated the element axis is constructed, then being able to determine these element names (internal relations). The model axis of spatial elements corresponds to the element axes of the three-dimensional model.

In Figure 6.6, each box represents a three-dimensional model, with the model axis painted on the left side of the box, and the element axis painted on the right side of the box. The model axis of three-dimensional model of the human body is an element, which describes clearly the general characteristics (size and direction) of the whole shape of the human body. The six element axes corresponding to the human body, head, limbs can connected with a three-dimensional model, which contains the additional configuration information parsing further the these element axes into smaller elements. Although the structure of a single three-dimensional model is very simple, but in accordance with this hierarchical structure to combine several models, we can constitute in any degree of precision the description grasping geometric nature of the shape. We call the hierarchical structure of the three-dimensional model as the three-dimensional model description of a shape.

The three-dimensional representation represents fully and clearly the object shape information. It is important to adopt the concept of generalized cylinders, but it is very simple. It can be regarded that an ordinary cylinder is generated by a circle moving along its center line. More general case, a generalized cylinder is generated by two-dimensional cross section moving along the axis. During moving process, the angle between cross-section and axis keeps fixed. Cross-section can be any shape, during the moving process its size may be changing, the axis is not necessarily a straight line.

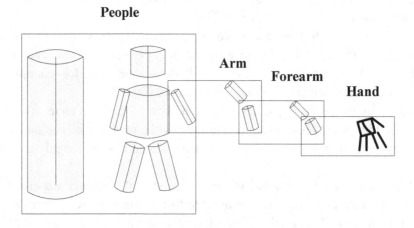

Fig. 6.6 The 3D model of human (Marr, 1982)

The three-dimensional representation represents fully and clearly the object shape information. It is important to adopt the concept of generalized cylinders, but it is very simple. It can be regarded that an ordinary cylinder is generated by a circle moving along its center line. More general case, a generalized cylinder is generated by two-dimensional cross section moving along the axis. During moving process, the angle between cross-section and axis keeps fixed. Cross-section can be any shape, during the moving process its size may be changing, the axis is not necessarily a straight line.

Complex objects are often composed by connecting several generalized cylinders. Considering mutual impacts of different levels, one probability is that information flow to each representation in bottom-up way, and the computation of each layer only depends on the description of the front adjacent layer. For example, the computation of 2.5 sketches needs only the information of primal sketches, neither to need direct information from the images, nor to use any clues what can be seen from the image. Each of the processes used in computation carries on in independent or quasi-independent manner.

Another possibility is that a wide variety of computing in the primary and 2.5D sketches is conducted by mixed constraint spread. For example, the information from the three-dimensional processing can be used to improve computing from gray-scale shadow to the direction of the surface, and vice versa. Information can flow in all directions. It is also possible that information flow top-down, so understanding of the image depends on controlled imagination to a large extent. In that case, the early vision is guided by the fixed forecast what should be seen.

## 6.5 Gestalt Vision Theory

Since the image data itself cannot provide sufficient constraints for spatial structure of the corresponding objects, that is to say this is an under-constrained problem. Therefore, to understand the content of the image need necessarily additive constraint conditions. The phenomenon of perceptual organization found by the Gestalt's psychologists is a very powerful additive constraint of pixel integration. This provides a basis for visual reasoning. Gestalt is a transliteration of the German Gestalt. It is often translated to form or shape in English. The research starting point of Gestalt psychologists is the "shape", which refers to the overall experience organized from the perceptive activities. In other words, the Gestalt psychologists believe that any "shape" are results or functions organized or constructed by percepton, rather than that the object itself has.

In vision research, Gestalt theory suggests that the gathering process that gathers point data into the overall characteristics is the basis of all other meaningful process. Human visual system has the ability obtain relative grouping and structure from the images of the scenes in case of no knowledge of the objects. This capability is called perceptual organization. The basic principle of perceptual organization, according to Gestalt theory, is known as the Pragmant, means "simple expedient." It comes from that Gestalt (Gestalt) psychologists found that some "shape" has given people very pleasant feelings. These are the "shape" which the visual stimulation are best organized most regularly (symmetry, unity, harmony), with a maximum of simpleness and clearness under certain conditions. For such shape, they invented a unique word, that is, Pragnant, and some people translate this word as "Gestalt." Human visual system has strong capacity detecting a variety of patterns and random, but also a significant feature of the picture element arranging. For example, people can from the random distributing image elements immediately detect symmetry, cluster, collinearity, parallelism, connectivity and duplicating texture, and so on. Perceptual organization converts point sensor data into objective representation. In these representation the describing words are not point-like gray-scale in images, but descriptions such as shape, form, movement and spatial distribution. The transformation completed by the perception organizations can be regarded as similar to performing Fourier transform on real functions. During performing Fourier analysis, a function is represented by the Fourier components of the Fourier domain. Using Fourier analysis, we can use a set of Fourier coefficients to describe a function. The advantages of doing so is using a set of limited coefficients to provide a good overall description, thus greatly reducing the complexity. Although no point value of this function is likely to be expressed correctly. Here as in the perceived, as though the part and the whole are mutual connected, but are essentially different. In short, the perceptual organization analyses sensor data whole, obtaining a set of macroscopical representation. Such macroscopical representations are the basic components that we use in cognitive activity, and we use them to be able to constitute a description of the outside world.

Gestalt theory reflects the nature aspects of human vision, but its basic principle of perceptual organization is a axiom description rather than a mechanical description. Therefore since proposed in 1920s it has not played a essential guiding role in vision research. However, the researchers have never stopped the study of perceptual organization principle. Especially after the

1980's, Witkin and Tenenbaum, Lowe, Pentland and others have made new important research results in the principles of perceptual organization and visual processing applications.

## 6.6 The Visual Model of Detection of Topological Properties

Marr extended the guiding ideology of functionalist of computing and expression the field of visual perception research. In his view, vision constitutes effective symbol description of the outside world. Those perceptions are composed by many different, but fixed representations. Each kind of representation reflects one aspect of the outside world scenes. To understand the vision first requires us to know what should be used to represent, and then to analyze needful computing accessing and operating each type of representation. Marr particularly emphasizes that how to select representation is crucial to establishing computing - representing model, however, for the early stages of visual process, what representation is selected depends on what is calculated from outside world images, rather than what is needed; only in the late stages of visual process, the selection of representation is more dependent on the specific demands of recognition process. Clearly, these arguments clearly reflect the Marr's theoretical premise, i.e., vision is essentially computing. Proceeding from this, he had come to the conclusion that in the early visual process, what are selected to be information representation is not an experiment issue, but a computing theory matter what is possible to be computed.

The overall computing framework of the Marr's visual information processing is discussed above. In the primal sketch level, there are mainly two types of visual information, the intensity changes and local geometric properties of images. The local geometric properties refer to parallel, relative position and direction, and so on. The vision initial process is to computing the representation of the local features and characteristics, which are no more than some simple and small parts of images, such as line, column, and the partial relations between them. Then, based on the computing results of the local characteristics, visual information processing enter a higher level, such as 2.5-D and 3-D computing. "What is the roughest representation of visual information?" It is the central issue of visual study, and is the issue that must be first answered to establish a visual image recognition model. From where visual systems starting to perceive the outside world images, the answer for the question will determine the whole direction of image recognition model. The answer to this question from Marr's primal sketches is simple graphical elements and their local features. Therefore, the Marr's visual computing system starts from the local features, being from computing of the local detail features to the overall large-scale computing.

A series of visual perception experiments show that, visual graphics perception has a function level, and the visual system can detect not only the large-scale topological properties, and the visual system is more sensitive to large-scale topological features rather than local geometry features, the detection of large-scale topological features dependent on the spatial adjacent relationship occurred in the initial stages of the vision time course (Chen, 1982).

Topology researches the features and relationship of pictures' keeping unvariable under the graphic change, and the features and relations are known as topology features. The so-called topology transformation is one-to-one connection transformation, and it can be vividly imagined as any deformation of rubber, as long as not to cut or not to agglutinate any two points. A rubber membrane can be arbitrarily deformed from a square into a triangle, and the triangle can be turned into a round or irregular arbitrary graphics (Figure 6.7), as long as they are not cut off. As a whole the feature of connectivity, namely, connectivity, still remain unchanged. Therefore, connectivity is a topological feature. In addition, a connected graph has no holes or a few holes; this feature is a typical topology one.

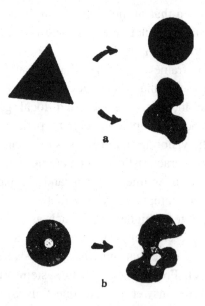

Fig. 6.7 The chart of topology transformation and topology features

The following typical experiments are selected as examples to show how to experimentally prove the function the early visual system extracting the topological properties (Chen, 1982). Experiment I, visual system's sensitivity to topology differences.

For the people's intuitive experience, round, triangle and square appeared to be very different graphics, but from the point of view of topology, which are topological equivalent, the same. Round and ring, one contains a hole whereas the other does not contain holes, so they are different topology. Although in normal visual observative conditions, from the similarity point of view in the people psychology, people will think that ring and round are more like comparing to round, triangular and square. But if the visual system has a primary function extracting topological features, we should expect that one can distinguish round and ring in short-term emerging conditions when one cannot distinguish round, triangle and square. Figure 6.8 shows the three groups of stimulating graphics for such experiments. They are a solid circle and solid square and solid triangle, solid circle and the ring. The experimentees were asked to gaze the black spot in the center of each image, and then each image emerges a short five milliseconds, and after removed it, another blank cover stimulation without graphics emerges immediately, to interfere with the visual system perception to the former graphics. The questions asked to the experimentees were not what graphics are that presented on both sides of focus points, but the two graphics are the same or different.

**True Positive Rate**

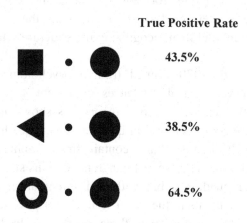

43.5%

38.5%

64.5%

Fig. 6.8 Visual system's sensitivity to topology difference

The experimental results are shown in Figure 6.8. The main experimental finding is that the visual system is indeed more sensitive to differences of the topology features, which is sensitive to the difference between a ring with a hole and a solid round without hole. The rate of correct reports to a group of rounds and rings stimulations is remarkedly higher than that of circles and squares. Moreover, for two pairs of graphics with equivalent topological features, round vs triangle and round vs square, and the difference of their correct report rate did not meet statistical significance, so which as control experiments strengthen the assumptions the sensitivity of the visual system to the difference of graphics is the one to topological differences between them. The experiments inconsistent with the day-to-day experiences but consistent with the interpretation of topology provides a more direct and convincing evidence to support topological structure assumption.

Experiment II, the advantage effects of closure and graphical structure. To establish any kind of image recognition model, one question that must be answered first and foremost is: What is the basic unit representing image information? The feature detection theory dominant n the visual system is always to seek some specific, simple graphical parts and their local geometric properties as the basic coding unit of graphical analysis. One of the most usual models regards line segments with a certain orientation as the most basic analysis unit representing visual image information. In view of feature detection theory, the graphics recognition is first to identify these basic analysis units, and then to identify the graphical structure formed by the basic units. For example, recognizing a triangle is interpreted as first recognizing the three line segments with different orientation, and then recognizing the structure relation of the three sides.

Olsen and Attneave in 1970 wanted from a psychological conduct level experiment to find psychological evidences consistent with the physiology experiments support the feature detection theory. As shown in Figure 6.9, the stimulating graphics are composed of four quadrants, each quadrant contains four small graphics, in which three quadrants contain small graphics that are exactly the same structure and order, and the rest quadrant contains small graphics that is the same as the other quadrants, but with a different arranging structure. In Figure 6.9, small line segments in the lower right corner have different direction with the small segments in the other three quadrants. In Figure 6.9, as a comparison, although the line segments included in each quadrant have, the same corresponding direction respectively, but the angle formed by line segments in the bottom-right corner quadrant has different direction compared with the angle included in the other three quadrants in the experiment. The experimentees are requested to report which is different to others quadrants as soon and correct as possible, and where each of stimulating graphics appears in the different quadrants is random. The time the experimentees spend to finish the task, that is the time interval from the moment stimulating graphics beginning to show to that the experimentee respond, was recorded as reaction time. The average response time in Figure 6.9A is just over 1400 ms, while for Figure 6.9B, a much more difficult task, the average response time closes to 2000 ms. The discovering is regarding as a support at action experiment level of the shape-coding feature detection theory regarding line as a basic unit. Because if line segments with the certain direction are the primary analysis unit of pattern recognition, then in terms of Figure 6.9A, the identification of different quadrant occurred in the most primary and basic line segment detector level; however, for Figure 6.9A, as the direction of the segments of each quadrant are the same, then the judge for the different quadrants need further and more processing, it takes a longer period of time.

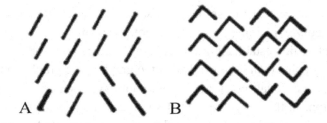

Fig. 6.9 Olsen and Attneave's stimulating graphics

Experiment III topology invariability features and apparent motion. Chen adopted the so called "motion competition technology", perform apparent motion experiment in 1983. The two stimulus graphics emerge successively. The first graphics has a single stimulus graphics located in the center, while the second graphics has two stimulus graphics equidistant to the center located on both sides. For each subject, adjusting the presentation time and time interval of the two stimulus graphics made the subject generating perception of apparent motion in this condition. The question the subject answered is the middle graphics contained in the first stimulus appears to move to which graphics included in the second stimulus, in a nutshell, is the middle graphics move toward left or right side of the graphics. The above mentioned motion competition experimental method has provided us with an objective measure to study the effect various graphics structural features impacting on apparent motion.

As shown in Figure 6.10, 7 pairs of stimulus graphs represent various the comparison of topological invariability. The middle of each pair stimulus graphs is included in the first stimulus presentation, the two side graphs are included in the following second stimulus. In order to help the reader easily grasp the rules of stimulus graphic design, in Figure 6.10 each middle graph is arranged with topology equivalent or the same simple topological connectivity invariability with the right graph, without equivalent to the left one. Of course, in actual experiments, any of the two graphs randomly presented on the left or the right when the second stimulus presented in order to avoid to impact the normal results of the experiment by the subjects' psychological bias. Below, we only selected part of the seven pairs of stimulus graphs for further clarification.

The first pair of three graphics are three identical line segments. The middle graph A is an arrow. And the left side graph b and the right graph c derive from the deforming of the middle grap, although there is a topological difference between them one is closed and another is not a closed, but they are derived from shifting one line segment of the graph a the same distance. Ullman proposed a representative theory explaining apparent motion mechanism, line segments are the basic characteristics establishing the coherence correlation of between two apparent motive graphs, then compared with the graph a, the graph b and c have the same coherence correlation, graph a should not have a superiority moving to graphic c direction. In this way, the pair of stimulus graphs provided us with an opportunity to verify topological feature detection or computing starting from local features works in apparent motion generating mechanism.

Experiment IV, the competitive organization of several factors working at the same time. Human visual perception has an important characteristic: the image perceiving is not a simple list of separate parts of the image, but with the characteristics of the overall organization. Graphs perceived are organized by the visual system spontaneously, under certain conditions, certain parts of graphics are seen as a whole. The phenomenon is known as group in visual perception research. Although a large number of experimental studies and theoretical analysis have been done for group issue, however, there is no perfect theory to explain what is the nature of group on earth.

Figure 6.11 shows a typical example perceptual grouping. Although Figure 6.11 is an array consisting of discrete points, but the points in each column their distances are shorter than row spacing are connected to form a whole perception. Psychology call the group as the adjacent organization, that is, the points adjacent in space will be perceived as a connected whole.

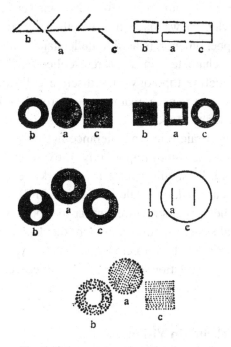

Fig. 6.10 Apparent motion stimulus graph

Fig. 6.11 Visual perceptual grouping phenomenon

Grouping is an important and difficult issue in visual perceptual organization research, how to understand the nature of grouping is also a difficult point using the topological invariability to describe visual perceptual grouping. The process of visual perception is essentially discrete, visual perceptual organization research are often aimed at some apparently discrete stimulating graphs, as shown in Figure 6.11 of the array of points. Therefore, the general topology cannot be directly used to describe large-scale features of the discrete collection. This is a serious obstacle using the topological mathematical tools to describe the visual issue, and a problem must be given a clear answer in theory. For obvious discrete collection, why do we have the overall perception? That is why the perceptual grouping phenomenon is hard to understand. The question is "how we can grasp large-scale characters in a discrete collection?" Using mathematical terms, "how can we define topology in a discrete collection, and not discrete topology?" The Tolerance Space mathematics proposed by Zeeman tells us exactly how to describe topological properties on a discrete collection systematically. The algebraic relation Tolerance not only represents the concept of minimum resolution and, more importantly, it expressed the smallest scale of perceptual grouping, in the smallest-scale framework the vision system neglects details in order to focus on large-scale characters. In Tolerance Space, we can establish a set of mathematical structure similar to topology. Grouping manifests the function the visual system ignores a certain tolerance details to extract large-scale tolerance character, such as tolerance connectivity, closure and hole. The nature of grouping is extraction of large-scale tolerance characters, that is, grouping is also a representation of topological character detection.

## 6.7 Regularization Theory in Vision

Low-level vision is made up of a group of processes during which three-dimensional physical appearance natures can be restored from two-dimensional light intensity arrays. The output of these processes is roughly corresponding to the Marr's 2.5-D graph. The computational theory of low-level vision mainly solves the two closely-related issues of appearance and process. It must clarify what kind of form or appearance the input and the expected output should have, and also provide an algorithm (processing procedure) of transforming one appearance to another.

The extract definition of low-level vision is the inverse problem of optical imaging. For classical optics or computer graphics, the fundamental problem is to determine the 3-D images while for vision it is facing this inverse problem of image reconstruction. Since a large amount of information is lost when three-dimensional real world is projected to two-dimensional images, it is only possible for vision to obtain the fixed output by virtue of some natural constraints (i.e.

hypotheses of the real world). How to find and use these constraints will be frequently encountered in analysis of special vision problems.

The calculation of motion and the detection of the changing of image intensity (physical edge) is the two most critical issues in vision, which fully manifest the difficulty of low-level vision problem. Measuring local motion can only provide normal component of velocity vector and the tangential component remains unknown, thus the problem of estimating the whole velocity field in general cannot be completely solved only by virtual of the measurements directly from the images. The measurement of vision flow is in essence undetermined. Edge detection is the process of finding physical boundaries from the gradients of image intensities. This problem is actually to make numerical differentiations on the image data. However, the unavoidable noises in the process of imaging and sampling make differential operations between wind and water. The differentiation also amplifies the noises, thereby leading to the procedure essentially unsteady.

T. Poggio et al. pointed out that a problem is well-posed if its solution is existent, unique and continuously dependent on the original data (Poggio et al., 1985). The ill-posed problem does not satisfy one or more of the above prerequisites. It is not difficult to prove formally that some problems in low-level vision such as stereo matching, structure restoration from motion, calculation of visual flow, edge detection are all ill-posed problems in the Hadamard's meanings. The reason why the calculation of vision flow is ill-posed is that the inverse problem of restoring the whole velocity vector from the normal velocity component of a contour line cannot satisfy the uniqueness condition; and the reason why the edge detection (i.e. numerical differentiation) is ill-posed is that the solution does not depend on data continuously. The main idea of solving ill-posed problem (i.e. restoring the well-posedness) is to introduce appropriate prior knowledge to constrain the set of possible solutions. We call the way of making ill-posed problem well-posed as regularization in general. Variation regularization is a regularization approach for re-formulating ill-posed problems under some variation principle. For instance, to find such ill-posed problem $z$ from the data $y$,

$$Az = y \tag{6.1}$$

For the sake of regularization, it is demanded that a norm $\|\bullet\|$ and a stabilizing functional $\|Pz\|$ should be selected. In the standard regularization theory, A is a linear operator, the norm is quadratic, and P is linear. The two kinds of methods available are:

(1) find the $z$ which satisfies $\|Az - y\| < \varepsilon$ and minimizes (6.2)

$$\|Pz\|^2 \tag{6.2}$$

(2) find the $z$ which minimizes (6.3), where $r$ is the regularization parameter.

$$\|Az - y\|^2 + \lambda\|Pz\|^2 \tag{6.3}$$

Currently most of the stabilizing functional used in low-level vision is Tikhonov, which is the linear combination of the first $P$-order derivatives of the expected solutions $z$.

Hildreth proposed more general smoothness constraints for velocity field. According to the work of Horn and Schunk, Hildreth proposed a more general smoothness constraint for velocity field. This constraint is based on the consideration that the real world is made up of the solid surface-smoothing objects and the projection velocity field of these objects is smooth as a rule. The first class of algorithm is to minimize (6.4) after the measurements of the normal component of the velocity vector, supposing that velocity component VN(s) can be measured precisely.

$$\|PV\|^2 = \int \left(\frac{\partial V}{\partial s}\right)^2 ds \tag{6.4}$$

Where $s$ is the arc length and the integration is calculated by the contour line. For the imprecise data, we can employ the second class of algorithm: find out the solutions by minimizing (6.5).

$$\|V \bullet N - V^N\|^2 + \lambda \int \left(\frac{\partial V}{\partial s}\right)^2 ds \tag{6.5}$$

Where N is the normal unit vector of the contour and r represents the reliability of data.

For the analysis of regularization, the most important thing is not the uniqueness of solutions but the physical reasonableness. The physical analysis of one problem and its main constraints plays a great role in regularization. In some special case, however, the regularization solution does not correspond to the solution with practical physical meanings and the assumed prior hypotheses for solving ill-posed problem will be violated. Under some very general conditions, smoothness assumption can give correct solutions as well. But for some kinds of motions and contours, the smoothness principle cannot generate correct velocity vector fields. In this situation, even human vision system seems to only give rise to the same incorrect velocity vector field. Therefore this kind of phenomenon will do us a favor to reveal the prior hypotheses that our brains make on the real world.

One of the most impenetrable mysteries in the biological vision is its high speed and people always come up with parallel processing as the reasons. However, the digital computational model is not satisfying, particularly considering that more and more evidence indicates the neural system is not a complicated device which is far different from the simple digital switch. Therefore it is very meaningful to analyze whether the regularization method of low-level vision should lead to a different type of parallel algorithms or not. As we point out, a linear analog network (electrical or chemical) is one natural way of solving the variational principles required by the regularization theory

The basic starting point of mapping from the variational principles to electronic or chemical networks is Halmiton principles of least action. The types of the variational principles that can be calculated by the analog networks are given out by the two laws: Kirchhoff's Current and Voltage Laws, which represent the conservative and continuity constraints respectively each circuit component satisfies. Generally speaking, there is not just one variational principled network, but a lot. For example, the cascade network proposed by Hopfield for solving associative memory problems can also be used in the standard regularization principles.

According to the Kirchhoff's law, for every quadratic variational problem in which a unique solution exists, there exists a corresponding electronic network which has the same solutions and is made up of electric resistance and voltage or current sources. From the current understanding of the biophysical properties of the neurons, neural membrane and synapses, this analog parallel computational model will have special meanings. One small piece of neural membrane is equivalent to the inductance under the meanings of electric resistant, electric capacity and phenomenology. The synapse of the apical dendrite is analog to the voltage source, and the huge dendrite or the synapse of the soma is analog to the current source. Therefore a single neuron or neural network can implement the analog solutions of the regulation principles.

This new theory framework of low-level vision clearly demonstrates the inner advantages and limitations of the standard Tikhonov regulation theory. Its major problem lies in the demand of learning about the smoothness degrees of the unknown functions. The foundation of the standard regularization is quadratic stabilizer and it only refers to linear problems. The result obtained from this is the minimization of the quadratic functional and linear Euler-Lagrangian equations. In order to add correct physical constraints, non-quadratic functional may also be required. Even in this case, the standard regularization theory may also be applicable, but the solution space is no longer convex. As a result, a lot of local minima may be found in the minimization process. Some people have already proposed a non-quadratic stabilizer which can keep the discontinuity point when reconstructing the surfaces from deep data.

The challenge facing the vision regularization theory is how to break through the constraints of the standard regularization methods. It may be solved by the quadratic functional, but the applicability is very limited. We can see it very clearly only if we have realized that the minimization of the quadratic cost functional can only generate one linear regularization operator, i.e. generate one linear mapping from input data to solution space. When all the data is in the regular lattice and satisfies the proper conditions, this linear operator will turn to a convolution operation, i.e. to make simple filtering processing on data. Similar to linear model in physics, the standard regularization theory is a very useful approximation method in many cases, however, it cannot all the complicated problems in vision.

Another strict way of implementing regularization is built on the basis of Bayesian estimation and Markov random field models. In this method, the prior knowledge is represented by the proper probability distribution while it generates the constraints for the solution space in the standard regularization method. In the calculation of Hildneth's motion, the hypothesis of smoothness is equivalent to assume that the variation of the velocity vector of two neighboring points on one contour line is a zero-mean independent Gaussian random variable. The link between stochastic methods and the standard regularization methods makes us to gain an insight into the truth of selecting constraints and stabilizers. The variational principle used for solving this inverse problem in vision corresponds to the Markov structures which can generate reasonable solution set.

In the future works, one research field related with regularization in vision is the regularization operators. Under the standard regularization conditions, mapping the data to corresponding linear operators in the solution space can be obtained via a kind of associative learning method. This learning method is proposed in the research of biologic memory.

## 6.8 Vision Theory Based on Models

One of the most distinguishing characteristic of human vision is selectivity. The observer always focuses on his attention on the things he is most interested in. In general the creatures pay special attention to frequently changed things in the environment and ignore those unchanged things because only by doing so can we quickly discriminate which is beneficial and which is harmful and make the reactions such as snatch or escape. Another important characteristic is that, as is found out by psychologist Gestalt, humans have the ability of organizing and inducing the image data, i.e. the ability of discovering such integrity attributes of image data as regularity, coherence and continuity. Experiments also show that human visual system has the ability of obtaining images' topological attributes in the low-level processing.

Marr's theory does not take the selectivity and integrity in vision into consideration. It takes the following as the research objectives of low-level vision: to restore the related appearances' attributes in the scope such as surface direction, depth and reflectivity according to the gray values and other measurements of the images with all sorts of physical models and additional constraints. However, since every pixel's gray value in the image is the collective result of a variety of different factors such as illumination, the reflection property of the surface materials and observation orientation, and also the distance information between each pixel in the imaging process is lost, to restore corresponding appearance's three-dimensional properties (e.g. depth, direction) from the measurements (e.g. gray values) of images is in essence an under constrained problem. That is to say, the measurement of images itself cannot supply sufficient information to afford the corresponding restoration of appearance's three-dimensional information. Thus it is necessary to add additional constraints for the sake of restoring the surface's three-dimensional information via Marr's theory. For example, restricting the objects in the range of rigid body, supposing that the surface is continuous and isotropic, or assuming some more special constraints like making surface as flat, setting illumination or reflectance of the materials as constant. These constraints can only be satisfied under some man-made environments (e.g. the so-called "block world"), and they are in general unsatisfying in the nature world. What's more, even we are equipped with these constraints, the performances of most of the solving methods, which are similar to the solution of the classical boundary problems, is comparatively weak. The difficulty of the Marr's theory has already shown up apparently since the late 80s.

As inferred from the above analysis, both of the two current vision information processing theories encounter severe difficulty. Neither of them can systematically and reliably process the vision problems. Therefore, some researchers have come up with all sorts of assumptions that make modifications to the above theories and tried to combine the two approaches in a complementary manner.

The vision theory based on models assumes that the concept of information is linked with the selection among a group of candidate objects. If we have no idea of a group of optional stimuli or responses, it is meaningless to mention the stimuli or responses. Furthermore, people must also know the properties or features of defining this group of candidate objects and discriminating the candidates' members. These features and properties may also differ with the tasks to be solved. For example, in our visual perception, stimulus invokes the selection of one state from a group of possible states on the retinal and generates an image. The selection is made according to constancies and parameters. If a baby can hear sounds, but his perception does not consist of "quietness" and "noise", then any music contains the same amount of information to him while the music contains abundant information for a well-trained musician.

Besides, this vision theory utilizes the concept of feature detectors as the bridge linking pixel-based image data with macro information (Pentland, 1986). Therefore the vision theory based on models embodies the selectivity and integrity in the Gestalt theory.

Fal's (Fal, 1972) INTERPRET programs use models in aid of interpreting incomplete line graph. It first analyzes a line graph and makes hypotheses about the class and orientation of the objects in the graph, then predicts the line graph of the assumed scene and finally tries to verify the hypothesized line graph. This method that actively applies models is called model-based, top-down, semantic and target-driven method. In some systems, models are simply used to verify the results whereas in other systems the models have dominant control of what objects, and when and where they can be seen. In the early 70s, the academic community commonly believed that the low-level vision processing which does not introduce top-down scene knowledge cannot generate plentiful and useful descriptions in essence, and that an intelligent vision system should learn a lot about the objects in the scene. The typical programs of this sort of method include Shirai's semantic edge detection method, Yakimosky's semantics-based area analysis method and Tenenbaum's interpretive bootstrapping segmentation method. However, these methods are confronted with severe difficulties in the interconnections of advanced semantic knowledge and low-level gathering process. They also unavoidablely introduce some unduly simple hypotheses.

Thus they do not gain huge success as expected. In this way, the researches on computer vision in the late 70s face a huge dilemma. On one hand, it is impossible to achieve perfect image segmentation and also image understanding if there is no prior knowledge of the objects in the image; on the other hand, we will encounter the above severe difficulties when using prior knowledge to bootstrap the image segmentation. Naturally a problem will be proposed: what information the two-dimensional gray images can provide on earth if we do not know what objects are in the images. For example, people obtain the depth information by use of binocular observation, but do people acquire the depth information before they recognize the objects they see? or can people obtain the depth information for any objects they see? Another example, can gray images provide the shape information of objects? To answer these questions, we have to refer to the researches on human vision.

## 6.9 Computer Vision

Computer vision is one of the most important parts in computer science and intelligence science. It focuses on the computational model of human vision and implements the similar visual perception functions by making processing on image data which describes the scenes via computers.

The human vision has an extremely strong ability, which can have a deep insight into the surrounding views without efforts. To make the computers own or approach the ability of human vision, we must be very familiar with our own vision perception mechanisms. Therefore one task of intelligence science is to reveal the mechanism of human vision.

By the aid of the analysis of images or image sequences, we can obtain the descriptions of the scenes completely and correctly as much as possible. The researches which accomplish the theory, method of the task and the implementation of software and hardware are called image understanding. Many people also regard it as the synonym of computer vision. Since so many factors such as geometric shapes of the objects, physical properties, camera properties, illumination and spatial relationship between objects and cameras are integrated in the imaging process and the imaging result is only represented as the gray value of each pixel, there is no doubt that it is very difficult for image understanding or computer vision which aims to solve the inverse problems. The computer vision is involved in the intersection and penetration of a multiple of sub-disciplines such as neuroscience, applied mathematics, image processing, pattern recognition and knowledge engineering. However, in the view of practical applications, there exist many approaches for solving the scene-related practical problems by extracting the image information rather than completely determine the three-dimensional structure of scenes. The researches on the design and implementation of application oriented computer vision system are called machine vision.

Computer vision has a more than thirty year long history. The early research works focused on the two-dimensional cases such as character recognition and chromosome image classification. In 1965, L. G. Robert devised and implemented a program that can understand the scenes of polygon block world, which is the earliest results of three-dimensional computer vision. In the program, a three-dimensional model library is built which contained cubes, cuboids, wedges and hexagonal prisms. The method for recognizing these objects from the line map is first to find the candidate three-dimensional models according to such simple features as the number of vertices, then to translate, rotate, scale transform and project the models to match the line graph to be recognized. In 1970s, computer vision gained success to some extent in the fields such as the interpretation of remote sensing images, the analysis of biomedical images, and the industrial automatic check. Along with the development of sensing techniques, the researches on the acquisition and analysis of distance images have begun, for instance, the analysis of image sequences obtained by the moving sensor to the static scenes or the static sensor to the moving objects have become a new valued direction. This kind of analysis of motions may determine the three-dimensional shapes and parameters of motion, which can be used for the navigation of the locomotive robots or the industrial robot vision systems. In 1978, H. G. Barrow and J. M. Tenenbaum proposed that the processing power of vision system can be improved by generating all sorts of inherent descriptive representations of scenes such as depth and direction. In the early 80s, D. Marr set up a comparatively systematic and complete vision computational theory based on this. The Marr's theory started a new flourishing stage for computer vision and dominated the whole researches all over the 80s. It is not until 1990 that a new hot research topic came into being when J. Aloimonos put up with a new theory framework such as object-oriented and qualitative active vision.

Computer vision has already endured several development stages. Before the 1980s, most of the research works only focused on the individual and constrained problems. Their basic methods were:

Acquire the gray images; Extract such features as the edges, circumference and moment of inertia; Find the best matched result from the feature bases.

However, the above method can hardly obtained good preferable performances in the complicated cases due to the lack of three-dimensional information. In the 1980s, computer vision developed into a new stage. According to the Marr's theory (see 6.4), vision is implemented through the three-layer bottom-up information processing procedure, i.e.

Make such low-level vision processes on images as edge detection and image segmentation;

Calculate the 2.5-D descriptions like depth information and direction. The main approach is to restore the three-dimensional configurations from the shadows, contours and textures, to restore the depth information from stereo vision, to analyze and determine the three-dimensional object shapes and the parameters of motion from image sequences, to acquire and analyze distance images and structured light techniques.

Model, represent and recognize the objects according to three-dimensional information. One commonly used method is the generalized cylinder based method; the other is to represent the object shapes as a set of planes or curve plane blocks (abbr. plane primitive). The parameters of each plane primitive and the interrelationship between these primitives can be represented by attribute-related structure, which converts object recognition problem into the attribute-related structural matching problem.

At the end of 1980s, although the computational theory, algorithms and representations, and even the hardware of the above three layer information processing modules gained huge success, it is still impossible to achieve the integrated general computer vision system. Hence some researchers have begun to find the new way of breaking through the Marr's theory. Flagged with the qualitative vision and active vision, proposed by J. Aloimonos in 1990, computer vision entered into a new stage. The core of the qualitative vision method is to regard the vision system as the sub-system of a larger system executing some task. The information obtained by the vision system is only to provide the demanded information in the accomplishment of large system tasks.

In many cases, the qualitative and incomplete descriptions of scenes are enough, not like the required complete quantitative description by Marr's theory. The description and recognition of scenes is not one-way bottom-up information processing procedure, but an implementation process in combination of top-down and bottom-up controlling strategies. The active vision method integrates perception, planning and control. It accomplishes the vision tasks in a more effective way by use of the dynamical invoke of these modules and the interactions between the procedures of information acquisition and processing. The core idea of this method lies in the establishment of active perception mechanics, which is to plan and control the types and positions of the sensors used for acquiring information in the next step according to current tasks, environments, the outcome of stage processing and the related knowledge. The implementation of multi-view and multi-sensory data integration is the key techniques.

The development of computer vision, which also improves the level of automation and machine intelligence, provides a key technique for developing intelligent robots and all sorts of intelligent systems. Along with in-depth researches on such new directions as active vision, qualitative vision and multi-sensory information integration and the increasing demand of practical applications, it is anticipated that computer vision will have more alluring development.

### 6.9.1 Image segmentation

Image segmentation is the process of dividing an image into several different parts or regions. It is an important step in digital image processing, image analysis and image understanding. Its purpose is to segment the image into some useful or meaningful regions so as to make image analysis and understanding further. There exist two common way of segmenting images into several areas with definite meanings (all sorts of objects or background): one is to make segmentation based on the different gray values or color components among the image pixels, which is called pixel-based image segmentation; the other is to make segmentation based on the discontinuity of different types of areas in the images, which is called area-based image segmentation. For example, we can make segmentation based on the fact that different regions have different textures (organized structure features). Besides, the discontinuity of images may lead to the boundary and we can segment the image by use of the boundary. Pixel-based segmentation method can be used to segment the images having white characters with white paper background, or yellow walls with brown doors. However, if the image to be segmented contains two kinds of figured cloth, we have to resort to area-based segmentation method. The pixel-based segmentation method can be further divided into the threshold and histogram based approach while the area-based segmentation method can also be divided into edge-based, region-based and edge and region based methods.

The edges in the images are the boundaries of two regions that have fairly large differences on the intensities (or colors). It is generally assumed that the intensities of the boundaries have rather sudden variation. From a mathematical point of view, the derivatives of the intensities on the boundaries to the space (two-dimensional image plane coordinates) will have relatively large absolute values. Therefore most of the edge detection techniques are based on the derivation method. The computers represent the images by use of some discrete values rather than the continuous functions, which makes it a must to utilize discrete difference algorithm to calculate the derivatives. (In image processing, the difference is represented by some feature extraction operators). In edge detection, the concept of intensity gradient is frequently used. The image's intensity gradient is a vector whose components are the partial derivatives calculated by the image intensity from two coordinate directions. When the image is represented by a continuous function $f(x,y)$,

$$G = \begin{bmatrix} G_x \\ G_y \end{bmatrix}, \quad G_x = \frac{\partial f(x,y)}{\partial x}, \quad G_y = \frac{\partial f(x,y)}{\partial y} \tag{6.6}$$

In the actual image, the two components of gradients can be calculated by using the following template operators:

$$\begin{bmatrix} -1 & 1 \\ -1 & 1 \end{bmatrix} \quad \text{and} \quad \begin{bmatrix} 1 & 1 \\ -1 & -1 \end{bmatrix}$$

The magnitude of the gradient is:

$$\sqrt{G_x^2 + G_y^2} \tag{6.7}$$

The direction of the gradient is:

$$\tan^{-1}(\frac{G_y}{G_x}) \tag{6.8}$$

The above motioned algorithm and the feature extraction algorithms all work on the isolated points by use of the information contained in a small neighborhood. Usually after using these algorithms, the jobs of further detection and connection are required to obtain meaningful object boundaries or the boundary lines of the surfaces. For the purpose of determining and connecting boundaries, there generally exist two methods: local analysis method and global analysis method.

(1) Local analysis method is the simplest method of determining connections. Taking a small neighborhood into consideration, for example 3*3 or 5*5, we connect the similar points in this neighborhood to form a boundary of some common properties. In general, two aspects are considered with regard to the similarity: one is the intensity (the magnitude of the gradient) obtained after the calculation with edge detection operators, the other is the ratio of the two derivatives which are calculated along two different coordinate directions (the direction of the gradient). In some image region, if the differences of the magnitude and the direction of the gradient of the detected two points are both below some given values, we think they belong to the same boundary and will be marked in the image. This process can be repeatedly made on the whole image in block;

(2) Global analysis method studies the inter-relationship of the possible detected boundary pixels on the whole image plane. Hough transformation can be used to make global analysis and determination.

The edge detection method can determine whether one pixel is on the edge or not by making local operations on the sub-window surrounding the pixel. In general, the operations are differentiation or correlation on the ideal edge. After that, a threshold operation is made on the obtained images to generate binary images. The detected edge points will be connected as one meaningful line. This can be implemented by tracking the edge points according to some kind of rule. There will encounter many special situations such as the gap between edges, the sudden change of curves and false edge points caused by noises in the tracking. It demands more complicated tracking rules.

Region based segmentation method accomplishes the segmentation through finding the regions in which the pixels have similar gray values (or properties). The two approaches are complementary and will get the same results in the ideal cases. Image region based segmentation is a image segmentation technique based on the differences of the properties of image regions. The basic idea of region based segmentation is to identify all the regions of similar features in the image. The similar features can be shape, pixel value or texture. In pattern recognition, clustering techniques are also used in the region based image segmentation.

(1) Template matching is to match the image region with a group of given templates so as to segment the objects satisfying the templates from the other parts of the image. The other methods are required in analysis of the left image. For example, template matching can be used to segment the graph-text manuscripts. Once the texts are found out by the template matching method, the

graphics are analyzed by other methods. The procedure of template matching is always depending on the correlation and convolution operations.

(2) Texture segmentation. When the object is in the background of apparent textures or has strong texture features in itself, the texture based region segmentation method is needed. Since the texture is some kind of pattern or alternately the repetition of patterns, designs and structures, it is hardly possible to describe by use of single pixel. Naturally it is impossible to employ the pixel based classification methods. There exist large amounts of edges in the textures. Therefore, we can hardly obtain desirable segmentation results on the images with abundant textures by use of edge tracking method unless the textures are filtered.

The descriptions of textures are the foundations of classification and segmentation. When we know that there exists some kind of texture in the image, it can be found by utilizing the known texture features (i.e. the descriptions of this texture in the frequency domain or spatial gray relation matrix). If no prior knowledge is known in advance, we can use region based clustering methods to segment the texture regions. One solution that can be easily thought of is to first divide the image into several small blocks, then to calculate the texture features of each block and lastly to decide to combine the blocks or not based on the features' differences.

(3) The region based clustering method in general can be divided into region growing method and splitting-merging method. Its basic idea is to grow the object in all directions starting from the points or regions which satisfy the detection criteria. The growth is based on that the region features of the same type such as gray values, colors and texture features make only a few differences. The neighborhoods which satisfy some merging conditions can enter this region. In the growing process, the merging conditions can also be adjusted. The growth stops until no more regions are available for merging. The basic idea of the splitting-merging method is to first divide the images into several "initial" regions, and split or merge these regions, then improve the criteria of region segmentation gradually until the image is segmented into the minimum approximately consistent (satisfying some requirement) regions. In general, the criteria of consistency can be measured by use of the property's mean square error. Compared with edge based image segmentation method, region growing method and splitting merging method are not very sensitive to noises but have high computational complexity.

### 6.9.2 *Image understanding*

For a digital image or a moving image sequence which is represented in the form of dot matrix (raster) and made up of all sorts of light-dark or colored pixel sets, we think that computers have already understood this image or image sequence if the computers know the semantics expressed by the image and answer the question about semantic contents proposed by human beings (for example, are there any people in the image? How many? What are they doing?) by means of analyzing and recognizing images. Image understanding is in general to integrate with such low-level processes as denoising processing, edge extraction, region segmentation, feature extraction, target extraction and inference analysis in high level. It can also starts from the high level prior knowledge or model assumptions and makes hypotheses testing on the low level processing in gradual. This process is the research directions set by us in the hope of further replacing advanced human vision and inference abilities through machine simulation. It is also regarded as the more advanced image processing than the general image analysis and recognition because recognition is basically equivalent to the classification and identification in pattern recognition while understanding demands the abstract of deeper meanings after thorough and repeated inferring and comparing. However, for the same image, it is not absolutely true that different persons will obtain the same understanding results. If we are interested in different problems, the focus on the same image will be different. In addition, different people have different levels and views of understanding the same objects, or even have the contradictory conclusions. Thus the so-called image understanding currently is an intentional proposition, which lacks of strict definitions or theory models. In practical applications, the expected results can be obtained only if we constrain the objects and the problems in a fairly smaller but definite range.

### 6.9.3 *Active vision*

In the mid 1980s, some American scholars in research of computer vision proposed a novel vision perception principle and a new approach for designing vision systems. The main idea is that system can actively change the intrinsic parameters (focus, focal length, diaphragm, vergence) of sensors (cameras) and the exterior parameters (position, direction, illumination condition) so as to simplify the vision calculation, eliminate the ambiguity of scene interpretation, and achieve the goals of real time and robust perception of the real world. The mechanism of active vision comes more close to the human vision system, for example, people will rotate eyeballs time after time, turn around the head or even move body's position to adjust his view and focus. Traditional computer vision theory (representative of the famous scholar D. Marr) regards the vision process as a information processing procedure. It emphasizes particularly on how to obtain the accurate geometric descriptions of three-dimensional scenes and the quantitative descriptions of objects in the scene from the two-dimensional images by use of the low-level to high-level representation and modularized vision calculation. Since the imaging processes of three-dimensional scenes are very complicated, many factors such as geometrical shapes, surface reflection properties, spatial relationship between objects and cameras will affect the gray values of the pixels in the two-dimensional images. Besides, the imaging processes will also introduce such problems as noise, distortion and occlusion. As the inverse process of imaging, it is really a very difficult task to acquire the accurate descriptions of three-dimensional scenes from the original two-dimensional images. Currently many algorithms are not only hard to compute but also less robust to noises. Sometimes they even hardly get the unique solution. The reliability and precision of the final results cannot be guaranteed, which leads to the slow progress made in the applications of computer vision. Since the mid-1980s, many scholars have come up with all sorts of new computer vision theory frameworks and thoughts. Similar to active vision, there also exist qualitative vision, purposive vision and animate vision. Although the terms used are different, the key ideas are the same which all closely link vision perception with the actions interacting with environments. According to the knowledge and requirements of the related tasks, it is required to take control of the procedure of acquiring images actively and purposely and make observations selectively (with respect to space, time and resolution). This provides more constraints for the vision processing, and thus simplifies the calculation, increases the robustness and eliminates the ambiguity. Finally the required qualitative descriptions in the completion of the tasks are obtained while no complete and qualitative descriptions of scenes are demanded. This idea does not completely deny the traditional computer vision theory. The differences only lie in that the algorithms and representations are more close to the natural thoughts. The tools used are all the same. No matter of whatever terms are employed (the current trend is active vision), this idea will open up a novel road for computer vision, in particular for the applications of vision systems. The early stage of active vision emphasizes on the camera sighting systems similar to the human eyes (multi-resolution, multi-degree) and the low-level vision processing problems which is related to the tracking and gazing. Along with the popularity of the experimental equipments used for active vision, the researches on active vision have expanded continually. On the other hand, the robotics systems, which interact with the external environments, are the main application areas of active vision. Robots can be regarded as agents integrating perception and actions, for example, hand eye system and locomotive robot system. Therefore in active vision how to integrate the active vision into robot systems is one of the most important aspects. In other words, the development of active vision is closely related with the researches of intelligent robots.

### 6.9.4 Stereo vision

Stereo vision, an important branch in computer vision, aims to reconstruct three-dimensional geometrical information of the scenes. The researches on stereo vision have significant values for applications such as autonomous navigation system of locomotive robot locomotive robot, measurements of aviation and remote sensing and industrial automatic systems. In general, there are three types of methods in the researches of stereo vision:

(1) Set up the approach for three-dimensional descriptions by use of range data obtained directly by range finder. Range data method reconstructs the surfaces with numerical approximation methods according to the given depth graph and implements image understanding based on the objects' descriptions modeled in the scenes. This is a kind of stereo vision method in an active manner, whose depth graph is obtained by the range finder such as structured light and laser range finder. This type of method is applied to the environments under strict control, for instance the applications of industrial automation;

(2) Infer three-dimensional shapes from the information of only one image. According to the perspective principles and statistical hypotheses of optical imaging, from shadows to shapes the objects in the scene can be inferred based on the object contours and surfaces derived by the gray variation. The understanding of line graph is one such typical problem, which once brought about widespread concerns in computer vision. All sorts of line label methods are thus generated. The method is qualitative and it cannot determine such quantitative information as positions. There exists extreme difficulty hard to

overcome for this method due to the limitations of the information provided by one single image.

(3) Reconstruct three-dimensional structures by use of the information provided by two or more images photographed at different time, or from different views. The methods of restoring three-dimensional information from multiple images are passive. It can be further divided into two main classes of normal stereo vision and generally called optical flow. The research on normal stereo vision is focused on the two images photographed by two cameras at the same time while that of optical flow is to do with the two or more images along the same track photographed in sequence by a single camera. The former can be regarded as a special case of the latter. They have the same geometrical configurations and common points in research techniques. Binocular stereo vision is one special case.

The researches on stereo vision are made up of the following parts:

(1) Image acquisition. The approaches for the acquisition of images used in the research of stereo vision are diverse and they have very wide variation range in time, views and directions, which is directly affected by the applications. The three main application areas of stereo vision lie in the interpretation of aviation images in automatic surveying and mapping, the guide and obstacle avoidance of automatic mobile, and the functional simulation of human stereo vision. Different application areas will refer to different scenes; two classes divided are in the view of scene features, one is the scenes containing civilized characteristics such as buildings and road, the other is the scenes containing features of nature such as mountains, water, plain and forests. The image processing methods for different classes of scenes are quite different and have their own specialties. The main factors related to the image acquisition are the type of the scene, timing, time of day (illumination and shadow), photometry (including special coverage), resolution, field of view and the relative camera positioning.

(2) Camera modeling. Camera modeling is the significant geometrical and physical feature representation of stereo camera groups. As a computational model, it is used for calculating the positions of the spatial points represented by the corresponding points according to the parallax of the points. The camera model not only provide the mapping from the point in the image to the corresponding point in actual scenes but also constrain the search spaces of finding the corresponding points so as to lower the complexity of matching algorithms and decrease the false matching rate.

(3) Feature extraction. The regions having no features and nearly the identical gray values are hard to make matching. Therefore, most of the works in computer vision include some kind of feature extraction process. What is more, the specific form of feature extraction is closely related with matching strategy. In stereo vision, the feature extraction process is the procedure of extracting the matching primitives.

(4) Image matching. Image matching, the core of the stereo vision systems, is the procedure of establishing the correspondences between images and thereby calculating the parallax. It is extremely important.

(5) Depth determination. The key points of stereo vision lie in the image matching. Once the accurate corresponding points are established, the distance determination is just a simple triangular calculation. However, the depth determination process also encounters notable difficulty, in particularly when the corresponding points are not very accurate and reliable. Roughly speaking, the errors of depth determination are proportional to the bias of matching and are inversely proportional to the length of the baseline of camera groups. Increasing the length of the baseline can decrease errors, but it also augments the parallax range and the differences between the features to be matched, which complicates the matching problem. In order to solve this problem, all sorts of matching strategies have appeared such as strategies from coarseness to fineness and relaxation methods.

In many cases, the fineness of matching is generally a pixel. However, both regional correlation method and feature matching method in fact can gain the higher fineness. It is required for regional correlation method to make interpolations on the related planes to achieve half-pixel fineness. Although some feature extraction methods may also get better features than one-pixel fineness, it directly relies on the types of operators used and there exist no commonly used methods.

Another way of increasing the fineness is to employ one-pixel fineness algorithms. It obtains the estimation of higher fineness through the statistical average results of multi-group matching with multi-image matching. The contribution each matching result makes to the final depth estimation can be processed by use of a weighting strategy according to the reliability and fineness of the matching result.

(6) Interpolation. In the application areas of stereo vision, one dense depth map is in general needed. Feature based matching algorithm is only a sparse and not uniformly distributed depth map. In this meaning, region based matching

algorithms are more suitable for obtaining dense depth map. However, the matching of the regions which hardly have any useful information (uniformly gray) is often unreliable. Therefore, the two classes of methods cannot get away from some kind of interpolation procedure. The most direct approach for interpolating sparse depth maps into dense depth maps is to regard the sparse depth map as one sampling from continuous depth map and approximate this continuous depth map by use of general interpolation methods such as spline approximation. When the sparse depth map is enough to reflect the important variations of depth, this method is perhaps the most suitable. For instance, it is fairly suitable by using this kind of interpolation for the processing of aero-stereo geomorphic photos. However, it is not suitable for many other application areas, in particular for the area where images have occluded boundaries.

Grimson pointed out that the missing degrees of matching features reflect the corresponding limited range of the variation of the surfaces to be interpolated. Based on this, he came up with an interpolation procedure. In other point of view, according to the single image's "from shadow to shape" techniques, we establish the contour conditions and the smooth connected surfaces by use of matched features, which ensures the validity of interpolation. Combining these methods can make interpolation more appropriate for the requirements. Another way of interpolation is to establish the mapping relationship from the given geometric model to the sparse depth map, which is called model matching. Generally speaking, for the sake of model matching, we should cluster the sparse depth maps in advance and form several subsets each of which corresponds to one special structure, then find the best corresponding model for each class that provides parameters and interpolation functions for this special structure (object). Gennery found the ellipse structure in three-dimensional images by using this method and Moravec employed it for the ground detection for the automatic mobiles.

The binocular stereo vision theory is based on the researches of human vision systems. Through the processing of binocular stereo images, three-dimensional information of the scenes can be obtained, which is represented as depth map. With further processing, the objects of the scenes in three-dimensional space can be interpreted, and thus the reconstruction from two-dimensional images to three-dimensional space is implemented. Marr, Poggio and Grimson proposed and implemented a kind of computational vision model and algorithm based on human vision systems. In binocular stereo vision systems, the method of acquiring depth information is more direct compared to others (e.g. method from shadow to shape). Since it is passive, the applied range is wider than active method, which is its most outstanding characteristic.

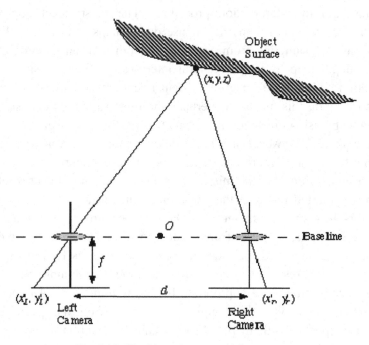

Fig. 6.12. The binocular stereo vision system.

In binocular stereo vision systems, the acquisition of the depth information is divided into the following two steps:

(1) Establish the point-to-point correspondence between binocular stereo images;

(2) Calculate the depth from the corresponding points' parallax.

The first part, corresponding point problem, is crucial to the binocular stereo vision; the second part is the camera model problem. In binocular stereo vision model, the two cameras have the same parameters with each other. Their optical axes are parallel and perpendicular to the baseline, which forms an epipolar structure. The purpose of doing so is to shrink the corresponding search spaces to the parallax of only horizontal direction, which simplifies the related procedures, as is shown in Figure 6.12.

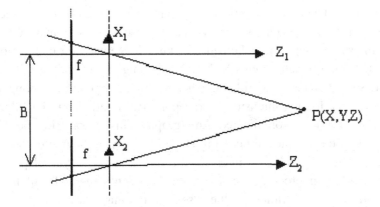

Figure 6.13. Depth determination.

As shown in figure 6.13, supposing that the point $P(X,Y,Z)$ in the space is projected into two image points $(x_1,y_1)$, $(x_2,y_2)$ for the two identical cameras placed in parallel, then we can calculate the depth given the length of the baseline $B$ and the focal length $f$.

$$Z = f \frac{B}{x_2 - x_1} = f \frac{B}{\Delta x}$$

It is the basic principle of binocular stereo vision, i.e. to restore stereo information according to the parallax.

### 6.9.5 Heuristic knowledge-based method

In image understanding, the first to use heuristic knowledge widely is A. Guzman (Guzman, 1968). His "see" programs can segment the line graphs into three dimensional objects. His method is to classify the vertices created by the interconnected lines in the line graph. He found that the local clues of the relationship between the object regions can be obtained according to the type of the vertices. For example, Psi vertices (see Figure 6.14) in which several lines intersect to form ψ shape often appear when two blocks are posed in alignment. This means the upper half two regions belong to one object and the lower half two regions belong to the other object. Guzman called the connection of two regions which belong to the same object as chain and use the chain to represent the heuristic rule with regard to the link relationship between regions. The "see" program connects every region according to the heuristic knowledge with regard to these vertices. The regions connected by many chains may belong to the same object while there exist no chains or few chains between the regions which do not belong to the same object. But the heuristic knowledge used for connections are still not able to finally determine which region belong to which object. Therefore Guzman designed a heuristic rule which can assign regions according to the number of chains, linking intensities and topological relationship. His algorithm is applied to a rather complicated line graph. This is one of the famous achievements in early vision processing stage by applying heuristic knowledge. It testifies that it is possible to interpret the line graph via symbol processing rather than matching process. However, the Guzman's method still has huge difficulty in essence. Although the "see" programs can recognize three-dimensional objects, the heuristic knowledge used is only limited to the field of two-dimensional images. Moreover, the heuristic knowledge is very specialized, which is not universal and short of physical foundations. These two problems are not intended for the Guzman's method but the common faults of the class of methods by use of heuristic knowledge.

## 6.10 Synchronization Responses

### *6.10.1 Outline*

Vision information processing is the most appropriate paradigm of setting up integral concept. In most of the regions of visual cortex, the neural processing information only comes from the limited part of the field of view. It also makes responses only to the limited range of feature conformations; thereby a large amount of the neurons' output must be combined to form the integral conformation of the special object. When the stored information are re-assembled in the period of memory and recall, a kind of integrally connected mechanism is demanded.

In the single cell theory advocated by H. B. Barlow (Barlow, 1972), it is supposed that the input from the elementary processing stage concentrates on the single cell with the characteristic of highly specialized responses (so called "bishop cell" or "grandmother cell") in order to solve the connection problems while the complicated varieties of the objective world make the number of cells increase in a combinatorially explosive manner, which hardly can get any experimental supports. After the long exploration, experimentation and rational

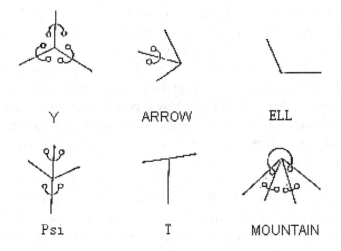

Fig. 6.14. The alignments of the chains surrounding the vertices.

thinking, research works returned to the view of D. O. Hebb (Hebb, 1949), i.e. representing visual objects via inter-connected neuron ensemble is more appropriate than the single cell liveness. This kind of ensemble assumption is made up of the neurons coded by the basic properties and complicated representations came into being in the elementary processing stage. Since neurons may join in different systems at different time, the difficulty facing Barlow theory in the explosively increasing number of cells can be avoided. However, according to the Hebb's hypothesis, only one ensemble will be activated in a specific cortex region at one time whereas the other ensembles will be restricted. The consequences are that if the neuron group A represents feature a and the neuron group B represents feature b, both a and b will disappear when A and B are overlapped to represent feature c. This is "overlapping disaster". Furthermore, many objects in natural scenes require that several ensembles should correspond to the same visual cortex region and be activated collectively. It is hardly possible to determine which cells belong to which specific ensembles, which thus generates the feature binding problem.

From the information processing point of view, the external stimuli are coded by the average neural pulsing firing rates whether for Barlow's hypothesis and Hebb's opinion. The former emphasizes the serial information processing and is thus possessed of hierarchical structure (i.e. the syntax structure linking contexts in knowledge representations), while the latter emphasizes the parallel information processing and naturally lacks of hierarchic structure. In the information integrating phase, the former resorts to "grandmother cells" while the latter is plunged into "feature assembling problem".

To investigate the root, how to understand the coding mode of neural systems becomes the key point of solving this problem and a feasible way of getting out of dilemma (Deadwyler et al., 1995). However it is facing more and more new challenges from experimental facts to regard the neurons as the integrators of the average pulsing firing rates. The neuron coding problem has already invoked the passion of the scientists from different fields.

Von der Malsburg was devoted to the exploration of the neural encoding problem in the whole 80s. He believed that the ensembles should be determined by the synchronized responses from the cortex neurons rather than the average firing rates. In this correlation model, the perceptional correlation attributes in the view are displayed by detecting the corresponding neural synchronized responses. The neurons corresponding to the same object fire synchronously while the neurons corresponding to the different objects fire in a non-correlational manner. In essence, this is time-correlated hypothesis (von der Malsburg et al., 1983), which relies on the way of dynamically connecting. The neurons can slightly change their firing patterns so as to rapidly make the conversion among the ensembles. In other words, the neuron group forms synchronized responses to the objects via time coding. Different neuron groups in the same ensemble are identified with the synchronization. In the noisy background, people can hear others' words attentively, and this is the famous cocktail party effect proposed by von der Malsburg, which is also the vivid description of the correlation theory (von der Malsburg et al., 1986).

The synchronized oscillation and synchronized responses of neuron groups is the most important progress made in the following of receptive field and lateral inhibition. The new theory created by rational thinking appears to be more brilliant in consideration of the rather late experimental support. That also manifests that the researches on vision and brain can hardly get away with the instructions of theory.

In 1989, the time-correlated theory showed a turning point. C. M. Gray et al. (Gray et al., 1989) found the $\gamma$ synchronized oscillation phenomenon (with the frequency from 30 to 70) stimulated by the activities of neuron groups in the cat's primary visual cortex, which bring about great concerns in the field of neuroscience. The following ongoing sets of neurobiological experiments discovered that this oscillation does not only exist in the human's brain, the mammalian brain, insect, snail and the limacine brain but also in the vision system (retina, lateral geniculate nucleus) and auditory system, whether the animals in the experiments are in the state of anesthesia, wake or activeness. Thus we can see that γ synchronized oscillation is one common phenomenon in the neural system.

The researches on vision and brain started from the classical hypothesis of neuron groups proposed by D. O. Hebb, and turned to the "single cell" opinion proposed by H. B. Barlow in 1972, and then developed into the temporal spatial coding hypothesis of dynamic neuron groups. It is really a long and winding road of exploration. We should learn a necessary and precious lesson from this so as to welcome the new era of the neural network, vision and brain research with the truly scientific attitude.

### 6.10.2 Neurobiological experiment

γ oscillation is initially found in the primary visual cortex of the anesthetic cat. It is observed in the local field potential and verified via the micro-electrode array records. The same observed experiment is also made in the primary visual cortex of the awake cat. The recorded neuron ensemble when stimulated by the correlation stimuli has the zero-phase delayed synchronization even though the spatial distance between neurons is up to 7 mm (Gray et al., 1989). Oriented to the synchronization of the neuron ensembles of different visual cortices such as area 17, area between 18 and 19 and the area between area 17 and PMLS, the area synchronization can also be observed in the experiment. If different cortices are representative of the different features of the same object, combining these features can be implemented by use of the synchronization between these cortical areas. It is also proved by the experiments that the visual object features can be linked with each other through the synchronized responses of the feature neurons in milliseconds.

The synchronized responses should also appear in two cerebral hemispheres because the hemispheric cortices directly receive the input signal of the retina from the half field of view. In order to combine the features of the objects which extend to two half fields of view, the synchronization of the two hemispheres are needed. The experiments found the synchronized responses of the two hemispheres and also the relationship between the intensities that are similar to the synchronization and average phases in the record of the cerebral cortex of area 17 of the left and right cerebral hemisphere (Engel et al., 1991).

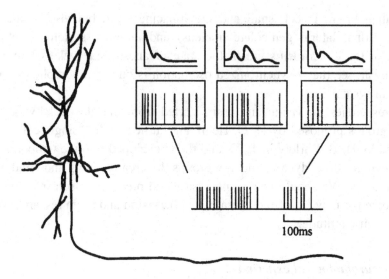

Fig. 6.15 The recorded three groups of pulse firing sequences in the neuron axon, the average pulse firing rates are the same and the temporal patterns are different (Ferster et al., 1995).

### 6.10.3  Temporal coding

After the discovery of the synchronized oscillation of neuron ensembles, the research works focused on the problem of how neurons encode the external world objects. Do the three patterns of figure 6.15 represent the same event of neural coding or different events in different temporal patterns? To answer this question, a series of experiments are done, which indicate that the synchronized firing of ganglionic cells in the retina neighborhood determines the overlapping area between the receptive fields approaching them. Compared with the firing rate coding of single ganglionic cell, the retina can build up more accurate representations of visual objects via temporal coding. The model of timely simulating the information coding via action potentials recently proposed by Hopfield (Hopfield, 1995) also supports the idea that the neural network processes the phase encoding information more effectively than the rate encoding information.

T. Sejnowski (Sejnowski, 1995) pointed out that this kind of temporal coding requires the precise timing at the pulsing starting point and the highly temporal consistent sensitivity of the pulses from different neurons. The experiments on the slicing samples of the neurons in the visual cortex indicate that if the precision of the responses repeatedly injected into the same noise current by the pulses is less than 1 ms, the cortex circuit may be able to process the continually increase of experimental evidence in a very high time precision, for example, the Malsburg synapse named by F. Crick is physiologically "fast" synapse, which is in millisecond magnitude. The time resolution of the new detection method for measuring the coherent activity (or synchronized firing) of the neuron ensembles proposed by A. Riehle et al. is in the magnitude of millisecond (Riehle et al., 1997).

In the previous researches, nearly all the neural network models start from the assumption that the firing rates are the S-type functions after summing the input signals. The brain needs to determine the precise properties of the stimuli by comparing the output of different neurons. In temporal coding, one neuron makes precise coding of the one characteristic changes of the stimulus by sending an instruction from the large list of so many temporal output patterns. The γ oscillation provides rich temporal structures for temporal coding. What is more, the temporal coding will make contributions to the integral problems of parallel and distributed information processing.

## 6.10.4 Neuron oscillation model in visual cortex

In order to make deep understandings of the biological significance of γ oscillation and its role in information processing, the researches on mathematical modeling are started in parallel with neurobiological experiments.

In 1990, H. G. Schuster et al. set up a neuron oscillation model in visual cortex (Schuster et al., 1990), in which the efferent synapses, excitatory or inhibitory, closely interconnect with each other to form a modeling neural network in the local scale. They are sparse in the wider range. The local fiber bundle can be described by use of the average activity of the excitatory and inhibitory neurons. Its corresponding differential equations determine a neuron oscillator. The equations are able to implement the on-off switch between active and non-active state, and also study the coupling of the two oscillators. H. G. Schuster et al. found that this kind of coupling is actively related, that is to say if two oscillators are in an active state, the coupling between them is of tight coupling relation; if one or two oscillators are in a non-active state, the coupling is weak. The activity related with the coupling is different from the directly connected activity. Direct connection is a kind of non dynamical permanent connection. The oscillator's properties are described by the phase of the limit cycle oscillators instead of the magnitude.

First of all, the single orientation functional column in visual cortex is modeled; the method is to specify two neuron ensembles and discriminate them according to the facts whether the ends of axons are excitatory or inhibitory. The activation rate of excitatory neurons is $e_k(t)$, that of inhibitory neurons is $i_l(t)$, the total number is $N_e$ and $N_i$ respectively, i.e. $k=1,2,...,N_e$, $l=1,2,..,N_i$. In cerebral structure, the neurons in the functional column are interconnected with each other, which is corresponding to the oscillators' coupling. In this way, the corresponding model can be built upon the functional columns as shown in Figure 6.16:

$$\frac{de_k}{dt} = -e_k + S[a_e(\frac{1}{N_e}\sum_{l=1}^{N_e}U_{kl}e_l - \frac{1}{N_i}\sum_{l=1}^{N_i}V_{kl}i_l - \theta_k^e + p_k)], k = 1,2,...,N_e,$$

$$\frac{di_k}{dt} = -i_k + S[a_i(\frac{1}{N_e}\sum_{l=1}^{N_e}W_{kl}e_l - \frac{1}{N_i}\sum_{l=1}^{N_i}Z_{kl}i_l - \theta_k^i)], k = 1,2,...,N_i.$$

(6.10)

To decrease the number of variables, the above equations can be replaced by the average field equations:

$$\dot{E} = -E + S[a_e(c_1E - c_2I - \Theta^e + P)],$$

$$\dot{I} = -I + S[a_i(c_3E - c_4I - \Theta^i)],$$

$$E(t) = \frac{1}{N_e}\sum_{l=1}^{N_e}e_l(t), I(t) = \frac{1}{N_i}\sum_{l=1}^{N_i}i_l(t), \Theta^e = \frac{1}{N_e}\sum_{k=1}^{N_e}\Theta_k^e, \Theta^i = \frac{1}{N_i}\sum_{k=1}^{N_i}\Theta_k^i,$$

(6.11)

$$P = \frac{1}{N_e}\sum_{k=1}^{N_e}P_k, S(x) = \frac{1}{1+e^{-x}}.$$

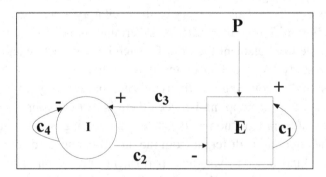

Fig. 6.16 The schematic diagram of the functional column made up of two coupled neuron ensembles.

This kind of substitution is correct up to 1/sqrt(Ni) order (Ni≈ 104 ). Make Taylor expansions and transformations to S(x) will lead to the phase equations of the coupled oscillation:

$$\dot{\varphi}_1 = w_1 - k_{12}\sin(\varphi_1 - \varphi_2),$$
$$\dot{\varphi}_2 = w_2 - k_{21}\sin(\varphi_2 - \varphi_1). \tag{6.12}$$

I: the inhibitory neuron, E: the excitatory neuron, c1and c4 represent the couplings, the symbols + and - represents the excitatory and inhibitory coupling respectively, p is the external input (Schuster et al. 1990).

Apparently, as the number of the state variables of the phase equations decreases to a large extent, the numerical integration becomes easier. The outcome of the numerical experiments successfully simulates the phenomenon found by C. M. Gray in the cat's visual cortex.

Why the model created by H. G. Schuster et al. gained huge success? The main reason is that this model is based on not only the neurobiological facts (for example, the neuron ensembles are regarded as excitatory and inhibitory) but also the typical structures of visual cortex. For the functional column, the neural network model is not local; for such large scale coupling network as super functional column, the model is local and sparse; for the case of long range synchronized oscillation of the cortical neuron groups with the distance between them up to 7 mm, the model is based on the phase descriptions of the coupled nonlinear oscillators between the neuron groups and thus it is possible to discuss the relationship between the synchronized oscillation and the pulse timing coding visual objects.

The significant meaning of this model also lies in the importance of mathematical modeling towards the researches on visual information processing.

### 6.10.5 *The representation and scale transformation in vision system*

When D. Marr founded the vision computational theory, he emphasized the extreme importance of the concept of representation over and over again because the idea that regarded vision as a perfect information processing system has been widely accepted by people. However, vision in general is not the traditional information processing system. The representation is the specific characteristic of regarding vision as information processing system, and also the core concept of computational vision theory. It specifies the problems to be solved in visual information processing and the constraints, decided by the general properties of the outer world, with which the problems can be solved. In this way, the so-called vision is the appropriate representation and algorithm selected by all sorts of visual information processing modules in the limited range of the computational theory. The calculation mentioned here is in essence a kind of simulation and implemented via the corresponding hardware (brain or computer). Therefore the outer world can be perceived such as what the objects are and where they are.

The three-layer internal representations proposed by D. Marr are: element graph (the images' representation), 2.5-D graph (visible surface representation) and three-dimensional representation (the representation used for recognizing the shapes of the three-dimensional objects), and the most critical is the 2.5-D graph. In general, the hierarchical structural descriptions and recognition of the objects' shapes are very complicated processes related to the human's knowledge, experience and memory, which will naturally be affected by the brain's other parts.

The reason for selecting graphical local geometric properties like line segment, parallelity, relative position and direction as the basic information of vision element graph is that there exist feature detectors composed of simple and complex cells and the functional columns which can re-assemble the input from retina and lateral geniculate body and analyze such spatial characteristics as lines, contours, directions and motions, and also that computers are possessed of the functions suitable for calculating local geometric properties.

D. Marr explicitly pointed out that one processing procedure of vision is to gain the mapping from one representation to another representation. For human vision, the primitive representation is made up of the image intensity arrays detected by the photoreceptors in the retina with no doubts.

This theory withstood the tests of a series of experiments and research developments since its creation and became a refined theory in exploring the actual information processing procedures in vision system. Its problem mainly roots in the 2.5-D graph although T. Poggio developed a whole set of regularization methods for low-level vision. Restrict the possible solution space and eliminate the ill-posed problem in restoring the three-dimensional objects' shapes from the image's intensity distribution by selecting a function that minimizes some proper functional. It is undoubtedly important for computer vision. However, for the understanding of biological vision, it is not true. In face of this kind of more and more complicated mathematical abstract processing, people cannot help but to ask is it the real procedure of vision?

Billions of neurons in cerebral cortex interconnect with each other in a special, complicated and accurate manner to form a network. The aim is to have the way of calculating and information processing for neurons dominated by "much" instead of "complexity" when perceiving the outer world. It is simple and the unification of harmony and beauty for vision system which processes information relying on numerous neural networks. The complicated structure reflects the simplification rules which adapt to the fast changing objective world.

The discovery of the synchronized oscillation phenomenon and that of the neuron pulsing firing with the resolution in milliseconds magnitude provide basis for studying and testifying regularization theory and also the other theories proposed for the same purposes.

The biological organisms of vision, the features of external objects and the imaging processes all are possessed of hierarchical structures, thus the visual representations must be able to express the images' properties clearly.

### 6.10.6 Nonlinear dynamic problems in neural network

The neural network in the vision-brain researches is a global viewpoint in spite of the S-type transmission characteristic of one single neuron or making neurons as oscillators. We can gain profound knowledge in the cellular global activities or evolutive final state by using nonlinear dynamic methods. In the early 80s, Hopfield's neural network set operation model is proposed for the sake of solving the subjects of how to solve the optimization algorithm and implement it with hardware for the neural network. Its biggest characteristic is to employ the energy function minimization techniques as the optimized operating output of neural networks, thereby linking it with the associative memory problem. The energy is universal quantity, and also the measurement of the whole system activity. Maintaining the minimized energy cost is the result of the evolution of the life system, so the global operation of using energy functional to gain the descriptions of the cerebral cortex more closely approaches to the true procedures happening in the brain.

In 1995, Hopfield proposed the pattern recognition principles of using action potential timing coding to represent external stimuli based on the synchronized responses of neuron ensembles. He suggested using time delay network and radial basis function to calculate the representation. These researches boosted the development of neural networks. Neural network is a typical nonlinear system, that is to say, the neurons of visual cortex are firing in cluster, and the neural network activity via complicated connection is highly nonlinear. In spite of the visual environment or any background noise in the brain environment, the optimal responses can be made to the input signal via stochastic synchronization so as to assign the functional role of noise in neural networks. The response of the summing network composed of N neurons to the stimulus of neurophysiologic perceptron systems is shown in Figure 6.17. It has a significant value on the research of the roles of the noises in detecting signals for vision system.

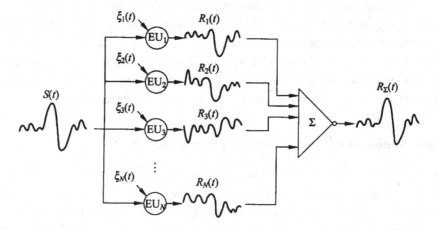

Fig. 6.17 The response of the summing network composed of N neurons to the stimulus

The summing network composed of N Fita Hugh-Nagumo model neurons. Its responses to the input signals obey the following equation:

$$\varepsilon\dot{V_i} = V_i(V_i - a)(1 - V_i) - W_i + \Lambda + S(t) + \xi_i(t), \dot{W} = \tfrac{dw}{dt} = V_i - W_i - b, \quad (6.15)$$

Where $\varepsilon=0.005$, $a=0.5$, $b=0.15$, $\Lambda$ is constant (tuned) activity signal; $S(t)$ is low-changing non-periodic signal, $V_i(t)$ is a fast variable, $W_i(t)$ is a low variable, $R_i(t)$ is the average firing rate signal of each unit, $\xi_i(t)$ is the zero-mean Gauss white noise.

At present the discovery of the phenomenon of synchronized oscillation of neuron ensembles has deeply changed the opinion people have on network. For the dynamically or functionally connected neural network, synchronized oscillation is a kind of selection mechanism, which makes the representation processing on the appropriate dynamic neuron groups selected according to the external stimulus. When the external objects change, the neuron groups formed in transient states will be substituted by the newly formed neuron groups. B. J. Richmond et al. researched on the problem of rotational invariability in visual information processing by use of Walsh functional diagram, and K. W. Konen solved the same problem by use of dynamically connected network.

## 6.11  Semantic Analysis and Understanding of Visual Information

### 6.11.1  Semantic analysis of visual information

Extraction of Semantic Features from Visual information is essential for meaningful content management in terms of filtering, searching and retrieval. Zhongzhi Shi have proposed a framework of semantic analysis for visual information shown in Figure 6.18, which presents a comprehensive approach with data-driven, model-driven and cognition driven together (Shi, 2009d).

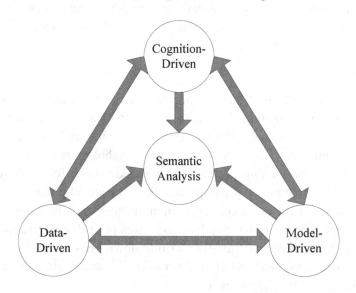

Fig. 6.18 The framework of semantic analysis

## 1. Data-driven

Data-driven is a bottom-up approach which extracts features form image, video. Data-driven techniques can be feature-space based and image-domain based. Feature-space based methods use only the features (color or intensity) of the pixels. Image-domain based techniques can be region-based or edge-based. Region-based techniques focus on the similarities between pixels in a region, where edge-based techniques focus on discontinuities. Marr's theory of visual computing is a typical data-driven approach. Many statistical learning methods are used for dealing with clustering, classification, such as

- Generative method-PLSA/LDA
- Boosting
- SVM / HSVM
- Max-Margin Markov Network

## 2. Model-diven

Model-driven is a top-down approach. Digital images are subject to a wide variety of distortions during acquisition, processing, compression, storage, transmission and reproduction, any of which may result in a degradation of visual quality (Wang et al., 2004). Natural image signals are highly structured: their pixels exhibit strong dependencies, especially when they are spatially proximate, and these dependencies carry important information about the structure of the objects in the visual scene. We can use structure similarity to asses the quality of image, object recognition and so on.

## 3. Cognition-driven

Since the visual data itself cannot provide sufficient constraints for spatial structure of the corresponding objects. Therefore, to understand the content of the visual object need necessarily additive constraint conditions. The phenomenon of perceptual organization found by the Gestalt's psychologists is a very powerful additive constraint of pixel integration. This provides a basis for visual reasoning. The fundamental principle of gestalt perception is the law of pithiness which says that we tend to order our experience in a manner that is regular, orderly, symmetric, and simple. Gestalt psychologists attempt to discover refinements of the law of pithiness, and this involves writing down laws which hypothetically allow us to predict the interpretation of sensation, what are often called "gestalt laws" (Sternberg, 2003). These include:

(1) Law of Closure — The mind may experience elements it does not perceive through sensation, in order to complete a regular figure (that is, to increase regularity).

(2) Law of Similarity — The mind groups similar elements into collective entities or totalities. This similarity might depend on relationships of form, color, size, or brightness.

(3) Law of Proximity — Spatial or temporal proximity of elements may induce the mind to perceive a collective or totality.

(4) Law of Symmetry (Figure ground relationships) — Symmetrical images are perceived collectively, even in spite of distance.

(5) Law of Continuity — The mind continues visual, auditory, and kinetic patterns.

(6) Law of Common Fate — Elements with the same moving direction are perceived as a collective or unit.

### 6.11.2 Visual understanding

Video event detection is an important case for visual understanding. We heve proposed a process of event detection shown in Figure 6.19 (Wang et al., 2010).

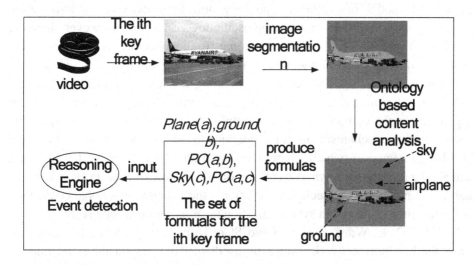

Fig. 6.19 The process of Event Detection

Figure 6.19 demonstrates the process of video event detection in $LTD_{ALCO}$ based event detection system. For a video clip $v$, the $n$ key frames are extracted from it. For each extracted key frame $k_i$, image segmentation techniques are applied to $k_i$ in order to separate $k_i$ into different parts. For each part, the object recognition techniques are applied to recognize the objects in that part. Then, a set of logic formula to describe the content of $k_i$ is produced according to the result of object recognition. Meanwhile, the object tracking techniques are employed to recognize the same object in different key frames. Finally, a logic set sequence is obtained. Then the logic set sequence is put into a $LTD_{ALCO}$ based reasoning engine to detect the specified video events from the logic set sequence. By video analysis, a logic formula set sequence $Seq_v=\{s_1,s_2,\ldots,s_n\}$ is produced to describe the content of video clip $v$. Each logic formula set $s_i \in Seq_v$ corresponds the logic description of the content of a key frame in $v$.

## 6.12 Prospect

The researches on visual information processing began in early 1970s in China, which is in parallel with overseas works. Several progress has been made in the fields such as motion perception, self-organized critical state of the neural ensembles in the hippocampus area, macro connected ensemble model of neural network, the regularization form of neural network dynamics, the meta-cell automation model of neural morphology and the modeling of information processing system of the synchronized oscillating visual path. However, there are still fairly large gaps from the international frontier whether in depth or width. From the development of the researches on current international vision-brain information processing, the trend of combining the temporal coding of neuron pulsing firing and the average pulsing firing rate coding is more and more apparent, and the combination is also helpful for the deep understanding of the neuron coding mechanism. In corresponding to this, there are the Hebb's and Malsburg's synapses which process information at different spatial-temporal scales. The former is the synapse connection of the slow time scale and forms the stabilized anatomical connections; the latter is the dynamic functional connection of the fast time scale and in synchronization of psychological time scale.

In 1995, D. L. Wang et al. in Ohio State University proposed the model of using the LEGION network formed by oscillators to segment the static images, which opens up new ideas for the applications of synchronized oscillation theory. However the LEGION network, based on the pixel positions and the gray-scale similarities, is not able to be used for segmentation. The scientists in China have already worked on the time correlation and synchronized oscillation model, for instance: A. K. Guo came up with a new model of solving the problem of motion vision processing by use of synchronized oscillation proposed by, solving the perception of rotational moving objects, and discriminating the static background and moving graphs (Guo, 2000). However the model is still in the theoretical modeling stage, which is far away from the actual use in the industrial applications.

# Chapter 7

# Auditory Information Processing

Auditory process includes the stages of mechanical, electrical, chemical and central information processing etc. The mechanical movement ranges from sound receiving of external ear to basilar membrane movement of inner ear. Stimulating the hair cells leads to the change of electricity, the release of chemical mediator, and the generation of nerve impulse etc. After the impulses are transmitted to the nerve centre, a series of complicate information processing takes place.

## 7.1 Auditory Pathway

The ear is composed of three parts: the external ear, the middle ear and the inner ear. The external ear collects sound stimulus while the middle ear transfers the sound vibration to the inner ear. The inner ear is the location of sound receptor cells, which transform the mechanical sound energy into neural energy.

The pathway from the cochlea to the auditory cortex is the most complicate one of all the sensory pathways. The information process and activity happening in every level of the auditory system have a certain effect on the activities of relatively higher and lower level. The auditory pathway is extensively intersected from one side of the brain to the other side.

The fibers bifurcated from the eighth cranial nerves terminate at the dorsal and ventral part of the cochlea nucleus. The fibers initiate from the dorsal cochlea, pass through the central line and rise to the cortex via lateral lemniscuses. The lateral lemniscus ends at the inferior colliculi of the mid brain. The fiber initiating from the ventral cochlea nucleus first establish connection with the homonymous and contralateral superior olivary complex by synapse. As the first stop in the hearing pathway, the superior olivary complex is the site where the interaction of the two ears occurs.

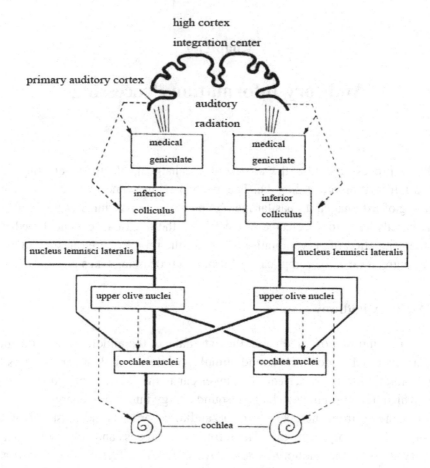

Fig. 7.1 The auditory pathway

The superior olivary complex is a part of the auditory system that attracts a lot of attention. It is composed of several nucleuses, of which the biggest are the inner superior oliva and the lateral superior oliva. Researches on several kinds of mammals have found that the size of these two nucleuses is related to the sensory ability of the animal. Harrison & Irving suggest that these two nucleuses are capable of different functions. They maintain that the inner superior oliva is related to the sound orientation of the eye movement. For all the animals that are equipped with advanced visual system as well as the ability of tracing sounds and making responses, the inner superior oliva has a conspicuous appearance. On the other hand, they infer that the lateral superior oliva is associated with the sound orientation that is independent of the visual system.

Animal with acute hearing but limited visual ability often has quite distinct lateral superior oliva. Bats and dolphins have quite limited visual ability, but they are blessed with sophisticated hearing system, as a result, they are completely lacking in inner superior oliva.

Fibers initiating from the superior oliva complex rise to the inferior colliculus via the lateral lemniscus. The inferior lemniscus then transmits the impulse to the medial geniculatum body of the thalamus. The fiber bundle linking these two areas is called brachium colliculi inferiors. The hearing-reflecting fibers conduct the impulse to the superior temporal gyrus (Area 41 and Area 42), which is also referred to as the auditory cortex. The auditory pathway is shown in Figure 7.1.

## 7.2  Central Processing of the Auditory Information

The central processing of information is such a complicate issue that until now a comprehensive understanding is still lacking. The regulations of general nerve physiological activity in the central nerve system apply largely to the auditory central activity as well. The impulse transmitted from the cochlea nerve has various temporal and spatial configurations with the different sound characteristics received, which is the general pattern of input information coding. What is clear is that the hearing eventually generated can accurately and subtly reflect all the complex characteristics of the sound. It is still unknown as to what happens between the input and output of the central information processing, which is the most heated topic in the auditory physiological research.

### 7.2.1  Frequency analysis mechanism

Since Helmholtz proposed the resonance theory 100 years ago, authors of different eras have put forward many theories to interpret the frequency analysis mechanism of the cochlea. Although opinions have different underpinnings, they can be grouped into two perspectives: one perspective maintains that sounds of different frequency stimulate sensory cells of different places in the basilar membrane and the stimulation place is the grounds for frequency analysis; the other perspective holds that sounds of different frequency cause the aroused nerve to give off impulse of different frequency and the impulse frequency is the foundation for sound frequency analysis. The former is called place principle or place theory while the latter is known as time principle or impulse frequency theory. Both perspectives are based on facts, whereas they are not exempted from shortcomings. Contemporary, it is generally accepted that the two perspectives are not mutually exclusive rather than mutually complementary. Auditory frequency analysis is more the process where the centre plays a decisive role in exact sound discrimination than a simple peripheral process.

## 1. Traveling wave theory

Through direct observation on the animal cochlea under a microscope and designed research on the cochlea model, Bekesy has found that the traveling wave on the membrane induced by sound sets off from the cochlea base and reaches the top of the cochlea gradually. During the course of the traveling, the amplitude of the traveling wave is changing. The amplitude maximum site and the distance that the traveling wave goes through also vary with the frequency of the sound. The amplitude maximum site is in the vicinity of the base cochlea when the stimulus is of high frequency. When the frequency gradually goes down, it departs from the base cochlea and moves towards the top of the cochlea. It then reaches the top of the cochlea when the stimulus is of low frequency. Having reached its peak, the amplitude starts to attenuate rapidly. When the traveling wave is of the largest amplitude, the sensory cells of the spiral organ receive the strongest stimulation. According to the place principle, the traveling wave theory argues that the amplitude-maximum place of the traveling wave is the grounds for sound frequency analysis. Specifically speaking, the base of the basilar membrane receives stimulus of high frequency while the top of the cochlea receives stimulus of low frequency. In between receives stimulus arranged according to the magnitude of the frequency. Therefore the basilar membrane becomes a preliminary frequency analyzer.

Another method is to use the microelectrode to record the frequency tuning curve of different auditory fibers. Every curve stands for the relationship between threshold and frequency of a single auditory fiber and each has its minimum threshold. The corresponding frequency of the minimum threshold is the characteristic frequency of the fiber.

## 2. The volley theory

Single fibers have limited power to repeatedly give off impulses, generally not more than hundreds times per second and not being able to catch up with high tone sound frequencies. This is the reason why in the early years the impulse frequency theory was under so much attack. Wever proposed the volley theory which provided a satisfactory explanation for it.

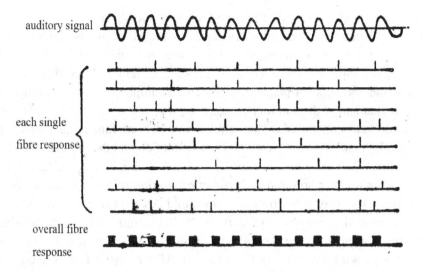

Fig 7.2 The configuration of the volley

The volley theory interprets from the following perspective: as several fibers simultaneously give off impulses along with the cycles of the sound wave, the firing frequency of every fiber is not high while the total firing frequency can still catch up with high frequency (Figure 7.2). The volley theory argues that the auditory nerve gives off impulses in a frequency identical to the frequency of the sound stimulus, which is the basis for frequency analysis. Experiments recording nerve impulses on the auditory nerves have shown that when the sound frequency is high, the nerve impulse of a single fiber is not exactly given off once every sound wave cycle, but it sticks strictly to a simultaneous relationship with certain phrase of the sound wave cycle, which is referred to as phrase lock relationship. This is the powerful experimental evidence supporting the volley theory.

## 3. The centre mechanism of frequency analysis

According to calculation, the cochlea is of low frequency resolution, estimating about 30 Hz around 1000 Hz. However, at around 1000 Hz, human being can discriminate 3 Hz or even smaller Hz difference. It is obvious that precise frequency analysis is undertaken in the centre. In animals, from the cochlea nucleus to certain parts of the centers at all levels in the auditory cortex, the nerve cells are aligned more or less in a distribution of frequency areas. As every part of the retina has corresponding projection area in the visual cortex, all the parts along the cochlea basilar membrane has systematic reflection area in the surface of the auditory cortex as well. The time lock relationship between the firing of the nerve units and the sound stimulus can be observed in the medial geniculate body and every level of auditory cortex below it, especially in the cochlea nucleus and the superior olivary nucleus. These facts demonstrated that the place principles and the time principles are of crucial importance to the frequency analytic mechanism of the auditory centre.

Psychophysical experiments have shown that certain functional relationship exists between man's accuracy of frequency resolution and the time course of the sound signal. When the time course of the signal is shorter than certain critical time, the accuracy of resolution is in direct proportion to the square root of the signal time course $t$, or the differential threshold $\Delta F$ is in inverse proportion to the square root of $t$, i.e. $\Delta F = Kt^{-1/2}$ if $t < T$. If the time course of the signal exceeds the critical time, the accuracy of resolution will remain at its best level and not change with the increment of time, i.e. $\Delta F = K$ if $t > T$. T is about 120-130 millisecond. This indicates that the auditory centre may accumulate the input information and process them statistically, for if certain quantum is measured repeatedly and statistical value of it is observed, the accuracy of the measure result is in exact proportion to the square root of the measure times.

### 7.2.2 The intensity analytic mechanism

There are relatively few researches on the analysis of sound intensity. According to the general rule, the excitability threshold of the sensory cell and nerve unit has both high value and low value. Strong stimulus arouses more sensory cells and nerve units; furthermore, the nerve impulses given off by every stimulated nerve units are in larger number as well. Intensity analysis can be based on the following three factors: whether the stimulated unit is of high threshold value or low threshold value; whether the number of the stimulated unit is large or small; whether the nerve impulse given off is in large amount or small amount. In the auditory nerve or auditory centre of animals, it is not difficult to find experimental findings supporting the aforementioned relationship between sound intensity and response. However, it has been shown that there is certain area distribution relationship between the auditory cortex and other auditory centers on one end and the sound intensity on the other end. That is to say, different sites respond to stimulus of different intensity. It seems like the place principle is at work too.

### 7.2.3 *Sound localization and binaural hearing*

Sound localization refers to the auditory system's judgment on the localization of the sound source. The foundation for sound localization is binaural hearing. As the distance from the sound source to the ears differs and the barrier condition in the pathway of sound transmission varies, a sound from certain location reaches the two ears with time difference and intensity difference, the magnitudes of which are related to the location of the sound source. The primary ground for sound localization is the time difference and intensity difference of the sound that the ears perceive. As to sounds of high frequency, the intensity difference is relatively more significant while for low frequency sounds, the time difference is more important.

Besides the important function of sound localization, compared with monaural hearing, binaural hearing has remarkable advantages. The common effort of the two ears can increase the loudness of the sound, uplifting 3-6 decibels compared with monaural hearing. The revolving ability of binaural hearing is better than that of monaural hearing; especially under the condition of noise distraction, binaural hearing has remarkably higher language identification ability than monaural hearing. Under the circumstance of binaural hearing, the right ear plays a more important role in the sensory of language signals while the left ear seems to account more for the sensory of non-language signals, which may be related to the labor division of the brain hemispheres.

### 7.2.4 *Analysis of complex sounds*

As to the issue of how the auditory system discriminate complex sounds, there are two distinct opinions:

(1) The sensory of complex sounds is based on the auditory system and its constituents. The neural activity of auditory centre induced by complex sounds is the sum of neural activities of all the constituents.

(2) The auditory system has special component units for detecting all the complex sounds and certain features of the sounds, which is referred to as detector or feature detector. They are only sensitive to specific sounds or specific sound features while not giving response to other sounds or sound features.

Currently it is not settled yet as to which of the two opinions is more convincing.

## 7.3 Speech Coding

The technique of speech digitalization can be generally classified into two kinds: the first is to model the waveform and code them digitally on the prerequisite that the waveform is strictly abided by. The second is to process the modeled waveform but code only those speeches that can be heard during the course of speech perception. Three frequently used methods of speech coding are impulse code modulation (PCM), difference PCM (DPCM) and delta modulation (DM). Normally, the digital telephones in the public switch telephone network adopt these three techniques. The second speech digitalization method is mainly related to the speech coder that is used in narrowband transmission system or capacity-limited digital facilities. Equipments adopting this digitalization technique are generally referred to as vocoder. Currently the vocoder is widely used, particularly in speech of frame-relay or IP.

Besides the technique of compressed coding, people also use many other bandwidth-saving techniques to minimize the bandwidth occupied by speech and optimize the network resource. The silence speech inhibition technique that people use in ATM and frame-relay network could eliminate the silent speech data in connection while at the same time not influence the transmission of other information data. The voice activity detection technique (SAD) can be used to trace the noise PWL and set up a sharing voice detection threshold for it. In this way, speech/ silent speech detector can dynamically match the user's background noise environment and minimize the audibility of the silent speech suppressed. To replace the audio signal in the network, these signals will not pass the network. The comfortable background noise is integrated into a signal path on either side of the network so as to ensure the speech quality and natural speech connection on both ends of the speech channel. The speech coding method can be grouped into the following three kinds: waveform coding, source coding and hybrid coding.

### 1. Waveform coding

Waveform coding is a relatively simple process. Before coding the sampling theorem quantifies the modeled speech signal and then quantifies the amplitude; finally binary coding is performed. After the decoder makes digital/analog conversion, the low pass filter restores the original modeled speech waveform, which is the most simple impulse code modulation (PCM), also called linear PCM. Data compression could also be realized by means of non-linear quantification, difference between prior and post sample value and adaptive prediction. The goal of waveform coding is that the modeled signal restored by the decoder should be identical as much as possible to the original waveform before coding, that is to say, distortion should be the minimum. The waveform coding method is quite simple and the digital ratio is relatively high. From 64kbit/s to 32kbit/s the sound quality is quite good. Nevertheless, when the digital ratio is lower than 32kbit/s, the sound quality would degrade remarkably and when the digital ratio is16kbit/s, the sound quality is extremely poor.

## 2. Source coding

Source coding is also referred to as vocoder. Based on the articulation mechanism of human, the vocoder analyzes the speech signal at the coding end and decomposes them into sounds and non-sounds. The vocoder analyzes the speech at regular intervals and transmits the corresponding analytic coding of sound/non-sound and filter parameters. The decoding end re-synthesizes the speech based on the parameters received. The code rate generated by vocoder coding can be extremely low, such as 1.2kbit/s, 2.4kbit/s. however, it has shortcomings too. Firstly, the quality of the synthetic speech is rather poor, with high intelligibility but low naturalness. Therefore, it is quite difficult to distinguish the speaker. Secondly, it is of high complexity.

## 3. Hybrid coding

Hybrid coding combines the principle of waveform coding and vocoder, with a digital ratio ranging from 4kbit/s to 16kbit/s. It generates sounds of high quality. Lately there is certain algorithm that can produce sound quality equivalent to that of waveform coding and yield complexity between waveform coding and vocoder.

The aforementioned three methods of speech coding can be grouped into many coding methods. The attributes of speech coding can be classified into four kinds, namely bit rate, time delay, complexity and quality. Bit rate is a very important factor of speech coding, ranging from 2.4kbit/s of confidential telephone communication to 64kbit/s of G.711PCM coding and G.722 wideband (7KHz) speech coder.

## 7.4 Prosodic Cognition

Prosody is the common feature of all the spontaneous speech, playing a significant role in verbal communication. Through the combination and contrast of segmental information, prosody enables the speaker's intention to be better conveyed and understood. As for artificial synthetic speech, the naturalness of the synthetic speech is largely determined by the sophistication of the prosodic manipulation model. The issue of prosody cognition is drawing more and more attention from experts of linguistics and speech engineering. A comprehensive understanding of the prosodic feature of the natural language is of crucial importance no matter for phonetic research or for improving the naturalness of the synthetic speech and enhancing the accuracy of speech identification. The information of speech involves two aspects: segmental information and prosodic information. Segmental information such as syllable is represented by tone quality while prosodic information is conveyed through the use of prosodic feature.

Previous research on speech focused primarily on syntactic and semantic processing, ignoring the issue of prosodic feature. It is not until 1960s that the systematic research on prosody started.

### 7.4.1 Prosodic feature

Prosodic feature comprises three dimensions: stress, intonation and prosodic structure (referring to the boundaries of prosodic elements). As prosodic feature can cover two or more segments, it is often referred to as suprasegmental feature. Prosodic structure constitutes a hierarchy resembling a tree structure. Although views differ on how the hierarchy should be classified, it is generally acknowledged to be composed of three levels: prosodic word, prosodic phrase and intonational phrase (Yang, 2004).

**1. The stress of Mandarin Chinese**
   (1) Word stress and sentence stress
   (2) The types of sentence stress
   (3) The distribution and rank difference of sentence stress
The prosodic stress of Mandarin Chinese is a complex phenomenon. In broadcasting speech, the means of contrast is frequently utilized, involving the contrast of pitch and syllable duration.

**2. The intonation of Mandarin Chinese**
The intonational contour is shaped from the combination of semantic stress. It is a kind of phonetic representation, which conveys the extra-grammatical meaning by means of information focusing. Based on the hierarchical structure of

language, rhythm utilizes the limited decomposition degree of the phonic element to arrange the rhythmic stress and constitute the hierarchical rhythmic units according to the required expression. Semantic stress and rhythmic stress manipulate the top line and the bottom line of the tonal pitch range respectively. Integrating the register features of all the parts of the intonational contour, we can distinguish different intonational types. Therefore, intonation is an important factor to re-manipulate the tonal pitch range, which, in turn is the most important phonic reference for functional intonation and mood intonation.

The basic frame of Chinese intonation can be divided into four parts: pre-head, head, nucleus, tail. The typical acoustic representations of the intonational contour can be described as follows (Shen, 1994):

(1) The head and the nucleus possess relatively strong semantic stress, while only unstressed syllables exist for the pre-head and generally no strong semantic stress for tail.

(2) The pitch top line after the nucleus has a tendency of falling, displaying abrupt discontinuity.

(3) Syllables after the nucleus are apparently weakened. If the tone of the nucleus is the original low tone, then the subsequent syllable will be unstressed and its pitch will be remarkably raised, followed by the abrupt discontinuity of the top line.

An abundant of evidence has proved that in the combination of unstressed syllables, the cadence of the top point is subjected to the variation of the semantic intonation. In the strong-weak combination, the top points of the subsequent syllable display a downward movement. As the semantic difference expands, the subsequent syllable will fall in a larger degree. However, if it is followed by another strong semantic stress, the top points will recover to certain pitch level.

In declarative sentences, the falling of the top points is accomplished rapidly. Hence, at the beginning of the tail or one or two syllables after the tail, the pitch top line falls to the bottom level, which is referred to as the abrupt falling of the top line. In interrogative sentences, the falling of the top line is accomplished step by step, i.e. the top line of the syllables after the tail assumes a contour of gentle falling, which is referred to as the gradual falling of the top line. As the top line and the bottom line are two independent factors, therefore, the intonational contour of the declarative sentence is a combination of the two features (i.e. the abrupt falling of the top line and the gradual decline of the bottom line) rather than the manipulation effect of a single register factor. Likewise, the intonational contour of the interrogative sentence is the combination of two features: the gradual falling of the top line and the gentle raising of the bottom line. Sorting out two factors will result in four combinations of them. Except declarative and interrogative sentences, phonetic evidence has provided support for the fact that the common kind of imperative intonational contour comprises the abrupt falling of the top line and the gentle raising of the bottom line while an important kind of exclamatory intonation contour is shaped by the gradual falling of the top line and the gradual decline of the bottom line. There are still variances for the four functional intonational contours, which are not covered in the above description. In addition to the functional contours, the global and local intonation manipulation is an underlying factor for all the mood intonation and other intonation phenomenon.

The marking of the intonation:

(1) The unmarked top line—abrupt falling of the intonation. The top line plummets after the nucleus, resulting in the possibility of unstressed syllables coming after the nucleus.

(2) The marked top line—gradual falling of the intonation. The top line gradually falls after the nucleus. It is possible for unstressed syllable to appear after the nucleus. Many researches have suggested that the low tone tends to fall abruptly or gradually after the nucleus.

(3) The unmarked bottom line—declination of the intonation. The bottom line fluctuates considerably and moves downward.

(4) The marked bottom line—rising of the intonation. The bottom line fluctuates slightly and moves upward, particularly in the nucleus and the tail.

Generally speaking, the bottom line rises remarkably for interrogative sentences and slightly for imperative sentences. There may still be some other unknown features. The classification of mood intonation agrees with the categorization of the functional intonation, taking into account similar acoustic features while adding the bandwidth feature. The fine-grained manipulation of the top line and the bottom line is functioning here. The implication of "mood" is relevant to the fundamental function (or meaning) of the functional intonation.

## 3. Prosodic constituent

(1) Prosodic word: the combination of two or three syllables reflecting the rhythm of Mandarin Chinese. The prosodic word is supposed to have no pause inside it, whereas in the boundaries of the prosodic words, it is not necessary to have pauses but there may be pauses.

(2) Prosodic word group: generally consisting of two or three closely-related prosodic words, amid which there is virtually no perceivable pause while in the end of the prosodic phrase there is bound to be a perceivable pause, which is not necessarily observable from the spectrogram.

(3) Prosodic phrase: comprising one or several prosodic word group. There is usually perceptible pause between prosodic phrases, which can be remarkably observed from the spectrum. An important characteristic of the prosodic phrase is that its bottom line declines gradually over the course of the phrase.

(4) Intonational phrase: including one or several prosodic phrases. Intonational phrase may be a single sentence or the clause of a complex sentence, mostly separated by punctuation. Usually there is a relatively long pause at the end of the intonational phrase.

From the definitions above we can see that the four prosodic units are involved in an inclusive relationship, i.e. the intonational phrase boundary must be the boundary of prosodic phrase, and the prosodic phrase boundary must be the boundary of prosodic word group; the prosodic word group boundary is rested on the boundary of prosodic words. Nevertheless, the boundary of prosodic word group is not necessarily the boundary of dictionary words, and vice versa.

### 7.4.2 Prosodic modeling

Prosodic features vary with the changes of context, which means that context and prosodic features are in close relation with each other. The parameter distribution of prosodic features is subjected to the influence of context information, which follows certain probability correlation relationship rather than a simple functional mapping relationship. From the perspective of probability, the corresponding prosodic parameters for a given sentence parameter would be the set of parameters that has maximum appearing probability of all the prosodic parameters, which can be illustrated in the following equation:

$$Y = \arg \max_n P(Y_n \mid A) \tag{7.1}$$

From the Bayesian formula we can derive the following equation:

$$Y = \arg \max_n P(Y_n \mid A) = \arg \max_n \frac{P(A \mid Y_n) P(Y_n)}{P(A)} \tag{7.2}$$

Since P (A) represents the statistical distribution of the context information, it can be seen as a constant and neglected. Then formula (7.2) can be transformed as follows:

$$Y = \arg\max_{n} P(Y_n \mid A) = \arg\max_{n} P(A \mid Y_n)P(Y_n) \qquad (7.3)$$

Formula (7.3) suggests that the derivation of the posterior probability $P(Y_n|A)$ can be transformed into the derivation of the priori probability $P(A|Y_n)$, whereas $P(Y_n)$ embodies the distribution of prosodic features per se, which is represented by the appearing probability and interaction of the prosodic features. Therefore formula (7.3) implies that prosodic features are not only subject to the impact of context information, but also subject to the influence of interaction between themselves. $P(A|Y_n)$ is a component of the priori probability. Theoretically, any model able to be trained numerically and capable of memorizing can be the basis of its realization.

### 7.4.3 Prosodic labeling

Prosodic labeling is to give a qualitative description of the linguistically functioning prosodic features in speech signal. Tonal variation, intonation pattern, stress pattern and prosodic structure are labeled as they are capable of signaling linguistic function. Intonation variations triggered by the influence of stress are labeled while the pitch variation of vowels and the tonal co-articulation between syllables are not labeled. Prosodic phenomena that can be quantitatively described are not labeled. Generally, prosodic labeling is divided into several layers. Prosodic segmentation is the foundation of prosodic labeling and thereby, an indispensable layer. The other layers are labeled according to the practical needs and the phonetic characteristic. The prosodic labeling system of Mandarin Chinese should include the following features:

(1) Reliability: the labeling results of different labelers should have high reliability.

(2) All-roundness: the important prosodic phenomena in natural language should be covered.

(3) Learnability: able to be learned in a short time.

(4) Compatibility: capable to be integrated with new methods of speech synthesis and speech identification and incorporated with the contemporary syntactic, semantic and pragmatic theories.

(5) Manipulability: the labeling symbols should be as simple as possible and close to the surface structure of the speech.

(6) Openness: allow the existence of uncertain labeling items.

(7) Readability: the labeling symbols should be identifiable to machines.

From the aspect of engineering application, prosodic labeling is the process of describing speech phonetically, whose relationship with linguistics and phonetics can be demonstrated in the following figure. Utilizing the labeling results, it is quite easy for speech engineering to model the corresponding relationship with linguistic information or phonetic information. Therefore, prosodic labeling is playing a more and more important role in speech identification and data-driven speech synthesis.

As the system of prosodic labeling is layer-divided, every layer is involved with different prosodic or relevant phenomenon. Generally speaking, it contains the following layers and the user is free to select the layer according to personal needs. The prosodic labeling system C-ToBI embraces the following layers:

(1) The syllable layer: for labeling the pinyin of Mandarin syllables. For instance, 1,2,3,4 are used to represent the four tones and 0 to represent the neutral tone in Mandarin Chinese. Tone is labeled after pinyin.

(2) Actual articulation layer: for labeling the actual articulation of initial consonants, vowels and tones. The IPA machine-readable symbol system SAMPA-C is generally adopted for labeling this information.

(3) The intonational layer: the intonational contour is determined by the prosodic structure and the stress structure. That is to say, if the stress structure and the prosodic structure are defined, then the intonational contour is established. Previous researches have showed that the intonational variation involves primarily the variation of tonal range and register, with the former focusing mainly on the pitch change and the latter concentrating on the variation brought about by the influence of the psychological state, the mood and the prosodic structure of the speaker. Therefore, it is essential that the intonational labeling reflect the expansion and contraction of the range, the variation of the register and the changing of the overall intonational contour (also referred to as the changing of the top line and the bottom line).

Prosodic segmentation is to segment every phonetic unit (including syllable, phonological units and phonetic units even smaller) from the utterance, and furthermore, make a detailed and truthful description of their timbre characteristics. The prosodic segmentation of Mandarin Chinese can be carried out layer by layer. The extended labeling is to label the actual articulation of the speech on the basis of the regular pronunciation and mark the phonetic change of both segmental units and suprasegmental units. The machine-readable segmental labeling system of Mandarin Chinese SAMPA-C (corresponding to the IPA system) can be used here. For speech corpora, paralinguistic and nonlinguistic phenomena should also be labeled.

SAMPA is a speech keyboard symbolic system that is machine-readable and popular internationally, which is widely used in corpus segmentation and labeling. A feasible SAMPA-C symbolic system has worked out for phonetic labeling of Mandarin Chinese. Here we would like to expand the system to incorporate all the dialects of Mandarin Chinese; therefore, a set of principles for SAMPA-C should be established first.

(1) Corresponding symbols of Mandarin Chinese are established in line with the SAMPA symbolic system.

SAMPA (http://www.phon.ucl.ac.uk/home/sampa/)

(2) Add additional symbols for Mandarin-specific phonetic phenomenon.

(3) It is an open system. As the knowledge of phonetic phenomenon enlarges, new symbols could be added and unsuitable symbols could be modified.

SAMPA-C focuses primarily on the segmental labeling of Mandarin Chinese. First, labeling systems such as consonants, vowels, tones and phonetic changes of Mandarin Chinese are given. Then symbolic systems of Putonghua are listed. Moreover, the phonological symbolic system of main Chinese dialects such as Guangzhou dialect, Shanghai dialect and Fuzhou dialect are provided. Other dialects fitting this pattern can be supplemented continuously.

### 7.4.4 Prosodic generation

Prosodic generation was first noticed as a part of phonological coding of syllable generation. With the development of research methods, the prosodic generation of phrase and sentence is also studied, which is mainly done from the perspective of information processing. Correlative models of prosodic generation include Shattuck-Hufnagel's duplication and reproduction model and the connective model of Dell. Unfortunately, these two models didn't go to lengths on the issue of prosodic generation. So far the most comprehensive prosodic generative model is the prosodic coding and processing model proposed by W. J. M. Levelt (Levelt, 1989).

Levelt maintained that during the course of speech production, the processing of all the stages is parallel and incremental. Prosodic coding comprises several processes. Some are processed during the categorization of words while others are processed during the categorization of sentences. As the syntactic structure of the sentence begins, the phonetic planning of the lexicon initiates almost simultaneously. Lexicon is generally processed in two stages: the retrieving of lemma (including semantic and syntactic features) and the retrieving of lexeme (including the morphological and phonological forms). The latter is implemented in the lexicon-phonology retrieving stage, which uses lemma as the input to retrieve the corresponding morphological and phonological structure. Therefore, segmental information is not indispensable for the generation of prosodic features. The morphological and phonological information is utilized in the segmental retrieving stage for retrieving the segmental contents of the lexicon (the phonemes embraced by the lexicon and their positions in the syllable), thereafter the prosody and segments are integrated together.

At the last stage, the prosodic generator implements the speech articulatory plan to generate the prosodic and intonational pattern. Specifically, the generation of prosodic involves two steps:

(1) To generate prosodic units such as prosodic word, prosodic phrase and intonational phrase.

(2) To generate the metrical grid of the prosodic structure.

Yet the metical grid does not convey the stress and time pattern of the speech. Firstly, the generation of the prosodic unit has to go through the following procedures: the processing outcome of the morphology-phonology retrieving stage is combined with the linking elements to generate the prosodic word. By scanning the syntactic structure of the sentence and integrating all kinds of relevant information, the extended elements of the grammatical phrase are enclosed to form the prosodic phrase. Then the speaker pauses at certain time spots to generate the intonational phrase. Secondly, based on the prosodic structure of the sentence and the metrical grid of the single words, the prosodic generator finally builds the metrical grid of the whole utterance.

In 1999 Levelt proposed a new concept on prosodic generation during the generation process of lexicon (Levelt, 1999b). He maintains that in stress language like Dutch, English and German, there is a primary lexical prosodic pattern: word stress falls on the first full-voweled syllable. Therefore, the stress of the regular word is generated automatically according to this rule during the course of incremental lexicalization, rather than being retrieved. Nevertheless, the stress of the irregular word is not generated automatically. Consequently, only the prosodic structure of the irregular word is stored as a part of the phonological code. The retrieved phonological structure of the irregular word is then used to instruct further prosodic processing of the irregular words, which leads to the generation of syllables and larger prosodic units.

It should be noted that these models are founded on the basis of research findings obtained from languages of English, Dutch and German. Compared with these languages, Mandarin Chinese is distinguished in two characteristics:

(1) Mandarin Chinese has a smaller amount of syllables, accounting for only one tenth of language like English.

(2) Mandarin Chinese is a tone language while language like English is a stress language without tones. Therefore, it is inevitable that the prosodic generation mechanisms of Mandarin Chinese differ from the models aforementioned. Nevertheless, scarcely little research on the prosodic generation of Mandarin Chinese has been done so far.

### 7.4.5 *Cognitive neuroscience mechanisms of prosodic generation*

Resorting to meta-analysis, Levelt analyzed the findings of 58 brain image researches (Levelt, 2001). He concluded that during the process of lexical production, the brain areas activated tend to be left-lateralized, including the posterior inferior frontal gyrus (the Broca area), the central superior temporal gyrus, the middle temporal gyrus, the posterior superior temporal gyrus, the middle superior temporal gyrus (the Wernicke area) and the left thalamus. The process of assimilating vision and concept involves the occipital lobe, the ventral temporal lobe, and the prefrontal area (0~275ms); then the activation is transmitted to the Wernicke area where the phonological codes are stored. This information is then transferred to the Broca area and (or) the left superior-middle temporal lobe to undergo the post phonological coding process (275-400ms); next it is coded phonetically, which is in close relationship to the sensorimotor area and the cerebellum, with the former activated to articulate.

In 2002 Mayer et al studied the brain activities of normal person during the process of prosodic generation by means of fMRI (Mayer etc. 2002). The results show that relatively small, non-overlapping, frontal-basal areas of both the right and the left hemisphere are involved in the generation of prosody. Furthermore, generating linguistically geared prosody revealed exclusively left hemisphere activation, while the production of affective prosody revealed right hemisphere activation only.

## 7.5 Speech Recognition

### 7.5.1 Overview of speech recognition

In 1981 Japan proposed the fifth generation of computer with the support of the state government, which is targeted at man-machine interaction of natural language. Although this goal has not been realized yet, it gives an enormous impetus and stimulus for the research and development of information technology in other countries. Researches on speech recognition and language comprehension have been greatly promoted. All the develop countries competed to invest a large amount of manpower and capital to tackle the problem. For instance, from the late 1980s to the early 1990s, 12 experts headed by H. Fujisaki in Japan Tokyo Imperial University hosted the Nation Program of Advanced Man-Machine Speech Interaction System. 185 researchers majoring in natural language processing and computer science took part in this program. Funds invested amount to 3 million dollars. The program focused on eight key projects: advanced language analysis, language feature analysis, speech recognition, language comprehension, language synthesis, knowledge processing of speech interaction and dialogue technique, language processing technique in noisy and intervening environment, man-machine interaction technique and technology evaluation. In the 1990s, national key projects on automatic telephone translation system and online Japanese-English translation system were put into research.

The US Defense Advanced Research Projects Agency started a ten-year DARPA project of strategy computational engineering, which included speech recognition, language comprehension and general corpus for military application. Organizations participating included MIT (the Massachusetts Institute of Technology), CMU (Carnegie-Mellon University), BellLab and IBM Company etc. Goals achieved were as follows: 100 words recognized by assigned person in intensive noisy environments resulted in an accuracy rate of over 98%. By means of the SPHINX system, 1000 words of continuous speech recognition under the condition of moderate grammar resulted in an accuracy rate of 91.1%. 997 words of continuous speech with grammatical constrain results in a recognition accuracy rate of 96.8%. Accuracy rate of phoneme recognition amounts to 73.8%.

Taking advantage of the INRS system and being speaker-dependent, recognition of 75000 words results in an accuracy rate of 89.5%. Utilizing the Tangora system and being speaker-dependent, recognition of 5000 words and 20000 words results in an accuracy rate of 97.1% and 94.6% respectively. In the late 1970s, F. Jelinek of IBM Company proposed the n-gram statistical language model and successfully applied the trigram model to the TANGORA speech recognition system. Later, Carnegie-Mellon University of the US applied the bigram model into the SPHINX speech recognition system, which greatly enhanced the accuracy rate of recognition. Thereafter some well-known speech recognition system started to adopt the bigram and trigram statistical language model. Currently, research on speech recognition is headed by the IBM institution (Thomas J. Waston Research Center) and the BellLab of AT&T. Both IBM and Belllab use methods based on the HMM statistical model. The reason why HMM is so successful in the field of speech recognition is that it has stronger modeling ability for time series. At present, IBM is more advanced in technique than Belllab, which may be attributed to the following reasons:

(1) Bell Lab employs the continuous parameter HMM while IBM uses the discrete parameter HMM. Researches has found that for small-or-medium-size vocabulary system ($\leq 10000$ words), continuous parameter HMM has a higher accuracy rate of recognition than discrete parameter HMM, whereas the reverse situation happens when it comes to large-size vocabulary system.

(2) It is relatively difficult to utilize mixture distribution using the continuous parameter HMM, while it is not a troublesome matter for discrete parameter HMM.

(3) To obtain the Robust statistical results, it is necessary to employ the Segment Models in the continuous parameter HMM. However, it is very difficult to obtain the Maximum Likelihood result of segmental boundary; hence it could not secure the segmental performance. Whereas for the discrete parameter HMM, the statistical Robust is realized by incrementing condition numbers.

(4) Employing the discrete HMM can effectively reduce the training dada, which saves the users from providing every articulation sample for every word.

Using the discrete parameter HMM, IBM constructed some basic acoustic models (fenone model which is smaller than the phone model) and then established word model by utilizing fixed and finite basic acoustic models. By this means, it is possible to obtain better statistical results by using less training data as well as finish the data training process automatically. In later use of the system, a new user can easily train the system with less registered data to improve the recognition accuracy rate of the system (the system allow registrations of many users). The training includes 254 sentences, with each sentence consisting of 10 to 20 words. It is of crucial importance that the user projects his articulation features to the parameter space of the system. With the help of this method, IBM is leading the way in the field of speech recognition.

As to continuous speech with temporal sequence, the recognition performance of HMM is far better than other methods. HMM is the method underlying most person-unspecified speech recognition system of large vocabulary and continuous speech. HMM is playing a significant role in speech recognition and it is booming with maturity. The success of HMM in the application of speech recognition is due largely to its advanced modeling method in temporal sequential structure. Nevertheless, HMM has weakness too. It is not designed to comprehend in the same way as human brain does and it has poor adaptability and unsatisfactory robustness, which is manifested in the fact that it has poor modeling ability for low-level acoustic phonemes, likely to confuse words similar acoustically and performs poorly in comprehend advanced phonemes or modeling semantics. All these drawbacks reduce HMM to be only applicable in simple occasions that has finite state or based on probabilistic grammar. First-order HMM has trouble employing model to describe coarticulation, which could be accounted for by several reasons: first, HMM is based on the prerequisite that outputs are independent of each other; second, HMM only relies on the current state and that it needs too many parameters and samples to be trained; finally, it is a necessity for HMM to make prior assumptions on the distribution of the states, which reduces it to be unsuitable for speech signals.

In the 1990s, neural network paved a new pathway for speech recognition. Artificial neural network (ANN) has the characteristics of adaptability, parallelism, nonlinearity, robustness, fault-tolerance and learning ability. It demonstrates its strength both in structure and algorithm. It takes advantage of the associative patterns to map the complex acoustic signals into phonetic and phonological representations with different granularity rather than stick to selecting special speech parameter. By training and recognizing the comprehensive input pattern, ANN is able to integrate the auditory model into the network model. Current research has found a more powerful model NN for speech signal, which is more adaptable for activated function, has more effective learning algorithm and more reasonable structure. Work done involves the following aspects:

(1) Dwindle the size of the modeling unit. Generally phoneme-based modeling is preferred to enhance the recognition accuracy of the system by improving the recognition accuracy of phonemes.

(2) Intensive studies into the acoustic model, auditory model, the functioning mechanism of the brain have been carried out. Context information should be utilized to lessen the influence of excessive phonetic variation on the speech signal.

(3) By extracting various features from speech signal, adopting mixed network model (e.g. NN+HMM) and applying all sources of knowledge (including phonology, morphology, syntax and semantics), research on speech recognition and comprehension should be carried out to elevate the performance of the system.

Japan is leading the way in neural network speech recognition. For instance, a hybrid method called TDNN-LR-DP has been put forward based on the features of the speech signal, which make improvements on Waibel' s Time Delay Neural Network (TDNN). Firstly, extend the training sets by means of maladjustment to enhance the ability of shift-invariant. Secondly, taking advantage of left-to-right parser, it makes overall prediction as to which phoneme is the legal one to appear next in a given dictionary. Finally, through dynamic temporal optimization of DTW, the output of TDNN and the predicted optimal phoneme is matched. This method results in a recognition accuracy rate of 92.6% for 5000 words. Miyatake et al. carried out a comprehensive training of the TDNN in large scale phoneme table. For 2620 words, the accuracy rate of phoneme location is 98.0%, which makes it possible for speech recognition of copious vocabulary while at the same time independent of the vocabulary. This method was used to predict the neural network model. For 5240 normal Japanese words, the recognition accuracy rate is 92.6%. Hild found that the neural network's recognition accuracy rate was 98.5% for 1000 time-delayed sentences with multiple models whereas for SPHIX the accuracy rate was 96.0%. Furthermore, for 120 unspecified people, the accuracy rate of 1680 words was 92.0% while for SPHIX the accuracy rate was 90.4%. The predictive neural network takes NN as the predictor, which is a neural-network speech recognition method that was emerging in 1990s. It is sophisticated in modeling and capable of being applied to speech recognition research of copious vocabulary, continuous speech and unspecified person. K. Iso applied this method to large-scale vocabulary with semi-syllable as the recognition unit. In order to enhance the discrimination ability, he introduced the reverse prediction pattern and improved the calculation method of predictive error. The result revealed a recognition accuracy rate of 97.6% for 5000 person-dependent words.

At present, almost all the man-computer interaction systems that are technically mature are domain-specified such as the airport booking automatic question-answering system, the tourist guide automatic question-answering system, the restaurant ordering automatic question-answering system etc. Researchers and developers of Chinese speech recognition include the following: IBM, Speechworks, Nuance, Philips, Microsoft, Infotalk, the China Science Pattern Recognition, TianLang, D-Ear Technologies, Anker Communication, ShengShuo Technologies.

China has launched research on speech recognition since 1950s, yet the research booming phrase began in the 1980s. Speech recognition is becoming a key factor for the man-computer interface in communication technology. Researches are shifting from experimental study to application study.

### 7.5.2 Chinese speech recognition system

In 1997, IBM developed a speech recognition system *ViaVoice* for Mandarin Chinese in China. It is a continuous speech recognition system for large-scale vocabulary without dependent on specified speaker, applicable for Windows'95, 98 series. It takes the IBM company 26 years to develop the system, which is a new speech recognition system developed after the language of American English, British English, French, German, Italian, Spanish and Japanese. Basing on the characteristics of Mandarin Chinese such as abundant in homophones, distinguished by tone, fuzzy in boundary, open up for new words etc, the system realizes speaker-unspecified continuous speech recognition with large-scale vocabulary. It has basic vocabulary of 32,000 words which could be extended to 65000 words including those common Chinese words for office usage.

The system is also equipped with an "error correction mechanism", which leads to an average recognition rate of over 95%. In 1997, the application of speech recognition dictating machine in some fields has been graded as one of the top ten events of computer development by the American media. IBM is one of the first to seize the Chinese speech market and its speech recognition product *Viavoice* enjoys the highest market share (over 900%) in China. After it made its official debut in 1997, *ViaVoice* has successfully broken through a couple of difficulties such as continuous speech, large-scale vocabulary and speaker-independency, furthermore, problems of Mandarin Chinese are tackled such as abundant in homophones, distinguished by tone and rich in dialects. *ViaVoice* speech recognition software has realized sentence-based character input and vocabulary-based command drive. Grounded on these two functions, people can make many applications such as sound control games, sound control edition, automatic speech query, speech-input online chatting and speech-aided teaching etc.

*ViaVoice* is the Chinese version of the Tangora system of IBM (IBM name every American English speech recognition system "Tangora", with a series of models). Every speech recognition system can be divided into two parts: Acoustic Processor and Linguistic Decoder. The acoustic processor of *ViaVoice* is quite qualified in resisting noises, which is achieved by employing the auditory model (in the IBM system it was referred to as the "*Ear Model*") and noise adaptive algorithm in VQ. In the acoustic processor, the speech signal is obtained through the Ear Model, then a 255 FFT was made and spectrum energy of 20 critical bands was extracted for longtime normalization. Finally, *VQ* clustering was performed on the basis of K-Means with the help of EM algorithm. After all these are done, the acoustic processor can be adaptive to noises. *ViaVoice* is based on a kind of discrete HMM called Fenonic Basefoms, which is a serial of FenoneModels. Each serial composes a word model (referred to as "Linguistic Models"). The HMM acoustic training was completed by 54 speakers (both male and female) of Mandarin Chinese. Every speaker articulated over 30,000 sentences which underwent an enormous amount of statistical training. Nevertheless, acoustic decoding alone is sufficient. A fine speech recognition model has to be established on the foundation of language models, which in turn could also be regarded as HMM and based on stochastic grammar (or referred to as statistical grammar). All the *n-gram* grammar probabilities are obtained from statistic results of 300 M Chinese authentic corpus texts. As *n-gram* model requires enormous computation expenses and has certain demands for storage space, it is generally limited to Tri-grammar. All the grammar probabilities are obtained from statistic results of a wealth of texts. The basic algorithm of *ViaVoice* is laid on the foundation of HMM, Context-Dependent VQ and Decision Trees. This algorithm can accurately retrieve the speech characteristics of different speaker in different context while at the same time contract the huge amount of system parameters to an irreducible minimum. The front end acoustic processing of *ViaVoice* is qualified to resist noises. For speech articulated by speaker with standard pronunciation, the system can achieve very high recognition accuracy, which impresses people with its excellent performance. As to speaker with accents, the system can improve its recognition accuracy after a period of training. In 1988, IBM Beijing development centre brought out an improved version of *ViaVoice* speech recognition system that is capable of identify Chinese dialects such as Cantonese or Sichuan dialect. At present, most speech recognition soft wares achieve user-specified speech recognition by the function of self-study and continuous training.

*ViaVoice* is in essence a dictation machine. The key part is composed of a word edition processor that is called "IBM Voice Pad". The other five auxiliary parts include: Microphone Setup Initialization Program, Vocabulary Manager, Enrollment, *ViaVoice* Properties and Online Help. It comprises the following sections: dictation system, realization of Chinese speech input, edition and print.

(1) Voice Pad: the main part of *ViaVoice*. Its primary function is to dictate texts with punctuations and editing symbols and then transmit the dictated text to the other applications.

a) It has a basic vocabulary of about 32000 words, including Chinese entries for office usage and most of the computer command words. The vocabulary can be expanded to 65000 words. *ViaVoice* processes the dictated input by using the basic vocabulary and the personal speech vocabulary.

b) It has an "error correction mechanism", which can be used to change the phonetic data of the user (the prior probability of the homophones) and in turn modify the language models of the system. Reasonable utilization of the "error correction mechanism" can enhance the recognition rate steadily.

c) It has a personal vocabulary of the user which can be extended to 65000 words. Meanwhile, for those words that are not included in the basic vocabulary (if there is any), the "error correction mechanism" will add them into the personal vocabulary of the user. Together with the personal phonetic files, it affects the language model of the system.

(2) Microphone Setup Initialization Program. *ViaVoice* provides a specialized microphone Setup initialization program, which ensures the normal operation of the microphone and the accuracy of speech recognition. The initialization program goes through the following procedures: test the linking state of the microphone; the program collects phonetic samples according to the input of the user; automatically adjust the volume of the microphone; carry out tests on speech recognition.

(3) Vocabulary Manager. If certain terms of the user can not be correctly recognized after error correction repeatedly, this item can be deleted from the vocabulary manager.

(4) Enrollment: the enrollment program enables the system to train the pronunciation characteristic of the user so as to improve the recognition rate of the system. The training comprises 254 sentences, each consisting of 10-20 words.

(5) *eViaVoice* Properties: in the same system, every user is specified with a name to store their personal speech files and personal vocabulary. In case that different users use the same system, properties should be changed first.

IBM *ViaVoice* Developers Toolkit has realized the interface between application soft ware and kernel of *ViaVoice*. This toolkit is qualified to develop the dictated command and manipulation application. It includes:

a) Dictation Engine (SMAP Interface): to realize the speech dictation function.

b) Navigator Engine: to realize the function of phonetic command.

c) Speech Recognition Data: to realize recognition command or manipulation that does not contain grammatical function or dictation that contains grammatical function.

The toolkit is capable of the following functions:

a) Establish dynamic command vocabulary and their corresponding pronunciation and tests.

b) Extend the grammar, grammar compiler and grammar testing tools.

c) Dictionary constructer and sound bank expansion.

d) Develop the application of dictation, which includes the speech application program interface (SMAPI)of C language, speech function call processing, sharing of speech engine, the header file and library function invoked by the parallel API and the AMAPI programming.

The Microsoft Company has obtained the use license of the speech recognition technique from the Speech Works Company, which specifies that text-based information (such as email, news or other dynamic contents) can be automatically read to the telephone caller. It can also be used in the speech start up system to make it possible for transaction dealing by phone. The Sun Micro-System Company has brought out a new series of products aimed at the telephone company. The "Voice Tone" software put forwarded by Sun is capable of helping the operator to provide the speech dial and speech email service to cell phone users.

## 7.6 Speech Synthesis

### 7.6.1 Overview of speech synthesis

Research on speech synthesis has been over two hundred years. However, modern speech synthesis technique that is of practical significance begins with the development of computer technique and digital signal processing technique, aiming at enabling the computer to generate continuous speech of high clarity and naturalness. The development of speech synthesis technique can be divided into two stages: the early stage mainly employed the parameter synthesis method while the latter stage primarily adopted the waveform splicing synthesis method with the development of computer technique.

In the development of speech synthesis technique, the early stage mainly used the method of parameter synthesis. What are worthy to be noted are the Parallel Formant Synthesizer (1973) of Holmes and the Series/ Parallel Formant Synthesizer (1980) of Klatt. As long as the parameters are meticulously adjusted, these two synthesizers can synthesize very natural speech. The most representative Text-To-Speech (TTS) system is the DECtalk developed by America DEC Company. Decades of researches and practices have revealed that due to the difficulty of extracting formant parameters, although synthesized speech of high naturalness can be obtained by employing the formant synthesizer, the overall quality of the synthesized speech is still far away from meeting the requirements of Text-To-Speech system.

Since 1980s, speech synthesis technique has been greatly advanced. Particularly with the advent of the PSOLA (in 1990) method, the timbre and naturalness of the speech synthesized by time-domain waveform splicing have been improved to a large extent. The early 1990s has witnessed the success of PSOLA-based Text-To-Speech systems of French, German, English and Japanese etc. These systems are of higher naturalness than those TTS systems based on LPC method or formant synthesizer. Furthermore, as the structure of the PSOLA-based synthesizer is capable of real-time realization, it has a bright prospect of business application.

China is a latecomer on the research of Mandarin speech synthesis. However, it has caught up with the international research since the early 1980s. Roughly speaking, China has also undergone the stages of formant synthesis, LPC synthesis and PSOLA-based synthesis. Nevertheless, similar to the TTS system of foreign languages, these systems yield machine-like speeches of sentence and discourse, which has a naturalness far from satisfactory to the mass of users, and therefore, becomes a obstacle for these systems to enter the market extensively.

In the 1960s, the English TTS system made its first appearance. In 1980s, China launched research on TTS system of Mandarin Chinese, which has made considerable progress in the past few years.

### 7.6.2 Methods of speech synthesis

The methods of speech synthesis have gone through a series of stages: from parameter synthesis to splicing synthesis, and finally to the combination of the two methods. The continuous stimulus for this development is the improvement of people's cognition and demands. At present, the common speech synthesis technique includes the following: formant synthesis, LPC synthesis, PSOLA splicing synthesis and LMA soundtrack modeling technique. All of them have both advantages and disadvantages, therefore, it is necessary that people integrate these techniques together or import the strength of one technique onto the other so as to overcome the shortcomings of the other technique.

### 1. Formant synthesis

The mathematical model of speech generation is the theoretical foundation for speech synthesis. The speech generation process can be described as follows: spurred by the stimulation signal, the sound wave goes through the resonator and radiates the sound waves through mouth or nose. Therefore, the sound track's parameters and its resonance characteristics have been the kernel of the researches. Figure 7.3 displays the frequency response of certain speech. In the figure, Fp1, Fp2, Fp3 ······ mark the peak of the frequency response, which suggests the time when the transmitted frequency response of the sound track reaches its utmost. Normally, these peaks of the frequency response in sound track transmission are referred to as formants. The distribution characteristics of the formant frequency (peak frequency) play a decisive role in the tone quality of the speech.

Speeches of different tone qualities differ in formant pattern; hence, formant filter can be constructed by taking the formant frequency and bandwidth as parameter. Next, several combinations of these filters can be used to simulate the transmission characteristics of the sound track (the frequency response) and adjust the stimulated signal. Then by applying the radiation model the synthetic speech can be obtained. This is the basic principles of formant synthesis technique. There are three practicable models based on formant theories.

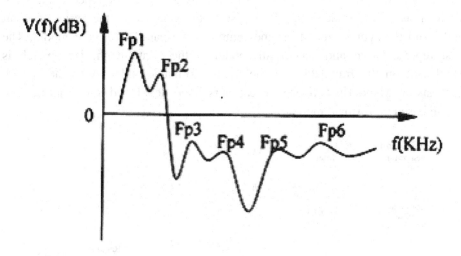

Fig. 7.3 Frequency response of certain speech

(1) Series formant model: in this model, sound track is regarded as a set of sequent second-order resonator. This model is mainly used for the synthesis of most vowels.

(2) Parallel formant model: many researchers argue that the aforementioned series formant model can not adequately describe and simulate special vowels (such as nasalized vowels) and most consonants, which lead to the birth of the parallel formant model.

(3) Hybrid formant model: in the series formant model, the formant filters are connected end-to-end. Whereas in the parallel formant model, the input signals have to go through amplitude adjustment first and then be added to every formant filter; after that, the outputs of all the circuits are added up together. Comparing these two models, we can see that for those speeches whose synthesized sound source locates at the end of the sound track (including most vowels), the serial formant model is more tallied with acoustic theories and moreover, it is free from the burden of making amplitude adjustment for every formant filter. However, for those speeches whose synthesized sound source locates in the middle of the sound track (including most tenuis and stops), the parallel model is more suitable. Nevertheless, it is very complicate to adjust the amplitudes in the parallel model.

Taking all these into consideration, people combined these two models together and yielded the hybrid formant model, which is shown in Figure 7.4.

In fact, all the three models aforementioned have obtained successful applications. For instance, the OVE system of Fant adopts the series formant model and the synthesizer of Holmes employs the parallel formant model. The most representative and successful model is the Klatt synthesizer which is established on the foundation of the hybrid formant model. A to the speech synthesis of Mandarin Chinese, researchers have developed some application system based on formant models.

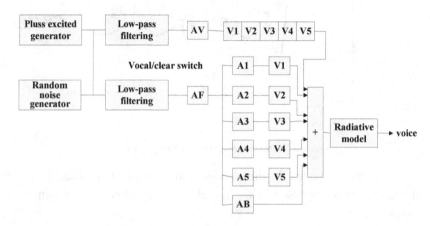

Fig. 7.4 The hybrid formant model

Formant models simulate the sound track accurately, which can be used to yield speech of high naturalness. Additionally, as the formant parameters have definite physical meanings which correspond directly to the sound tract parameter, it is easy to use the formant models to describe the various phenomena in natural speech and summarize the acoustic rules, which ultimately leads to its application in the formant synthesis system.

However, people have also discovered that this technique has conspicuous shortcomings. Firstly, as it relies on the simulation of the sound track, inaccurate simulation of the sound track will definitely affect the synthetic quality. Secondly, practical applications have demonstrated that although the formant models describes the most important and basic part of the speech, it can not represent other delicate speech signals that influence the naturalness of the speech. Finally, it is very complicate to manipulate the formant synthesis model. For a refined synthesizer, manipulation parameters can be as many as dozens, which make it difficult for realization.

As a result, researchers went on to find and develop other new synthesis techniques. Inspired by direct recording and playing of waveform, people came up with the synthesis technique of waveform splicing, which can be represented by LPC and PSOLA synthesis technique. Different from the formant synthesis technique, waveform splicing synthesis relies on splicing the recorded waveform of the synthesized element rather then relying on the simulation of the articulation.

## 2. LPC parameter syntheses

The development of speech coding and decoding technique has close relationship to the development of waveform splicing, of which the development of LPC technique (Linear Prediction Coding) has shed enormous impact on the development of the waveform technique. LPC synthesis technique is in essence a coding technique of time waveform, with its purpose to slow down the transmission rate of the time signals.

Institute of Acoustic, Chinese Academic of Science has done a lot of work applying the LPC synthesis technique to researches on the speech synthesis and Text-To-Speech of Mandarin Chinese. They introduce the multiple-pulse excitation LPC technique in 1987, the technique of vector quantization in 1989 and the technique of coding excitation in 1993. They have made significant contribution to the application of LPC synthesis technique in the synthesis of Mandarin Chinese.

LPC synthesis technique has the advantage of being simple and straightforward. Its synthesis process is in essence a simple process of decoding and splicing. Additionally, as the synthetic unit of LPC splicing technique is the waveform data of the speech and all the speech information is preserved intact, it is possible to obtain signal synthetic unit of high naturalness.

However, natural speech flow differs greatly from the speech in isolation. If it is so simple as to splice all the isolated speech together bluntly, then the quality of the overall speech is bound to be unsatisfactory. Whereas, LPC technique is essentially the process of recoding and replaying, therefore it is inadequate to yield continuous speech satisfactorily using LPC technique. Hence LPC technique has to be integrated with other techniques for the sake of improving the quality of the synthesized speech. The principles of a typical TTS system based on single syllable and VQLPC (Vector Quantization LPC) are illustrated in Figure 7.5.

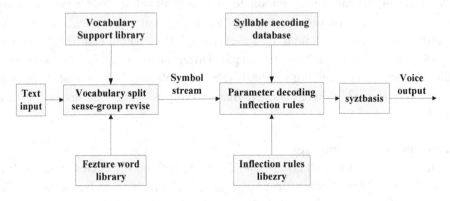

Fig. 7.5 PSOLA synthesis techniques

The PSOLA synthesis technique (Pitch Synchronous Overlap Add) put forward in 1980s has infused new life into the waveform splicing synthesis technique. PSOLA concentrates on the manipulation of suprasegmental features of speech signal such as F0, syllable duration and intensity, which are of crucial importance to the manipulation and modification of speech. Therefore, PSOLA technique has the advantage of being more revisable over LPC technique, which makes it possible to yield speech of high naturalness.

The main features of PSOLA technique are as follows: before splicing the speech waveform segments, it is necessary to adjust the prosodic features of the spliced segment to the context using PSOLA algorithm, which preserves the primary suprasegmental features of the original speech while at the same time enables the spliced segments to be in line with the context so as to produce speech of high naturalness and intelligibility.

Universities and institutions in China have done extensive researches on how to apply the PSOLA technique to the TTS system of Mandarin Chinese. Based on research on the PSOLA technique, Mandarin TTS system has been developed and moreover, measures to improve this technique and the naturalness of the synthetic speech have been proposed.

PSOLA technique inherits the strengths of the traditional waveform splicing technique, being simple, straightforward and fast. Furthermore, PSOLA is able to control the prosodic parameters of the speech signals conveniently and is ready for synthesizing continuous speech. All these characteristics have made it widely applicable.

However, PSOLA technique also bears disadvantages. Firstly, PSOLA technique is based on fundamental tone synchronous speech analysis/synthesis technique, which requires accurate identification of the fundamental tone cycles and their starting points. Any erroneous identification of the cycle and its starting point will affect the outcome of the PSOLA technique. Moreover, PSOLA is in essence simple mapping and splicing of the waveform. It is not yet settled as to whether this splicing can achieve smooth transition and how it affects the frequency parameter. Therefore, it is likely to yield unfavorable outcome in the course of the synthetic process.

## 3. LMA model

As people are becoming more and more stringent in the naturalness and quality of the synthetic speech, the PSOLA algorithm has been found with shortcomings, namely, it is weak at adjusting prosodic parameters and it cannot handle the case of co-articulation. Therefore, people proposed another speech synthesis method that is based on LMA sound track model. Similar to the traditional parameter synthesis, this method can agilely adjust the prosodic parameter, and moreover, it can produce better synthetic qualities than the PSOLA algorithm.

At present, the main speech synthesis techniques are formant synthesis technique and waveform splicing synthesis technique based on PSOLA algorithm. Both techniques have their advantages. The formant technique is more mature and has a lot of research findings to rely on while PSOLA technique is relatively new and has a bright prospect of development.

In the past, these two methods are basically developed independently. Nowadays many scholars start to investigate the relationship between them and try to combine the two techniques efficiently for the sake of generating more natural speech. For example, researchers in Tsinghua University have done research on applying the formant revision technique to the PSOLA algorithm and the improvement of the Sonic system. They have yielded Mandarin TTS system of higher naturalness.

TTS system that is based on waveform splicing has to meet at least the following four requirements during the course of splicing and prosodic manipulation so as to ensure better outcome:

a) The frequency spectrum has to be smooth in the boundary of the synthetic units.

b) Frequency should be kept constant during time scale modification (TSM).

c) Time should not be changed during pitch scale modification (PSM).

d) Modification on the amplitude of the synthetic unit should be linear.

### 7.6.3 Concept to speech system

Many problems have to be settled if authentic man-machine conversation is to be realized. The first problem is the overall process of the dialogue such as the completeness and the default of the dialogue, the comprehension of the speaker's intention, and the most suitable expression for the scene. The second problem is the treatment of the man-machine interaction such as the recovery after a speech recognition error and the prosodic generation of the output speech. These problems not only depend on the process of the IPS, but also depend on the dialogue per se. Therefore, it is necessary to design a speech interface that can handle these problems agilely and independent of IPS. Nevertheless, natural speech is very complicated and full of expression; moreover, representations vary with context. It is very difficult to modify natural sentence automatically in the interface. In short, the representation of information description is playing a decisive role.

Japan Osaka University has developed a Concept to Speech (CTS) system, which is a system with speech output from case structure representation (SCOS: http://www.zzrtu.com/jsj/).

The input of CTS is a concept description based on case structure and phrase model. The output of CTS is synthetic speech. Research of this level includes natural speech generation, prosodic modification and speech synthesis. First of all it has to generate prosodic-modified sentences from concept description and convert the sentences into speech output.

### 7.7 Auditory Scene Analysis

Auditory scene analysis was found by Cherry in 1953, which suggests that the auditory system of human can select and chase efficiently the voice of a certain person from the background of mingling sounds (the cocktail party effect). In the early 1990s, the famous hearing psychologist A.S. Bregman of Canada McGill University proposed this notion (Bregman, 1990). In 1995, B. Markus of Ruhr University & Bochum put forward a binaural model CASA method based on the binaural auditory characteristic of human (Markus, 1995). Researchers put the model in the front end of speech recognition in noisy environment and the result revealed that the front-end processing greatly improved the speech recognition outcome. In 1999, D. Godsmark & J. Brown of Britain Sheffield University brought forward the black board architecture for computational auditory scene analysis. Since 1990, scholars in China have started to do research on computational auditory scene analysis.

Auditory scene analysis aims to study how the auditory system organize and process the external stimulation. It has two tasks: one is to find out what can blend the spectrum elements together or sever them into separate auditory flows or acoustic features of representation; the other is to investigate the method of auditory grouping. Scene analysis comprises two stages: the first stage is the preliminary analysis based on gestalt principle, which classifies different sensory elements into its corresponding groups; the second stage is schema processing, which verifies and revises the perceptual organization. These two stages correspond to the bottom-up processing and top-down processing respectively.

### 7.7.1 Preliminary analysis

Preliminary analysis is an innate process which requires no participation of the conscious attention. The strategies of preliminary analysis are: first, the auditory signals are segregated into many independent units which correspond to the specific time domain and frequency domain in the spectrum. Then, these independent units were grouped together or separated. Grouping refers to the process that the auditory system perceives those speeches that are similar or contiguous in time as a whole and extract them from the complicate sound environment. Separation is to identify different sources of the sound or distinguish different sounds from the complicate sound environment. Grouping and separation are two sides of one coin. If there is the processing of grouping, then there is bound to be separation between flows. Preliminary analysis includes sequential integration and simultaneous integration. The former brings all the spectrums that appear in sequential order into a perceptual flow so as to calculate the serial characteristic of the sounds while the latter separates the elements that appear together and put them into different flows.

### 1. Sequential integration
In accordance with the proximity and similarity principle, sequential integration classifies the sounds that are adjacent in time or frequency into the same group.

There are two kinds of sequential integration: the first kind is the integration of sound series that are composed of two simple sounds of different pitch and appearing alternatively. The listener will perceive the sounds into two flows that are of different source and composed of low pitch and high pitch respectively. The other kind is the integration of sounds which have quite complicate frequency relationships. The two frequency-varied sounds are aligned in certain sequence so as to make a sound series. Whether the sound series can generate melody depends on the frequency relationship of the sounds. When the two sound sets are identical in frequency, the melody will disappear. However, if they belong to two non-overlapping frequency domains, then the melody generated will be perceived as an independent flow. There are two factors that play a decisive role in flow separation: the first is the alternating rate and the second is the frequency difference between the two alternating sounds. The series rate depends on the time span of the sounds. Bregman (Bregman, 1990) suggested that the time span is 35ms for the grouping effect. Darwin (Darwin, 1989) found that when a harmonic wave is advanced or lagged for 32ms, this harmonic wave will separate with the other harmonic wave. Dai et al  even maintained that listeners could follow commands to manipulate the time integration span in accordance with the specific task (Dai etc., 1995). Nevertheless, it is not yet settled as to which one is more important, the time span of frequency-identical sounds or the time span between two frequency-different sounds? Researches are still called for to solve this problem.

Other factors influencing sequential grouping are fundamental frequency, time proximity, shape of the spectrum, intensity and spatial location etc. these factors cooperate while at the same time compete during the course of grouping. If all the factors contribute to the grouping, it will be reinforced. For instance, the most remarkable effect happens when the spatial difference integrates with other factors. For another example, two sounds that only differ in loudness will not result in separation. However, if other differences are added, loudness may play a significant role.

## 2. Simultaneous integration

The harmonic wave of the sound are aligned linearly in the frequency domain while in the corresponding location of the basement membrane it is aligned in logarithmic distribution. In the logarithmic frequency units, there is a relatively long distance between the two low-frequency harmonic waves while the distance is relatively short between the two high-frequency harmonic waves. Therefore, the capturing of harmonic wave conforms to the following rules:

(1) in complex sounds, low-frequency harmonics are easier to be captured than high-frequency harmonics;

(2) spectrum units that contain odd harmonic are easier to be captured than spectrum units embracing continuous harmonic;

(3) it is easier to capture the harmonic that are rejected from the neighboring harmonic. Hereby, the bigger differences between the harmonic frequencies, the easier to capture the harmonic from the complex sounds.

Duifhuis et al. (Duifhuis etc., 1982) found that in pitch perception, the auditory system can reject the extra sounds from the complex sound, which works like a sieve to filter the information. This processing mechanism was referred to as harmonic sieve. Those harmonics that have similar frequencies can pass the sieve while the extra sounds are rejected. This effect manifests itself more prominently when it comes to low signal to noise ratio. The harmonic sieve serves as one mechanism for the formation of the flow, and it is functioning in a gradual manner rather than all-or-none. Under the condition of low imbalance ratio (3% $-8\%$), the harmonic wave can still pass the harmonic sieve. The harmonic sieve only works on discernable harmonics, which means that it can not totally reject the extra sound from the first formant frequency domain of the vowels. That is why the two can achieve partial integration.

Frequency modulation (FM) and amplitude modulation (AM) also affect the simultaneous integration. In FM, the auditory system perceptually disintegrates the simultaneous sound by using the range difference of FM. FM has two kinds: the first is arithmetical modulation, which adds the same frequency to every harmonic. After this is done, the harmonic relationship disappears, resulting in the separation of different components of the sound. The other kind is geometric modulation, i.e. every harmonic is multiplied by the same integer, which doesn't change the harmonic relationship but enlarge the distance between them. AM changes the amplitude of different spectrum location. This change, together with the time difference of arrival and vanishing, sheds impact on the flow separation. The simultaneous change of the amplitude can part the spectrums, which is in line with the neural activities. The simultaneous activities of the neurons, which correspond to different locations of the spectrum, last for a fairly short time. In every segment of the spectrum, corresponding neurons keep pace to pace while they are not in the same pace between segments. The recognition of sounds is realized by the perception of these synchronous changes in the segments. The processing of the space location information and frequency information is likely to be independent. Physiological research has found that if a cat's auditory cortex is impaired, it will lose the ability of space location judgment for certain frequency sound while it may still fairly judge the space location of other frequency sounds. The same phenomenon occurs in the human brain too. Additionally, man can simultaneously perceive two pure tones from different locations of different frequencies without confusing them. For instance, in the frequency range from 250 to 4000 Hz, it will not cause confusion when the biggest frequency difference is over 7%. Although the listeners perceive sounds of the two ears as two different sounds, they may integrate sounds of the two ears when the frequencies of the two sounds are rather approximate.

The difference between simultaneous integration and sequential integration is quite obvious. However, both integrations involve the basic feature of sound: time domain and frequency domain. Therefore, they are in isolation. In the perception of complex sounds, the two integrations work mutually and affect each other.

### 7.7.2 Perceptual organization based on schema

Listeners commit the specific sound signals of an environment (such as speech, music and other familiar sounds) into their memories, which establish themselves as cognitive units referred to as cognitive schemas. When the information pattern obtained by the auditory system is identical to the schema, the schema will be activated which may automatically lead to the prediction on the rest part of the pattern. Schemas may also be activated by other relevant patterns. Schema processing is a top-down process in which knowledge and attention play a crucial role.

### 1. The role of attention and knowledge
Schema processing requires selection of information, which is closely related to the state of attention. Voluntary attention is able to control the schema so that as long as the task requires the participation of attention, the schema will take place, which in turn result in schema-based separation. The auditory system can make use of the frequency cue to focus the attention on a specific range of frequency. Process with the participation of attention can easily disentangle a information flow while it is not qualified to integrate the information between the flows since

attention can only focus on one flow. The process of schema formation equals the process of obtaining knowledge about the stimulus. Taking advantage of the knowledge obtained, the listener can make predictions on the developing trend of the stimulus. If we listen to the same sound repeatedly, we will grasp its rule and form the schema. The knowledge of this rule will prepare us psychologically and integrate the series into the successive mental representation. Since the rule could easily attract one's attention, it shed considerable impact on the state of the contra flow. The trace rule effect has been most conspicuous in task with the participation of memory and likewise, trace-based organization effect increments with the increasing presentation of the stimulus. Auditory pattern recognition coexists with the activation of schema, with the latter affected by temporal rules and other regulations.

## 2. The processing of speech

The organization of speech can be classified into two forms: serial integration and simultaneous integration. Serial integration process integrates all the sequential parts of the word (or vowel) together, which forms the basis of word recognition. The prerequisite of serial integration is that the neighboring parts of the acoustic features (such as pitch, formant and fundamental frequency) come in continuity and demonstrate little difference. Speech flow separation is similar to the flow separation of non-speech, which is affected by the speech of the series, i.e. the faster the speed, the larger degree of flow separation. The other kind of speech organization is simultaneous integration. Generally, we are not dealing with a single sound while it frequently happens that we are only aware of one of the sounds. The reason for this is that our auditory system is capable of making simultaneous integration of many sounds to form a perceptual flow. In the course of simultaneous integration, fundamental frequency (or pitch) is an important cue. The greater they differ, the easier the separation. The same rule applies to the formant. In addition, the space location of the sound also plays a non-trivial role in simultaneous integration. Sounds from different locations are easier to be distinguished. Compared with the pattern of single sound, speech signal is not very stable since not only its fundamental frequency varies with the change of time, but the resonance sound in the oral cavity change synchronously with the fundamental frequency. Therefore, speech processing is more complicated than the speech perceptual process. During the course of the processing, there are both preliminary analysis and schema processing. Some preliminary analyses are only applicable to simple vowels or sounds that are similar to vowels, while complicate process like "cocktail party effect" is beyond their ability to explain. It will be much easier to explain from the aspect of schema process, i.e. the familiar sound or content activates the corresponding schema in the memory.

### 7.7.3 *The relationship between preliminary analysis and schema processing*

Preliminary analysis and schema processing are likely to compete with each other rather than functionally independent. Bregmanl (Bregman, 1990) suggested that:

(1) schema processing comes after preliminary analysis;

(2) information can be represented by schema through training and learning;

(3) schema does not take part in the flow formation process of auditory analysis;

(4) schema describes the typical attributes of the perceptual element no matter for consonants, vowels, syllables or other speech elements. Perceptual grouping based on gestalt principles is the outcome of low level processing. Information input of the auditory system is mostly messy, while this unordered fluctuation will be maximally undermined in the later stage of auditory information processing.

The two processes shed different impact on perception. Preliminary analysis separates the sensory information while schema processing selects the information rather than removes them from the compound sound. The grouping of preliminary analysis is symmetrical such that when it separates the treble from the bass, two independent flows take shape. Likewise, it can also separate two sounds from different locations and distinguish that one sound comes from the left while the other comes from the right. Nevertheless, schema processing does not possess this symmetric characteristic. In a noisy environment, we can easily discriminate our names while we can not tell when they appear and what the background sounds are. Therefore, the asymmetry of separation can be used to judge whether schema-based separation has appeared. The temporal scope of preliminary analysis and schema analysis are different too. Schema processing involves a larger time scope than preliminary analysis. Hence, we can safely conclude that preliminary analysis and schema analysis belongs to two different processes. The former is the first stage of scenario analysis and when it fails to interpret the speech organization process, the latter will take part. Combining the separation resulted from preliminary analysis and the schema processing can avoid or reduce the errors resulted from preliminary analysis and speech familiarity. The two process deals with the same sensory information while they differ in processing difficulty, with preliminary analysis more difficult than schema processing.

### 7.7.4 General evaluation of scenario analysis

Traditional hearing theories interpret the hearing process of human from the perspective of physiology such as the location theory, the traveling wave theory, the volley theory etc. however, scenario analysis applies the gestalt principle and schema process to the processing of auditory information from the aspect of psychological model. It treats auditory organization as a hierarchical processing course, enriching the theory of auditory organization. Scenario analysis also adopts the ecology concept to interpret the auditory organization process, therefore increments the eternal validity of the theory and makes it easier for actual application. Nevertheless, the theory still has some limitations both in the theory per se and its method.

### 1. The limitation of gestalt principles
The gestalt principles are effective when the grouping principles conflict with each other and could not lead to fusion. In contrary, if all the gestalt principles manipulate the separation process and thereby result in perceptual fusion, then non-gestalt principles will be bound to take part for the perceptual organization to be successfully completed. As the sounds articulated by every person has their unique characteristics, speech perception is more the process of recognizing complex sounds articulated by the vocal organ rather than grouping those simple sound pattern together. Additionally, former speech schema and other perceptual experiences should be resorted to so as to comprehend the meaning.

### 2. The role of schema
Bregman et al only summarized the research findings favorable for scenario analysis while ignoring negative research findings. It is very easy for the gestalt principles to be demonstrated in experiments while illustrating the role of the schema is quite a difficult job. Scenario analysis takes the schema process as omnipotent such at under whatever circumstance, all the phenomena that could not be explained by gestalt principles can be satisfactorily accounted for by it. This exaggerates the role of schema while at the same time neglects the

important characteristics of the schema per se. Moreover, the characteristics of schema such as level, size and interrelation are still waiting to be further exploited.

The resource of schema has a direct bearing on the knowledge of schema function. Compared with preliminary analysis, schema is obtained by learning. Chomsky maintained that it is extremely difficult to reinforce the speech of children, if not impossible. Therefore, schema may be totally the result of acquisition.

# Chapter 8

# Computational Linguistics

Language acquisition and language development is not only the precondition for man to acquire knowledge and accumulate experience but also the prerequisite for him to develop his mentality, particularly his abstract thinking. Language, the "material coat" of abstract thinking, comes out of human labor and hence is a social phenomenon. Labor together with language serves as the primary driving force of the generation of human thinking. Language is composed of speech sound (pronunciation), vocabulary and grammar. From various perspectives of language study, people have developed many branches of linguistics, such as sociolinguistics, pragmatics, psycholinguistics, neurolinguistics, mathematical linguistics and fuzzy linguistics, and so on.

## 8.1 The Properties of Language

A language is such a system in which speech sound serves as its material shell, vocabulary its construction material and grammar its structure rule. Generally speaking, we have spoken language and written language. Patterns of spoken language are sounds and those of written language are graphics. Spoken language is far more archaic than written language; people also first learn to speak and then write. The grammar of spoken language is simpler than that of written language, and spoken language has a smaller vocabulary accordingly.

Language is a most complicated, systemic and widely used symbol system. Language symbols can not only represent concrete things, status or action, but also denote abstract concepts. For example, "pen" and "book" refer to certain concrete things, "eat" and "drink" certain concrete actions, and "cold" and "hot" certain status. Concepts are thinking forms of special attributes used to characterize things. There is a close relation between concepts and words; the generation and existence of concepts must depend on words. Representation of things using words is based on the corresponding concepts stored in people's knowledge. So, words are the linguistic forms of concepts, and concepts are the contents of words. The word "people" show the concept of an animal that can make and use tools, can speak, can think and can walk upright by two feet. In different trades, areas and social settings, there are different terms which may not be understood completely. The meaning of language symbols changes greatly if different word order and combination happens. For example, the combination of "tooth" and "brush" is "toothbrush" which means a type of tool, but if we reverse the word order, "brush teeth" will be a certain movement. With the continuous development of social practice and man's improvement of his thinking power, our language is bound to have an increasingly abundant vocabulary with many new words and terms coming into being and some concepts and words being added new content as well.

As a special social phenomenon, language belongs to neither the economic base nor the superstructure. It comes into being for people's need of exchanging ideas in the process of productive labor. There is always a close relation between language and society. Sociolinguistics is a branch of leaning which studies the correlation between variation of language structure and change of social structure, and its main research contents are the following:

(1) Language and society. Explore the impact of social factors on language, and the impact of language factors on society.

(2) Variant of language. Explore how the change of the society causes the change in such aspects as vocabulary and grammar of a language.

(3) Variant of utterance. Find out various characteristics and differences of utterances in particular communication environment.

(4) Bilingual phenomenon. Explore the effect and restriction of factors such as society, psychology on language selection in the situation of using more than two languages alternatively by a community.

(5) Discourse Analysis. Analyze dialogues or conversations in communication; explore the conversational structure from the social, psychological, linguistic and situational perspectives and the inner relation between them, so as to expand the language study to the field of utterance study.

(6) Function of Language. Mainly explore the various functions of language in society, such as communicative function, ideational function and informative function, etc.

(7) Language policy. Make scientific language policy according to the need of social development, and build the discipline of language.

## 8.2 Language and Thinking

Thinking, as well as sensation and perception, is what the human brain reflects the objective reality. However, what the human brain reflects is not a specific feature, but rather the essential features shared by of a kind of things. The so-called indirect reflection means reflecting an objective thing through the media of other things.

The problem of relation between language and thinking is one of the most interesting and controversial topics in language study. Major views on it are listed below:

Behaviorism psychology thinks language and thinking are the same. Watson thinks there is no difference between talking to oneself and thinking; and he just regards thinking as the silent language. Later on, the new behaviorist Skinner thinks thinking is silent or obscure or faint speech act.

Another view is that language determines thinking. The psychologists who hold this view emphasize that factors such as activity, language and thinking are interwoven and moving forward as a whole. In other words, work and language generated in it are the main driving force of the outcome of thinking and human consciousness. Various activities and languages form the foundation of individual thinking. The thinking referred to here is the language thinking, which is a reflection of the intermediary with word to reality.

In 1930s, Ivan Pavlov, the famous Soviet Union physiologist, who studied the nervous system of reflective mechanism, put forward a theory that there are two kinds of signal systems in human brain. Pavlov divided the reaction namely reflex of human body with the participation of nervous system to the stimulation both in vitro and in vivo. In conditioned reflex, the various stimuli acting on people are divided into the first signal system and second signal system. All those concrete conditional stimuli which cause the temporary nervous connection are called the first signal. Temporary nervous connection system witch is caused on the cerebral cortex by the first signal is called the first signal system. Feeling hungry once smelling the appetizing dish is a first signal system activity. The first signal system is common in both people and animal. But people have second signal systems as well; it is the temporary nervous connection system which is caused on the cerebral cortex by the kind of signal such as languages. If one feels sour while eating red bayberry, he will feel sour when hearing others talk about red bayberry. This is the second signal system activity. Here, the reason of language substitution is there exist the above mentioned two kinds of signal systems in man's brain and the interaction between them. He says "if our sensation and presentation of the surrounding environment are the first signal in the reality for us, the concrete signal, the speech, first especially the sports stimulation go from speech organ to cerebral cortex are the second signal, namely the signal signals. They are the abstract of reality, and can be summarized. And this makes up man's peculiar advanced thinking, which creates common human experience first, and science finally, i.e. the tool which man uses to understood his surroundings and himself deeply."

Swiss psychologist Piaget (Jean Piaget) finds the emergence of logic thinking is earlier than the that of the language and speech by studying the origin history, the relation between language and thinking, trend of speech and thinking and comparing deaf-mute children to normal children. So he claims thinking determines language, and language consists of logic, while logical operation is belong to ordinary movement coordinating law, which controls all activities, including language itself. Piaget also admits the language plays an important role in turning movements into representation and thinking, but just one of many factors of influencing internalization.

We think that thinking and language are different concepts, but a close related entity. Thinking is a subjective image of the objective world, while language is the expression of this image. Man produces language for the need of cooperating in the process of work, and with the development of work and social interaction, human language develops and improves gradually, which leads to man's increasingly developed and improved thinking. The generalization of thinking is realized with the aid of word and language. People think by means of concepts, judgments and reasoning, thus to reflect the essence and laws of the nature. On the basis of sensation, perception and impression, people can form concepts reflecting the world by using the abstract function of language. Because we often use the same words to express the specific things in the same class, we could abstract the characterized attributes of these specific things. Such as "microcomputer" is a kind of small, low power dissipation, simple structure, easy-to-use and low price computer. For the language of generalizing, not only a generation can be connected, but different generations can be connected, thus to form the knowledge system, which make people's thinking is not merely a kind of general reflection, but a kind of indirect reflection with knowledge as intermediary.

## 8.3 Language Acquisition and Development

Language acquisition means the course of acquiring language, that is, how do children learn to use language. Behaviorism psycholinguistics with American psychologist Skinner as the major representative think that children's acquiring language is a course of response to the speech stimulus in the condition of outside reinforcement. And based on this, American linguist Bloomfield further proposes that speech habits of children's acquiring language are gradually formed in the repeated connection of material objects and speech stimuli. These scholars who explain language acquisition course from the basic principle of behaviorism psychology are generally known as the school of associationism.

Skinner thinks all behaviors from simple to complicated, including language, are acquired by study. Mankind has no behavior of doing things easily and naturally. According to the principle of Skinner's study theory, Jensen divides man's development of language into 6 stages.

(1) The study of connection between language stimulus and body response. Babies within one year old learn to respond to others' speech by making body movements. For example, a mother lets her child put down the ball in the hand, and s/he puts it down immediately. This is obviously the study of recognizing language stimulus. Babies in this stage make responses of movements to speech sound much more rapidly than to other sounds. This is the first step of language learning.

(2) The study of connection between object stimulus and speech response. Infants about 2 years old begin to learn to make speech response to various object stimuli. For example, infants like naming specific objects to prove that they have learned how to distinguish objects using different speech sounds.

(3) The study of connection between speech response and movement response and that between language thinking and movement response. Children of 3 years old begin to cultivate the language habit of doing when saying and doing when

thinking. For example, if a child says "chase", he chases accordingly. Children in this stage can use the sound or silent language to directly control their own behaviors, and in daily life, they can do as they tell themselves.

(4) The study of the connection between environment stimuli, language thinking and body responses etc. Children about 3 or 4 years old first learn to say to themselves while facing objects and then take action accordingly. After acquiring this kind of link, children can further add language to confirm whether their response to language thinking is correct or not. For example, a child finds there are crayon and paper on the desk, he thinks he can draw a picture. He will say "very excellent!" with smile after drawing on the paper with the crayon. This indicates that he is able to employ language response confirmation.

(5) The study of the chain of environment stimuli with the language thinking and body response etc. After learning to recognizing the stimulus, children of 4 years old will use language thinking to respond to the previous one, and then make body movement response. The response of one kind of language caused by another kind of language is called language association. Language association is a result of study, for example, people will think of "grass" when seeing "flower", think of "dish" when seeing "meal".

(6) The study of language stratum. This is the most complicated language study stage. Children learn to summarize words or sentences of lower stratum by using words or sentences of the higher stratum. For example, children begin to refer to apple, pear, banana and grape etc with the word "fruit" in general.

Is the language ability innate or acquired? Obviously, language acquisition can not go without learning. However, the anatomy oriented research of the language function and the study of children's language development suggest that language acquisition to a great extent is innate. The American linguist Chomsky studied the process of children's learning language, and refuted behaviorism theory with lots of evidences. He thinks, children are born with creative ability to develop their native language, i.e. linguistic competence. They can not only speak out but also understand sentences that they have never heard. He claims that linguistic competence is born, not made through the process of stimulus and response. In other words, language is a kind of structure with priori grammatical rules. He assumes man has an innate mechanism of acquiring language called language acquisition mode, which can be shown in Fig. 8.1. Linguistic competence in the figure refers to the ability of understanding and producing sentences.

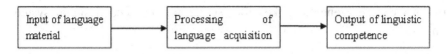

Fig. 8.1 Language acquisition mode

Chomsky thinks some priori grammatical rules can form our daily utterances via transformational programs. So, language is "deep structure", while utterance is "surface structure". "Surface structure" can perceive sound directly, while "deep structure" includes the basic grammatical relation and sentence meaning. There is a transformational rule between "deep structure" and "surface structure". For example, the active sentence "I use computer" and the passive sentence "The computer is used by me" has different surface structures with different utterances, but their deep structures are the same and express the same meaning. In Chomsky's eyes, man is born with the "language acquisition mechanism" in his brain. This mechanism can generate infinite sentences induced by few language materials. The foundation of proposing this innate mechanism is:

(1) Children can learn their native language not only unusually fast but also perfectly;

(2) Children have the same experience in grasp phonemes, especially order of sentence structure and the time of acquiring is roughly the same, but they live in different language environments;

(3) Though there are infinite utterances, there exist some basic and universal linguistic forms;

(4) Children are born with the ability of acquiring language by realizing or analyzing language program.

Chomsky holds that language develops from instinctive language into transformational grammar which comes from heredity. The variety of language behaviors is derived from this transformational rule.

Russian scholars consider language as motile, purposeful speech activity, and regard the speaking and listening course as an integral component in all systems of human activity, combining the psychological factors with social factors at the time of speech activity. In the research of speech acquisition, they base their study on Pavlov's conditioned reflex theory, especially his "two kinds of signal systems". They study how a word can replace a concrete object signal to obtain the function of "the signal of the signal", and how a speech system can be formed between words. It generally takes four stages for the second signal system to form and develop:

(1) Direct object stimulus →direct response
(2) Word stimulus →direct response
(3) Direct object stimulus →word response
(4) Word stimulus → word response

Russian psychologists think the speech communication between children and adults plays an extremely important role in children's speech development. Children grasp speech in the course of communicating with adults, and they gradually acquire their own speech independence, which in turn becomes a powerful tool to regulate their behaviors.

## 8.4 Language Processing in Brain

Man uses language to exchanges ideas, to think and to reason. It is confirmed now that language function is orientated in the left hemisphere of the brain. The asymmetry hemisphere structure related to language function appeared as early as 300,000 years ago in the history of human evolution. Man's language potential seems to have already existed when he is born. The universal features of language are thought to partly originate from the special structure of the area of language relevant cortex in the left hemisphere. Biologically speaking, commanding a language is not a single ability, but a group of abilities, such as understanding and expressing. The ability of understanding and expressing is located in the different areas of left hemisphere pallium.

Language is formed by limited groups of sounds ordering according to meaning array in law. Man can emit a variety of sounds, but each of the language in the world is only based on a few of these sounds. The sound that each language uses is by no means the same. The sound which makes up the language is called the phoneme. The pronunciation difference between phonemes can be very slight, such as d and t. In the natural language, phonemes combine together and form words (morphology); words combine together and form phrases and sentences (grammar). In the simple symbol system, the meaning of symbols is related to the highly particular situation. But language is different. It offers the approaches of modeling and exchanging abstract concepts, and these abstract meanings are independent of the instant situation. Language contains the content of emotion, and is supported by some extra-linguistic devices such as gestures, tones, facial expressions and postures etc. Different languages have their different content structures. Basically speaking, language is a tool for social communication. Language is not only the neutral media of exchanging outside world facts and phenomena but is also used to organize sensory experience, and express thought, emotion and expectation.

How human language originated always remains a question that people are interested in. There are two kinds of hypothesis about the origin of language i.e. the gesture hypothesis and pronunciation hypothesis. The gesture hypothesis claims that the language is evolved by the gesture system. When some anthropoids begin to walk upright, their hands are liberated and engaged in social communication, thus the gesture system appears. Subsequently, the appearance of sound communication liberates hands out to serve other purposes. Pronunciation hypothesis holds that the language is evolved by various instinct cry (for example, those cries to show depression, happiness and sex awakening etc). About 100,000 year ago, the structural changes of anatomy such as mouth and sound channel, make it possible to consciously control various sound production. And then, in theory at least, sounds can be combined and used creatively. The ancestors of mankind scatter in different inhabited regions, and the separation of these regions results in the development of different pronunciation systems. Language may happen at once in human being evolution. This can explain why there are so many features shared by all human languages. In addition, language may come from the common evolution of gesture and pronunciation. This kind of possibility may explain why verbal language and gesture orientate in the same side of cerebral hemisphere (left hemisphere).

It is believed by linguists and psychologists that the universal mechanism of language acquisition is determined by the human brain structure. According to this view, the development of the brain makes people have the ability of learning and using language, and specific languages, dialects and accents that people use are decided by social environment. Figure 8.2 provides the Wernicke-Geschwind model of language information processing of the brain (Mayeux etc. 1991).

Wernicke-Geschwind model A provides us with the main gyrus and area related to language in the left hemisphere. Wernicke language area lies at the back of superior temporal gyrus, close to the auditory cortex. Broca language area nears the face representing area of sport cortex. The access which joins Wemicke area and Broca area is called arcuate fascicle. Wernicke-Geschwind model B provides us with the Brocdmann area of left hemisphere. Area 41 is elementary auditory cortex, area 22 Wernicke language area, area 45 Broca

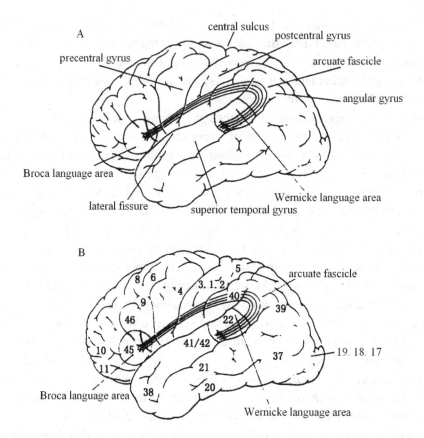

Fig. 8.2 Wernicke-Geschwind model of language information processing of the brain

language area and area 4 elementary sport cortex. According to the initial Wernicke-Geschwind model, when people hear a word, the information reaches the corpora geniculatum internum through the acoustic nerve from basilar membrane, then reaches to the elementary auditory cortex (the Brodmann area 41), then to senior auditory cortex (area 42), and then transfers to gyrus angularis (area 39).

The gyrus angularis is a particular area of vertex - temporal - pillow cortex, and is thought to be related with information integration of the incoming of hearing, vision and feeling. Therefore, the information reaches to Wernicke area (area 22), and then reaches to Broca area (area 45) through arcuate fascicle. In Broca area, the perception of language is translated into grammatical structure of phrases, and the memory of how to sound the word clearly is stored. Then, messages of the voice mode of the phrase is transmitted to the facial expression of sport cortex about controlling pronunciation, thus the word can be spoken out clearly.

According to Wernicke-Geschwind model, very useful predictions of clinically can be made:

(1) Prophesy the consequence caused by Wernicke area damages. Language information reaching to audition cortex can not activate Wernicke area, therefore it cannot be understood. If the damage expands to the rear and below and exceeds Wernicke area, processing of visual language input will be influenced. As a result, the patient is unable to understand spoken language or written language.

(2) This model has prophesied correctly that the damage of Broca area will not influence the understanding of spoken language and written language, but it can cause serious obstacles of generating sentences and words, for the sound mode and structural mode of language can't reach to the sport cortex.

(3) This model prophesy that damage of arcuate fascicle will cut off the connection between Wernicke area and Broca area, and thus affect words generation, for the hearing inputs cannot be transmitted to the brain area which participate in language generation.

Though Wernicke-Geschwind model is still useful on clinic, the research of cognition and brain imaging carried out by Damasio, Raichle and Posner etc shows Wernicke-Geschwind model is too simple. Language function involves many brain areas with complicated connection between them, which can not be generalized by Broca area and Wernicke area with their connection. Language obstacle is never as simple as what Wernicke-Geschwind model predicted. So far, Figure 8.3 is a relatively ideal model (Mayeux etc. 1991).

A research group of Tokyo University in Japan found that a special part of the Broca area in the front of brain cortex is responsible for grammar, and another area administers the disposal of vocabulary. At the time of testing of 16 university boy students' grammar and vocabulary, researchers used zeugmatography (MRI) to observe their brains' activity. They find that a part close to left temple of Broca area is in an active state when judging the grammar and an even farther area is stimulated on the occasion of memorizing words. The part of human brain responsible for grammar contains organization which does not exist in the monkey brain, and this may help to explain why only man can use the complicated language. This discovery will help people to understand diseases such as aphasia and dementia deeply.

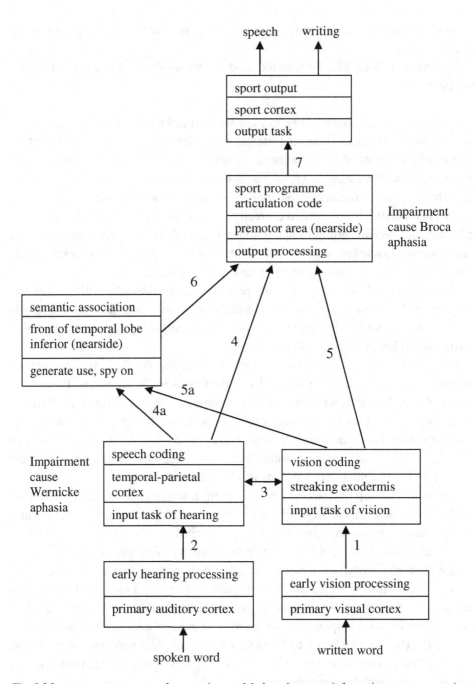

Fig. 8.3 Language message neural processing model about language information nerve processing

Only the cognitive part of language is discussed above. However, human communication has important emotion compositions too. These compositions include music syntax and emotion posture. Some emotion compositions of language depend on the special disposal of the right hemisphere. The lose of language emotion compositions caused by damage in the right hemisphere is called prosody deletion. The organization of prosody disposal in the right hemisphere corresponds to the organization of cognitive respect of language in the left hemisphere. Whether patients with damage in the front of their right hemisphere are sad or happy, their intonations are always singsong when speaking. And patients with damage in the back of their right hemisphere can't understand others' emotion composition in language.

## 8.5 Cognition of language

Psycholinguistics is new branch of science developing from the combination of psychology and linguistics, and it has a history of only half a century so far. Its initial research was mainly dominated by behaviorism thought, and most researches were explorations of human language behaviors from the view of stimulus – response. It was believed that language behavior is nothing but a set of habits formed gradually through stimulating, responding and reinforcing. In 1960's, Chomsky (N. Chomsky) put forward his theory of transformational-generative grammar and the concepts of surface structure and deep structure. Later on, the study on psychological reality to prove Chomsky's sentence structure theory became the mainstream in psycholinguistics research.

In 1970s, researchers began to pay attention to studying the sentence meaning while continuing to study how sentence structure cognizes and processes. The research focus gradually shifted from single sentence to paragraph or text. "Sentence processing" and "text processing" form two major biggest sub-fields of psycholinguistics. Current research focuses on the following problems.

### 8.5.1 The probability and restraint problems in sentence processing

From the beginning of 1970s to the end of 1980s, most guiding ideology of sentence processing research is: The syntax processing of sentence is prior to and independent of its semantic processing. Research with various sentence structures does not take the influence of other factors into consideration. At that time, the central issue of psycholinguistics was: How does syntactic representation of sentence form? Its purpose is to build a kind of model that can produce the syntactic structure of sentences.

1990s witnessed new viewpoint, that is, the computational process of syntactic structure utilizes "restriction" of different information, including semantic information and information about the frequency of syntactic structure appearing in the real language (Trueswell etc., 1994). This restraint model assumes that each entry of the psychological dictionary has the following information:

(1) The presumable parameter of a certain word, i.e. the particular compositions related to the word;

(2) The possible type of sentence structure, such as transitive and intransitive;

(3) The frequency of certain parameter and sentence structure taking place in the real language behavior.

For example, the word "eat" may have an agent who eats and a theme, that is, what to be eaten; and there are two possible sentence structures, i.e. transitive and intransitive. Frequency is related to each parameter or each sentence structure; for example, "eat" is often used in transitive structure, and seldom in the intransitive structure.

As to the model based on restriction of syntax processing, the appearing frequency of syntax structure is an important theoretical foundation. The more a structure appears in the language, the easier it is to be processed. But, how it works in fact remains unclear now.

The probability and restriction problems of language processing initiated many scholars' thinking over theoretical questions concerning language. For over 30 years, the study about language nature and theory was dominated by Chomsky's thought all the time. Chomsky's supposition of "linguistic competence" claims that the language knowledge that people have is grammar. This kind of knowledge is often tacit, and we know what is but do not know why it is so. This kind of tacit language knowledge is called "linguistic competence". This view excludes other factors which influence the language activity, such as the properties of sensory system, memory ability and the function of reasoning ability. It also excludes the function of statistical probability in the cognitive processing of language. The supposition also thinks language acquisition must be explained through how children obtain this kind of language ability. Why children can learn language so quickly and why they can speak out what never have been heard lies in that grammatical knowledge is innate in nature, and the function of acquired experience is only to make children grasp the vocabulary and set up the particular parameter.

The appearance of neural network promoted the study on statistical probability of language; the neural network emphasizes extracting the structural regularity from the random data and considering the weight as the code of probability restriction to prior experience, which determines the activity mode of the network. This characteristic is in fact related to how children obtain language in natural condition. The applying statistical approach to speech recognition and machine translation, etc, has also promoted people to pay attention to the statistical probability of language. The psycholinguists begin to pay more attention to studying of connection between statistical probability information and language acquisition, as well as language comprehension. For example, sentence ambiguity is a very complicated problem, but the ambiguity can often be solved quickly through utilizing various probability restrictions which are got from previous language experience. For example, in sentence "The plane left for the east coast", there are multiple meanings of both the word *plane* and *left*, but when the two words appear together in the same sentence, the former is very likely to be *plane* , while the latter the past tense of *leave*.

So, there appeared a new point of view. It denies that the idealized grammatical ability should be the starting point of language study, but emphasizes that we should explain the nature of language by making it clear how language is acquired and used to represent facts in brain (Seidenberg, 1997). This view holds the following to be true. First, children are learning and using language instead of recognizing and identifying the inborn grammatical ability. Second, children can automatically encode the statistical characteristics of the speech uttered by people around them. Third, the mechanism of multiple probability restrictions plays a key role in children's grasping language. This view means that we get back to empiricism again; however, it does not deny that children are born to have certain condition that makes it possible to learn a language. For example, brain tissue with its function instead of grammatical knowledge can restrain language acquisition.

### 8.5.2 Text representation and memory

In the 1970s and 1980s, most researches about text processing involve the problem whether certain reasoning is encoded when the text is read. For example, while reading "the frog sits on the plank, and the fish swims below the plan", we are asked "Does the fish swim below the frog?", a reasoning question. But here methodology remains as a question, i.e. we can not distinguish the reasoning is carried out while reading or testing. In order to ensure the reasoning happens in the course of reading, the researcher needs to design new experimental procedure. For that purpose, two views from memory study are introduced:

(1) Memory depending on clue of E. Tulving, i.e. the clue activates the information of long-term memory directly, and selectively (Tulving, 1974);

(2) M.I. Posner's dividing of the fast, automatic cognitive processing and the slow, tactful cognitive possessing (Posner, 1978).

Therefore, people adopt the fast single word recognition procedure to examine the reasoning process. Its typical experiment situation is: After reading a sentence, the tested is shown a test word and is asked to confirm as soon as possible whether the word appears in the sentence or not. For example, given the sentence "the cleaner sweeps the floor in the classroom" and a test word "broom", if the reasoning of the cleaner using the broom to sweep the floor is encoded, the tested will generate a fast positive response. In the process, the tested is not given any particular purpose to encode a particular type of information, so it is strategy-free. Therefore, this kind of response reflects the encoded information in reading, not the reasoning formed in the course of slow tactics while being tested. The ongoing reasoning is based on the information in memory being activated quickly, concurrently and automatically. In the 1990s, the study of text processing is characterized by distinguishing the instant and passively formed reasoning from the reasoning which needs reader's processing tactics.

The term resonance is originally used to describe Tulving's view of abstraction depending on clue, and J. L. Meyers et al. use it to describe the way of a word or phrase activating relevant information from general knowledge (lexical knowledge, world knowledge) (Meyers, 1994). In fact, a word not only activates its own meaning, but also the information of its relation with other concepts. For example, "stuff" means we can't fill in other things any more, but "fill" doesn't have this meaning. Some verbs imply causality, such as "irritate" and "envy". The former hints the agent of the verb is the cause of "being angry", while the latter implies the cause of "envy" is the object of the verb. Recent research indicates that this kind of causality verbs can quickly and automatically activate the lecical information of the parameter that may be regarded as its cause.

The context integration model put forward by W. Kintsch is a concrete example of this kind of thought (Kintsch, 1988). This model holds that words in the text activate the relevant concepts in memory, and the activations go back and forth among these concepts; if the concepts in text and memory possess multiple strong connections, the concepts will be highly activated; if there are only weak and few connections, the concepts may not be activated or decline themselves. As a result, the information in text and the relevant information in long-term memory are combined fast, and automatically to form the meaning representation of text. So, this is a kind of comprehension course based on memory.

### 8.5.3 Module theory and language processing

Fodor (J.A. Fodor) put forward the module theory (Fodor, 1988), and it has attracted people's attention just as physical symbol theory, artificial neural network theory, psychological. Ecology theory has done. The cognitive module is defined as a kind of fast, compelling and closed information process. The most prominent feature of the cognitive module is the closeness of information process, i.e. module activity and its output are not affected by other information. In the view of cognitive module theory, language processing system is composed of a series of modules separating from each other in function; each module is an independent processing unit; processing is automatic and compelling; this course is free of other modules. For example, the lexical processing or syntactical processing is independent; its processing is not affected by high-level factors such as sentence or context etc.

The main basis of the module theory comes from the modularity of the language cognitive processing. For example, the lack of inanimate effect can be considered as an example to show syntactical analysis is a kind of cognitive module process (Ferreira etc., 1986):

(1) The evidence examined by the lawyer......
(2) The defendant examined by the lawyer......

These two compound sentences include compressed relation clauses. The animality or inanimacy of the main nouns in the sentence may hint whether they can be the subjects of the following verbs or not. In sentence (1), if inanimacy information is involved in the syntax analysis, readers will confirm the following verb not to be the main verb of the sentence easily, but the verb of the compressed clause. So, the appearance of the following "by" phrase is natural, causing no difficulty in understanding. But relevant experiments indicate that the time readers spend reading this "by" phrase is the same as the time that readers spends in reading the phrase "by" in sentence (2), which suggests that the inanimacy of main noun does not enter into the syntax analysis process of the verb. Certainly, there is dispute for this in some way. In addition, the special language damage phenomenon observed in neurolinguistics also supports module theory.

The cognitive module theory can easily connect psychology with neurophysiology, and neuroanatomy, and it also connects certain cognitive process with particular brain structure and function course, but it ignores the interaction with environment and context. The modularity of psychology is a noticeable question for understanding the relation between cognition and brain. The relation of the calculation and modularity of cognition in theory and practice is a question that asks for the experiment study of psychology and cognitive nerve science to answer. And psycholinguistics may have significant contribution in this respect.

### 8.5.4 Inhibition mechanism in language understanding

The structure building framework proposed by M.A. Gernsbacher is a comparatively famous language understanding model (Gernsbacher, 1990), which believes that the purpose of understanding is to build a coherent psychological token or structure, and the building material of the token is memory cells. This building process includes three steps. First, laying a foundation, namely form a cadre according to initial input information. Second, mapping, namely when new input information is consistent to the foregone information, then mapping it into the foundation to develop the former structure. Third, transferring, namely when new input information is not consistent to the foregone information, then begin to build a new substructure. Thus, most of psychic structures are composed of substructures of some branches. During the process of building structure, there are two kinds of mechanisms to control the activation level of memory cells. One is strengthening, namely the improvement of the activation level of the information whose structure is consistent to the structure which is being built. The other is inhibition, namely the voluntary decline of the activation level of the information whose structure is not consistent to the structure which is being built. This theory emphasizes that inhibiting inappropriate information and interferential information are the foundations of effective comprehension. The efficiency of inhibition mechanism may be the important reason of the individual differences in the ability to understand language.

Relevant researches preliminarily show that inhibition mechanism is different in two cerebral hemispheres. The inhibition for inappropriate information may be mostly happen in the left cerebral hemisphere. The left cerebral hemisphere maybe lead the integration process, which inhibits inappropriate meaning according to the contexts and selects appropriate meaning to realize the integration with the former information. The responsibility of the right cerebral hemisphere is to make many kinds of information keep activated so that the left cerebral hemisphere can choose appropriate meaning (Faust, 1996). Thus, each of the two cerebral hemispheres maybe has a relatively independent semantic system. If that is true, some existing language understanding models need to be revised. But at present the evidences are still insufficient, we need to carry out further experimental studies.

At present there are still many disputes in the important issues studied by the above contemporary psycholinguistic. Recently some scholars advocate the research on Large Corpora. They claim to check up all kinds of theoretical systems using empirical data which is offered by large corpora. And they emphasize the importance of the frequency of language structure and concept combination in language processing. They also highlight to keep the naturality of the materials used during the experiments as much as possible. This is also a trend of the research development of psychological linguistic.

## 8.6 Chomsky's Formal Grammar

In computer science, formal language is a set of some finite strings in a certain alphabet. But formal grammar is a method to describe the set. Formal grammar is so named just because that it is similar to the grammar of human natural language. The most common classification system of grammar is Chomsky hierarchy developed by Chomsky in 1950s. The classification hierarchy divides all grammars into four types: phrase structure grammar, context sensitive grammar, context free grammar and regular grammar. Any language can be expressed by the unrestricted grammar. And the language classifications corresponding to the three remaining grammars are recursive-enumerable language, context free language and regular language respectively (Chomsky, 1957). According to the ordering, the four grammars have stricter and stricter production rules in turn. The language which can be expressed is also less and less. Context free grammar and regular grammar are the most important grammars for their high-efficiency realization, though the express ability of the above two grammars is weaker than phrase structure grammar and context sensitive grammar.

### *8.6.1 Phrase structure grammar*

Phrase structure grammar (Type-0 grammar) is an unrestricted grammar. It is an important grammar in formal language theory. Phrase structure grammar is a quadruple $G = (\Sigma, V, S, P)$, where $\Sigma$ is a finite alphabet of terminals, $V$ is a finite alphabet of non-terminals, $S (\in V)$ is a begin symbol, $P$ is a finite non-empty set of productions, the form of productions in $P$ is $\alpha \rightarrow \beta$, where $\alpha \in (\Sigma \cup V)^* V (\Sigma \cup V)^*$, $\beta \in (\Sigma \cup V)^*$. Phrase structure grammar is also called Type-0 grammar. There is not any restricting for $\alpha$ and $\beta$, so phrase structure is also called unrestricted grammar. The language which is produced by Type-0 grammar is the same as the language which is accepted by Turing machine. This language is called Type-0 language ($L_0$) or recursively enumerable language (Lre).

For example, $G = (\{a\}, \{, [, ], A, D, S\}, S, P)$, where $P = \{S \rightarrow [A],$ $[\rightarrow [D, D] \rightarrow], \ DA \rightarrow AAD, [\rightarrow \wedge,] \rightarrow \wedge, A \rightarrow a\}$. Obviously, G is phrase structure grammar, and the language produced by $G : L(G) = \{a^{2^n} \mid n \geq 0\}$ is Type-0 language.

The closure property of Type-0 language in some algebraic operations is shown in Table 8.1. Some results of decision problems are shown in Table 8.2, where D denotes decidable, U denotes undecidable, G denotes grammar, L denotes language.

The standard form of phrase structure grammar is: $A \rightarrow \xi, A \rightarrow BC, A \rightarrow \wedge,$ $AB \rightarrow CD$, where $\xi \in (\Sigma \cup V)$, $A, B, C, D \in V$, $\varnothing$ is an empty word.

Some restrictions are made on productions in phrase structure grammar to get context sensitive grammar, context free grammar and regular grammar.

Table 8.1 The closure property of $\pounds_0$, $\pounds_1$ in algebraic operation

| Algebraic operation \ Language | $\pounds_0$ | $\pounds_1$ |
|---|---|---|
| union | √ | √ |
| link | √ | √ |
| closure | √ | √ |
| complement | × | ? |
| intersection | √ | √ |
| intersect with regular grammar | √ | √ |
| inversion | √ | √ |
| permutation | √ | × |

Note: √ denotes closure, × denotes not closure, ? denotes unresolved.

Table 8.2 The decision problem of $\pounds_0$, $\pounds_1$

| Decision problem \ Language | $\pounds_0$ | $\pounds_1$ |
|---|---|---|
| $\forall x \in L(G)$? | U | D |
| $L(G_1) \subset L(G_2)$? | U | U |
| $L(G_1) = L(G_2)$? | U | U |
| $L(G) = \varnothing$? | U | U |
| $L(G) =$ infinite set? | U | U |
| $L(G) = \sum{}^{*}$? | U | U |

## 8.6.2 *Context sensitive grammar*

Context sensitive grammar is an important grammar in formal language theory. It is a quadruple $G = (\Sigma, V, S, P)$, where $\Sigma$ is a finite alphabet of terminals, $V$ is a finite alphabet of non-terminals, $S(\in V)$ is a begin symbol, $P$ is a finite non-empty set of productions, the form of productions in P is $\alpha A\beta \rightarrow \alpha\gamma\beta$, where $A \in V$, $\alpha, \beta \in (\Sigma \cup V)^*$, $\gamma \in (\Sigma \cup V)^+$. Context sensitive grammar is also called Type-1 grammar. The intuitive meaning of productions is that $A$ can be replaced by $\gamma$ in the context whose left is $\alpha$ and right is $\beta$. The language produced by context sensitive grammar is called context sensitive language or Type-1 language, which is often denoted by L1.

**Monotone grammar**

If all the productions of grammar $G = (\Sigma, V, S, P)$ is $\alpha \to \beta$ and $|\alpha| \le |\beta|$, where $\alpha \in (\Sigma \cup V)^* V (\Sigma \cup V)^*$, $\beta \in (\Sigma \cup V)^+$, then we call it monotone grammar. Monotone grammar can simplify the right maximum length of any productions in P to 2, namely if $\alpha \to \beta \in P$, then $|\beta| \le 2$. It has been proved that the language which is produced by monotone grammar is the same as Type-1 language, namely it is the same as context sensitive language. Thus some literatures take the definition of monotone grammar as the definition of context sensitive grammar. For example,

$$G = (\{a, b, c\}, \{S, A, B\}, S, P)$$

where $P = \{S \to aSAB \mathbin{/} aAB, BA \to AB, \quad aA \to ab, bA \to bb, bB \to bc,$ $cB \to cc\}$, obviously, $G$ is monotone grammar, so it is also context sensitive grammar. The language produced by $G : L(G) = \{a^n b^n c^n \mid n \ge 1\}$ is context sensitive language.

The standard form of context sensitive grammar is: $A \to \xi$, $A \to BC$, $AB \to CD$, where $\xi \in (\Sigma \cup V)$, $A, B, C, D \in V$. Context sensitive language is the same as the language which is accepted by linear bounded automat. The closure property of operation and some results of decision problems in Type-1 language refer to Table 8.1 and Table 8.2 introduced in phrase structure grammar. We need to point out specially that if complementary operation has closure property in Type-1 language is an unresolved problem hitherto.

### 8.6.3 Context free grammar

Context free grammar is an important transformational grammar in formal language theory. It is called Type-2 grammar in Chomsky layers. And the language produced by context free grammar is named context free language or Type-2 language, which has important applications in grammar description of program design language.

Context free grammar (CFG for short) can be transformed to one of two kinds of simple normal forms. Namely any context free language (CFL for short) can be produced by either of the two kinds of standard CFG. One is Chomsky normal form whose production form is $A \to BC$ or $A \to a$. Another is Greibach normal form whose production form is $A \to aBC$ or $A \to \alpha$, where $A, B, C \in V$, is Non-terminals; $a \in \Sigma$, is Terminal; $a \in \Sigma^*$, is Terminal string.

There are a variety of derivation manners to generate language from grammar. For example, there maybe are two kinds of derivations for $\{S \to AB, A \to a, B \to b\}$: $S \Rightarrow AB \Rightarrow aB \Rightarrow ab$ and $S \Rightarrow AB \Rightarrow Ab \Rightarrow ab$. If every time we choose the leftmost non-terminals to derive, such as previous form of last example, then it is called left derivation. If we can get the identical result by two different left derivations, then we say that the grammar is ambiguous. On the contrary, we say the grammar is unambiguous. We may find an equivalent unambiguous grammar to generate identical language for some ambiguous grammar. The language without unambiguous grammar is called essential ambiguous language. For instance, $\{S \to A, S \to a, A \to a\}$ is an ambiguous grammar. $L = \{a^m b^n c^n \mid m, n \geq 1\} \cup \{a^m b^m c^n \mid m, n \geq 1\}$ is essential ambiguous language. The automata accepting CFL is called push down automata. The languages accepted by certain and uncertain push down automata are called certain CFL and uncertain CFL respectively. The former is a real subset of the latter. For example, $L = \{a^n b^n \mid n \geq 1\} \cup \{a^n b^{2n} \mid n \geq 1\}$ is an uncertain CFL rather than a certain CFL.

For arbitrary positive integer n, let $\Sigma_n = \{a_1, \cdots, a_n\}$, $\Sigma_n' = \{a_1', \cdots, a_n'\}$, Chomsky transformational grammar $G = (\Sigma, V, S, P)$ is defined as $(\Sigma_n \cup \Sigma_n', \{S\}, S, \{S \to S_{a_i} S_{a_i}' S \mid 1 \leq i \leq n)$. The language generated by this grammar is called Daike set. If regarding $a_i$ as an opening parenthesis, and regarding $a_i'$ as a closing parenthesis, then n-dimensions Daike set $D_n$ is a matched sequence set which is composed of n kinds different parentheses pairs. Such as, $a_1 a_2 a_2' a_2' a_1'$ and $a_1 a_1' a_2 a_2' a_1 a_1'$ both belong to $D_2$.

Daike set is a tool which enlarge regular language family to context free language family. For arbitrary context free language L, there must exist two homomorphic mapping $h_1$ and $h_2$ and a regular language R, which make $L = h_2[h_1^{-1}(D_2) \cap R]$ hold, where $D_2$ is two-dimensions Daike set, and vice versa.

Furthermore, context free language family is a minimum language family which contains $D_2$ and has closure property in three kinds of algebraic operations: homomorphism, inverse homomorphism, and regular language intersection.

Since context free grammar is widely used to describe the grammar of program design language, so what's more important is to get sub-grammar of context free grammar from the angle of mechanism implementation grammar decomposition.

The most important kind is unambiguous context free grammar, because unambiguity is vital for decomposing grammar of computer language. In unambiguous context free grammar the important subclass is $LR(k)$ grammar. It only demands to look ahead k symbols so that it can make correct left-to-right grammar decomposition. $LR(k)$ grammar can describe all the certain context free language. But, for arbitrary $K > 1$, because the language generated by $LR(k)$ grammar is sure to be generated by an equivalent $LR(1)$ grammar, the language generated by $LR(0)$ grammar is a proper subclass of the langrage generated by $LR(1)$ grammar.

### 8.6.4 Regular grammar

Regular grammar rooted from the study of natural language by N. Chomsky in 1950's. It is Type-3 grammar in Chomsky phrase structure grammar layers. Regular grammar is the proper subclass of context free (Type-2) grammar, which has already been applied in design of compiler in computer programming language, lexical analysis(the text mode to describe the triggering process action in text-processing, file type, and scanner, standard base of text tool), design of switched circuit, syntactic pattern recognition and so on. Regular grammar is a thesis which cannot be ignored by Computer and Information Science, engineering, physics, chemistry, biology, medicine and applied mathematics.

Regular grammar has many kinds of equivalent definitions. We could use "left linear regular grammar" or "right linear regular grammar" to equivalently define regular grammar. "Left linear regular grammar" demands that the left of production only contains one non-terminal, and the right of production only contains empty string, a terminal or a non-terminal followed by a terminal. "Right linear regular grammar" demands that the left of production only contains one non-terminal, and the right of production only contains empty string, a terminal or a terminal followed by a non-terminal.

Left linear regular grammar is a quadruple $G = (\Sigma, V, S, P)$, where $V$ is a finite set of variable, $\Sigma$ is a finite set of terminals, $S \in V$, $S$ is beginning symbol, $w \in \Sigma^*$ ($w$ is a string connected by a finite terminal or a word, and may be empty string or empty word $\varepsilon$). When $A, B \in V$, $P$ is a finite set which is composed by the productions: $A \rightarrow w$ and $A \rightarrow wB$ ($A \rightarrow Bw$). Right linear regular grammar and left linear regular grammar are equivalent, namely they can generate the same language class (word set).

The structure and complexity measure of regular grammar are decided by variable, number of productions and height of grammar digraph, number of nodes in every layer. $S \overset{*}{\underset{G}{\vdash}} w$ shows that using productions in P within limited times can derive word w. Regular grammar G could be used as generator to generate and describe regular language $L(G) = \{w \in \Sigma^* \mid S \overset{*}{\underset{G}{\vdash}} w\}$ . For example, $G = (\{S, A, B\}, \{0,1\}P, S), P = \{S \to 0A \mid 0, A \to 1B, B \to 0A \mid 0\}$ , G is a regular grammar (right linear regular grammar), $L(G)$ contains word 0, $(S \to 0)$ , $01010(S \to 0A \to 01B \to 010A \to 0101B \to 01010)$ . Regular language is also called regular set, and it may be expressed by regular expression. For arbitrary regular expression, we can construct non-deterministic finite automata (NFA) with ε action to accept it in linear time, and we also can construct deterministic finite automata (DFA) without ε action to accept it in quadratic time. The language generated by regular grammar can be also accepted by bidirectional deterministic finite automata (2DFA). NFA, DFA and 2DFA are equivalent, namely they accept the same languages.

The recursive definition of regular expression is that, let Σ is a finite set,

(1) $\varnothing, \varepsilon$ and $a(\forall a \in \Sigma)$ are regular expressions on Σ, they express empty set, empty symbol $\{\varepsilon\}$ and set $\{a\}$ respectively;

(2) If α and β are regular expressions on Σ, then $\alpha \cup \beta$ , $\alpha \bullet \beta = \alpha\beta$ and $\alpha^*$ are also regular expressions on Σ , they express word set $\{\alpha\}$ , $\{\beta\}$ , $\{\alpha\} \cup \{\beta\}$ , $\{\alpha\}\{\beta\}$ and $\{\alpha\}^*$ respectively, operator $\cup, \bullet, *$ respectively express union, link and power. Power closure $\{\alpha\}^* = \{\bigcup_{i=0}^{\infty} \alpha^i\}$), their priority is $*, \bullet, \cup$ ;

(3) Only the expressions decided by limited using (1) and (2) are regular expressions on Σ. Only word set expressed by regular expressions is regular set on Σ. For example 1, the word set generated by regular grammar, its regular expression is 0. For simplifying regular expression, we usually use following equations:

a) $\alpha \cup \alpha = \alpha$ (idempotent law);

b) $\alpha \cup \beta = \beta \cup \alpha$ (commutative law);

c) $(\alpha \cup \beta) \cup \gamma = \alpha \cup (\beta \cup \gamma)$ (associative law);

d) $\alpha \cup \varnothing = \alpha$, $\alpha \varnothing = \varnothing \alpha = \varnothing$, $\alpha \varepsilon = \varepsilon \alpha = \alpha$ (zero one law);

e) $(\alpha \beta) \gamma = \alpha (\beta \gamma)$ (associative law);

f) $(\alpha \cup \beta) \gamma = \alpha \gamma \cup \beta \gamma$ (distributive law);

g) $\varepsilon \cup \alpha^* = \alpha^*$;

h) $(\varepsilon \cup \alpha)^* = \alpha^*$.

We say that $\alpha$ is similar to $\beta$ if we can change $\alpha$ to $\beta$ by using equation a) to d).

It is convenient to use regular expression equation $X_i = a_{i0} + a_{i1} X_1 + \cdots + a_{in} X_n$ to process language, because such equation $\Delta = \{X_1, \cdots, X_n\}$ (set of unknown quantities) and $\Sigma$ intersect at $\varnothing$. $\alpha_{ij}$ is regular expression on $\Sigma$. when $\alpha_{ij}$ is $\varnothing$ or $\varepsilon$, it is respectively corresponding to coefficient 0 or 1 of ordinary linear equation group, so that we can solve the linear equation group by Gauss elimination. Certainly, this answer is a set, namely the answer is not unique. But this algorithm can accurately ensure an extremely small immobile point as answer.

It is reflected by generated regular language. If $R$ is regular language, then there exists a const n which makes all words w whose length not less than n can be expressed by the form of $xyz$ ($y \neq \varepsilon$ and $|xy| \leq n$), and for all nonnegative integers $i$ must satisfy $xy^i z \in R$. This is Pumping Lemma. It is a powerful tool of to prove that some language is nonregular, and it is helpful to construct algorithm to judge language generated by a given regular grammar is finite or infinite.

## 8.7 Augmented Transition Networks

In 1970, W. Woods, the artificial intelligence expert of U.S.A., studied a language automated analysis method named Augmented Transition Networks (ATN for short). ATN is developed after important expansion on the basis of finite-state grammar. Finite-state grammar can be expressed by state diagram, but the function of this grammar only lies in generating. If beginning with the angle of parsing sentence, we may use state diagram to vividly express the parsing process of a sentence. This state diagram is called finite state transition diagram (FSTD). An FSTD is made up of many finite states and arcs from one state to another state. We can only mark final symbol (namely concrete word) and word class symbol (such as, <Verb>, <Adj>, <Noun> and so on) on the arcs. The analysis begins with start state, then according to the direction of arrowhead in finite state transition diagram, scans input word from one state to another state, check up if the input word match the symbol on the arc. If scanning the end point of input sentence, FSTD goes into the last state. Then FSTD accepts the input sentence and the analysis is completed. (See Figure 8.4)

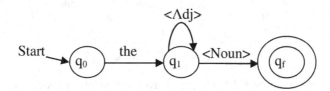

Fig. 8.4 Transform diagram of Augmented Transition Networks

Augmented Transition Networks can only identify finite state language. We know that the rewriting rule of finite state grammar is A→aQ or A→a. This grammar is relatively simple. FSTD has enough capability to identify the language generated by finite state grammar.

Finite state grammar is unfit to deal with quite complicated natural language, so it is necessary to expand FSTD, and offer a recursive mechanism for it to increase its identification ability, so that it can dispose context-free language. Therefore, Recursive Transition Networks (RTN) are proposed. RTN is also a finite state transition diagram, but in which the marks on the arc not only contain final symbol (namely concrete word) and word class symbol, but also contain phrase type symbol (such as, NP, S, PP and so on). Because every phrase type symbol can be also expressed by another finite state transition diagram, RTN then have recursive ability. Whenever the phrase type is scanned, RNT may temporarily transfer to another finite state transition diagram corresponding to the phrase type, so that it can control analysis procedure temporarily. In this way, RNT can identify not only finite state language, but also context-free language, and expand the identification ability of FSTD. (See Figure 8.5)

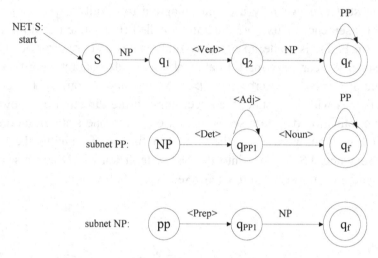

Fig. 8.5 RTN network

The operation mode of RTN is similar to the operation mode of FSTD. If the mark on the arc is final symbol or word class symbol, then it can deal with the arc like FSTD. For example, ball, the word, matches the arc marked <Noun>, but does not match the arc marked <Adj>. If the mark on the arc is phrase type symbol and the phrase type symbol is corresponding to another finite state transition diagram, and then make the current analysis state into stack, transfer the control to finite state transition diagram with corresponding name, and deal with this sentence continuously. When process is end or fails, turn the control back again, and return to the former state to process continuously.

For example, let RTN is made up of a net named S and two subnets named NP and PP. Here, NP shows noun phrase, PP shows preposition phrase, <Det> is definitive, <Prep> is preposition, <Adj> is adjective, and <Noun> is noun, the last state is marked with $q_f$. If input symbol string is the little boy in the swimsuit kicked the red ball, RTN will be analyzed according to the following sequence:

   NP: the little boy in the swimsuit
   PP: in the Swimsuit
   NP: the Swimsuit
   Verb: kicked
   NP: the red ball

In net S, start from S, scan to NP, then the control goes into the subnet named NP to process this NP—the little boy in the Swimsuit. After scanning the little boy, PP can be scanned in subnet, namely in the swimsuit. Upon that, the control goes into the subset named PP to process the PP—in the swimsuit. In this subnet after scanning <Prep>, namely in, Np the swimsuit should be scanned. Then, the control goes into the subnet named NP again to process the NP, the swimsuit, and goes into the last state of this subnet named NP. So, noun phrase, the little boy in the swimsuit, is processed. The control goes back to net S, goes into state $q_1$ and scans the verb kicked, then goes into state $q_2$ and scans noun phrase NP again in state $q_2$. Upon that, the control goes into subnet named NP to process the noun phrase, the red ball. After processing this noun phrase, just come into the last state $q_f$, the analysis of sentence is ended.

RTN can process context-free language, but we know that it is still imperfect for processing natural language by context-free grammar which can generate context-free language. Hence, we need to further expand RTN to make it have superior identification ability. In this way, Woods put forward Augmented Transition Networks, namely ATN. ATN is formed by expanding RTN in following three facts:

(1) Add a register to store information. For example, it is possible to form some derivation trees locally among different subnets. Such derivation trees may be stored in the register temporarily.

(2) The arc in the net can not only be marked with final symbol, word class symbol, phrase class symbol, but also check if the condition of coming into the arc is satisfied.

(3) Execute some actions on the arc, and rearrange the structure of sentence.

Because of adding register, condition and action, the function of ATN is raised to the level of Turing machine. In theory, ATN has enough ability to identify any language which may be identified by computer.

The operation mode of ATN is similar to RTN. The differences are as follows. If marking "check" on the arc, then this "check" must be executed at first; Just after "check" succeeding, this arc can be scanned continuously. In addition, if the actions relative to it on the arc will be executed, then after scanning this arc execute these actions again. At present, ATN is successfully applied to the study of man-machine conversation, and also applied to generate sentence.

ATN also has some limitations. It depends on syntactic analysis excessively, which limits its ability to process some languages, semantic but not completely asyntactic.

## 8.8 Conceptual Dependence

R.C. Schank put forward Conceptual Dependence theory in 1972 to express the meaning of phrase and sentence (Schank, 1972), which provide common sense knowledge for computer to help reasoning, and achieve automatically understanding of language. The rationales of concept dependence are as follows.

(1) For any two sentences with the same meaning should only have a kind of expression of concept dependence meaning regardless of the language.

(2) The expression of concept dependence is composed of very slight semantic primitive. Semantic primitive contains primitive action and primitive state (relative to attribute value).

(3) Any information in implied sentence must form explicit expression which indicates the meaning of that sentence.

Concept dependence theory has three aspects:

(1) The aspect of concept dependence $\rightarrow$ action primitive, include:
  • Basic acts in physical world = {GRASP, MOVE, TRANS, GO, PROPEL, INGEST, HIT}
  • Basic acts in spiritual world = {MTRANS, CONCEPTUALIZE, MBUILD}
  • Basic acts of means or instrument = {SMELL, LOOK-AT, LISTEN-TO, SPEAK}

(2) Drama $\rightarrow$ describing some base fixed complete sets of actions (composed of action primitive) in common scene.

(3) Plan $\rightarrow$ its every step is composed of drama.

Then, we introduce Schank's concept dependency relationship. He divided concept into following categories:

a) PP: a kind of concept noun, only use for physical object, also named image creator. Such as, character, object and so on, are all PP. It still contains natural wind, rain, thunder, lightning and human brain which is thinking (regarding brain as a production system).

b) PA: attribute of physical object, it and its value together describe physical object.

c) ACT: actions carried out by one physical object to another physical object, or actions carried out by itself, including physical action and spiritual action (such as criticism)

d) LOC: an absolute position (determined by universal coordinate), or relative position (relative to a physical object)

e) TIME: a time point or time slice, also divided into two kinds: absolute time and relative time.

f) AA: the attribute of an action

g) VAL: the value of all kinds of attributes

Schank adopts following methods to form new conceptualization:

(1) An actor (active physical object), adding an act.

(2) The above concepts adding arbitrarily following modification:

a) An object (If ACT is physics action, then is a physical object; if ACT is spiritual action, then it is another concept)

b) A place or a receiver (If ACT happens between two physical objects, it shows that transmitting a certain physical object or concept system to another physical object. If ACT happens between two places, it shows the new place of object. )

c) A method (itself is also a concept)

(3) An object adding the value of a certain attribute of the object.

(4) Forming new concept by composing concept and concept in some method. For example, composed together by causation.

Originally, R.C. Schank's goal was to make all concepts atomized. But in fact, he only made ACT atomized. He divided ACT into eleven classes.

(1) PROPEL: applying physical forces to an object, including push, pull, hit, kick and so on.

(2) GRASP: an actor grasping a physical object.

(3) MOVE: a part of body of actor alternating space positions, such as hand up, leg kick, stand up, sit down and so on.

(4) PTRANS: physical object alternating positions, such as walk into, run out, go upstairs, dive and so on.

(5) ATRANS: change of abstract relations, such as transfer (holding relationship changes), present (possession relationship changes), revolute (governing relationship changes) and so on.

(6) ATTEND: getting information by some sense organ, such as search with eyes, listen with strained ears and so on.

(7) INGEST: actor making something inhale his body, such as eat, drink, dose and so on.

(8) EXPEL: actor making something send out his body, such as vomit, shed tears, relieve the bowels, spit and so on.

(9) SPEAK: actor producing a kind of voice, such as sing, play music, cry loudly, and scream and so on.

(10) MTRANS: the transmission of information, such as talk, discuss, phone and so on.

(11) MBUILD: forming new information by old information, such as angry from mind, evil from gallbladder, bend brows, stratagem comes to mind, and so on.

When defining these eleven kinds of atomic action, R.C. Schank has a basic thought, these atomic concepts are not mainly used for expressing movements themselves, but for expressing the results of actions, and the essential results, so we can think it is the inference of these concepts. For example, "X transfers Y to Z from W through ATRANS" contains the following inferences.

(1) Y originally located in W.

(2) Y reaches Z now (no longer in W).

(3) A certain purpose of X is realized through ATRANS.

(4) If Y is a kind of good thing, then it implies that thing changes toward direction in favor of Z, but not in favor of W. Otherwise on the contrary.

(5) If Y is a kind of good thing, then it implies that X makes this action for interests of Z. Otherwise on the contrary.

A kind of important sentence is causal chain. R.C. Schank and his fellow workers worked out some rules used in concept dependence. Five kinds of important rules are as follows:

a) Action can cause the change of the state.

b) The state can start action.

c) The state can eliminate action.

d) State (or action) can start the spiritual incident.

e) The spiritual incident can be a reason of action.

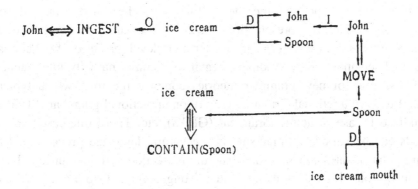

Fig. 8.6 Expression of the implicit information

These are the basic part of the knowledge about the world. Concept dependence contains each kind (and combination) shorthand expressions called causal connection. In concept dependence theory, any information in implied sentences must form explicit expression which shows the meaning of that sentence. For example, concept dependence of the sentence "John eats the ice cream with a spoon", is expressed as Figure 8.6. In the figure, vectors D and I respectively express direction and instruction dependence. Note, in this example, mouth as conceptualization part comes into the figure, even if it does not appear in the original sentence. This is the basic distinction between concept dependence and derivation tree produced by sentence syntactic analysis.

## 8.9 Language Information Processing

### 8.9.1 Overview

Studies on natural language information processing had been started when the electronic computer appeared, and the test of machine translation had been carried out at the beginning of the fifties of the 20th century. The research approach at that time can't be recognized as "Intelligence". Chomsky's transformational-generative grammar was widely approved by the 1960s. The core of the generative grammar is a phrase structure rule. The procedure of analyzing sentences' structures is that rules are used to generate syntactic trees from top to down or from bottom to up.

Because of realizing that generative grammar is lack of the means of expressing the semantic knowledge, with the prosperity of cognitive science in the 1970s, it has expressed the theory that researchers had proposed some theories of semantic representation, such as semantic network, concept dependence theory, case frames. After their own development of the theories of syntax and semantics, they gradually began to become mutually integrated. By the 1980s, a set of new grammar theories come to the fore, which typically include Lexical Functional Grammar (LFG), one functional grammar (FUG) and Generalized Phrase Structure Grammar (GPSG), etc. These rule-based analysis methods can be called "rationalism" in the natural language processing. Basic starting point of rationalism is to pursue the perfection and attempt to solve the problem absolutely by thinking and distinguishing. Chomsky, a famous American linguist, proposed the standard theory in the 1960s, the standard theory of expansion in the 1970s, government and binding theory in the 1980s, minimalist program in the 1990s, and has been studying on universal grammar (Cook, 2000; Radford, 2000). Pursued goal of rationalism is to keep the abstract to find the grammar general rule across different languages similar to the periodic table of elements in studies on the cognition of language or pure linguistics theory. Although existing means have basically grasped the analytical technology of the single sentence, it is still very difficult to cover the overall language phenomenon, especially understanding of the whole paragraph or the chapter.

Research ideas of "empiricism" relative to "rationalism" are mainly for studies on large-scale corpus. The corpus is the sets of a large number of texts. After the computer appears, the corpus can be stored conveniently, and queried easily. With the appearance of the electronic publication, it becomes no longer difficult to collect the corpus. As early as the 1960s, Brown and the LOB corpus of computer had been worked out the scale of 1 million vocabularies respectively. By the 1990s, there are dozens of corpora and their scales reach the magnitude of $10^9$ at most, like DCI, ECI, ICAME, BNC, LDC, CLR, etc.

The studies on corpus are divided into three areas: The development of tool software, tagging of corpus and corpus-based language analysis method. The collection of the raw corpus can't directly offer various knowledge about language; knowledge acquisition becomes possible only when multi-level processing is used, such as morphology, syntax, and semantics. Processing way is to tag various marks in the corpus, whose content include the speech of each word, the semantics, the phrase structure, sentence patterns and inter-sentence relations, etc. With continually deepening the degree of tagging the corpus, it is gradually ripening, and becomes a distributed knowledge source of statistical meaning. A lot of language analytical work can be carried out by using the knowledge source. For example, according to the law of frequency summed up in the tagged corpus every word in new text can be gradually tagged, and sentence elements can be divided, etc.

The knowledge provided by the corpus is expressed by statistical strength, rather than certainty, which aim at covering the language phenomenon with the expansion of the scale. But the basic certainty rules in the language are still judged by the size of statistical strength, which runs counter to common sense. The shortages in studies of "empiricism" are made up for by methods of "rationalism" which come remedy. The integration of the two kinds of methods is exactly the development trend of present natural language processing too.

U.S. cognitive psychologist G. M. Olson proposes the criteria for language understanding (Olson, 1981):

(1) Can successfully answer the relevant question in the language material, namely the ability to answer questions is one criterion for language understanding.

(2) There is an ability to make the summary from a large number of materials offered.

(3) Can use one's own language, i.e. repeat this material in different words.

(4) Translate from a kind of language to another.

If computer can do the above points, it can be used in the following in these places:

a) Machine translation: Translation of the multilingual; 10000 vocabularies; Accuracy of machine translation is 90%, manual intervention is 10%; In the integrated system, the computers are served as the interpreter, and participates at all levels from editorial to printing; The total cost of translation is 30% of the manual translation or lower.

b) The understanding of the file: Machine can read, and digest the contents of the file to make the summary or on the basis to answer the concrete question.

c) The generation of the file: Machine can generate natural language based on some kind of store messages in computer with some form languages.

d) The application of the other places: Natural language interface for the big system.

## 8.9.2  Developing stage

The development of nature language understanding system can be divided into two stages: the first-generation system and the second-generation system. The first-generation system which is based on the fact that speech and order of words is analyzed often uses statistical methods while analyzing; the second-generation system begins to introduce the factors of the semantics and even pragmatics and linguistic context, and statistical technology is in the secondary position.

The first-generation nature language understanding system can be divided into four types:

## 1. Special format system

Early most nature language understanding systems are special format systems which adopt the special format to carry on man-machine dialogue according to the characteristic of the interactive content. In 1963, R. Lindsay designed SAD-SAM system with the IPL-V form processing language in American Carnegie technological institute, which used the special format to carry on the man-machine dialogue about relative's relation. The system in which a database about relative's relation established can receive the English sentence of questions about relative's relation, and answer in English.

In 1968, D. Bobrow designed STUDENT system in American Massachusetts Institute of Technology. This system generalized some basic modes from the English sentence in algebra applied problems of high school, and used the computer to understand the English sentence in the applied problems, list the equations to ask and solve and provide the answer. The initial stage of the sixties, B. Green set up BASEBALL system in American Lincoln laboratory which used IPL-V form processing language and could answer some questions about baseball match, in which the database stored the data about scores of U.S. federal baseball match in 1959. The ability to analyze sentence structure of this system is relatively bad. Sentences inputted of this system are very simple and have no conjunctions, adjective and adverbial words of the comparative forms. This system mainly identifies words by a machine dictionary, using the 14 speech categories, and answers all questions with a special kind of normative expressions.

## 2. Text based system

Some researchers are unsatisfied with the limitations of all sorts of formats in the special format system. As to a special field, it is the most convenient that the system with no limitations of special format structure is used to carry on man-machine dialogue, which made system based on text presented. For example, PROTOSYNTHEX-I system designed by R. F. Simmons, J. F. Burger and R. E. Long in 1966, worked by means of storing and search of text information.

## 3. Limited logic system

The limited logic system has further improved the system based on text. In this kind of system, the sentence of the natural language is substituted for some formalized marks which make up a limited logic system, can do some reasoning. In 1968, B. Raphael had set up SIR system with LI SP language in American Massachusetts Institute of Technology. In the system, 24 match modes of English are proposed. Inputted English sentences match these modes to identify their structures. In the process from storing knowledge into the databases to answering the questions, some commonly used concepts in people's dialogue can be treated, such as the inclusion relation of sets, and spatial relation, etc, and some simple logical reasoning can be carried on. The machine can study in dialogue, remember studied knowledge, and be engaged in some preliminary intelligence activities.

In 1965, J. R. Slagle set up DEDUCOM system for deductive reasoning in information retrieval. In 1966, F. B. Thompson set up DEACON system which manages a fictitious military database by English, and uses the ring structure and the concept similar to English to deduce in the design. In 1968, C. Kellog set up CONVERSE system on IBM360/67 computer, which can deduce based on the files of 1000 facts about 120 cities in U.S.A.

## 4. Generally deductive system

Generally deductive system use some standard mathematics symbols (such as predicate calculus symbols) to express information. Based on all achievements made in proof of theorem by the logicians, the effectively deductive system is set up which can express any question in the way of theorem proving, deduces out the information needed actually, and answers in natural language. Generally deductive system can express those complicated information which it is not easy to express in limited logic system, and further improve the ability of nature language understanding system. Between 1968 and 1969, Green and Phil set up QA2 and QA3 systems which use the way of predicate calculus and the formatted data to carry on deductive reasoning, solve questions, and answer in English. These systems are typical representative of generally deductive system.

Since 1970, a certain number of the second-generation nature language understanding systems had appeared, the majority of which are programming deductive system that carry on a large number of semantic, contextual and pragmatic analysis. More famous systems among them are LUNAR system, SHRDLU system, MARGIE system, SAM system, PAM system.

LUNAR system is a natural language information retrieval system designed by W. Woods in 1972. The system adopted formal question language to express the semantics of the question, thus make semantic interpretation for the sentence questioned, finally make the formal question language carry out in the database and produce the answer to the question.

SHRDLU system is a system that robots' movements are commanded in natural language, which is set up by T. Winograd in American Massachusetts Institute of Technology in 1972. This system combines analysis of the sentence structure, semantic analysis, and logical reasoning to greatly strengthen its ability in the respect of language analysis. The object of dialogue is a simple toy robot that has "Hands" and "eyes", and can operate toy building blocks with different color, size and form in desk, for instance cube, pyramid, box, etc. the robot can follow the operators' commands to pick up these building blocks and move them to form the new building blocks structure. In the process of man-machine dialogue, the operators can acquire the various visual feedbacks from the robot, and real-timely observe the situation that the robot understands languages and carries out the orders. On the television screen the simulated image of this robot and vivid scene in which it freely talks with a real person in English on the telex can be displayed.

MARGIE system is developed by R. Schank in the artificial intelligence laboratory of Stanford in U.S.A. in 1975. The purpose of this system is to offer an ocular model of nature language understanding. The system transforms English sentences into the expression of conceptual dependency at first, and then deduces a large number of facts according to the relevant information in the system. Because while people are understanding sentences, more contents than external expression of sentences are involved, this system has 16 types of reasoning such as causes, effects, descriptions, functions, etc., finally, transforms the result of reasoning into English to output.

SAM system is set up by R. Abelson in Yale University in U.S.A. in 1975. This system adopts Method of script to understand the story written in natural language. The so-called script is a standardized series of events used for describing the people's activity (going to restaurant, seeing the doctor).

PAM system, another system of understanding the story, is set up by R. Wilensky Yale University in America in 1978. PAM system can explain the plot of the story too, answer the question, carry on the inference, and make the summary. Except for series of events in the script, the system also proposed "plan" regarded as the basis of understanding the story. So-called "plan" is a means adopted to realize the purpose of the characters in the story. If you want to understand the story by "plan", it is necessary to identify characters' purpose and the action taken to accomplish this purpose. There is a plan box in the system, in which the information about various purposes and various means is stored. In this way, while understanding the story, as long as the coincident part about the plot in the story and information stored in the plan base is found out, what the purpose of this story is can be understood. While the obstacle appear one by one in the process of matching from plots of the story and the script, it does not result in a failure to understand the story because general information of purpose can be offered in plan base. For example, we rescue a person snatched away by a ruffian. This total purpose of "rescue" consists of several sub-purposes including reaching the ruffian's nest and various methods to kill the ruffian. The next behavior can be expected. The purpose can be deduced according to theme at the same time. For example, there is an inputted story of "John loves Mary". Mary has been snatched away by a ruffian. "PAM system can expect that John will take action to rescue Mary at once". The story doesn't have such content, however, according to "the love theme" in plan base, "John wants to take action to rescue Mary" can be deduced.

Systems described above all are written nature language understanding systems, which use the written characters to input and output. Oral nature language understanding systems still involve complicated technology such as phonetic recognition, speech synthesis, etc. It is obviously a more difficult subject. The research of oral nature language understanding system is developed in recent years.

### 8.9.3 Analytical methods based on rules

From the view of Linguistics and cognitive science, a group of linguistics rules are set up to make the machine be able to correctly understand the natural language. Method based on rules is a theoretical approach. In ideal conditions, the rules form a complete system that can cover all the language phenomena, so the use of Method based on rules can interpret and understand all the language problems.

Natural language understanding systems involve Syntax, Semantic and Pragmatics to varying degrees. Syntax is a kind of rules which can binds the words into phrases, clauses and sentences. The analysis of Syntax is one solved best so far in three fields described above.

The same word serves as different parts of speech according to different linguistic contexts respectively, and the meaning is also different. These examples can illustrate even while the syntax is analyzed, in order to obtain correct analysis as soon as possible, often some semantic information or even the intervention in knowledge of the outside world is needed. In dealing with the question of analysis of the syntax and semantics, there are the following two different methods on the whole at present:

(1) The serial treatment of separating syntax and semantic analysis.
(2) The integrated treatment schemes of syntax and semantics.

Since the 1980s, the semantic knowledge engineering in the field of natural language processing both at home and abroad has been studied. Every semantic knowledge base describes the content with focusing on semantic relation; The category of semantic knowledge has obvious characteristics of relativity; Semantic knowledge as the main constraints play a role in the computer doing various operations for changes of the language form; Pay attention to defining the semantic category by the varying means of the language form of the system, and draw semantic constraints. Therefore the semantic knowledge acquired, can more directly and better serve for natural language processing.

In 1972, T. Winograd combined the linguistics methods and reasoning methods to appropriately deal with the interaction among the grammar, semantics and pragmatics, and succeeded in developing the natural language processing system SHRDLU on PDP-10 computer. It is a kind of relatively living theoretical model of human language understanding, which has caught great interests of a lot of researchers (Winograd, 1972).

SHRDLU system includes: An analysis program, a systemic grammar of English, a semantic analysis program, as well as a problem solver. The system is written in LISP language and MICRO-PLANNER language which is one kind of programming languages based on LISP. The systematic design is based on one such faith that the program must deal with syntax, semantics and reasoning with a kind of the whole idea in order to understand language. Only when Computer system can understand what it discusses, it can reasonably study language and provide an exhaustive model about one special field and a simple model about its one's own intelligence, for example it can remember and discuss its plans and actions. Knowledge is expressed by way of course, but not by rules table or mode in the system. Because each section of knowledge could be a course, it can be reflected by special course of syntax, semantics and reasoning. It can transfer any other knowledge in the system directly, so SHRDLU system has the ability to reach the unprecedented performance level at that time.

Therefore, grammar information is an abstract information level; Semantic information is the result of interrelation between grammar information and the corresponding objects; Pragmatic information is the result of interrelation among grammar information, semantic information and the cognitive subjects, therefore is the most concrete level. Grammar information and semantic information only relate to situation of the object of things, but pragmatic information still relates to situation of the subject. As can be seen, the whole information concept is an organic system.

### 8.9.4 Corpus-based statistical model

Linguistics of corpus studies collecting, storing, tagging, searching and counting the readable texts of natural language machine etc. The purpose is to support the studies on Linguistics and development of the robust natural language processing system by quantitative analysis to language facts in the large-scale true texts of the objective existence. The application areas include: econometric analysis of language, linguistic knowledge acquisition, style analysis, lexicography, full-text retrieval systems, natural language understanding systems, and machine translation systems etc.

The origin of linguistics of modern corpus can trace back to the linguistics era of structural doctrine on later stage of American Leonard Bloomfield in the fifties when the linguists thought the corpus is a language database of big enough scale under the influence of views of scientific positivism and behaviorism. Because these languages data happen naturally, they are essential and sufficient for studies on the task of linguistics, but intuition evidence is only a poor second resource at best. On later stage of the fifties Noam Chomsky who advocated intuition is reasonable but any natural corpora are distorted established the transformational generative grammar. His idea of rationalism constitutes the contemporary theoretical linguists' orthodox idea, thus curbed the development of linguistics of early corpus to great extent. But the facts have proved from practice, which is impossible to cover various language facts appearing in the large-scale true texts simply by such knowledge. The advancing by leaps and bounds of the computer and computing technology make the scale of the corpus which has expanded thousands of times among 30 years which rise from 1 million word times in the sixties to rapidly (1-10) hundred million word times in the 1990s. The early corpus linguists in the fifties who refused the intuition methods and the formulation linguists in the sixties who refused the corpus method have not predicted with that. This fact makes the vocabulary of a kind of language and syntactic phenomenon can be carried on the open investigation by the corpus.

In 1959, there are some scholars who proposed the imagination of setting up the corpus about the investigation in the usage of modern English. At the beginning of the 1960s, American Brown University set up Brown corpus of modern American English, which marks the beginning of the second period of linguistics of corpus. The Brown corpus by way of inputting with keyboard and LOB corpus of modern British English established in the 1970s are known as the 1st-generation corpus, whose capacity are all 1 million words times. In the 1980s, Optical Character Recognition (OCR) Technology substituted the artificial way of keyboard input of corpus, which made the scale of corpus increase rapidly. COBUILD corpus, 20 million word times and Longman/Lancaster English corpus, 30 million word times set up in this period are called the second-generation corpus. By the 1990s, as a result of popularization of the word processing and editing software and the desktop printing system, the enormous machine-readable texts have already become the inexhaustible resources of corpus, which make the third-generation corpus appear that the scale reaches (1-10) hundred million words times such as ACL/DCI corpus proposed Computational Linguistics Society of the United States, and Oxford Text Archive base etc. According to this kind of growth of the scale of corpus over the past 30 years, G. Leech predicted the super large-scale corpus which is 1,000 billion word times, which will appear in A.D. 2021.

The scale of the corpus and the principle of distribution on selecting suitable materials are very important, because they will directly affect the reliability of statistical data and the applicable scope. However, as supporting environment of studies on linguistics of corpus, processing depth of corpus has more impacts on the function of corpus. Take Chinese as an example, the primitive "raw" corpus can only be used for statistics of word frequency (including several adjacent word co-occurrence frequencies) and length of sentence, and offer simple keyword-retrieval (KWIC). In order to achieve word-level statistics and retrieval, it is necessary to add sub-word tags to the original corpus. In the subsequent processing, we can also tag the corpus at different levels such as part of speech, syntactic relations and semantics etc, which makes the stored corpus progressively change from "raw" to "mature". As the corpus is increasingly full of all kinds of information, the corpus will eventually become full-fledged language Knowledge base.

The main contents of studies on linguistics of corpus include:

(1) The construction of the basic corpus;

(2) The studies on the tools of processing corpus, including automatic segmentation system, part of speech tagging system, syntactic analysis system, semantic tagging system and discourse analysis system etc;

(3) Set up various "mature" corpus with the tagged information by processing the corpus;

(4) Technology and method on acquiring language knowledge from the corpus.

At present, hundreds of corpora on various languages, which are important resources that researchers of various countries are engaged in linguistics research and the development of natural language processing system, have already been set up in the world. Meanwhile, the topic of Construction and use of the corpus has become an important content of the academic international journals and conferences. in July 1993, the British scholar pointed out in the special report, which made at the fourth meeting of a high-level conference on machine translation, that since 1989, the whole world had already entered the research in third-generation machine translation systems, whose main symbol is to introduce the corpus methods in the regular traditional methods, including statistical methods, case-based methods and processing the corpus which makes the corpus transform into a language knowledge base etc.

In order to make Chinese corpus have universality, practicability and the times as a shared infrastructure, and provide an important resource for natural language processing, the multi-level Chinese corpus should be built that consists of finishing corpus, basic corpus and network corpus. The research of Building the corpus will shift to focus on how to obtain resources of three level corpora and effectively utilize them. The finishing corpus can offer good, a large number of norms and examples of language processing for studying on various languages. The basic corpus is a wide-coverage, large-scale raw corpus that can offer a more detailed data of language analysis. The network corpus is a kind of language resource that can realize dynamic update including a lot of new words, new mixes and new usages, and be used in the following research of network language, new words, popular words, and for observing the usage mode of the language with the change of time. The issues of traditional corpus on data sparse and language material upgrade can be overcome by the multi-level Chinese corpus based on Internet. The scale of corpus decreases from bottom to up gradually, but the corpus on quality (the processing depth) is improved gradually. The finishing corpus maintains at the scale of 10 million word times, and the basic corpus is more rational at above 100 million word times. The network corpus at the bottom level is online open resource.

### 8.9.5 Machine learning method

Machine learning is a calculation model or cognitive model of the human learning process which is set up based on the understanding of mechanism scientifically about the mankind of physiology and cognitive science and so on. Various learning theories and learning methods are developed. The common learning algorithms are studied and analyzed in theory. The task-oriented learning system for specific application is set up. These goals of research mutually reinforce interaction. Machine learning methods are applied to language information office extensively at present.

### 1. Text classification

The purpose of classification is to learn a classification function or classification model (often called Classifier) which can map data item of database to one of the given classes. Classification and regression can all be used for predicting. The purpose of prediction is to automatically derive the extended description of the given data from historical data records, thus can predict the next data. Different from regression, the output of classification is a discrete value, but the output of regression is a continuous value. We will not discuss the regression method here.

A data set of training samples as inputting is needed for construct classifier. The training set consists of one group of database records or tuples. Each tuple is a characteristic vector consisting of relevant fields (also called attributes or characteristics). In addition, training samples have a tag of category. The form of a concrete sample can be: $(v1, v2, ..., vn; c)$; among them $vi$ expresses the value of this field, $c$ expresses the category.

The creation methods of classifier have statistical methods, machine learning methods, neural network methods, etc. Statistical methods include Bayesian and non-parameter methods (Neighbor learning, case-based learning), whose corresponding expression of knowledge are discriminative function and prototype examples. The machine learning methods include decision tree and rule induction. The former is expressed as the decision tree or discriminative tree correspondingly, the latter generally as production rules. The neural network methods are mainly BP algorithm, whose model is a neural network model of feedback forward (a kind of architecture made up of node representative of Neurons and edge representative of Connection weight values). BP algorithm is one kind of non-linear discriminative function in essence. In addition, a new method has risen again recently: rough set whose knowledge is expressed by production rules.

## 2. Text clustering

Data is divided into different clusters according to its different characteristics. The purpose of clustering is to make distances among data in the same clusters small as far as possible, but make distances among data in the different clusters big as far as possible. Clustering methods include statistical methods, machine learning methods, neural network methods and database-oriented method.

In statistical methods, clustering is called cluster analysis, which is one of three major methods of the plural data analysis (other two kinds are regression analysis and discriminative analysis). Its main research is clustering based on geometry distances such as Euclidean distance and Minkowski distance, etc. Traditionally statistical methods of cluster analysis include Hierarchical clustering, decomposing clustering, adding clustering, dynamic clustering, clustering for orderly examples, overlapping clustering and fuzzy clustering etc. The clustering method is a kind of clustering based on that the overall comparison, which needs investigate all individuals to determine which clusters individuals are divided into; so it requires that all data must be given definitely in advanced, but the new data can't increase dynamically. Cluster analysis method does not have linear calculation complexity, so it is difficult to be suitable for the situation of very great database.

Clustering is called unsupervised learning or induction with no teacher in machine learning. Because examples in classification learning have tags of category, but examples in clustering have no tags of category which need be determined by clustering algorithm automatically. In many artificial intelligence literatures, clustering is called conceptual clustering too. Because the distance here is no longer the geometric distance in statistical methods, but is determined according to the description of the concept. When objects of clustering can increase dynamically, conceptual clustering is called concept forming.

In the neural network, there is an unsupervised learning method: self-organizing neural network method such as Kohonen Self-organizing feature map network and competitive learning network etc. In data mining field, neural network clustering in the papers is mainly Self-organizing feature map method, especially which is mentioned and used to cluster database in IBM's the White Paper about data mining.

## 3. Case-based machine translation

Case-based machine translation was proposed by Japanese scholar Makoto at first at the beginning of 1990s. This method is on the theoretical basis of Case-based Reasoning (abbreviated as CBR). In CBR, facing problems or situations at present are called goal examples, and problems or situations in memory are called source examples. Briefly speaking, Case-based Reasoning is a kind of strategy that the goal examples are guided to solve by source examples which in memory are obtained through suggestion of the goal examples. So the general idea of case-based machine translation is: Construct the corpus made up of the bilingual translation units in advance, then choose an algorithm of searching and matching in process of translation to look for the units of optimum matching in the corpus, finally construct the translation of the units translated at present according to the translation structure of the example sentence.

Assuming we translate the source language text S, we need to find out translation example S' similar to S in the stored bilingual corpus at first, thus construct translation T of S by analogy according to reference translation T' of S'. In general, the case-based machine translation system includes several steps such as searching modes of candidate examples, calculating similar degree of sentences, alignment of bilingual words and constructing by analogy. How to find out the most similar translation examples S' according to the source language text S is a key to case-based translation methods. So far, researchers have not found a simple and common method to calculate similar degree between sentences yet. In addition, the issue of evaluating similar degrees between sentences requires some knowledge such as human engineering, linguistic psychology, etc.

The case-based machine translation methods hardly need to analyze and understand the source language, and only need a relatively large sentence-aligned bilingual corpus, so its knowledge acquisition is relatively easier. The system can bootstrap from zero-knowledge, combining the technology of translation memory. If the sentences similar to translated sentences exist in the corpus, very good translation can be got by the case-based method, and the more similar the sentence is, the better translation quality is.

Another advantage of case-based translation method is to easily and conveniently express a large number of the ambiguous phenomena of human languages which the accurate rules difficultly deal with by the knowledge expression of the case modes.

However, the shortcoming of case-based translation method is obvious. While not finding the enough similar sentences, the failure of the translation will be announced. This method will require the corpus to cover the extensive language phenomenon, for example, the corpus of PanEBMT system [61] of Carnegie Mellon University has more than 2,800,000 pairs of English and French sentences. Though the researchers who set up PanEBMT system also thought of a lot of other methods at the same time, for opening text test, the translation coverage rate of PanEBMT is about 70%. In addition, it is not easy to set up a high-quality large-scale two-sentence-aligned corpus, especially for the small language.

So, a main respect of the research on the case-based machine translation is how to make the translation system improve the coverage rate of translation under the condition of relatively small-scale base of case mode, or how to reduce the scale of base of case mode under the premise of keeping the effect of translation of the system. For achieving this purpose, we need to draw automatically linguistic knowledge from the base of case mode as many as possible, including grammar knowledge, Lexical knowledge and semantic knowledge etc, and study the expression of its corresponding knowledge and so on.

# Chapter 9

# Learning

The learning ability is a fundamental characteristic of the human intelligence. People learn from objective environment constantly in the whole life. Person's cognitive ability and wisdom to lifelong learning is the gradual formation, development and improvement.

## 9.1 Basic Principle of Learning

Learning and training has always been the main research contents of psychology. The definition of learning is being developed constantly too. In 1983, Simon gave a better definition of learning: A certain long-term change that the system produces in order to adapt to the environment, makes the system can finish the same or similar work next time more effectively (Simon, 1983). Learning is the change taking place in a system; it can be either the permanent improvement of the systematic work or the permanent change on the behavior of organism. In a complicated system, the change of learning is due to many aspects of reasons; that is to say, there are many forms of learning process in the same system, and its different parts will have different improvement. People can get new production rules and set up new behaviors.

The principle of learning is that the learner must know the last result, i.e. whether its behavior can be improved. It is better he can also get the result that what part satisfied in behavior of him, what parts are the information unsatisfied. The knowledge of accepting the learning results is a kind of remuneration or encouragement, and this knowledge can produce or strengthen learning motivation. The interaction of information and motivation of learning result is called reinforcement in psychology, and their relation is as follows:

$$\text{Reinforcement} = \text{Resulting Knowledge} + \text{Reward}$$
$$\text{(information)} \qquad \text{(motivation)}$$

Reinforcement is possibly extrinsic as well as internal. It can be positive, also can be passive. There must be a positive learning motivation when learning. Reinforcement can support learning motivation. The teacher should pay attention to the choice of the learning material in education, in order to attract students' attention and encourage them. If learning material is too simple, it can not attract students, and students are easily sick of them; if learning material is too complicated, it is difficult for students to understand and students are also sick of them. Therefore, factors influencing learning motivation are various, including property and composition of learning material, etc.

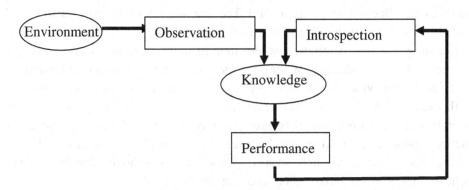

Fig. 9.1 Learning system model

The author has proposed a kind of learning system model (see Fig. 9.1), where the ellipse denotes information unit, the rectangle denotes processing unit, and the arrow denotes the main direction of dataflow in the learning system.

The most important factor influencing learning system is environment that provides the system with information, especially level and quality of this kind of information. Entironment provides learning unit with information; learning unit uses these information to improve knowledge base; execution unit then utilizes the knowledge base to carry out its task; finally, the information obtained can be feedbacked to learning unit. For human being's learning, utility information is produced through internal learning machine in order to feedback to learning unit.

Learning theory is about learning the essence of the learning process, learning the rules and constraints to study the various conditions to explore the theory and explanation. Learning theory must provide knowledge in the field, analyse and explore learning methods and means, it must make it clear which aspects of learning is the most worthy of learning, which independent variables should be controlled, and which the dependent variable should be analyzed, which methods and techniques can be used, what kind of terms should be used to describe the results of the learning, so as to provide educators with a framework for research and learning. From this sense, learning theory is the guidelines and resources that people learn to conduct scientific research and thinking. It is to summarize to a large amount of knowledge about learning the rules and systematize and standardize them. However, any theory in the abstract and general a large number of specific knowledge of the process, will inevitably lose a certain degree of specificity and accuracy, precisely because of this, theories that have the general guide. Learning theory should explain how learning work, why some learning methods are effective, some are invalid. The learning rules tells us "how to learn" and learning theory then tells us "why to learn like this".

Learning is a kind of process, where individuals can produce lasting changes on the behavior by training. What does the change denote on earth? How does individual's behavior change? The psychologists have not come to an agreement with these problems so far. Therefore there are various learning theories. For over 100 years, the psychologists have provided all kinds of learning theoretical theory schools due to difference between their own philosophical foundation, theory background, research means. These theory schools mainly include behavioral school, cognitive school and humanism school.

## 9.2  The Learning Theory of Behavioral Schools

Behavioral psychologists interpret learning as the formation of habit by using relationship between stimulus and response by training. In their options, an unprecedented relation can be established between a certain stimulus and related response, and such establishing process is so-called learning. Then this kind of learning theory is called stimuls-response theory, or behavioral school. The learning theory of behavioral school emphasizes the behavior that can be observed. According to this theory, behavioral numerous happy or painful consequences can change the individual's behavior. Pavlov's classical conditioned reflex theory, Watson's behaviorism view, Thorndike's connection doctrine, Skinner's operation conditioned reflex theory, etc., classically belong to behavioral school.

Some other psychologists do not agree with that learning is the process of the formation of habits. In their options, learning is a cognitive process of individual cognizing relation among the things in its environment. So, this kind of theory is known as the cognitive theory.

### 9.2.1 Learning theory of conditioned reflex

Russian physiologist Ivan Pavlov is the founder of the classical conditioning reflex theory (Pavlov Website). Pavlov was studing dog's digestive physiology phenomenon. The food presented in front of the dog, and measure the effect of saliva secretion. Usually the dog will salivate when food to be eaten. However, Pavlov accidentally discovered the dog not to eat food, only heard of food breeder's footsteps, they start to salivate. Pavlov did not spare this phenomenon. He began to do an experiment. Try giving the dog to listen to a ring, the dog did not respond, but in the dog show ring immediately after the food, and repeated many times by the combination, a separate ring while listening without food, the dog also "learn" the secretion of saliva. Ringtones and unconditional stimulus (food) from the repeated combination of a neutral stimulus becomes a conditioned stimulus secretion of saliva caused the conditions of sexual response, this phenomenon known as Pavlovian conditioning reflex, that is, classical conditioning reflex. Pavlovian conditioned reflex that the physiological mechanism of the formation of neural connection is temporary, and that learning is a temporary formation of neural connection.

The impact of Pavlov's classical conditioning theory is enormous. In Russia, the theory based on Pavlov's classical conditioned reflex theory had dominated in the circle of psychology for a long time. In the United States, behavioral psychologists Watson, Skinner, etc. are all impacted by the Pavlov's conditioned reflex theory.

### 9.2.2 Learning theory of behaviorism

Behaviorism is founded by America psychologist J.B. Watson in 1913 (Watson, 1913). Behavioral popular in the United States, affecting extended to the whole world, the 20th century, 20 to 50 years, during 40 years, and nearly all of psychology dominated by behaviorism. Behaviorism, also known as behavioral psychology. Behavioral changes later, due to a different point of view to explain behavior, another radical behaviorism (radical behaviorism) and the new behaviorism (neo-behaviorism) distinction.

Watson is the first American psychologist who regarded Pavlov's classical conditioned reflex theory as the theoretical foundation of learning. He believes that learning is a stimulating place to another to create conditions to stimulate the process of reflection, in addition to birth with the concentrated conditioned reflex (such as sneezing, a knee-jerk reflex), the adoption of all human behavior is conditioned the establishment of new stimulus - response association (ie, S - R link) formed.

Watson used the principle of conditioned reflex, making the formation of a baby fear experiments to prove his point. Experiment object is the original pairs of rabbits without any fear, baby. In the experiment, when the rabbits appear in front of the baby at the same time presented a terrible voice. After repeated many times, the baby felt fear once he saw a rabbit, even any with hair.

### 9.2.3 Association learning theory

From the end of 19th century to the beginning of 20th century, Thorndike's learning theory had occupied the leadership in American psychological circles for nearly 50 years. Thorndike is the pioneer of animal psychology. Since 1896, he systematically studied animal's behaviors by using the chicken, cat, dog, fish, etc. in Harvard University, thus first putting forward the most intact learning theory in learning psychology. Through the scientific experiment method, he found that individual's learning is via a kind of "try to be successful accidentally with the mistake". In this way, a kind of connection or combines between stimulus and response is established through repeated responses to a stimulus. In Thorndike's view, the essence of learning lied in forming the association between situation and response. So this kind of learning theory is known as association theory.

Situation, denoted by S, is called stimulus sometimes, which includes cerebral internal situation, such as external situation, thought and emotion. Response, denoted by R, includes internal response, such as "the activities of muscles and gland", and internal response, such as idea, will, emotion and attitude. The so-called connection includes association, relation, inclination, meaning that a certain situation can only arouse a certain response, and can not arouse other responses. By the symbol "$\rightarrow$" we mean "arouse". The formula of association is expressed by: $S \rightarrow R$.

The relation between situation and response is the causality. The relation is a directed association without any intermediary. Thorndike thought that the

association is an instinctive combination. He applied such association to human being's learning. In his terms, all the thoughts, behaviors and activities of human being can resolve into the connection of basic unit stimulate with response. The difference between the learning of human being and animal lies in: "the learning process of the animal is blindfold", and "do not need the idea as media", while human being's learning needs the idea as media and is conscious. But their essential distinction only lies in simpleness and complexity as well as the number of association. The law of animal's learning is still suitable for human learning.
The association between stimulus and response subjects to three following principles:

(1) Number of the practice;
(2) Individual's own preparation state;
(3) Result after the response.

The above three principles is known as Thorndike's famous three laws: practice law, prepare law, result law. Practice law means that the more an individual responses to a certain stimulus, the stronger the association is. Prepare law is in fact motive principle. Motivation is an inherent process that causes individual activity and maintains this activity. Result law, the core of association theory, its main content is emphasizing that the power of association is determined by the result of response. If individual obtains satisfied result, association is strengthened after response, otherwise is weakened.

After 1930, Thorndike had modified the practice law and result law. He thought that practice can not strengthen the association between situation and response unconditionally. Practice is helpful just when being accompanied by the satisfactory sense. For result law, unsatisfactory sense can not directly weaken the association, but just admits that satisfaction can strengthen the association. In Thorndike's terms, association is built by trial and error. Learning is a gradual and blindfold process. In this process, with the gradual increase of right response and the gradual reduction of error response, the firm association between stimulus and response is finally formed. Thorndike carried on the experiment with different animals, and the result is quite identical. Therefore, he thought that the forming of association followed certain law. Thorndike still proposed accessional laws of learning, including ① selection response law; ② multiple response law; ③ fixed response law; ④ apperception response law; ⑤ associative transference law.

Thorndike's learning theory is the first comparatively intact learning theory in the history of educational psychology. It is a great progress that he used the experiment, instead of the argument method, to study learning. His theory has caused the academic controversy about learning theory, promoting the development of learning theory. Association theory helps to establish the key position in the theoretical system, and helps accordingly to set up the discipline system of educational psychology, promoting the development of educational psychology.

Association theory is based on instinct, and the association between situation and response is interpreted as the supreme principle of learning. It is determinism of heredity and instinct doctrine. But it obliterates the sociality, consciousness and dynamic role of human being, and fails to open out the essence of human being and the essential distinction between animal's learning and human being's learning. It is mechanical doctrine. It ignores the roles of cognition, idea and understanding in learning process and does not accord with the reality of learning. But test-error theory is still regarded as a kind of the form of learning until today, especially playing an important role in the learning of motor skill and social behavior. Thorndike's learning theory seems a bit simple and can not explain the essential law of learning. But there are some corrections too. Even in today, their some laws are still of directive significance.

### 9.2.4 Operational learning theory

Operational learning theory proposed by the U.S. new behaviorist psychologist B. F. Skinner in the "Verbal Behavior". This theory is based on the operat conditioning reflex experiment that is carried on the animal. During this operating, the organism encounters a special kind of stimulus, called a reinforcing stimulus, or simply a reinforcer. This special stimulus has the effect of increasing the operant, that is, the behavior occurring just before the reinforcer. This is operant conditioning: the behavior is followed by a consequence, and the nature of the consequence modifies the organisms tendency to repeat the behavior in the future. By this theory, the power of children's speaking owns to acquired learning. Like studying other behaviors, it is acquired by operational conditioned reflex.

Skinner thought that there are two kinds of conditioned reflex: Pavlov's classical conditioned reflex and operational conditioned reflex. Pavlov's classical conditioned reflex is responsive conditioned reflex. The process of conditioned reflex is a response caused by already knowing to stimulate the thing first and is a combination of enhancing things with stimulating things. Enhancing is to strengthen enhancing stimulus. Skinner's operational conditioned reflex is reactive conditioned reflex. There is no known stimulus. It is caused by spontaneous response, and is the process of combination of enhancing stimulus with reaction. This enhancing is to strengthen reaction.

Skinner thought that all behaviors were made up of reflect. There are two kinds of behaviors and then two kinds of behaviors: responsive behavior and operational behavior. Therefore, there are two kinds of learning: responsive learning and operational learning. Skinner paid more attention to operational learning. He thought that operational behavior could more reflect human being's learning in reality, which were all operational learning. Therefore the most effective method to study behavioral science is to investigate the forming of operational behavior and its law.

In Skinner's terms, reinforcement is an important means by which the operational behavior is formed. Reinforcement plays an extremely important role in Skinner's theory. It is the foundation stone and core of Skinner's theory. So it is also called reinforcement theory or reinforcement doctrine. Its basic law is as follows: if reinforcement stimulus appears after an operation happens, the strength (the probability of reacting) of this operation is increased. The change of learning and behavior is intensive results and behavior can be controlled by controlling enhancing. Reinforcement is the key to moulding the behavior and keeping behavioral intensity. The process of moulding behavior is learning process and education is to mould the behavior. As long as we can control the intensity of behavior well, it is possible to optionally mould people and animal's behaviors.

In 1954, the traditional teaching has been criticized Skinner in his paper "The Art of Teaching Science and Learning", according to his reinforcement theory (Skinner, 1954). Hence Skinner strongly maintained that class teaching should be reformed by performing procedure teaching and machine teaching. The learning content should be programmed to be a procedure, which was installed in a machine, according to the operat conditioning reflex principle. Students could finish their learning by using the installed procedure. The process of procedure learning is to divide big problem into several small questions with presenting to them in certain order, asking students to answer each question. In this way, students can receive related feedback information. The question is equivalent to "stimulus" in the forming process of conditioned reflex while student's answer is then equivalent to "response" and feedback information is equivalent to "reinforcement". The key of procedure learning is to program good procedure. For this reason, Skinner had proposed five basic principles to establish a procedure:

(1) Small step principle: divide whole learning contents into teaching materials that consists of pieces of knowledge, which are sorted in an ascending order by knowledge's difficulty, such enabling students can learn step by step.
(2) Positive reaction principle: in order to make positive response to what students learn, the view of "although there is no response, they really understand".
(3) Reinforcement in time (Feedback) principle: the response to student should be reinforced in time, such that they can get feedback information.
(4) Making the step by oneself principle: students determine their learning progress by themselves according to their own learning situation.
(5) Low wrong rate: student must make the correct response each time as much as possible and the wrong rate must be minimized the most.

Skinner thinks that the procedural teaching has the following advantages: step by step; learning speed and learning capacity of the same; correct student's mistake in time, speed up the learning; conducive to improving student learning initiatives; students self-learning abilities and habits. procedural teaching is not perfect. Since it mainly to acquire knowledge as the goal of individualized learning styles, so that people criticized it mainly in three aspects: to make students more rigid knowledge; the lack of collective classes in interpersonal contacts, is not conducive to the socialization of children; neglect the role of teachers.

### 9.2.5 Contiguity theory of learning

Edwin R. Guthrie had been agreeing to the view of behaviorism in psychology very much. In the work of 1921, he explained behaviors mainly by the association between stimulus and response. In his view, there are two kinds of the form of learning. The first one is active adaptation, that is to say, the organism will react constantly in order to adapt to the environment. But this is just the reprint of Watson's theory. The second one is the condition function. This is similar to Pavlov's learning theory. Guthrie thought that all responses were initially caused by a certain unconditioned stimulus. Such stimulus also may be existing neutral stimulus. The essence of condition function is to replace unconditioned stimulus with neutral stimulus in order to cause response. In a sense, this formula is suitable for all learning. So, condition function had become the synonym of learning in fact. This was nearly all theoreticians' creed at that time.

By 1935, Guthery published his book "psychology of learning" (Guthrie, 1935). In this book, he had proposed the learning theory with his own characteristics. Guthrie's contiguity theory specifies that a combination of stimuli which has accompanied a movement will on its recurrence tend to be followed by that movement. According to Guthrie, all learning was a consequence of association between a particular stimulus and response. Furthermore, Guthrie argued that stimuli and responses affect specific sensory-motor patterns; what is learned are movements, not behaviors.

In contiguity theory, rewards or punishment play no significant role in learning since they occur after the association between stimulus and response has been made. Learning takes place in a single trial (all or none). However, since each stimulus pattern is slightly different, many trials may be necessary to produce a general response. One interesting principle that arises from this position is called "postremity" which specifies that we always learn the last thing we do in response to a specific stimulus situation. Contiguity theory suggests that forgetting is due to interference rather than the passage of time; stimuli become associated with new responses. Previous conditioning can also be changed by being associated with inhibiting responses such as fear or fatigue. The role of motivation is to create a state of arousal and activity which produces responses that can be conditioned. Contiguity theory is intended to be a general theory of learning, although most of the research supporting the theory was done with animals. Guthrie did apply his framework to personality disorders (Guthrie, 1938).

### 9.2.6 Need reduction theory

American psychologist and behaviorist Clark Leonard conducted research demonstrating that his theories could predict and control behavior. His most significant works were the *Mathematico-Deductive Theory of Rote Learning* (1940), and *Principles of Behavior* (1943), which established his analysis of animal learning and conditioning as the dominant learning theory of its time. Hull created the "hypothetic-deductive" systematic method, after the observation and elaboration of hypotheses. This method brought him precise definitions and conceptualised axioms which helped him develop his theories. He believed that behavior was a set of interactions between an individual and their environment. He analysed behavior from a perspect of biological adaptation, which is an optimization of living conditions through need reduction.

Hull's need reduction theory emphasizes the learning process consists of four elements: motivation, tips, response and reward. Motivation is a driving action of the internal stimulus produced an individual, and some incentives are biological in nature, non-academic, such as pain, thirst, hunger, etc.; also some are learning to manage, such as fear, social needs. Motivation is the basis of behavior, without incentives, individuals do not act, there would be no learning.

Tips lead to individual responses, and decide when and where the individual, as well as what the reaction. The value of tip is that it has character. Tip action can be an individual goal is to achieve goals can also be inspired, you can also combine the above two functions.

Incentives to promote the individual according to prompt the reaction if the reward was paid after reaction. The same reaction will continue to be generated, if the continue to receive remuneration, habits can be formed. If the reaction is not to be paid, the reaction will reduce the tendency to repeat. Therefore, incentive reward reduction due to the reaction because of remuneration to reproduce, so that constitutes learning. Incentives for the reduction is the need for individual satisfaction, are also said to meet the needs of their needs, the extent of reduction, so this theory is known as the need reduce theory.

Hull's theory system displays in three main works: "Behavioral Principle", "Behavioral Foundation" and "Behavioral System". There are 17 formulae and 17 inferences as the most basic form of this system. These forms are used for the symbol units, which expound the following questions:

(1) The association between stimulus and response and feel ability that organism take to learning situation;
(2) The process of motivation and the state of inner drive that can effectively strengthen behaviors;
(3) The law of forming habit;
(4) The elements that influence no-association caused by response;
(5) Reverse condition inhibition that response trends to;
(6) The elements that causing both habit strength and response trend complicated;
(7) When more than one stimulus appear at the same time, the elements that

causing excitability of stimulus complicated is greater than constant alteration in formula caused by the individual difference. Enhancing principle is the foundation of this system.

The strengthen principle is the cornerstone of this system. In its initial form, Hull strengthened the hypothesis that a response to basic needs or driving force due to a tendency to be met and enhanced.

## 9.3 Cognitive Learning Theory

In opposition to the behaviorism theory, derived from the Gestalt school of cognitive learning theory, after a period of silence. After mid-50s of the 20th century, with the appearances of much creative work of a lot of cognitive psychologists, such as Bruner, Ausubel, the learning theory entered a brilliant period since Thorndike. They believe that learning is the face to the present problem situation, in the heart through the active efforts of organizations to form the and development of the process of cognitive structure, emphasizing the link between stimulus-response is mediated consciousness, emphasizing the importance of cognitive processes. So that cognitivism learning theory in the study of learning theory began to dominate.

Cognitive refers to the process of cognition and the cognitive process analysis. American psychologist G. A. Gilbert think that a person's cognitive understanding of the objective world experienced by the general term for several processes. It includes the perception, understanding and reasoning, several relatively unique process, containing aware of the meaning of the term. Cognitive structure has become a modern educational psychologists trying to understand the core issue of the student's psychology. Learning is the cognitive school of thought within the cognitive changes, learning is an S-R association than the much more complex process. They focus on the middle to explain the process of learning behavior, that is the purpose, meaning such that the study of these processes is the control variable. The main contribution of cognitive school's learning theory is as follows:

(1) Pay attention to people's subject value in the learning activities and affirm fully the learner's conscious dynamic role;

(2) Emphasize the important position and function of consciousness activity in learning, such as cognition, understanding, thinking independently;

(3) Paid attention to people's preparation state in learning activities. This means that the result of a person's learning depends not only on outside stimulus and his subjective efforts but on a person's existing knowledge level, cognitive structure, non-cognitive factor. Preparation is the precondition of any meaningful learning.

(4) Emphasize the function of reinforcement. Cognitive learning theory pays much attention to the inherent reinforcement function caused by inner motive and learning itself;

(5) Advocate the creativity of people's learning. Bruner's discovery learning theory emphasizes the flexibility, initiative and finding of student's learning. It requires student's observing, exploring and experiment. Students should develop the spirit of creation, think independently, reorganize materials, find knowledge and grasp the principle by oneself. Bruner recommend an exploratory learning method. He insisted that student's intelligence potentiality should be developed through discovery learning theory, and the learning motive should be regulated and enhanced so as to grasp the knowledge and then form the ability of innovation.

The weak point of the cognitive learning theory is that it can not open out the mental structure of learning process. In our view, learning psychology consists of the mental structure of learning process, including intelligence factors and no-intelligence factors. The intelligence factor is a psychological foundation of the learning process, which plays an important role in learning. The no-intelligence factor is the psychological condition of learning process, which plays an indirect role in learning. Only closely combining the intelligence factors with no-intelligence factors could enable the learning to achieve the purpose desired. But the cognitive learning theory pays little attention to the research on the no-intelligence factors.

Gestalt school's learning theory, Tolman's cognitive purpose theory, Piaget's diagrammatic theory, Bruner's discovery learning theory, Ausubel's meaningful learning theory, Gagné's information processing learning theory and the learning theory of constructivism are all considered the representative theory of cognitive school. This school's representative persons are Piaget, Newell, etc.

### 9.3.1 Learning theory of Gestalt school

Early 20th century theorists, such as Kurt Koffka, Max Wertheimer, and Wolfgang Köhler from Germany established Gestalt school. The school's learning theory is to study the perception issue for Thorndike's learning theory put forward. They stressed that the integrity of experience and behavior against the behavior theory of "stimulus – response" formula, so they redesigned the learning experiment of animal.

Gestalt theory is well known for its concept of insight learning. They think that learning is not a gradual test-error process, but the reorganization of perceptual experience and the insight of the situation relation. The basic standpoints of Gestalt school are as follows:

(1) That learning is a kind of whole form organization. Gestalt views that learning is a kind of whole form organization which refers to the style of things and relationships awareness. The learning process to resolve the problem is due to the situation in the understanding the relationship of things and constitute a kind of whole form to achieve. Chimpanzee can find the relationship that the pole is a tool for it to grasp the banana, such filling the gap and constitute a whole form. According to Gestalt's school, motor learning, sensory learning, perceptual learning all lie in generating whole form organization, not a link between the various parts.

(2) Learning is achieved through insight. Gestalt school holds that learning success and the achievement is entirely due to "insight" result, that sudden understanding, rather than "test-error", "trial and error." Insight is the overall perception of situations, and understanding the relationship of things in the problem situation, that is, the process of whole form organization.

Gestalt justifies the learning process is insight rather than trial and error using the main evidence: ① sudden transformation from "no" to "yes"; ② learned can be well maintained, and not duplicate the error. They pointed out that, as set by Thorndike problem situation is not clear, resulting in a blind trial and error learning.

The evaluations to Gestalt's school's theory are as follows:

(1) Gestalt theory has a dialectical study were reasonable factors, mainly in that it confirmed the role of consciousness, emphasizing the cognitive factors (Gestalt organization) in the learning role. This makes up for learning theory of Thorndike defects that the relationship between stimulus and response is an indirect, not direct, and takes consciousness as intermediary. Gestalt school criticized test-error, also promote the development of the theory of learning.

(2) Gestalt insight was affirmed at the same time, denying the role of test-error is one-sided. Test-error and the insight are at different stages of learning process or different types of learning. Test-error is often a prelude to insight, insight is often the inevitable result of test-error, the two are not mutually exclusive opposites, but should be complementary. Gestalt theory of learning were not complete and systemic enough. Its impact was far less than Thorndike's association theory at that time.

### 9.3.2 Cognitive purposive theory

Edward Chace Tolman thinks that he is a behaviorist. He amalgamated each school's theory and is famous for learning wildly from other's strong points. He did not only appreciate the link to send the objectivity and simple method of measuring behavior, but also by Gestalt view of the impact of the overall study. His learning theory has many names, such as symbol learning, purpose learning, latent learning, expecting learning. He insisted that theory should be completely objective method of testing. However, many people think he is a study of animal learning behavior of the most influential cognitive activists. Affected by the Gestalt school, he stressed that the integrity of behavior. He considered that the overall behavior is pointing to a definite purpose, while the organism is to achieve awareness of the environment means to an end. He did not agree with a direct link between the situation (stimulus) and response, or S - R. He put forward the "intervening variable" concept, that the variables are intermediary between experimental variables and behavior variables and to link the two factors. In particular, the intermediate variable is the psychological process, from the psychological process to link their stimulus and response. Therefore, S - R of the formula should be S - O - R, where O represents an intermediary variable. His learning theory is from the above point of view, through the whole process of animal learning behavior study put forward.

Tolman is best known for his studies of learning in rats using mazes, and he published many experimental articles, of which his paper with Ritchie and Kalish in 1946 was probably the most influential. His major theoretical contributions came in his 1932 book, *Purposive Behavior in Animals and Men* (Tolman, 1932), and in a series of papers in the *Psychological Review*, "The determinants of behavior at a choice point" (Tolman, 1938). The main viewpoints of Tolman's cognitive purposive theory are as follows:

(1) Learning is purposeful. In Tolman's terms, the learning of animal is purposeful, which is to get food. He disagreed with Thorndike's viewpoint that learning is blind. The "test-error" behaviors are guided by the goal (food) in the labyrinth of animal, and they will not give up without reaching the purpose. He believed that learning was to acquire expectation. The expectation is individual's idea about the goal. The individual sets up the expectation of the goal with the existing experience through observation of the amazing situation.

(2) Awareness of the environmental conditions is a means or way to achieve the goal. Tolman thought that the organism would meet all kinds of the environmental condition during the process of achieving the goal. Only understanding the condition, it can overcome the difficulty and achieve the goal. Therefore, the cognition of the environmental condition is a means or way to achieve the goal. Tolman used symbol to denote the cognition of the environmental condition of organism. Learning is not a simple, mechanical reflect the formation of movement, but to learn to achieve the purpose of symbols, form a "cognitive map." The so-called cognitive map is formed in the minds of animals in a comprehensive representation of the environment, including the route, direction, distance, and even time, and more. This is a relatively vague concept.

In a word, the purpose and cognition are two important intermediary variables in Tolman's theory, which is then referred to be cognitive purposive theory.

Tolman's cognitive purposive learning theory pays attention to behavioral integrity, purpose and put forward the concept of intermediary variable, emphysizing the psychological processes between stimulus and response, emphasizing awareness, purpose, expectations of the most used in the study is a progress, and should be affirmed. Tolman theory, some of the terminology, such as "cognitive map" is not clearly defined; did not distinguish between the human learning and animal learning, therefore it is mechanical attention, which makes his theory can not be a complete rational system.

### 9.3.3 Cognitive discovery theory

Bruner (T. S. Bruner) is a prominent contemporary American cognitive psychologist. In 1960, he, together with George Miller, has established the cognitive research center of Harvard University. He is a main representative person of USA's cognitive theory.

Bruner's cognitive learning theory is influenced by Gestalt's theory, Tolman's idea and Piaget's epistemology. He thought that learning is a cognitive process, where the learner forwardly forms the cognitive structure. But Bruner's cognitive learning theory is different with Gestalt's theory and Tolman's theory. The major difference is that Gestalt and Tolman's theory are based on the research on animal learning, and related cognition is a conscious cognition. Bruner's cognitive learning theory then is based on human learning, and related cognition is a abstract thought cognition.

Bruner's Discovery Learning model states learning occurs through exploration, in which students discover the unknown or gain interchangeable knowledge. Students develop processes for attainment of information from their experience. Bruner believed that the student's first growth is through stimulus, which represents how the knowledge is gained though related experiences. This enables the student to attain information that has been stored for later recall. Bruner also discusses how the mental process of the person's mind projects stimulus-response through discovery learning. Discovery learning can be defined as an independent practice on the learner's part to maintain information, without memory, with much self-confidence. Students who complete individual discovery learning tend to recognize the connections within themselves, and what was learned with this type of discovery is placed in high value. In discovery learning, Bruner makes note that students become individual thinkers and encourage the youth attitude of wanting to discover newness of ideas and the unknown (Bruner, 1966). Its basic viewpoint is mainly as follows:

## 1. Learning is active in the process of the formation of cognitive structures

The cognitive structure refers to an internal cognitive system that reflects the relationship between things, or is all the contents and organizations of a learner's idea. People's understanding activity is organized by certain order. In Bruner's terms, human being initiatively acquires knowledge and initiatively selects, changes, stores and employs the sensory information. That is to say, human being initiatively selects knowledge and is the learner who remembers knowledge and transforms knowledge instead of a passive recipient of knowledge. In Bruner's views, learning is generated on the basis of original cognitive structure. No matter what form will be token, individual learning is always to connect the newly acquired information with existing cognitive structure and to actively establish new cognitive structure.

Bruner points out that people represent knowledge in three ways and these emerge in developmental sequence: enactive, iconic and symbolic (Bruner, 1964). Enactive representation includes use of motor skills. In this representation, people manipulate objects. They learn to do things like drive a car or use a computer. Babies would learn that a bottle is something that they suck on to get mil. Iconic representation has to do with images and things that can be altered. For example, we can imagine a bus station that is empty or a station that is crowded with many people. We think about the differences in these two situations separately. Symbolic representation implies using symbols to change knowledge into a code.

## 2. Emphasize the learning of the basic structure of discipline

Bruner paid much attention to curriculum setting and teaching material construction. He believed that no matter what discipline the teacher selected to teach, he did not fail to make students understand the basic structure of discipline, i.e., the basic principle or thought which had been summarized. That is to say, students should understand the structure of the things with meaningful connection method. Influenced by knowledge concept and cognitive concept, Bruner paid attention to the learning of basic structure discipline. In his terms, all knowledge constitutes a kind of structure with level. The knowledge with such structure can be shown through code system or structural system (cognitive structure). The connection of the cognitive structure of the human brain with the basic structure of teaching material will produce a strong learning benefit. If getting a good grasp of the basic principle of a discipline, it is not difficult to understand the special subjects about this discipline.

In teaching, the teacher's task is to offer the best coding system of student, so as to ensure teaching materials have the greatest generality. Bruner thought that it is impossible for teacher to tell student each thing. So teacher should ensure the students acquire the generalized basic thoughts and principles to a certain extent. These basic thoughts and principles constitute the best knowledge structure for students. The higher the generalization level of knowledge is, the easier to be understood and moved knowledge is.

## 3. The formation of cognitive structures through active discovery

Bruner found that the teaching on the one hand have to consider people's knowledge structure, the structure of teaching materials, on the other should pay attention to people's initiative and intrinsic motivation to learn. In his view, the best motivation to learn is what they have learned the material interests, rather than external incentives to stimulate competition, and the like. Therefore, he advocated discovery learning method in order to make students more interested and more active learning with confidence.

The feature of discovery learning is concerned about the learning process is better than care about learning outcomes. Specific knowledge, principles, laws, etc. so that learners themselves to explore, to discover, so that students will actively participate in the learning process to go through independent thinking and the restructuring of teaching materials. "Learning in the discovery does affect the students, making it a 'constructivist'." Learning is a cognitive structure of the organization and reorganization. He emphasized that it has both the knowledge and experience of the role, but also stressed that learning materials for their intrinsic logical structure.

Bruner thought that the discovery learning has the following several functions: (1) increasing intellectual potential. (2) to enable the external motivation becomes intrinsic motivation. (3) good at discovery. (4) helps to keep memory of the learning materials.

Therefore, cognitive discovered that is worthy of special attention as a learning theory. Cognitive discovered that emphasize learning initiative, emphasized that it has cognitive structure, the structure of learning content, students the important role of independent thinking. The right to cultivate a modern talents are positive.

### 9.3.4 Cognitive assimilation theory

D. P. Ausubel is a psychology professor in Academy of New York State University. He is one of proponents of cognitive school. He has developed the learning and maintenance of the meaningful speech materials since the middle period of 1950's. His theory was put forward in the 1960s and was well accepted by the teachers in primary and middle schools. In 1976, He got "Thorndike's award" of Amercian Psychological Association.

Ausubel describes two orthogonal dimensions of learning: meaningful versus rote and reception versus discovery. Assimilation theory seeks to describe how rote learning occurs and the pitfalls of learning material by rote. The theory also explains how concepts might be acquired and organized within a learner's cognitive structure in a meaningful fashion through a broad range of teaching/learning strategies on the receptive - discovery dimension (Ausubel et al., 1978).

Ausubel believed that student's learning is mainly accepting learning instead of discovery learning. Accepting learning means that teacher directly presents students with learning content in the form of conclusion. Since practising classroom education, accepting learning has been the main form of classroom learning. But this kind of learning has been misunderstood as mechanical learning. In Ausubel's terms, accepting learning is both meaningful and mechanical. Because some teachers make his students carry on mechanical learning while they themselves apply accepting learning, accepting learning is considered mechanical learning. Likewise, discovery learning can be considered meaningful learning and mechanical learning. Only the discovery learning that can find a few facts but can not understand it is mechanical discovery learning. In Ausubel's terms, the learning in the school should be meaningful accepting learning and meaningful discovery learning. But he paid more attention to meaningful accepting learning, and believed that it could make students obtain a large amount of systematic knowledge in short time, which is exactly primary goal of teaching.

Ausubel thought that the essence of meaningful learning is the process of establishing non-human and substantive association through the new idea used symbol as its representation and intrinsic proper idea in learner's cognitive structure. The cognitive structure defined by Ausubel is all the content of one's idea and organization or partial content of one's idea in a certain field. Intrinsic knowledge in cognitive structure is idea's frame, or is called the idea with fixed role. The meaningful learning is to assimilate the idea with fixed role in cognitive structure; and intrinsic idea changes at the same time, and new knowledge is brought into intrinsic cognitive structure, such obtaining the meaning.

The meaningful learning is to assimilate the new idea with the old one. Ausubel called his own learning theory assimilating theory. The original idea assimilates the new one through three ways: subsumptive learning, superordinate learning, combinational learning. The subsumptive learning, is to properly combine the new idea with original idea in cognitive structure and make them associate with each other.

In subsumptive learning, original idea is the total idea while the new idea is subordinate one. So it is also called subsumptive learning. This learning has two kinds of form: derived subsumptive learning and relevant subsumptive learning. In derived subsumptive learning, the new idea just makes the original total idea expand, but not changes the original total idea in essence. In relevant subsumptive learning, the new idea can deepen, decorate and limit the original total idea, such leads to the fundamental changes of the original total idea through assimilation.

Superordinate learning is to induce a total idea based on several existing subsumptive ideas. For instance, after grasping the concepts of pencil ($a_1$), rubber ($a_2$) and notebook ($a_3$), the original superordinate idea $a_n$ may serve the total idea A if learning the more advanced total idea "stationery" A. The formed total idea in superordinate learning is higher than some already existing ideas in summarizing and forgiving intensity. So this learning is called superordinate learning.

Combinational learning refers to the general connection between the new idea and the whole content in original cognitive structure, but not the subsumptive relationship between as well as not superordinate relationship. For example, suppose that the new idea is "relation between quality and energy" (A), the original idea is the relation between "heat and the volume" (B), "heredity and variation" (C), "demand and price" (D). Under this condition, the new idea neither belongs to a special relation nor totally generalizes original relation. But they possess a certain common attribute. Because of this, the new idea can be assimilated by already existing knowledge.

### 9.3.5 *Learning theory of information processing*

R. M. Gagne is a education psychology professor in Florida State university. His learning theory is based on behaviorism and cognitive learning. It was established by using modern information theory and a lot of experimental research in the 1970s. In his terms, the learning process is receiving of the message and using information. Learning is the result of interaction of objects with environment. Learner's internal state and external condition are interdependence, inalienable entity.

Gagne thought that learning is the complex of different course taking place in learner's nervous system. Learning is not a simple association between stimulus and response. The stimulus is dealt with central nervous system through different methods, so understanding learning is to point out how the information processing plays role. According to Gagne's theory, learning is also regarded as the relationship between stimulus and response. Stimulus reacts on events of learner's sense organ while response appears with sense input and its subsequent conversion. Response can be described by way of operating changes. But there are some basic elements such as "learner" and "memory" between stimulus and response. The learner is a real person. They have sense organs and receive stimulus through sense organs; they have brains and receive the information from sense organ. The information is transferred by various complicated ways; they have muscles, by which the learned contents are showed. The learner is accepting various stimulus constantly, which are input into the neural activities with different form. Some are stored in memory. When reacting, the content in the memory can directly be transferred into external behaviors. Gagne regarded learning as a process of processing information. In 1974, he depicted a typical structural mode of learning (see Fig. 9.2).

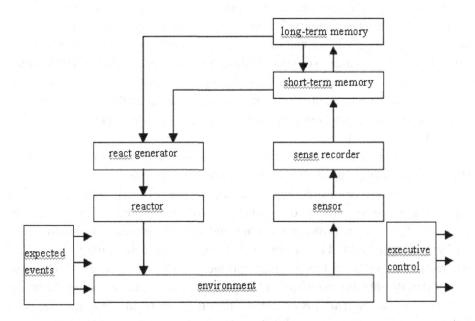

Fig. 9.2 Learning structural mode

Gagne's learning structural mode is divided into two parts: one is the structure on the right, called operative memory; the other is an information flow. The stimulus originating from external environment reacts on sensor and then related information is generated and is put into sense recorder. Here information is dealt with preliminary choice. After staying no more than one second, the information then enters into short-term memory. Here the information stays only a few seconds and then arrives at long-term memory. Later if needing remembering, the information is drawn out and returns back to short-term memory and then is put into generator. Here the information is processed and turned into behaviors, which react on environment. Learning generates in this way. The second part is the structure on the left. It includes expected events and executive control. The expected link plays a directional role such that learning activities go on along certain direction. The executive link plays a regulating, controlling role such that learning activities can be realized. The function of the second part causes learner learn, changes learning, strengthens learning and promotes learning, and information flow is activated, weakened and changed in direction at the same time.

Gagne had put forward basic model of learning according to information processing theory. He believed that learning is a process of information rocessing. That is to say, learner cognitively processes the information from environment, and he had concretely described the typical information processing mode. In his terms, learning can differ external condition from internal condition. The learning process is in fact learner's internal activities in the mind. Accordingly, learning process is divided into eight stages: motive stage, understanding stage, obtaining stage, keeping stage, remembering stage, summarizing stage, operating stage and feedback stage (see Fig. 9.3).

Gagne's learning theory pays attention to the internal condition and hierarchy of learning, and emphasizes the systematic teaching of systematic knowledge and teacher's progressive instructing function. It has offered certain basis for controlling teaching. His theory directly involves the classroom instruction. Therefore there are a positive meaning and certain reference value to actual teaching. Gagne used the viewpoint and method of information theory and cybernetics to explore the learning problems. He has attempted to some viewpoints in both behaviorism and cognitive school's theory to establish his own learning theory. This has reflected a development trend of the west learning theory. In his learning theory, the ability (energy) is just come down to a large amount of organized knowledge. This is unilateral and has ignored the function of thinking and intellectual skill and its cultivation.

### 9.3.6 Learning theory of constructivism

Constructivism is the outcome of the further development of behaviorism and cognitivism. The key of constructivism is: first, understanding is not a simple,

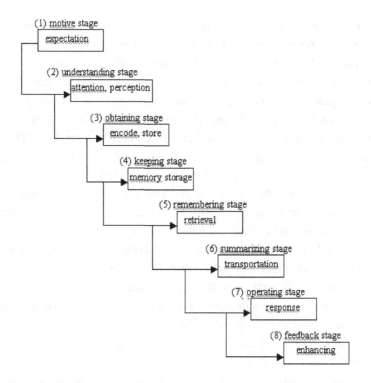

Fig. 9.3 Gagne's eight stages and corresponding mental process

passive response to objective being but an active course of construction, i.e. all knowledge is obtained through construction. Secondly, in the process of construction, the already existing cognitive structure of subject has played a very important role during the process of construction, and the cognitive structure of subject is also in constant development. Piaget and Vygotsky are all the pioneers in constructivism. Though Piaget highly emphasized each individual's innovation and Vygotsky paid more attention to the transition of knowledge's tool, i.e. culture and language, they were all constructivist in terms of the basic orientation.

Modern constructivism can be divided into extreme constructivism and society constructivism. The extreme constructivism has two essential features: first, put emphasis on constructive property of understanding activity and believe that all knowledge is the construction of subject. We can not directly sense the outside world. Understanding activity is in fact a process of sense making, i.e. subject uses its own already existing knowledge and experience to make a sense to the outside world. Secondly, absolutely affirm "individual properties" of understanding activity and believe that each subject has different knowledge background and experience (or different cognitive structure). Hence even for understanding of the same subject, corresponding understanding activity can not be totally identical, but has individual's particularity undoubtedly. For extreme constructivism, individual construction has its abundant independence, i.e. a kind of highly independent activity. That is to say, "there are 100 subjects and 100 different constructions if there are 100 persons". Just in this sense, extreme constructivism is usually called individual constructivism too. The core of society constructivism lies in definite affirmation of society property of understanding activity. Social environment and social community play important roles in understanding activity; the individual's understanding activity can be realized in certain social environment. The so-called sense making implies the meaning of "culture inheriting". That is to say, the "individual meanings" generated through individual constructive activity implies the inheritance and understanding of corresponding "social cultural meaning" in fact.

By constructivism, learner uses their own experience to construct significant understanding, but not to understand the already organized knowledge that is passed to them. Learner's understanding of outside world is his or her own positively constructing result, but not something that passively acceptable. Constructivist believes that knowledge is formed through individual's constructing the real world. According to this kind of view, learning appears by constantly constructing rule and assumption, in order to explain observed phenomenon. When consistency appears between the original idea and new observation, the original idea loses it balance and then constructing new rule and assumption is needed. Obviously, learning activity is a creative understanding process. For general understanding activity, it is mainly an "acclimation" process, i.e. constant change and recombination of cognitive structure, which is just a direct result of interaction of new learning activity and cognitive structure.

According to constructivism, "acclimation" or change and recombination of cognitive structure is subject's main constructive activity. Constructivism pays attention on learner's go-aheadism, association between new knowledge and old one and emphasizes the understanding that is obtained by applying knowledge to real situation. The American psychologist Wittrock (M. C. Wittrock) has presented a production process of student's learning, which well explains such constructive process of learning. In Wittrock's terms, the production process is the process of interaction of original cognitive structure and sense information (new knowledge), and the process of forwardly choosing information and constructing information.

The theory of constructivism is a kind of newly developing theory. This theory emphasizes the positive initiative and the understanding of construction of meaning of new knowledge and originality. This theory emphasizes that learning is of societal properties and pays attention to the influence of interactions between teacher and student and among students for learning. By this theory, learning is divided into elementary and advanced learning with emphasizing student's constructing network knowledge structure through advanced learning. A set of novel and creationary opinions are put forward in teaching goal, teacher's function and teaching method and design etc. These opinions have some positive significance in relation to further realizing learning's essence, revealing learning's law and deepening teaching reform.

The theory of constructivism flourished on the basis of absorbing all kinds of learning theories. However, there are some contradictions in this theory, which betrays its shortcomings, so it needs to further develop and improve.

## 9.4 Humanistic Learning Theory

Humanistic psychology is a psychological thought rosen in fifties or sixties of the 20th century in the United States. Its main representatives are A. Maslow and C. R. Rogers. Humanistic view of learning and teaching profoundly affected the world-wide education reform, with the programmed instruction movement, the subject structure of movement par the 20th century, one of the three major education campaign.

Humanistic psychologist thought that to understand human behavior, one must understand the sense world of behavior person. When understanding human behavior, an important one is not the external fact, but a meaning of the behavior. If we want to change a person's behavior, we should change his faith and perception at first. When ways that he looks at problem are different, his behaviors are just different. In other words, the humanism psychologist attempts to explain and understand the behavior from behavior person himself instead of observer. Below we will introduce Rogers's learning theory, who is a representative of humanism learning theory.

Rogers thought that learning could be divided into two kinds. One is similar to the learning with insignificant syllable in psychology. In Rogers's terms, this kind of learning involves only the mind, and is the learning that takes place "above the cervix". It does not involve the emotion or personal meaning, and has nothing to do with the whole person. The other is meaning learning. The so-called meaning learning refers to the learning that individual behavior and attitude, individuality change greatly in further choosing the course of action, but not to the one that only involving the cumulating of fact. This is not only a learning of growth knowledge, but also a kind of learning merging with every part of experience of everybody together.

Rogers though that the meaning learning mainly includes the following four elements:

(1) Learning is of the property of personal involvement. That is, the whole person, including emotion and cognition, puts into the learning activities;
(2) Learning is self initiated, even if the stimulus or driving force comes from external world, but the acquired sensation must comes from internal world.
(3) Develop in an all-round way. That is, it ensures the all-round development of student's behavior, attitude, personality, etc.
(4) Learning is evaluated by the learner. Because students know whether this kind of learning meets one's own need, whether it facilitates causing him to know what he wants to know.

Rogers thought that the key to promote their learning does not lie in the teacher's teaching skill, professional knowledge, course project, guidance material of seeing and hearing, demonstrating and explaining, abundant books, etc. but lie in the particular psychological atmosphere factor between teacher and student. Then, what does a good psychological atmosphere factor include? Rogers provided his own explanation:

(1) Sincerity and reality. As a promoter, the teacher displays real self, and has no namby-pamby, sham and recovery;
(2) Respect, attention and admission. The teacher respects the learner's opinion and emotion, cares about the learner's every aspect and admits each individual's values and emotional expression;
(3) Empathy-key of understanding. The teacher can understand the learner's inherent response and students' learning process.

The learning that is carried on under such psychological atmosphere regards student as the centre and the teacher as the promoter, cooperator or partner. Students are the key to the learning and the course of learning is the purpose of learning.

In a word, humanistic psychologists such as Rogers, proceeding from their human nature and self-actualization theory, advocate student-centered "meaningful freedom learning" in teaching practice. This has assaulted the traditional education theory and has promoted the development of educational reform. This kind of impact and promotion is manifested in the following ways: stress the position and function of emotion in teaching; form a new teaching model that uses emotion as the basic motive forces of teaching activity; emphasize the importance of interpersonal relationship in teaching with student's self-perfect as the core; the emphasis of teaching activity is transferred from teacher to student and student's thought, emotion, experience and behavior are regarded as the body of teaching, such promote the growth of the individualized teaching.

Therefore, a lot of viewpoints in humanistic theory are worth our using for reference. For example, the teacher should respect students and deal honestly with students; let student discovery the joy of learning and actively participate in teaching; the teacher should understand the learner's inherent response, and find out student's learning process; the teacher is the promoter, cooperator or partner, etc. However, we also can find that Rogers denies the teacher's function excessively, which is not very correct. In teaching, we stress the subject position of student, as well as do not ignore the leading role of teacher.

## 9.5 Observational Learning

The remarkable contribution to psychology of Albert Bandura lies in that he had explored the ignored learning form, observational learning, and provided the observational learning with related position and attention. Observational learning is much more complex than simple imitation. Bandura's theory is often referred to as "social learning theory" as it emphasizes the role of vicarious experience (observation) of people impacting people (models). The proposed model of observational learning, together with the classical conditioned and operating reflex, are called the three major tools of observational learning. The observational learning is called societal learning theory sometimes. Bandura's learning theory does not avoid behavioral internal reason. On the contrary, it pays attention to the function of the symbol, substitute, self-regulation function. Hence Bandura's theory is also called cognitive behaviorism.

In the research of Bandura, he pays attention to the influence of the social factors, changes the trend that the tradition learning theory emphasizes individual but despises society, and combines the research of learning psychology with that of social psychology. Hence he has made great contribution to the development of learning theory. Bandura has absorbed the research results of cognitive psychology, and has organically combined enhancing theory with information processing theory and then changes the inclination of emphasizing "stimulus and response" and despising intermediate process.

Because he emphasizes social factors in learning process and the function of cognitive process in learning, Bandura must pay attention to the experiment with person as measurand on methodology. His theory has changed the method that animal is used as measurand and corrected the wrong inclination of extending the result obtained from animal experiment to human learning. Bandura thought that by observing the behaviors of important people in their life, children can learn the societal behaviors. These observations are expressed in the form of mental imagery or other symbol and are stored in the mind. This theory has accepted the most principles of behavioralism theoreticians, but pays more attention to the function of the clue on behavior, inherent mental process. The theory emphasizes the interaction of thought and behavior. His viewpoint has provided the bridge between behavioral school and cognitive school, and has made an enormous contribution to the treatment of "cognition-behavior".

The concept and theory of Bandura are built on solid and rich experiment data. His experimental method is more rigorous and the conclusion is more convincing. His opening theory frame adheres to behaviorism position as well as actively absorbs the research results and methods of modern cognitive psychology. At the same time, under the enlightenment of some idea of humanism learning theory, his theory involves some important subjects such as observational learning, interaction, self-regulation, self-efficiency, etc. It stresses the initiative and sociality, and is met with general acceptance. Social learning theory explains human behavior in terms of continuous reciprocal interaction between cognitive, behavioral, and environmental influences.

Necessary conditions for effective modeling:

(1) Attention — various factors increase or decrease the amount of attention paid. Includes distinctiveness, affective valence, prevalence, complexity, functional value. One's characteristics (e.g. sensory capacities, arousal level, perceptual set, past reinforcement) affect attention.

(2) Retention — remembering what you paid attention to. Includes symbolic coding, mental images, cognitive organization, symbolic rehearsal, motor rehearsal

(3) Reproduction — reproducing the image. Including physical capabilities, and self-observation of reproduction.

(4) Motivation — having a good reason to imitate. Includes motives such as past (i.e. traditional behaviorism), promised (imagined incentives) and vicarious (seeing and recalling the reinforced model)

By this theory, individual, environment and behavior are all linked and influenced together. The size of influence of the three is determined by the environment and behavioral property at that time. The theory has often been called a bridge between behaviorist and cognitive learning theories because it encompasses attention, memory, and motivation.

Besides this kind of direct reinforcement, Bandura also proposed other two kinds of reinforcements: alterative reinforcement and self-reinforcement. The alterative reinforcement refers to the reinforcement that is tasted because the observer is tasting a reinforcement. For instance, when a teacher enhances a student's an act of giving aid, the other students in the class will spend certain time helping each other too. In addition, the other function of alterative reinforcement is he arousing of emotional response. For example, a star shows charming way because of wearing a kind of clothes or using a kind of shampoo in TV advertisement; at this time, if you feel or experience the happiness because the star is noticed, this is a kind of your alterative reinforcement. The self-reinforcement depends on the result that is transmitted through society. When the society transmits a certain behavioral standard to an individual and the individual behavior suits even exceeds this standard, he will reward himself with his own behavior. In addition, Bandura had also provided the concept of self-regulation. Bandura supposed that people can observe their own behaviors and make a judgment according to his own standard, such reinforcement or punishing himself.

## 9.6 Introspective Learning

The introspection refers to investigating a person's own thought or emotion, i.e. self-observation; it also refers to observing sensation and perception experience under the control of experiment condition. The introspection is opposite to appearance. The appearance is to investigate and observe the situation of the exclusion of oneself. Introspection method is early a psychological research approach. It investigates the psychological phenomena and process according to the report of the tested person or the experience described by himself. The introspection learning is to introduce introspection concept into machine learning. That is to say, by checking and caring about knowledge processing and reasoning method of intelligence system itself and finding out problems from failure or poor efficiency, the introspection learning forms its own learning goal and then improves the method to solving problems.

The mankind often improves himself through self-observation. People may conscientiously and unconsciously carry on introspection learning. For example, a long-distance runner, who participates in match of 10000 meters, may meet the problem of improperly distributing the physical power. It is possible to influence the achievement that either the physical power is depleted greatly or he is too conservative to dash late. After several unsuccessful experiences, he will find out the unsuccessful reason constantly, so as to avoid the same problem in the new match again. So he will rationally adjust physical power and tactics and therefore each match is better than the last. Only not from some instances we find that introspection learning is a good way to improve the ability to solve problem, but also from a lot of psychological results we can verify that the human is of the ability of introspection learning.

A learning system with the ability of introspection learning will improve learning efficiency too. When a system is in a complicated world, it is difficult to tell all possible relevant information and deduce method of the system in advance. A very difficult question is to predict the situation that the system will face, what information will be important and what response condition will be needed. Hence better flexibly and adaptability are required for the system, so as to seasonedly deal with various situations. The system should be of the ability to improve system's knowledge and know how to operate. But most learning systems do not possess the ability to change knowledge processing reasoning method. In a learning system with multi-policy, a central issue is to choose and arrange the learning algorithms for the particular situation. It requires the intelligence system to automatically choose and arrange the appropriate algorithm from the algorithm storehouse. By using introspection learning, the learning system can determine its goal based on analyzing successes and failures of executed task. In other words, its goal is not the one that the designer of the system or user provides. The system can determine clearly what is needed and what should be learned. In other words, introspection learning system can understand the causes of the failure and related reasoning and knowledge in the process of operating system. The system has its own knowledge and the ability to check its reasoning. In this way, the system can effectively learn. And the learning is less effective without such introspection. Therefore introspection is necessary for effective learning.

The introspection learning involves four sub-problems:

(1) There are standards that determine when the reasoning process should be checked, i.e. monitoring reasoning process;

(2) Determine whether failure reasoning takes place according to the standards;

(3) Confirm the final reason that leads to the failure;

(4) Change the reasoning process in order to avoid the similar failure in the future.

To be able to find and explain the failure, introspection learning system is required to be able to visit the knowledge about its reasoning process until present moment. It needs a rough or clear expectation about the field result and its internal reasoning process. It is able to discovery the failure of expectation in the reasoning process and problem solving. In addition, it also can use reasoning failure to explain expectation failure and determines how to change the reasoning process and then corrects the error hereafter. The introspection learning process includes three steps:

(1) Judge a failure. Determine whether disappointed expectation should be generated;

(2) Explain the failure. Introspection learning system can find out the cause of error of reasoning line before the failure and give the explanation to the reasoning failure. The system provides the definite goal of introspection learning so as to change its knowledge and reasoning process;

(3) Correct the failure. The system carries out the tactics of introspection learning according to the goal of introspection learning.

From the above, an introspection learning system must possess itself intact learning structure, such as knowledge base, algorithm base and inference engine, etc. In addition, it requires a set of meta reasoning representation in order to track and confirm the realized process of reasoning; the system also requires a set of evaluation standard of reasoning, including explanation, efficiency analysis, mistake, failure, etc.; it requires an introspection mechanism that is used to check the reasoning, form goal and execute policy too.

M. T. Cox applied explanation pattern (XP) to explain anomaly and then created an accident understanding system (Cox et al., 1999). It is a goal-driven learning system. The system chooses algorithms from algorithm toolbox and combines them with multi-learning method, so as to repair the erroneous part that leads to the failure of the system. The input of the system is dataflow of incident concept entity; the executing task is to generate an interaction model of person and incident. As a system prophesies a certain explanation is tenable in an incident but a different explanation appears after the incident, a failure will happen. The system will explain why the system fails and form knowledge learning tactic which can change the failure. Such the system can learn through failures.

When Meta-AQUA has not succeeded in understanding a story passage, it then uses the introspective Meta-XPs (IMXPs) to repair its reasoning process. An IMXP describes the tactics that are related to reasoning failure and repairing reasoning. An IMXP can be consider the template matched with the description of real reasoning process. It determines whether the reasoning will fail. But the real reasoning process is expressed by Trace Meat-XPs (TMXPs). For different reasoning failure, Meta-AQUA has summed up failure's symptom category, reason type and goal type. The symptom of reasoning failure can be used to confirm the reason of the failure, and the reason of the failure also can be used to confirm related learning goal.

ROBBIE is a route planning system proposed by S. Fox (Fox, 1996). Its task is to produce a route planning from place to another place under the conditions of several streets, possessing limited map knowledge and a small amount of initial samples. It examines the quality of planning by carrying out the planning in one simulation world. ROBBIE is a case-based system. Its knowledge can accrue from increasing cases: when the cases increase, it will understand the map better. ROBBIE's introspective unit monitors the reasoning of the planning device and compares the expected performance of real reasoning process with that of case-based reasoning process. When expectation failure takes place, introspective unit will stay planning task and will attempt to explain the failure and correct the system. If there is enough information to prove that failure may generate, the system will continue carrying out the task. When necessary information is ready, explanation and modification will resume from the suspended place. The feature of ROBBIE's system is to apply introspection learning in case-based retrieval reasoning module, and realize the refining of case index. When retrieval fails, the reason of failure can be found through introspective unit and retrieval process is corrected. In addition, the system has provided the frame for applying introspection learning to intact process of case-based reasoning.

### 9.6.1 General model of introspection learning

The general introspection course is divided into three parts: judge the failure, explain the failure and correct the failure (Shi et al., 2005).

(1) Judge the failure: based on the establishment of definite and finite expectation of reasoning process, compare the expectation with the real executing process of the system and then find out the difference. The difference between expected behavior and real behavior is explanation failure. To determine whether the failure takes place means that there is a group of definite expected value about the reasoning state of the system. Expectation failure is monitored in the process of reasoning. When going on every step of the reasoning process, compare the related result with related expectation. If expectation is found, then failure will take place.

(2) Explain the failure: according to the standard of expectation failure and the trace of reasoning, explain the failure. After finding out the reason, a definite correcting suggestion related to the reasoning process should be presented, in order to avoid the same failure again.

(3) Correct the failure: related corrective action of the reasoning process can be appended to a particular expectation. Such, when an expectation failure takes place, the appended method also can be presented at the same time. The description of corrective method is not able to be detailed enough. So the system should also include forming the mechanism of the revision tactics. The revision module carries out the real revision tactics and the real modification according to the description of failure and the suggestion of revision.

The general model of introspection learning is shown in Fig. 9.4. Besides judging the failure, explaining the failure and correcting the failure, the model also includes knowledge base, reasoning trace, reasoning expectation model and monitor protocol, etc. The monitor protocol is used to standardize the monitor of reasoning process. It prescribes where and how the reasoning process should be monitored and the control of the system should be transferred. The knowledge base includes the knowledge relevant to reasoning. It is not only the foundation of reasoning but also the grounds for judging and explaining the failure at the same time. The reasoning trace has recorded the reasoning process. It is specially used in introspection learning, also is the important grounds for judging, explaining and correcting the failure. The reasoning expectation model is an ideal model of system's reasoning process. It has provided the standard for reasoning expectation, and therefore is the main grounds for judging the failure. The introspective learning unit of the system uses monitor protocol, already existing background, reasoning expectation and reasoning trace to check whether the current state appears expectation failure.

The emergence of expectation failure includes two cases: one is that when a model expectation about the current ideal state of reasoning process does not fit the current real reasoning process, expectation failure will take place. Another one is that when the system can not continue because of disastrous failure, expectation failure takes place certainly. If there is no expectation failure in reasoning unit, then all the expectations fit the real process and the system is informed that everything is all right and then the system regains the control power again. If a failure is found, the reasoning will use background, reasoning trace and ideal expectation model to look for the initial reason for the failure and explain the failure. It is possible that the obtained information possible is not enough to diagnose and correct the failure when a failure is found. At this time, the introspection learning unit can suspend its explanation and revision tasks until there is abundant information. When the necessary information is already obtained, the explanation and revision tasks will resume from the suspended place. The explanation of the failure can provide clue for correcting the failure. After explanation, the learning goal of correcting failure is generated and revision method is also formed according to the learning goal. After revision, the system will regain control power.

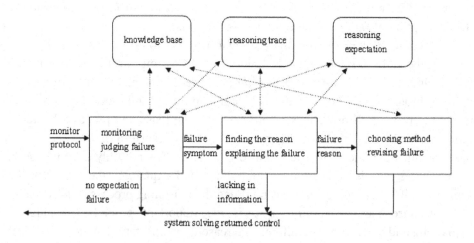

Fig. 9.4 Introspection learning model

## 9.6.2 *Meta-reasoning of introspection learning*

Meta-reasoning originates from the concept of meta-cognition in cognitive process. It is also called self-monitor cognition. The meta-cognition is viewed as the cognition of cognition. It refers to a cognitive process about oneself and the knowledge of all the related things. It includes two kinds of ability of awareness and control. The former refers to knowing one's own ability limiting, concept, knowledge and cognitive strategy. The latter refers to appropriately controlling and applying one's own knowledge and strategy. The past learning system paid more attention to knowledge acquisition and processing. It emphasized the exactness of knowledge as well as that of reasoning process. This makes a demand of reasonably expressing reasoning process based on knowledge representation. Similar to the meta-data of warehouse, i.e. data about the data, meta-reasoning is used in introspection learning system. By using meta-reasoning, the learning system can acquire the cognition of knowledge and knowledge processing, and further finishes the proper control and usage of its own knowledge and tactics.

Meta-reasoning involves reasoning about the reasoning. Because one of the main goals of introspection learning is to revise reasoning process according to reasoning failure or execution, expressing the reasoning process through the basic level is a basic condition of introspection learning. The introduction of meta-reasoning requires reaching two goals. The first goal is to record the reasoning process of the system and form the reasoning trace. The second one is to explain the reasoning process and provide a causal chain for reasoning failure. And the final goal is to offer expressing for reasoning process of monitoring and offer essential information for explaining and revising reasoning failure.

The expression of meta-reasoning can be realized by both external and internal ways. The external way is to establish one ideal model for reasoning process, and design different evaluation standard at different stages. The internal way is to use the expression with meta-explanation to internally record reasoning process, and explain anomaly. For instance, the Meta-AQUQ system applies XP theory to express the transition of mind state, and names this kind of expression structure as the meta-explanation pattern. Its meaning is a explanation pattern of one about another explanation mode. Because the standard explanation mode is the expression method of a cause and effect structure, meta-explanation pattern can explain its own explanation process. According to the difference of functions, there are two kinds of meta-explain patterns. One is used for tracking explanation process, and it is called trace meta-explanation pattern (TMXP). Another one is to use introspective explanation, and it is called introspective meta-explanation pattern (IMXP).

### 9.6.3 Failure classification

Another important problem of the introspection learning system is failure classification. Meta-AQUA system has listed the types of symptom, reason of the failure and related learning goal. The failure symptom is classified according to whether actual value (A) and expected value (E) exist and are the same or not, including contradictory, unexpected, deadlock, strange affair, false proposition, expect proposition, degradation, etc. Each symptom is expressed by the associations of various failure marks. The system has proposed two kinds of wrong marks, such as inference expectations failure and amalgamation failure, and four kinds of omission marks, such as overdue prophecy, search failure, structure failure and input failure. ROBBIE system classifies the abnormity according to different module in the model, and combined with related assertion, which is the main ground for explaining failure. The failure is divided by reasoning process. The reasoning process is divided into several stages, such as index example, search case, adjusting case, second retrieval case, executing case, keeping case. The failure is also divided into several stages.

The failure classification is a key element of introspection learning. It is the ground for judging failure and provides a important clue for explaining failure and forming corrected leaning goal at the same time. The failure classification also determines the ability of introspection learning to a certain extent. So it is necessary to set up a rational failure classification for introspection learning system. Failure classification requires considering two important factors. One is the granularity of failure classification; the other is association among failure classification, failure explanation and the goal of introspection learning. The failure classification with granularity can settle the contradiction of classification which is too thin or too thick. For failure big classification, we can abstractly describe the failure as well as can finish the thickly classifying according to different stage of reasoning process. In this way, we not only can include some unpredictable situations and increase the adaptability of the systematic introspection, but also can accelerate contrasting process according to different stage. The thin classification can describe the failure in detailed. This way can provide valuable clue for failure explanation. Appropriately dealing with association between failure classification and failure explanation will also raise systematic introspection ability. The system not only requires finding out the failure reason through failure symptom and forming introspective learning goal, but also has the ability (adaptability) to deal with all kinds of different problems. The failure explanation also can be divided into different levels. The granularity of failure classification facilitates forming reasonable relationship between failure symptom and failure explanation.

The method of failure classification includes failure common approach and reasoning process module approach. The failure common approach proceeds with common characteristic of failure and finishes the classification. For instance, lack of input information can come down to input failure; inference machine's failing to induce or create a solution to a problem comes down to creation failure; knowledge failure is regarded as knowledge contradiction, and so on. The common approach considers the failure classification from the whole respect of the system. This approach is suitable for introspection learning in the distributed environment. The module approach is to classify reasoning process into several modules and creates a partition according to the module. For example, case-based reasoning can be divided into several modules, such as retrieval, adjustment, evaluation, storage. Retrieval failure refers to the anomaly appearing in retrieval process. The module approach is suitable for the reasoning in modular system. In some cases, two kinds of approaches can be combined.

### 9.6.4 Case-based reasoning in the introspective process

The case-based reasoning is to obtain the source case in memory through suggestion of the goal case and then to guide the goal case by using the source case. In this reasoning, the facing problems and situations is called goal case, and the question or situation in memory is called source case. Its advantage lies in simplifying knowledge acquisition, improving the efficiency and quality of problem solving. The process of case-based reasoning is to form case's retrieval characteristics according to current goal and then search related case in the memory case base by using retrieval feature. Then it selects a case that is the most similar to current situation, judges the case in order to suit the current situation, forms a new case and evaluates the new case, finally stores the new case to the base for further usage. The case-based reasoning and model-based reasoning are important way to realize introspection learning. On the contrary, introspection learning also can improve the process of the case-based reasoning.

A key link in the introspection learning process is to find out the reason for failure according to failure features. Introspection not only concerns about executing failure or reasoning failure, but also should contain less effective execution or reasoning process. Besides finding the error, the system needs to evaluate reasoning.

Form the perspective of expectation, the failure judgment is also called supervision and evaluation. The expectation value is considered as the criterion of supervision and evaluation. At the same time, evaluation factor can be used for quantitative evaluation. Supervision is oriented to reasoning process while evaluation is oriented to reasoning result. A series of processes, such as case-based reasoning retrieval, adjustment, evaluation and storage, to finish judgment failure and explanation failure may the effectiveness of judgment and explanation. So case-based reasoning is an effective way. In the Meta-AQUA system, the process from checking error to forming learning goal is a case-based reasoning process. The system can find out the reason of failure and then form learning goal by failure symptom. On the other hand, the usage of introspection learning in different modules of case-based reasoning, such as retrieval and evaluation, has improved the adaptability of the system and accuracy. The evaluation of case is an important step in case-based reasoning system. Quantitative case evaluation enables case to automatically modify case weight, so as to improve the effectiveness of case retrieval.

## 9.7 Scientific Discovery

Science discovery is defined as a complete and scientific cognitive process in which humans inherit the knowledge from the predecessors and practice with it, reveal the internal disciplines among objects and phenomena, form new concepts, principles, patterns and theories from these disciplines, and put them into use in the practice to solve problems in the reality. In human history, scientific discovery always appears as an exciting event, and is seen as the bloom of human intelligence. In the development of society, it always brings happiness to humankind and contributes greatly to both the material and the spiritual civilization. 19th Century is considered as the true beginning of the era of science. Michael Faradoy's electromagnetic experiment has led to the invention of the dynamo. J. C. Maxwell's discussion on the properties of the electromagnetic wave delivers the invention of radiotelegraphy and wireless telephone. In around 1838, Cagniard de Latour found in fermentation, the yeasts were actually some extremely small plant cells, whose living activities were the cause of the chemical changes in the fermentation liquid. In 1855, Louis Pasteur proved both fermentation and decay were caused by the action of living microorganism. These discoveries have great impact on the industry and medicine. British naturalist Charles R. Darwin introduced the theory of evolution on the basis of species selection, and hence gave an explicit explanation variation and biological adaptation of the species, which brought the concept of development and change into biology. Friedrich Engels thought that the evolution theory was one of the three greatest discoveries in natural science of the 19th century (the other two were the law of conservation and transformation of energy and the cell theory, providing the natural science foundation for the emergence of Marxist philosophy.

### 9.7.1 Discovery theory

There are many different theories providing different explanations to the general mechanism or pattern of the new knowledge generation, which consists of problems such as the essence, origin, motivation, certainty and truth. To date, empiricism, rationalism, transcendentalism and structuralism are most influential, and we'll briefly introduce the basis for each of them in the following.

### 1. Empiricism

Empiricism considers the experience as the only source of all cognition, which means new knowledge is delivered from experience and can only be delivered from it. Both materialistic and ideal comprehensions are available for empiricism, and as a result, there are both materialistic and idea empiricism. But only materialistic empiricism will be discussed in more detail here as it is related to the scientific discovery.

The founder of materialistic empiricism is Francis Bacon. Bacon believed all knowledge was produced by the perceptual experience and was escalated to the universal law eventually. Because of this, he paid particular attention to the acquisition of facts and emphasized the importance of experiment in induction. He contrived an inductive methodology to represent the specific steps of scientific induction. When use it, not only do the positive facts (Table of Presence) required consideration, but also negative facts (Table of Absence) and the facts of difference degrees (Table of Degrees). Afterwards the general principle can be obtained by using elimination to exclude those non-essential things. Bacon's inductive methodology was a summary of the experimental research methods in the natural science of that time.

Bacon made some interesting comparison to the three different scientific methods: ants', spiders' and bees'. Ants only acquire facts or evidences, and accumulate them. Spiders only produce theories just like they spin. Ants don't produce any methods like spiders do, but spiders totally ignore the evidences. Bees collect evidences, and use them to produce methods, and use those methods to change the evidences. Bacon considered the methods of ants' or spiders' to be wrong, while the bees' were correct. This means from Bacon's view, the true scientific knowledge is the cognition of the cause and result of things, which can only be acquired by laboratory observation, rational exploration and the arts of discovery. Moreover, the goal of humans pursuing scientific knowledge is to apply it to the real life, and thus the criterion of the scientific knowledge correctness is its usability.

Empiricism was not able to explain the transition of knowledge from the experience level to the theory level, or the upgrade from perceptual experience to theory knowledge. Therefore Bacon didn't fully recognize the complexity, relativity or tortuosity of the process of scientific cognition.

## 2. Rationalism

From the point of view of rationalism, the development of new knowledge starts from self-evident axioms, and general scientific principles are gradually deduced from them. The essence of scientific discovery was the self invention of the rationality. Perceptual experience is the correspondence with the theories at most, which are invented by this kind of rationality.

Contrast to empiricism, rationalism only admits the reliability of rational knowledge, but denies perceptual knowledge's dependence on rational knowledge. Rationalism has both ideal and materialistic forms. The representative individual of the former is René Descartes, while the latter can be represented by Baruch Spinoza. Descartes insisted, the knowledge source was the "innate idea" of the rationality. Only the knowledge provided by the rationality is reliable, while that from experience was not. The criterion of truth is the clarity of the concept itself.

When Descartes was building his system of metaphysics, he proposed "I think; therefore I am" based on his universal doubt theory, and with a series of complicated reasoning, he introduced the three entities: mind, god and matter, and the natural and relation among them. He pointed out, the natural of mind was thought, and matter's was extension; Extension couldn't think, while thought didn't have extension. Hence the natural of mind and matter are mutually different, incompatible, and indecisive. Based on the metaphysics, dualism was created and was a typical philosophy in modern Europe.

Baruch Spinoza founded materialistic in the process of his criticism to the Descartes dualism. He opposed Descartes' two entities, insisting there was only one entity in the universe, i.e. natural or substantial world; Knowledge was the correspondent effect on human cognition, which was caused by the external objects. He classified knowledge and knowledge acquirement into 3 categories: opinion, reason and intuition. The first one was that obtained from perceptual experience, the second was inductive knowledge, and the last was intuitive. He asserted the intuition was the highest level of knowledge and the acquirement of knowledge was using the rational intuition to obtain the tool of gift – "intuitive sense" and using it to deduce other knowledge.

Regarding to scientific discovery, in 1637 Descartes published his famous work *Discourse on the Method*, which has since made enormous impact to the westerners on the way of thought, concept and methods of research. The 4 precepts introduced in this book are very enlightening.

(1) The percept of doubt: "...never accept anything for true which I did not clearly know to be such; that is to say, carefully to avoid precipitancy and prejudice, and to comprise nothing more in my judgment than what was presented to my mind so clearly and distinctly as to exclude all ground of doubt."

(2) The percept of analysis: "...divide each of the difficulties under examination into as many parts as possible, and as might be necessary for its adequate solution."

(3) The percept of generalization: "...develop my thoughts in order, beginning with the simplest and easiest to understand matters, in order to reach by degrees, little by little, to the most complex knowledge, assuming an orderliness among them which did not at all naturally seem to follow one from the other."

(4) The perceptual of entirety: "...make my enumerations so complete and my reviews so general that I could be assured that I had not omitted anything."

Descartes emphasized heavily on rationality, advocating the concept of "clarity" being the starting point of fragmentation. He was against blind faith, and took doubt as his weapon of choice against scholasticism.

Gottfried Wilhelm Leibniz, the famous German scientist from 17$^{th}$ century, was also a rationalist. He asserted the task of cognition was to obtain the universal and necessary knowledge. This kind of knowledge couldn't be acquired from perceptual experience, or displayed in human mind as a concept of gift. It appears as a "orientation, intuition, habit or natural potential" in our mind which is given by God. It became clear and occurred in our mind with the assist of external "opportunities". He was against John Locke's empiricism, and did not completely agree on Descartes' rationalism either. He saw the human mind as a marble with stripes instead of a blank slate. Those stripes were not a completed statue, but the completed statue would be determined by them innately.

Leibniz divided knowledge into deducted knowledge and factual knowledge, and highly valued the latter and the universal and inevitable knowledge. From his point of view, if a "universal symbolic language" can be established, we can make the "calculation of thought" like math. And arguments can be correctly judged by "let's calculate it". Leibniz attempted to create an accurate, universal language of science, and establish such a deduction or calculation that can be used to settle debate and arguments. This idea of his not only has great influence on the development of modern mathematical logic, but also significantly affected the development of computer science, artificial intelligence and cognitive science. During creative thought, once the inner mechanisms and formalities are made clear, their deduction and development will transform to logic, even algorithm. Rationality, logic and algorithms are somehow internally related.

## 3. Transcendentalism

Transcendentalists start from the premise that spirit is the origin of the world, and materials are produced by spirit. They insist on the cognitive path -- from mind or spirit to objects, asserting human knowledge and ability is prior to objective things, social practice and perceptual experience because it's innate and autogenic..

Immanuel Kant is the first ever philosopher that publicly claims his epistemology to be transcendental idealism. He blended rationalism and empiricism to create his own "critical philosophy". In rationalistic perspective, Kant was mainly influenced by Leibniz, while in empiricist perspective his influence greatly came from David Hume. Kant stated, neither the inevitability and universality of Leibniz's gift, nor David Hume's perceptual experience could construct knowledge alone. Any knowledge was the combination of perceptual material and universality and necessity. Any knowledge had two parts, the material and the form. The material (the content of knowledge) was generated from experience, while the form (various categories) was inherently transcendental in our mind. Only after being collated by the innate form could the material have its order and regularity. His logical foundation was the innate categories, thus his logic was named "transcendental logic". Kant believed the transcendental logic mostly focused on clarifying the source, limit and objectivity of human knowledge.

Kant realized the active function of concepts and categories in the process of scientific discover, but he overly emphasized the capacity of consciousness generating concepts automatically. He also took many basic logic categories, and philosophical concepts like causality, possibility and inevitability as transcendent, and thus split the connection between rationality and perception. Kant divided human understanding ability into perception, intellectuality and rationality. Kant admitted there was a "thing in itself" existing outside us. This "thing in itself" would stimulate our organs to generate senses. The so called perceptual understanding is the combination of the stimulating material and the innate time and space. It took time and space as an intuitive priori of the perception. However, in the stage of perception, the perceptual material has the properties of space and time after some collation, but it's still scattered, lacking the universality and inevitability, so understanding must move from this stage to the stage of intellectuality. Intellectuality further collates and synthesizes the perceptual material process by time and space. And the synthesized form is the 12 intellectual categories including entity, causality, inevitability, etc. This synthesis is made by the "cogtio", i.e. the "transcendent apperception". Kant asserted the intellectual category was innate. Only through this kind of innate category of intellectuality, can the perceptual material obtain its universality and inevitability to provide strictly scientific knowledge. Intellectuality is the understanding of things that are infinite, relative and conditional, but rationality is not. Rationality requires infinite and unconditional knowledge. It needs the master of the absolute entity, i.e. theory. Kant's view on scientific knowledge as the combination of perceptual intuition and abstract thought admits the effect that the synthesis of intellectual categories has on perceptual experience. It also sees the mutual connection between perceptual understanding and rational understanding, as well as the active function of thought. These should be acknowledged. Moreover, he introduced a different logic from traditional formal logic, namely transcendental logic, which contributed to the foundation of dialectic logic. Kant separated analytical judgment from synthetic judgment, and this has particular influence on western science and philosophy.

## 4. Falsificationism

In 1968 Karl Popper's publication *The Logic of Scientific Discovery* was a classic of falsificationism. The book mainly discussed two problems of knowledge and theories: demarcation and induction. According to the author, criterion of demarcation was falsifiability instead of verifiability and the scientific method was deduction and verification instead of induction.

Falsificationists admit observation is under the guide of theories, as theories are the precondition of observation. They are also willing to give up any points of view insisting theories could be verified as true or possibly true simply by observation. According to their explanation, theories are freely made, speculative and tentative hypotheses. Once a speculative theory is introduced, it needs laboratorial, strict and cruel observation and verification. The theories which can't survive such observation and verification must be eliminated, replaced by the more speculative hypotheses. By trial-and-error, science develops with these hypnosis and refutation. Only the most adequate ones will last. Though a theory can never be fully proved to be true, it's possible to say it is the best, at least better than any previous theories.

Falsificationists hope to discard the ad hoc hypotheses and encourage the daring ones that can be improved the falsified theories. These daring hypotheses may lead to some innovative and verifiable predictions that can't be made by the previously falsified theories. However, despite the fact that a new hypothesis may possibly result in some new verification, making it worth further study, only after it goes through some of the verification, can this hypothesis be considered to replace the theory in question as an possible improvement. In other words, before a newly proposed daring hypothesis can be considered as appropriate replacement for an already falsified theory, some innovative predictions must be made and verified. Many hasty and ruthless speculations can't stand the verification afterwards, so they can't be considered as contributions to the scientific knowledge. Somehow once in a while, one of the hypotheses of this kind may cause seemingly impossible predictions, which are later observed and verified by experiments, and thus wrote a glorious page in the book of science history. The evidence of the innovative predictions caused by the daring speculation plays a significant role in the growing theory of falsificationism.

## 5. Structuralism

Structuralism was first introduced in the early 20<sup>th</sup> century. To the 1960s, it had already gained wide significance. First appearing the linguistics, structuralism has developed in various subjects, including ethnology, sociology, psychology, history, aesthetics, literature and art. The foothold of structuralism is that objects have their own structures, and the essences of objects are determined by their structures. The structuralist methodology was:

(1) Understand an object by its structure, finding out a pattern or frame of it first.

(2) Search for the structure outside the scope of experience with observation. Studying the appearance within experience is strictly opposed.

(3) Take the object as an entity, with its own structural elements. But in logic the entity has priority of pseudo-importance over its components.

(4) The relation among the structural elements is highlighted, requiring attention and description. And methods of simple analysis shall not be applied.

(5) Focus on the synchronic structure, opposed to diachronic structure. Emphasize on the synchronicity against the diachrony.

Swiss psychologist Jean Piaget thinks that structuralism is a method of inquiry based on the triple principles of wholeness, transformation and self-regulation (Piaget, 1970b). In Piaget's view, these three critical principles are mutually connected. The concept of wholeness inevitably has the understanding of the essence and the form of structuralism involved, thus is an overall principle about the structuralism. The concept of transformation is also important to structuralism. Concepts such as generation, series, and time course can be derived from transformation, and without these concepts, structuralism would have a static and fixed form. Self-regulation enables us to see a structure as a hierarchy and orderly operation control system, which helps the understanding of the structure, the sub-structures, and the relation among the sub-structures.

Piaget attempted to overcome the theoretical difficulties that the explanations of empiricism, rationalism and transcendentalism encountered in epistemology. He proposed knowledge was originated from actions; the essence of intelligence was adjustment; and all human intellectual activities had certain cognitive structures. He insisted, the acquirement of knowledge must be explained with a theory that closely connects structuralism and constructivism. That is to say, every structure was a result of psychological occurrence, and psychological occurrence was a process transforming a primitive structure to a not so primitive (more complicated) one.

As a methodology, structuralism has its reasonable parts, like the emphasis on the entity and structure. However its fatal defect appears in its idealistic explanation of the essence of the structures, as well as in the explanation of cause and effect.

### 9.7.2 Discovery strategies

Generally there are two types of scientific discovery strategies: one is that a theory is proposed first. Predictions will be made on the basis of the theory and the predictions will be verified by checking the facts. At last, other scientists and experts will evaluate this theory. An example of this process is the theory of relativity by A. Einstein. This process of discovery is named as theory-driven. The other way is that massive data is collected by scientists and analysis is made for them to find out a pattern. Later an explanation will be made for the pattern. Such process is data-driven.

### 1. Data-driven strategy

A scientific theory is the systematic description for the cognitive findings of scientific discovery. It's supposed to be a coherent and autonomous system of concepts, and has logical completeness, unity and simplicity. A specific conclusion derived from this theoretical structure needs a purification process that is from a hypothesis to an established law. A theory is originated from the needs of social practice, and such needs mostly start from explaining new facts or new contradictions. For instance, the pioneer of the quantum theory, N. Bohr went through such a process to introduce the theory of atomic structure.

The BACON discovery system was invented by Herb Simon, Pat Langley and Gary L. Bradshaw from Carnegie Mellon University, United States. It is able to simulate the process of scientists making scientific discoveries, and thus re-discover some important scientific disciplines. In 1974, Prof. Simon introduced the induction machine of general rules. As an implementation of the idea, BACON.1 system was proposed in *the Second Biennial Conference of the Canadian Society for Computational Studies of Intelligence* in 1978. BACON.1 was a tool that was only able to use general induction rule (Langley, 1978). By solving sequential extrapolation tasks, the program was able to prove considerable general problems. It was capable of learning of concepts of conjunction and disjunction and re-discovery simple disciplines in physics. BACON.2 system was issued in 1979 with the addition of a heuristic program to handle sequential information. This program could examine the difference to annotate symbolic loop sequence and discover some complex polynomial functions. BACON.3, which was introduced in 1981, reached a higher level, as it could describe the disciplines of higher complexity and explain more original data. This enabled the system to treat its assumptions as new data, and thus apply the heuristic program to them recursively. BACON.3 succeeded in re-discovering the Ideal-gas law, Coulomb's law of electric attraction, Kepler's $3^{rd}$ law, Ohm's law, Galileo's law of simple pendulum and the law of uniformly accelerated motion.

BACON.4 is a production system, which is able to discover and generalize the descriptive law of data (Langley et al., 1989). It uses a small group of heuristic programs to search for the conservation and trend of data and describe hypotheses, and theoretical items will be defined this way. These heuristic programs could be expressed as "condition-behavior" rules, which are called productions and written in OPS4 language designed by Forgy. BACON.4 is a general development system. When it's still being designed, BACON's data-driven property has been considered as the goal of the heuristic programs. BACON system series were named after philosopher Francis Bacon (1561-1626), due to the reason that he discovered a data-driven property similar to the heuristic method used by this kind of program.

The standard analysis of scientific methodology decomposes the world into data or observational material, and explains or generalizes the hypotheses and disciplines about these data. BACON.4 replaces the dichotomous approach with a continuous one, in which information can be represented as different levels of description. The lowest level is the data, while the highest is the hypotheses. And the intermediate levels are actually the hybrids of these two. To facts of a specific level, the higher levels are their hypotheses, and conversely, the lower levels are data to them.

## 2. Theory-driven strategy

Theory-driven uses theories to instruct the scientific researches to discover new disciplines. A theory is a combined system of concepts, principles and viewpoints. It's the result of human thought processing and transforming the perceptual cognitive material. A scientific theory is the accurate reflection of the essence of objective things, and their disciplines. It is the kind of theory that originates from the social practice and always gets verified and proven back in the social practice. However, although it originates from social practical activities, and develops in them, it has the function of instructing these activities.

Theory and practice is a dialectic unity. Theory is concluded from practice, and theory is used to instruct practice, and then again, theory gets verified and proven on the basis of the new practice. Thus theory and practice reach their dialectic unity. A theory without practice is empty, while a practice without the instruction of theory is blind.

Electromagnetic waves are a form of electromagnetic fields in motion. Their existence is due to the mutual effect and dependence of alternative electric fields and magnetic fields. That means they are the wave motion of electric fields and magnetic fields. Such motion propagates in the velocity of light in vacuum or slightly slower in matter. Electromagnetic waves have a prominent role in the modern transmission of information or energy, supporting as the basis of technologies such as communication, broadcasting, television, remote control, telemetry, remote sensing, radar, radio navigation and guidance possible. Also, it acts an important choice of approach in the exploration of universe space and the microscopic world. All these great achievements will not occur without the theory of electromagnetic waves. In 1864, James C. Maxwell comprehensively synthesized the basic disciplines of electromagnetic down to a set of equitation, which is now widely known as Maxwell equations. By doing this, he first predicted the existence of electromagnetic waves, and the corresponding theory of light as electromagnetic waves. But not until 1887 did Heinrich Hertz successfully prove its existence and it verified of the theory for the very first time.

The law of conservation and transformation of energy is one of the most important disciplines in natural science. This law explains that the energy in natural phenomena can't be "created", or "eliminated". They can only be transformed from one form to another, or transmitted from one object to another, while the total amount stays constant the whole time. The basic idea of the conservation of energy was first proposed by Descartes in his 1644 work *Principia Philosophiae (Principles of Philosophy)*. During the 1840s, a few scientists including J.R. Mayer, James P. Joule, at el carried out experiments and calculations respectively, and confirmed the discipline. The establishment of the law of conservation of energy brought massive new points of view and methods into scientific researches, mainly as in a closed system a prediction of the final stage could be made in many occasions, with intermediate stages ignored due to the equality of energy in the whole progress.

Modern physics is defined by two great theoretical discoveries: theory of relativity and quantum mechanics. The theory of relativity is the natural scientific theory about the relation between the motion of matter and time and space. It reveals the connection between time and space, their connection with the motion of matter, and the connection between the mass and energy of matter, etc. Quantum mechanics has made a historical leap concerning the unified description of the wave and corpuscular property of matter. It provides a reasonable explanation to the atomic, nuclear and sub-nuclear structure of matter. The foundation of quantum mechanics has led to various new discoveries and inventions, such as release of nuclear energy, transistor, laser, etc.

In the history of science, the discovery or establishment of the scientific theories has many different ways, but they all represent the dialectic process of human cognition. This process starts from the study on the external appearance and phenomena of the object and gradually advances to the research on its internal mechanism. Then some hypotheses, model or theories are likely to be proposed, get verified by the practice and keep improving. The history of the foundation of quantum mechanics clearly shows the whole process of theory-driven discovery:

1890: Janne R. Rydberg discovered the general expression of the spectral line wavelengths of alkali metals and hydrogen atom, which required the explanation of the internal structure and microscopic motion of atoms.

1893: Wielhem Wien discovered the displacement law of blackbody emission, which is about the product of absolute temperature and the peak wavelength of a blackbody emission being a constant. It needed further study and explanation of the blackbody emission.

1898: Walter Ritz' combination principle of spectral line frequencies asked for the explanation of the pattern displayed by spectral lines from the perspective of internal atomic structure and microscopic motion.

1899: Max Planck assumed that an object did not emit energy constantly. Instead, the emission was discrete, and the discrete energy of emission was named quantum, thus introducing the discreteness into the description of the motions of matter. This assumption was made on the actual facts to support his formula of blackbody emission, but back when the accurate structure of atoms was still unknown.

1905: Albert Einstein proposed the theory of photons, which explained the photoelectric effect and revealed the wave-particle duality of microscopic objects.

1905: Neils H. D. Bohr proposed the theory of atomic structure, which explained the atomic spectra with the hypothesis of atomic transition. However this theory was still not able to explain the microscopic motions inside the atoms with complex structures.

1923: Louis V. de Broglie founded the matter wave theory, marking the beginning of wave mechanics.

1925: Werner K. Heisenberg attempted to use to an explicitly mathematic method to analyze the atomic spectra. He introduced the uncertainty principle on the basis of the interference that the observation process inevitably had on the observed object. This brought the concept of probability into quantum theory and started a new era.

1926: Erwin Schrodinger officially founded wave mechanics and successfully proved its equality to the matrix mechanics. Wave mechanics is a specific and visual expression, while matrix mechanics is an abstract and formal one. From this moment on the interior of atoms could be described with wave functions x and j, which was another significant advance in quantum mechanics.

## 9.8 Granular Computing

Granular computing (GrC) is an emerging conceptual and computing paradigm of information processing. Information granules are collections of entities that usually originate at the numeric level and are arranged together due to their similarity, functional adjacency, indistinguishability, coherency, and so on, which arise in the process of data abstraction and derivation of knowledge from information. Zadeh proposed the concept of granularity in 1979 (Zadeh, 1979). He thought that many circumstances could not meet the demand of continuity because of measuring method and restricted acquisition method. At this time, information is of granularity. That is to say, all the data in a granule should be treated with as an entirety. The reasons for proposing the concept of information granularity are that by the common consent of the researchers of artificial intelligence cognitive science, people can observe and analyze the same question from extremely different granularity. People not only can solve the problem at different granular world but also can quickly jump to another granular world with no difficulty. The ability to treat with different granular world is exactly to manifest human powerful problem-solving. Zadeh thought that there were three basic concepts providing the base for human cognition: granularity, organization and causation. On the whole, the granularity refers to resolving the whole into parts; the organization combining parts into a whole; the causation the relationship between cause and result.

Granular computing may be considered as a label of a new field of multi-disciplinary study, dealing with theories, methodologies, techniques, and tools that make use of granules (i.e., groups, classes, and clusters) in the process of problem solving. A granule is usually composed by elements, which are indiscernible, similar, adjacent or functional. The essence of information granulation is approximation. Suppose $K=(U, R)$ is an approximate space, and $R$ is a partition of $U$, then the granularity of knowledge $R$ can be defined as:

$$GK(\ R\ )=(1/|U|^2)*(\ |R_1|^2+|R_2|^2+\ldots\ldots+|R_m|^2)$$

Granular computing is an umbrella term which covers any theories, methodologies, techniques related with granularities. At present, there are four methods of GrC. One is computing with words (CW) proposed by Zadeh; the second one is Pawlak's rough set (RS); and the third one is quotient space (QS) proposed by Bo Zhang and Ling Zhang; another mothod is tolerance granular space model *TGSM* proposed by Zhongzhi Shi and Zheng Zheng.

### 9.8.1 Computing with words

Zadeh thought that language was used for consideration, judgement and reasoning by Human being, while language was a kind of very coarse "granularity". For example, we say "the scenery in Jiu Zhaigou is very beautiful", where the term "very beautiful" seems very "general". That is to say, its granularity is very coarse. How to use language to deduce and judge is in fact to use "computing with words". Early in 1960s, Zadeh have proposed the fuzzy set theory, which is the precursor of Computing with words (CW). Based on fuzzy set theory, using the methods of fuzzy mathematics to study the method and theory of GrC is a very important direction of GrC (Zadeh, 1996). This is a method that people are relatively familiar with too.

### 9.8.2  Rough set theory

In 1980s, Polish scholar Z. Pawlak has proposed rough set theory (Pawlak, 1982). He gave an assumption: People's intelligence (knowledge) is a kind of classification ability. This assumption is not complete but very concise. In this way, a concept can be expressed with subsets of universe. From mathematics, to give a partition on subset $X$ is equivalent to give an equivalent relation $\mathbf{R}$ on $X$. Pawlak called it a knowledge base $(X,\mathbf{R})$ on a given universe. Such, for a general concept $x$ (a subset of $X$), the problem of how to express x with the knowledge in $(X,\mathbf{R})$ becomes how to express $x$ with the union of subsets in $(X,\mathbf{R})$. For the subsets which can not be expressed with the union of subsets in $(X,\mathbf{R})$, he used the concepts of kernel and closure in topology and introduced lower approximation $\mathbf{R}(x)$ (equivalent to a kernel of $x$) and upper approximation $\mathbf{R}^{\cdot}(x)$ (equivalent to closure $x$). When $\mathbf{R}(x){\neq}\mathbf{R}^{\cdot}(x)$, $x$ is called a rough set. In this way, he created rough set theory. At present, rough set theory has be widely applied in all fields, especially in data mining.

Related granular computing with rough set theory Pawlak et al. did many researches on them (Peter, 2002). In Yiyu Yao's work uses decision logic language (DL-language) to describe the granularities of sets (that is, use the sets of objects satisfying formula $\varphi$ to define equivalence classes $m(\varphi)$), and then utilize the lattices constructed by all partitions to solve consistent classification problems. Moreover, Yao pointed out that researchers can make use of multilayer granulation to explore the approximation of hierarchical rough sets. Lin and Yao researched on granular computing with the help of neighbor systems.

### 9.8.3  Quotient space-based GrC

Bo Zhang and Ling Zhang think that concepts with different granularities can be represented by subsets, and concepts with different granularities can be expressed by subsets with different granularities. A cluster of concepts can constitute a partition of universe – quotient space (Zhang et al., 1990). Different concept clusters can construct different quotient spaces. Therefore, given some knowledge bases, the research on granular computing is to find the relations and transformations among various subsets. The model of quotient spaces can be described by a triplet $(X, F, T)$, where $X$ denotes a universe, $F$ denotes a attribute set, and $T$ denotes the topology structure on $X$. When choosing coarse granularities, that is, giving an equivalence relation R (or a partition), we say that a quotient set is related with R is generated, which is denoted by [X]. The corresponding triplet of [X] is ([X], [F], [T]), called as the quotient space related with *R*. The research on Quotient space theory is to explore the relations, composition, synthesis, decomposition of quotient spaces and also the inference on quotient spaces (Zhang et al., 2005).

The above three different kinds of GrC theories are not completely the same from the starting point of considering problem and the task of solving problem and have their own characteristics. But they have a common characteristic: they all simulate a mechanism of human intelligence, which is to consider problem with different granularity. How to combine their advantages and form a more powerful method and theory of GrC is an important subject for further research.

### 9.8.4 Tolerance granular space model

In 1962, Zeeman proposed that cognitive activities can be viewed as some kind tolerance spaces in a function space. The tolerance spaces, which are constructed by distance functions based tolerance relations, is used for stability analysis of dynamic system by Zeeman. In our work, tolerance spaces based on distance functions are developed for the modeling and analysis of information granulation, which is defined as tolerance granular space model (Shi et al., 2007).

The aim of describing a problem on different granularities is to enable the computer to solve the same problem at different granule sizes hierarchically. We can use a tolerance space to describe a problem (Zheng et al., 2005). A tolerance granular space model *TGSM* can be formalized as a 4-tuple (*OS, TR, FG, NTC*), where *OS* denotes an object set system and is composed by the objects processed and granulated in tolerance granular space, which can be viewed as the object field; *TR* denotes a tolerance relation system and is a (parameterized) relation structure. It is composed by a set of tolerance relations. It includes the relations or coefficients that the granular spaces base on; *FG* denotes transformation function between tolerance granules; *NTC* denotes a nested tolerance covering system. It is a (parameterized) granular structure, which denotes different levels granules and the granulation process based on above object system and tolerance relation system. It denotes a nested granular structure to express the relationships among granules and objects. *NTC* defines a nested granular structure to represent:

- Relations among granules and objects;
- The composition and decomposition of granules.

# Chapter 10

# Memory

Memory is defined as the function of human brain to reflect the things that took place in the past and keep newly acquired behavior. Because of the existence of memory, people could retain past responses, make present reactions on the basis of the past, and enable the reflections to be deeper and more comprehensive. That is to say, memory could make people accumulate and expand experiences. Memory is the temporal continuation of mental activity, and builds the bridge between the former and later experiences to enable the mental activity to be the developmental process and the unified process, which is beneficial for forming his own psychological characteristics. Memory is an essential aspect to reflect the function.

## 10.1 Ebbinghaus's Memory Research

Memory is an advanced mental process, which is influenced by lots of factors. Old associationism only made inference from results to reason, paying no scientific demonstration. But Hermann Ebbinghaus broke through Wundt's assumption that memory and other advanced mental process can not be studied with experimental methods. Observing the result and strictly controlling the reason, carrying on quantitative analysis to the memory course, he specially created the pointless syllable and save law for the study of memory.

Although there is much disputation among old associationism, they never analyze association's own mechanism. Ebbinghaus spelled letter into pointless syllable as experimental material, which made associative content and structure unified, and got rid of adults' interference of meaning association to the experiment. It is a great job to quantify memory experimental material. It is a very good means and tool. For instance, he spelled the letter into a pointless syllable in form of a vowel and two consonants, such as zog, xot, gij, nov, etc.

and about 2300 syllables, then formatted a syllable group by several syllables, made up an experiment material by several syllable groups. Such a pointless syllable can only be remembered by repeated reading aloud. This created material unit for various memory experiments, and made the memory effect identical and convenient to statistics, compare and analysis. For example, studying different length syllable group (7, 12, 16, 32, 64 syllable groups of syllables, etc.) influence on knowing and remembering, retention effect and learning times (or over learning)' relation with memory.

In order to quantitatively measuring the learning (memory) effects, Ebbinghaus created saving method. He asked subjects to read the recognition material aloud again and again, until subjects can recite it out smoothly and errorless for the first time (or twice continuously). He wrote down number of times and time needed from reading aloud to reciting. After certain time (usually 24 hours), he required the subjects to learn and recite the material again, to compare the number of times and time of the second time with the first time, to see how many number of times and time it will save. This is named saving method or relearning law. Saving method created a quantitatively statistical standard for the memory experiment. For instance, Ebbinghaus' experimental result proved: 7 syllable group of syllable, subjects were able to recite by reading aloud once. This was generally acknowledged as the memory span later. 12 syllable group of syllable need to be read 16.6 times to recite, and 16 syllable group of syllable take 30 times to recite. If one had to memorize the same material, the more number of times to read aloud, the deeper memory is consolidated, and then (the next day) more read aloud time or number of times is saved while relearning.

Table 10.1 Memory performance after different time intervals

| Time Interval | Rehearsal Time Percentage Saved by Relearning |
|---------------|----------------------------------------------|
| 20 min | 58.2 |
| 1 hour | 44.2 |
| 8 hour | 35.8 |
| 1 day | 33.7 |
| 3 days | 27.8 |
| 6 days | 25.4 |
| 31 days | 21.1 |

In order to make learning and memory hardly influenced by past and daily working experience, he had employed the pointless syllable as the material of studying memory. He made, and tried with himself, learning the material until just being able to recite. After a certain time, he relearned the material again, and made the time and number of times of reading aloud saved as the index of memory. He generally made a word form with 10-36 syllables. He successively learned thousands of word forms within seven or eight years. His research production 《memory》 were issued in 1885. Table 10.1 is one example which provides his experimental result. Utilize the table material; one can draw a curve, call forgetting curve (Figure 10.1) generally.

We can see from Ebbinghaus' forgetting curve, it seems obvious that the course of forgetting is unbalanced: within the first hour, the information kept in long time memory reduces rapidly, then after, the forgetting speed is slackened gradually (Ebbinghaus, 1913). In Ebbinghaus' research, even after 31 days, there is still a certain intensity of saving; the information is still kept in some degree. Ebbinghaus' original work initiated two important discoveries. One is to describe forgetting process as the forgetting curve. The psychologist replaced the pointless syllable with various materials such as word, sentence even story later on, finally found that, no matter what material to be remembered was, and the developing trend of the forgetting curve was the same as Ebbinghaus' results. Ebbinghaus' second important discovery was how long the information in long time memory can be kept. Research found that, information can be kept in long-term memory for decades. Therefore, thing learned in childhood, which has even been not used for many years, once have an opportunity to be learned again, will resume original level very shortly. If things had not been used any longer, which might be considered to be totally forgetting, but in fact it is not totally thorough to forget definitely.

Amnesia and retention are the two respects of memory contradiction. Amnesia is that memory content can not be retained or difficult to be retrieved. Take things once remembered for example, they can not be recognized and recalled in certain circumstance, or mistakes happen while things being recognized and recalled. In various situations of amnesia: incomplete amnesia is the moment that you can recognize things but can not retrieve them; complete amnesia is that you can not recognize things and can not retrieve them. Temporarily can not recognize things or recollect them called temporary amnesia, otherwise called perdurable amnesia.

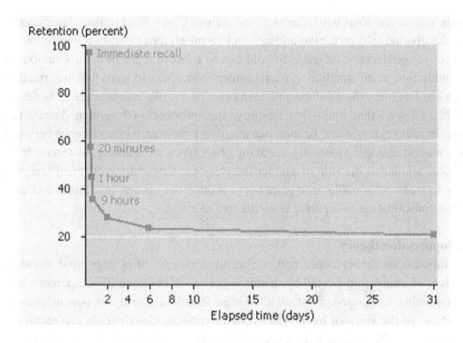

Fig. 10.1 Ebbinghaus' forgetting curve (From Ebbinghaus, 1913)

The reason why amnesia happens, there are many kinds of viewpoints, they are summing up as follows:

## 1. Decline theory

In decline theory, amnesia is due to that memory traces can not be strengthened but gradually weakened, so the information disappears finally. This statement is easy to be accepted by us, because some physical and chemical traces tend to decline and even disappear. At the circumstance of sensory memory and short-term memory, the learning material without paid attention or rehearsal, may be forgotten because of declining in trace. But decline theory is very difficult to verify with experiment, because of the decline of retention quantity within certain time, perhaps due to the interference of other materials, thus not due to the decline of memory traces. It has already been proved that even in case of short-term memory; interference is also an important cause of amnesia.

## 2. Interference theory

Interference theory holds that long-term memory of the forgotten information is mainly due to learning and memory is subject to interference by other stimuli.

Once the disturbance was removed, the memory can be resumed. Interference can be divided into proactive and retroactive interference and two interferences. Proactive interference refers to the old has to learn to learn new information on the inhibition of information, proactive interference was to learn new information refers to has been the inhibition of memories of the old information. A series of studies showed that long-term memory, the information forgotten despite the spontaneous regression of factors, but mainly by the mutual interference between information caused. Generally speaking, two types of learning materials have become similar to the role of greater interference. Content for different learning how to make reasonable arrangements to reduce the mutual interference effects in the consolidation of learning is worth considering.

## 3. Suppression theory

As suppression theory concerned is, forgotten as a result of depressed mood or the role of motivation caused by. If this suppression has been lifted, memory will also be able to resume. First of all, Freud found this phenomenon in clinical practice. To the spirit of his patients found hypnosis, many people can recall the early years of life in many things, but these things usually are not up memories. In his view, these experiences can not be recalled because of memories of when they will make the suffering of people not happy and sad, so he refused to enter their consciousness, its stored in the unconscious, which is suppressed by unconscious motives. Only when the mood weakens in Lenovo, which has been forgotten can be recalled with the material. In daily life, emotional tension as a result of the situation caused by forgotten and is often. For example, the examination, as a result of excessive emotional tension, with the result that some of the content learned, not remember how. To suppress that, taking into account individual needs, desires, motivations, emotions, such as the role of memory, which is not in front of the two theories involved. Thus, while it does not have the support of experimental materials, it is still a theory worthy of attention.

## 4. Retrieval failure

Some researchers believe that long-term memory is stored in the message is never lost. We can not remember things, because we extract the relevant information at the time of extraction did not find the right clues. For example, we often have the experience that we are obviously aware of each other's names, but can not remember what the name is. Extraction of the phenomenon of the failure suggests that long-term memory from the extracted information is a complex process, rather than a simple "all-or-none" issue. If there is no one thing about a memory, even if many of us we also leads the extract have no idea. But it is equally, if not properly extract the evidence, we can not think of have to remember information. It's like in a library to find a book, we do not know its title, author and retrieval code, although it is on the book, we can hardly find it. Therefore, a word in memory at the same time, try to remember the words of the other clues, such as word shape, word sound, phrase and the context and so on, will help us to make word into sentence.

In normal reading, the information extraction is very rapid, almost automatic process. But sometimes, the need to extract information extracted through special clues. Extraction of clues enables us to recall what has been forgotten, or re-identified is stored in the memory of things. When memories can not afford one thing, it is in many ways to search for clues. A clue to the effectiveness of extraction depends on the following conditions:

(1) Coded information associated with the close degree

In the long-term memory, information is often organized semantics and, therefore, closely linked with the information significance of the clues are often more conducive to the extraction of information. For example, the sight stirs up one's feelings, the reason why we returned to the imagination because the plants are closely linked with the past, they arouse memories of the past.

(2) The interdependence of situation and status

Generally speaking, when the efforts of memories are paid in a learning environment, people tend to remember more things. In fact, we learn not only what will be coding in mind, also occurred in many of the environmental characteristics at the same time into a long-term memory. An environmental characteristic of these memories in the future is becoming an effective clue of retrieval. The similarity of the environment that facilitate or hinder the phenomenon of memory called context dependent memory.

With the external environment, the study of the internal mental state will be incorporated into the long-term memory, as an extract clues memory is called a state of interdependence. For example, if a person in the case of alcohol to learn new material, but also alcohol test conditions, the results are usually recalled better. Circumstances in a good mood, it is often more beautiful memories of the past; mind when poor people are often more remembered the troubles.

(3) The role of emotions

Emotional state and learning the contents of the match also affects memory. In one study, a group of subjects were told to read a variety of exciting and sad story of the incident, and then under different conditions in their memories. The results showed that when people are happy when more memory is out of the story of a happy situation, and in sorrow when the opposite is true. Research has shown that effects of the existing state of mind is consistency of coding of information also included in the extraction of information in. Emotional intensity of the impact of memory depends on the mood of the type, intensity and has to bear in mind the information content. In general, positive mood than negative mood is more conducive to memory, a strong sense of emotional experience can lead to abnormal vivid, detailed, lifelike lasting memory. In addition, when the material must bear in mind and to maintain long-term memory does not have much contact information, the mood of the largest memory. This may be due to emotional in such circumstances is the only clues available to extract.

Ebbinghaus' study was the first time in the history of experimental research on memory; it is a pioneering work, for experimental psychology has opened up a new situation, that is, the experimental method with the so-called high-level psychological processes, such as learning, memory, thinking and so on. Sought in the methods of experimental conditions to control and measure the results; aroused psychologists' study memory States boom, contributed greatly to the development of psychology and memory. Although Ebbinghaus' memory experiments made historic contributions to psychology, it also likes any other new things, can not be perfect. The main shortcomings are as follows: Ebbinghaus only carried on a quantitative analysis of memory developing process, the contents of memory were not included in the design and analysis; his meaningless syllables are used in artificial, divorced from reality, there are significant limitations; his memory as a result of mechanical repetition, does not take into account the complexity of memory is an active process.

## 10.2 Memory Process

Memory is the psychological process which contains accumulation, preservation and extraction of individual experience in the brain. Using of information processing terms, that is, the human brain to the outside world enter the information coding, storage and retrieval process. Perception of the things people have to think about the questions raised, experienced the emotional and engaged in activities, will be left in people's minds the impression that to varying degrees, this is the process in mind; under certain conditions, according to the needs of those stored in the minds the impression that they can be aroused, to participate in the ongoing activities, to be applied again, and this is the process of memory. From storage to the brain to extract the application again, the integrity of the process referred to as memory.

Memory consists of three basic processes: the information into the memory systems - coding, information stored in memory - storing, the information extracted from memory - extraction. Memory encoding is the first fundamental process that information from the sensory memory system becomes able to receive and use the form. In general, we have obtained through a variety of external sensory information, it is first necessary to convert a variety of memory code, that is, the formation of an objective mental representation of physical stimulation. Coding process requires the participation of the attention. Attention to the processing of different coding standards, or to take different forms. For example, a character, you can pay attention to shape its structure, word pronunciation or the meaning of the word to form a visual code, sound code or semantic code. Encoding has a direct impact on the strength of the length of memory. Of course, a strong emotional experience will also enhance the memory effect. In short, how the information is encoded has direct impact on memory storage and the subsequent extraction. Under normal circumstances, the information will be encoded using a variety of memory effects better.

The information that has been encoded must be preserved in their minds, after a certain period of time may be extracted. However, the preservation of information is not always automatic, in most cases, the application for the future; we must strive to find ways to preserve information. Information has been stored may also be undermined, there forgotten. Psychologists study memory is the main concern of the factors that affect memory storage in order to fight against oblivion.

The information saved in memory, only to be extracted in the application, be meaningless. Extraction, there are two ways: recall and recognition. Day-to-day said, "remember" refers to the memories. Recognition is easier because the original stimulus presented in front of us, do you have a variety of clues can be used only to determine the need for familiarity with it. Some of the materials studied can not be recalled or re-identified. Are they completely disappear in the minds of the case? Not. Memory traces will not completely disappear; with further study can be a good example of this. That is, to enable subjects to learn the same material twice, each time to achieve the same proficiency level of learning required to practice the number or time must be less than the initial study, twice the number used in the difference between the time or means of preserving the number.

## 10.3 Memory System

According to the temporal length of memory operation, there are three types of human memory: sensory memory, short-term memory and long-term memory. The relationship among these three can be illustrated by Figure 10.2. First of all, the information from the environment reaches the sensory memory. If the information is attentioned that they will enter the short-term memory. It is in short-term memory, the individual to be the restructuring of the information and use and respond to. In order to analyze the information into short-term memory, you will be out in the long-term memory storage of knowledge. At the same time, short-term memory in the preservation of information, if necessary, repeat can also be deposited after long-term memory. In Figure 10.2, the arrows indicate the flow of information storage in three runs in the direction of the model.

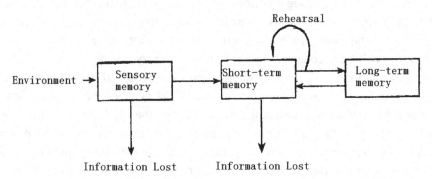

Fig. 10.2 Memory system

R. Atkinson and Shiffrin carried out their expanded memory system model in 1968, and the expansion of the model was shown in Figure 10.3 (Atkinson etc., 1968). From the figure we can see that the memory system by the feel of the model of the sensory memory (register), short-term memory and long-term memory of three parts. The difference is that they joined the contents of the control process, and the controlling of the course of the process is stored in the three works. The model also has a point of concerning its long-term memory of

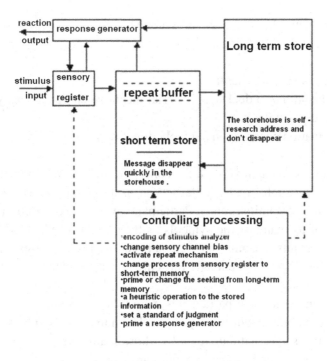

Fig. 10.3 Memory system model

information. Model of long-term memory that the information will not disappear, their information is not dissipated library of self-address.

### 10.3.1 The sensory memory part

Information impinging on the senses initially goes into what is called sensory storage. Sensory storage is the direct impression that the sensory information comes from the sense organ. The sensory register can only keep between dozens of and several hundred milliseconds of information from each sense organ. In the sensory register, information can be noticed, and obtain the meaning by encoding, then enter the next processing. If they can not be noticed or encoded, they will disappear automatically.

All kinds of sensory information continue keeping for some time and working in its characterized form in the sensory register. These forms are called iconic store and echoic store. Representation can be said to be the most direct, most primitive memory. Mental image can only exist for a very short time, if the most distinct video only lasts dozens of seconds. Sensory memory possesses the characteristics of the following:

(1) Memory is very transient;
(2) Have the ability to deal with material incentive energy as many as handled in anatomy and physiology;
(3) A information encoding in a quitely direct way.

George Sperling's research verified the concept of the sensory memory (Sperling, 1960). In this research, Sperling flashed an array of letters and numbers on a screen for a mere 50 milliseconds. Participants were asked to report the identity and location of as many of the symbols as they could recall. Sperling could be sure that participants got only one glance because previous research had shown that 0.05 seconds is long enough for only a single glance at the presented stimulus.

Sperling found that when participants were asked to report on what they saw, they remembered only about four symbols. The number of symbols recalled was pretty much the same, without regard to how many symbols had been in the visual display. Some of Sperling's participants mentioned that they had seen all the stimuli clearly, but while reporting what they saw, they forgot the other stimuli. The procedure used initially by Sperling is a whole-report procedure. Sperling then introduced a partial-report procedure, in which participants needed to report only part of what they saw.

Sperling found a way to obtain a sample of his participants' knowledge and then extrapolated from this sample to estimate their total knowledge of course material. Sperling presented symbols in three rows of four symbols each. Sperling informed participates that they would have to recall only a single row of the display. The row to be recalled was signaled by a tone of either high, medium, or low pitch, corresponding to the need to recall the top, middle, or bottom row, respectively. Participants had to recall one third of the information presented, but did not know beforehand which of the three lines they would be asked to report.

Using this partial-report procedure, Sperling found that participants had available roughly 9 of the 12 symbols if they were cued immediately before or immediately after the appearance of the display. However, when they were cured 1 second later, their recall was down to 4 or 5 of the 12 items, about the same as was obtained through the whole report procedure. These data suggest that the iconic store can hold about 9 items, and that it decays very rapidly. Indeed, the advantage of the partial-report procedure is drastically reduced by 0.3 seconds of delay and is essentially obliterated by 1 second of delay for onset of the tone.

Sperling's results suggest that information fades rapidly from iconic storage. Why are we subjectively unaware of such a fading phenomenon? First, we are rarely subjected to stimuli that appear for only 50 milliseconds, then disappear, and that we then need to report. Second and more important, however, we are unable to distinguish what we see in iconic memory from what we actually see in the environment. What we seen in iconic memory is what we take to be in the environment. Participants in Sperling's experiment generally reported that they could still see the display up to 150 milliseconds after it actually had been terminated.

### 10.3.2 The short-term memory part

Information encoded in sensory memory will enter into short-term memory, through further processing, and then entering into the long-term memory in which information can be kept for a long time. Information generally only keeps in short-term memory for 20-30 seconds, but if repeated, it can continue keeping. Repeating guaranteed the delaying disappeared. It was the information that is using that stored in short-term memory. It was a very important function in the psychological activity. First of all, short-term memory is acting the part of consciousness, making us know what ourselves is receiving and what is being done. Secondly, short-term memory can combine some sensory message into a intact picture. Third, short-term memory functions as register temporarily while thinking and solving the problem. For example, before making the next step while do the calculation question each time, people will deposit one step of upper results of calculation for utilizing finally temporarily. Finally, short-term memory is keeping present tactics and will. All of these enable us to adopt various complicated behaviors until reaching the final goal. Just because we found these important functions in short-term memory, most present researches rename it as working memory. Comparing with sensory memory which had a large number of information could be used, the ability of short-term memory is quite limited. Participants were given a piece of figure bunch, such as 6-8-3-5-9, he can recite immediately. If it is more than 7 figures, people can't recite completely. In 1956, George A. Miller, an American psychologist proposed clearly that our immediate memory capacity for a wide range of items appears to be about 7 items, plus or minus 2. Chunk means several little units were united into a familiar and heavy unit of information processing, also means the unit that made up like this. Chunk is a course and a unit. Knowledge experience and chunk: The function of the chunk is to reduce the unit in short-term memory, and increase information in each unit. The more knowledge that people owns the more messages in each chunk. Similar with chunk, but it is not divided by meaning. There is no meaning connection between all kinds of composition. In order to remember a long figure, we can divide figures into several groups. So, it is an effective method that we can reduce quantity of independent element in figures. This kind of organization is called a chunk, which plays a great role in the long-term memory.

Someone pointed out that, information was stored in short-term memory according to its acoustical characteristic. In other words, even if a message received by vision, it will encode according to the characteristic of acoustics. For example, when you see a group of letters B-C-D, you are according to their pronunciation [bi:]-[si:]-[di:], but not according to their shape to encode.

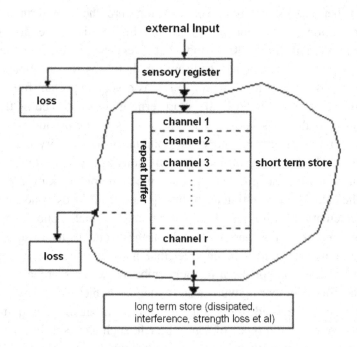

Fig. 10.4 Repeat buffer in short term memory

Figure 10.4 provides short-term memory buffer. Short-term memory is Short-term memory encoding of human maybe have strong acoustical attribute, but can't get rid of the code of other properties either. Monkey who can't speak, can do the work of short-term memory too. For example, after seeing a figure, they will select one of two colorful geometric figures, consisted of several troughs. Every trough is equivalent to an information canal. Informational unit coming from sensory memory enters into different troughs separately. The repeating process of buffer selectively repeats the information in the trough. The information was repeated in the troughs will be entered into the long-term memory. The information which not be repeated will be cleared out from the short-term memory and disappeared.

The time of information in every trough keeps differently. The longer that the time of information keeps in the trough is, the more chances may enter in the long-term memory, and the more chances may be washed and squeezed out by new message coming from the sensory memory. Comparatively, the long-term memory is a real storehouse of information, but information can be forgotten by subsidising, interference and intensity.

It is quite complicated to retrieve the course of short-term memory. It involves a lot of questions, and arose different hypothesis. There is no identical view so far.

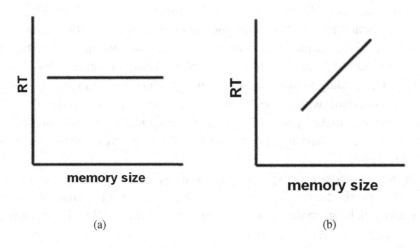

(a) (b)

Fig. 10.5 The scanning test of Sternberg

## 1. Classical research of Sternberg

Saul Sternberg's research indicates that the information retrieval in short-term memory is through the way of series scanning which is exhaustive to realize. We can interpret it as the model of scanning (Sternberg, 1966).

Sternberg's Experiment is a classical research paradigm. The suppose of the experiment is: until participants scan all items in the short-term memory, they will judge the items of test is "yes" or "no", then the reaction time of participants' correct judges should not change with the size of memory (Fig. 10.5 (a) showed). The experimental result is shown in Fig. 10.5 (b), the reaction time will be lengthened with the size of memory. It means, the scanning of short-term memory does not carry on parallel scanning, but carry on serial scanning.

Sternberg's Theory must solve another problem is: if the information retrieval in short-term memory is serial scanning instead of parallel scanning, then, where the scanning begin, and how expire. He thinks, the information retrieval is serial scanning even though participants are busy enough with their own affairs. Meanwhile, the course of judgment includes comparing and decision-making process. So, when participants are judging, they will not be self-terminating.

## 2. Direct a access model

W. A. Wickelgren do not think that retrieving items in short-term memory is through comparing. People can lead to the position of items in short-term memory directly, and retrieve directly.

Direct access model (Direct Access Model) think, the retrieval of information does not by scanning in short-term memory (Wickelgren, 1965). Brain can directly access to the position where items are needed to draw them directly. This model thinks, each item in short-term memory has certain familiar value or trace intensity. So, according to these standards, people can draw a judgment. There is a judgment standard within the brain, if the familiarity is higher than this standard, then will make "yes", if lower than this standard, then will make "no". The more between familiarity and standard is, the faster that people can give a yes or no response.

Direct access model can explain serial position effect (primacy and recency effect). But how short-term memory know the position of the items? If retrieval of information belongs to direct access, why reaction time will be linear increase when the numbers of items increased?

## 3. Double model

R. Atkinson and J. Juola think the retrieval of information has already included scanning and direct access in the course of short-term memory. In brief, both ends are direct, and middle is scanning.

Search model and direct access model both have their reasonable aspects, while there is a deficiency also. So, someone attempts to combine the two together. Atkinson and Juola put forward that information retrieval of the double model in short-term memory is a attempt (Atkinson, 1973). They imagine that each of words was input can be encoded according to their sensorial dimensionality, called sensory code; the words have meanings, called concept codes. Sensory code and concept code form a concept node. Each concept node has different level of activation or familiar value.

There are two standards of judging within the brain; One is "high-standard" (C1), if the familiar value of a certain word is equal or higher than this standard, people can make a rapid "yes" response; another one is a low standard (C0), if the familiar value of a certain word is equal or lower than this standard, people can make a rapid "deny" response. Atkinson and Juola seem this is a direct access course. However, if a survey word which familiar value are lower than a "high-standard" and is higher than "the low standard", it will carry on serial search and to make a reaction. So the reaction times will spend more.

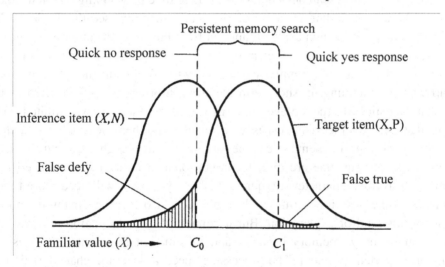

Fig. 10.6 Double model

The research of short-term memory finds that processing speed and materials properties or information type of information have some relationships. The speed of process raise with increasing of the memory capacity, the bigger capacity of the material has, the faster it will scan.

Table 10.2 The processing speed and memory capacity in different types of materials

|  | Processing speed (ms) | Memory capacity (item) |
|---|---|---|
| Figure | 33.4 | 7.70 |
| Color | 38.0 | 7.10 |
| Letter | 40.2 | 6.35 |
| Words | 47.0 | 5.50 |
| Geometric figure | 50.0 | 5.30 |
| Random figure | 68.0 | 3.80 |
| Pointless syllable | 73.0 | 3.40 |

The experimental result indicates, processing speed in short-term memory has the relationship with materials properties or information type. In 1972, Cavanaugh through caculating the average experimental results to some kind of material in different researches obtain the average time of scanning one item, and contrast the corresponding capacity of short-term memory, see the Table 10.2. An interesting phenomenon can be found out from the table: the processing speed is raised with increase of the memory capacity. The bigger capacity of the material is, the faster of scanning is. It is difficult to explain this phenomenon clearly. Once imagining, in short-term memory, information was signified with the characteristic. But the storage space of short-term memory was limited, the larger that each average characteristic in quantity is, then the smaller that the quantity of short-term memory can be stored is. Cavanaugh then think, each stimulus' processing time are directly proportional to its average characteristic quantity. If average characteristic quantity is heavy, then it will need more time to process, otherwise fewer time will be needed. Also there are many doubtful points in this kind of explanation. But it connected the information retrieval of short-term memory, memory capacity and information representation. This is really an important problem. The processing speed reflects the characteristic of the processing course. Behind processing speed difference of different materials, the cause may be because of memory capacity and information representation etc. has different course about information retrieval.

Through Peterson-Peterson method discover the information which was forgotten in short-term memory.

(1) Information can keep 15-30S in short-term memory;

(2) If can't be repeated, then the information in short-term memory will be forgotten rapidly (see Figure 10.7);

(3) So long as quantity in short-term memory does not change, the change of material property has no influence on short-term memory.

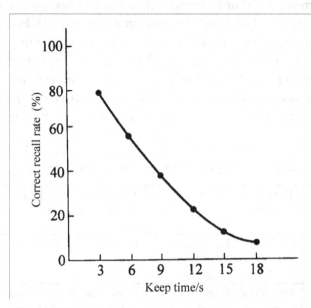

Fig. 10.7 Forgetting rate in short-term memory without repeat

### 10.3.3 Long-term memory part

Information maintained for more than one minute is referred to as *long-term memory*. The capacity of long-term memory is greatest among all memory systems. Experiments are needed to illustrate the capacity, storage, restore and duration of long-term memory. The result measured that how long one thing can be memorized is not definite. Memory can not last for long time because the attention is unstable; if accompany with repetitions, however, memory will be retained for long time. The capacity of long-term memory is infinite. Eight second is needed to retain one chunk. Before recovered and applied, information stored in long-term memory need to be transferred into short-term memory. During the phase of long-term memory recover, the first number needs two seconds, then every followed number needs 200-300 seconds. Different figure numbers such as 34, 597, 743218 can be used for the experiment to measure how long each number needs to recovery. The result indicates that two-figure number needs 2200 milliseconds, three-figure number needs 2400 milliseconds and six-figure number needs 3000 milliseconds.

The Bluma Zeigarnik effect means instruct subject to complete some task (Zeigarnik, 2007), while the other tasks are unfinished. Some time later, the subjects can remember unfinished work better than finished when they are asked to remember what they had done. It reveals that if stop a task before finish, the task will be continuing activity on in another space. Some things are easer to retrieve than others in long-term memory, because their threshold is lower. Other things with high threshold need more clues to retrieve. The unfinished task's threshold is low and can activate and spread easily. Activation spread along the net until the location stores information, and then the information will be retrieved.

Table 10.3 Comparison of three kinds of memory system

| Memory system | Time interval | Capacity | Type of organization or encode | Mechanism of forgotten |
|---|---|---|---|---|
| Senory memory | Less than one second | Depend on capacity of receptor | Direct outcome of stimulation | Passive decline |
| Short-term memory | Less than a minute | Only several items (5-9) | Indirect encode include a lot of auditory organization | Passive decline |
| Long-term memory | One minute to several years | Almost infinite | Complicate encode | Interference and forgotten, constrain, productive forgotten |

A lot of psychologists agree that sensory memory and short-term memory will disappear fast and passive, but few psychologists agree there is same simple decline mechanism in long-term memory, because it is difficult to explain why some materials are forgotten a bit faster than others? Does it relate to completion intensity of the original study material to forget? Will forgotten be affected by something happens during the time between study and remember? Many psychologists in this area believe that long-term memory disappear because of interference. This is a passive point. There are some points about forgotten propose an active process as a supplement or substitution of interference. Floyd thinks forgotten is result from constraining. The material will be difficult to remember, if it is extremely painful and threatening in mind. Another standpoint comes from "productive forgotten" proposed by Bartlett. If you have not received accurate memory, you will create something similar to the memory, and then you will get the real memory. The characteristics of three kinds of different memory system are provided in Table 10.3.

The memory system of human is extremely similar to that of computer. Computer memory layers consist of cache, main memory and auxiliary memory, which speed is from fast to slow and capacity is from small to large, with the optimum control deployment algorithm and reasonable cost compose an acceptable memory system.

## 10.4 Long-term Memory

The storage form of long-term memory means the internal representation of information in human brain. There are certain difficulties in the research in this respect, because the internal structure where information stores can not be observed, and only can be studied by indirect method. We can study the internal structure of information with computer simulation to strengthen the understanding of human mind gradually.

### 10.4.1 Type of the long-term memory

Human memory can be divided into procedural memory and declarative memory. Procedural memory keeps the skill about operating which mainly consist of perceptive-motor skill and cognitive skill. Declarative memory stores the knowledge represented by symbol to reflect the essences of the things. Procedural memory and declarative memory are the same memories that reflect someone's experience and action influenced by previous experience and action. Meanwhile, there are different between them. First, there is only one way for representation in procedural memory which need skill research. The representation of declarative information can be various and is different from action completely. Second, with respect to true or false question of knowledge, there is no different between true and false to skilled procedure. Only the knowledge of cognation of world and relationship between the world and us has the problem of true or false. Third, the study forms of these two kinds of information are different. Procedural information must take through certain exercise, and declarative information needs only a chance practice. Finally, a skilled action works automatically, but the reparation of declarative information needs attention.

Declarative memory can further to be divided into episodic memory and semantic memory. Episodic memory is one's personal, biographical memory. Semantic memory stores the essential knowledge of the incident that individual understands or in some other words-the world knowledge. Table 10.4 shows the different between these two kinds of memory:

Table 10.4 Comparison of episodic memory and semantic memory

| Characteristics of distinction | Episodic memory | Semantic memory |
|---|---|---|
| Information domain | | |
| input source | sensory | understand |
| unit | event, episodic | truth, concept |
| system | time | conceptive |
| reference | oneself | world |
| facticity | belief of personal | consistent of social |
| Operation domain | | |
| content of memory | experiential | symbol |
| symbolization of time | yes, direct | no, indirect |
| feeling | important | not very important |
| reasoning ability | low | high |
| context dependent | high | low |
| susceptible | high | low |
| store and read | depend on intention | automatically |
| retrieval method | according to time or place | according to object |
| result of retrieval | memory structure changed | memory structure unchanged |
| retrieval principle | concerted | open |
| content recalled | past memory | knowledge represented |
| retrieval report | feel | know |
| order of develop | slow | fast |
| children amnesia | hindered | no hindered |
| Application domain | | |
| education | independent | dependent |
| generality | low | high |
| artificial intelligence | unclear | very good |
| human intelligence | independent | dependent |
| experience proven | forgotten | semantic analyze |
| lab topic | given scene | generic knowledge |
| legal evidence | yes, witness | no, surveyor |
| memory lose | dependent | independent |
| binary | no | yes |

Episodic memory is proposed by Canadian psychologist Endel Tulving. "Elements of Episodic Memory" written by Tulving was published in 1983 which discussed the principle of episodic memory specially (Tulving, 1983).

The base unit of episodic memory is a personal recall behavior that begin with event or reproducing (remember experience) subjectively of experience produced by scene, or change to other forms which keep information, or adopt the combination of them. There are a lot of composition elements and the relation among the elements about recall. The composition elements which are elements of episodic memory can be divided into two kinds, one observes the possible incident, and another kind is composition concepts of the hypothesis. The elements of episodic memory consist of encode and retrieval. Encode is about the information of the incident of the experience in a certain situation at some o'clock and points out the process of transform to the traces of memory and retrieval is mainly about the form and technique of retrieval. The elements of episodic memory and their relations are proposed in Figure 10.8.

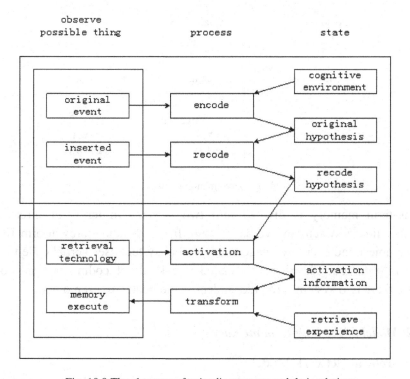

Fig. 10.8 The elements of episodic memory and their relations

Semantic memory proposed by M. Ross Quillian in 1968 is the first model of semantic memory in cognitive psychology (Quillian, 1979). Anderson and Bower, Rumelhart and Norman all had proposed various memory models based on semantic network in cognitive psychology. In this model, the basic unit of semantic memory is concept that has certain characteristics which are also concept in fact, but they are used to explain other concepts. In the semantic network, information is represented as a set of nodes which are connected with each other by arc with mark that represent the relationship between nodes. Figure 10.9 is a typical semantic network. ISA link is used to represent layer relationship of concept node and to link the node represented specific object with relevant concept. ISPART links the concepts of global and partial, such as Figure 10.9, Chair is a part of Seat.

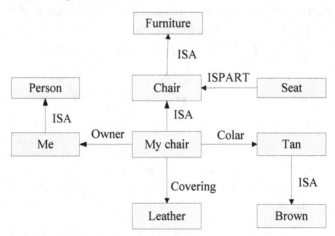

Fig. 10.9 Semantic network

Long-term memory is divided into two systems in terms of information encoding: image system and verbal system. Image system stores information of specific object and event by image code. Verbal system uses verbal code to store verbal information. The theory is called two kinds of coding or dual coding because these two systems are independent while related to each other.

### 10.4.2 Model of the long-term memory

### 1. Hierarchical Network Model
Quillian etc. proposed hierarchical network model-that the basic unit of long-term memory is concept which has relation with each other consist of a structure

with hierarchical-of semantic memory. In Figure 10.10, the dot is a node represent concept and the line with arrow point expresses the dependence between the concepts. For instance, the higher hierarchical concept of *bird* is *animal*, while its lower hierarchical concepts are and *ostrich*. The lines represent the relation between concept and attribute to designate attribute of each hierarchical, e.g. *has wing, can fly* and *has feather* are features of *bird*. Nodes which represent each hierarchical concept, concept and feature are connected with lines to construct a complicated hierarchical network in which lines are association with certain significance in fact. This hierarchical network model stores feature of concept in corresponding hierarchical which only store the concepts with same hierarchical, while the common attributes of every concept in same hierarchical are stored in higher hierarchical. There is a fragment of concept system in Figure 10.10, *canary* and *shark* in the lowest level called zero level concepts, *bird* and *fish* called first level concepts and *animal* called second level concepts. The higher and more abstract hierarchical of concept, the longer that time needed for processing is. Only the particular attributes of each hierarchical concept can be stored in that layer, so the significance or connotation of a concept is depend on features of that concept and others connected.

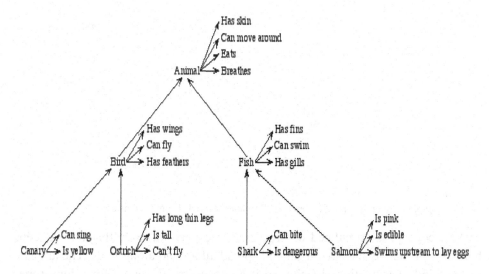

Fig. 10.10 Hierarchical Network Model of semantic memory (From Collins etc. 1969)

## 2. Spreading Activation Model

Spreading Activation Model proposed by Collins etc. is also a network model (Collins etc., 1975). Different with Hierarchical Network Model, this model organizes concepts by semantic connection or semantic similarity instead of hierarchical structure of concept. Figure 10.11 reveal a fragment of Spreading Activation Model. Those squares are nodes of network represent a concept. Lines, length of which means compact degree of relation, e.g. shorter length indicate that the relation is close and there are more common features between two concepts, or if there are more lines between two nodes by common features means their relation is compact, connected concepts denote their relations.

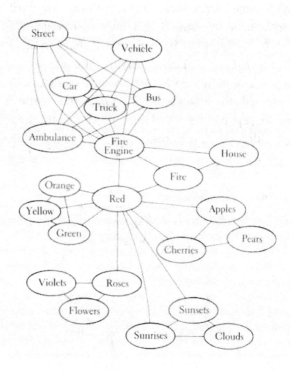

Fig. 10.11 Fragment of Spreading Activation Model (From Collins etc., 1975)

As a concept is stimulated or processed, the network node that this concept belongs to is active and activation will spread all around along lines. The amount of this kind of activation is finite, so if a concept is processed for a long time, the time of spread activation will increase and familiarity effect may be formed, on the other hand, activation also follows the rule that energy decreased progressively. This model is a modification of Hierarchical Network Model, which consider attributes of every concept may in same or different hierarchies. Relation of concept-length of lines illustrate category size effect and other effects-is the form of spreading activation. This model may be humanized Hierarchical Network Model.

## 3. Set-theoretic Model

Set-theoretic model is proposed by Meyer (Meyer, 1970) in which the basic semantic unit is concept too. Every concept is represented by a set of information or factors which can be divided to example set and attribute set or feature set. Example set means several examples of a concept, e.g. example set of concept *bird* include *robin, canary, pigeon, nightingale, parrot* etc. Attribute set or feature set mean attribute or feature of a concept, e.g. feature of *bird* include *is an animal, have feathers, have wings and can fly* etc. These features called semantic feature, so semantic memory is constructed by innumerability information like this. But, there is no made relation in these information set or concepts. When information intend to be retrieved from semantic memory to judge sentence, e.g. when judging the sentence "canary is bird", attributes set of *canary* and *bird* can be retrieved respectively, then compare these two attribute sets and make a decision depend on overlap degree of these two sets. The more common attributes of two sets, the higher overlap degree they have. As overlap degree is

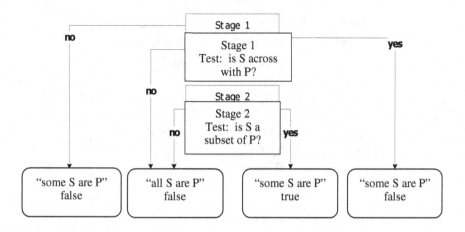

Fig. 10.12 Predicate-cross model (Meyer, 1970)

high, affirm judgment can be made, or vice versa make a negative judgment. Because attribute sets of *canary* and *bird* overlap highly, affirm judgment can be made speedy. While the judgment of "canary is animal", because feature sets of *canary* and *animal* overlap highly too, this judgment is also affirmed. But, this decision needs more time because common attributes of *canary* and *animal* are less than *canary* and *bird*. So, set-theoretic model can also illuminate category size effect. But it is different with logic level or line used by hierarchical network model and spreading activation model that this model illuminate category size effect by overlap degree of attributes set of two concepts.

## 4. Feature Comparison Model

Feature comparison model is proposed by E. E. Smith etc, which also considering that concepts in long-term memory are represented by a set of attributes or features (Smith etc., 1974). But, there is a large difference with set-theoretic model that whether distinguish attributes or features of a concept or not depend upon their importance and consider their importance are equal in fact. Feature comparison model divides every semantic feature of a concept into two kinds. One kind is defining feature that is necessary feature for defining a concept. The other is specificity feature, which is not necessary for defining a concept while has some representation function. Figure 10.13 shows features and

|  | robin | bird |
|---|---|---|
| defining<br>features | Is animal<br>Has feathers<br>Red chest<br>————<br>————<br>———— | Is animal<br>Has feathers<br>Red chest |
| special<br>features | Can fly<br>Sylvatic<br>Wildness<br>small<br>————<br>———— | Can fly<br>————<br>————<br>————<br>————<br>———— |

Fig. 10.13 Features of concept

their comparison of *robin* and *bird*. Features in the figure are ranged top down defining features of superior concept (bird) are less than subordinate concept (robin). But, defining features of subordinate concept must include all of those of superior concept besides their particular features. Defining feature and specificity feature can be seen as two ends of a semantic feature continuum. Degree of defining or importance of semantic feature is changed continuously. Any point can choose to separate an important feature from others not very important. Feature comparison model emphasizes the action of defining feature.

Feature comparison model consider that if the more common semantic features are, especially features between concepts, the closer the relation would be. The two information processing stages in the "feature comparison" model are illustrated in Fig. 10.14. At the first comparison stage, lists of features for the instance and category are retrieved, including features drawn from characteristic as well as defining dimensions. These two lists are compared, with respect to all features, to evaluate their similarity. A high level similarity would cause positive response (true), and little similarity would call for negative response (false). A second comparison stage is necessary for a middle level similarity. This second stage separates the more defining features from the characteristic ones on the basis of feature weights and then compares the set of defining features of the category to those of the test instance. A positive response can be made if the comparison result was match, otherwise, a negative response would be made. Note that the first stage of the model may be characterized as holistic, intuitive and error prone, whereas the second stage is selective as it considers defining features, logical in that it bases its decision on a procedure that evaluates only defining features, and relatively error free.

The feature comparison model could provide reasonable explanation for the typicality. It is clear and effectual to explain various experiment results based on the similarity of semantic characteristics. However, it raises a new problem, that how to distinct the features drawn from characteristic from those drawn from defining dimensions. Additionally, there is counterexample that question the validity of this model. Main difficulty for the semantic memory model research is that this model could not be observed directly. Therefore, all the conclusions are drawn from passive operation. Such operation could be performed in two parts, structure or process. These two parts have different concerns, leading to a plenty of different models.

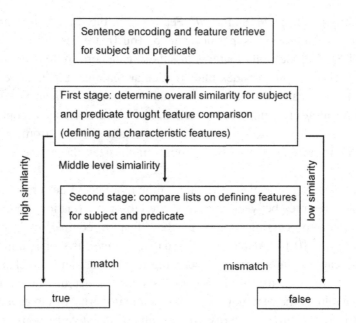

Fig. 10.14. Information processing stage for the feature comparison model

## 5. Human Association Memory

The greatest advantage of the Human Associative Memory model is this model could represent semantic memory as well as episodic memory; it could process the semantic information and the non-verbal information. What is more, this model could make proper explanation of the practice effect and imitated through computer very well. But it could not explain the phenomenon of familiarity effect. The comparison process is composed of several stages and figures that the basic unit of semantic memory is proposition, rather than concept.

Proposition is composed of associations, which in turn, are composed of two concepts. There are four different kinds of association.

(1) Context - fact construction. The context and fact are combined into associations, in which facts refers to events happened in the past, and context means the location and exact time of the event.

(2) Subject - predicate construction. Subject is the principle part of a sentence, and the predicate is intended to describe the specialties of the subject.

(3) Relation - object construction. This construction served as predicate. Relation means the connection between some special actions of subject and other things, while object is the target of actions.

(4) Concept - example construction. For instance, furniture-desk is a concept-example construction.

Proper combination of the above constructions could make up a proposition. The structures and processes of HAM can be described by the propositional tree. When a sentence was received, for example, "The professor ask Bill in classroom", it could described by a propositional tree, see Figure 10.15. It is composed of nodes and labeled arrows. The nodes are represented by lower case letters and the labels on the arrows by upper case letters, while the arrows represented various kinds of association. Node A represents the idea of proposition, which is composed by facts and associations between contexts. Node B represents the idea of the context, which could be further subdivided into a location node D and a time code E (past time, for the professor had asked). Node C represents the idea of fact, and it leads by arrows to a subject node F and a predicate node G, which could in turn by subdivided into a relation node H and an object node I. At the bottom of the propositional tree are the general nodes that represent our ideas of each concept in the long term memory, such as classroom, in the past, professor, ask, Bill. They are terminal node for their indivisibility. The propositional tree is meaningless without these terminal nodes. Those concepts are organized to a propositional tree according to the propositional structure, rather than their own properties or semantic distance. Such organization approach possesses a network quality. The long term memory could be regard as a network of propositional trees, which also demonstrate the advantage of the HAM model that it could represent both semantic memory and episodic memory and combined them together.

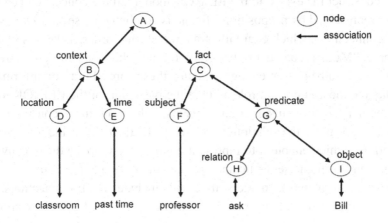

Fig. 10.15. Propositional tree of the HAM model

This propositional tree could comprise all kinds of personal events as long as the episodic memory information is represented with proposition, which is absent in those memory models that mentioned above. HAM propositional structure enables one proposition implanted into another, and combined into a more complicated proposition. For example, the two propositions, that 'Professor asked Bill in classroom' and 'it makes the examination over on time', could be combined into a new proposition. In this situation, these two original propositions become the subject and predicate of the new proposition, respectively. This complicated proposition could also be represented with propositional tree.

According to the HAM model, four stages are needed to accomplish the process of retrieval information to answer a question or understand a sentence. These stages are sentence input, sentence analysis and propositional tree generating, searching from each related node in long term memory until a propositional tree that matched the input proposition to be found, to match the input propositional tree with that found in the long term memory.

## 6. ELINOR model

ELINOR model is named after its founder: Lindsay, Norman and Rumelhart. According to this theory, three kinds of information are stored in long term memory, including concept, event, and scene. Concepts refer to some special idea that defined by kinds of relations: is, will be, be kind of. Memory is organized around events. Event is a scene that composed of actions, actors, and objects. Thus an event could be regarded as various relations that around actions. Concepts construct the evens. In the ELINOR model, all the concepts, events and scenes are represented by propositions. Scene is combined by several events with temporal connections, which could illustrate the events' order. Take this sentence for example, 'Mom prepared the breakfast for her child and the child went to school with schoolbag after eating'. Among these three kinds of information, events play the most important role and are the basic unit of the ELINOR model. Human memory is organized around events, which in turn, constructed by concepts. Except the three relations of concept, ELINOR also includes another more relations, which enable it to represent complex item, make deep analysis of information and combine semantic and episodic memory into together.

ELINOR is a network model. It could include multi-connections, and represents various kinds of information. However, it is still not clear about its operation process and to predict output, thus it is difficult to make reasonable comparisons with other models.

### 10.4.3 Information retrieval from LTM

There are two ways of information retrieval from long term memory, recognition and recall.

### 1. Recognition

Recognition is knowledge of feeling that some one or some thing had been perception, thinking or experiencing before. There is no essential difference between recognition and recall process, though the recognition is easier than recall. From the point of personal development, recognition appears prior to recall. Infants have the ability of recognition in the first half year after their birth, while they could not obtain the ability of recall until a more latter stage. Shimizu, a Japanese scholar, had investigated the development of recognition and recall among child in primary school by using pictures. The result indicated that the performance of recognition was better than recall for child in nursery or primary school. This recognition advantage, however, would diminish, and child in the fifth year class and senior had similar recognition and recall performance (table 6-6). There are two kinds of recognition, perceive and cognitive, in the form of compact and opening, respectively. Recognition at perceive level always happened directly in the compact form. For instance, you could recognize a familiar band just through several melodies. On the contrary, recognition at cognitive level depended on some special hints an including some other cognitive activities, recalling, comparison, deduction, and so on. The recognition process probably causes mistakes, such as fail to recognize the familiar item or make wrong recognition. Different reasons could be responsible for the mistakes, such as incorrect received information, fail to separate similar objects, or nervous and sickness.

Several aspects determine whether the recognition process would be fast and correct. The most important factors are following below:

(1) Quantity and property of the material. Similar material or items would confound and cause difficulty to the recognition process. The quantity of the items would also affect recognition. It has been found that another more 38% time would demand as a new English word added during recognition process.

(2) Retention interval. Recognition depends on the retention interval. The longer the interval is, the worse the recognition would be.

(3) Initiative of the cognitive process. Active cognition would help to the comparison, deduction, and memory enhancement when recognize strange material. For instance, it might be difficult to recognize an old friend immediately whom you had not met for a very long time. Then the recalling of the living scene in past time would make the recognition easier.

(4) Personal expectation. Besides the retrieval stimuli information, the subject experience, mental set, and expectation would also affect recognition.

(5) Personality. Witkinet and his colleagues divided people to two kinds: field-independent and field-dependent. It had been demonstrated that people of field-independent would less affected than the people of field-dependent by the around circumstance. These two kinds of people showed significant difference in recognize the embedded picture, namely to recognize simple figures form a complex picture. Generally speaking, people of filed-independent always have better recognition than people of field-dependent.

## 2. Recall
Recall refers to a process of reappearing of past things or definitions in human brain. For instance, people recalled what they have learned according to the content of an examination; the mood of a festival leading to recalling of some relatives or best friends who is at a distance.

Different approach used in the recalling process would lead to difference memory output.

(1) Recalling is based on associations. Everything in the outside word is not isolated while dependent on each other. Experiences and memories kept in human brain are not independent; rather, they are connected with each other. The rise of one thing in the brain would also be a cue to recalling other related things. A cloudy day would remind of raining and a familiar name would remind us of the voice and appearance of this friend. Such kind of mind activity is called association, which means the recalling of the first thing would induce the recalling of another thing. Association has some characteristics: Proximity, elements that are temporal or spatial closed each other are tended to be construct together. For instance, the word of 'Summer palace' would remind people of 'Kunming Lake', 'Wanshou Mountain' or 'The 17-Arch Bridge'. A word would associated with its pronunciation and meaning, and the coming of New Year's Day would remind of the Spring Festival. Similarity, items that similar in form or

property would be associated together. For example, the mention of 'Spring' would lead to recalling of the revival and booming of life. Contrast, the opposite characteristic of items would form associations. People would think of black from white, short from tall. Cause and effect, the cause and effect between elements would form construction. A cloudy day would be associated with raining; snow and ice would be associated with cold.

(2) Mental set and interest would influence recalling process directly. Due to difference prepared state, mental set would have great effect on recalling. Despite same stimuli, people would have different memory and associations. Additionally, interest and emotional state would also prefer some specific memories.

(3) Double retrieval. Finding useful information is a very important strategy. During the recalling process, representation and semantic would improve the integrity and accuracy. For instance, when answer the question of 'how many windows are there in your home?' the representation of windows and the retrieval of the amount would help the recalling effect. Recalling the key point of the material would facilitate the information retrieval. When ask what letter is after B in the alphabet, most people would know it is 'C'. But it would be difficult if the question is 'what letter is after J in the alphabet'. Some people recall the alphabet from A and then know K is after J, while most people from G or H, for G has an outstanding image in the whole alphabet, thus could become a key point for memory.

(4) Hint and recognition. When recalling unfamiliar and complex material, the presentation of context hint would be helpful. Another useful approach is the presentation of hints that related with the memory content.

(5) Disturbance. A common problem during recalling process was the difficulty of information retrieval result from interference. For instance, in an examination, you may fail to recall the answer of some item due to tension, although you know the answer in fact. Such phenomenon is called 'tip on the tongue' effect, namely you could not speak it out even if you know it. One way to overcome this effect is to give up the recall and try to recall later, and then the memory would come into your mind.

## 10.5 Dynamic Memory Theory

Dynamic memory theory was proposed by R.C. Schank in 1982 (Schank, 1982), which described how the information organized into together, and how the memory changed and accumulated form past experience. The process of confirming useless of past experience was also a process of generating and storing new experience, which is learning from experience. Dynamic memory is dependent on the persistent neural activity or the metabolism in the neural cells. The mechanism of dynamic memory may be the connectivity of neural closure. Each memory item depends on the activity of special neural closure of neural network. In fact, the amount of long term memory is greater than the amount of neurons. Therefore, different memory would share part of pathways. If the impulse left no long term trace, then the memory would disappear inevitably and completely.

To illustrate the dynamic memory system, we compare the way an expert stores knowledge about books to the way a library catalog system. In a library, an initial set of categories is chosen to describe a domain of knowledge. Within those categories, titles, authors, and subjects of the books area recorded. Such a system is not dynamic. Eventually, the categories will have to be changed; over utilized categories will require updating; other categories will have to be created to handle subjects and subjective divisions. A library does not have a dynamic memory. It changes with great difficulty. More important, to change it requires outside intervention.

An expert has neither of these problems. He can change his internal classification system easily when his interests change, or when his knowledge of a particular subject matter changes. The expert is conscious. He could describe what he knows and may be able to alter the memory structure that catalog what he knows. He has a dynamic memory.

Category is not the only problem for a library. Libraries require physical space, and different theme would require their own room or floor. Some theme might be neglect at first but rearranged latter, while other themes have enough space but never been filled up with anything. Knowing where you want to put a book, or information about this book, requires having some preconception of the possible places available for it in the library. However, those preconceptions would be useless as soon as the original organization had been modified. People, on the other hand, seem to be able to cope with new information with ease. We can readily find a place to store new information in our memories as well as find old information.

Based this, dynamic memory is a flexible, open-ended system. It could change its own organization when new experiences demand it, and abstract general rules on the basis of mounts of old experience.

Schank presented a memory structure named MOP (Memory Organization Package). MOP is both a memory structure and a processing structure. It could provide a place to store new inputs. At meantime, it could offer expectations on the basis of event previously encountered. It makes anticipation according to the previous events with similar structure.

MOP is a particular scene-based order. Scene is a memory structure, which combines a setting and activities in pursuit of a goal relevant to that setting. Scene provides an order of general events. It also comprises all kinds of particular memories, and marks the sign to differentiate them from general actions. MOP included a group of scene that directed to predefined targets. However, in the MOP, there is always a main scene, whose target is the subject of the events in the MOP.

MOP is the scene-organizer and in turn the scene is the memory-organizer. Memory could be stored in the scene. MOP could provide the information about how the different scenes were constructed into together, as well as the specific content of the scene, named render. Multiple MOP could share a same scene, which offers a mechanism of making general conclusion. The event and corresponding anticipation would be stored in this mechanism when the anticipation was proved to be a failure, since the event was share by multiple MOP. When similar situation encounters, the previous failure also emerge even another MOP was used, because this failure was stored in the sharing mechanism. The anticipation failure would help to construct new MOP through changing the render or order of scenes in the old MOP.

The dynamic memory system describes how the memory was organized, and how the memory change and accumulate based on the previous experience. New memory would be formed when the old experience leading to failure, that is to say, learning from experience, using associative and deductive approach to rearrange the structure to response to the anticipation failure.

## 10.6 Working Memory

In 1974 A. D. Baddeley and Hitch put forward the concepts of working memories based on the experiments which imitated short-term memory deficit (Baddeley etc., 1974). In traditional Baddeley model working memory is composed of a central executive system and two subsidiary systems including phonological loop and visuo-spatial scretch pad (Baddeley, 2001). The phonological loop is responsible for the information storage and control on the foundation of voice. It consists of phonological storage and articulatory control process, which can hold information through subvocal articulation to prevent the disappearance of spoken representation, and also switch from the written language to the spoken code. Visuo-spatial scretch pad is mainly responsible for storing and processing the information in visual or spatial form, possibly including the two sub-system of vision and space. The central executive system is a core of working memory and is responsible for each subsystem and their connection with long-term memory, the coordination of attention resources, the strategy choice and the plan, etc. A large amount of behavioral researches and a lot of evidences in neural psychology have shown the existence of three sub-compositions, the understanding of the structure about working memory and then the function form is enriched and perfected constantly.

### 10.6.1 Working memory model

All working memory models can be roughly divided into two big classes, one is European traditional working memory model, among which the representative one is the multi-composition model brought forward by Baddeley, which divided the working memory model into many subsidiary systems with independent resources, stress modality-specific processing and storage. The other one is North American traditional working memory model, which is represented by the ACT-R model, emphasizing the globality of the working memory, general resource allocation and activation. The investigation of the former mainly focuses on the storage component of the working memory model, i.e. phonological loop and visuo-spatial scretch pad. Baddeley pointed out that short-term storage should be clarified clear firstly for its being operated easily before answering more complicated questions of processing, whereas the North American class emphasizes the working memory's role in complicated cognitive tasks, such as reading and the speech comprehension. So North American working memory model is similar to European general central executive system. Now two classes of researches are approving some things each other more and more, and exert a mutual influence in respective theory construction. For example, the concept of episodic buffer is very similar to proposition representation of the Barnard's Interacting Cognitive model. So the two classes already demonstrate certain integrated and unified trend.

Baddeley developed his working memory theory in recent years on the basis of traditional model in which a new subsystem-episodic buffer is increased

(Baddeley, 2000). Baddeley suggested that the traditional model don't notice how the different kinds of information is combined, and how the combined results maintain, so it can't explain that the subjects could only recall about 5 words in the memory task *in random word* lists, but they can recall about 16 words in the memory task according to the prose content. Episodic buffer represents a separated storage system which adopted a multi-modal code, offered a platform where information combined temporarily among phonological loop, visuo-spatial scretch pad and long-term memory, and integrated information from multiple resources into the intact and consistent situation through the central executive system. Episodic buffer, phonological loop, and visuo-spatial scretch pad, are equally controlled by the central executive system. Though integration of different kinds of information is executed by central executive system, it maintained and supported subsequent integration by the episodic buffer. Episodic buffer is independent of the long-term memory, but it is a necessary stage in long term episodic learning. The episodic buffer can explain following questions such as the interference effect of serial position recall, the mutual influence question among speech and visuo-spatial processing, the memory trunk and unified consciousness experience, etc. The four-component models of working memory including the newly-increased the episodic buffer is shown in Fig. 10.16.

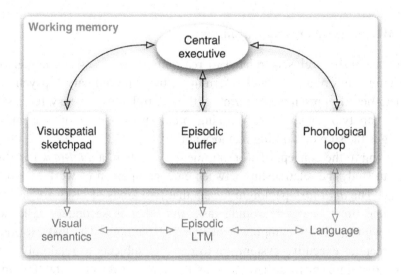

Fig. 10.16. The four-component model of working memory (Baddeley, 2000)

ACT-R model from Lovett and his colleagues can explain a large number of data with individual difference (Miyake etc., 1999). This model regards working memory resources as one kind of attention activation, named source activation. Source activation spreads from the present focus-of-attention to the memory node related to present task, and conserves those accessible nodes. ACT-R is a production system, and process information according to the activation production regularity. It emphasizes that the processing activities depend on goal information, the stronger the present goal is, the higher the activation level of relevant information is, the more rapid and accurate information processing is. This model suggests the individual difference of the working memory capacity actually reflects total amount of "source activation" expressed with the parameter W. And it is field-universal and field-unitary. This source activation in the phonological and visuo-spatial information is based on the same mechanism

The obvious deficient of this model lies in such a fact that it only explains with a parameter of the individual difference in the complicated cognitive task, and neglects that individual difference of working memory might be related with processing speed, cognitive strategy and past knowledge skill. But ACT-R model emphasizes the singleness of working memory, in order to primarily elucidate the common structure in detail, thereby can remedy the deficient of the model emphasizing the diversity of working memory.

### 10.6.2　Working memory and reasoning

Working memory is closely related to reasoning and has two functions on it: maintaining information and forming the preliminary psychological characteristics. Representation form of the central executive system is more abstract than two subsystems. Working memory is a core of reasoning and reasoning is the sum of working memory ability.

According to the concept of working memory system, a *dual-task* paradigm is adopted to study the relationship between each component of work memory and reasoning. The *dual-task* paradigm means that two kinds of tasks are carried out at the same time: one is reasoning task, the other is secondary task used to interfere with the every component of working memory. The tasks to interfere with the central executive system are to demand subjects to randomly produce the letter or figure, or to utilize the sound to attract subjects' attention and ask them to do corresponding response. The task to interfere with the phonological loop cycle is to ask subjects pronounce constantly such as "the, the…" or to count the number in certain order such as 1, 3, 6, 8. The task to interfere with visuo-spatial scretch pad is a lasting space activity, for example typewriting blindly in certain order. All the secondary tasks should guarantee certain speed and correct rate, and conduct the reasoning task at the same time. The principle of the *dual-task* is that two tasks compete for the limited resources at the same time. For example the interference to the phonological loop is make reasoning task and the secondary task takes up the limited resources of the subsystem in the phonological loop of working memory at the same time. If the correct rate of reasoning is decreased and response time is increased in this condition, then we can confirm that the phonological loop is involved in reasoning process. A series of researches indicate that the secondary task could interfere the components of working memory effectively.

K. J. Gilhooly studied the relationship between the reasoning and working memory (Gilhooly etc., 1993). In the first experiment it was found that the way of presenting the sentence influenced the correct rate of the reasoning: the correct rate was higher in visual presentations than hearing presentation, which of the reason is that the load of memory in visual presentations was lower than hearing presentations. In the second experiment, it was found that the presented deductive reasoning task visually was most prone to be damaged by the *dual-task* paradigm (memory load) used to interfere with the executive system, next by the phonological loop, and least by the visuo-spatial processing system. This indicates representation in deductive reasoning is a more abstract form which is in accordance with the psychological model theory of reasoning and has caused the central executive system to be involved in reasoning activities. Probably the phonological loop played a role too, because the concurrent phonological activities with the reasoning activity slowed down, which indicated two kinds of tasks may compete for the limited resource. In this experiment, Gilhooly and his coleagues found that the subjects may adopt a series of strategies in deductive reasoning, and that which kind of strategy is adopted can be inferred according to the result of reasoning. Different secondary tasks force the subjects to adopt different strategy, so their memory load is different too. Vice versa. Increasing the memory load will change the strategy too because the changing strategy will cause the decreased memory load.

In 1998 Gilhooly and his colleagues explored the relationship between each component of working memory and deductive reasoning in presenting the serial sentence visually using the dual-task paradigm. Sentences presented in serial way require more storage space than those presented in simultaneous way. The result showed that visuo-spatial processing system and phonological loop were all participated in deductive reasoning, and the central executive system still plays an important role among them. The conclusion can be drew that the central executive systems are all participated in deductive reasoning no matter in serial or simultaneous presentation; When memory load increases, visuo-spatial processing system and phonological loop may participate in the reasoning process too.

### 10.6.3 Neural mechanism of working memory

The development of brain sciences in nearly a decade have already found two kinds of different working memory are involved in the thinking process: One is used for storing the speech material (Concept) with the speech coding; the other is used for storing the visual or spatial material (imagery) with the figure coding. Further research indicates, not only concept and imagery have their own working memory, but also imagery itself has two kinds of different working memory. There are two kinds of imagery of the things: One represents basic attribute of the things used for recognize them, generally called "attribute imagery" or "object image"; The other one used for reflecting the relationship of spatial and structural aspect of the things (related to visual localization), generally call it "spatial image", or "relation image". Spatial image does not include the content information of the object, but the characteristic information that used to define required spatial position information and structural relation of the objects. In this way, there are three kinds of different working memory:

(1) working memory of storing speech material (abbreviated as the speech working memory): suitable for time logical thinking;
(2) working memory of storing the object image (attribute image) (Abbreviated as the object working memory): suitable for spatial structural thinking which regarded the object image (attribute image) as the processing target, usually is named idiographic thinking;
(3) working memory of storing the spatial image (related image) (abbreviated as the spatial working memory): suitable for spatial structural thinking which regarded the spatial image (relation image) as the processing target, usually is named intuitive thinking.

The contemporary neuroscientific researches show that these three kinds of working memory and their each corresponding thinking processing mechanism have their corresponding area of the cerebral cortex, though the localization of some working memory is not very accurate at present. According to the new development of brain science research, S. E. Blumstein in Brown University pointed out (Blumstein et al., 2000), the speech function is not localized in a narrow area (according to the traditional idea, the speech function only involves Broca's area and Wernicke's area of left hemisphere), but widely distributed in the areas around *lateral fissure* of the left brain, and extend toward anterior and posterior regions of frontal lobe, including Broca's area, inferior frontal lobe close to face *movement cortex* and left precentral gyrus (exclude the frontal and occipital pole). Among them, the damage of Broca's area will harm the speech expression function, and the damage of Wernicke's area will harm the speech comprehension function. But the brain mechanism related with the speech expression and comprehension function don't merely limited to these two areas. The working memory used for maintaining speech materials temporarily is regarded as generally relating to left prefrontal lobe, but the specific position is not accurate still at present.

Compared with the speech working memory, the localization of object working memory and the spatial working memory are much more accurate. In 1993 J. Jonides and his colleagues in Michigan University investigated the object image and the spatial image with PET (Positron emission tomography) and obtained some achievement about their localization and mechanism (Jonides etc., 1993). Positron emission tomography (PET) detects pairs of gamma rays emitted indirectly by a positron-emitting radionuclide (tracer), which is introduced into the body on a biologically active molecule. Images of tracer concentration in 3-dimensional space within the body are then reconstructed by computer analysis. Because of its accurate localization and non-invasive, this technique is suitable for human subject studies.

## 10.7 Implicit Memory

The psychological study on memory was launched along two lines: One is traditional research—pay attention to the explicit, conscious memory research; the other one is on implicit memory, the focus and latest tendency of present memory studies.

In 1960s, Warrington and Weiskrantz found that some amnesia patient can't recall their learned task consciously, but showed an facilitating memory performance through implicit memory test. This phenomenon was called priming effect by Cofer. Afterwards, it was found that priming effect is ubiquitous in normal subjects through many studies. It is a kind of automatic, unconscious memory phenomenon. The priming effect was called implicit memory by P. Graf and D. L. Schacter (Graf etc., 1985), whereas the traditional and conscious memory phenomenon was called explicit memory.

In 1987 Schacter pointed out implicit memory was a type of memory in which previous experiences is beneficial for the performance of a task without consciousness of these previous experiences. In 2000 K. B. McDermott defined implicit memory as "manifestations of *memory* that is occurred in the absence of intentions to re-collect" (McDermott etc., 2000). In recent years, there are great improvement in the explanation and modeling of the implicit memory. The most prominent one is that the past model of implicit memory is descriptive and qualitative, and its efficiency depends on their qualitative predictability on the results of experiments, whereas the recent model is computable and the fitting between the model and experimental data which can be quantified. Here we introduce two quantitative models of implicit memory: REMI and ROUSE.

The full name of REMI is "Retrieving Effectively from Memory, Implicit". This model is supposed that people represent the items in study in vector form of characteristic value, and there are two the characteristics represented: content information and environmental information. In the task of perceptive recognition, without priming item, people will represent environmental information of the goal item as the same with the interfering item. So people's responses depend on the basis of content characteristic and their decision is optimized according to Bayesian inference. REMI further supposes that this kind of optimization inference is based on "Diagnostic characteristic" or difference among the alternative item. Firstly, calculating each item separately to judge if it is in accordance with the diagnosis characteristic of the perception content, then searching which item has more matching characteristic, the winner item will be the response of perception recognition.

But with the priming item joined, the goal items have the representation of environmental information additionally besides the representation of content information in the recognition task (if the priming item is an alternative one in the recognition task). The additional environmental characteristic information can match the environmental information of testing condition, so the amount of diagnostic characteristic of priming item will increase to make the recognition response bias to the priming one.

REMI can predict how the long-term priming changes along with the similar extent of between the goal item and interference item. This model predicts that less similar among the items is, the more diagnostic characteristics are. As a result, the amount deviation of the diagnostic characteristics matched successfully in two optional items will have a larger possible range. If the abscissa is the amount deviation of matched diagnose characteristic, the ordinate is incidence, then high similar item will produce one high and narrow distribution, and the low similar task is produced flat distribution. So REMI predicts that similar item will be influence by priming effect, and this prediction is validated by the real experimental result.

ROUSE means "Responding Optimally with unknown Sources of Evidence" and explain the mechanism of the short-term priming. This model includes three parameters: the priming stimulus activate each correlated diagnostic characteristic in the goal item and the interference item by α-probability (each characteristic value is 0 or 1, the initial value is 0); the perception discrimination of stimulus activate each characteristic of the goal item by the β-probability; the neural system and environmental noise activate the characteristic of the goal item and the interference item by the γ-probability. ROUSE's supposes:

(1) The activation by the priming stimulus will be confused with the activation by the flash of goal stimulus, that is so-called "unknown origin's evidence";

(2) On the premise of this confusion, the subject will estimate subjectively the size of α-probability in order to give a optimal reaction, and will remove the priming stimulus' influence from the comparison of diagnostic characteristic according to this revision.

By analogy, if α-probability is overestimated, then the subjects' reaction will choose the non-priming item; if it is underestimated, the subjects will choose the priming item.

Then what will happen when the goal item and interference item are primed all or not primed all? According to the prediction of ROUSE, because goal item is in the equal position with interference one, the subject don't continue to estimate α-probability and optimize judgment, but judge directly. In this way, in all-priming condition, α-probability added simultaneously to the goal item and interference item by the priming stimulus is not different from such noise of the γ-probability, whereas the strengthened noise will decrease the correct rate of the goal recognition.

In the experiment to examine model of D. E. Huber and his colleagues (Huber etc., 2001), in the passive priming group two priming words were presented 500ms, subsequently a goal word flashed briefly, then the forced choice discrimination task between the alternative word is asked to be completed; And in the active priming group the subjects maintained priming stimulus until they gave "is there a life" judgment on the priming word, subsequently completed the perception discrimination program. The result is very close to ROUSE's prediction; More processing cause the overestimate to the priming word , so the subjects prefer the primed item in the passive condition and prefer the non-primed word in the active condition; in two conditions, the decreased correct rate was found when the predicted goal and the interference item were both primed.

In the overall direction of implicit memory studies, constructing quantitative model is an important way to investigate implicit memory, even in generalized perception, learning and memory.

## 10.8 Physiological Mechanism of Memory

Some perception test demonstrated that per one-tenth second is an experience unit of human brain, within these 1/10 seconds it may receive 1000 bit of information. In the seventy years of lifetime, without regard to information input during the sleep time, the figure of information entering and being stored into brain is up to 15 trillion bits, is 1000 times larger than the number of neurons in the brain. So the memory of the human brain is very rather complicated.

"Where and how the memory does the brain store its memory" is a question brought out by E. G. Boring in his classical work "History of Experimental Psychology" (Boring, 1950). Though more than 30 years had already passed from 1950 to now, it still is a question being solved so far. Conjecture at that time was all on the basis of the simpler electric fields or reflection circuits in the nerve tissue. But now, it is recognized that the physiological mechanism of memory is extremely complicated, the cooperation of researcher and theoretician in many scientific fields is demanded to explore this problem.

### 10.8.1 Brain area associated with memory

At the beginning of the 20th century, Simon and Heling propose memory is "the ability to keep trace", is "general attribute of the material". The research of the neurophysiology has already shown, when the target stimulation is administrated repeatedly and reaches certain intensity (called threshold value), it will leave "the traces of memory" in the brain cell. And when its frequency is higher, this threshold value is lower, and its memory is firmer.

The human brain is constituted of 10 billion nerve cells which are reciprocated by various ways. Every cell can be firing or not, which may be the basis of the behavior and the spiritual activity, and all memory phenomena must be explained from the spatial and temporal pattern of the cell firing. Behavioral changes brought by experience must be accompanied with subsequent changes of neural activities, so the following general problems about the trace of neural system should be put forward:

(1) Whether memory depends on lasting stimulating, or some static traces or changed structure left by the past stimulation?

(2) The structural trace of certain memory is confined to the particular area, or distributed widely in the brain?

Dynamic memory depends on the continuous nerve impulses, or some active metabolic and electric potential changes in the neuron. If the close circuit consisted of the contacting neuron is the mechanism of such dynamic memory, then every memory project depends on the particular neuron circuit. In fact people's memory capacity is much more than the figure of neurons, so different memory must share some common pathways. However, this kind of memory device is costly in view of metabolism, and memory is lost completely and irreversible if nerve impulses can't leave the long-time and lasting trace when it stopped.

The experiment indicates memory is not dynamic purely. However, this never can get rid of its initial dependence on the nervous pulses. The nervous pulses are surely involved in the initial experiences shaping memory trace. The fact that repetition produce better memory suggests the nervous pulses must be flowed circularly in its circuit in order to leave persistent physical changes. Indeed, it takes time to consolidate the traces of memory in the brain.

Then what is such lasting static trace? According to the learning mechanism, it may be the structural changes of synapses, or the change of the nerve protein. These changes essentially are the given synapse of a neuron inoperative originally, may become to work, even work continuously because of outside stimulations. The 10 trillion synapses in brain roughly match the amount of the information bit stored in one's lifetime. If in this case, every memory has its accurate, atomic point in the brain, stay in the fixed position in all one's life. This puts forward how the memory localizes.

Orientation is a key problem in memory. In Von Neumann's computer system, the main storage is encoded and then becomes to be a memory system with uniform number. For example, there are four storages by each one with 4096 bytes. The address code of the first storage is from 0 and 4095, the second one is from 4096 to 8191, the third one is from 8192 to 12287 and the forth one is from 12288 to 16383. The address code and the character code will be provided by the computer order when we need and be changed to virtual address of information. If that storage unit is destroyed the content in the storage will be disappeared. But when one part of the brain is injured, the special memory doesn't be destroyed, the memory still works well. Therefore, we suppose that the given memory is represented by various parts—a fully redundant model instead of specific part. If one part of it is destroyed the rest is still representative of memory.

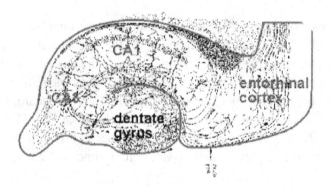

Fig. 10.17 The structure of hippocampus

In neurophysiology, the general method to study memory is damaging the brain in part to observe the functional disorder. M. Mishkin removed monkey's bilateral hippocampus and amygdala simultaneously in order to cause the memory disorder. J.O' keefe recorded the activity of a single neuron in rat's hippocampus and proposed spatial memory hypothesis. D.S. Olton and his colleagues then provided another hypothesis about working memory related to hippocampus based on lesion results. Hence, there are closed relationship between memory and hippocampus.

Hippocampus body is a large neural tissue inside the brain, which is located in the joint between interior cortex of hemisphere and brainstem. It is composed of hippocampus, dentate gyrus and hippocampus flat. Hippocampus organized in layer structure has many branches without climbing fiber. There are two types of cells in hippocampus: pyramidal cells and blue cells. In hippocampus, the body of pyramidal cell constitutes the layered and paralleled pyramidal cellular layer, which of dendrite is extended to hippocampus sulcus. The blue cells are arranged in strict order. Fig 10.17 indicates the structure of hippocampus.

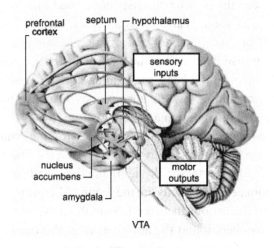

Fig .10.18 Amygdala

Amygdala or exactly the amygdaloid nuclear complex, is composed of several nerve nucleus, which is a center for the meeting of brain areas. Amygdala has direct connection with all sensory systems in cortex, which is along part of the memory system and also connected with the thalamus network. Finally, amygdala assembles sensory message into the same parts and its neural fibers are sent into the inferior thalamus in the brain, which is shown in Figure 10.18.

Amygdala is thought to be served as structure relevant to memory. The nervous fiber from cortical sensory system goes to the amygdala, which initiated the sensory in this memory loop. This loop relies on the connection between the amygdala and the thalamus: the link between these two structures makes it possible to combine the experience and the emotion. These links connect the amygdala and the sensory path repeatedly, which make the learning being influenced by emotion and could provide an explanation that single stimuli evoke various memories. For example, when the smell of a familiar food is perceived, the memories of its appearance, quality and the taste are evoked naturally.

One is from the hippocampus and the other is from the amygdala in above mentioned two memory loops, which are responsible for various cognitive learning—recognition of familiar objects, recall the unperceived character of sensory, memorize the previous location and adding emotionality into the objects.

In addition to the above memory loop, there is "second system" used for learning, which of the key component is repeated stimulus. This kind of learning is called "habituation", which is the unconscious combination between stimuli and response. The scientist of behavioralism confirmed this combination was the basis of all learning in early years. In their views, there are no terms such as "mind", "cognition" or even "memory". Learning relies on two different systems: one is from non-cognitive habituation; the other is the base of cognitive memory. So this view could mediate the behavioralism and cognitive approach. Behavior is possibly the combination between unconscious response to the stimuli and action under the control of cognition and anticipation.

The structure contributed to the habit might be striatum, which is a complex structure in forebrain. Striatum receives many nervous fibers projected from cortical cortex (including the sensory system) and then send the fibers to different regions which dominate movements in the brain. Therefore, it provides more direct link among all the actions included in stimuli and habit in view of anatomy. Actually, some researchers found the ability to form the habit was weakened in object recognition task for monkeys with injured striatum.

Paul D. MacLean from NIH pointed out that striatum is an old part in evolution of human brain, even elder than the limbic cortex. Simple animal learns how to respond to the stimuli at the unconscious level, which indicated that the habit is formed by primitive structure.

In a matured brain, it needs to confirmed further that how the memory interact with the habit. Most learning behaviors seemingly utilize these two systems; however, researchers found effortlessly that there are always conflicts between cognitive memory and non-cognitive habit. How does brain judge the issue between the formation of habit and cognitive learning? Does every unit in memory system communicate with striatum to influence the development of habit? The studies into the areas involved in memory and habit are still in further exploration.

Prefrontal lobe seems to be important in working memory, during which the input message and the ongoing behavior are influenced by individual's view, perception or rule. These internal resources accumulated for a lifetime constitute human's inner world, which could offer some kind of weights to deter large number of sensory information into the brain.

### 10.8.2 *The storage of memory*

How does a fact or an event store in our brain? Do short-term memory and long-term memory work by a completely parallel or independent way? It is well known that some patients could not recall the things happened lately and seems to have the symptom of total amnesia, their ability of short-term memory, however, are as the same with that of the healthy people. So it is clear that these two processes could be separated. But could somebody keep long-term memory when his short-term memory is damaged?

A good case to be studied towards the association between the short-term memory and the long-term memory is from a patient H.M. He is a young man suffered with severe epilepsy, which sometimes leaded to the loss of consciousness. This disease happened frequently and he leaded a bad life. In 1953, when he was 27 years old, his doctor removed a part of his brain in an attempt to control epileptic seizures. Although the symptom of his epilepsy disappeared absolutely, such a surgical operation was not used any more for serious consequences: H.M. could only recall the things occurred in two years ago. Since he finished operation H.M's consciousness was only kept in the moment. He could not recognize his friends or his neighbors. And he could not tell his age exactly although he could tell his birthday. Also he thought he was younger. At night, he asked his nurse where he was and why he stayed here. On another occasion he remarked, "Every day is alone in itself, whatever enjoyment I've had, and whatever sorrow I've had." There was no yesterday for him, who could only finish some easy activities in present. So he did the invariable things such as fix the cigarette or lighter on the display board. He could not describe where he worked, what he did and could not tell the way which people sent him.

The removed part of brain was medial temporal lobe, which is located besides the brain and near the temple, above the ears. This area also included the subcortical area called hippocampus.

If there is no hippocampus in the brain, then what happened? In a study with the monkey, the researchers removed its hippocampus after it remembered the things, which leaded to its failure to recall these things. The temporal lobe, however, still worked and the facts it memorized were in storage. Some other clinic evidences and studies confirmed the same results. Therefore, the researchers presumed that the function of hippocampus is controlling memory but not storing. The area stored information is the temporal lobe. The information from the environment is sent to the hippocampus by the temporal lobe before being kept in it for a period of time, and then sent back to the temporal lobe, where the information stored. The hippocampus played a key role of "management" according to the importance of information. Therefore, not all of the information is sent to the temporal lobe. The information which is approved by the hippocampus is sent to the temporal lobe whereas others will be deleted automatically.

No one really knows how the hippocampus and the medial thalamus work. These two areas might be combined with the cortical cortex in several years to store the memory, and eventually the memory does not depend on the integrity of subcortical structures anymore. An attractive view explains that memory is composed of the unit in random way, which gathered together when a fact or event appear for the first time. What the hippocampus or the medial thalamus do is to associate the isolated and irrelevant units and organize them into the combined memory. As we observed in the experiment by Ross it is only the simple situation about the color or the shape of the beard, which also involved the participation of different parts of the cortex. Therefore, a certain mechanism is necessary to recruit different, isolated neurons to form a kind of network.

We can imagine that the convergence of cortical network about memory depends on the constant dialogue between cortical structure and the hippocampus or the medial thalamus. However, subcortical cortex seems to be no more important when the memory network established (it might takes several years), which leaded to the fact that the established memory could ultimately isolate from the hippocampus and not affected by it, and absolutely independent of it.

### 10.8.3 The storage and enhancement of memory

Memory is divided into different processes, each of which relied on the different combination of brain areas. The most mysterious is that there are common points for these memory components. We know that some people could recall the things happened 90 years ago, but every molecule in the body updated for many times within 90 years. Then how could they maintain if the long-term change of media memory is successively occurred in the brain.

It is thought that constant stimulation would change the synapse of neuron. For instance, the axon terminals of neuron become to be enlarged, the dendrites increase and longer, and the synaptic gap grows to be narrower. The adjacent neurons are likely to be influenced by this biochemical change in synapse. Someone supposed that this structural change is the substrates of long-term memory. During the memory, two irrelevant neurons activate simultaneously, which of this coupling activity could cause some kind of lasting effect and the time is much longer than the initial activity of individual cell. Hebb assumed that when an axon of input cell $x$ is active enough to excite a neighbouring target cell $y$ and the synapse between x and y is enhanced. What he stressed is that compared with other silent inputs near $y$, this synapse is more efficient in transfering the chemical signals. The view is duplicated for explaining the development: the most activated neuron could form the most efficient association.

The second updated speculation is about the enhancement of association, that is, the involvement of association is realized via the third cell $z$ instead of reaching to the target cell $y$. This third cell influenced $x$ before sending to cell $y$. So this enhancement occurred in presynaptic cell but not postsynaptic cell in Hebb's rule. If cell $z$ and cell $x$ activate at the same time and cell $z$ modulates the activation of cell $x$, then more transmitters would release to the target $y$. $x$ release more transmitters to $y$ only if $x$ and $z$ activated at the same time.

This successful case is proved in scollop, which is well studied for its much simpler nerve system and even easy identification of single neuron. In scollop's simple nerve system, the combination of top-down strategy with bottom-up strategy doesn't exist at all. The activity of neural circuit could translate into observed behavior. For example, if a neuron $z$ (it is compared to the above $z$) responds to a natural noxious stimuli from the tail, $y$ affects sensory neuron x which is responded by innocuous stimuli. This sensory neuron is associates directly with motor neuron $y$ being responsible for gill-withdrawal reflex.

The established conditioned reflex make scollop withdraw the gill when a neutral stimuli appears, which is like the establishment of conditioned reflex between blink and ring. When $z$ and $x$ activated simultaneously, that is, the innoxious stimuli and noxious stimuli appear at the same time, $z$ evoked successive chemical reaction in $x$ neuron, which caused the closure of potassium channel. When this outflow of positive charge ion is repressed, the cross-membrane potential becomes more positive, which just change the voltage being necessary for opening the special channel and calcium's entering the cell. More calcium enters into the cell, more transmitter release. Sensory neuron $x$ releases more transmitter to motor neuron, which means activation of motor neuron increased and the observed behavior-gill withdrawal becomes more enhancing.

Neuron $x$ could keep this enhancement even when neuron $z$ doesn't activate. Therefore, this conditioned behavior is established successfully.

Likely, the enhancement of activity in synapse could be found in mammalian's brain. Such highly activated efficiency exists in many synapses of brain areas involved in memory. This key mechanism of this case is called long-term potentiation (LTP). LTP is benefited from target receptor (NMDA) of certain neurotransmitters (glutamate). Unlike the normal situation, this receptor could trigger the opening of the channel only when two conditions are met. The first condition is the same with the normal condition, that is, the input cell is activated and then relevant transmitters (glutamate in this case) is released and combined with the receptor. The second condition is quite a special requirement, that is, this cell must have more positive voltage. Only when these two conditions are met, the critical receptors permit the influx of large number of calcium into target cells.

These two requirements could be realized only do the neurons activate at the same time. This coincidence could be occurred by two ways. One way is that two input cells activate simultaneously, each of which met one of the above conditions: one cell releases the glutamate and the other decreased voltage by releasing another transmitter. The other way depends on the cell releasing the glutamate. At the beginning, the critical channel could not open until the voltage of the cell changed to negative level although the glutamate is released. In general, the glutamate only works at the subtype of its receptor. If the releasing of the glutamate is lasting the voltage of the target cell will be decreased for the activation of critical receptor, which just meet the second requirement. In this case, critical glutamate could make calcium channel open, which is necessary for the influx of calcium. So the lasting activity and simultaneous activity of the input cell could evoke the change of LTP of the target cell.

Such this activity of input cell working as the lasting or simultaneous way could be found in memory. The influx of a large member of calcium triggering a chain of chemical response will cause the release of another chemical substance, which get across the synapse and enter into the cell to evoke more releasing of transmitters. The target cell is getting activated, which means the enhancement of synapse. When the enhanced input cell is stimulated (in proper power), the following response gets stronger. It is like the enhancement of gill withdrawal of scollop, which called potentiation.

It provides good explanation for short-term memory. However, it is known that the short-term memory lasts for no more than one hour. In order to explain the long-term memory, we suppose that more permanent change will occur at the cell level. LTP is a necessary factor for mammalian's brain, which is similar to LTP in scollop. But it is not the sufficient factor. If the releasing of transmitter is durative, then the transmitter has to send the signal to the target cell in another side so as to get the response for a short period stronger and more activated. But it is not enough. Actually, this durative effect of enhancement occurs within the target cell.

Clearly, durative change doesn't simply rely on the mass releasing of present chemical substances. Even certain enzyme gets activated automatically and enhances the efficiency; the life of this molecule only lasts for as short as several minutes or weeks. Although the cellar change during memory is a mystery, some evidences are provided. As we observed, whatever for the LTP of the scollop or that of the mammalian, the common fact of these phenomenon is that the influx of calcium into the neuron.

The influx of calcium works as a trigger, which activated certain genes with the help of the protein with short life as short as 30 minutes. The production of these genes then activates other genes, which could be expressed with various ways to modify the neurons for a long time. One function of the gene activated by this neuron is to increase the efficiency of the transmitters and the numbers of the receptors, and even increase the efficiency of opening the ion channel. However, the other function, which is the essential one, is to alter the neuron for the change of gene expression.

Experience effect does not significantly alter the neuron itself but to change the association between them. Generally speaking, more experience, more association. It is known that some important proteins are excited within one hour when finishing a given task. There are two good examples among these proteins, one is cell adhesion molecules-CAM, the other is growth associative protein-GAP-43. CAM seems to play an important role in cell recognition and stable ephapse. The glucide will combine with the CAM produced in the brain. If proper medicine is injected to deter the combination with the glucide, people will suffer from amnesia, which indicated the importance of CAM in memory.

GAP is another protein example which played a role in memory. Just like its name, it is involved in the growth of neuron and included in growth cone. We know that the synthesize speed of GAP is improved as the neuron extend its axon. During LTP, GAP is obviously activated. Therefore, an attractive hypothesis is the influx of calcium prompts the development of ephapse with the help of GAP and maintains these ephapses at a stable level with the help of CAM when the ephapse is enhanced during memory task.

New synapse connection is produced by this way during the growth, which is also the attractive way to reflect the environment by brain. It is no wonder that the process such as memory modulated by the experience echoed the development in our brain during our life time.

It is difficult to answer the question that how this increased connection between the neurons evokes the memory. Because it means we should build the bridge between the bottom-up function and the top-down mode in cell level in mammalian. Then how do we associate the events in microcosm with the memory in macrocosm. Although it is straightforward to translate a certain neural circuit of scollop into a kind of automatic behavior (such as gill withdrawal), it is impossible to contribute some memory into a specific neuron for human's brain. Nevertheless, some characters in memory indicate that the character of connection is very important for neurons. Though the connection is rather difficult and not be identified at present, this echo loop is thought be the mechanism of memory based on the studies of EEG and neural structures. Echo loop is defined as the closed neural circuit between cortical cortex and subcortical cortex in nervous system. When certain part of the loop is stimulated, the loop produces the nervous pulse. And the pulse doesn't stop when the stimulation disappears. It is delivered in the loop back and fro and lasts for a period of time. It is supposed that the echo effect in brain might be the substrate of short-term memory.

Recently, with the development of molecular biology, especially the discovery of transmission mechanism of genetic message, DNA transmits the genetic code with the help of RNA, which causes some scientists assume that RNA in the neuron is responsible for the memory. The nervous activity by learning could change the relevant subtle chemical structure of RNA in the neuron, which just like the subtle structure of RNA could be reflected by inherited experience. In the beginning of 1960s, Cohen, an American physiologist, trained dugesia gonocephala, which is a kind of invertebrate with RNA, and removed its memory of acquired behavior. Later, H. Hyden, a Sweden neurobiological chemist trained mouse as the ropewalker and found RNA relevant to the neural cells increased significantly in their brain and the components were changed. Hence, Hyden and his colleagues regarded macromolecule as the storage of message and suppose that RNA and DNA might be the carrier of chemical molecule in memory.

# Chapter 11

# Thought

Thought and thinking are mental forms and processes respectively, but thought has both meanings. Thinking allows beings to model the world and to deal with it according to their objectives, plans, ends and desires. Thinking is the reflection progress of the objective reality. This progress constitutes the advanced stage of human cognition. Thought provides the essential knowledge of characteristics about the objective reality, the connections and relations, and realizes the transformation of "From phenomenon to essence" in the progress of cognition. Different from sensation and perception which are directly perceptual reflection progress, thought is an indirect, complex and mediated reflection. Thought has sensation as its only source, but it is beyond direct perceptual cognition. It enables humans to acquire knowledge of those characteristics, progresses, connections and relations existing in reality, which cannot come from sensory perception of reality directly.

## 11.1 Introduction

Thought is spontaneous, indirect and generalized reflection of the essential attributes and internal regular of the objective reality made by the "conscious brain". The essence of thought is the reflection of objects made by the conscious brain. "With a conscious mind" means there is knowledge of brain, but also with a conscious knowledge of the habits of acquiring knowledge spontaneously. "For the object reflect" reflect the intrinsic linkages and the nature of the object properties, rather than the superficial reflection.

The human brain is highly organized special material, is so far the most complex substances known, through sensation and perception, a direct reflection of objective reality. This reflection is not necessarily conscious, and in many cases reflect the objects spontaneously. The thought, as consciousness drive, it must have the object reflect the varying degrees of consciousness.

The most notable feature of thought is generalization. Thought has been able to reveal the nature of things and the inherent regularity of the relationship, mainly from the process of abstraction and generalization, that thought is a reflection of generality. The so-called general reflection is that does not reflect the individual things or of their individual characteristics, but a category of things, the nature of the common features.

As the thought develops, generality of higher level gradually forms. In 1777, Antoine-Laurent de Lavoisier, the French chemist introduced the concept of oxidation for the first time. At that moment it simply meant the chemical combination of oxygen and other substances. 100 years later, it expanded along with the development of chemistry, to adding substances losing hydrogen into its original meaning. Nowadays, oxidation generally means elements losing their electrons. It's clear that this concept had a great advance in a century and a half. A concept develops as cognition deepens. Regarding a certain kind of objects, in the beginning humans can only cognize its external characteristics. But as the practical activities keep going further, the internal essence and the decisive and unique attributes of this kind are gradually revealed. A full concept is not formed until this point. The developing progress of human thought starts from the external attributes of objects and ends with in the decisive and unique attributes of those. The developing progress of concept goes from a preliminary concept to a deeper concept. Since the essences of objects and the essential relations among them are not external, and instead they are internal, human reflection of objects develops from direct and perceptual to indirect and non-perceptual along with the gradual cognition of these relations.

An indirect reflection is to say, objects are not directly reflected and are reflected through other intermediaries. Firstly, by using knowledge and experience, thought can reflect those objects not directly perceived by the sensation, their attributes, and the relation among them. For instance, in traditional Chinese medicine, a doctor can tell the symptoms and physical signs of the patient by using just hearing, sight, touch and asking. That is, seeing the essence of objects and their internal regular relations through the surface phenomena.

Due to the generality and indirectness of thought, by thought humans can cognize those objects that don't directly affect them and the attributes of these. Also humans can predict the development progress of objects. Humans cannot perceive the velocity of light directly, but can calculate indirectly that it is 30,000 km/s. Humans can master the knowledge beyond direct senses, so thought has a much larger field of objects than direct senses. Assumption and imagination are based on the indirectness of thought. Such indirectness can affect the practical activities and guide them into the formation of science and theories, and also reveal the possibility of the future development of objects.

In 1879, Wilhelm Maximilian Wundt set up the first psychological laboratory in Leipzig, Germany, and founded the experimental psychology. He used the introspective method, i.e. statements based on self-observation to study psychological phenomena. He insisted mentality is the subjective and autogenous experiences inside the subject, which cannot be experienced by others. It can only be known via the self statements and observation of the subjects. Wundt studied on sensation, perception, attention, emotions, and wills. He also researched on views and associations, but he never really studied on thought. His experimental psychology tried to find the elements of consciousness, and their relation or regular pattern, but denied the existence of substantial world, which is outside the consciousness. As for thought, an advanced element of psychology progress, he insisted it couldn't be found in the lab. He couldn't reveal the regular pattern of thought progress through the objectives existence of external behaviors either. Thus, Wundt excluded the research on thought from his psychology laboratory.

During the same period, associationistic psychologists, including Hermann Ebbinghaus tried to explain thought by using the associationism. Associationistic psychology was popular during the 17th-19th century. Plato pointed out that recalling is a progress of association, and Aristotle further analyzed three kinds of association: similarity, comparison and proximity. However, it was T. Hobbes and J. Locke, both British, that created the associationism, which used association to explain the basic discipline of memory and learning. The phrase association of ideas was first introduced by Locke. After explaining the subjective and objective causes for the formation of simple ideas, he pointed out the importance of associations in the progress of complex ideas.

In the history of psychology, the first one that literally studied thought as a subject of psychology was O. Kulpe, who was a student of Wundt. He and his students heavily studied on thought psychology in Wurzburg University, and formed Wurzburg School, also known as thought psychology school. Under the direction of Kulpe, his students made many researches on thought.

Gestalt psychology studied thought particularly, and started the study on children's thought. They made the view on the effect of the subject in the thought activities. They insisted thought is a progress, which is generated by the nervousness in the problem situation. Whether the nervousness can be generated or not, that is, whether the subject of the thought progress can be constructed, acts as a key role in the thought activities. Insight theory is one of the important theories of learning. Gestalt psychology insisted thought progress, from nervous to not nervous, is eventually solved by the constant reorganization of problem situations. In their terms, the constant reorganization of the "gestalt" does not stop until the internal relations among the problems are mastered, which leads to "insight".

Behaviorism looked on thought as an inaudible language. Watson believed thought is self talking. B. F. Skinner insisted thought is just a behavior, words or non-words, open or concealed. Behaviorism doesn't admit thought as a function of the brain. Instead, it takes thought as the implicit behaviors of body muscles, especially throat muscles. On methods used in studies on children's thought and learning, behaviorism opposed self observation and encouraged experiments. Behaviorism used conditioned reflex to study the development of children's reproductive thought, which led to the conclusion that thought, learning, etc were learned by conditioned reflex.

Lev Vygotsky is the founder of Social-Cultural-Historical School of the Soviet Union (USSR). His book "thought and language" is directional work in USSR. In this book, he pointed out the Constraints of life on thought and the decisive effect of objective reality on thought. He also pointed out thought is using the experience from the past to solve the new problem emerged. It is analysis and synthesis by the brain in the form of language. Again, in this book, he provided some opinions on children's, especially preschool children's formation of thought. He believed children's brains have the possibility of a natural development of thought. It is realized in the progress of constant guide from adults and interactions with the surroundings. Children's relation with the objective world is mediated by the relation with the people who educated them. Mainly depending on language and socializing is the special condition for the development of children's thought. Vygotsky pointed out, the development comprehended by students appears in the perfection of the concept forming progress, and the true formation of concepts seemingly begins from teenage period. He noticed the relation between thought and other psychological phenomena, especially the one with feelings and emotions. Social-Cultural-Historical School studied on genetic epistemology by Jean Piaget. Vygotsky recognized Piaget's contributions to the theory of children's development of language and thought, but criticized his point on children's egocentric speech. Vygotsky cooperated with his students А. Н. Леонтъев and А. Р. Лурия to conduct experiments and Clinical Research on children's egocentric speech, and found out the reason and function of egocentric speech, pointing out egocentric speech served for difficulty solving, and it's a combination of a formal external language and a functional internal language. This egocentric language transits from external language to internal language via the mode of "social language – egocentric language – internal language". It has a great importance in children's orientation in surroundings and the adjustment of themselves' activities.

Jean Piaget, the founder of School of Geneva, Switzerland, is one of the most important contemporary child psychologists and experts of genetic epistemology. Piaget spent his whole life on the research of children's thought activities. He published 30 titles and over 100 other works. He took cognition, intelligence, thought and mentality as synonyms. He founded his own structuralistic child psychology and genetic epistemology by aggregating researches on biology, mathematical logic, psychology, philosophy and others. In 1955, he convened many famous experts, such as psychologists, logicians, mathematicians and physicists to study on the generation and development of children's thought. At the same time he also founded International Center of Genetic Epistemology in Geneva.

In cognitive science, information processing theory was deployed to study on the thought progress from different aspects, including perception, presentation, memory and thought, etc., with thought as the core. Currently, people are integrating information processing and neurophysiology to further discover the essences and regular patterns of thought.

## 11.2 Hierarchical Model of Thought

Human thought mainly involves perceptual thought, imagery thought, abstract thought and inspirational thought. Perceptual thought is the primary level of thought. When people begin to understand the world, perceptual materials are simply organized to form self-consistent information, thus only phenomena are understood. The form of thought based on this process is perceptual thought.

Perceptual thought about the surface phenomena of all kinds of things can be obtained in practice via direct contact with the objective environment through sensories such as eyes, ears, noses, tongues and bodies, thus its sources and contents are objective and substantial.

Imagery thought mainly relies on generalization through methods of typification and the introduction of imagery materials in thinking. It is common to all higher organisms. Imagery thought corresponds to the connection theories of neural mechanisms. AI topics related to imagery thought include Pattern Recognition, Image Processing, Visual Information Processing, etc.

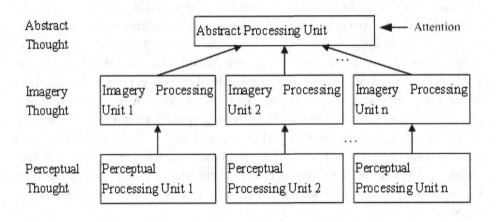

Fig. 11.1  Hierarchical model of thought

Abstract thought is a form of thought based on abstract concepts, through thinking with symbol information processing. Only with the emergence of language is abstract thought possible: language and thought boost each other and promote each other. Thus, physical symbol system can be viewed as the basis of abstract thought.

Little research has been done on inspirational thought. Some researchers hold that inspirational thought is the extension of imagery thought to sub-consciousness, during which a person does not realize that part of his brain is processing information. While some others argue that inspirational thought is sudden enlightenment. Despite all these disagreements, inspirational thought is very important to creative thinking, and need further research.

In the process of human thinking, attention plays an important role. Attention sets certain orientation and concentration for noetic activities to ensure that one can promptly respond to the changes of the objective realities and be better accustomed to the environment. Attention limits the number of parallel thinking. Thus for most conscious activities, the brain works serially, with an exception of parallel looking and listening.

Based on the above analysis, we propose a hierarchical model of human thought, as shown in Fig. 11.1 (Shi, 1990a; Shi 1992; Shi 1994). In the figure, perceptual thought is the simplest form of thought, which is constructed from the surface phenomena through sensories such as eyes, ears, noses, tongues and bodies. Imagery thought is based on the connection theories of neural networks for highly parallel processing. Abstract thought is based on the theory of physical symbol system in which abstract concepts are represented with languages. With the effect of attention, different forms of thought are processed serially most of the time.

The model of thought studies the interrelationships among these three forms of thought, as well as the micro processes of transformation from one form to be other. Presently, much progress has been made. For example, attractors of neural networks can be used to represent problems such as associative memory and image recognition. Yet there is still a long way to go for a thorough understanding and application of the whole model. For example, further research is needed on the micro-process from imagery thought to logical thought.

## 11.3 Abstract Thought

Abstract thought is the understanding of the activities of people in the use of concepts, judgments, reasoning and other forms of thought, for objective reality indirectly, the general reflection process belonging to rational knowledge stage. Abstract thought reflects the essences of objects and the long-term development by using scientific abstract concept. It enables humans to acquire much more knowledge than that got from the sensoria directly. Scientific abstraction reflects the internal and essential thought of the natural or social substantial progress. It is based on the analysis, synthesis and comparison of the essence of the objects. It abstracts the essential characteristics from the objects and upgrades the concreteness to the abstract definition, and thus forms the concepts. An empty, fabricated and intangible abstraction is an unscientific one. Scientific and logic abstract thought is formed on the base of social practice.

Abstract thought is a profound reflection of the external world. On the condition of the cognition of objectives laws, it enables humans to foresee the trend of the developing objects and phenomena, and predict those natural phenomena and their characteristics, which are not provided by the vivid immediacy but existing outside the consciousness.

A process is called an abstract thought, if it reveals the internal connections between the objects by using concept, judgment and reasoning and based on the perceptual knowledge. Concept is a form of thought that reflects the essences of objects and their internal connections. Concept is not only the result of practicing, but also the result of abstract thought. A concept is formed by abstracting the essential characteristics from the objects on the base of analysis, synthesis and comparison.

Judgment was the form of thought which approves or negates the stage of objects. Judgment is an extended concept, it indicates the connections and relations among concepts. Objects are always concrete, so to make a proper judgment, attention must be paid to the time, place and conditions the object is in. Human practice and cognition always keeps advancing, so the form of judgment must keep changing along to adjust to it. It goes from lower level to higher level, from simplex to special, and then transforms to general judgment.

From judgment to reasoning is a deepened progress of cognition. Judgment is the expansion of the conflicts among concepts, so it reveals the essences of concept profoundly. Reasoning is the expansion of the conflicts among the judgments, and it reveals the necessary connections among each of the judgments, i.e., deducing the new judgments or conclusions from current ones. Judgments compose the reasoning, and constantly advance in the reasoning. This is to say judgment, concept and reasoning are connected and reinforced each other.

Reasoning is the form of thought that obtains new knowledge from that already existed. Human thought's creativity is clear to see in the progress of reasoning. When one uses the methods of reasoning to cognize those reality progresses which can be observed directly, if he can confirm those important steps in the complex chain of reasoning through the actual practice, and deduces logically, the new conclusions, judgments, or concepts obtained should be scientific. Autonomic reasoning will be briefly introduced as below:

### 11.3.1 Deductive reasoning

Deductive reasoning is the reasoning on the implication relation between the premises and conclusions, or rather, the reasoning on the necessary connection between the premises and conclusions, from the general to the specific.

Rule-based deductive systems are often classified as forward, backward, and two-way integrated systems. In the rule-based forward deductive systems, implications used as rule F keep operating the factual database until a terminal condition of the goal formulations is produced. In the rule-based backward deductive system, implications used as rule B keep operating the goal database until a terminal condition of the facts is produced. In the rule-based two-way integrated systems, implications should use different rules (Rule F or B) to operate from both directions. This type of system is a direct proof system, not a resolution refutation system.

### 11.3.2 Inductive reasoning

Inductive reasoning is the reasoning that starts from particular objects or phenomena and eventually concludes the general principles of these. This type of reasoning indicates the necessary connections between premises and conclusions. It's a specific-to-general thought progress. In the recent decades, studies on the inductive logic from overseas are mainly carried in 2 directions. One is based on classical meaning of Francis Bacon's inductive logic, trying to find out the logic route to produce the universal principles from related experiences and facts. The other deploys the probability theory and other formal and reasonable methods from the limited experiences and facts available, to explore the "support" and "validation" of a universal proposition about certain fields. The latter is actually logic of theoretical evaluation.

Main points of Bacon's inductive methods are:

(1) Senses must be guided to overcome the partiality and superficiality of the perceptual cognition.

(2) Proper inductive procedures are needed when form the concept.

(3) Escalation must be used for the construction of axioms

(4) In the inductive progress, the importance of inversion method and exclusion method must be emphasized on.

These points are also the basis of the 4 rules of the inductive method, proposed by John S. Mill. Mill also introduced the method of agreement, difference, concomitant variation and Residues in his book "A System of Logic, Ratiocinative and Inductive". He thinks that "induction can be defined as the operation of discovering and proving the general propositions."

Probabilistic logic bloomed in 1930s. Hans Reichenbach used probability theory to calculate the frequency limit of a certain proposition from the Relative frequency, and used this to predict future events. During 1940s and 1950s, Rudolf Carnap founded the probabilistic logic based on the rational belief. Using the same standpoint as the Bayesianism, he described the rational belief as a probability function, and took the probability as the logic relation between two evidential statements. Bayes' theorem can be written as:

$$P(h \mid e) = P(e \mid h)\frac{P(h)}{P(e)} \tag{11.1}$$

where $P$ is the probability, $h$ is a hypothesis, $e$ is the evidence. This formula stated that the probability of $h$ to $e$ equals to the likelihood value of $h$ to $e$, or rather, the probability of $h$ when $e$ is true multiplying the prior probability of $h$, then divided by the prior probability of $e$. Here the prior probability refers to the probability known before the current experiment. E.g., if $A_1$, $A_2$... and so on are the "causes" of the effect of the experiment, $P(A_i)$ is called the prior probability. But if the experiment leads to the event $B$, and this information is useful to the discussion about the "cause" of the event, conditional probability $P(A_i/B)$ is called the posterior probability. Therefore, Carnap needed to make a reasonable explanation of the prior probability, since he used the same standpoint of Bayes'. However, Carnap didn't agree on the interpretation of the prior probability being the personal and subjective degree of belief, and tried to explain rational belief objectively.

Carnap interpreted his logic concepts of probability as the degree of "confidence". He used $C$ to present his own interpretation of probability, as $C(h, e)$ stands for "the degree of confidence of the hypothesis $h$ to the evidence $e$", and further introduced credit function item *Cred* and belief function item *Cr* to apply inductive logic to the reasonable decision. Degree of confidence $C$ is defined as

$$C(h, e_1, e_2,...,e_n) = r \tag{11.2}$$

This means the joint probability of statements (inductive premises) $e_1, e_2,...,e_n$ contributes the logic probability $r$ to the statement (inductive conclusion) $h$. In this way, Carnap defined belief function item and other items by the expectation an observer *x* gives to the value of a conditional probability at the time *h*. Cr, which is the belief item for hypothesis *H* to evidence *E*, is defined as:

$$C_{rx,t}(H/E) = \frac{Crx,t(E \cap H)}{C_{rx,t}(E)} \tag{11.3}$$

Further, he introduced credit function item *Cred*. Definition is, if *A* is all knowledge known by an observer *x* at the time *T*, his degree of credit to *H* at the time *T* is *Cred(H/A)*. Belief function item is based on the credit function item, and that is:

$$C_{rT}(H_1) = Cred(H_1/A_1) \tag{11.4}$$

Carnap believed that with these 2 concepts, the transition of the regulated decision theory to the inductive logic can be achieved. He also thought the belief function item and credit function item could correspond to the pure logic concepts. What *Cr* was corresponded to was called *m-* function item, i.e., inductive measurement function item, while *c-* function item, i.e., inductive validation function item, corresponded to *Cred*. In this way, the axioms for probability calculation can also be used as the axioms for inductive logic. He pointed out: "In inductive logic, *C-* function item is more important than *M-*, because *C* stands for the degree of reasonableness of the belief and it helps to decide in the reasonable decision. *M-* is more of a tool for the definition and evaluation of *C-*. In the sense of axiomatic probability calculation, *M-* is a universal (absolute) function item, while *C-* is conditional (relative)." He stated if we used *C* as the initial item, axioms for *C* could be described as:

(1) The axiom of the lower limit: $C(H/E) \geq 0$      (11.5)
(2) The axiom of self validation: $C(H/E) = 1$      (11.6)
(3) The axiom of complementation: $C(H/E) + C(-H/E) = 1$      (11.7)
(4) The axiom of general multiplication: If *EHH* is possible, Then

$$C(HHH'/E) = C(H/E)*C(H'/EHH) \tag{11.8}$$

These axioms are the basis of Carnap's formal system of inductive logic.

The reasonableness of logic has always been controversial in the history of philosophy. David Hume raised his problem of induction with the key point that future couldn't be inducted from the past, and the general couldn't be inducted from the specific. Hume insisted "every induction from experiences are the result of habits, instead of results of ration." So he had the conclusion that the reasonableness of inductive method was improvable, and there's no reasonable agnostic conclusion in the related empirical science.

K. R. Popper described the problem of induction in his book *Objective Knowledge: An Evolutionary Approach* as:

(1) Is the induction provable?

(2) Is the principle of induction provable?

(3)Are some inductive theories like "the future is the same as the past", i.e., the uniformity of nature's laws, provable?

### 11.3.3 Abductive reasoning

In abductive reasoning, we give out the rule of $p \Rightarrow q$ and the rational belief of $q$. Then we hope to obtain that predicate p is true with some explanations. Abductive reasoning is unreliable, but still called the best explanation because of $q$.

The method based on logic is set up on the more advanced concept of explanations. Levesque defined the phenomenon set $O$ which cannot be explained earlier as the minimal set of items in $H$ and background knowledge set $K$ in 1989. Hypothesis $H$ together with background knowledge $K$ must be able to entail $O$. A more formal description:

abduce$(K,O)=H$, if and only if

(1) $K$ is unable to entail $O$

(2) $H \cup K$ is able to entail $O$

(3) $H \cup K$ is consistent, and

(4) No subsets of $H$ exist with properties (1), (2) and (3).

It is necessary to point out that, generally speaking, there could be many hypothesis sets, which means there could be many potential explanation sets for one given phenomenon.

Definition of abductive explanation based on logic suggests that explanations of the content in discovery knowledge base system have corresponding mechanisms. If an explainable hypothesis must be able to entail phenomena $O$, the way to set up a complete explanation is reasoning backward from $O$.

### 11.3.4 Analogical reasoning

If there are similarities or certain relations between 2 objects, a property of one of these 2 can be speculated from the related property of the other. This progress of speculation is called analogical reasoning. The mode of analogical reasoning can be described as:

If   A has attributes of a, b, c, and d
And B has attributes of a, b, and c
Then  B has the attribute of d

Therefore, analogical reasoning is a method using the information of one system to speculate the information of another similar system. The objective basis of analogical reasoning lies in the universal relation among the objects, progresses and elements in different systems, and their comparability.

How the theory of analogical works is shown in Figure 11.2. Here $\beta_1$ and $\alpha$ are the established facts in $S_i$. $\beta_i'$ is the established fact in $S_2$. $\varphi$ is the relation similarity between the objects. The analogical reasoning is that, when $\beta_i \varphi \beta_i'$ ($1 \leq i \leq n$) exists, $\alpha \varphi \alpha'$ in $S_2$ leads to $\alpha'$. To achieve this, the conditions given below are necessary:

(1) the definition of similarity $\varphi$
(2) the procedure to produce $\varphi$ from given objects $S_1$ and $S_2$
(3) the procedure to produce $\alpha'$ in $\alpha \varphi \alpha'$

Firstly, the definition of similarity $\varphi$ shall be relevant to the form of the object and its meaning. Here the object of analogy is the finite set of judgment clauses $S_i$. Define clause $A$, $\beta_i$ as literal constants to form the "if then rule". Item $t_i$ doesn't include any variables from $S_i$, and it presents the individual object. Predicate symbol $P$ presents the relation among the individuals, e.g., atom logical expression $P(t_i,...,t_n)$ stands for the relation among $t_i$. (From now on atom logical expression will be called "atom" for short.) The set which consists of all the atoms is denoted as $\beta_i$. The minimum model $M_i$ is the set of atoms logically deducted from $S_i$.

Object $S_1$:  premises $\beta_1, \ldots, \beta_n \rightarrow$ conclusion $\alpha$

Similarity $\varphi$

Object $S_2$:  premises $\beta'_1, \ldots, \beta'_n \rightarrow$ conclusion $\alpha'$?

Fig. 11.2 The principle of analogical reasoning

$$M_i = \{\alpha \in \beta_i : S_i \cong \alpha\} \tag{11.9}$$

where $\cong$ stands for logical reasoning in predicate logic. Moreover, the individual of $M_i$ is called the fact of $S_i$.

## 11.4 Imagery Thought

Imagery thought is the thought activity that uses the images stored in the brain. Such thought activities occur in the right sphere of the brain, because this sphere is responsible for the direct, generalized, geometric and drawing thought, cognition and behavior. Imagery thought uses typification to achieve generalization, and use image materials to thought. Images are the cells to imagery thought. Imagery thought has 4 following characteristics:

(1) Imagery. It's the key characteristic of imagery materials, that is, that is, the specific nature of intuitive. This is obviously different from the concepts, theories, numbers, etc. used by abstract thought.

(2) Generality. It means to master the common characteristics owned by a group of similar objects through corresponding typical or general images. Techniques such as sampling, analysis of typical cases, scientific modeling, etc., which are used widely in scientific research, all have the generality feature.

(3) Creativity. The materials used by creative thought and its products are mostly the processed, reformed, and re-created images. The personae created in literature, or the new products designed have this characteristic. Since all creativity and remake shows in the imagery reformation, the designer must create or reform the images in his thought when he is making a design. The creation of something new works in this way, so does the cognition of something by visual thought. When physician Ernest Rutherford was studying on the internal structure of atoms, by observing the particle scattering experiment, he imaged the interior of the atom as a microcosmic Solar system: the nucleus was the center, with electrons circling in various orbits around it. This is the origin of the famous planetary model of atom.

(4) Mobility. As a rational cognition, related thought materials are not still, isolated and invariant. It provides a lot of imagination, association and creativity, to promote the motion of thought, analyze profoundly the images, and acquire needed knowledge.

These characteristics make imagery thought expand from perceptive cognition into the scope of rational cognition. However it's still different from abstract thought, just another kind of rational cognition. Pattern recognition is a typical imagery thought. It uses computers to process the information about the patterns, classifying, describing, analyzing and interpreting the texts, sounds, images and objects. Currently pattern recognition has been applied directly or indirectly in some areas, and many systems of the pattern information have been made, like optical character recognition (OCR), cell or blood corpuscle recognition, voice recognition etc. The researches of the analysis of sequence images, computer vision, speech or image understanding systems, with their implementations, have become a wide interesting.

## 11.5 Inspirational Thought

Inspirational thought is also known as insight. It is intuitive that people with the sudden burst of inspiration as a form of thinking, insight or understanding. Poets, writers of "flash in the pen," the military conductor of the "surprise move" ideological strategist "suddenly link up", scientist, inventor of the "The filled cogongrass open at once", etc. All these show that the inspiration of this characteristic. It is after a long period of thinking, the problem is not resolved, but suddenly inspired by a certain thing, the problem was immediately resolved way of thinking. "Everything takes its time to ripe, give a birth in one day", is a figurative description of this approach. Inspired by the information from the induced accumulation of experience, the advance of association and the boost of motivation.

In general, abstract thought occurs in significant awareness, by means of the concept of strict logical reasoning, from a premise, step by step reasoning continues, until the conclusion. The performance of the whole reasoning process as a linear, one-dimensional. Imagery thought mainly occurred in significant awareness, unconscious from time to time engaged in activities. Thinking in images, is to use images to think and express. Image of the place of thinking processes, not only can not do without sensitivity, intuition, imagination and other non-logical thinking, inspiration, and ultimately, similar to laws in accordance with the control law and other methods of inference; place complicated process than the abstract thinking, and is a face, and two-dimensional. Inspiration occurs mainly in the subconscious mind, which is a remarkable blend results between conscious and unconscious. The process of inspiration breeds, performance information for the perceptual experience, fresh information on the subject, and brain high-level of the nervous system "construction" activities conducted in these three aspects would be integrated with the structure formed by topology. Inspirational thought is non-linear, three-dimensional. Thus, the inspiration thought has different characteristics with abstract thought, imagery thought. Here, we list the characteristics of inspiration thought as follows.

(1) Abruptness. Abruptness is the situation that a long pondered problem is suddenly solved by a strike of something else, such as walking, chatting, flowers, tourism and so on. This was the inspiration thought performances from time and place of the state. The abruptness of inspiration means that regarding to time, it happens in a sudden; regarding to the effect, it's unexpected and unpredictable. However all these are related to the subconscious inference, which is an integrated reasoning of information isomorphism and the functional constructing of the neuro system. The result of this kind of reasoning goes from implicit to explicit. The essence of this thought activity is the precise isomorphism that occurs between the source and sink of information, which is to say, 2 things share some rare but precise intercommunity deep inside (in the information essence) and information essence transits from this basis to a higher level. It is accompanied by the transition of EEG power that occurs in the mutual effect of between conscious and sub-conscious mind.

(2) Occasionality. From space point of view, inspiration was suddenly evoked by something else, and this lasts so short that it's to trace. That's what occasionality means. Engels pointed out: inevitability has the occasionality as its supplement and manifestation. This kind of occasionality must comply with the law of causation. Although the sub-consciousness can't be realized by us, but inspiration, from the start to the end, occurs with the participation of the conscious mind. Regarding to the pondered subject, it provides information related to the subject in a divergent manner. It's possible that some information will lead to the inspiration. Therefore, the inspiring information has some kind of occasionality regarding to the time, location, conditions and chances. But this occasionality has some kind of inevitability hidden inside.

(3) Originality. Originality is the essential characteristic of inspirational thought that differs from other form of thought. Inspiration appears in every important invention or discovery in the whole history of humankind. From literature to poetry, from military actions to scientific creation, inspiration exists everywhere.

(4) Vagueness. Inspiration Thought comprehensive survey produced by the new clues, new results, new conclusions, will find inspiration ideas often come with a certain degree of ambiguity. From fuzzy to clear, with precise description of vague, it is the world's diversity and complexity of performance. The development of modern science and the overall trend shows that the deepening of science require more precision. However, the deepening of science itself implies that the problem more complicated, but complicated and difficult to precise. Thus, with the complexity of things just do not accompany the accuracy of that ambiguity.

According to human experience, the mechanism to produce inspiration roughly has 5 stages: conditions, enlightenment, transition, insight and validation. They are briefly discussed as below.

(1) Conditions refer to the necessary and sufficient conditions that can lead to the burst of inspiration.

(2) Enlightenment refers to the random information by chance which intrigues the occurrence of inspiration. Epistemologically speaking, enlightenment is a universal form to intrigue inspiration, connecting different information of thoughts. It's the "golden key" to the new discovery.

(3) Transition is that the non-logical way of the qualitative change at the moment inspiration occurs. When the conscious and subconscious mind mutually effect each other, different thoughts appear in the brain, and this is the result of the thought transition. This kind of transition is a characteristic of sub-thought, is a noncontiguous way of the qualitative change that is beyond reasoning procedures.

(4) Insight means the manifestation at the moment when the matured but not yet shown inspiration communicates with the conscious mind. Ancient Chinese philosopher Zhu Xi described enlightenment as "to see everything suddenly in a clear light" or the scales fall from one's eyes. This proves at this moment, inspiration can be realized by humans.

(5) Validation is the scientific analysis and evaluation of the product of the inspirational thought. Along with the advance of inspiration, new concept, theory and view start to emerge. However, intuition may be vague, so it's possible that there are flaws in the insight. Therefore, not every conclusion is valid, and proper validation is need.

The human brain is a complex system. Complex systems often taken to constitute a hierarchical structure. Hierarchical structure is composed of interrelated subsystems, each subsystem is hierarchical in structure type, until we reach a certain minimum level of basic subsystems. In the human central nervous system where there are many levels, while the inspiration may be more than self. The problem is solved when the different parts of the brain suddenly connect at work.

## 11.6 Problem Solving

Problem solving is a mental process and is part of the larger problem process that includes problem finding and problem shaping. Considered the most complex of all intellectual functions, problem solving has been defined as higher-order cognitive process that requires the modulation and control of more routine or fundamental skills. Any operation sequences towards certain goals by the cognition are called problem solving. The solving processes requiring new procedures are called creative problem solving, and otherwise, those using current available processes are called regular problem solving.

### 11.6.1 Problem domain

The thought process always occurs in certain activities, and those activities have the problem solving as its main form. Thus, the thought process can be examined through the analysis of the problem solving process. In the whole process of problem solving, many factors are involved, such as memory, learning, skills, emotions and motives. As a complex psychological activity, it is a "psychological process of higher level". Whether this higher level process can be explained by discipline like "rote learning" or "stimulus-response" has always been and still is a controversial topic. Similarly, so is whether knowledge obtained from laboratory environment can explain problems such as humans being able to solve complicated and difficult problems in real life or to cognize and adjust to the complicated surroundings.

In artificial intelligence (AI), the basic form of problem solving is described as 5-tuple format, which consists of two sets: $S$ and $A$, the partial function: $f$ from $S \times A$ to $S$, and two elements from $S$: $s_i$ and $s_g$, is called the problem. Here $s_g = f(f(\dots (f(f(s_i, a_1), a_2)a_3)\dots), a_n)$ is called the problem solving, as it describes the sequential operation on $a_1 a_2....a_n$.

In above definition, $S$, $A$, $f$, $s_i$, $s_g$ is called status space, operation set, status shift function, initial status and target status separately. Status means that a group of variations $q_0, q_1,..., q_n$ constructs an orderly group $<q_0, q_1,..., q_n>$, and the variation of $q_n$ represents the difference or change of the object. Each $q_n$ is called a component. Finitude of $N$ is not enforced, $N$ could be infinite too. The variation of some components could lead to the transition from one status to another, and this is called an operation.

In this way, a graph of all possible status and the relation among them can be used to represent a problem. This method is called status space notation. When use it, the process of problem solving transforms to finding the routine from the initial status $s_i$ to the target status $s_g$. The operational sequence from $s_i$ to $s_g$ is described as:

$$a = a_1, a_2, \dots a_n$$
$$s_g = f(f(\dots(f(f(s_1, a_1), a_2)a_3)\dots), a_n)$$

To solve the status space problem, first should transform an informal problem to the formal description according to the following requirements:

(1) Define a status space, which contains the possible combination of related objects and maybe unrelated objects. Certainly, the definition has no need to enumerate all the possible statuses in the status space.

(2) Determine one or more statuses belonging to this status space to describe the possible initial conditions, which are called the initial statuses.

(3) Determine one or more statuses belonging to this status space, and they're the solutions to the problem, which are called target statuses.

(4) Set up a group of rules, which describes the applicable behaviors or operations. To do this, the following should be considered.

a) In the informal description of the problem, which are explicit assumptions?

b) What level of the regularity should be applied for the rules?

c) What work should be done and expressed in the rules before the problem solving?

The next step of problem solving is the application of the rules and its control strategy to traverse the problem domain, until a routine from an initial status to a target status is found. Search is the basis of the problem solving. Under the condition of no more direct methods being available, the search can be a framework, which enables the usage of the more direct methods for the sub-problems to be embedded into it.

### 11.6.2 Problem-solving techniques

Problem solving occurs when an organism or an artificial intelligence system needs to move from a given state to a desired goal state. So far there are a lot of methodologies and algorithms have been proposed, such as:

Heuristic search
Divide and conquer
Hill-climbing strategy
Means-ends analysis
Trial-and-error
Brainstorming
Morphological analysis
Lateral thinking
Analogy
Reduction
Hypothesis testing
Constraint examination
Root Cause analysis
Working backwards
Forward-Looking strategy
Simplification
Generalization
Specialization
Random search
Split-Half method
TRIZ
Wu's method

Here we take heuristic search as an example. In order to solve problem effectively, we need to balance two different requirements: flexibility and systematicness to construct a control strategy. This strategy cannot guarantee the most optimal solution, but usually it can find a better solution. Heuristic search is frequently used, as it improves the effectiveness of search process at the cost of the completeness.

The practical problems intelligent system faces mostly belong to the uncertain problems in partial information settings. As the system doesn't know all information about the problems, it doesn't know the entire state space of the problems. Therefore it is impossible to solve all problems with only one algorithm. We can only solve some of the problems with the partial state space and some special empirical rules. Although some problems are in complete information settings, algorithm cannot be implemented because of the low efficiency of the algorithm. To improve the efficiency of problem solving, some empirical heuristic rules must be used. Some heuristic methods are universally applicable to many problem fields, while some only represent some specific knowledge related to some specific problems.

There are two expression modes of heuristic information:

(1) Rules. For example, rules of chess playing system not only can describe a group of legal steps, but also can describe a group of "brilliant" steps confirmed by the one who wrote the rules.

(2) Heuristic function. The heuristic function can estimate a single problem state, to determine its degree of the conformation with the requirements.

Heuristic function is a mapping function. It maps problem state description to the desired degree, which is usually described by numbers. The aspects of the problem state that should be considered, the estimation of those aspects and the choice of the unilateral weight and so on all depend on the heuristic function value of a given node during the searching process, which makes a as good as possible estimation about whether that node is on the expected route of problem solving.

## 11.6.3 Wu's method

As two mainstreams in mathematics, mathematics axiomatization and mechanization have played an important role in the development of mathematics. After a deeply study of ancient Chinese mathematics and decades of research in mathematics, Wu Wenjun finally formed his idea of mathematics mechanization, well-known as Wu's method (Wu, 1996).

Wu's method, also known as mechanized method of geometry, is mainly in two steps. The first step is to express the premises and conclusions of the theorem to be proved in algebraic equations by introducing coordinates. This is applicable only to theorems whose algebraic relations can be encoded in polynomial equations, such as parallel, perpendicular, intersection, distance, etc. This step may be called the algebra of geometry. The second step is the resolution of coordinates in the equations encoding conclusions with the help of the polynomial relationships in the equations encoding premises. The theorem is proved if all coordinates in the condition equations can be eliminated, and should be checked further. This step is entirely algebraic. The above two steps can be carried out in a mechanical and rigid manner. There are no significant difficulties in realizing the above method in computers. Its principle runs as follows (Wu, 1996).

Assume a supply of variables $x_1, \dots, x_n$, and a domain $k$ with the characteristic $O$. The following polynomials are from $k[x_1, \dots, x_n]$. A group TPS = $(f_1, \dots, f_n)$ of polynomials is a triangle, if $x_1, \dots, x_n$ are can be divided into two parts, i.e., $u_1, \dots, u_s$ and $y_1, \dots, y_r$, ($r + s = n$), such that $f_i$ has the following forms:

$$f_1 = I_1 y_1^{m_1} + o(y_1^{m_1}),$$
$$f_2 = I_2 y_2^{m_2} + o(y_2^{m_2}),$$
$$\cdots \cdots \cdots$$
$$f_n = I_n y_n^{m_n} + o(y_n^{m_n}).$$

subject to the following conditions:

c1) the coefficient of each $y_i$ in $f_i$ is a polynomial in $k[u, y_1, \dots, y_{i-1}]$;
c2) the exponent of each $y_i$ ($j<i$) in $I_i$ is less than $m_j$.

For any polynomial G, we can identify the following equation:

$$I_1^{s_1} \cdots I_n^{s_n} G = \sum Q_i f_i + R,$$

where $s_i \geq 0$, $Q_i \in k[x_1, \dots, x_n]$, $R \in k[x_1, \dots, x_n] = k[u, y_1, \dots, y_n]$, and the exponent of each $y_i$ in $R$ is less than $m_i$. $R$ is referred to as the remainder of $G$ w.r.t TPS, in symbols, R=Remdr (G/TPS).

The polynomial triangular group TPS is irresolutionable, if each $f_i$ is irresolutionable w.r.t $y_i$ in the expansion domain of $k=[u, y_1,...,y_{i-1}]$. The number of $u$ is the dimension $n$ of TPS, in symbols, dimTPS.

For any polynomial group PS and another polynomial H, we denote by Zero (PS / H) the set of elements in $k$'s expansion domain such that PS = 0 and H ≠ 0. Wu Wenjun's mechanized method is based on the following two theorems:

(1) Ritt's Principle:

For any polynomial group PS, we can mechanically produce a polynomial triangular group TPS (not unique), called the characteristic set of PS, such that:

(a) Zero(TPS/J) ⊂ Zero(PS) ⊂ Zero(TPS);

(b) Zero(PS) =Zero(TPS/J) +ΣZero(PSi).

where J refers to the product of all $I_i$ of TPS, and $PS_i$ is the resulting polynomial group by adding $I_i$ to PS.

(2) Zero Decomposition Theorem:

For any polynomial group PS and another polynomial H, we can mechanically compute a decomposition (not unique) such that:

$$Zero(PS/H) =\Sigma Zero(IRR_i/R_i),$$

where each $IRR_i$ is a irresolutionable polynomial triangular group with Remdr $(R_i/IRR_i) \neq 0$.

These two theorems can be naturally generalized to the case of differential polynomial groups. The mechanization method based on the above two theorems can be applied in solving, but not limited to, the following problems:

The machine proof of theorems in the elementary geometry;
The machine proof of theorems in the differential geometry;
The mechanical derivation of unknown relationships;
The solution to high exponent algebraic equations;
The factorization problems.

## 11.7 Decision Making

Decision making is the process of sufficiently reducing uncertainty and doubt about alternatives to allow a reasonable choice to be made from among them. Usually Decision making is a nonlinear, recursive process, which most decisions are made by moving back and forth between the choice of criteria and the identification of alternatives.

### 11.7.1 Decision making procedure

Decision Making Process is the systematic process of identifying and solving problems, of asking questions and finding answers. Decisions usually are made under conditions of uncertainty.

### 1. State the problem

A problem first must exist and be recognized. What is the problem and why is it a problem. What is ideal and how do current operations vary from that ideal. Identify why the symptoms (what is going wrong) and the causes (why is it going wrong). Try to define all terms, concepts, variables, and relationships. Quantify the problem to the extent possible. If the problem, not accurately and quickly filling customer orders, try to determine how many orders were incorrectly filled and how long it took to fill them.

### 2. Define the objectives

What are the objectives of the study. Which objectives are the most critical. Objectives usually are stated by an action verb like to reduce, to increase, or to improve.

### 3. Develop a diagnostic framework

Next establish a diagnostic framework, that is, decide what methods are going to be used, what kinds of information are needed, and how and where the information is to be found. Is there going to be a customer survey, a review of company documents, time and motion tests, or something else. What are the assumptions (facts assumed to be correct) of the study. What are the criteria used to judge the study. What time, budget, or other constraints are there. What kind of quantitative or other specific techniques are going to be used to analyze the data. (Some of which will be covered shortly). In other words, the diagnostic framework establishes the scope and methods of the entire study.

### 4. Collect and analyze the data

The next step is to collect the data Raw data is then tabulated and organized to facilitate analysis. Tables, charts, graphs, indexes and matrices are some of the standard ways to organize raw data. Analysis is the critical prerequisite of sound business decision making. What does the data reveal. What facts, patterns, and trends can be seen in the data. Many of the quantitative techniques covered below can be used during the step to determine facts, patterns, and trends in data. Of course, computers are used extensively during this step.

## 5. Generate alternative solutions

After the analysis has been finished, some specific conclusions about the nature of the problem and its resolution should have been reached. The next step is to develop alternative solutions to the problem and rank them in order of their net benefits. But how are alternatives best generated. Again, there are several well established techniques such as the Nominal Group Method, the Delphi Method and Brainstorming, among others. In all these methods a group is involved, all of whom have reviewed the data and analysis. The approach is to have an informed group suggesting a variety of possible solutions.

## 6. Develop an action plan and implement

Select the best solution to the problem but be certain to understand clearly why it is best, that is, how it achieves the objectives established in Step 2 better than its alternatives. Then develop an effective method (action plan) to implement the solution. At this point an important organizational consideration arises - who is going to be responsible for seeing the implementation through and what authority does he have. The selected manager should be responsible for seeing that all tasks, deadlines, and reports are performed, met, and written. Details are important in this step: schedules, reports, tasks, and communication are the key elements of any action plan. There are several techniques available to decision makers implementing an action plan. The PERT method is a way of laying out an entire period such as an action plan. PERT will be covered shortly.

## 7. Evaluate, obtain feedback and monitor

After the Action Plan has been implemented to solve a problem, management must evaluate its effectiveness. Evaluation standards must be determined, feedback channels developed, and monitoring performed. This Step should be done after 3 to 5 weeks and again at 6 months. The goal is to answer the bottom line question. Has the problem been solved?

## *11.7.2 Decision making strategies*

As you know, there are often many solutions to a given problem, and the decision maker's task is to choose one of them. The task of choosing can be as simple or as complex as the importance of the decision warrants, and the number and quality of alternatives can also be adjusted according to importance, time, resources and so on. There are several strategies used for choosing. Among them are the following:

### 1. Optimizing

This is the strategy of choosing the best possible solution to the problem, discovering as many alternatives as possible and choosing the very best. Note that the collection of complete information and the consideration of all alternatives is seldom possible for most major decisions, so that limitations must be placed on alternatives.

### 2. Satisfying

In this strategy, the first satisfactory alternative is chosen rather than the best alternative. If you are very hungry, you might choose to stop at the first decent looking restaurant in the next town rather than attempting to choose the best restaurant from among all (the optimizing strategy). The word *satisfying* was coined by combining *satisfactory* and *sufficient*. For many small decisions, such as where to park, what to drink, which pen to use, which tie to wear, and so on, the satisfying strategy is perfect.

### 3. Maximax

This stands for "maximize the maximums." This strategy focuses on evaluating and then choosing the alternatives based on their maximum possible payoff. This is sometimes described as the strategy of the optimist, because favorable outcomes and high potentials are the areas of concern. It is a good strategy for use when risk taking is most acceptable, when the go-for-broke philosophy is reigning freely.

### 4. Maximin

This stands for "maximize the minimums." In this strategy, that of the pessimist, the worst possible outcome of each decision is considered and the decision with the highest minimum is chosen. The Maximin orientation is good when the consequences of a failed decision are particularly harmful or undesirable.

Maximin concentrates on the salvage value of a decision, or of the guaranteed return of the decision.

## 11.8 Creative Thinking

Creative thinking is the process which we use when we come up with a new idea.

This creative thinking process can be accidental or deliberate. Without using special techniques creative thinking does still occur, but usually in the accidental way; like a chance happening making you think about something in a different way and you then discovering a beneficial change. Other changes happen slowly through pure use of intelligence and logical progression. Using this accidental or logical progression process, it often takes a long time for products to develop and improve. In an accelerating and competitive world this is obviously disadvantageous.

Using special techniques, deliberate creative thinking can be used to develop new ideas. These techniques force the mergence of a wide range of ideas to spark off new thoughts and processes. Brainstorming is one of these special techniques, but traditionally it starts with unoriginal ideas.

The research of creativity can be traced back to over 100 years ago. It is generally believed that the earliest systematic and scientific work on this matter is British physiologist Francis Galton's book *Hereditary Genius*, which was published in 1869. But as the core of creativity, creativity thought wasn't systematically studied with scientific methods until much later. The true mark of the opening of this field was Graham Wallas' book *The Art of Thought* in 1945, where Graham made an intensive research on the creative thinking related psychological activity process. Based on his research, he introduced the general model of the creative thought, which includes 4 stages: preparation, incubation, illumination and verification.

In 1945, German psychologist Max Wertheimer published his book *Productive Thought*, explicitly created the concept of "productive thought". The major achievement of this book is the analysis of creative thinking process with the Gestalt theory. It has a wide range of content. From an easy math lesson, to the genius Einstein, all is carefully analyzed in the thought psychological way. Wertheimer believed the process of the thought activities are not the step-by-step operations in formal logic, or the blind connections in idealism. Instead, it's the structural information theory in the gestalt. He further indicated this Gestalt structure did not come from mechanical exercises or the repeats of the past experience. It's acquired from the enlightenment.

American psychologist Joy Paul Guilford introduced the tri-dimensional model of intelligence in 1967 (Guilford, 1967; Guilford, 1971). Guilford's Structure of Intellect (SI) theory comprises up to 180 different intellectual abilities organized along three dimensions—Operations, Content, and Products. Guilford claims that the core of creative thinking in the three-dimensional structure in the second dimension of "divergent thinking." So he and his assitants focused on divergent thinking was more in-depth analysis, in this based on the divergent thinking on the four main features:

- Fluency: in a short time be able to continuously express a number of concepts and ideas;
- Flexibility: from different angles and the flexibility to think in different directions;
- Originality: has a unique ideas and inventiveness in problem-solving ideas;
- Elaboration: be able to imagine and describe the details of things or events.

Guilford believes that this is the main features of creative thinking, and developed a set of specific methods to measure these characteristics. They then apply the theory of educational practice again this date on the above indicators to develop divergent thinking (according to Guilford's theory, which is to develop creative thinking), so that the cultivation of divergent thinking becomes the operationable teaching procedures.

In 1988, Professor Robert Sternberg from Yale University, US, has proposed a triarchic theory of intelligence, based on the usage of analytical methods of implicit theories and the in-depth analysis of the creative power. Sternberg categorizes intelligence into three parts, which are central in his theory, the triarchic theory of intelligence (Sternberg, 1988):

(1) Analytical intelligence, the ability to complete academic, problem-solving tasks, such as those used in traditional intelligence tests. These types of tasks usually present well-defined problems that have only a single correct answer.

(2) Creative or synthetic intelligence, the ability to successfully deal with new and unusual situations by drawing on existing knowledge and skills. Individuals high in creative intelligence may give 'wrong' answers because they see things from a different perspective.

(3) Practical intelligence, the ability to adapt to everyday life by drawing on existing knowledge and skills. Practical intelligence enables an individual to understand what needs to be done in a specific setting and then do it.

Sternberg claims that successfully intelligent individuals have the ability to achieve success according to their own definition of success, within their social and cultural environment. They do so by identifying and capitalising on their strengths, and identifying and correcting or compensating for their weaknesses in order to adapt to, shape, and select their environments'. Furthermore, individuals with successful intelligence often have a 'can-do' attitude, learn from past experiences and apply their mental abilities to achieve their goals and ambitions in real-life situations. He also proposed a propulsion theory of creative contributions, which states that creativity is a form of leadership (Sternberg, 1999).

Creative thinking is the combined usage of various thought methods, thus it requires to well handle relations between abstract and concrete, analysis and synthesis, induction and deduction... to reveal the relations existing among the objects in the natural world and discover the new facts and knowledge.

Creative thinking consists of six thought factors: divergent, imagery, intuitive, logical, dialectical and stereoscopic thought (He, 2000). In the creative thinking of the six elements of the structure, divergent thought is mainly responsible for goal and direction of thought, i.e., directional issues. Dialectical and stereoscopic thought provide the principles of philosophical guide and psychological process to the highly complicated problems. Imagery thinking, intuitive thinking and logical thinking are three basic ideas of human form, but also to achieve the main process of creative thinking. On the basis of the discussion above, the 5 stages of the cultivation of creative thinking are:

Stage 1: The emphasis on the cultivation of divergent thinking
Stage 2: The emphasis on the cultivation of intuitive thinking
Stage 3: The emphasis on the cultivation of thinking in images
Stage 4: The emphasis on the cultivation of logical thinking
Stage 5: The emphasis on the cultivation of dialectical thinking

## 11.9 Model of Logical Thought

In 1995, Nina Robin, et al from University of California published a paper *Relational Complexity and the Functions of Prefrontal Cortex* (Robin et al.,

1995), which attempted to discuss the relation between the most advanced human thought model and the neurological mechanism, on the basis of the neurobiology of the most advanced thought of human beings. Robin et al has postulated that, the human-thought-made reflection of the essential properties of objects and the internal connections among objects can be seen as a response to the various connections existing among objects. According to the predicate logic expression in mathematical logic, the essential properties of objects can be seen as the simplest form of relation, a 1-place relation; The connections among objects, however, is an n-place relation. Here n is the dimensionality of the relation. The larger n is, the more complex the relation is. In other words, n can be used as the indicator of the complexity of a relation. A theoretical framework based on this was further introduced to determine the complexity of the relation. They also used the achievements of modern neurology and the new discoveries about the structure and function of the prefrontal cortex to connect the process of different levels of complexity with the functional mechanism of different parts in the prefrontal cortex. This establishment has become a more scientific and more solid part of the foundation for our understanding of advanced thought process of human beings, as it was not only built on the psychological perspective, but also rooted in the internal mechanism of our brain and nervous system. The term "creative thought" was not used in the paper. Instead, they chose concepts like "the most advanced form of thought", "the most unique form of thought" and "advanced cognition". Considering that the paper attempted to cover the most complex kind of relation and its emphasis on "the most advanced" and "the most unique", the authors should have meant "creative thought" with "the most advanced thought". However, regarding to the actual meaning of "the most advanced thought" in the paper, the theoretical framework to process the relation complexity is in fact a logical thought based on neurology. Although it was not precisely the model of creative thought, it was somehow enlightening to the true establishment of the creative thought model.

The model proposed by Nina Robin and his colleagues is built on their theoretical framework of "relational complexity". So-called "relational complexity" is determined by the dimensionality $n$ of the relation, with different values of $n$ representing the different levels of relational complexity.

- *level 1*. A function of 1 dimension describes a certain property of an object (Called "attribute mapping" by Robin).

- *level 2*. A function of 2 dimensions describes a 2-place relation between two objects ("relational mapping").
- *level 3*. A function of 3 dimensions describes a 3-place relation among three objects ("system mapping").
- *level 4*. A function of n dimensions (n > 3) describes a n-place relation among n objects ("multiple system mapping").

Nina Robin etc. claim that there are 2 categories of knowledge for humankind to solve all kinds of actual problems: explicit relational concepts and implicit relational concepts. Explicit relational knowledge is based on the thought that is conscious and capable of further reasoning and processing; Implicit relational knowledge is based on the thought process that is, in contrast, non-conscious (or namely sub-conscious), relatively rapid and effortless. Robin and her colleagues have proved the major function of prefrontal cortex is to learn about and reason with the "explicit relational knowledge" by using neuroanatomy and electrophysiology. In another word, prefrontal cortex is the neurobiological foundation of the implementation of logic and reasoning. The theory of "relational complexity" is specialized for "explicit relational knowledge", so in the following we will only discuss this kind of knowledge.

According to the definition given by Nina Robin, explicit relational knowledge is what differentiates roles from their fillers, and hence relates the latter to the former. The so-called "role" here is an abstract concept, which represents the objects generalized by certain properties. For example, a "red thing" is a role of objects (the abstract concept generalized by the property of "red"). As for its specific meaning of a red apple, toy, shirt or other things, that is the filler of the role. Explicit relational knowledge differentiates roles from their fillers, and thus relates the latter to the former. The example, an unary relation (attribute mapping) is listed as below:

red (apple)

It can differentiate the role and its fillers and also establish the relation between them. Meanwhile, it indicates that a property of the apple is its red color. Another example below is a binary relation (relational mapping):

Greater than (A, B)

It explains the difference and relation between the role and the relation that one thing is greater than another, and it also points out the specific "greater than" relation between A and B.

On the basis of the "relational complexity" framework, Robin and others referred to the evidences from neuroanatomy and electrophysiology, and carried on a more perceptive study on the structure and function of the prefrontal cortex. Results show that prefrontal cortex can be divided into the dorsolateral/periprincipalis region, periarcuate region and orbitofrontal religion. Every region functions as an indefensible part in the processing of complex relation among objects and the implementation of logical thought:

(1) The dorsolateral area, including the principal sulcus and its surrounding area (i.e., the periprincipalis region), is associated with planning, concentration, and working-memory and learning contingencies between stimuli and responses separated in time. Thus damage to this region will impair or even suspend these psychological operations that are closely connected with logical thought.

(2) The periarcuate region (the arcuate sulcus and its surrounding area) is important for learning conditional contingencies between stimuli and responses, especially in situations with no significant delays.

(3) The orbitofrontal region controls environmentally cued responses and emotional inhibitions. Insult to this region may lead to incapability of selective processing (The ability to select the goal object from the environment and resist distractions) and affective disturbances, including personality changes, mood swings, and socially inappropriate behavior resulting from decreased inhibitions.

For the operation control with timing sequence and goal-directness, the cooperation of the three regions is required. Robin, etc also analyzed the detailed complexity levels of different kinds of processing in human thought. For instance, if various types of information need to be integrated in order and within a period of time, the complexity level will rise: First, succession, or rather separation in time hinders the chunking of different information, so segmentation is required to divide the information into distinct but related units for the processing, which leads to appear binary relationships (relational mapping), ternary relationships (system mapping) or even n-relations (multi-system mapping). Meanwhile, during the thought processing, working memory must be supplied to the information of every dimension in order to prepare for the arrival of the last dimensional information (Not until when the n-relations can be fully processed). Obviously, this will bring in extra heavy burden of working memory and attention distribution to the prefrontal cortex. Additionally, Robin and colleagues made a quantitative comparison between the relational complexity levels of "ordered recall tasks" and "unordered recall tasks", and the conclusion is the former is much greater than the latter.

In summary, if Nina Robin, who established the framework of the relationship between complexity theory based on the model of high-level thinking, because of neuroanatomy and electrophysiological evidence of strong support for measurement, so that the whole logic of human psychological operation with the more profound understanding. This is by far, in the logic of science-based brain model of a model gives the impression of deep.

# Chapter 12

# Intelligence Development

In this chapter, we will first explain the essences and the differences of intelligence, intelligence quotient, and the characters of intelligence development. Then introduce how different psychologists treat intelligence, and discuss the question of does intelligence can be measured and how to make accurate and objective evaluation of intelligence. And at last, we will discuss what factors determine the level of intelligence and what extent intelligence depends on the hereditary gene or the condition of living environment.

## 12.1 Introduction of Intelligence

What is intelligence? Psychologist could not put forward a clear definition until now. Some think that the intelligence is an ability of abstract thinking. And some others define it as adaptive capacity, learning ability, and the integrated ability of perceive activities. What's more, some pioneers of intelligence tests insist that intelligence is just intelligence tests. However, psychologists' definitions of intelligence can be divided into three kinds roughly:

(1) Intelligence is individual's ability of adaptability. A person who adapt living environment more easily, especially a newly flexible environment, he will own a higher level of intelligence.

(2) Intelligence is individual's capability of learning. The faster and easier can someone learn new things, and can solve problems by using experience, the higher level of intelligence he owns.

(3) Intelligence is individual's ability of abstract thinking. People who obtain new conceptions from concrete things and do logical reasoning through the conceptions show their relatively high intelligence.

Contemporary well-known test scientist Weissler integrated the above three kinds of views, intelligence is defined as: intelligence is the individual intentional action, rational thinking, and effective comprehensive ability to adapt to the environment.

All of the above definition, although some stressed that a certain aspect, and some emphasis on the whole, but there are two aspects in common:

(1) Intelligence is an ability, and belongs to potential capability.

(2) This capability through behavior. Expression, or adapt to the environment, learning, abstract thinking, such acts of individual performance or behavior of the resulting three kinds of overall performance. In other words, intelligence can be seen as an individual performance of various aspects to things, objects and scene features, and such functions are performed by behaviors.

## 12.2 Theory of Factors Effects on Intelligence

### 12.2.1 The two main factors of intelligence

English psychologist named Spearman began his research for the issue of intelligence at the very beginning of 20th century and found there always was a positive relation in any psychological test. Spearman put forward that the common relations build on every kinds of psychological missions are decided by a very usual factor of psychological ability. Above all psychological missions, there all include general factor (factor g) and special factor (factor s). The former is the common foundations of people's intellectual activities, while the latter only relates to particular intellection. The reason why the testing results of a certain person are positively related is they both share the same factor-factor (g). But they would not be identical because they enjoy a different factor-factor(s). Spearman insists that general factor determines one's intelligence. Intelligence is not determined by any single test, but can be estimated by numerous tests' average results.

### 12.2.2 Theories of fluid intelligence and crystal intelligence

After the mid-term of 20th century, Raymond Cattel introduced the theories of fluid intelligence and crystal intelligence to deep explore the general factor and the special factor. Fluid intelligence, which reflects the ability of study and

behaves, is measured by the tests of velocity, energy and adapting new
environment quickly, such as: logic reasoning test, memory span test, abstract
problems solving test and velocity of information processing test. And crystal
intelligence is judged by one's knowledge and craftsmanship such as vocabulary
and ability to ratiocinate and solve social problems.

The key function of fluid intelligence is to obtain new knowledge and solve
new and different problems, he thinks, and this ability is strongly influenced by
biological factors; crystal intelligence measure knowledge experiments which
indicate things people already learned whose key function is to handle familiar
and already-solved problems. A part of crystal intelligence is determined by
education and experience, but other parts are consequences of the early
development of fluid intelligence.

From the early 1980s, further research found that fluid intelligence and crystal
intelligence would experience different courses as age increasing. The same as
some other biological ability, the diversification of fluid intelligence follows the
movement of physiological growing curve which reaches its peak at around
20 years old and stays in that high level during the period of maturity
before declines. While the reverse is true for crystal intelligence, it goes up as we
grow older. Because fluid intelligence effects on crystal intelligence, they are
interacted with each other. So, we can suppose that no matter how many abilities
man own and what's the character of the task, all the marks or testing results
come are derived from the ability from general intelligence .Thus, there are two
board types of subject about fluid intelligence and crystal intelligence in most
intelligence tests.

### 12.2.3 Multifactor intelligence

L. L. Thurstone, an American psychologist, put the students of Chicago
University in practice for his 56-ability research. And he found 7 of 56 are highly
related and seem to have less relation to others. These 7 abilities include
coherence and comprehension of words and phrases, sense of space, speed of
consciousness, ability of counting, reasoning and memory. Since this testing
group could not be explained by "the two main factor of intelligence" and
emphasizing general factor cannot reach the purpose to distinguish the individual
difference, so Thurstone proposed that any group formed by 7 or above 7 kinds
of individual mental abilities, will be marked as multifactor intelligence case.
With this foundation, Thurstone did the framework of general mental ability

testing. And research shows that positive-relations have been found in the 7-ability group, so it seems that a higher class of psychological factor which indicate the general factor has also been abstracted.

## 12.3 Theory of Multi-element Intelligence

Theory of Multi-element Intelligence proposed by the U.S. psychologist Gardner. In his view, the connotation of intelligence is diverse, relatively independent from the seven kinds of intelligence components of the composition. Each element is a separate mental functional systems, these systems can interact to produce explicit intelligent behavior. This is seven kinds of intelligence as follows:

(1) Speech intelligence infiltrate in all ability of speech, including reading, writing and daily communication.

(2) Logic-mathematical intelligence, involves mathematical operation and logic thinking ability, such as doing the proof question of mathematics and reasoning from logic.

(3) Space intelligence, including navigation, the understanding of environment such as reading maps and painting.

(4) Music intelligence, including distinguish a sound and expressing a melody such as playing violin or writing some melodies.

(5) Body mobility intelligence, including govern your body to accomplish some accurate jobs, such as playing basketball or dancing.

(6) Relation intelligence, including the ability to affiliate with people friendly such as knowing other people's feeling, motivation and mood.

(7) Introspection intelligence, which means to one's inside world's condition and ability possess high level of sensitivity, including contemplate oneself and the ability of choosing one's own way of life.

## 12.4 Intelligence Structure Theory

American Psychologist J. P. Guilford thinks that the intellectual ability can be divided into three different dimensions, those are content, operation and result, and these dimensions make up a three-dimensional structural model (Guilford, 1967; Guilford, 1971).

According to Guilford's Structure of Intellect (SI) theory, an individual's performance on intelligence tests can be traced back to the underlying mental abilities or factors of intelligence. SI theory comprises up to 180 different intellectual abilities organized along three dimensions—Operations, Content, and Products.

(1) Operations dimension

SI includes six operations or general intellectual processes:

Cognition—The ability to understand, comprehend, discover, and become aware of information.

Memory recording—The ability to encode information.

Memory retention—The ability to recall information.

Divergent production—The ability to generate multiple solutions to a problem; creativity.

Convergent production—The ability to deduce a single solution to a problem; rule-following or problem-solving.

Evaluation—The ability to judge whether or not information is accurate, consistent, or valid.

(2) Content dimension

SI includes five broad areas of information to which the human intellect applies the six operations:

Visual—Information perceived through seeing.

Auditory—Information perceived through hearing.

Symbolic—Information perceived as symbols or signs that have no meaning by themselves; e.g., Arabic numerals or the letters of an alphabet.

Semantic—Information perceived in words or sentences, whether oral, written, or silently in one's mind.

Behavioral—Information perceived as acts of an individual or individuals.

(3) Product dimension

As the name suggests, this dimension contains results of applying particular operations to specific contents. The SI model includes six products, in increasing complexity:

Units—Single items of knowledge.

Classes—Sets of units sharing common attributes.

Relations—Units linked as opposites or in associations, sequences, or analogies.

Systems—Multiple relations interrelated to comprise structures or networks.

Transformations—Changes, perspectives, conversions, or mutations to knowledge.

Implications—Predictions, inferences, consequences, or anticipations of knowledge.

Therefore, according to Guilford there are 6 x 5 x 6 = 180 intellectual abilities or factors. Each ability stands for a particular operation in a particular content area and results in a specific product, such as Comprehension of Figural Units or Evaluation of Semantic Implications.

Guilford' took the content, process and result of intellectual activities into consideration in his 3-D intelligence structure model, which has boosted the work of IQ testing. Nearly 10 tens of functions of the 3-D intelligence model had been proved into use in 1971 and this action has been marked as one of the greatest exciting achievement to not only theoretical but also practical areas of IQ testing.

## 12.5 Preyer's Genetic Epistemology

The German physiologist and psychologist W. Preyer published his famous book named Children's mentality in 1882, which urge a new study of children psychology. And during the next 100 years, psychologists from different countries have made many researches on the study of the growth of children's intelligence. They were A. Gesell and his edition of Natural Maturating Theory, S. Freud and his psychoanalysis Theory, J. B. Watson and his behaviorism, E. H Erikson and his Personality Development Epigenesis. Those researchers' works promoted people's understanding on Children intelligence development and formed the main stream of children's mental development today. The influence is enormous and far-reaching.

Jean Piaget, a psychologist, had his distinctive view on psychology in both experiment and theory. The Piaget School made great efforts to explore children's language, judgment, deduce, cause and effect view, world outlook, moral concept, symbol, time, space, number, quantity, geometry, probability, conservation and logic. Those put forward a brand-new theory for children psychology, cognitive psychology or thinking psychology, which make broad and deep influence on contemporary children psychology.

According to Jean Piaget's deduce, our mankind was born with the ability to organize and adapt to new environment. How we organize stuff systematically and rigorously is what we call organized inclination. While how we meet and adjust a new environment calls meeting inclination. It is the same as we digest the food and transform them into our energy needed that we transform our experiences to the construction of our cognitive structure. Moreover, both of the transform need balance and equilibrium which can be treated as regulating action that make the concepts one obtains stable. Adjusting and assimilating cooperate reciprocally is a method of meeting inclination, the former one means to change the cognitive structure and mode oneself in order to adjust to new experience, while the latter one mix the new experience with the old. During Jean Piaget's long exploring on how children make mistakes, he found it is much enlightening to analyze the incorrect answers than correct ones. By using the clinical method, Piaget observed his three children and then did the same to tens of thousand of children with other researchers. Well, they proposed the distinctive theory of children's periodic development by finding the differences between different-aged children in their intellectual activity. This action lastly came into a revolution of views on children's intelligence, but still with so many controversies. Some psychologists pointed out that, it is the most complete and systematic cognitive development so far.

### *12.5.1 Schema*

Piaget thinks intelligence has a structural foundation, and schema is what he used to describe cognitive structure (Piaget, 1954). He defined schema as organized and repeatable behavior or way of thinking, or things that are repeatable and summarizing. In short, schema is the structure or framework of any action. Also, it is a part of cognitive structure as we can divide one's cognitive structure into many schemas. Like new born babies have abilities of sucking, crying, looking, hearing and grasping, which are innate that helped them to survive. Those are inborn genetic schemas. The synthesis of all genetic schemas composes a baby's intelligence structure. Genetic schema is formed with the long period evolution of schema. Based on those inborn genetic schema, with the rise of age and the maturity of enginery, young children's schemas and cognitive structure developed constantly through assimilation, adaptation and balance with interaction with environment. There are different schemas in different stages of the development of children's intelligence. For example, the schema is called perceptive activity schema in the stage of perceptive activity, and operation thinking schema in the stage of thinking.

As a psychological structure of intelligence, Schema is a biological structure based on physical condition of nerve system. Current studies can hardly explain the physical and chemical quality. On the contrary, the existence of those schemas in people's brain can be speculated from people's behaviors. Actually, Piaget analyzed the intelligence structure based on a large number of clinical cases using biology, psychology, Philosophy and logic and mathematical concepts (group, throng and grid). Since this intellectual structure accords with Principles of logic and epistemology, it is not only a biological structure but more importantly is a logical structure (computing schema). The neuro-physiology basis of the pre-described visual prehension action is nerve pathway myelin sheath, which seems to be a product of genetic procedure. Natural maturity which includes genetic factors really plays an indispensable role in the sequence that the development of children's intelligence follows a consistent stage. However, maturity does not play a decisive role in the schema development from enfant to adult. Evolution of wisdom as a functional structure is the outcome of many factors. The whole development of intelligence structure during children's growing does not decided by the inherited program. The factor of inheritance mainly provides the probability for development or approach for structure, and nothing will be evolved in structure until the probabilities are provided. However, between the probability and reality, there are some other factors plays a crucial role in changing the structure, such as practice, experience and society.

We still need to point out that the structure of intelligence proposed by Piaget has three factors, integrity, conversion and automatic adjustment. Integrity of structure refers to internal coherence while every part is interacted with each other by inherent laws in which every schema has its own law and the sum of all is not the children intelligence structure; Conversion of structure shows that structure is not still but developing with the effect of assimilate, adapt and balance. Automatic adjustment of structure means self-adjustment based on the discipline of structure. It also means that the change of one component in the structure will result in changes of other component. Therefore, only view a self-adjust system as a whole, then it is a structure.

Assimilation and acclimation are terms Piaget uses to describe the basic process of development of Children intellectual schema. He believes that assimilation is a forming or formed structure which integrates external factors. In another word, take the environment into consideration is aim to enrich the main action, or say, to obtain new knowledge using existing one. For example, an infant, who knows how to grab, will try to get toy by grabbing repeatedly when he sees the toy on his bed. When he is alone and the toy is too far to get, this baby will still try to get it by grabbing. This action is acclimatization. In this case, the infant used his old experience to meet the new situation (a toy far away from him). So we can see that acclimatization applies to not only organism's life but also actions from the explanations talked about above. Acclimation is "the format and structure of assimilability will change according to the influence of assimilated elements". i.e., change the action of subject to adapt to objective changes or improve the cognitive structure to deal with new problems. And let us suppose that, if that baby accidentally got that toy by drawing the sheet or something like that. This action is acclimation.

Piaget used Assimilation and adaptation to explain the relationship between main cognitive structure and environmental stimulation. Acclimation makes the stimulation a part of the cognitive structure. A main body will response to certain environment stimulations only when those stimulations be assimilated in its' cognitive structure (schema). In other words, it is the assimilation structure that makes the main body responds to stimulation. The story in acclimatization is quite different, because the cognitive structure is changing rather than stays the same. Simply, filter or change of input simulation is called assimilation, and change of internal structure to adapt reality is called adaptation. The balance between the assimilation and acclimatization is the understanding of adaptation and the essence of human wisdom.

Assimilation does not change or improve the schema, but the acclimation does. Piaget thinks assimilation plays an important role in formation of intelligence structure. Structure changes due to adaptation; however, it is formed during the procedure of assimilation through repeating and abstraction.

Mental operation, which is one of the main concepts of Piaget's theory, is internalized, reversible, conservational and logical. So we can see four characteristics of operation or mental operation from this:

(1) Psychological operation is a sort of psychological and internalized action. For example, pouring water of a thermos bottle into a cup, we can see in this action a series of characteristics, which are explicit and can be appealed directly to sense. However, as for adults and children of a certain age, there is not need to carry out this action but just imagine finishing it and predicting its result in mind. This process of pouring water in psychology is the so called "internalized action" or one of the factors that such actions can be called operation. It is observed that this kind of operation is an internalized thought that caused by external actions or

an action directed by thoughts. The actions by newborn baby, such as cry, sip, grip and so on, are non-thought reflex which should not be treated as operation. In fact, because operation based on some other conditions, the actions by children will never have such so-called operational actions until they reach a certain age.

(2) Mental computing is an internal reversible action. This leads to the concept of reversibility which can be explain by the process of pouring water. We can imagine pouring water into a glass from a thermal bottle. In fact, we can also imagine that water in glass returning to the thermal bottle, and this is the concept of reversibility, which is another factor makes actions become operation. If a child has a reversible way of thinking, it can be considered his wisdom of action has reached the level of computing.

(3) Computing is an action that has the prerequisite of conservation. An action is not only an internalized and reversible one but also has the premise of conservation once it has the meaning of thinking. The so-called conservation means that amounts, length, area, volume, weight, quality etc. stay unchanged although they present in different ways or different forms. For example, 100 ml water in big glass is still 100 ml after it is poured into a smaller glass. And also weight doesn't change when a whole apple is chopped into 4 parts. Conservation of energy, momentum conservation, charge conservation in nature are concrete examples. When children can recognize conservation which means children's intelligence has developed and reached the level of computing. Conservation and reversibility are inner-related, they are two forms of expression of the same process. Reversibility means the turn of a process can be forward direction or negative direction while conservation means that the quantity in a process stays unchanged. If children's thoughts have the feature of reversibility or conservation, we can almost say that their thoughts have the quality of conservation or reversibility. Otherwise, neither of them will exist.

(4) Operation is an action of logical structure. As we previously mentioned, intelligence has its structural named foundation-schema. As long as children's intelligence has developed into the level of computing, or say, their intelligence structures have already been equipped with internalization, reversibility and conservation, the structure begin to become the computing schema. Computing schema or computing exists in an organized operation system which is not separated. A single internalized action does not mean computing but just a simple instinctive representation. However, action is not separated and alone but coordinated and organized in fact. For example, in order to reach a certain goal, an ordinary person need organic coordination of goal and action, and the

structure is formed during the procedure of goal attainment. In the introduction of schema, we have mentioned that computing schema is a logic structure, the reason of this fact not only because the biologic basis of computing is not clear and it is reasoned by people, the most important reason is that the view of structure conform to the principle of logic and epistemology. Computing is a logic structure; therefore, psychological computing is an action with logic structure.

Taking computing as a symbol, children's development stage can be divided into the pre-operational stage and operational stage. The former one includes the sensor motor stage and representative stage; the latter one distinguishes the concrete computing stage and formal computing stage.

### 12.5.2 Stages of children's intellectual development

Jean Piaget proposes that there are four distinct, increasingly sophisticated stages of mental representation that children pass through on their way to an adult level of intelligence. These four stages have been found to have the following characteristics: (1) Even the timing may vary, the sequence of the stages does not. The development of stages is universal to every child and which experiences unalterable order. The appearance of each specific stage lies on the level of intelligence rather than age. In order to show the various stages of the age range that may arise, Piaget used the approximate age in the concrete description of each stage. Whereas, the average age appeared in the stages are quite different because of the dissimilarities of social culture or education. (2) The unique cognitive structure of each stage determines the common characteristics of child behavior. When the intelligence developed to a certain stage, the children can engaged in various kinds of activities at the same level. (3) The development of cognitive structure is a process of continuous construction. Every stage is an extension of the previous stage, and it forms a new system after reorganizing the previous stage. So, the structure of the former stage is the prerequisite of the latter one and will be replaced by it.

### 1. Sensorimotor period (0-2 years old)

From birth to 2 years old is the sensorimotor stage. Not much reflective actions can be found in children by this stage. In this stage, infants construct an understanding of the world by coordinating sensory experiences (such as seeing and hearing) with physical, motoric actions. And the cognitive structure of action format is formed. Piaget divided the sensorimotor stage into six sub-stages, from actions by new born babies, such as crying, sucking, hearing and seeing, to a more organized and meaningful actions with the maturing of brain and organisms at the end of this stage.

*The first sub-stage* (practice of reflexive behaviors, birth-1 month): New born baby adapts to the new environment with the innate unconditional reflexes, including reflexes of sucking, swallowing, grasping, embracing, crying, seeing and hearing. The development and coordination of these inherent reflexes lies on repeated practices and which implies the functions of assimilation and accommodation. By observing the way how an infant sucks, Piaget discovered the development and change of sucking reflex. For example, if we give a breast feeding infant a feeding-bottle, we'll find that it is quite different for the movement of the mouth between the sucking of the breast and the bottle. Since it is easier to suck the feeding-bottle than the breast, sometimes the infant may refuse to suck the breast or becoming upset once given the chance to suck the bottle. From which we can generalize the development of children's intelligence, that is, he is willing to suck the laborsaving feeding-bottle rather than the breast.

*The second sub-stage* (formation of habits and perception, 1-4 months): Based on the first sub-stage, children connect their actions and make them into new behavior through the integration of the organisms. As long as an infant learn a new action, he or she would try to repeat it again and again, for example, sucking the finger, grasping and opening up the hand constantly, finding sound source and gazing the movement of an object or a person. The repeating and modeling of behavior indicates its assimilation and then forming behavior structure, whatsmore, the reflex is transformed to intelligence. We don't call these activities intelligence ones because they are aimless and determined only by perceptual stimulus. Accommodation, however, has taken place in this phase, for all these actions are not as simple as reflex actions.

*The third sub-stage* (formation of formation of, 4-9months): From the fourth month, the infants begin to form a good coordination between the movements of seeing and grasping. Then the infants become more object-oriented, moving beyond self-preoccupation and the influenced objects lead to more subjective movements in turn. So, a relation between action and the outcome of it circulates, and then polarization between the schemes and intentionality of actions will emerge, eventually, the movements exerted for a special purpose come forth. For example, the shaking of a rattle can attract the children's attention by its special sound. Repeating this attraction, we'll find that the infants would try to grasp or kick the rattle which is hung on the cradle. Obviously, children grow wisdom is this stage as they begin to act purposefully rather than accidentally. But the polarization of schemes and intentionality appeared in this phase is neither complete nor clear.

*The forth sub-stage* (coordination of schemes and intentionality, 9-12 months): This stage can also be called as coordination of schemas. In this phase, the schemes and intentionality of the infants begin to polarize and intelligence activities are shown up. This means, some of the schemas will be used as purpose and the rest as means, such as a child who pulls the adult's hand to the toy which is out of his reach or demanding the adult to uncover the cloth with toy below. This indicates that before the conducting of these actions, the children have intentions already. The more practice, the more flexible they are in operations of all kinds of action models. Just the same as we use concept to understand the world, infants use grasp, push, pull and some other actions to get acquainted with the new world. With accommodation to the new environment, children are acting to become wiser. But, in this phase, creativity and innovative thinking have never been found.

*The fifth sub-stage* (perceptual intelligence period, 12-18 months): According to Piaget, infants in this phase could manage to achieve their purposes by way of testing. When a child accidentally finds an interesting movement, he would try to make some change in the repeating of the previous action or resolve a new problem for the first time through experiencing mistakes. For example, an infant wants to catch the toy on the pillow out of his reach, without parent around, who has been trying but failed. Accidentally, he grabbed the pillow and eventually caught the toy with the movement of the pillow. There after, he could easily get the toy on the pillow by way of pulling the pillow first. It is a big step in the development of children's intelligence. However, it is not a way thought out by him but found accidentally.

*The sixth sub-stag* (intelligence synthetic phase, 18-24 months): In this phase, an infant can not only find out but also "think out" some new ways with his body and external movements. What we say "think out" is to resolve new problems by way of "inner connections", for example, a child would try to get the strip in a matchbox even if it isn't opened big enough for him to take the strip out. He would look at the box over and over again or try to put his finger into the open slit, if it is not useful, he would stop the action and then gaze at it with his mouth open and shut, suddenly, he undrew the box and took out the strip. In this process, the open and shut of his mouth is an indicating of the internalized movement of the open of the box because a child isn't good at representation ability. The action can be "thought out" by the child if he saw the similar action conducted by his parent before. Infants develop the ability to use primitive symbols and form enduring mental representations, which indicates the intelligence development running to a new stage.

The sensorimotor period marks the development of intelligence in three functions: Firstly, with the development of infant language and memory, the consciousness of conservation gradually comes into being. The concrete manifestation of which is that: When there is something (parents or toys) in front of him, he is conscious of it; vice versa, he is still convinced the existing of it even if it is not in front of him. Parents leave, and he believes that they will appear again; toys disappear, they should be found again somewhere in the drawer or under the sheet. The cases described above indicate that the format of the stable cognitive object is made up. According to recent studies, the permanent consciousness of mother is related to the maternal and child attachment, so it appears earlier than any other consciousness. Secondly, with the construction of the permanent cognitive schema of the stable object, the spatiotemporal structure also attains a certain level. Before he looks for an object, he must locate the object in space; then the continuity of time is constructed because the space location occurs following a certain sequence. Thirdly, the emergence of cause and effect cognition, the construction of permanent cognitive schema and the level of spatiotemporal structure are inextricable linked. The original cause and effect cognition is the outcome of children's movements, the polarization of movements and the relations among the objects caused by the movements. If a child can realize a special purpose (such as taking a toy by pulling the pillow) with a series of coordinated actions, it predicts the formation of cause and effect cognition.

## 2. Preoperational stage (2-7years)

Compared with sensorimotor stage, pre-operation stage has a big change in qualitative. In sensorimotor stage, children only think of matters they can currently feeling. In the middle and late phases of the stage, permanent awareness and early internalization have been formed. Till the pre-operational stage, the awareness of permanence has been consolidated; moreover, the actions have become more internalized. With the rapid development and improvement of the linguistic ability, more and more symbolic expressions have been used for external objects. In this stage, children are gradually liberated from concrete actions, paying attention to external activities and processing "pre-sensitive thought" by means of symbolic format. That's the reason why is called as pre-sensitive thought stage. The internalization is of great significance in this new stage. To describe internalization, Piaget told us his personal experiences: once, he took his 3-year-old daughter to visit one of his friends who has a one-year-old little boy. As the boy played in the play-pen, he fell to the ground, and consequently, crying aloud with angry. Piaget's daughter saw that with a surprise and muttered to herself. More importantly, 3 days later, his daughter mimicked the scene she saw 3 days ago. She tried to fall repeatedly and cackled since she was just experiencing the fun of the "game" that she had seen and never experienced. Piaget pointed out that, the action of the little boy has been internalized into his daughter's mind.

In the process of pre-sensitive thinking, children mainly use the symbolic function and vicarious function to internalize the objects and actions. Not as easy as accept everything like photography or transcript, this internalization means reconstruction of experienced sensual activities in mind neglecting some unrelated details (Piaget's daughter didn't cry when she fell.) and then the presentation comes into being. The internalized action is in mind while not carried out concretely. This non-physical action boosts the development of children's intelligence.

The Preoperational Stage can be further broken down into the Pre-conceptual stage and the Intuitive stage.

*(1) Pre-conceptual stage (2-4 years)*
The symbol of this stage is that children begin to use symbols. In game, for example, wooden bench has been treated as car, a bamboo pole has been considered as a horse, so wooden bench and bamboo pole are the symbols of car and horse respectively. In addition, there must be something in their mind that we called differentiation, connecting the objects with symbols. Piaget thinks it is the occurrence of cognition and symbolic system.

Language is also a symbol that produced by social activities and widely used in the society. Children's symbolic thinking develops by creating pre-sensitive symbols and mastering linguistic symbols. In this stage, the children's words are only the combination of linguistic symbols and words which are lack of general conception. As a result, they can only conduct a special-special deduction while not a special-general one. It can be concluded by the mistakes often made by kids. For example, when they see a cow for the first time, they know that a cow is an animal with four legs. Or, he will say "It is my hat" when he saw someone wearing the same hat as his. Also he will think there are two moons, since he saw it from the window of his room and then saw it outside when he walked on the road.

## (2) Intuitive stage (4-7years)

The intuitive stage is a transition of children's intelligence from pre-conceptual stage to operational stage, and its typical characteristics are still the lacking of conservation and reversibility; however, it begins to transit from single-dimensional focus to two-dimensional focus. Conservation is about to form and then mental operation followed, which can be proved by the following example: A father who took two bottles (in a same size) of cola (same quantity) and was ready to give them to his 6 and 8 year child respectively. At the beginning, both of the kids knew that the quantity of cola in the two bottles is the same. Then, the father poured the cola into 3 glasses (one bottle into a bigger glass and another into two smaller ones), and let the kids to choose.

The 6-year-old kid first picked the bigger glass, looked hesitated, and then took the two smaller glasses. Not decided yet, he took the bigger glass at last and muttered, "This glass does contain more." The kid made the last choice with hesitation. When waiting for the younger brother's decision, the older brother looked impatient and cried with a scorn voice, "Ah, dummy! They are the same quantity. You'll find this if you try to pour them back." Then he demonstrated it. From this case, we can see the improvements and limitations of children's intelligence in this stage. Several weeks ago, he chose the bigger glass without hesitation, which explains the lack of conservation and reversibility. He judges the quantity by the size of container. However, his hesitation this time indicates that he starts to take notice both of the size and numbers of the glass. His last choice reveals that conservation and reversibility are still not formed while the intuitive thinking is transit from single-dimensional focus to two-dimensional focus. The hesitation showed in the process of picking cola described above is the contradiction (or imbalance) of the children's inner world, i.e., an imbalance of assimilation and accommodation. The present problem cannot be resolved by the existing cognitive schema (assimilative cognitive structure) when the new one does not exist. The situation of imbalance can't last for a long time when the equalization factor takes effect and will develop toward balance, which is decided by the accommodation function. As a result, the preoperational cognitive structure is evolved to mental operation ones, which is symbolized by conservation and reversibility. The 8-year-old boy's cry and demonstration proves that.

To summarize, the characteristics of children's cognitive activities are as follows: (1) Relative concreteness. Thinking lies on presentation while not operation. (2) Without reversibility and conservation structure. (3) Self centered. Children have no realization of thinking process and his understanding of the world is by reference of himself, the specific one. The topic of his conversation is mostly on himself. (4) Stereotypy. It means when thinking a current problem, his attentions can neither be distracted nor distributed and he has no concept of rank when generalizing the nature of things.

The thinking of this stage is called as semi-logical thinking by Piaget, which is a big progress compared with that in the sensorimotor stage without logical and thinking.

## 3. Concrete operational stage (7-11 years)

This stage, which follows the preoperational stage, occurs between the ages of 7 and 11 years and is characterized by the appropriate use of internalized, reversible, conservative and logical actions.

We say this operation is a concrete one because children begin thinking logically about concrete events, but have difficulty understanding abstract or hypothetical concepts. For example: Edith's hair color is lighter than Susan's but darker than Liza's, when the question "whose hair is the darkest" is asked, it is a difficult one for children in the concrete operational stage. However, if we take three dolls with black hair of different degree and make a comparison between two of them, then raise the same question. This time, there is no difficulty for the children to give the answer: Susan's hair is the darkest.

The most important manifestation of children's intelligence development in this stage is the acquirement of the concepts conservation and reversibility. The concept conservation consists of conservation of quality, weight, corresponding quantity, area, volume and length. The children do not acquire these conservations at one time but gradually with the growth of age. In the year 7-8, the quality conservation is acquired, then the quantity one in the year 9-10 and followed by volume conservation in the year 11-12. Piaget believes that the beginning of concrete operational stage is the obtaining of quality conservation and ended by the volume conservation which is the beginning of the following stage.

The achievements of children's intelligence in this stage are as follows:

(1) On the basis of the formation of reversibility, with the help of transitivity, children can sort objects in an order according to size, shape, or any other characteristic. For example, if given sticks of different length, say, from the longest one to the shortest one in the order of A, B, C, D. Children will put them together and pick out the longest one and then the less longer one and so on. By doing this, they can sort out the length order (that is A>B>C>D...) of the four sticks even if they don't use algebraic signs to express their ideas.

(2) The ability to name and identify sets of objects according to appearance, size or other characteristic, including the idea that one set of objects can include another. For example, they know the quantity of sparrows (A) is less than that of birds (B), and birds less than animals (C), and animals less than creatures (D). The ability to classify belongs to mental operation.

(3) The ability to make correspondence (complementary or non-complementary) of objects in different categories. The simple correspondence is one-to-one. For example, if the students are given a series of numbers, each student matches a number and vice versa. There are also some more complicated correspondences, such as duplicate correspondence and multiple ones. For example, the group of people can be divided by either complexion or nationality and every one in the group is duplicate corresponding.

(4) The weakening of egoism. In the stages of sensorimotor and preoperational, child is self-centered and takes himself as the reference when looking at the external world. The idea of taking his own inner world as the only existence of psychological world impedes him looking at external things objectively. With the interactions of the external world, children's self-centeredness is gradually faded away in this stage. There is a case studied by a scholar: Two boys, one is 6 year old (preoperational stage) and another is 8 year old (concrete operational stage), are sitting in a room against the wall side by side. There are four different pictures (A, B, C, D) (see figure...) hung on the four sides of the wall, then the pictures are completely photographed and made four photos (a, b, c, d) respectively. The two kids are required to look at the pictures first and then presented the four photos. After that, they are asked which photo is the one hung on the wall they lean against; both of them give the right answer after a hard thinking. Then, the two kids are asked, "If you lean against that wall, which

picture will be the one opposite to that wall?" The answer of the 6-year-old boy is still the same (photo a) while the 8-year-old boy correctly gives the answer (photo c). To make the 6-year-old boy understand that correctly, the 8-year-old boy was asked to sit down oppositely. Then the researcher asked the younger boy, "What's the picture on his opposite wall?", however, the answer is the same (photo a) as before.

To generalize, children would acquire the abilities of systematic logical thinking, which including reversibility and conservation, categorization, seriation and corresponding, grasping the concept of numbers in operational level and the fading of self-centeredness.

## 4. Formal operational stage (12~15years)

In the previous part, we have discussed that children have acquired the ability of thinking or operation with concrete objects while not those described in words. Children are incapable to make a correct judgment with only words, such as the example of the hair color given above. Whereas, when entering the stage of formal operation, the children can resolve a problem only with words by reconstruction the object and its process through thinking and imagination. That is the reason why children can give the answer without taking reference of dolls. The child who needs to draw a picture or use objects is still in the concrete operational stage, whereas children who can reason the answer in their heads are using formal operational thinking. And the ability to resolve problems with reconstructing objects and its process is what we call formal operation.

Besides words, children in this stage can also take conception or hypothesis as premise, and then deducing and making conclusion. Therefore, formal operation is also called as "hypothetical priori operation". The hypothetical priori thinking is the basis of all formal operations including logic, math, natural and social science, so it is an important measurement of children's IQ.

According to Piaget, children in the formal operational stage are able to do not only hypothetical priori thinking but also the "basic operations" needed in the fields of technology. Besides the operations in the concrete operational stage, "basic operations" also include the consideration of all possibilities, separated and controlling variable, eliminating outlying factors, observing the functional relations of variables and organizing the relating elements an organic one.

Formal operational stage is the last period of children's intelligence development. Here we want to give a further explanation: (1) not all children gain the ability of formal operation at the age of 12+. It was found by recent studies that in the United States nearly half or more college students' IQ are still in the stage of concrete operation or between concrete operation and formal operation. (2) People's intelligence is still developing at the age of 15+. Totally speaking, it is in the stage of formal operation which can be sub-staged. Piaget thinks that the development of intelligence is influenced by many factors and there is no inevitable relation between age and intelligence. So, children who enter a stage (divided by age) but are quite different in the development of their intelligence doesn't contradict Piaget's theory.

From the discussions above, we can generalize that operational thinking structure of Piaget's genetic epistemology is the main one in cognitive or intellectual activities. Piaget indicates that operational structure is not only a biological one; moreover, it's a logical structure. The basic character of operational thinking is conservation, meaning the internalized and reversible actions, and it's realized by the realization of reversibility and reciprocity.

Presently, children's and adolescents' intelligence development is divided into three stages both at home and abroad. They are periods of: a) intuitive action thinking; b) concrete imaginable thinking; c) abstract logical thinking. It can be sub-divided into primary logic thinking, practical logic thinking and theoretical logic thinking.

The topic of cognition is complicated since each cognitive subject lives in a complex social relation, which unavoidably restricts the appearance and development of cognition. So, the limitation of Piaget's Genetic Epistemology is the failure of taking the study of children's intellectual development into social relations.

## 12.6 Intelligence Test

From the viewpoint of intelligence tests, intelligence displayed through behavior is an importance view. Therefore, some psychologists simplified the definition of intelligence as follow: Intelligence is the object of an intelligence test. If questioned further: what is the object of the test? Although it's not so easy to answer that question, one point is certain, that is, instead of being measured by intelligence itself, the object is measured by an individual's external actions. Indirect measurement of individual behavior characteristics which acted externally, then quantified it in order to estimate the level of their intelligence, which is the basic principle of intelligence test. Intelligence is an abstract concept and can not be directly measured, which is the similar case as "energy" in physics since it must be measured by the work generated by the movement of objects.

In the early 20th century, the French psychologist Binet was entrusted by the education authorities of Paris to produce a set of tests to identify students with mental deficiency, so that they can enter the schools which do not teach standard curriculum. Since then intelligence tests is used to predict the ability of children and students and the benefit of "intellectual" training. Now there is an increasing tendency to establish and apply intelligence tests to measure different aspects of a person's capabilities. The main request of intelligence tests is to categorize people according to the level of capacity, which also depends on the studies of intelligence theory and the establishment of new intelligence tests.

We can categorize intelligence tests into many sorts. For instance, they can be divided into individual test and group tests according to the number of people tested; the speed test is in reference to the score which is determined by the number of reaction correctly in limited time, and the capacity test is in reference to the score determined by the difficulty of the mission completed successfully; the verbal test which requires testee's response verbally, on the contrary, tasking test requires non-verbal reactions. No matter what type of intelligence test it is, generally speaking, there are a large number of test items or assignments which have different contents. The score is decided by the numbers of assignment completed successfully.

Each item of the intelligence tests can provide the level of age which fits it. When a child is tested, the scores he got is based on the items he passed. So his scores can be indicated by age. For example, Terman-Merrill's test requests defining each word, and sixty percent of the 13-year-old children can make it, so it is given to the 13-year-old child.

Given this, a child not only had past all the items of the 10-year-old child tests, but also the items of the 11-year-old and 12-year-old child tests. First of all, giving scores of his items of the age 10-. According to the half items of the 11-year-old tests, and a quarter items of 12-year-old tests past then, his scores should plus six months (11-year-old) and three months (12-year-old), so the score is ten year and nine months, which is Month Age (MA). Therefore, MA is based on the scores derived from intelligence test, it is determined by the difficulty level of passing the tests.

Intelligence quotient (IQ) is defined as MA divided by the chronological age, then multiply it by 100, the formula is as follow:

$$IQ = \frac{MA}{CA} * 100 \tag{12.1}$$

Multiplying the formula by 100, on the one hand, eliminates decimals, so that the IQ obtained as a integrated; on the other hand, shows the level of intelligence .To determine IQ ,this approach assumes that mental age grow together with the growth of actual age. On the contrary, if the intellectual age no longer grows at a certain actual age, so if a person was at this age, after which he re-growth of the age, he received intelligence on getting smaller and smaller. However, his intelligence has not diminished. After his or her arriving a certain age, the development of mental age stays at a relatively stable level. Because of intelligence no longer grow with the actual age in direct proportion at the age of 15, so the formula is used to test the intelligence of 15-year-old and over is as follow:

$$IQ = \frac{MA}{15} * 100 \tag{12.2}$$

But we can't get satisfactory results by using this approach. D. Wechsler proposes the Adult Intelligence Scale, the main component is as follow:

(1) Property and content: in property, items of the test are divided into language and assignment. The former contains 84 questions and can be divided into six subtests: common sense, comprehension, arithmetic, analogy, memory span and vocabulary. The latter contains 44 questions, including allocation of object and its form, chart filling, line up of picture series, building blocks according to the designed picture and symbol substitution. The 128 questions cover wide range of people's general abilities.

(2) Sphere of application: at the age of 16+.

(3) Implementation of procedure: implement individually, all of the tests consume about one hour.

(4) Score and criterion: the original scores of each sub-test process into a weighted score through conversion. The weighted score of the first six sub-tests is the total scale of verbal. The sum of the later five weighted scores of the sub-tests is the total scores of assignment. Check the total sum of the two scale scores to the standard table and then get the standard scores of IQ.

The criterion of this test is based on the standardized sample made up of 700 representational persons. There are appropriate consideration about many aspects such as gender, age, district, race, occupation, and educational background, in this sample, so it is of high representativeness.

(5) Reliability and related coefficient: the multiple coefficient got by midpoint subdivision is: the scale of verbal is 0.96, the scale of assignment is 0.93, and the total scale is 0.97. The research of related coefficient is base on the Stanford-Binet scale, the related coefficient is: the scale of verbal is 0.83, the scale of assignment is 0.93, and the total scale is 0.85.

Table 12.1 IQ's Distribution

| IQ | Category | Percentage |
|---|---|---|
| 140 and above | extremely good | 1 |
| 120——139 | excellent | 11 |
| 110——119 | nakagami | 18 |
| 90——109 | medium | 46 |
| 80——89 | middle-lower | 15 |
| 70——79 | critical | 6 |
| 70 and below | mentally retarded | 3 |

There is difference in individual intelligence. For most person chosen randomly, the IQ distribution shows in the Table 12.1. It is introduced by the Stanford-Binet scale revised edition in 1973. The result is 2904 person who is between 2 to 18 years old to get the intelligence test. From the table, we can conclude that, the person of highest or lowest IQ is minority; most of people are of medium IQ.

American psychologist Terman had done research on ability development of children whose intelligence is extraordinary. He chose 1528 children whose IQ was above 130, of which 857 boys, 671 girls. He made a visit to school investigation and family, got detailed appraisement of the teachers and parents, and made a personality inspection in a third part of those people. He made a visit to the schools and families of those people to inquire the development and change of their intelligence when they were adolescent. In 1936, those people had grown up, and got different jobs. Termen went on doing a random survey by letters, got the information of the development of their ability. In 1940, he invited them to Stanford University, and made a psychological test. From then on, he stacked to make a letter survey every 5 years, until the year of 1960.

After Terman's death, American psychologist Hills continued his research. At 1960, the average age of those research subjects was up to 49 years old. Hills made a letter survey, the number of people was 80% that of before. He made a survey again in 1972, people investigated stay 67% that of before. Till then, the average of them was above 60 years old.

Above research lasts about half century, storing lots of valuable materials. The research indicates that superior in the early age does not guarantee the outstanding ability in adult life. The ability of a person does not have much to do with the intelligence at early age, the capable and intelligence person is not always the smart child in the eyes of teacher and parents, but the persistent person who seek for greater perfection. The researcher received a Distinguished Contribution Award in 1999 for its groundbreaking achievements in psychology.

How to distinguish the prominent child and student? American scholar Laze proposes 17 items of psychology criterion to identify as follow:

(1) Knowledge and technical ability: the ability to possess primary knowledge and technical ability, solving practical problems by those technical abilities.

(2) Concentration: not tend to distract, can focus on one problem then get the solution.

(3) Interest of study: be favor of investigation, and doing homework.

(4) Persistence: take the assigned task seriously; make the best of them to make it eagerly.

(5) Responsively: liable to get inspiring, can response to the advice and questions of adult positively.

(6) Sane curiosity: get satisfaction from the process of solving problem, can propose new problem by self.

(7) Reaction to challenge: readily to solve problems and assignments which are relatively difficult, and to debate them.

(8) Sensitive: possess intelligence beyond actual age and sensible insight.

(9) Level of oral expression: be good at using numerous vocabularies.

(10) Fluency of thinking: can propose lots of concepts, do well in adapting to new and profound concept.

(11) Thinking flexibility: can get rid of own prejudice, approach a problem from the point of view of others.

(12) Originality: can approach problems through a novel way.

(13) Ability of imagination: can take independent thinking, be a man of imagination.

(14) Ability of inference: can extend given new concept to broader relationships; comprehend given material in integrated relationship.

(15) Wide interests: have interests in a lot of knowledge and activity, for instance, drama, handwriting, reading, mathematics, science, music, sports, common sense.

(16) Be concerned for the collective: be willing to take part in various kinds of collective activity, be ready to help others, be not fastidious to others.

(17) Be emotionally stable: Stay confident, happy, serene, have sense of humor, can adapt to the change of daily life, be not in violent rage

## 12.7 The Influence Factors of Intelligence Development

However, what are the influence factors affect the evolvement of children intelligence from low-grade to high-grade? There are three classical factors: maturation, material environment and experience, and the transmission of social environment. Piaget affirms the importance of those factors on children's intelligence development adequately, thinks them are essential. But at the same time he puts forward the fourth kind of factor named balance (also called modulation), which means reciprocities between the constantly matured internal organizations and the external environment. He also points out that the equilibrium and self-regulation are the crucial factors of intelligence development. Then we introduce those four factors separately as follows.

### 12.7.1 The factor of maturity

Maturity means the gradually developmental process of the organism, the neural system and the endocrine system under the control of hereditary procedures. In the view of some scholars, with the increasing age, children's behaved psychological and intelligent development is the result of maturity. It means the genotype of human inheritance decide the development level of their psychology and intelligence. It seems that the time and the development level children could reach have been arranged early, and the acquired behave is the gradual appearance of congenital inherent factors. Such extreme standpoint is "The determinism of heredity", whose representative figure is the founder of eugenics called F. Galton. However, the "The naturally mature theory" (whose representative figure is Gajser) represents firmly that although we would not ignore the influence of environmental factors, the development of children's intelligence has certain inherent program of organism.

Piaget thinks the maturity of the neural system has an important effect on development of intelligence. Because as a kind of human advanced function, intelligence must depend on physiological foundations of certain neural and the endocrine system. So the maturity of the physiological function will become the essential factor of development of intelligence undoubtedly. Such maturity factor plays an indispensable role in making children's psychology and intelligence development follow the continuous stage without changing. For example, the physiological function of new born baby's sucking and embracing reflection is a reflex arc, which without reflecting will not have such reflections. When the neural fiber in the cone of the neural system after the myelin (it is equivalent to half a month and four of a baby), the baby has a coordination of the vision and the grasping reflection (this is the third stage of the perceiving stage). But Piaget don't think maturity is the determined condition in the growth course of intelligence. The maturity of the neural system can only determine the possibility and impossibility of a certain designated stage. The environmental factors for realizing those possibilities can not be lacked. We can think so, even in the primary stage of the psychology or intelligence development and though the restriction factor of hereditary maturity is relatively great, some simple function of elementary psychological (such as perceiving, movements and initial speech) need practicing experience and functional practice at minimum extent. And the acquisition and development of some more complicated advanced psychological functions will be more influenced by the result of the dynamic interaction between the environmental factor and the maturity factor of the organism. Piaget says: "We can't imagine the existence of a hereditary procedure as the development foundation of human intelligence". Maturity can't explain the ability of calculate $2+2=4$ and how the deduction take shape. Intelligence is not innate, neither the conception. Take the language that has the close relation with age for example, if a child is not in the human society, he will not acquire the human language at any age.

To sum up, maturity is a factor which can influence the development of intelligence. It is possible for it offers the chance for the evolution of the intelligence structure, but between possibility and reality, there must be some other factors, such as practice, experience and interacts with the society.

### *12.7.2 The factor of experience*

Experience is the second factor of the development of perceiving from the traditional point. Piaget thinks experience is indispensable in human's intelligence development. The experience factor includes the physical environment and natural environment. Piaget who pays much attention to experience points out experience which is the source of knowledge and is the important condition for the increase of intelligence. But the experience factor is insufficient, which can't determine the development of psychology and intelligent. The so-called physical experience draws from the object through a kind of simple abstract course, such as children's experience of weight, color, the intensity of smooth, the level of voice, wood floating in surface of water and water forming ice draws from the sense of touch, vision, and hearing. The most essential characteristic of this kind of experience is stemming from the object itself. The properties of these objects (weight size, height of sound) are objective. Even children do not see, feel or act on them, these objects properties still exist.

The experience of logic mathematics and physics is although in the interaction of main body and object, this kind of experience is stem from the movement and coordination that the main body and object not taken out by the object. Piaget has given one example to explain the experience of such logic mathematics and physics: One of his friends is a mathematician. When he was young, he played with the cobble on the sandy beach, making 10 cobbles into one line and finding that no matter where begin to count, it will be 10. Then he arranged the cobbles into other shape, such as a circle, square, but the figure counted out does not change yet. So he reaches the conclusion that "the total is nothing to do with the order". Piaget thinks it is extremely normal for an adult, but for a child it will be an amazing discovery. When play with the cobble, you can experience the weight, form and size, etc., this is called the physical experience. "Nothing to do with the order" is also the experience, which neither gets from the perceived intuition, nor the reflection of the physical properties of the cobble. So, this experience is not the physical experience. Children receive this kind of experience through counting cobbles, which is a concept about the exchangeability with figures. This is the experience of logic mathematics and physics.

The physical experience and the experience of logic mathematics and physics are two kinds of experience with totally different essences. We can realize the physical property by physical experience, but the physical property does not depend on physical experience. Some object has physical property without physical experience. The experience of logic mathematics and physics stems from movements, but does not depend on the physical property. Without movements, there will no logic experience which stems from it. And the physical property does not rely on the object. Without movements, there will no experience of logic mathematics and physics. Two experiences include two abstract courses with different properties. The physical experience is a simple original meaning abstract, which only consider a certain property (Such as weight) of the object not the others. It means only abstract the "Weight". However, the logic mathematics and physics experience is introspection abstract. Because it is the abstraction of the movement itself, this kind of abstract is not only does not consider other characteristics, but needs a new reconstruction course.

As introduced before, all operations are movements. The formed experience is all the experience of logic mathematics and physics. The experience of logic mathematics and physics has extremely important meanings for the forming of the cognitive structure. Intelligence mainly shows the most essential experience of logic mathematics and physics. Any movement can take physical experience and experience of logic mathematics and physics out, but people can easily pay attention to the acquirement of physical experience not to the experience of logic mathematics and physics. Therefore in the cultivation of children's intelligence, on one hand, we should rich children's life by supplying various natural environment materials to make them obtain physical experience; on the other hand, perhaps more important, we should guide children through analyzing, synthesizing, considering and probing into inner links and laws between the things to make them get the experience of logic mathematics and physics during the activity environment described above.

But Piaget proposes two reasons to argue that experience neither prove everything nor determine the development of children's intelligence. (1) Some concepts can't be taken out from experience, which means the concept does not totally depend on experience. For example, children often obtained the concept of conservation of mass first, and then obtained weight and volume conservation concept. The weight and volume can be understudied by measuring the object, but children have not obtained the conservation concept through experience. Piaget asks, where does the concept of conservation of mass come from without the antigravity conservation and volume conservation? (2) The concept of experience is ambiguous and not clear.

### 12.7.3 The factor of environment

The social environmental factor mainly involves aspects such as the social life, education, study and language, etc. Obviously, those factors affect on the development of children's intelligence enormously. Firstly, it is the social life. People's life is soaked in the social living environment. Socializing one's life begins at the moment he was born. It is obvious that social life impact on the children's intelligence development. For example, by studies, someone finds that the relation (or call the family emotion atmosphere) between child and his parents 2 years old ago presents positively correlate with intelligence at the age of 18. The better relation, the higher intelligence. On the contrary, it will be low. In addition, from the development of children's view of self-centre, we can find out that as the communication with his family, little partners and teachers, children will appear to dispose self-centre, which is a behave of the development of children's intelligence. Secondly, it is education. In fact, when we emphasize the function of the experience factor which makes positive effect on the advance of children's thinking, it has already accumulated and bred the attention to the educational factor. Because the systemic education (study and train) can make children experience external world better, obtaining experience (physical experience and logic experience of mathematics and physics). Just because of this too, the educational factor could promote children's intelligent development.

Piaget puts emphasis on educating must accord with children's cognitive structure. He says "Even under social transmission which seems very passive of the subject such as situation of school education, if lacking children's initiative assimilation, such social function is invalid. Children's initiative assimilation is taking appropriate operation structure as prerequisite". He also says "Only the things which taught to children could make them do some creative works actively, the things could be assimilated by children effectively." To a certain extent, education can accelerate the transition of children's intelligence development, but can not surmount or change the order of development. Any child (including the talent) is definitely without exception too. We should pay full attention to this when conducting education during the early age of children.

Let's discuss languages again. The language plays a leading role in internalizing movements in presentation and mentality. We have already found out the influence of language which affected on children's intellective development by the introduction of the operational stage in children's thinking development. But the language is not the only factor of working, which is a kind of symbol system. But it is not the only symbol system. Though it may be the best symbol system, the ones that remain with symbol system are as follows, picture, model, imitating movement, internalizing imitation, peculiar gesture and posture, etc. Although the language is in close relation with intelligence, the development of the two is not parallel. Some people with fluent languages have ordinary intelligence. However, some people have extremely excellent thinking ability, but not well at speaking.

We can say that all science and culture of human society will not be inherited and developed without social transmission. Piaget emphasizes the important function of the social environmental factor which affects on the development of children's intelligence. But the social environmental factor is not the sufficient factor with the continuity of children's intelligence development. We can achieve this point through the analyses of language, education and so on above.

### 12.7.4 The balanced factor

The maturity of physiology, natural environment and social environment are the essential prerequisites and conditions for the development of children's intelligence. But each of them is not the sufficient factor. The growth of children's intelligence is not the result of the simple mechanical summation of these factors. Piaget has put forward the concept of the balanced factor and claimed that this factor is the decisive factor of children's intellective development. In Piaget's view, since maturity, experience and social environment can't totally explain the essential reason of development separately; there must be some other factors. This factor plays a corresponding and regulating role among the three kinds of original factors. This coordinator or conditioner is the equilibration.

Piaget's intelligence view has already been stated. He thought "intelligence is a special behave of the adaptability of creatures". Intelligence is one of the forms in which all cognitive structure prone to the equilibrium. Intelligence has structural foundation. The rise of intelligence goes with the constant development of the intelligence structure. Assimilation and acclimation are two pieces of basic course during the development of the constantly built intelligence. When individual meets outside stimulation (natural environment and social environment), it is the existent schema has an effect at first. When a baby come into being, this kind of schema is an inborn schema which determined by heredity. Then with maturity and the interaction which between the mature organism and the external world, this kind of schema becomes an existent schema. According to the existent schema, organism absorbs external information and makes a response, which means the course of assimilation. Repeated assimilation makes the schema or cognitive structure consolidated. When people get to know something and solve some problems, they always use the existing thinking and behavior pattern which is the exhibition of assimilation. When a new stimulation comes, the organism still uses the old or existing schema to handle, but the result may not be successful (children feel perplexed and hesitated while selecting coke beverage from preoperational stage to filterable stage of concrete operation). So while the new stimulation is absorbed by the cognitive form which is assimilated by the main object, this will make the cognitive form change which means acclimation. Changing the assimilating cognitive form does not be finished in a moment, but needs a period of time. Assimilation and acclimation are in an imbalanced state during the process. The old schema conflicted with the new-forming schema, which manifest the struggle of old idea and new idea in cognitive respects of people. If the new schema is been built at last, it means the imbalanced state of assimilation and acclimation is over. The equilibrium has already been realized, and children's intelligence has got development. Based on the new schema, children begin new assimilation, which construction in, and meet new stimulation which brings about new acclimation. Like this, children's intelligence is developing from low-grade to high-grade step by step. Maturity, natural environment and social environment all work in developing, but the balanced factor makes children's intelligence develop towards a certain direction by regulating these three factors.

## 12.8 Intelligence Developmental Artificial System

With the development of computer science and technology, people try to make a further understanding of the biologic mechanism by the computer or other artificial systems, and use computer to replicate the phenomenon and behavior of nature and natural lives. In 1878, the new subject, artificial life, was established (Langton, 1987). Artificial life is a simulation system or model system, which is constructed by computer and precise machinery and shows the natural life behavior, and reflects the process of organization and behavior. Its behavior characteristics and dynamics principle present as some basic properties, such as self-organize, self-repair and self-replicate, which are formed by chaotic dynamics, environmental adaptability and evolution (Shi et al., 1995).

Researching on the artificial life intelligence development, it will become more and more brightness as human self learning. The most essential or the most intrinsic problem is that artificial life system possesses ability of learning as the human. This problem has proven difficult. Over the past several decades, scientists have taken 4 approaches.

(1) Knowledge-based approach, an intelligent machine is directly programmed to perform a given task.

(2) Behavior-based approach, the world model is replaced by the behavior model, and the intelligent programmers compile program according to different layers behavioral status and desired behavior. This is a hand-modeling and hand-programming method.

(3) Genetic search approach, robots have evolved through generations by the principle of survival of the fittest, mostly in a computer-simulated virtual world. Although notable, none of these is powerful enough to lead to machines having the complex, diverse, and highly integrated capabilities of an adult brain.

(4) Learning-based approach, a computer is "spoon-fed" human-edited sensory data while the machine is controlled by a task-specific learning program. However, the process is non-automatic, and the cost is higher on training the system.

The traditional manual development paradigm can be described as follows: Firstly, starting with a problem or task, understood by the human engineer, then designing a task-specific representation, programming for the specific task using the representation, finally, running the "intelligent" program on the machine. If, during program execution, sensory data are used to modify the parameters of the above pre-designed task-specific representation, we say that this is machine learning. In this traditional paradigm, a machine cannot do anything beyond the pre-designed representation. In fact, it does not even "know" what it is doing. All it does is ruled by the program.

The autonomous development paradigm is different from the traditional manual development paradigm (Weng, 2001), and it is described as following: Firstly, design a body according to the robot's ecological working conditions (e.g., on land or under water), then design a developmental program, finally, at "birth," the robot starts to run the developmental program. To develop its mind, humans mentally "raise" the developmental robot by interacting with it in real time. According to this paradigm, robots should be designed to go through a long period of autonomous mental development, and the essence of mental development is to enable robots to autonomously "live" in the world and to become smart on their own.

For agent owning ability of self learning, we introduce the self learning mechanism into it, and Figure 12.1 shows its structure (Shi et al., 2004), where autonomous mental development (AMD) is agent root, and knowledge database, communication mechanism, inductor and effecter are absolutely necessary subassembly, then control main center is similar to the neural center of brain, which can control and coordinate others, and also it displays the agent function. AMD is intelligence agent's self learning system, which embody an ability of self learning. The communication mechanism interacts with the agent's environment, which is a special inductor or effecter. The inductor is sensory organ as eye and ear, and sense the environment around it. The effecter is another organ as hand, feet and mouth, and finishes the tasks required by agent. The agent enriches the knowledge and improves itself by automated animal-like learning algorithm, and reflects in increasing the module quantity and function. The knowledge database is a part as the memory of brain, and stores the information. How to store automatically is an important for the intelligence developmental artificial system, and the key of AMS is to organize effectively and store automatically all kind of the information, for example, image voice and text, and so on.

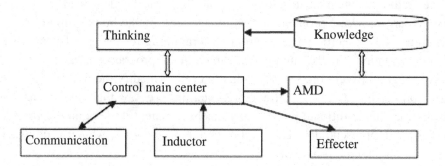

Fig. 12.1 Self Intelligence Development

# Chapter 13

# Emotion and Affect

Persons are living in the society. People's cognition is result not only from cognitive ability but also from integrated effect of multiple factors, such as affect, emotion, will, personality, etc. So, in the research of artificial intelligence, should simulate human advanced ability to the utmost extent, must also take account of the effect of affect. Machine intelligence will be able to recognize human emotion and express affect of itself only if it has affective ability. By this way we can make human-computer interaction more effective. Emotion is a multielement combinational, multidimentional structured, multilevel integrated mental activity process and psychological motive power which interact with cognition in order to adapt organism's survival and effective human communication.

## 13.1 Introduction

Subjective experience such as joy or sadness, happiness or pain, love or hate will occur when mankind cognize external things. The attitude experience and corresponding reaction toward objective things is defined as emotion and affect.

In general, emotion is considered to contain three aspects and most of emotion researchers give the definition of emotion according to the three aspects which are as follows: Subjective experience on cognitional aspect, physiological arousal on physiological aspect and external behavior on expressional aspect. Above three aspects interact when emotion occurs and thus form a complete emotional experience course.

The subjective experience is a person's self-awareness, i.e. a kind of feeling state of brain. People have many kinds of subjective experience such as joy, anger, sadness, happiness, love, fear, hate etc. The attitudes toward different things will produce different feeling. Certain attitude will occur toward certain

499

thing which may be oneself, other people or objective things. These attitudes could be sympathy for the misfortune of friend, hate for fierceness of enemy, happiness for success in undertaking or sadness for failing in examination. This subjective experience could be felt just by one's own heart: for instance, that I know "I am very happy", I feel "I am very sad", I realize "I am very guilty" and so on.

Physiological arousal is a kind of physiological reaction arise from emotion and affect. It related to many neural elements, such as brain stem, central gray, thalamus, amygdala, hypothalamus, locus coeruleus, pineal and prefrontal cortex which in central nervous system, and also include peripheral nervous system, endocrine gland and exocrine gland. Physiological arousal is an physiological activation level. Physiological reaction model aroused by different emotion and affection is different too. Cardiac rhythm is regular when people is satisfied or happy. Whereas cardiac rhythm will accelerate and the blood pressure will elevate when people are in the mood of fear or fury, at the same time respiratory rate will increase and even turn to be intermittent or pause. In a similar way, vascular volume will reduce when people are pain. Physiological index such as pause rate, muscle tensility, blood pressure and blood velocity is representative of inner physiological reaction circs. They always change along with emotion.

External behavior will appear when people are in a mood. This is emotional expression cause. For example, one will cry bitter tears when he is sad, flourish when excite, laugh a hearty laugh when happy etc. These body gestures and facial expressions are emotion external behaviors. People always judge and deduce one's emotion by these index. But sometimes external behavior and subjective experience will be inconsistent because of the complexity of people psychology. For instance, although one person is very nervous when he addressing lots of audiences, he must pretend to be perfectly calm and collected.

Subjective experience, physiological arousal, external behavior is the three necessary aspects of emotion. None of them can be dispensed with when estimate one's emotion. A emotional process will be complete only if the three parts of them exist and play at the same time. For example, when someone pretend to be anger, only external behavior is presented, but his authentic subjective experience and physiological arousal are lost, so it is not a complete emotional process. So any emotion must has the above three aspects and these aspects must be consistent, if not, the emotion cann't be identified. When we research and give definition of emotion, that is where the rub is.

In real life emotion and affect are well connected, there are some differences between them.

## 1. Difference Lies in Requirement

Emotion refers chiefly to attitude experience which relate to material requirement and spirit requirement. For example, one will be happy when his requirement of thirsty is satisfied, one will be scared when his safety is under threat, these are both emotional reaction. Whereas affect relates mainly to people's spirit or social demand. For instance, sense of friendship due to the meeting of our communication demand, sense of achievement is come from one's success. Sense of friendship and sense of achievement are both affect.

## 2. Difference Lies in Occurrence Time

In terms of development, emotion happen before affect. One could have emotional reaction at birth, but haven't affect. Emotion belongs to both human and animal but affect is only the character of human. Affect develops with one's growing. One couldn't have sense of moral, sense of achievement and sense of beauty at birth. These affect reactions is forming along with children's socialization process.

## 3. Difference Lies in Reaction Characteristics

Emotion and affect are different in reaction characteristics. Emotion has the trait of irritability, temporality, superficiality and explicitness. We will be very fearful when we encounter danger. But the feeling will disappear when the danger past. Whereas affect has the trait of stability, persistence, profundity and implicitness. For example, most people will not change their national self-respect whatever the frustration they meet. Elder's Warm Expectations and deep love to their next generation reflect the trait of profundity and implicitness of affect.

Emotion and affect are different, meanwhile they are fairly relevant to each other. They are always interdependent and blend in with each other. Stable affect is form based on emotion and be expressed by emotional reaction. So there will be no affect without emotion. The change of emotion reflect the deepness of affect. The changing process of emotion is filled with affect.

Human has four basic emotions, such as joy, anger, fear and sadness. Joy is an satisfied experience when people pursue and achieve the goal. It is a positive emotion with hedonic tone. It has high hedonic dimension and certain dimension. It can make one has the sense of transcend, freedom and acceptance. Anger is a kind of experience which occurs when one cann't achieve his goal for disturbance. One will get angry suddenly when he realize that something is unreasonable or vicious. Fear is a kind of experience which occurs when one try to escape from danger. Lack of the ability and means to deal with danger instance is the main cause for anger arousal. Sadness is a kind of experience which occurs when one lost his love or fail to satisfy his desire and expectation. The experience degree depend on the importance and value of object, desire and wish. Many complex emotions such as disgust, shame, regret, envy, favor, compassion etc. could derive from the four basic emotions.

## 13.2 Emotion Theory

### 13.2.1 *James - Lange theory of emotion*

19th Century American psychologist William James and the Danish physiologist Carl Lange respectively put forward a similar theory of emotion in 1884 and in 1885. The theory is based on the direct connection of emotional state and physiological changes, and proposing that the emotion is the perception which is the sum of the feeling of a variety of body organs in body. James thinks that when we perceived the object that we moved, our physical immediately changes. When these changes occur, we feel these changes that is emotional. Langer thinks that any role in a wide range of blood vessels can cause nerve system changes, there will be emotional expression. James – Lange's theory of emotions emphasize on physiological changes to the role of emotions. This theory has historical significance, but it one-sided exaggerates the impact role of external environment change and neglects the leading role of central nervous system to emotions.

### 13.2.2 *Emotional assessment - Exciting theory*

In the 1950's, American psychologist M. B. Arnold presented emotional assessment - exciting theory, stressed that the environmental impact which from the outside world engender to a feeling must through the evaluation and assessment which come from the cerebral cortex of people (Arnold, 1970). For example, in the forest, you would cause fear when see a bear. But in zoon, when see a bear in a cage we would not afraid, which is the awareness of individual to the situational and the evaluation's affection. Arnold defines that emotions is a tendency of experience that draw on the advantages and avoid disadvantages. He believes that emotional responses, including the body's internal organs and changes in skeletal muscle, and that feedback on the changes in the external environment is the basis of emotion. Arnold believes that the cortex's excited is the primary mechanism for emotion.

### 13.2.3 The three factors of emotion

The 1970's, the U.S. psychologist S. Schachter proposed three factors of emotion (Schachter, 1971). He thinks that emotion is not a simple decision to the external stimulus and the body's internal physiological changes, and attributes to the emergence of emotional in the role of three factors that stimulate the factors, physiological factors and cognitive factors. In his view, the cognitive factors play an important role in the context of the current estimates and past experience to the formation of emotional memories. For example, a person faced a dangerous situation in the past, but he safely went through, when he experienced such a danger again, the memories from past experience will make him to be ease. In other words, when the real life experience is same with the model established in the past, believe it can be deal with, there is no obvious emotional to person; when the real life is inconsistent with the expectations and people feel unable to cope, tension would be produced. This theory emphasis on human's regulation in the process of cognitive.

### 13.2.4 Basic emotions theory

Basic emotions theory thinks that there are a number of basic prototype form of pan-human emotions, each type has its own unique characteristics of experience, physical wake-up mode and explicit mode, the combination of different forms compose to all human emotions. In the point of individual development, the emergence of the basic emotional maturity is the result of natural organisms, rather than learned. From the point of biological evolution, the prototype of emotional is a product of adaptation and evolution, but also a means of adaptation and evolution; from ape to human, from the ancient cortex cortical to the new cortex cortical, the division of facial muscle system and distribution of facial blood vessels, as well as the occurrence and differentiation of emotional are simultaneously carried out and obtained. The most commonly mentioned is the aversion, anger, happiness, sadness, fear and so on, which are the basic emotions for different views.

The most famous study which supports the basic theory of emotion is the response to facial expressions and movement carried out by Ekman and Izard (Ekman, 1983). Ekman requested student assume himself as a character in some story and as much as possible to show facial expressions of characters. At the same time, researchers video-recorded their facial expressions; Finally, they required students to see their face and asked to identify, as a result, American students identified four types of expression (happiness, anger, disgust, sadness) from the six. Meng Shaoran's experiment also proved that Chinese infant and the standardization of basic emotional expression in Western model is the same; Similarly, Chinese adults and Chinese infant are the same in emotional expression of the basic model, and the socialization of the adult face still retains the basic expression model. Levenson and other young people as a test of the west of Sumatra, guided them to move facial muscle in order to outside the marked basic emotions, and had a series of physiological measurements, finally, compared the results of the measurements with the United States college students' result and found that the autonomic nervous physiological responses of the system model associated with the underlying sentiment has great cross-cultural consistency, such results tend to confirm that the basic emotions exist specific physical wake-up mode of pan- human.

The main objections of basic emotions theory contain: (1) Notwithstanding the above experiments confirmed the pan-cultural patterns of emotion, but the study has also shown some cross-cultural differences. (2) Studies in psychology and linguistics have found that the basic meaning of emotional words have a significant difference between different languages. (3) There haven't sufficient evidence to prove that the basic emotions have different neurophysiologic mechanisms. (4) The basis of recognition to facial expression may not be the basic type of emotions, but may be the location of bipolar dimensions of facial expressions in the emotional experience, or acts preparatory mode induced by facial expression.

### *13.2.5 Dimension theory*

Dimension theory thinks that several dimensions can construct all the human emotions; the distance in the dimensionality space presents the similarity and dissimilarity among the different emotions. They take the emotion as a gradual and calm change. The last two decades, dimensions means a number of researchers favor, but there are many controversies in using which dimension. The most widely accepted model is the the following dimension composed of two-dimensional space: (1) Valence, or hedonic tone, its theory is based on the separation of positive and negative emotional activation; (2) Arousal or the activation, refers to the degree of activation energy associated with emotional states, and the function of wake-up is to call to mobilize the body's functions, so as to prepare for action. At present we have a tendency to make the activate dimensions linking with the integrated wake-up call or the intensity of emotional experience. In the early 1970's, because of the impact of information processing theory, Mandle put forward that the autonomy wake-up of perception decides the intensity of emotional experience, cognitive evaluation decides the nature of emotional, which when integrated rose to awareness, resulting in emotional experience (Mandler, 1975). International Affective Picture System (IAPS) good reflects the two-dimensional space (Lang et al., 1988). In the two-dimensional coordinates space with pleasant and wake-up degree the average assessed value of tested objects for emotional pictures showed regular distribution.

The study of brain imaging confirmed that the positive and negative emotions are separate, that is to say both their own have specific processing system in brain, and link with the left hemisphere and right hemisphere activity, or the left hemisphere advantage and the right hemisphere. Study of electrophysiological have shown that when the film evokes you feel disgust and fear, the activity of right frontal lobe and temporal lobe are increasing, and the positive emotion showed by the strengthen of left hemisphere's activity. Study of PET have shown the similar results, when tests to be induced their specific emotions by emotional picture, the metabolic rate of right frontal lobe brain regions increasing when having negative emotion while the left shows advantage when having positive emotion.

Bradley gave tests pictures (from IAPS), at the same time measured their physiological responses, the grade of pleasure, activation and dominance after each picture had been shown. The experimental results show that, although not all of the physiological responses consistent with the changes of emotional self-evaluation, but overall, the model of physiological responses same with the model of two-dimensional self-report to emotional. For example, the startle reflex is closely related to the evaluation of emotion: the intensity of startle reflex decline with the increased degree of happiness when positive value, vice versa. But the responses of skin consistent with the wake-up degrees: when the degree of awaken declining, the conductivity of skin is decreasing. To some extent, this explains show that the startle reflex is the indicator of pleasant, and the response of skin-electrical is the physiological indicator of wake-up degree.

The limitations of two-dimensional emotional space with pleasure degrees and wake-up degree is they can not distinguish all of the emotions, because their locations in space are closely, so anger and fear which have same wake-up value can not be clearly distinction. In recent years, people keen on using approach-withdrawal to instead of pleasure. The superiority of approach-withdrawal is: (1) It based on biological. The behavioral responses of all life to events on the environment can be expressed as approach-withdrawal, and behavioral responses are closely related to emotional responses; (2) The approach-withdrawal can distinguish anger and fear which unable to be distinguished by pleasure. Anger same with the positive emotion lead to approach things, while fears lead to escape. Anger and positive emotions are related to approach behavior, which is puzzling, because anger is a negative emotion. However, we must remember that when we facing with a harmful incident, our anger emotion will lead to offensive, which consistent with the adaptation meaning of biological. In line with the fact anger is belong to reaching-dimension, the research of Harmon proved the activities of left prefrontal cortex is involved with anger. But opponents of approach-avoidance dimension think that the different between the reaching-dimension and the happy-dimension show that the reaching-system unfully associates with positive emotional, emotion and behavior are two different things. In a narrow definition of the emotion, the approach-avoidance behavior does not belong to the scope of emotions, at least it does not belong to the scope of emotional experience always, but it is the motives and behavior trends after the emotional experience. Positive emotion does not always lead to approach-behavior, for example, although scary movie let you feel terrified and detest, but which doesn't obstruct addiction of some people; while speak to negative emotion or unfamiliar stimulate, it is probability to take approach-active, which has advantages to exploring the unknown world and is also in line with the natural law of survival. The different views of dimensions approach are:

(1) The evaluation of emotional has individual differences, some people report and experience emotion in the way of dimension, while some people' manners to experience and report emotional more accord with the theory of basic emotions.

(2) Although some researches have shown that the hemispheric has differences to positive and negative emotions, but there are also some studies which did not receive similar results. Tor D. Wager comprehensively analyzed the 65 different brain imaging studies from 1992 to February 2002, and the conclusion is: there is no adequate and consistent experimental evidence to support the positive and negative emotional have differences in hemispheric; the analysis also think that hemispheric differences in emotional activities is very complex and largely has regional specificity.

(3) There is evidence that the activation dimension and strength of experience are not completely related.

### 13.2.6 Nonlinear dynamic strategy

Emotion is a multi-dimensional phenomenon and evolves with time, so with a simple linear model to express this multi-dimensional systems will inevitably loss certain information, and that prevents us to understand the mood of a complex process, so Tracy put forward a strategy for nonlinear dynamics to study emotion.

Emotional not only includes interrelation subsystems each other, but also the actions of these subsystems are dynamic. Emotion is an integrated process of the neurophysiological, explicit expressions and internal experience. The neural basis of emotions including the activities of central nervous system, peripheral nervous system and autonomic nervous system. For example, when we feel fear, associating with experience, we will also show the expression of fear, as well as a series of physiological responses, such as muscle tension, pale, empty in abdomen, blood more flows to limbs. So in our study of mood, not only from one side to study the emotions and could not think that only by a measurement method to reveal the scientific laws of emotion, we must combine these three aspects.

Emotional is a process rather than a state. People's emotional responses to the same events are dynamic changing with time, for example, speak to a new thing, our initiate reaction of closing to things because of our curiosity, but with the deepening of understanding, we gradually have love or hate emotion. Schere thinks that emotion is the simultaneously activities and dynamic linking of various subsystems. Tracy did synchronous dynamic measurement to blood pressure, facial expression, and fear of experience as a result fear-induced emotional of seeing a snake. The measurement result is the three aspects shown a certain waveform, and finally return to the steady state. These reactions is not isolated, linking with and affecting each other. As Marshall and Zimbardo had proved, the physiological activation can lead to fear experience; emotional behavior (especially facial expression) can lead to physical waked-up and emotional experience. Emotion is a huge complex system, just to understand the various components of the system can not explained the whole system.

Different emotions are susceptibility and interactions each other, emotion could be impacted by the previously occurred every time, and may affect the next. In studies of psychological physiological, have introduced the law of initial value (LIV), and for emotional events, an important initial condition is the state of mind. State of mind is closely related to the previous emotional event and it's primary function is working on the a threshold of specific excitement. A cold stimulus to the skin there will be two kinds of different situations, if the skin is over-heated, the cold-induced would stimulate the happy emotions, and physiological responses perform the extent of skin capillary largely; on the contrary, if the original skin is cold, then the cold stimulate would became negative stimulus, and the contraction of skin capillaries become less; if the temperature of cold stimulate is higher than the initial skin temperature, then it will lead to diastolic capillary. Likewise, when a fortuitous event (such as some people carefully tread your foot) occurred in a happy mood, the system of mood will not be activated. However, if the incident occurred in angry mood, the system of mood will be activated. These have shown the dynamical of emotion depends on the initial state.

## 13.3 Panksepp's Emotional Brain System

Panksepp is an advocate of a biologically-based basic emotions theory, claiming that there are distinguishable brain bases for a set of "biologically given" emotion systems (Panksepp, 2000). There are several areas of resistance to the specifics of Panksepp's proposals. These are based in part on:

(1) Panksepp focuses on neural systems that originate in the brainstem to a much greater extent than other physiologically-oriented theorists, who tend to focus on forebrain structures of the so-called "limbic system". This makes his

assignations difficult to study in humans, because deep brain structures are nearly impossible to study with neuroimaging techniques.

(2) Panksepp differentiates his basic emotion systems neurochemically, as he finds considerable overlap in the neuroanatomically defined areas he specifies as important to each emotion. This, too, makes it difficult to study his theories in humans.

(3) Panksepp relies largely on data from animal studies. Animal studies allow more direct exploration of brain/behavior relationships. However, many human emotion theorists question whether animals have "true" emotions, and many more question the validity of behavioral variables used to index emotions in animals (especially in rodents).

Panksepp described a small set of 'hard-wired' emotion systems found in mammalian brains (Panksepp, 1998). The first four emotion systems appear shortly after birth in mammals (Panksepp, 2006):

(1) Fear: The world has abundant dangers some of which can arouse the major FEAR system of the brain. The system which responds to pain and threat of destruction and leads to the well-known flight, fight, or freeze behavior. It is based primarily in the central and lateral nuclei of the amygdala with connections to the medial hypothalamus and dorsal periaqueductal gray matter (PAG) of the midbrain.

(2) Seeking: This remarkable system mediates all appetitive desire to find and harvest the fruits of the world. The underlying system is the one that mediates our intense appetitive motivation to obtain resources from the environment and promotes goal-directed stimulus-bound appetitive behavior and self-stimulation.

The concept of the seeking system includes classical reward pathway in the brainstem as well as other subcortical areas. The primary reward pathways in mammals include mesolimbic dopamine pathway and mesocortical dopamine pathway. Mesolimbic dopamine pathway consists of dopaminergic neurons that origenate in the ventral tegmental area (VTA) of the brainstem terminate at the nucleus accumbens in the forebrain. Mesocortical dopamine pathway consists of dopaminergic neurons which project from VTA to orbitofrontal cortex.

(3) Rage: This system mediates anger and is aroused by restraint, frustration and various other irritations, as well as directly by brain stimulation. The associated mammalian brain areas include medial amygdala to bed nucleus of the stria terminalis (BNST) and perifornical hypothalamic to PAG.

(4) Panic: The system that responds to cry and call caused by sadness or shyness. The associated mammalian brain areas include anterior cingulate, BNST and preoptic area, as well as dorsomedial thalamus, PAG.

In addition to the four basic emotion systems, three other special-purpose systems come on-line at different stages of mammalian development. We briefly describe them as follows:

(5) Care: The care-giving system promotes social bonding and nurture each other. The associated mammalian brain areas include anterior cingulate, BNST, as well as preoptic area, VTA, PAG.

(6) Play: The system supports laughter and joy. Associated brain areas include dorsomedial hypothalamus, as well as parafascicular area, PAG.

(7) Lust: The system coordinates sexual behavior and feeling. Associated brain areas include cortico-medial amygdala, BNST, as well as preoptic area, VTA, PAG.

Since each of above emotional systems has its own wiring-diagram, so emotion in the brain is quite complex system.

## 13.4 Affective Computing

Scientific research shows that: Affect is a part of intelligence, rather than separation between Affect and intelligence, and therefore the field of artificial intelligence may be the next breakthrough is to empower the affective capacity of computers. Affective capacity is essential important for natural interaction between human and computer. Traditional human-computer interaction, primarily through the keyboard, mouse, screen, etc., and only the pursuit of convenience and accuracy, all of that cannot understand and adapt to one's mood or state of mind. But if the lack of such understanding and ability to express affect, it is difficult to count on the same computer with similar intelligent people, we can hardly expect the human-computer interaction so as to realize the harmony with nature. Due to human communication and exchange are natural and full of feelings, and so in the course of human-computer interaction, it is also natural to expect with the affective capacity of computers. Affective Computing is to be given to the computer, like similar to the observation, understanding and affective characteristics of the various generation capacities; ultimately leading to the computer like human beings can be natural, warm and lively interaction.

As early as the late 19th century the in-depth study of human affect has carried out. However, in addition to science fiction, in the past, there were very few people to linked "feelings" with the machine. So that the computer has the affective ability from the MIT University of the United States Minsky putting forward in 1985, the question is not whether intelligent machines have any feelings, but rather at how intelligent machines cannot be affective (Minsky, 1985). Since then, the affective capacity to give the computer and let the computer can understand and express feelings of the study on the computer industry caused by the interest of many people. The United States MIT Media Lab Professor Picard term affective computing and gives the definition, that is, affective computing is about the feelings, emotions and the impact of emotional arising from the calculation of million surfaces (Picard, 1997). Let the machine (computer) also have "feelings" to extract the signal from the perceived emotional characteristics, analysis of a variety of emotional and perceptual signals related to the international community, in recent years, which is just emerging research directions (see Figure 13.1).

Affective Computing is the focus of the study through a variety of sensors to obtain from the person's feelings caused by physiological and behavioral characteristics of the signal, to establish a "model of affect", in order to create the capacity of awareness, recognition and understanding of human affect and feelings and personal computing systems can do for a smart, sensitive and friendly response to the users ,which shorten the distance between the machine and create a truly harmonious man-machine environment.

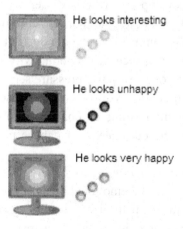

Fig. 13.1 Intelligence with affect

Affective Computing is a highly integrated technology-based field (Minsky, 2006), the main research contents include:

(1) *Mechanism of affection*: this is about affective determinate and the relationship between physiological and behavior, which related to psychology, physiology, cognitive science, etc., in order to provide a theoretical basis for affective computing. Research on human affection has been a very old topic, psychologists, physiologists has been done a lot of work in this regard. Any kind of affective state may be accompanied by several physiological or behavioral characteristics of the change; and some affective or behavioral characteristics may also be due to a number of emotional states. Therefore, to determine the state of affective and physiological or behavioral characteristics is a fundamental premise of the theories of affective computing, these relationship is not very clear and need for further exploration and research.

(2) *Affective signals acquisition*: this research is to develop various kinds of effective sensors, it is the most important in affective computing, there is no effective sensors, can be said that there is no study of affective computing, because all the studies are based on sensors received signal. Various types of sensors should have the following basic features: the use of the process should not affect the user (such as weight, volume, pressure, etc.), should be subject to medical tests without injury to the user; data privacy, security, and reliability; sensor has low prices, and is easy to manufacture. MIT Media Lab developed the sensor at the front, has developed a variety of sensors, such as pulse pressure sensor, current sensor skin, sweat and muscle current sensors. Skin current sensors can be real-time measurement of the conductivity coefficient of the skin, through measurable changes in electrical conductivity coefficient of the user's level of tension. Time monitoring of pulse pressure sensor can be changed by the cardiac pulse pressure caused by changes. Sweat Sensor is a band and can be scalable through its time monitoring of changes in the relationship between respiration and sweat. Muscle current sensor can be measured voltage value at the time of the weak.

(3) *Affective signal analysis, modeling and recognition*: once the sensor from all kinds of effective access to the emotional signals, the next task is to affective signal and aspects of the mechanism of corresponding counterparts, and here to get the signal modeling and identification. As a result of affective states is an implicit in a number of physiological and behavioral characteristics that can not be directly observed in the volume, not modeling, some can use mathematical

model, such as hidden Markov models, Bayesian network model. MIT Media Lab is given a hidden Markov model, based on changes in the probability of human affection to draw the appropriate inference to the affection. How to measure the depth of artificial affection and intensity, qualitative and quantitative measure of the theoretical model of affection, indicator system, the calculation methods, and measurement techniques.

(4) *Affective understanding*: through the affective acquisition, analysis and identification, the computer will be able to understand their affective state. The ultimate goal of affective computing is to have an appropriate response, then adapt to changing user affection on the basis of users understanding the emotional states. Therefore, this part of the main study is how the identification of affective information in accordance with the results of changes in the user's emotional response to the most appropriate. Within affective understanding and application of the model, we should note the following: affective signal is real-time tracking and maintaining records of a certain period of time; the expression of affective is based on the current affective state, timely; affective model is for the personal life of in a particular state which may be edited; affective model has self-adaptive capacity; through understanding of the situation feedback the identification of regulation model.

(5) *Affective expression:* previous research infers affective states from the physiological or behavioral characteristics. Affective expression is to study its anti-process, that is, given a particular affective state research how to make this affective state in one or more physical or behavioral characteristics reflected, for example, how to reflect the speech synthesis and synthesis of facial expressions, make the machinery with emotion, and users can exchange feelings. The expression of affective feelings provide the possibility of interaction and exchange, for a single user, the affective exchanges include man and man, man and machine, man and nature and human interaction their own exchange.

(6) *Affect generation:* in the basis of affective expression, the further study is how the computer or robot to simulate or generate emotional patterns, develop virtual or physical or affective robot with artificial affection and applications of computer equipment to generate emotion theory, methods and techniques.

So far, the study has made progress in the facial expression, gesture analysis, speech recognition and expression of emotion. Here we give examples to illustrate:

## 1. Facial Expressions

In life, it is difficult to maintain a rigid facial expression, through facial expressions to reflect the common sentiment is the performance of a more natural way, the affective performance of the region includes the mouth, cheeks, eyes, eyebrows and forehead, and so on. In the expression of affection, only through a slight change of the local facial features (for example, about wrinkle eyebrows), this can reflect a state of mind. In 1972, the well-known scholars Ekman proposed the method of facial expression of affection (facial movement coding system FACS). Coding and movement through different combination of modules that can be formed in the face of complex changes in expression, such as happiness, anger, sadness and so on. The results have been accepted by most researchers, and facial expressions used in the automatic recognition and synthesis (Figure 13.2).

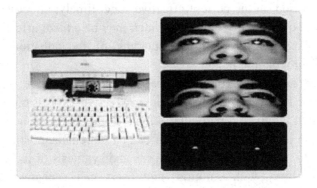

Fig. 13.2 Facial expressions recognition and synthesis

With the rapid development of computer technology, in order to meet the needs of communication, it will further blend the work of face recognition and synthesis into the communications code. The most typical is the MPEG4 V2 visual standards, which define the parameters of three major sets: Face the definition of parameters, interpolation transforms face and facial animation parameter. Expression of specific parameter values representative the size of the degree of emotion, facial expressions can be combined to simulate a variety of mixed expressions.

## 2. Gesture Change

The general gesture of people accompanied by a change in the interactive process, they express some of the information. For example, the gesture is usually reflected in an emphasis on mood, the mentality of a certain part of the body kept swinging; you generally have the tendency to nervousness. Compared with the voice and facial expression changes, the gesture changes in the discipline more difficult to obtain, but because of changes in people's gesture would be more vivid expression, therefore people still express a strong concern. Scientists researching the physical movement designed a series of sports and physical information to capture device, such as motion capture device, data gloves, seats and so smart. Some well-known foreign universities and multinational companies, such as the Massachusetts Institute of Technology, IBM, etc. are the basis of the equipment to build a smart space. At the same time the seat was also used in intelligent vehicle driving seat, which monitor the driver's emotional state dynamically, and dispatch a timely warning. Some scientists in Italy hold automatic sentiment analysis for the staff of the Office through a series of posture analysis, to design a more comfortable office environment.

## 3. Speech Understanding

In the course of human interaction, voice is the most direct channel of communication; it is clear that through the voice people feel each other's emotional changes, such as through special word tone, the tone changed and so on. In people's phone, although people do not see each other, from the tone can feel each other's emotional changes. For example, the same sentence, "for you", in the use of a different tone, you can make an appreciation, also can make it so ironic or jealousy.

At present, the international research on affective speech focused mainly on the affective characteristics of the acoustic analysis in this area. Generally speaking, the voice of the affective characteristics of voice often manifested through changes in rhythm. For example, when a person is angry, the rate of speech will become faster, the volume becomes large, the pitch becomes higher, while a number of phonemic features (formant, channel cross-section function, etc.) can also reflect the affective changes. Experts from Chinese Academy of Sciences State Key Laboratory, Pattern Recognition Institute of Automation, first put forward the affective focus generation model for the phenomenon of language in the focus. Speech Synthesis for the affective state of the automatic forecast provides a basis, combined with high-quality acoustic model, the emotional speech synthesis and identification reach the level of practical application firstly.

## 4. Multi-modal Affective Computing

Although the human face, gesture and voice, etc can be a certain degree of independence sentiment, but in the process of exchange has always been overall performance through the above information. Therefore, only the realization of multi-channel interface, the computer is the most natural way of interaction, it focus on natural language, voice, sign language, face, lip reading, the first potential, and many-body potential channel. These channels of information hold coding, compression, integration and integration to focus on image, audio, video, text and other multimedia information. At present, the multi-modal technology itself is becoming a hot research on human-computer interaction, and affective computing and multi-modal integration processing technology, you can achieve more than the characteristics of emotional integration, can effectively increase the depth of affective computing research, and promote high quality, make human-computer interaction become more harmonious system.

## 5. Affective Computing and Personalized Service

Further research about affective Computing, it has been more than satisfied with its application in a simple human-computer interaction platform, but develop a wide range of interface design, psychological analysis and behavior investigation in all aspects, in order to improve the quality of services and to increase the content of personalized services. On this basis, it was the beginning of the main devoted to the Affective Agent study with a view to adopting the behavior patterns of affective interaction, and build an affection identification and generating type of life, and this model replace the traditional calculation of this model in some applications model (for example, the role of computer games, etc.), so that the application of computers become more alive, so that people can produce a number of similar acts or thinking. The study will have a greater promoting role in the side of the overall study of artificial intelligence.

## 6. Affective Understanding Model

Affection state of recognition and understanding, which is given to the computer to understand affection and make appropriate response are the key step. The steps usually include from the people of affection to extract information used to identify the characteristics, for example, from a smiley face, such as to distinguish between the eyebrows, and then allow the computer to learn about these characteristics in order to be able to accurately identify their feelings.

In order to better accomplish computer tasks of affection recognition, scientists have been clear to a reasonable classification about the state of human affection and proposed the basic affection categories. At present, the methods of affective recognition and understanding use a large number of research results of pattern recognition, artificial intelligence, and voice and image technology. For example: based on the acoustic analysis of voice affection, they use linear statistical methods and neural network models of emotion based on voice recognition prototype; through facial movement coding regions, using different models such as HMM, establish the characteristics of facial affection identification methods; through human posture and movement analysis, explore the affective type of motor and so on.

However, by impact of technology of the information captured by affection and the lack of large-scale data resources of the affection, the multi-feature integration model of affective understanding have yet to be thoroughly. With future technological advances, they put forward more effective mechanism for machine learning.

Affective computing and intelligent interaction attempt to establish a precise nature interactive between the computer and human, which will be an important means from computer technology to infiltrate human society comprehensive. With the future breakthroughs in technology, the application of affective computing is imperative, and its impact on daily life in the future will be in all aspects, we can be expected are:

Affective computing will effectively change the past, mechanical computer interactive services to enhance human-computer interaction of accuracy and the kind. A computer with affective capacity, is able to carry out human affection of the acquisition, classification, identification and response, to help users feel warm and efficient and effective to reduce the use of computer frustration, and even easier to help people understand themselves and emotional world of others.

It can also help us increase the use of safety equipment (for example, when using such technologies, it can detect the driver who can not focus on to change in a timely the status of and response vehicles), make the experience become humanity, the function that the computer as a medium for learning get the best, and collect feedback from us. For example, a research project using the computer in the car drivers measure the level of perceived pressure to help resolve the so-called drivers of "road rage disorder" problem.

Affective computing and related research are also able to involve the field of enterprise e-commerce benefits. Some studies have shown that different images can arouse different emotions of human. For example, the picture of snakes, spiders and the gun can cause fear, and a large number of dollars in cash and gold bullion make human have a very strong positive response. If shopping sites and sites in the design of stock research, they consider the significance of these factors, the increase in traffic will have a very positive impact.

In information appliances and smart devices, adding auto-perception of people's emotional state features, can provide better service. In information retrieval applications, through the analysis of the concept of emotional analytic functions, intelligent information retrieval can increase the accuracy and efficiency. In distance education platform, the application of affective computing technology can increase the effectiveness of teaching.

Using multi-modal affective interactive technology can be closer to people's lives of build a smart space or virtual scene and so on. Also used in affective computing, robotics, intelligent toys, games and other related industries, in order to build a more anthropomorphic style and more realistic scenes.

## 13.5 Affective Intelligence

The intelligence quotient (IQ) tests can not measure a person's comprehensive standard. For people with high IQs, his other smart does not necessarily mature and other aspects including emotional intelligence, arts and sports and so on. In other words: a high IQ does not guarantee that he will have promising future. Too much emphasis on the innate wisdom, the day after tomorrow will be an important part of capacity-building ignored.

The main shortcoming of intelligence tests is too focused on the logic of language and mathematical ability. In fact, intelligence is diverse, it should at least include the following seven kinds of different intelligence: a) verbal intelligence; b) mathematical logic intelligence; c) spatial intelligence; d) musical intelligence; e) mental fitness; f) interpersonal intelligence; g) intellectual insight. This is a preliminary concept of emotional intelligence summary by Jiandena, in order to explore the emotional intelligence after the effective bedding.

With the development of the times, psychology is increasing importance, from Skinner's behavioral psychology to the late 1960's cognitive psychology, and finally to the present relatively perfect study about psychology. Affective intelligence includes the following five aspects:

(1) The ability of understanding and expressing their affection and really know their own really feel.

(2) The ability of controlling their own affection and desire to slow down to meet their own.

(3) The ability of understanding other people's affection and respond appropriately to emotions of others.

(4) The ability of whether adopting an optimistic attitude toward the challenges.

(5) The ability of dealing with interpersonal relationships.

As IQ has been used to reflect the traditional sense of the intellectual, the emotional quotient (EQ) was also used to measure a person's level of emotional intelligence. If IQ scores more have been used to predict a person's academic achievement, then the EQ scores were considered to be used to predict whether a person to access to career success or the success of living things more effective, it is better to reflect the individual and social adaptation.

IQ tests can not absolutely know the EQ. Why are schools the best student was difficult to successfully into society? In 1990's Daniel Goleman pointed out that the level of intelligence is not to determine a person's key to victory or defeat, and himself with the EQ is the most important factor. Because EQ performs the degree of consciousness, impulse control, adhering to endurance, charisma infection, flexibility and ability in all aspects of doing things.

In general, the high IQ will be hired, but a high EQ are often easier to upgrade. Especially in the United States, many large companies have numerous students graduating from top university. However, all these people, as they have been excellent, so it is too easy to own arrogant, it is difficult to get along with others. So when upgrading, of course, those who are approachable, understanding the priority of his subordinates will be considered. First, they observe around and people, second, they are coordinated to fit their own state.

High EQ people can control their own emotional, but not seek the fun and meet; know how to inspire their own efforts; are good at understanding other people's hinted with human interaction, understand and honor the success or failure encountered in life. If the parents have these qualities and give guidance, children can easily have these qualities. Parents foster the children's emotional intelligence from the following areas:

(1) Cultivate children's the right affective responses, make children's the format correct emotional habits ahead.

(2) Learn accurate expression of their feelings. Communication often results from prejudice and misunderstanding. Because they can not accurately express their feelings and ideas.

(3) Help children learn to control their own desires. Through examples of life, Parents can let children know that a person would like to realize their aspirations to make unremitting efforts to overcome difficulties, otherwise it is impossible.

Study of the emotional intelligence can read the book written by G. Matthews (Matthews et al., 2004).

# Chapter 14

# Artificial Immune System

## 14.1 Introduction

The immune system is to protect the body's own defensive structure, mainly by lymphoid organs (thymus, lymph nodes, spleen, tonsils), the lymphoid tissues in other lymphocytic organs and lymphocytes, antigen presenting cells (APC) around whole body. It also includes the other leukocytosis in blood, plasma, mast cells in connective tissue in a broad sense. The main component of the immune system is lymphocytes. It makes the immune system be capable of recognition and memory. Lymphocytes travel around the whole body through blood and lymphocytic, from one lymphoid tissue to another lymphocytic organ or lymphoid tissue. It makes lymphocytic organs and lymphoid tissues dispersing around the body connect as a whole. Immune system gradually comes into being in the constant struggle with various disease-causing factors. It needs the stimulus of the antigen to completely develop in the ontogeny. The function of the immune system mainly has two respects:

(1) Identify and eliminate invasive micro-organisms, allogeneic cells or macromolecular substance (antigen) invading into body;

(2) Monitor stability of organism, clean infected cells (tumor cells and virus-infected cells, etc.).

The structures on the surfaces of two types of immune cells are very important among the cells of recognizing self and nonself cells or antigens. One type is specific antigenic receptor on T cells and B cells. Another one is organism histocompatibility antigen. A group of genes coding these antigens are called major histocompatibility complex (MHC). So this type of antigen is also called MHC. MHC is different among different kinds of animals and different individuals of the same kind of animal. So it has high-level specificity. MHC antigens can be divided into two types: MHC-I antigens, distribute extensively on

521

the surfaces of all cells of individual. MHC-II antigens, only distribute on the surfaces of some cells of the immune system. They are useful for mutual functional cooperation of cells, such as recognizing antigens, etc. The structure of the biological immune system is shown in Figure 14.1.

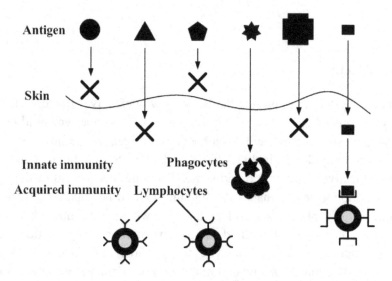

Fig. 14.1 Structure of the biological immune system

The biological immune system is a kind of highly evolved biological information process system. It has many kinds of mechanisms to identify and eliminate pathogens. The main function of immune system is to identify all cells in the body to classify nonself cells from self ones. In order to induce suitable defense mechanism, nonself cells are classified in further. Through evolution learning, the immune system distinguishes infectious pathogens and self cells. In one word, the biological immune system is a highly evolved intelligent system. It has the following characteristics:

(1) It is a distributed system. The biological immune system has no central controller. It is composed of cells which distribute extensively in whole body. These immune cells realize various immunological functions by distributed network structures on time and space.

(2) It is a kind of adaptive system. The kinds of antigens existing in nature are much more than those in organisms. So the antigens invading in the organism has no predictability. But the immune system can produce new antibodies constantly

by proliferating and differentiating. And it produces suitable antibodies finally to eliminate antigens. Thus it adapts to the changes of external environment dynamically.

(3) It is a dynamic equilibrium system. When the immune system responds to pathogens, interaction among every immune cell, antigens and antibodies, antibodies and antibodies forms a dynamic equilibrium network system.

(4) It has the functions of learning and memory. The biology immune system has two types of immune response: the primary response and the secondary response. When antigens invade the organism for the first time, the primary response will be initiated. And it makes the immune system produce antibodies to eliminate the antigens. In this process, the immune system produces memory cells by learning the antigens. When the antigens of the same class invade the body again, the secondary response is initiated. The immune system wakes memory cells up and produces a large number of antibodies to eliminate the antigens in shorter time than that of the primary response.

(5) It has recognition function. The biological immune system has the special ability of recognizing 'self' and 'non-self'. For non-self antigen, it can start immune response to exclude them. For self cells, it can keep no response, that is, immune tolerance. Thus, it can keep the stability of internal environment of biological body.

## 14.2 Immune Mechanisms

The immune system is the network that immune cells interacted with the soluble components. Its function is to distinguish non-self from self. Microorganism is main non-self material. But implanted organs and some foreign matters (i.e. some toxin) belong to non-self. In order to finish these tasks, immune system has two types of mechanisms: non-specific immunity and specific immunity. They relate to each other and has influence each other.

### 14.2.1 Non-specific immunity

Non specific immunity is immunity of phylogeny. It exists at birth and is also called innate immunity. It needs not to meet antigen material in advance. And it does not develop memory. The innate immunity includes barrier, such as the skin; chemical protection, such as gastric acid. It has two types of cells: a) Phagocyte system. Its function is to ingest and digest microorganisms.

b) Natural killer cell (NK). Its function is to kill some tumors, some microorganisms and infected cells.

Soluble material is composed of complements, and cytokines. Phagocyte includes neutral cells, the monocyte (in the blood) and macrophages (in organism). Phagocyte is the polypeptide of some non-immunoglobulin (Ig). It is secreted when monocytes and lymphocytes interact with specific antigen, non-specific antigen or some non- pecific stimulations (such as endotoxin, other cell factors). They influence the size of inflammation or immune response. Cytokines has no antigenic specificity, therefore they are the bridge between innate immunity and acquired immunity.

### 14.2.2 Specific immunity

The function of the antigenic receptor is realized by surface immunoglobulin (Ig). B lymphocytes will have a series of changes (such as hyperplasia, differentiate) after they are combined with soluble antigens through surface immunoglobulin (Ig). They secrete immunoglobulin (Ig), which is the specific antibody against antigen finally. At present, it is believed that the internal antibody table is caused by the recombination of the Ig genes in the maturation process of B lymphocytes before exposed to antigens. In order to understand the properties of recombination of Ig genes, we need to find out the structure of Ig.

It is composed of two heavy chains and two light chains. Each chain has constant region and variable region. Antigen is combined with variable region. On the genetic level, the constant region is encoded by the genes of C region. The variable region of light chain is encoded by genes of V and J regions. The variable region of heavy chain is encoded by genes of V, D and J regions. The embryo gene segments make a reservation on chromosomes discontinuously. They may be arranged together in the process of B cell maturation. Therefore, in order to form a heavy chain, one of D segments (12 segments at least) is combined with one of 6 J segments (lie in the upper reaches of C genes). Then the resulted segments are combined with one of several hundreds (may be thousands of) genetic segments of V genes. At last, they make up a unit that can totally transcript the heavy chain of Ig.

According to the requirements, special segment of each gene can be adopted. Thus it can get a large number of different types of specific Ig molecules. On the junctures of V, D and J, some nucleotides are added at random. Somatic hypermutation and inaccuracy adding various segments expand the potential variety of genes in further.

There is no Ig on the surface of T lymphocytes. But they can recognize antigens by T lymphocytes receptor (TCR) and some other assistant adhesion molecules. The genes of encoding TCR are the super family belonging to Ig. Similar to Ig genes, they can also be recombination. Therefore, a large number of clones of T lymphocytes will be obtained. Each one can response to a type of specific antigen.

The combination part for antigen of TCR is composed of 2 chains ($\alpha\beta$ and $\gamma\delta$). Each chain has a constant region and a variable region. Different from Ig, each chain of TCR can exist on the surface of B lymphocytes independently. TCR combines with CD3 molecule. This whole unit is called TCR, CD3 complex. Although TCR chain is determined by recombination of genes and it can change, CD3 chain (made up of 5 chains at least) does not change. And there is no antigen specificity. Some anti-CD3 antibodies activate T cells directly by the bypass without antigens. Therefore, CD3 is important for transmitting the signal of activation through the membranes of lymphocytic cells. Lymphocytes can be divided into subvarieties according to functions or surface marks.

The subvarieties of lymphocytes can be identified by combining with its certain surface molecules .These surface marks are named cluster of differentiation (CD). 166 CDs have been identified. The materials about CD antigens can be found in the international network (<http://www.ncbi.nlm.nih.gov/prow>).

### 14.2.3 T cells and cells immunity

T lymphocytes mature in the thymus and obtain their functions and learn to recognize self. Thymus has double functions of positive selection (Clones recognizing antigen proliferate, mature and move to around) and negative selection (exclude those clones which response to self).

T-stem cells that derives from bone marrow moves to in embryo's development. In thymus, it learns to recognize self and mature at last. After the selection of thymus, matured lymphocytes are permitted to leave thymus. They can be seen in peripheral blood and lymphous tissues. All matured T cells only express one type of CD4 or CD8.

Usually, T cells which express CD4 belong to T helper lymphocytes (TH). These cells can be divided two main parts according to the ability of responding to different cytokines and secreting cytokines. Now, it is believed that Th cells originate from predecessor cells which are be able to secrete IL-2. After the first stimulus, these cells develop into THO cells. It can secrete several kinds of cytokines, including IFN-γ, IL-2, IL-4, IL-5 and IL-10. According to the functions of cytokines, THO cells can develop into TH1 or TH2 cells. IFN-γ and IL-12 are useful for the development of TH1. IL-4 and IL-10 are useful for the development of TH2. TH1 cells secrete IFN-γ. TH2 secretes IL-4. But these subvarieties equally secrete some other kinds of cytokines (such as IL-3, GM-CSF, TNF-α). Generally speaking, TH1 is favorable to strengthen the cell immunity, and TH2 helps to strengthen humoral immunity.

Response of TH1 and TH2 has changed the view about the relation between immune system and diseases. Not only a kind of immune response should be vigorous, but also be appropriate to the infection or disease.

Compared with TH subvarieties, T cells which express CD8 have not been well fixed yet. Similar to CD4, according to the cytokines that CD8 secretes, CD8 can be divided into two types, too. The proposed types of lymphocytes are called type I and type II (T1, T2), not TH1 and TH2, because the classified types of CD8 can be seen as the same class.

Cytotoxin T cells belong to the antigenic specificity. The cytotoxin T cells are restricted by MHC. Both CD4 and CD8 cells have functions of CTL. They can be distinguished according to recognizing MHC II antigens or MHC I antigens respectively. Only several kinds of cells can express CD8 or CD4 marks in many kinds of identified cytotoxin lymphocytes and killer cells.

According to MHC restriction and requirement of sensibilization, specificity of target cells and response to cytokines can appraise a kind of killer cells. Although macrophages can be activated by some cytokines and become toxic lymphocytes, this toxin is not specific. Different kinds of killer cells can be simplified into MHC restriction (such as CTL) and none MHC restriction (such as NK cells). All of them do not need antibodies, complements or phagocytosis of target cells. In other words, they can send the dissolved signal through the target cell membrane after cells contact closely.

Cytotoxin T lymphocytes (CTL) is a kind of killer cells. They are produced only when there is sensibilization of specificity. This kind of sensibilization may be caused by the cells of expressing variant MHC with the same kind of resulted production or can be infected by virus, or due to self cells changed by chemical haptens. There are three stages in CTL's life: One is predecessor cells, they become the toxic cells through appropriate stimulus. One is effect cells, which can differentiate and dissolve appropriate target cells. One is resting cells, which are not stimulated for a longer period. They become effect cell again after simulated by original cell again. Intact cells produce the strongest CTL stimulus, but soluble antigens are invalid.

The variant CTL is easy to produce in the following cases. That is, normal lymphocytes and the parts of isotope handling or all variant stimulating cells with different MHCs are cultured together. This kind of CTL may play an important role in organ transplant repel. It needs two kinds of signals to produce CTL: Antigenic signal (stimulate cells) and amplifying signal. If these two kinds of signals are on function effectively, it needs antigen presenting cells (APC), T helper cells and predecessor of T killer cells. Amplifying signals are mediated by cytokines which work before and after it. The most important ones are IL-1, IL-2 and IL-4. The other cytokines (including IL-6, IL-7, IL-10 and IL-12) are sure to participate the production of CTL outside the body at least.

The other types of CTL are called antigen specific CTL (homologous CTL). It plays an important role in removing antigen causing diseases within cells (especially the antigens that the virus infects). Homologous CTL only distinguishes target cells which can express antigens, combine with MHC and cause sensibilization. This produced CTL can confront with self cells changed by virus infect or chemical haptens. Production of virus expressed on the surface of cells or haptens combine with MHC, and start chain reaction of differentiation of cells and release of cytokines. Its response is similar to allosome CTL. These two kinds of CTL adopt TCR/CD3 complex to discern target cells.

### 14.2.4 B cells and humoral immunity

B cells account for 5%-15% of peripheral blood lymphocytes. It is difficult to distinguish with T cells from the shape. B cell can be divided into different phenotypes (sIgM exist on mature B cells. SIgM and sIgD exist on B cells which are mature and not stimulated. SIgG, sIgA or sIgE can be seen on transformed B cells) according to their surface immunoglobulin (Ig). It can also be classified following CD19, CD20, CD21 (CR2), CD49C, CD72 and CD80. B cells also express production like MHC II and the other different CD antigens. This kind of CD antigen is not specific to B cells.

B cells seem to develop in certain order. In bone marrow, they begin from the stem cells of bone marrow. Through early and later stage, early B cells (with rearrangement of D-J heavy chain genes), former B cells (with successful rearrangement of V-DJ heavy chain genes and presenting μ chain on the surface of cells and cytoplasm). They become immature B cells at last (with rearrangement of V-J light chains and IgM on the surface of cells). In this developing process, the function of antigens is not clear. But the reactive of antigens with immature B cells can result in deactivation or tolerance. B cells which are not deactivated continue to develop into mature B cells without stimulation. Then they leave the bone marrow and enter into the lymphous organs around. In these organs, B cells which are not stimulated react with exogenous antigens and sIgG and change into lymphoblasts. Through differentiation, B cells become the plasma cells which secrete the single type antibody.

B cells in surrounding tissues can response to small amount of antigens. The reaction between such initial antigens and B cell are mutual. It is called the primary response. B cells have gone through differentiation and clone proliferation. Some become memory cells, the others become mature plasma cells which can produce antibodies. The main characteristic of primary response is that there is a incubation period before antibody appears. It produces only a small amount of antibodies. It is IgM at first. After that, there is the conversion (assisted by T cells) of different kinds of immunoglobulin (Ig), IgG changes to IgM, IgA or IgE. And it produces a lot of memory cells which response to the same antigens.

Enhanced immune response or the secondary response takes places while the immune system encounters the same or similar antigens again. Its main characteristic is that B cells proliferate quickly and differentiate into mature plasma cells, and they produce a large number of antibodies rapidly, which are mainly IgGs released into blood and other tissues. When these mature cells encounter antigens in these places, they will response effectively.

IgM, IgG and IgA can response to the same antigens. Therefore, mono, immature B cells which are not stimulated can be divided into a B cells department. They form specific antibody of the monovalent in genetic order, and can produce representative clones for each kind of immunoglobulin (Ig) (such as IgM, IgG, IgA).

B cells response to antigens by the way of non-T cell dependence or T cell dependence. T cell non-dependence antigens has antigenic determinant. And it can well resist the degradation of internal enzyme. T cell non-dependence antigen mainly causes the response of a kind of IgM.

Most natural antigens are T cells dependence and they need to be offered antigens by APC. These APCs present antigens to T and B cells. T cells release cytokines to make B cells response to antigens by producing antibodies. While the antigen stimulates B cells, the production of IgG change to produce IgM. This kind of conversion depends on T helper cells (TH), and it needs different subvarieties of TH cells and specific cytokines.

### 14.2.5 *Antigen and antibody*

The antigen is a kind of material that can cause the specific immune response. Once the antibody comes into being, it can combine together with the specific antigen. What antibody recognizes is superficial specific configurations (epitope) of some macromolecules (such as proteins, polysaccharide and nucleic acid). A kind of antigen has a molecule made up of one epitope at least. Because matching area of antigen and antibody on surface of each molecule are relatively big, it needs to put joints of antigen and antibody closely by strong affinity. When some epitopes on antigen surface are very similar to original epitope, the same antibody has cross reactive with the antigen, too.

Antigen of immunogenicity substance means the substance which is recognized as foreign matter by immune system and the amount of its molecule is great enough. Hapten means a kind of substance, the amount of molecular of which is smaller than that of antigen. It can specifically response to antibody. But it can't induce the forming of antibody, unless it is absorbed on the other molecules. It is usually a kind of protein (carriers albumens).

Antibody is immunoglobulin (Ig). It has special amino acid arrays and three-dimensional structure. It can combine with the complementary structure of the antigen. Although all Igs may be antibodies, it is usually impossible to know the antigen that each Ig is against. Reactive between antigen and antibody plays a peculiar function, which can protect the host against virus, bacterium and other pathogens.

Various immunoglobulins (Ig) have obvious heterogeneity. They can combine with limitless variety of antigens. They have the same specialty. In each type of Ig, monomer Ig has similar structure: Each molecule is made up of 4 peptides chains, the same two light chains of and the same two heavy chains. The molecular weight of each heavy chain is probably 50000 Doulton to 70000 Doulton. And the molecular weight of each light chain is probably 23000 Doulton. The disulfide bond joins these molecules to form Y configuration that are recognized usually.

Ig of Y shape is divided into the variable region (V) and constant region (C). Variable region lies in the far end of Y arm. It is named because amino acids in this region are highly different. The changes of these amino acids determine the combination ability of Ig with antigen. The constant region is near antigen combining area. It has relative constant arrays of amino acids. But this kind of array is different for every kind of immunoglobulin (Ig).

There is idiotype in the highly variable part of variable region. Anti-idiotype of nature antibody combines with it. The combination of anti-idiotype antibody and its idiotype is very important in regulating the response of B cells. On the contrary, allotype determinant can produce allotype antibodies. Each B cell clone will produce its own special Ig, which has peculiar amino acid arrays, and can combine with particular antigenic configuration. However, a B cell can converse the classification of Ig, but light chain region and variable region are still kept.

## 14.3 Immune System Theories

The immune system is a complex system composed of cells, molecules and organs. It is mainly for limiting foreign matter to infringe body. Thus, antibodies are produced and the immune response is initiated. The foreign material invading human body is known as the antigen (Antigen, is abbreviated as Ag) shown in 14.2a. The immune response is finished by the combination of antigenic determinant and antibody. A kind of response is to produce the antibody (Antibody, is abbreviated as Ab) by B cell or B lymphocyte. As Fig. 14.2b "shows, the antibody is "Y" shape. It mainly make use of similar shape to recognize and tie antigen.

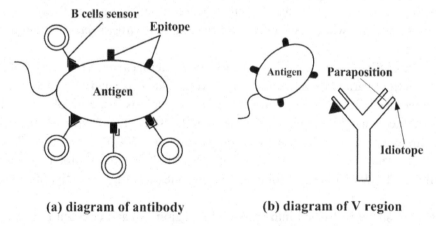

(a) diagram of antibody        (b) diagram of V region

Fig. 14.2 B cells, antigen, antibody, antigen determines, paraposition and coordination

Immune system was defined initially as a huge complex system recognizing the relation between antigen determinant and paraposition. In the immune system, relevant incidents are not only molecules themselves, but also among molecules. Immune cells can produce the positive or negative reaction to the recognized signals. The positive reaction will enable the proliferation of cells, and secrete antibodies. Negative reaction will result in suppression. In 1991, Varela and Countinbo proposed the immune network model, i.e. the second generation of immune network. It had emphasized three main characteristics of the immune network: structure, dynamic characteristic and steady state characteristic. Network structure had described the interaction among molecules and cells, and the structural form of connection. The immune dynamics means the density of network connection and affinity vary with time. And the steady state characteristic means that the immune system produces antibodies continuously and eliminates the cells which receive no stimulation at the same time.

Since the end of 1950s, two theories of immunology have occupied the leading position: antibody clones selection theory and immune network theory. The main points of clones selection theory is that the outside antigens choose the complementary cell originally in resting state to clone. The activation, proliferation and effect function are the cytology process of immune response. The clones of cells which response to self molecules will be suppressed or eliminated, Therefore the reorganization to foreign antigens is the key factor. The view of the immune network theory is set up in recognizing self. It is thought that the variable region of specific antigenic receptor (V) distributes on lymphocytes, and they can construct a network. The immune system realizes the function by recognizing epitope on V region by immune cells. The response is based on recognizing self antigens. They reflect three major functions of the immune system from different angles: The immune defense, immunity monitor and immune homeostasis.

### 14.3.1 Clone selection

The principle of clone selection is proposed by N. K. Jerne at first (Jerne, 1973), and then explained completely by F. M. Burnet (Bernet, 1978). When lymphocytes realize the recognition (i.e. affinity of the antibody - antigen exceeds certain threshold) to antigen, B cells are activated and proliferate to produce B cells clones. Subsequently, clone cells go through the process of mutation to produce specific antibodies to the antigen. Clone selection theory describes the basic characteristic of acquired immunity, and it declares that only those cells which succeed in recognizing the antigen can proliferate. After mutation, the immune cells differentiate into two types of cell, the effect cell antibody and memory cell.

The main characteristic of clone selection is that stimulated immune cells produce clone proliferation. After that, they differentiate into diverse effect cells and memory cells through genetic muatation. Clone selection corresponds to a process of affinity maturation. That is, the individual which has low affinity against antigen will gradually mature after undergoing proliferation and mutation operation under the effect of mechanism of clone selection. The nature of affinity maturation is a process of Darwin selection and mutation. The principle of clone selection is realized through adopting the genetic operators of crossing, mutation and corresponding to colony controlling mechanism.

### 14.3.2 Immune network model

The key characteristic of immune network theory is to define the consistency of independent molecule. It is shown that the network organization make the system develop through learning the relation between molecule and environment. In fact, such a dynamic characteristic is identical with capacity of memory. Such memory is not in memory cells, but distributed into a kind of mode. The study interest of immune network lies in developing the computer tool, because it provides a series of appealing characteristics, such as learning and memory, scale controlling and diversity of cells.

Based on immunology theory, we can construct artificial immune system models which have similar relations with biological antigen and antibody, antibody and antibody. The structure of most network models is usually described as:

Rate of change = inflow of new cells

+ death cells without stimulation

+ replicated stimulated cells

where, the last term includes antibody - antibody recognition and the new antibodies produced by the stimulation of antigen and antibody.

## 1. Idiotype network model

Based on clone selection, Jerne established the idiotype network theory and provided the mathematics frame of immune network. On the foundation of Jerne's work, Perelson had proposed the probability description for idiotype network [Perelson 89]. Immune network theory makes systemic hypothesis for immune cellular activity, antibody production, immune tolerance, self-nonself recognition, immune memory and evolution process of immune system, etc. And the immune system is regarded as the regulation network composed of immune cells or molecules. Immune network is based on reaction among antibodies and communication each other among different kinds of immune cells. Antigen recognition is finished by immune network formed by antigenic interaction.

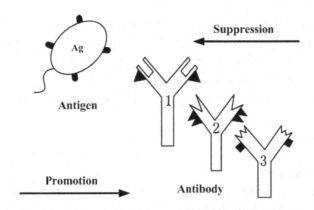

Fig. 14.3 Idiotype immune network

According to idiotype immune network theory, there are two types of immune reaction of recognizing signals, positive reaction and negative reaction. The former can produce cells proliferation, cells activation and antibody production. The later causes immune tolerance or suppression, as shown in Figure 14.3. By establishing the mathematics modeling to immune cells or molecules, immune network theory can be used for describing emergence attributes of immune system very conveniently, for instance, learning and memory, etc. Inspired by immune network theory, many researchers proposed many kinds of artificial immune network models, such as interconnected coupling network, multi-value immune network, antibody network, etc., and they are applied to data cluster, data analysis, robot control and so on.

The dynamics equation for the idiotype network model is as follows:

$$S_i(t) = S_i(t-1) + \left( \alpha * \frac{\sum\limits_{j=1}^{N}(m_{ij}a_j(t))}{N} - \alpha * \frac{\sum\limits_{k=1}^{N}(m_{ij}a_k(t))}{N} + \beta g_i - k_i \right) * a_i(t)$$

$$a_i(t) = \frac{1}{1+\exp(0.5 - S_i(t))} \qquad 0 \le a_i(t) \le 1$$

where: $S_i$ shows the number of the antigen that antibody $i$ receives and the other antibodies linked with it;

i, j = 0, N-1, N is the total number of antibody types in the network;

$m_{ij}(t)$ express the connection weight value among the antibody $i$ and j;

$g_i$ shows the antigen stimulates the intensity, i.e. affinity to the antibody;

$k_i$ shows the natural death coefficient of the antibody $i$;

$a_i(t)$ utilize the Sigmoid function to deal with the normalization to the antibody density;

$\alpha$, $\beta$ is a constant.

## 2. B cell network model

In the biological immune system, B cells secreted by the bone marrow can produce the immune cells of the antibody. Linking each other and forming B cell network among B cells. According to F. M. Burnet, cells proliferate after the antigens invade the organism. B cells in B cell network are activated. But B cells that can only produce the antibody with the high affinity to the antigen will be proliferated, differentiate. These new B cells will added into B cell network, but B cells that produce those antibodies which can't combine to the antigen will die, and be eliminated from B cell network. Their models are shown in Fig. 14.4. The B network model is suitable for solving the problem of optimization.

## 3. Multi-value immune network model

In the process of immune response, after T cells recognize antigen, B cells will be activated to proliferate, differentiate and produce antibodies. When the concentration of antibodies reaches the degree that can suppress antigens, T cells will suppress the reproduction of B cells conversely. Draw lessons from this principle, Z. Tang, etc. had proposed a kind of multi-value immune network model, which was applied to distinguish characters. The results were compared to those of traditional binary network recognition model. This model has the advantages of better memory, high capacity, less classification, strong noise immune, etc.

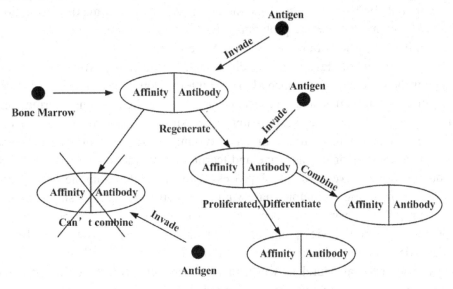

Fig. 14.4 B cell network model

Besides three kinds of typical artificial immune network models described above, there are artificial immune models of interconnected coupling, symmetrical network, immune reactive network, and the network model and so on.

## 14.4 Artificial Immune Systems

More and more researchers began to draw lessons from the way of information processing in the natural immune system to solve the problems of engineering and science. In 1973, the U.S. Nobel laureate N. K. Jerne proposed artificial immune network theory (Jerne, 1973). Subsequently, J. D. Farmer, etc., who were theory immunologists, published relevant paper inspiring the application of immune system to actual engineering. Among them, the research about immune system and machine learning of J. D. Farmer is creative and pioneering work.

Their research work opens the road (Farmer et al., 1986) to the development of effective computing system and intelligence system based on the immune principles. F. Varela discussed the convergence of immune network by a certain way and immune system can adapt to new environment by producing different antibodies and mutation. All of them had made the enormous contribution (Stewart et al. 1989) in order to make the immune system become the inspiration source of solving engineering problems effectively. Therefore, a new developing research field--Artificial Immune System, AIS emerges.

From the view of developed principles and applications, artificial immune system is the general name of many kinds of information processing technologies, computing technologies and intelligence systems applied in engineering and science which utilize the information processing mechanisms of biological immune system (mainly human immune system). Artificial immune network has similar abilities of self adaptive and learning to neural network. But it is set up on the cooperative of a lot of processes dynamically. Immune algorithms based on immunology principles have similar evolutionary mechanism to genetic algorithms. But it can realize accurate control of diversity and specificity of population. From the viewpoint of information processing system of living beings, AIS belongs to information science. It parallels with intelligence theories such as the artificial neural network, fuzzy theory, etc. But there are different properties, functions and potential applications in science and engineering.

There are several kinds of different definitions to artificial immune systems. The definition given by D. Dasgupta is that artificial immune system consists of intelligent strategies inspired by biological immune systems. They are mainly used for information processing and problem solving (Dasgupta et al., 1997); The definition provided by J. Timmis is: The artificial immune system is a kind of computing paradigm inspired by theory immunology. It has drawn lessons from the function, principles and models of immune system and is used for the solving complex problems (Timmis et al., 2001).

Since 1998, IEEE collected the research results of the artificial immune systems at conferences on artificial intelligence, evolutionary algorithms and magazines respectively. The first international meeting of artificial immune systems was held in Britain Kent university in September 2002. It had promoted the development of Artificial Immune Systems greatly. Because of realizing the potential applications of AIS in the information safety, machine learning and data mining, etc., the researches of AIS had been paid much attention by a lot of universities, research institutions and industries.

From the viewpoint of computing, natural immune system is a kind of parallel, distributing and self-adaptive systems. Immune system solves the problems of recognition and classification by learning, memory and association thinking. The immune system learns to recognize relevant modes, remembers the mode seen in the past, builds detection pattern high-efficiently by combination. Natural immune system is the inspiration source for developing intelligence technologies to solve problems. Researchers had already developed a lot of algorithms based on artificial immune network and computing system and model based on immune system.

(1) Develop new methods of computing intelligence according to the principles of biological immune system, including negative selection algorithm, clone selection algorithm and immune genetic algorithm and other algorithms used for optimizing problems. These are called immune algorithms.

(2) Set up immune computing system model, including artificial immune network model, according to the principles of biological immune system. Various immune network theories, for example idiotype network, interconnected coupling immune network, immune reaction network and symmetrical network, etc. They can be used for setting up the cognitive model of artificial immune network. Idiotype network is the model which is the most widely used at present.

(3) Combine with artificial neural network, fuzzy system, genetic algorithm, etc. to establish hybrid intelligence systems. For example, artificial neural network, fuzzy system and artificial immune system can be merged together to establish new intelligent computing system. The diversity of antibodies of immune system can be used for improving search optimization performance of genetic algorithm. At present, many methods of computing intelligence had been used to combine with immune algorithms, such as ant colony, particle swarm optimization and so on.

(4) Theoretical research of artificial immune system. For example, with the aid of mathematics, nonlinear, complexity, chaos, computing intelligence, intelligent agent, the mechanisms of artificial immune systems can be further investigated. What is more important is that new mechanisms of immune system should be investigated in further to research new methods of artificial immune systems. It is relatively slow in this respect.

(5) Applications research of artificial immune systems, for example, applications of immune computing intelligence in engineering. A certain characteristic or some characteristics of biological immune system should be

utilized to solve particular engineering problems. Many kinds of security systems, diagnosis system of diseases, computer security system and network invading detection system, fault detection system can also be researched on the basis of the immunology principles. It is developed quite extensively in this respect.

## 14.5 Biological Basis of Artificial Immune Systems

From the viewpoint of information processing, immune system has the strong ability of recognizing, learning, memory and characteristics of distribution, self-adaptive, diversity. These prominent characteristics are attracting researchers to select useful metaphor mechanisms from the immune system constantly and develop corresponding artificial immune system models, algorithms, which can be used for information processing and problem solving. Figure 14.5 provides the main contents that are used for design artificial immune systems.

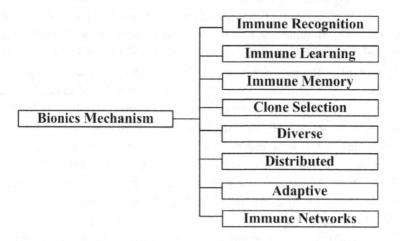

Fig. 14.5 The biological mechanisms of artificial immune systems

### 14.5.1 Immune recognition

Immune recognition is the main function of immune system, but also the core of one of the artificial immune system, while the recognition is the essence of the distinction between "self" and "nonself." Immune recognition is realized by the combination of antigen receptor on lymphocytes to antigen. The intensity of combination is called affinity. Negative selection is one of the important mechanism of immune recognition. That is, T cells which match with self cells cannot leave the thymus. Only those T cells which cannot match with self cells can carry out the task of immune response. Thus it prevents immune cells from attacking self.

Correspondingly, the recognition of the antigen of artificial immune system is realized by feature matching. The core of it is to define a match threshold. It can be measured by adopting many kinds of methods, for example, Hamming distance, Euclidean and R continuous location and so on. The principle of negative selection can correspond to the negative selection algorithm in the artificial immune system. The key is to encode the recognized object according to its features. A self set is defined and a series of detectors are produced to detect the changes of self set. According to its principle, if detectors match with nonself, the task of matching is finished.

### 14.5.2 Immune learning

The process of immune recognition is also a process of learning at the same time. The result of learning is that the affinity of individuals of immune cells is higher and size of population is expanded. And the optimum individual is kept in the form of immune memory. The immune learning can roughly be divided into two types: One happens during the primary response, i.e. when the immune system recognizes a kind of new antigen for the first time. The response time is relatively long. And when the organism meets the same or similar antigen again, because of the immune memory mechanism, the response speed of the immune system to this antigen is improved greatly. And it produces antibodies with high affinities to remove antigens. This process is the second type of learning in immune system, a enhanced learning one.

The immune system not only can realize the recognition of the same type of antigen, but also the antigen which has similar structures. This is a great characteristic. In general, the learning ways that the immune system adopts are as follows:

(1) Learn the same antigen repeatedly. It belongs to the reinforcement learning.

(2) Affinity maturation. It corresponds to the process that the affinity of individuals in artificial immune systems is raised progressively after genetic operation. It belongs to genetic learning.

(3) The low degree repeated infection. It corresponds to iterate training process of artificial immune systems.

(4) Cross reaction to the endogenous and internal antigens. It belongs to association learning and corresponds to the associative memory mechanism.

Study mechanisms are used widely in models of machine learning and algorithms design. In fact, the evolution of the immune network is a learning process too.

### 14.5.3 *Immune memory*

When the immune system meets a type of antigen for the first time, lymphocytes need some time to adjust in order to recognize the antigen better and keep memory information of this antigen in the form of optimum antibody after recognition. And when the immune system meets the same or antigens with similar structures again, because of the associative memory, its response speed is improved greatly. Immune memory corresponds to second immune response and cross immune response.

Immune memory belongs to associative memory. It is one of the important characteristics that is different from other intelligent systems except brain. Farmer pointed out that immune memory could be regarded as a kind of associative memory model at first. Smith had compared the associative memory model to the sparse distributing memory model. It was pointed out that the primary immune response corresponds to the process of storing information in memory of sparse distributing memory model. The second response and cross immune response can be regarded as corresponding to the process of reading stored information of sparse distributing memory model (Smith et al., 1998).

The immune memory mechanism had been applied in optimization and reinforcement learning at present. It can accelerate the process of optimizing and searching to improve the quality of learning. In a word, immune memory is a kind of very effective way that improves the efficiency of the immune algorithm.

### 14.5.4 *Diversity of individuals*

The immune system probably contains $10^6$ different proteins. But the potential antigens outside or patterns to be recognized are $10^{16}$. It needs effective generating mechanisms for producing diverse individuals to realize the recognition of antigens which have greater order of magnitude than self. The mechanisms of diversity of antibodies mainly include recombination of immune receptor libraries, somatic mutation and genes translation. The acknowledged mechanism of diversity production is the recombination of the gene parts of the antigenic receptor libraries. Gene segment is one of units that make up antibody.

It can be seen that diverse antibodies which can recognize antigens are produced by the recombination of genetic parts. According to this principle, De Castro had developed the model SAND of diversity production (De Castro et al., 1999). The diverse mechanisms of immune system can be used widely for optimization of searching, especially, peak function optimization and combination optimization. This diverse mechanisms used for genetic algorithm can improve local convergence performance and find the global optimum, or keep some local optimums for optimization of peak value function. In addition, the diversity generation mechanism can provide the reference for the researches which need diverse data sets, for instance, the integrated neural networks.

### 14.5.5 Distribution and adaption

The immune system consists of cells, tissues and organs distributed in organism. Firstly, the distribution of the immune system depends on the distribution of pathogens. That is, pathogens are dispersed within the organism. Secondly, the distribution of the immune system is benefit to strengthen the robust of the system. Thus the immune system will not be influenced on the whole function because of local damage of tissues.

Lymphocytes which disperse in every part of body recognize special antigens by the way of learning. The antibodies which finish recognition mutate at 10 times probability of normal mutation cells. Thus, the probability of improving affinity is increased greatly. Lymphocytes would differentiate into effect cells and memory cells to remove antigens effectively and keep the memory information respectively. In fact, this process is the process of adaptive response. Since the mechanisms of response act on by interaction among cells without centralized control, so the distributive of system strengthens its adaption in further.

The characteristics of distribution and adaption had been applied in promoting the systematic working efficiency and the ability of fault-tolerant. Since the working load is distributed on a lot of different working units, systematic working efficiency is improved effectively. Meanwhile, its distributed characteristic can also reduce adverse effects to whole systems caused by some failure working units. Forrest had studied the distributive, adaptive system of virus and network intrusion detection. In addition, the adaptive of the immune system had offered very good reference for automatic control.

## 14.6 Immune Algorithm

In the field of Artificial Immune System, there are mainly three types of immune algorithms, including the general immune algorithm, negative selection algorithm, clone selection algorithm.

### 14.6.1 General immune algorithm

At present, the general immune algorithm mostly adopts the searching strategy of genetic algorithm. The operators of crossover, selection and mutation (some include mutation only) which are often used by genetic algorithm are also designed in immune algorithm. But it is different from GA in the respect of population searching strategy, expression of solution and memory unit set .etc. About search strategy, genetic algorithm adopts fitness function to direct the searching process. General immune algorithm adopts affinity (such as Hamming distance, information entropy) metric. Genetic algorithm adopts the binary or floating string to express an intact solution. While general immune algorithm mostly adopts part encoding, i.e. the encoding individual is only correspondent to a part of solution. In addition, the control strategies of population of general immune algorithm and genetic algorithm are different to some extent. Genetic algorithm has no obvious memory unit, but general immune algorithm keeps memory information of optimum individual. It can be used for accelerating local search or suppressing premature convergence. Thus, the algorithm converges to global optimum quickly.

There is not a unified frame yet at present in the immune algorithm. But it has shown strong ability of searching optimization in solving combination optimization. From the essence of immune algorithm, it can be regarded as the improvement of genetic algorithm. S. Endoh proposed the immune algorithm (Endoh et al., 1998) based on two kinds of memory modes. It fully utilized the function of memory in the process of optimizing and iteration. Experimental results show that the efficiency was better than that of genetic algorithm.

The most natural immune algorithm is divided into three steps as follows:

(1) Produce diversity;
(2) Establish self tolerance;
(3) Remember nonself.

There are 6 steps in the general immune algorithm employed engineering shown in Figure 14.6:

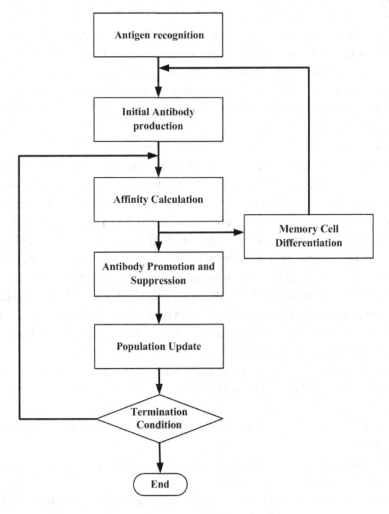

Fig. 14.6 The general immune algorithm

(1) Recognize antigens: the immune system confirms the invading antigens.

(2) Produce initial antibody population: memory cells are activated to produce antibodies to remove the antigens that appeared in the past. Select some antibodies from the database which includes the optimum antibody.

(3) Calculate affinity: calculate the affinity between antigen and antibody.

(4) Memory cells differentiate: The antibodies which have the biggest affinity with antigen are added into memory cells. Because the number of memory cells is limited. The produced antibodies with higher affinity to antigen replace the antibodies with lower affinity.

(5) Promotion and suppression of antibodies. The high affinity antibodies are promoted, and the high concentration antibodies are restrained. It is usually implement by calculating the expected value that antibody survives.

(6) Production of antibodies. New lymphocytes produced in bone marrow replace the antibodies removed in (5). This step produces many types of antibodies by crossover operator.

According to the concrete problems, researchers carry on different improvements or changes to the immune algorithm described above in employing, for example, it is combined with genetic algorithm and utilizes genetic operators to produce diverse antibodies etc. While using the general immune algorithm to solve problems, each step has the corresponding form: The antigen corresponds to the input data of problems, such as the goal and restrains of problem. The antibody corresponds to the optimum of optimization problem. Affinity corresponds to the evaluation of solution, combining intensity. Memory cells differentiation corresponds to keep the optimizing solution. The promotion and suppression of antibody corresponds to the promotion of optimizing solution, non optimizing solution deletion. The corresponding contents are different because of the different problems to be solved.

Compared to determinacy of general optimizing algorithms, most of immune algorithms have the following prominent characteristics:

(1) It searches for a series of points in solution space at the same time, and not only one point;

(2) The object who deals with is the encoding string expressing the parameter to be solved, but not parameters themselves;

(3) What it used is goal function, not its derivative or other additional information;

(4) Its change rules are random, not confirmed.

## 14.6.2 Negative selection algorithm

On the basis of choosing the principle negatively, D'haeseleer provides one kind to choose the algorithm negatively (D'haeseleer et al., 1996), is used in the monitoring data to change. Among them the antibody question answers the match with the antigenic question and adopts and matches the rule partly. The procedure of this algorithm is as follows:

(1) On the limited characters table, define a set of string S representing self. Its length is A. It is used for detecting.

(2) Produce the detector set R, according to the negative selection principle, examine each detector. Part match rule is adopted, i.e. two string match if and only if at least r pieces of continuous location among them are the same.

(3) Monitor the change of S by comparing detectors in R with S continuously. If the detector is matched, then the change takes place.

The advantage of this algorithm is simple and convenient, easy to realize. The main problem is computing complexity grows by exponential. It is difficult to deal with complex problems. It is applied to pattern recognition, virus detection and network intrusion, anomaly detection, etc. This algorithm does not utilized self-information directly, but generates detectors set by self sets through negative selection principle. And it possesses distribute detection, robustness, parallel, etc.

## 14.6.3 Clone selection algorithm

Based on the principle of clone selection, de Castro proposed the clone selection algorithm (de Castro et al., 2000). The core is that the operators of proportion duplicates and proportion mutation. It can be used in machine learning and pattern recognition, etc. The algorithm procedure is as follows:

(1) Produce candidate set S $(P)$ of scheme .This set is the total of a subset of memory cell $(M)$ and the surplus population $(P_r)$. $P = P_r + M$;

(2) Confirm $n$ best individual $P_n$ in the population $p$ based on affinity;

(3) Clone (duplicate) $N$ best individuals in the population. Produce temporary population $C$. The size of $C$ is the monotonically increasing function of antigenic affinity;

(4) Mutate the cloned population. The mutation rate is inverse proportion to affinity. Thus it produces a mature antibody population ($C*$);

(5) Reselect improved individuals to make up memory set. Some members of P can be replaced by the other of $C*$;

(6) Replace antibodies with low affinity in population. Thus maintain the diversity of antibodies.

It had been applied in algorithms in binary character recognition, multi peaks functions optimization and combination optimization. Compared with genetic algorithm, clone selection algorithm is basically identical on encoding scheme and construction of evaluation function. But the steps and search strategies are different to some extent. And through the immune memory mechanism, this algorithm can keep every local optimum. It is very important for optimizing multi-peak function.

### 14.6.4 Immune learning algorithm

J. D. Farmer explored the learning of immune system at first. It was pointed out that immune learning is similar to Holland classifier. Hunt proposed a kind of supervised learning algorithms based on immune network theory. Ishida had proposed a kind of artificial immune learning algorithm based on PDP model, and it was applied to the fault detection.

J. Timmis had studied unsupervised learning strategy based on artificial immune system and had set up a machine learning model RLAIS (Timmis et al., 2001). This model can find complex interaction relation from the studied data. Compared with neural network, AIS is improved greatly on the expression of the studied object, and the network size can be controlled. RLAIS adopts population control strategy to control the population growth and judge the stop of algorithms. Artificial Recognition Ball (ARB) had been defined to represent B cells. B cells are assigned based on the stimulation level by ARB. When ARB doesn't need B cells again, it is removed. Thus, it can realize the effective control of population. Through concentrating similar ARBs, RLAIS can realize pattern drawing and cluster analysis from the data. This model can also be used for strengthen learning. At the same time, it has potential value in data analysis and knowledge discovery.

## 14.7 Applications of Artificial Immune Systems

In recent years, different kinds of models and algorithms based on the principles of immune system are developed widely and applied to science research and engineering. Some typical applications are introduced as follows:

### 14.7.1 Information security

With the popularization of Internet, The trend of virus growing through the computer network is increasing tension. And the software of killing virus finds out and eliminates the virus by scanning characteristic database of computer virus. Thus, it can only kill the known virus passively. But it can't find and eliminate the unknown computer virus voluntarily. We must seek new methods from the principles of biological immune system to eliminate the viruses. T. Okamato had proposed a kind of distributed antiviral system based on agent. It consists of immune system and resume system. The function of the immune system is to identify nonself information by grasping self information. The function of resume system is to copy and cover the infected files on the virus infected file by network. Based on the same principle, the artificial immune system is used for preventing the network from hacker's invading, network security maintenance and system maintenance.

### 14.7.2 Data mining

At present, the task of data mining based on AIS mainly concentrates on cluster analysis, data concentration, classification. Hunt et al. researched unsupervised learning algorithm based on artificial immune network. It was used for the classification of DNA sequences. Compared with cluster analysis, self organization network, Timmis pointed out that artificial immune system is valid and effective in data analysis (Timmis et al., 2001). In fact, it is a method of cluster analysis based on unsupervised machine learning analysis. And RLAIS (resource limited Artificial Immune System) was proposed and used in data analysis, such as network faulty prediction.

### 14.7.3 *Pattern recognition*

The recognition ability of immune system is widely used in pattern recognition. The principles of clone selection, immune network, negative selection are involved. Forrest proposed the binary model of immune system and studied the pattern recognition and learning mechanism on the level of individual and population. Antibody and antigen are represented by binary string. Pattern matching adopts partial match rule.

Hunt proposed a frame of AIS -- Jisys based on Java and used it for pattern recognition. The principles of immune system included antibody heredity, clone selection, affinity maturation, immune memory, match mechanism and self-organizing characteristic, etc. The model had integrated classifier system, neural network, machine deducing and search based on instances, etc. It has the advantages of noise free, the ability of unsupervised learning, and can express the learned content externally.

### 14.7.4 *Robotics*

Based on the principle of the dynamic equilibrium of immune system, D.W. Lee proposed DARS method for the control of distributed robot (Lee et al., 1997). Each robot is regarded as a B cell and each environmental condition is regarded as an antigen. The behavioral strategy that the robot adopted was regarded as the antibody. The control parameters of the robot are regarded as T cells. In this way, under different environmental conditions, each robot will choose a group of behavioral strategies which were adaptive to environmental condition at first. Thus, this group of strategies were communicated with the around robots one by one. Then some behavioral strategies would be stimulated, some be suppressed. The most stimulated behavioral strategy would be adopted by the robot finally. In the immune system, the principle of interaction of cells is used for the control of self-containment and moving robot. The main idea of this strategy is to design basic actions for the control of action strategy of the robots in advance. Each basic action is regarded as an Agent. It can follow the environment around and make its own action decision, and send control command to the system. And then the action of the robots is determined according to the cooperation and competition states among Agents.

## 14.7.5 Control engineering

Based on the response to foreign pathogens rapidly and being stability quickly, a kind of new feedback controller can be designed. It was applied to the car tail collision system (RCAS). It can control the corresponding action of each executer by integrating the signals transmitted from each sensor. K. Takahashi had also designed a PID immune feedback model. It had the activation item of controlling reactive speed and suppression item that controls stabilized result. By the simulation of discrete, single input, single output, K. Takahashi had verified the validity of this controller. In addition, AIS was also used in order controlling, trends control and so on.

## 14.7.6 Faulty detection

Distributed detection system combined with immune network and learning quantization of vector (LVQ) can be used to detect the fault sensor in detected object. This system had two kinds of modes: Training mode and diagnosing mode. Under the training mode, it was trained by LVQ and the data of normal sensors. Under the diagnosing mode, the immune network confirmed the fault sensor according to the knowledge obtained by LVQ. The experiment showed that this system can find out the broken sensors in a group automatically. But in the past, this could be done only by measuring the output of each sensor independently. Immune learning can be applied to computer hardware monitoring system. Once computer hardware system is broken down, the monitoring system will mark the trouble region and take the corresponding recovery measure. The artificial immune system is also applied to the management of building roads, production schedule, bank mortgage defraud, associative memory, etc.

The study on artificial immune system is still at the starting stage, and immune system mechanism is too complicated and huge. There are few achievements in practice that the artificial immune system at present. So, artificial immune systems are difficult to describe abstractly by linear or non-linear model like artificial neural network, etc. Existing immune system non-linear model uses immunology of experiment. It is still difficult to be used in the artificial immune system in practice. Numerous computing models have just imitated some functions of immune system from the single angle, and the existing immune algorithms concentrate on utilizing immune mechanism to improve the other existing algorithms, especially the improvement of evolution algorithm.

Mechanisms of immune system have shortcomings too. For constructing the defense system, it needs to compute very much to get the initial antibodies (samples of solution features). The standard artificial immune system does not often fully utilize priori knowledge for the research object. In data processing, the artificial immune system can only generally concentrate the data samples (the characteristic obtained in the sample space). It can't optimize the composition of sample space. (Reduce the dimension of the sample space rationally). We should continue to develop various new immune intelligent methods and improve the shortcomings of existing intelligent algorithms. New optimization algorithm can be developed based on the mechanisms of learning, adaptive, organization diversity of immune system. All kinds of existing immune algorithms still exist a lot of problems. For example, clone selection algorithm are lack of ability of dealing with dynamic problem. Negative selection is too simple to deal with complex problem in practice, etc.

The field of artificial immune system does not have systematic mathematics foundation. Most artificial immune systems use the ideas from genetic algorithm, cell automata and artificial neural network, etc. to express some hybrid and heuristic algorithms. It is urgent to establish the theoretic foundation of artificial immune system. On one hand, it is necessary to study non-linear characteristics, such as the chaos of the immune network and steady state, etc., describe some dynamic behaviors of the immune system through the automata machine. Nonlinear dynamics of the immune system can be studied through the non-linear research. On the other hand, we need to strengthen the theoretical research of artificial immune system, including general principle, method, mathematical model, for example, convergence property, convergence speed, parameters set, encoding way of immune algorithm, etc. In biological theory, the research of interaction among nervous system, immune system and endocrine system should be strengthened in the hope of inspiration from it, and thus we can develop the new type of biological computer system.

**Chapter 15**

# Consciousness

The origin and essence of consciousness is one of the most important scientific problems. In intellectual science, the consciousness problems have special challenge meanings. It is not only the theme studied by philosophy, but also the important subjects of contemporary natural scientific research that existing how about determine consciousness and how the objective world reflects to subjective world. Consciousness involves advanced cognitive processes such as the consciousness, attention, memory, signifying, thinking, language, etc., its core is awareness. In recent years, because of the development of cognitive science, neural science and computer science, especially the appearance of the intact experimental technique, the research of consciousness is mentioned once again the schedule, and become the common focus of numerous subjects. In the 21st century, the consciousness problems will be one of the forts which the intellectual science tries hard to solve.

## 15.1 Concept of Consciousness

Consciousness is a complex biological phenomenon, the philosopher, physician, and psychologist have not common concept of consciousness. There is no final conclusion about consciousness so far. Contemporary famous thinker Dennett believes (Denett, 1991): Human consciousness is probably the last mystery difficulty to resolve. About consciousness, we puzzled so far, even to today, consciousness is the unique topic that wise and farsighted thinker loss words, confused thinking.

In the philosophy, consciousness is the highly improves and the highly organized special material--the function of the human brain, and it is the reflection of the objective reality correctly that owned by people only.

Consciousness is also the synonym of thinking, but the range of consciousness is relatively wide, including the cognition of emotional and rational stage, but think only mean the cognition of rational stage. Dialectical materialism believes that consciousness is the result of high development of material, and it is the reflection of existing. There is also play a huge activism role on existing.

On medical science, the understanding of consciousness of different disciplines has some difference too. In the field of clinical medicine, the consciousness refers to patient's understanding and reaction ability under surrounding and oneself, it is divided into different consciousness levels such as consciousness clearing, consciousness fuzzy, lethargy, coma; In spiritual medical science, consciousness has difference between ego-consciousness and environmental awareness. Consciousness obstacle performs as clouding of consciousness, somnolence, stupor, coma, delirium, twilight state, oneiroid state and confusion.

The view on consciousness in psychology is awareness or experience of objective things on external environment and one's psychological activity, such as feeling, consciousness, attention, memory, thought.

From the view with scientific intelligence, consciousness is the experience integration with external world, one's own body and mental process. Consciousness is "instinct" or "function" what the brain inherent, it is a "state", and it is many biological "combination" of a lot of brain structure. Generalized consciousness is the life phenomenon that higher organism and low organism all have. With the evolution of biological, it is continuous evolution that the organ of processing consciousness. It is mainly a brain that the organ of human consciousness activity. In order to reveal the scientific law of consciousness, building the brain model of consciousness, it not merely need to study the conscious cognitive process, and need to study the unconscious cognitive process, that is, the automatic information process of brain, and the transformation mechanisms of two processes in the brain. The consciousness research is the indispensable content in cognitive neuroscience, the research of consciousness and brain mechanism is important contents of the natural science. Philosophy involved the problems such as the origin of consciousness and the authenticity of consciousness exist etc., key problem of intellectual scientific research of consciousness is the brain mechanism of consciousness produce—how become consciousness the move of object.

## 15.2 Research History of Consciousness

The first one used this word "consciousness" is Francis Bacon in history. His definition of consciousness is that the consciousness is a person's understanding that what has happened in his thought. So, the consciousness problem is the field that the research of philosopher all the time. German psychologist Wundt established the first psychology laboratory in 1879. He clearly proposed that consciousness research is the major study in psychology, using physiological methods to study the consciousness, reporting the consciousness state under sitting quietly, working and sleeping. Psychology enter a new historical period with an identity of scientific experiment from then on, researches of a series of psychological phenomena develop rapidly, but there is slow progress in consciousness study, because it lacks the non-conscious of direct objective indicators. James proposed the concept of the stream of consciousness in 1902, and point out consciousness is rises and falls, its origin is constant, just like flowing water. Freud believes that person's feeling and behavior is influenced by consciousness need, hope and conflict. According to view of Freud, the stream of consciousness has depth; they have different level of understanding between the process of consciousness and the process of non-conscious. It is all or none phenomenon. However, because science was not developed enough at that time, it used introspection method, but it lacked the objective indicators, and only remain descriptive primary level but unable to advance. But since Watson declared psychology is a behavior science, the consciousness problem has been shelved. So in a very long time, no one study neuroscience because it is too complex, psychology is unwilling to become a forgotten science.

In 1950s-1960s, the scientists understood the neurophysiology foundation of the state of consciousness by anatomy, physiologic experiment. For example, Moruzziz and Magoun have found the reticular activation system of awareness in 1949; Aserinsky and Kleitman have observed the consciousness state of rapid eye movement sleep in 1953; in 1960s-1970s, they studied on the split-brain patient, it support that there are independent consciousness systems in two hemispheres of brain. Result of study described above has been opened and established the foundation of cognitive neuroscience research of consciousness.

Modern cognitive psychology started in 1960s, for cognitive psychologists, it is always a long-term challenge that to expound the neural mechanism of objective consciousness. The direct research about consciousness of objective experience and neural activity relation is still very rare so far. In recent years, with the rapid development of science and technology, using modern electrophysiological techniques (electroencephalography (EEC), event-related potential (ERP)) and radiation imaging technology (Positron Emission Tomography scan (PET), functional Magnetic Resonance Imaging (fMRI)), the consciousness study already become the new born focus of life sciences and intelligence scientific.

The research of on the brain mechanism of consciousness is very complex, the task is arduous, but the effect is great significance, it has caused the great interest of scholars all over the world in many domains, such as cognitive science, neuroscience of neural physiology and the neural formation of representation and neural biochemistry, social science, computer science. Association for the Scientific Studies of Consciousness is found in 1997, and had already held the international academic meeting of consciousness problem for 5 years in succession, meeting themes are: The relation of latent cognitive and consciousness (1997); Neural relevance of consciousness (1998); Consciousness and self-perception and self-representation (1999), consciousness joint (2000), the content of consciousness: Consciousness, attention and phenomenon (2001).

## 15.3 Consciousness Theory

### 15.3.1 Farber's view of consciousness

I. B. Farber and P. S. Churchland discussed the consciousness concept from three levels in the article in "Consciousness and the Neurosciences: Philosophical and Theoretical Issues" (Farber, 1995).

The first level is sense of awareness, including: feel awareness (by sensory channel with external stimulate), generality awareness (refer to a feeling that without any connect to channel, the internal state of the body aware, such as fatigue, dizziness, anxiety, comfort, hunger etc.), metacognitive consciousness (it refers to aware of all things of one's cognitive range, including thinking activity in the present and the past), conscious remember (can aware of the thing that happened in the past), etc. Here, we can aware of some signs of thing and report this thing in language. This method is convenient to measure, at the same time can exclude the animal who can not speak.

The second level is the advanced ability, it is advanced functions that not only passive perceive and awareness of information, also has activity of function or control, these functions including attention, reasoning and self-control (For example, physiological impulse was inhibited by reason or morals).

The third level is a consciousness state, it can be interpreted as a person's ongoing psychological activity, including link of the most difficult and the most common-sense in the consciousness concept, this state can be divided into different levels: consciousness and unconsciousness, comprehensive regulation, rough feeling etc.

The definition that first two levels of Farber for consciousness is an enlightening one, but the third level lacks the substantive content.

### 15.3.2 Psychological consciousness view

The cognitive scientist mainly wants to make contributions for understanding consciousness by standard psychological method. They regard the brain as an opaque "black box", we only know its output (behavior which it produces) within various input (Such as feeling input). According to the common-sense understanding about spirit and some general concepts, they build the model. This model expression spirit by using the project and calculation term (Crick, 1994).

Philip Johnson-Laird at the psychology of Princeton University is remarkable British cognitive psychologists. His main interest is to study languages, especially the meanings of the word, sentence and paragraph. Johnson-Laird convinced that any computer must have an operating system in order to control (Even not the thorough control) other part of work especially the highly parallel computer, in his view, them exist close connection between the work of operating system and the consciousness in the advanced position of the brain.

Rav Jackendoff is a professor of linguistics and cognitive in Brandeis University. He is a famous American cognitive scientist. He has special interests in language and music. Similar to most cognitive scientists, he would rather put the brain as an information processing system. But different from most scientists, he regard "how produce about consciousness" as a psychological most basic problem (Jackendoff, 1987). The middle level theory of his consciousness believes that consciousness is not from the consciousness unit of not processed, and not from high-level thinking too, but from an expression level between the minimum perimeter (similar to feeling) and the highest centre (similar to the thought). He has stressed appropriately the very novel views. He also believes that there are close connections between consciousness and short-term memory. It expresses this view that a sentence of his said "Consciousness needs the support of the content of short-term memory". But we should also add that short-term memory involves the rapid process; there is not the direct effect of phenomenology in the slowly process. Talking about attention, he believes that calculation result of attention is the material of attention experience more in-depth and detailed processing. He believes that it can explain why the capacity of attention is so limited.

Bernard J. Baars is a professor in the Wright Institute in University of California at Berkeley. He wrote a book of "A Cognitive Theory of Consciousness" (Baars, 1088). Baars is a cognitive scientist, but he cares more than Jackendoff and Johnson-Laird about people's brain. He calls his basic thought as global workspace. He believes that the information existing in this workspace at any moment is the contents of consciousness. As the workspace of central information exchange, it has contacts with a lot of unconscious receiving processors. These specialized processors have high efficiency only in their own field. In addition, they can obtain workspaces through collaboration and competition. Baars has improved this model in a number of ways. For example, the receiving processor can reduce uncertainty through interaction, until they accord with an effective explanation. Broadly speaking, He believes that consciousness is extremely active and the control mechanisms of attention can enter consciousness. We are aware of the some projects of short-term memory but not all.

These three cognitive theoreticians have roughly reached three points consensus about the attribute of consciousness. They all agree not all activities of the brain relate to consciousness directly, and agree consciousness is a initiative process; They all believe that attention and short-term memory involved in awareness process; They probably also agree that the information in consciousness can enter the long-time scene memory, can enter the level of high-level plan of the sport nervous system too, in order to control voluntary movement. Apart from this, their other ideas have more or less difference.

### 15.3.3 Reductionism

The Nobel laureate, the DNA double helix structure of the author, Crick is a typical representatives in this respect. He believes that the consciousness problem is a key problem in the whole advanced function of nervous system, so he published an advanced popular science book in 1994, is called "The Astonishing Hypothesis", the book's subtitle is "The Scientific Search for the Soul" (Crick,

1994). He boldly proposed "The Astonishing Hypothesis" based on the "reductionism". He believes that "People's spiritual activity completely determined by the behaviors of nerve cell and glial cells and the property of compositions and affects from their atoms, ions and molecules". He firmly believes that consciousness the psychological difficult problem can solve using the nerve scientific method. He believes that the consciousness problem relates to short-term memory and the shift of attention, he also believes that the consciousness problem involves many people feel, but he would like to work from the visual sense, because, human are vision animals, visual attention is easy to make psychophysical experiments, and neural science has accumulated a lot of materials in research of the visual system. At the end of the 20th century 80's early 90's, there was a great discovery in visual physiological studies: The phenomenon of synchronous oscillations recorded in shaking from different neurons, this around 40 Hz synchronous oscillations is considered to contact the neural signal between different picture characteristics. Crick proposed the 40Hz oscillation model of visual attention, and inferred that 40Hz synchronous oscillations of neurons may be a form of "bundling" that different characteristic in visual. As for the "Free Will", Crick believes it relates to consciousness; it involved execution of behavior and plan. Crick have analyzed the situation of some persons who lose "Will", and believes that a part of the brain for deduct "Free Will" lie in anterior cingulate gyrus (ACG), it close to Brodmanm area (area 24).

The bold assumption has undoubtedly pointed out a road to the research of consciousness that is we will find the answer to the consciousness problem finally by studying the material base of every level such as neural network, cells, and the molecule. But this assumption faces a key problem--Who have "Consciousness"? If it is the nerve cell, so who is "Me"?

Another Nobel laureate, Eccles was keen to the research of the consciousness problem. He is a neuroscientist, and makes the great achievement by study synaptic structure and function of nerve cell, so his consciousness view is worth paying attention to. He would not speak up his consciousness view is the dualism. He co-authored with philosopher Popper's "The Self and Its Brain" have published the "three worlds" of philosophy view. World 1 consists of the physical world (brain is inclusive too), world 2 consists of the mental or psychological world of human, world 3 consists of various activities such as social, language, science, culture etc. In his later works, according to structure and function of the nervous system, he propose a hypothesis of "sub-dendritic", it is a basic structure and function unit of nervous system, and formed by top of dendritic about 100. It is estimated that there is 400,000 sub-dendritics in human brain. Then he proposes a hypothesis of "sub-psychological", the "sub-psychological" in world 2 corresponding to the "sub-dendritic" in world 1. The dendritic microstructure is similar to the scale of quantum, so quantum physics may use to solve the consciousness problem.

### 15.3.4 Theatre hypothesis

About the consciousness problem, the most classical assumption is a metaphor of "bright spot in dramaturgical". In this metaphor, we aggregate into a conscious experience from a lot input of feelings, it compare to that, a spotlight shows a light to somewhere in dark theater, then spread to a large number of unconscious audiences. In cognitive science, most of assumption about consciousness and selective attention are come from this basic metaphor. B. J. Baars is the most important persons to inherit and carry forward about "dramaturgical assumption" (Baars, 1997).

In 1984, Crick borrowed it to propose the "searchlight" hypothesis in selective attention. This hypothesis means the thalamus-cortex interaction and its function in selective attention. The cerebral cortex divided into some areas such as visual, hearing, physical sense, movement, and the prefrontal areas. The thalamus has corresponded to nerve nucleus groups, so "searchlight" works in their interaction. In this hypothesis "Audience" Mean the unconscious brain area, such as a part of the cortex, hippocampus, basal ganglia, amygdala and implementation systems and interpretation system of movement.

"Assumption about dramaturgical" of consciousness implying that there are a lot of roles to perform on the stage at the same time, exactly as the human brain accepts many kinds of stimuli of internal and external receptors at the same time, but a few roles can receive the shining of the spotlight. There is a choice problem in this, and the spotlight does not stay on a place or a role, but it flow over time, the audiences represent the unconscious part of the brain.

The dramaturgical metaphor of consciousness has been opposed by some scholars. For example, Denett believes that, there must be "stage" could have "Consciousness" to performance in this assumption, mean, there is a stage as consciousness of special place in the brain, this assumption is easy fall into white case that the hypothesis of Descartes about the source of the soul of spirit "the

Pineal Gland" in the 17th century. The opposition believes that there isn't a special place to concentrate all input stimulus in the brain.

### 15.3.5 *Active model and receptive model of consciousness*

In 1977, R. E. Ornstein proposed the two modes of consciousness exist: active-verbal-rational mode and receptive-spatial-intuitive-holistic mode, abbreviated as the active mode and the receptive mode (Ornstein, 1977). He believes that two modes are controlled separately by the side of cerebral hemisphere, the evaluation of active mode is carried out automatically, and the human has limited the automation of awareness in order to block the experience, events and incentives that they do not correlate with survival ability directly. When people need to strengthen the ongoing to be summed up and judged, it increases the normal of awareness by the receptive model. According to the view of Ornstein, it can also contribute to learn using receptive mode to balance active mode that sit quietly, biofeedback, hypnosis, and even test some specific drugs. Intellectual activity is the initiative, and has a left hemisphere advantage. However the intuitive behavior is sensitivity, and has advantage of right hemisphere. The integration of two modes forms the foundation of the human advanced function.

### 15.3.6 *Microtubule hypothesis*

The most famous is Penrose about Microtubule hypothesis. He is a contemporary famous mathematical scientist, once proposed a kind of complex geometric figure can be completely covers the entire plane without leaving gaps, and make the creative work in black hole and gravitation. He successively published 2 works in computer, thinking and consciousness. In his view: "consciousness originated from the process of quantum physical that the special protein structure (microtubule) in the neuron". Penrose believes that the cytoskeleton plays an important role in transmitting information in the cell tissue of the neuron, cytoskeleton is composed of "microtubule", because its spatial scales is very small, should consider with quantum mechanics, the electromagnetic wave probably travels among them.

We think, the microtubule in neuron may be the site of the electromagnetic wave propogation and procession, but in the view of consciousness, this spatial scales is too small, the level is too low, in the view of system theory, using such a small spatial scales and low level, it is unable to make the perfect explanation for the complex and high-level function.

### 15.3.7 Quantum consciousness

Because of quantum characteristic and consciousness characteristic have common properties that beyond the limits of conventional computation, we can expect to solve the self-evident problem of consciousness through the quantum computing technology. In other words, we can use quantum characteristics such as superposition, entanglement, uncertainty etc, to provide the quantum algorithm that can achieve consciousness computation (Hameroff, 1998).

Perhaps there are about 10 fabric level between quantum mechanics and consciousness: such as chemical bond, molecule and its self-organization, molecular biology, genetics, biochemistry, membrane and its ion channel, synapse and its neurotransmission, neurons themselves, neural circuits, cortex column and module, extensive cortex's dynamic activity etc. There is strong competition among neuroscientist working on the adjacent level, so people are always aware of these levels in neuroscience research.

The accidental consciousness changes relate to some types of extensive stop in synaptic activity. However, a more reasonable level to explore consciousness should be the fabric level adjacent with perception and planning level, such as the cerebral cortical circuit and constantly changeable stamp sized cortexes in the discharge pattern of the level of dynamic self-organization. Although "Consciousness" has many meanings, it can't be explained by the low chemical level or the lower physical level.

### 15.3.8 Neural Darwinism

Neural Darwinism is proposed by G. M. Edelman in The Rockefeller University of American. The main idea drawn on Darwin's natural selection theory, he think neuron group composed of close inter-linked is the brain's neural structure and function of the mode of the selective main activities. And it is dynamic Darwinian process that our consciousness activity and mind activity. All behavior phenomenon was decided by space-time mode of neural cellular activity, the winner in the space-time mode at every moments will become apparent mind activity, especially consciousness activity. Finally, consciousness activity is a result of a large number of neural activities in the modes selection -- "Winner-King".

### 15.3.9 Constructivism theory

It is referred by A. M. Turing in "Computing Machinery and Intelligence" in 1950, he believes that the computer with thinking can be made in the end the 20th century (Turing, 1950). M. Mmsky believes that consciousness activity includes recognizing and purposeful behavior (Minsky, 1985). We have characterization ability and can control action and make a plan, predict the future, use languages; Processing information, the state of perception. All these are the general functions of the consciousness can be realized by a computer with cleverly designed. The consciousness activity is a behavior of complicated operation by the brain. So, it is out of question that the computer has conscious functions.

A. W. Burks is philosopher and computer expert, he proposed the constructivism theory (Burks, 1986) and defined consciousness like this:

(1) Consciousness should have intention, it means that choosing a goal and searching directional.

(2) Consciousness should have direct experience, such as feeling pain.

(3) Consciousness should have correction and restore function. When breaking down in some computer system, it can turn into another system automatically, or design a new procedure automatically, in order to reach its own completion.

(4) Consciousness should have awakens functions. People are in inactive period while sleeping and when they have conscientious consciousness while awakening. Likewise, computer have protecting system, it can run in the inactive period.

(5) Consciousness can make short-term control and long-time plan. According to constructing view, consciousness is a particular computer control system and a relatively simple real-time control organization, when the system is awakening, it can guide in short-term activity and implement long-time plan.

According to the conditions, if a system can make a short time and long-term plan, input, output, know result of its activity, correction mistake of its activity in working state, when we say this is a conscious system. If this definition is feasible, then we can produce the robot that can carry out all human's cognitive functions in one day.

### 15.3.10 Consciousness model

Descartes put forward the direct relationship between consciousness and brain (Specific brain district) on the interaction between the body and mind about the pineal body. D. L. Schacter proposed the block model of consciousness in 1988 (Schacter, 1988). Figure 15.1 gives the block model abut the brain system diagram.

In Figure 15.1, Schacter has not given a specific reservation to the Conscious Awareness System (CAS), but he believes that there is a conscious awareness system. In this system, its activity is necessary for consciousness experience and separated with the relevant brain districts such as consciousness, cognition and action. Under this theory, unconscious visual can be explained by visual system and conscious awareness system. The conscious awareness system has played advantage role in the consciousness media of leading, and carried out other functions at the same time.

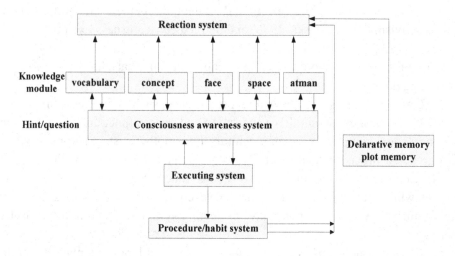

Fig. 15.1 Block model of consciousness of the brain system

## 15.4 Neural Correlation of Consciousness

Consciousness is a complicated problem, we should look for a starting point and study deeply with the current available technical means. Studying consciousness can regard awareness and non-awareness as starting point, find out the difference of neural correlates of consciousness in the brain activity.

Neural Correlates of Consciousness has been discussed as a special topic at the international consciousness conference in 1998. The natural scientists prefer to discuss this question, especially the neuroscientists. They attempt to explain the procedure of consciousness (phenomenon) in the view of neuroscience. The neural correlates are not only the material base of consciousness research, but also methods and processes of generate awareness. According to D. J. Chalmers, simply said the neural correlates is "a nervous system that directly related to the state of consciousness" (Chalmers, 2000). More detailed, "the neural correlate of consciousness is a minimum nervous system, and the state in this system can be mapped to the consciousness state, under certain condition, the state of this minimum nervous system is enough to reflect the state of consciousness". Certainly, studying the definition deeply, there are many questions, no repeat them here. Currently, the hot research of the neural correlates of consciousness is that the internal representation of things, the problem of feature binding, the problem of attention, the problem of neural coding etc. In a word, the study of the neural correlates of consciousness research is on the site and nature of consciousness.

In academia, many believes that in sensory channel (especially the visual channel) it forms the concept of an intact object by 40Hz synchronous oscillations integration (binding) them for the same object neuron with different sensitive characteristics. In Nikos Logothetis' experiments on the monkey (Logothetis etc. 1989), they train monkeys to press different poles and record the response of the neuron of different position in brain district, when appearing different figures, such as horizontal stripe presses the left pole or vertical stripe presses the right pole. They arranged another experiment called "binocular competition", which made the animals observe different graphics by two eyes. In human's perception it will present alternate phenomenon that turns by horizontal stripe and vertical stripe. This phenomenon is verified in the experiment of the monkey, it presses the left pole and the right pole alternately. There are different response of the neuron in different brain position, in area 17 (primary visual cortex), both were released in the whole process, to which the cells reacting to horizontal stripe and cells reacting to vertical stripe. In the inferotemporal area (the advanced area of visual perceives) the response of neuron are not identical with the perceptual react (monkey's action of press pole). It proves that the vision perception (a form of awareness consciousness) occurred in inferotemporal area.

## 15.5  Explicit Consciousness Thinking and Potential Consciousness Thinking

It is easy to understand what is explicit conscious thinking and potential conscious thinking after understanding the essence of consciousness. In narrow sense, consciousness is to detect, adjust or control time logical thinking and space logical thinking (including representation thinking and intuition thinking). To judge whether there is consciousness, thinking process must be "detected" at least. Any thinking process (no matter what form of thinking process) must have four key elements: thinking processing object (namely thinking material), thinking processing means or method (such as analysis, synthesis, abstract, summary, judgments, reasoning, imagination, etc.), thinking processing buffer memory area (called "working memory" too, used for keeping thinking in to process to the object and process the result) and thinking processing mechanisms. In other words, the absence of any one of the four elements will result in that the thinking process can not be sniffed out because of starting the thinking process. Hence it much simpler to judge whether there is consciousness or unconsciousness, i.e. just sense the thinking process. Because sensing a certain thinking process does not mean to analyze carefully each element of the four, but to catch the simplest one which is directly related to the sense. This element is known as "working memory" (the buffer memory area where thinking is processed). This is because that unlike long-term memory, the content in working memory is not kept for a long time and it only plays a buffer role: temporarily store processing objects and processing results in the process of thinking processing. After the processing, its content will disappear promptly. So, we can perceive whether the thinking process takes place so long as we consider whether there is content in working memory (but needn't consider what kind of content) and its duration, but needn't consider the way and mechanism of processing as well as processing object.

With the development of the research on brain science in many years, especially in recent 10 years, it has found that thinking processing involves two kinds of different working memory: one is to store language material (concept), using language coding; the other is to store visual or spatial material (representation), using representation coding. The Further research indicates that not only concept and representation possess their own different working memories, but also representation itself also possesses two kinds of different working memory. This is because that there are two kinds of representation of the things: one is to express the basic attribute of things, used for discerning the representations of things, usually called "attribute representation" or "object representation"; the other is to reflect the representation of spatial structural relationship (related to visual location), usually called "spatial representation" or "relation representation". Spatial representation just contains some feature information that is used for determining the position and structural relation of object space, but does not contain the information of the object content. Such, there are three kinds of different working memory:

(1) Working memory for storing language material (language working memory): it is suitable for time logical thinking.

(2) Working memory for storing object representation (attribute representation): it is suitable for the spatial structure thinking which uses object representation (attribute representation) as processing target, i.e. representation thinking.

(3) Working memory for storing spatial representation (relation representation) (spatial working memory): it is suitable for the spatial structure thinking which uses spatial representation (relation representation) as processing target, i.e. instinct thinking.

Contemporary brain science research has proven that these three kinds of working memory and their respective corresponding processing mechanism of thinking can be found its own corresponding area of the cerebral cortex (Though the localization of some working memories have not been very accurate so far).

According to the new development of research on brain science at present, S. E. Blumstein, which come from Brown University, pointed out that the speech function does not make a reservation on a narrow and small area (according to traditional concept, speech function only involves the left brain Broca area and Wernicke area), but widely distributed in the left lateral fissure on the surrounding region to the anterior frontal and rear extension including the Broca area, closing to the face motor cortex of the frontal lobe and the left side of the central pre-back (but not including the amount of polar and occipital pole). The damage of Bullokar district will influence the expression function of the speech and that of fertile Nick district will influence the understanding function of the speed. However, verbal understanding and speech-related processing mechanisms are not limited to these two districts (Before this, people believed that the two districts completely determined human speech function, and this traditional had dominated psychological circles more than a century). Working memory which is used to store verbal materials is usually considered to be "the left forehead leaf". But it is still difficult to accurately locate the specific position. According to M. Petrides etc., people incline towards Loyd's area 6 in the left frontal cortex (Petrides, 1993).

Compared with the verbal working memory, the localization situations of Object working memory and spatial working memory are relatively accurate. Jonides, etc., who worked in department of psychology, Michigan University, the most advanced brain scientific measuring technology, positive electron launch fault scan skill (PET), to deeply study the formation process of object representation and spatial representation, and obtained valuable result about the formation mechanism of the two representations and the location of working memory. PET uses the isotope of the positive electron as marker, which is put into brain's a certain area so as to participate in metabolism. And then by using PET, the metabolic process is expressed in the form of representation. Therefore, PET has the advantages of accurately locating, no damage to the brain, and is suitable for a large amount of measurement.

The formation and processing mechanism of object distributes in the inferior temporal gyrus in the left hemisphere (concentrate on Loyd's area 37, stereotactic coordinates is 48, -58, -11), the parietal lobe in the left hemisphere (concentrate on Loyd's area 40, stereotactic coordinates is 35, -42, 34) and the anterior cingulate gyrus in the right hemisphere (concentrate on Loyd's area 32, stereotactic coordinates is -1, 14, 43); object's working memory then situates in the prefrontal cortex in the left hemisphere (concentrate on Loyd's area 6, stereotactic coordinates is 39, 3, 29).

It should be pointed out that in the above testing results of each group, when a hemisphere is explicitly activated, the corresponding position of the other is also activated. But the activation does not reach the remarkable criterion in statistics.

The above results show that the mechanism of processing visual information which is related to discerning objects mainly situates in the left hemisphere (only anterior cingulate gyrus is not in the left hemisphere) as well as working memory situates in the left hemisphere too; the mechanism of processing visual information which is related to spatial representation, including spatial working memory, all situates in the right hemisphere.

It should be pointed out that what Jonides had adopted is nondestructive PET technology. Its test objects are a group of ordinary voluntary university students instead of mentally damaged patients (18 persons are tested for spatial representation testing and 12 persons for object representation). The experiment record includes 6 kinds of scanning, and e each kind of scanning carries on 20 experiments; each tested PET representation is transferred into a stereotactic coordinates. It is required to calculate measure's average value under a certain condition, standardize the tested data and then use Bonferroni's method to make multiple comparisons and corrections of the results. Therefore, the test result is relatively reliable and scientific.

The time logical thinking is based on language symbol sequence, so have order and constant characteristics. That is to say, when applying language symbol-based concepts to judge and deduce, we just operate step by step in the order they are found. The process is usually long in duration, especially in analyzing the complicated relationship between things. In a word, in case of logical thinking, its working memory's duration is relatively long, and each step is very clear and definite because of working in an linear order manner. So this kind of thought process is very easy to be aware, and each step can also be expressed through language, such that potential mind operation process becomes explicit language activity. In this sense, the time logical thinking is usually called "explicit consciousness thinking". In other words, the explicit consciousness thinking refers to that its process is not only sniffed out but also described with language.

The characteristic of structural thinking of space is not quite alike. The materials of spatial structural thinking are representation instead of linguistic concept. As stated above, representation is divided into object representation and spatial representation. The processing characteristics of the both representations are different too.

As to object representation (including the information of the basic attribute of the things, used for discerning different things), its processing method is usually analysis, synthesizing, abstract, summarization, imagination (be divided into creating imagination and re-creating imagination), etc. But intact representation, instead of fragmentary word, is used for the unit of thinking processing in the occasion of spatial structural thinking. Because in such occasion, although the representations are analyzed, synthesized, abstracted, summarized and imagined step by step (such process is also called representation thinking) too, processing units are fewer and the steps are relatively simple. So working memory is of short duration. Sometimes the analysis and synthesizing of object representation can be finished instantaneously. This kind of thinking can be decomposed into several operating steps, so it can be described with language too and then has the features of representation thinking. That is to say, the spatial structural thinking occasion (commonly referred to as representation thinking occasion) that uses object representation as its processing object usually belongs to explicit consciousness thinking. But there are two kinds of situations which are not the case:

(1) The one is that working memory is too short in duration (such as no more than one second), while the thinking subject nerve center is assigned with attention in advance. This thinking process possibly can not be sniffed out, and then becomes potential consciousness (also called "unconscious") thinking.

(2) At the stage of "creating imagination", there is a section of potential consciousness process. Unlike re-creating imagination, creating imagination has no available representation. So "something must come from nothing" and this requires recreating an unpredictable new representation. Therefore there is a section of blank in working memory before the recreation. When working memory is null, thinking process can not go on as well as be sniffed out in general because of the absence of thinking processing objects. It even can not be described with language. So it is the thinking process of real potential consciousness. However, if there is time logical thinking that coordinates with it in the meantime, this thinking process possibly goes on and then recreating imagination process can be finished. As to the coordination of time logical thinking with creating imagination, we will show the coordinating method in detail in the next section ("interactive mechanism of explicit conscious and potential conscious").

Compared with the processing of thing representation, the processing of spatial representation (used in the spatial vision location) has a lot of new characteristics. The processing unit of thinking is the whole representation. Except that this is common of the processing of the things representation, other respects are all different compare with the processing of the things representation: It can not make the judgment on structural relation of order step by step about spatial representation by means of analyze, synthesize, be abstract, summarize, imagining etc; It is considered especially with the relation (the relation of spatial position, or other structural relations) between the things, it is not considered especially with concrete attribute of each things. In a word, this is different with time logical thinking, and different with spatial structural thinking (imagery thinking) what representation of things as process of object, it is structural thinking of another kind. It is not slow rhythm to process with line shape and order, but it rapid made intuition judgment on the basis of synthesizing wholly and intuitive perspective. Therefore, this kind of thinking (it regard spatial representation as the thinking of processing object) has been called "intuition thinking".

The intuition thinking usually has two kinds: Simple intuition thinking and complex intuition thinking. The processing object of simple intuition thinking (thinking material) is the spatial position representation that related to the spatial vision location, that is, the above-mentioned spatial representation; The processing object of complex intuition thinking is "relationship representation" (relationship representation is a subclass of spatial representation, their full names should be "spatial structures relation representation", it and "spatial position representation" belong to two subclass of spatial representation, usually, the spatial position representation referred to "spatial representation" already at present, "spatial structures relation representation" referred to "relationship representation") that it used for describing structural relation between complexities. On state about spatial vision location (in the process of simple intuition thinking), there must be initial characteristic value about the position of object in working memory, according to value of these characteristics, we determine the spatial position of the object by thinking processing mechanisms; On state about judge, deal with the complexity relation (in the process of complex intuition thinking), the implicit complex relation remains to be found between the things, so there is no initial value in working memory. These are very big difference of two kinds of intuition thinking.

In addition, we should care that intuitive thinking should not be understood as the thinking of an intuitive feeling or no reason and no any basis, it is not subjective imaginary, but it is fast thinking that set up in the foundation of solid theoretical foundation, abundant practical experience, deep investigations, and sharp outsight and high-level generalization. This is because, if we don't possess the condition such as theory, experience, surveys and studies, observes, summarized etc, then we can not find out the overall complex problem or the internal relations of complex relationship in the twinkling of an eye, and catch the main key among them, thus we can "fully confident" quickly to determine more accurate. Certainly, the intuitive judgment has not been analyzed and deduced by tight logic after all. Therefore, it is unavoidably not overall enough sometimes, even it possible is mistake, so under the state of having more abundant time, we should use time logical thinking to prove, to ensure there is not supposition.

It can be concluded from the above analysis, about the spatial structure thinking (intuition thinking) that its processing object is spatial representation, its characteristic is the fast thinking of the overall integrated and intuition judge (No the slow thinking of linear, sequential, step by step analysis), its working memory must be short, therefore, this kind of thinking process is more difficult to be detect; In addition, its thinking process have not a clear step generally, so it is difficult to describe in speech. In other words, if this kind of intuition thinking does not specially offer attention, it is difficult to be detect, and often shown as "potential conscious thinking". Especially among complex intuition thinking, thing's inherent relation is complex, we hold it very much difficult for the moment, and can not find this kind of relation even considers longer time. It will appear the phenomenon that similar to the process of create imagine, the content of working memory is blank some time. The differences of the process of create imagine: create imagine constructed the unprecedented representation of new things, the complex intuitional judgment find a certain obscure relation between the things that others have never announced. It is obvious, the complex intuition thinking and create imagine are the same real potential conscious thinking, even if the nerve center pays sufficient attention in advance (There is expectancy), it is unable to be detect of its thought process, it is unable to describe this process in speech.

Through the above discussion, about conscious thinking and potential conscious thinking, we can get the following understanding:

(1) Time logical thinking, its thinking process is easy to be detected, and can describe in speech, so it is conscious thinking.

(2) About the relation of spatial structure thinking and conscious, potential conscious, they appear many kinds of different situations:

a) To thing representation (the object representation) as processing object (also known as "thinking in representation"), its thinking process can be noticed generally, and can describe in speech, so it belong to conscious thinking (Except two case Short-term working memory of no attention and its stage in the "create imagine");

b) To spatial representation as processing object (also known as "the simple intuitive thinking"), Its thinking process is difficult to detect generally, and difficult to describe in speech, so it should be the potential conscious thinking, however, if we prior to the attention of, and can not be converted space visual representation into the sequence of events on the timeline, this kind of thinking can turn into conscious thinking;

c) To relation representation as processing object (also known as "the complex intuition thinking"), this kind of thinking is difficult to detect (even we pays sufficient attention, still of no avail), and can't describe in speech, so it is the real potential conscious thinking;

d) To among two exception of thinking in representation, the first could become potential conscious thinking under certain condition (it is short-term time working memory and we pay attention to), the second (create imagine) is the unconditional real potential conscious thinking.

On the basis of the above various situations, the following conclusions can be summarized:

* Time logical thinking is the unconditional conscious thinking; thinking in images belongs to conscious thinking too generally;
* Complex intuition thinking and creative imagination all belong to unconditional potential conscious thinking;
* Thinking in images can be the potential conscious thinking under certain condition. The simple intuition thinking can be the conscious thinking under certain condition.

Such as music, painting, literary creation, this kind of creative activity mainly depends on a combination of "creative imagination" and "time logical thinking", and about discovery of law various movement in nature and human society (to explore the theory of the natural and social sciences), this kind of creative activity mainly depends on a combination of "complex intuitive thinking" and "time logical thinking", creative imagination and complex intuitive thinking belong unconditional potential conscious thinking, time logical thinking belong unconditional conscious thinking. It is obvious, there is really a decision meaning is unconditional potential conscious thinking and unconditional conscious thinking, for creative thinking. So, they refer to these two kinds of unconditional situations when we mention unconditional potential conscious thinking and unconditional conscious thinking in the future, except especially explain.

## 15.6 Attention

Attention is a subject for research, which is old and youth. As early as more than 100 years ago attention was already paid attention to by experiment psychologist as the control centre of the human behavior and psychological activity. But subsequently its dominant position has occupied position gradually because of the behaviorism and psychological school of Gestalt, which make attention study fallen into the low point. Behaviorism school denies initiative of human behavior, but Gestalt regards notice and consciousness as integration. Until the middle period of the 50th, with the rise of cognitive psychology, the importance of attention in the information processing of human brain has been re-recognized by people. In the past more than ten years, with the rapid development of brain imaging technology, cranial nerve physiology and theory brain model theory, attention is not only a psychological concept, but also has a visible neural network and measured cognition and neural physiological effect. Now, attention studying has become breach which announces the brain secret and hot subject for neural scientific research.

Attention involving many kinds of sensory systems such as the sense of vision, hearing and touch. Here we just discuss vision notice function network of mechanism, dissect –position and cooperative effect mechanism.

### 15.6.1 Attention network

Though the studies on attention mechanism have a history of more than 100 years, it has been an undecided problem that if an independent attention system exists in the brain. This is because , attention mechanism cannot cause unique and qualitative feeling experience like touch sense, at the same time it cannot generate muscle action response automatically like the system of action muscle either. We really have the ability to choose feel stimulating, memory information or muscle action response, but all these do not meant there was a independent attention system in the brain, because the whole brain has participated in the course of choice.

Recent years, with the rapid development of the technology of brain imaging and nerve physiological research, it has become true that isolate attention network from other information process system. Take the advantages of the positive electronic fault scan (PET)and the function magnetic resonance imaging (fMM) technology, it can measure the change (rCBF) of brain blood flow regional while finishing the specific attention task more accurately ,and then confirming each function structure dissect location of attention sub-network. At present, though the knowledge about attention network dissection still incomplete, but the brain imaging of existing brain and neural physiology proved that attention mechanism is not the characteristic of the single brain district, it is also not the function of the whole brain. There was really an independent attention network (Posner, 1994) in the human brain, there are three reasons: first, attention system and data handling system are separate in dissecting, though it interacts with the other parts of the brain, it still keeps its own characteristic. Second, attention composed of several dissection areas network, it is not a characteristic of the single centre, and it is also not the general function of whole operation of the brain. Third, there are different functions among the attention each of network dissect area, and it can be described in academic language of cognition.

According to the existing study results, Posner divides attention network into three subsystems: anterior attention system, posterior attention system, vigilance attention system. The anterior attention system involves frontal cortex, anterior cingulate gyrus and basal ganglion. The posterior attention system includes frontal-parietal cortex, pulvinar and superior colliculus. The vigilance attention system then mainly involves the input form the locus coeruleus norepinephrine in the right hemisphere to the cerebral cortex. The functions of these three subsystems can be summarized as orientation control, guiding search and keeping vigilance respectively.

## 15.6.2 Attention function

### 1. Orientation control

Orientation control means that brain leads the focus-of-attention to the place of interest the place of interest, and then realizes the ability of space choosing. There are two kind methods of choosing space information: first, attention mechanism involves eyes. Urged by the outstanding goal in the visual field or personal will, the observer's eyes move to the place of interest, and watch the corresponding goal. Eyes enable the goals representation in retina central concave through watching mechanism, thus obtain more detailed goal information. This kind of orientation control and attention shift system which rely on eyes move to realize is called explicit attention shift system. The second kind of attention shift mechanism occurred between two big beating eyes and turn attention to a certain place outside the watch point by implicit way, which dose not involve any hole move or head move. This kind of attention shift system is called implicit shift attention system. Posner holds, implicit attention may involve three kinds attention operating: Remove attention from the present focus-of-attention (involve the brain terminal leaf); Move the attention pointer to the area where the goal is (in the charge of midbrain district); Read the data in the place of attention point (the function of thalamus' pillow). The human has ability of implicit attention shift system. Through the experiment when turn attention to a certain place outside the watch point implicitly by attention clue, the person tested has not only improved the simulating response speed to this place, reduced threshold value of measuring, but also strengthened the corresponding electric activity of scalp. The directivity of attention explains that we can't pay attention to many goals in the visual field at the same time, but move attention point sequentially one by one, that is to say that we can only adopt the serial way of moving. But we can choose corresponding input processing yardstick with the vision. Attention point can focus finely and scatter in wider space range. In the attention cognitive model, regarding the attention point as spotlight of the variable focus, reflect this kind of characteristic vividly.

The directional alternative of attention is related to the limited information handling capacity of the attention system. The enhancement of the place information processing efficiency takes non-attention information place being inhibited as cost.

Clinical observation proves that the patient whose right terminal leaf of brain is injured, when attention clues appears in right visual field, and the goal appears in the left visual field, the directional control ability is damaged seriously; But in other situations, the harm is little. This indicates that the ability is damaged, of which remove attention from the inducing clue place. From PET data got through the normal tested person, when attention moving from a place to another, whether this kind of movement is driven by the will or stimulated by the external world, the area mainly concentrates the terminal leaf on left and right sides where the blood flow obviously increases. This is the unique area activated by attention shift. The record from sober terminal leaf cell that makes of monkey proves that terminal leaf neuron involves attention orientation control. P study reveals that the dissection network modulating the exodermis of other lines selectively crosses thalamus' pillow core; Strain, lose, interfere with or strengthen operation of goal cause the obvious effect among thalamus pillow core too.

PET measures and clinical observation indicates that the attention functions of two hemispheres of brain are asymmetric. The attention move in two visual fields of left and right sides can enhance the blood flow of the terminal leaf on the right side; and the enhancement of blood flow in the left terminal leaf only relates to the attention move of right visual field. This find could explain why right brain damage of hemisphere causes more attention damage than left. But for the person with normal brain, when equal amount disturbance targets distributing in left and right visual fields, it can not accomplish the mask quickly than concentrate on single vision. But to the patient resected callosum, when disturbance targets distributing in double visual fields, the speed of searching for the targets are two times faster than disturbance targets concentrate on single vision. It means that when callosum is damaged, the attention mechanism of left and right hemisphere relieve the connect of each other.

## 2. Guiding search

In the task of s vision searching, the guidance function of attention is obvious. Generally speaking, the time that the tested finds the goal increases with the disturbance targets' number with the linear increase. However, find out a certain goal, will not need to search for all goals. There are conclusive evidence prove that search can go on under the guidance of the characteristic of position in goal. These characteristics include color, form, sport, etc.

The experiment proves that when paying attention to the color, form or sport, the neural activity of the brain frontal lobe district is obviously strengthened; but there was not enlarging effect in the brain terminal leaf district. It means that guiding search is the duty of the before attention.

In preceding attention system, anterior cingulate gyrus's function is called 'execution function'. "Execution" includes two meaning. First, the brain interior organizing must notify "the executor" the process course what is taking place; then, "the executor" implement attention control to the whole system. The experiment finds that neural activity number in this area enhances with the increase of target number and the reduction on the training number. This is identical with attention's cognitive theory. In dissecting, anterior cingulate gyrus has pathway between after parietal and prefrontal cortex. Prefrontal cortex played a key role in keeping the representation of the past things. And anterior cingulate gyrus involves clear feel and control of the target. These finds indicates that before attention system is the neural basic of the will attention and the central of issuing orders by brain (Crick&Koch, 1992). This kind of conjecture may be reasonable, because the frontal lobe district of the human brain's cortex area is exactly the cortex which related to make plan, it is a psychological supreme control centre.

The experiment also found that it is happened coincide to choose through the position or characteristics such as the color, form, etc., interfere with each other less. So someone guess that it before attention system and after attention system may take the measure that like time share or time division.

### 3. Keeps vigilance

The function of vigilance system is to make the brain ready and keep vigilance, in order to deal with the signal with supreme priority fast. Keep vigilance closely related with attention, it involves a sub network of attention.

The positive electron fault scans reveal that when requiring tried keeping the vigilance state, the blood flow of right frontal lobe district strengthened; and when this area is damaged, the mankind loses the ability to keep vigilance. It means that keep the vigilance state involving an attention subsystem lying in the right side of brain.

### *15.6.3  Inhibition-enhancing effect of attention*

The great activity can be inhibited or enhanced selectively through the regulation and control that is paid attention to. An enhancement effect of inhibition of noticing is three results of paying attention to cooperative effect of the sub network.

When having a large number of interference goals in visual field, how does the brain find the correct place to finish the goal and measure? The experiment proves, the brain is through enlarging or inhibiting the neural activity of every brain district selectively, finish the goal and measure. PET measurement reveals, when the person tried of the instruction pays attention to amazing a certain attribute, the brain area that specially runs with this attribute is enhanced selectively. This kind of effect is especially obvious in the systematic line exodermis of vision. The experiment finds, though the amazing picture in the visual field of person tried is all the same, but different one instructs the language to cause the activity of different brain districts to enhance. Let the person tried pay attention to a certain attribute with amazing vision through guiding languages (such as the movement pace) With observing physics with this attribute to stimulate directly by the person tried (such as the movement goal) Can cause the activity of the same brain district to enhance. Generally speaking, any brain area can all be enhanced through function of noticing.

Measure to the enhancement effect paid attention to too by method to record electric potential of human brain scalp. In some search tasks, can not find the goal only according to single characteristics such as the orientation or form, etc.; it must be combining two or more characteristics with a place to accomplish the task of searching for. At this moment, try, need, carry on serial to search for, notice one move to another place from first place. If does not allow the eyes to move at this moment, then can only rely on obscure attention to shift. In the experiment, obscure attention shifted driven by the induction clue appearing in different places. Experiment find, when noticing the clue appearing in the position of goal, afford to conceal focus-of-attention, will cause the enhancement of the electric potential of scalp of carrying area after the person tried. It is all the same that the place where this kind of enhancement effect takes place and positive electron fault scan and studies the cortex area where the blood flow of midbrain enhancing.

### 15.6.4 Theory and model of attention

With the development of cognitive psychology, several attention-based models were arose in the mid-20th century. Some representative ones were attention-based filtration model and recessionary model which belong to conscious model of choice. These two kinds of models laid the attentive mechanism in the information-processing stage of consciousness, which made a choice of information before recognising. By contrast to the conscious model of choice is react and choose model, which shows that the function of noticing is not choosing but the response to stimulus. This model thinks, all information can enter highly handling stage, but only the most important information will cause the response of the centre system. The emphasis points of these two kinds of models are different, conscious model of choice emphasize centralized attention while react and choose model pay attention to distributing attention. The focus of the dispute is the position of the mechanism in information processing. The centre energy model of noticing is produced under this background. The theoretical foundation of this model is the limited processing ability of information system. It has avoided paying attention to the problem in the position of the mechanism in information processing which made the experimental result of the two models to be unified in form; but the disadvantage is not paying attention to the concerning information processing.

In the early 1980s, the characteristic integration model put forward by A. Treisman integrated noticing and the internal course of consciousness processing, It also compared the space choice of noticing by "the spotlight", which was spoken highly by cognitive psychologist, neural physiologist and neural computation of Jurists (Treisman, 1982). According to this model, visual processing is divided into two associated stages which called pre-attention stage and focus attention stage. The former handle the simple characters such as color of visual stimulating, orientation and movements in parallel, various characters were recoded in brain, produced the corresponding "characteristic map". Each character forms representation of pre-attention. Pre-attention processing is a "From bottom to top" information course without focus attention. Each character in the characteristic map is uncertain on the position. It need depend on concentration of attention if wanting to obtain object consciousness, by "the spotlight" to scanning of "position map" and integrating each character belonging to the searching target organically and equipping the character dynamic equipment of the characteristic. This is a slow serial processing. So, when the difference of goals and disturbance goals were shown as the single character, the goal can jump out form be hit from the visual field at once and finish the goal checking, to measure, the search time was not influenced by the number of the disturbance goals figure without interruption; while the difference of goals and disturbance goals were shown as the integration of various characters. It needs to use focus attention, scan to each goal position by order. At this moment, the search time will linear increased by the numbers of interfacing items.

The recent experimental evidence shows that according to comparative complicated attribute such as the three-dimensional surface, which can realize attention assigning too. The very interesting one is that the idea of characteristic assembling in characteristic combines model has already confirmed partly in physiological research of the visual nerve. There is not one-to-one numerous cortex neural unit like the object that we see in the brain, on the contrary, after the object enters the visual system, it was resolved into different characteristics or attribute, such as color, orientation, sport, etc. These characteristics are dealt with respectively by different visual passways and cortex area. How to releasing all attribute to signify the same goal in unison with different regional neurons, or whether we could find the common mark which carries on the relevant neurons for releasing, the so-called "the assembling question". The electricity physiological experiment indicates that concentrating attention to synchronization release, with which being paid attention affairs relating with neurons. This kind of synchronous releases displays vibration which is usually shown as about 40 weeks in step. This discovery has offered physiological evidence of the nerve for attention characteristic integration model. However, for "spotlight" of attention how to move it to another position, this remains a problem remained to solve.

The attention model of "spotlight" is a cognitive psychology model with extensive influence. However, it has not been generally accepted by neural physiologists. Some theories are put forward doubtful point for the objective reality. For example, the competition theory of attention thinks, attention mechanism is not "spotlight" scanned in the visual field fast, but the neural mechanisms of the brain characteristic for solving object competition and behavior control.

At present, though the attention theory has not been generally acknowledged, but attention involving a bottleneck question that everybody is generally acknowledged, this is the alternative question for attention. Its basic idea is that elementary information processing is fast and parallel on the whole; while at a certain or some stages in information processing there should be a bottleneck to control information process. Only one thing can be processed in a moment, at the same time the things out of the attention point will be restrained. Then move to another thing fast, and so on. This is a serial process which needs long time to finish (Crick, 1994).

# Chapter 16

# Symbolic Logic

Symbolic logic is an area of logic or formal logic studied with mathematical methods, and therefore is often called mathematical logic. There are very close relations between symbolic logic, computer science and intelligent science. In the 20th century, research works on the foundation of mathematics brought about five branches: the logical calculus, the model theory, the axiomatic set theory, the recursive theory, and the proof theory; these five branches form the main parts of modern mathematical logic. Logical calculus is the most fundamental part among these branches, and is also the prime part of mathematical logic. This chapter is devoted to logical calculus, model theory and recursive theory. Some topics on proof theory will be discussed in the next chapter.

## 16.1 Introduction

Logic as a formal science was founded by Aristotle. Leibniz reaffirmed Aristotle's logical developing direction of mathematics form and founded the mathematical logic. From the thirties of the last century, various mathematical methods were extensively introduced and used in the mathematical logic; with the result that mathematical logic becomes one branch of mathematics and is as important as algebra and geometry. Mathematical logic has spread out many branches such as model theory, set theory, recursion theory, and proof theory.

Logic is a primary tool in the study of intelligence science as well as in the study of computer science. It is widely used in many domains, such as the semasiology, the logic programming language, theory of software specification and validation, theory of data base, theory of knowledge base, intelligent system, and the study of robot. Objective of the computer science is essentially coincident with the goal of logic. On the one hand, the objective of the computer science is to simulate with the computer the function and behaviour of the human brain, and bring the computer to be an extension of the brain. Here the simulation of the function and behaviour of the human brain is infact to simulate the thinking process of persons. On the other hand, logic is a subject focused on the discipline and law of human's thinking. Therefore, the methods and results obtained in logic are naturally selected and put to use during the research of computer science. Furthermore, the intelligent behavior of human beings is largely expressed by language and character; therefore, simulation of human natural language is the point of departure for the simulation of human thinking process.

A formal system is completely determined by its symbol sets, production rules of formulas, axioms, and inference rules. The formal system itself is a pure syntax object. Its interpretations or means are defined by semantics. Generally, a formal system has its own background of logical inference system or mathematical axiom system.

In order to study the consistency problem of a mathematical system, it is necessary to take the concepts, propositions and proofs of this mathematical system as studying objects, and carry out studies on the logical structures and the disciplines of proofs. It then brought about other branches of mathematical logic, such as the proof theory, the recursive theory and the model theory. Recursive theory mainly studies the calculability and is closely connected with the development and application of computer. Model theory mainly studies the relation between formal systems and mathematical models.

According to Leibniz's idea, mathematical logic, mathematics and computer are all developed towards a unified target, i.e., calculating and computing of the thinking process and implement it by computer. As early as 1930s, reasoning process has been transformed into some simple and mechanical operations according to mathematical logic; Turing machine was proposed as an abstract model of computer, and the existence of universal Turing machine was also proved. These works provided a theoretical prototype for the stored-program computer (i.e., the Von Neumann machine) which appeared in 1940s.

Formal methods advocated by symbolic logic are extensively permeated into every fields of computer science, such as the software specification, formal semantics, program transformation, proof of program correctness, and the synthesis and validation of hardware. In the formal method, logics such as the programmed logic, the algorithmic logic, the dynamic logic, and the temporal logic are all frequently used. In the intelligence science, nonmonotonic logics as well as other mathematical methods are also used in the study nonmonotonic inference, with the target of simulating human's thinking by computer. It is believed that symbolic logic will continue to make critical contribution for the development of science and technology.

## 16.2 Predicate Calculus

In propositional calculus, each atom (such as $P$, $Q$ and so on) can only describe a proposition with certain degree of complexity, and cannot access every part of the assertion. Predicate calculus overcomes this problem. With predicate calculus, a sentence such as "It rained on Tuesday" is no longer represented as a single proposition $P$, but described as a formula *weather* (*Tuesday*, *rain*), where a predicate *weather* is introduced to described the relationship between days and weathers. Expressions of predicate calculus are manipulated according to inference rules; every part of a expression can be accessed, and new sentences can be deduced.

Predicate calculus supports variables. For example, it can be stated that the formula *weather* (*x*, *rain*) holds for any $x$, where $x$ represents one day of some week. The universal quantifier $\forall$ and the existential quantifier $\exists$ can also be used to quantify variables, where $\forall$ states that the subsequent sentence holds for any values of the quantified variable, and $\exists$ states that the subsequent sentence holds for at least a value of the quantified variable. For example, the above statement can be described as $\forall x$ *weather* (*x*, *rain*).

First-order logic is built on predicate calculus, where quantifiers are only used to quantify individual variables. First-order logic is the most developed part of symbolic logic and acted in the core position during the formalization of languages and inferences of mathematics. First-order logic is also called predicate logic.

Predicate calculus organizes logically valid formulas into a completely formalized system of axioms. A predicate calculus system consists of some axioms, which are selected from logically valid formulas, and some inference rules; based on these two parts, other logically valid formulas can all be deduced. Many predicate calculus systems have been built by researchers. The following is one of these systems. It consists of 7 axiom schemas and two inference rules:

$A \rightarrow (B \rightarrow A)$

$(A \rightarrow (B \rightarrow C)) \rightarrow ((A \rightarrow B) \rightarrow (A \rightarrow C))$

$(\neg B \rightarrow \neg A) \rightarrow (A \rightarrow B)$

$x = x$

$x = y \rightarrow (A \rightarrow A[x/y])$, where variable $y$ is free to be substituted for $x$ in $A$

$\forall x\, A \rightarrow A[x/t]$, where term $t$ is free to be substituted for $x$ in $A$

$\forall x\, (A \rightarrow B) \rightarrow (A \rightarrow \forall x\, B)$, where $x$ is not free in $A$

Inference rule has the following two:

(1) Modus ponens: $B$ can be deduced from premises $A$ and $A \rightarrow B$;
(2) Generalization rule: $\forall x\, A$ can be deduced from the premise $A$.
Theorem of predicate calculus is defined as follows:

(1) Every axiom is a theorem;
(2) If $A$ and $A \rightarrow B$ are theorems, then so is $B$;
(3) If $A$ is a theorem, then so is $\forall x\, A$;
(4) Every theorem can be obtained according to finite application of (1)~(3).
If formula $A$ is a theorem, then write this briefly as $\vdash A$.

Axioms of predicate calculus are all logically valid. Furthermore, inference rules guarantees that if all premises are valid with respect to a structure, then the conclusion is also valid with respect to this structure. Therefore, theorems of predicate calculus are all logically valid. This property is called the soundness of predicate calculus. Conversely, every logically valid formula must be a theorem of predicate calculus; this property is called the completeness of predicate calculus and was established by K. Godel in 1930. It has been proved that validity of first-order formulas is semi-decidable.

## 16.3 Modal Logic

As a branch of non-classical logic, modal logic deals with modalities such as necessity and possibility. It studies the formal inference between different modal propositions as well as the inference between modal propositions and non-modal propositions. Research topics on modal logic include formal systems of modal logic (different systems reflect different understandings about the concept "necessity"), semantics, properties of the metalogic of modal logic systems (such as consistence, soundness, completeness, and decidability), and relationships between modal logic and other branches of modern logic (Wang, 1987).

Traditional modal logic was born as early as the ancient Greece. Driven by the development of mathematical logic, modern modal logic was proposed and developed. After the establishment of the classical logic in the early twenty century according to Russell, many researchers were not satisfied with the material implication of the logic since many daily references schemas cannot be described by it. Therefore, C. I. Lewis, an American logician and philosopher, proposed the strict implication and built the earliest five modal logic systems which are named $S_1$, $S_2$, ..., and $S_5$. The so-called "p strictly implicate q" means that q can be logically deduced from p, in another word, "p materially implicate q" is a logical necessity. In such a way, concepts such as necessity were introduced into logic and consequently a new branch of modern logic was set up. Until now there are two climaxes for the research of modal logic. The first climax was about the building and research of modal systems, as well as the formalization of some kinds of operators which are similar with necessity and possibility. The second climax of research was start from the discovery of relationships between modal logic systems.

There are four basic modal propositional logic systems which are respectively named as T, $S_4$, B and $S_5$. System T is composed of the following four parts.

**Primitive symbols, including**
   a) Propositional variables: $p_1$, $p_2$, ...;
   b) The connectives ¬(negation), →(material implication), L(necessity), and the parenthesis "(" and ")".
   **2. Formation rules of formulas**
   a) Every propositional variable $p_i$ (i=1,2,...) is a formula;
   b) If $A$ and $B$ are formulas, then ¬$A$, ($A{\rightarrow}B$) and L$A$ are formulas.
   **3. Axioms: (where A, B and C represents any formulas)**
   a) $A{\rightarrow}(B{\rightarrow}A)$;
   b) $(A{\rightarrow}(B{\rightarrow}C)){\rightarrow}((A{\rightarrow}B){\rightarrow}(A{\rightarrow}C))$;
   c) $(¬A{\rightarrow}¬B){\rightarrow}(B{\rightarrow}A)$;
   d) $LA{\rightarrow}A$;
   e) $L(A{\rightarrow}B){\rightarrow}(LA{\rightarrow}LB)$.

**4. Inference rules: (where A, B and C represents any formulas)**

a) Modus ponens: $B$ can be deduced from premises $A$ and $A{\to}B$;

b) Necessity rules: L$A$ can be deduced from $A$.

Based on the system T, system $S_4$ can be built by introducing one more axiom L$A{\to}$LL$A$. System B and system $S_5$ can also be built by introducing the axiom ML$A{\to}A$ and M$A{\to}$LM$A$ in to the system T respectively, where M is called *possibility operator* and is defined as $\neg$L$\neg$. Some interpretations of intuitionism can be introduced for the system B, i.e., $\neg$M of the system can be interpreted as the negation of intuitionism.

There are two basic systems of modal first-order logic: T+BF and LPC+T, both of which are built on the modal propositional logic system T and classical first-order logic system LPC. Research results of modal logic proposed the development of many subdisciplines such as temporal logic and deontic logic, all of which are also called generalized modal logic. Furthermore, as one research result of modal logic, the Kripke semantic theory of possible worlds was adopted in the logic of natural language and in many subdisciplines of the modern logic. Modal logic is more and more importance for the study of artificial intelligence.

## 16.4 Temporal Logic

Temporal logic is a kind of modal logic that deals about some dynamic variables (called temporal variables) whose values are changing with time. Besides logical connectives and quantifiers of classical logic, some temporal operators are also introduced into temporal logic (Venema, 2001).

Temporal logic can be divided into propositional temporal logic and first order temporal logic. Furthermore, different temporal logic systems can be built according to the application of different temporal operators. The propositional linear-time temporal logic PLTL, which was proposed by A. Pnueli and Z. Manna, is extensive used in computer science. Primitive symbols of PLTL are a countable infinite set of propositional variables, the logical connectives $\neg$(negation), $\wedge$ (conjunction), $\vee$ (disjunction), $\supset$ (implication) and $\equiv$(bi-implication), as well as the temporal operators $\square$(means "any time"), $\diamondsuit$(means "some time"), $\circ$(means "the next time") and **Y**(means "until"). Based on these primitive symbols, well-formed formula of PLTL is defined inductively as follows:

(1) Any proposition variable P is a well-formed formula;

(2) If $w_1$ and $w_2$ are well-formed formulas, then $(\neg w)$, $(\wedge w)$, $(\vee w)$, $(w_1 \supset w_2)$ and $(w_1 \equiv w_2)$ are all well-formed formulas;

(3) If $w_1$ and $w_2$ are well-formed formulas, then $(\square w)$, $(\diamondsuit w)$, $(\circ w)$ and $(w_1 \mathbf{Y} w_2)$ are all well-formed formulas;

(4) Every well-formed formula is formed according to the application of (1), (2) and (3) with finite times.

There are 10 axioms and 3 inference rules for PLTL:

Axiom 1: $\neg \diamondsuit w \equiv \square \neg w$

Axiom 2: $\square(w_1 \supset w_2) \supset (\square w_1 \supset \square w_2)$

Axiom 3: $\square w \supset w$

Axiom 4: $\circ \neg w \equiv \neg \circ w$

Axiom 5: $\circ(w_1 \supset w_2) \supset (\circ w_1 \supset \circ w_2)$

Axiom 6: $\square w \supset \circ w$

Axiom 7: $\square w \supset \circ \square w$

Axiom 8: $\square(w \supset \circ w) \supset (w \supset \square w)$

Axiom 9: $(w_1 \mathbf{Y} w_2) \equiv (w_2 \vee (w_1 \wedge \circ(w_1 \mathbf{Y} w_2)))$

Axiom 10: $(w_1 \mathbf{Y} w_2) \supset \diamondsuit w_2$

Tautology rule: if u is a tautology, then $\vdash u$

Modus ponens rule: if $\vdash u \supset v$ and $\vdash u$, then $\vdash v$

Introduction rule on $\square$: if $\vdash u$, then $\vdash \square u$

Formulas which can be deduced by these axioms and inference rules within finite steps are called theorems of the system.

There are different structures of time for the construction of temporal logics. The structure can be either linear or branching, either discrete or continuous, and either point-based or interval-based. These structures can be selected according to concrete application. The structure of time adopted in PLTL is linear, discrete and point-based. A semantic interpretation of PLTL is an infinite sequence $\sigma = s_0, s_1, s_2, \ldots$, where each $s_i$ represents a valuation for propositional variables. Use $\sigma^{(i)}$ to denote the sequence $s^i, s^{i+1}, \ldots$ and use $\sigma \models w$ to denote that the value of formula w under valuation $\sigma$ is truth; semantics of temporal operators is defined as follows:

$\sigma \vDash \square w$ iff $\sigma^{(i)} \vDash w$ for any $i \geq 0$

$\sigma \vDash \Diamond w$ iff $\sigma^{(i)} \vDash w$ for some $i \geq 0$

$\sigma \vDash \circ w$ iff $\sigma^{(1)} \vDash w$

$\sigma \vDash w_1 \mathbf{Y} w_2$ iff there is some $i \geq 0$ such that $\sigma^{(1)} \vDash w_2$ and $\sigma^{(j)} \vDash w_1$ for any $0 \leq j < i$

Development of temporal logic is closely related to specification and validation of programs. The behavior of programs is in fact a family of dynamic phenomenon. During the execution of a program, states are changing with time as well as the environment is affected by the execution. Dynamic behaviors, especially for reactive and concurrent programs which will not terminate, are out of the specifying ability of classical logics as well as the Horn logic. Therefore, in 1974, it is firstly proposed by R. Burstall to specify and reason about programs with modal logic. A temporal logic system which can be used to specify and validate programs was firstly built by A. Pnueli and Z. Manna.

Properties of programs, including safety properties (such as partial correctness, invariant, mutual exclusion, and absence of deadlock), liveness properties (such as termination, total correctness, and response) and precedence properties, can all be described with temporal logic. Therefore, temporal logic provides a powerful formal tool for the study of reactive and concurrent programs which will not terminate (such as operation systems, network communication protocols, etc.). It has been extensively used in the specification, validation and development of programs, as well as in almost every topic related to the development of concurrent programs, such as synthesis of programs and combination of specifications. Temporal logic can also be used to specify and validate real-time systems, with the help of introducing a global clock or adding some restrictions of time to temporal operators.

## 16.5 Nonmonotonic Logic

Driven by the development of the intelligence science, various non-classical logics were preposed and studied since the eighties of the last century. Nonmonotonic is one of these logics (McDermott, 1980).

The human understanding of the world is a dialectical developing process which obeys the negation-of-negation law. During the cognitive process, man's understanding of the objective world is always uncertain and incomplete; it will be negatived or completed as while as some new knowledge is acquired. As pointed by Karl Popper, the process of scientific discovery is a process of falsification. Under certain condition and environment, every theory always has its historical limitations. Along with the increase of human understands of the world and along with the development of scientific research, old theories will not meet the new needs and will be overthrew by the new discovery; upon that, old theories are negated and new theories are born. In this sense, the growth of human knowledge is in fact a nonmonotonic development process.

Classical logics such as the formal logic and the deductive logic are all monotonic in their dealing with the human cognitive process. With these logics, new knowledge acquired according to rigorous logic inference must be consistent with the old knowledge. In another word, if there is a knowledge base A and it is known that A implies the knowledge B, i.e. A→B, then the knowledge B can be inferenced by these logics. However, as stated above, human cognitive process is in fact nonmonotonic and is not consistent with such a process at all.

Nonmonotonic reasoning is characterized by the fact that the theorem set of an inference system is not monotonic increased along with the progress of inference. Formally, let F be the set of knowledge holded by humans at some stage of the cognitive process, and let $F(t)$ be the corresponding function on time t. Then the set $F(t)$ is not monotonic increased along with the progress of time. In another word, $F(t_1) \subseteq F(t_2)$ is not always holds for any $t_1 < t_2$. At the same time, human understanding of the world is in fact enhanced. A basic reason for such a phenomenon is the incomplete knowledge base used in the reasoning process. Nonmonotonic logic is a family of tools for the processing of incomplete knowledge.

Inference rules used in monotonic logics are monotonic. Let $\Gamma$ be the set of inference rules of a monotonic logic, then the language $Th(\Gamma) = \{A \mid \Gamma \rightarrow A\}$ determined by these rules holds the following monotonicity:

(1) $\Gamma \in Th(\Gamma)$
(2) if $\Gamma_1 \subseteq \Gamma_2$, then $Th(\Gamma_1) \subseteq Th(\Gamma_2)$
(3) $Th(Th(\Gamma)) = Th(\Gamma)$    (idempotence)

Where (3) is also called as fixed point. A marked feature of monotonic inference rules is that the language determined by them is a bounded least fixed point, i.e., $Th(\Gamma_1) = \cap \{s \mid \Gamma_1 \rightarrow S \text{ and } Th(S) = \Gamma_2\}$.

In order to deal with the property of nonmonotonic, the following inference rule is introduced:

(4) if $\Gamma \neg \not\vdash P$, then $\Gamma \mid\sim MP$

Here M is a modal operator. The rule states that if $\neg P$ can not be deduced from $\Gamma$, then P is in default treated as true.

It is obvious that a fixed point $Th(\Gamma) = \Gamma$ can not be guaranteed any more as while as the inference rule (4) is incorporated into monotonic inference systems. In order to solve this problem, we can first introduce an operator NM as follows: for any first-order theory $\Gamma$ and any formula set $S \subseteq L$, set

(5) $NM\Gamma(S) = Th(\Gamma \cup AS\Gamma(S))$

Where $AS\Gamma(S)$ is a default set of S and is defined as follows:

(6) $AS\Gamma(S) = \{MP \mid P \in L \wedge P \in S\} - Th(\Gamma)$

Then, $Th(\Gamma)$ can be defined as the set of theorems that can be deduced from $\Gamma$ nonmonotonically, i.e.,

(7) $Th(\Gamma) =$ the least fixed point of $NM\Gamma$

Rule (7) is designed to blend the inference rule (4) into the first-order theory $\Gamma$ so that reasoning can be carried out with a closed style. However, since the definition of $Th(\Gamma)$ is too strong, not only the calculation but also the existence of $Th(\Gamma)$ can not be guaranteed. Therefore, definition of $Th(\Gamma)$ is revised as follows:

(8) $Th(\Gamma) = \cap(\{L\} \cup \{S \mid NM\Gamma(S) = S\})$

Now, let L be the language determined by these rules, then L must be a fixed point according to $NM\Gamma(L) = L$.

Furthermore, according to these rules, $\Gamma$ is inconsistent if $Th(\Gamma)$ does not exist. The definition of $Th(\Gamma)$ presented in (8) can also be rewrited as follows:

(9) $Th(\Gamma) = \{P \mid \Gamma \mid\sim P\}$

where $\Gamma \mid\sim P$ represent $P \in Th(\Gamma)$. We also use $FP(\Gamma)$ to denote the set $\{S \mid NM\Gamma(S) = S\}$ and call each element of this set as a fixed point of the theory $\Gamma$.

There are three major schools on nonmonotonic reasoning: the circumscription theory proposed by McCarthy, the default logic proposed by Reiter, and the autoepistemic logic proposed by Moore. In the circumscription theory, a formula S is true with respect to a limited range if and only if S cannot be proved to be true w.r.t. a bigger range. In the default logic, "a formula S is true in default" means that "S is true if there is no evidence to prove the false of S". In the autoepistemic logic, S is true if S is not believed and there are no facts which are inconsistent with S.

Various nonmonotonic logic systems have beed proposed by embracing the nonmonotonic reasoning into formal logics. These nonmonotonic logics can be roughly divided into two categories: nonmonotonic logics based on minimization, and nonmonotonic logics based on fixed point. Nonmonotonic logics based on minimization can again be devided into two groups: one is these based on the minimization of model, such as the logic with the closed world assumption and the circumscription proposed by McCarthy, and the other is these based on the minimization of knowledge model, such as the ignorance proposed by Konolige. Nonmonotonic logics based on fixed point can be devided into default logics and autoepistemic logics. The nonmonotonic logic NML proposed by McDermott and Doyle is a general default logic and was used for study the general foundation of nonmonotonic logics, and the default logic proposed by Reiter is a first-order formalization of default rules. Autoepistemic logic was firstly proposed by Moore to solve the so-called Hanks-McDermott problem on nonmonotinic logics.

## 16.6 Dynamic Description Logic

### *16.6.1 Description logic*

Description logic is a kind of formalization of knowledge representation based on object, and it is also called concept representation language or terminological logic (Baader et al., 2003). Description logic is a decidable subclass of first-order logic. It has well-defined semantics and possesses strong expression capability. One description logic system consists of four parts: constructors which represent concept and role, TBox subsumption assertion, ABox instance assertion, and reasoning mechanism of TBox and ABox. The representation capability and reasoning capability of description logic system lie on aforementioned four elements and different hypothesis.

There are two essential elements, i.e. concept and role, in description logic. Concept is interpreted as subclass of domain. Role represents interrelation between individuals, and it is a kind of binary relation of domain set.

In certain domain, a knowledge base K = <*T*, A> consists of two parts: TBox T and ABox A. TBox is a finite set of subsumption assertions, and it is also called terminological axiom set. The general format of subsumption assertion is $C \sqsubseteq D$, where $C$ and $D$ are concepts. ABox is a finite set of instance assertions. Its format is $C(a)$, where $a$ is individual name; or its format is P(a,b), where P is a primitive role, $a$ and $b$ are two individual names.

In general, TBox is an axiom set which describes domain structure, and it has two functions: one is to introduce concept name, the other is to declare subsumption relationship of concepts. The process of introducing concept name is expressed by $A \doteq C$ or $A \sqsubseteq C$, where $A$ is the concept which is introduced. The format of subsumption assertion on concepts is $C \sqsubseteq D$. As to concept definition and subsumption relation definition, the following conclusion comes into existence:

$C \doteq D \Leftrightarrow C \sqsubseteq D$ and $C \sqsubseteq D$.

ABox is an instance assertions set, and its function is to declare attribute of individual or relationship of individuals. There are two kinds of format: one is to declare the relationship of individual and concept, the other is to declare the relationship of two individuals. In ABox, as to arbitrary individual a and concept C, the assertion which decides whether individual a is member of concept C is called concept instance assertion, i.e. concept assertion. $a \in C$ is denoted as $C(a)$; $a \notin C$ is denoted as $\neg C(a)$.

Given two individuals $a$, $b$ and a role $R$, if individual $a$ and individual $b$ satisfy role $R$, then $aRb$ is role instance assertion, and it is denoted as $R(a, b)$.

In general, according to the constructor provided, description logic may construct complex concept and role based on simple concept and role. Description logic includes the following constructors at least: intersection ($\sqcap$), union($\sqcup$), negation($\neg$), existential quantification($\exists$), and value restriction($\forall$). The description logic which possesses these constructors is called ALC. Base on ALC, different constructors may be added to it, so that different description logics may be formed. For example, if number restrictions "$\leq$" and "$\geq$" are added to the description logic ALC, then a new kind of description logic ALCN is formed. Table 16.1 shows the syntax and semantics of description logic ALC (Schmidt-Schauß et al., 1991).

Table 16.1 Syntax and semantics of ALC

| Constructor | Syntax | Semantics | Example |
|---|---|---|---|
| Primitive concept | A | $A^I \subseteq \Delta^I$ | Human |
| Primitive concept top | P | $P^I \subseteq \Delta^I \times \Delta^I$ | has-child |
| | T | $\Delta^I$ | True |
| Bottom | | $\Phi$ | False |
| intersection | C⊓D | $C^I \cap D^I$ | Human ⊓ Male |
| Union | C⊔D | $C^I \cup D^I$ | Doctor ⊔ Lawyer |
| Negation | ¬$C$ | $\Delta^I - C^I$ | ¬Male |
| Existential quantification | ∃$R.C$ | $\{x \mid \exists\, y, (x, y) \in R^I \wedge y \in C^I \}$ | ∃has-child.Male |
| Value restriction | ∀$R.C$ | $\{x \mid \forall\, y, (x, y) \in R^I \Rightarrow y \in C^I \}$ | ∀has-child.Male |

An interpretation $I = (\Delta^I, \cdot^I)$ consists of a domain $\Delta^I$ and an interpretation function $\cdot^I$, where interpretation function $\cdot^I$ maps each primitive concept to subset of domain $\Delta^I$, and maps each primitive role to subset of domain $\Delta^I \times \Delta^I$. With respect to an interpretation, concept of ALC is interpreted as a domain subset, and role is interpreted as binary relation.

(1) An interpretation I is a model of subsumption assertion $C \sqsubseteq D$, if and only if $C^I \subseteq D^I$;

(2) An interpretation I is a model of $C(a)$, if and only if $a \in C^I$; an interpretation I is a model of $P(a, b)$, if and only if $(a, b) \in P^I$;

(3) An interpretation I is a model of knowledge base K, if and only if I is a model of each subsumption assertion and instance assertion of knowledge base K;

(4) If knowledge base K has a mode l, then K is satisfiable;

(5) As to each model of knowledge base K, if assertion $\delta$ is satisfiable, then we say that knowledge base K logically implicate $\delta$, and it is denoted as $K \vDash \delta$;

(6) As to concept C, if knowledge base K has a model $I$, and $C^I \neq \varnothing$, then concept C is satisfiable. The concept C of knowledge base K is satisfiable if and only if K $\nvDash C \sqsubseteq \bot$.

The basic reasoning problems of description logic include concept satisfiability, concept subsumption relation, instance checking, consistency checking and so on, where the concept satisfiability is the most basic reasoning problem, other reasoning problem may be reduced to concept satisfiability problem.

In description logic, reasoning problem may be reduced to concept satisfiability problem through the following properties. As to concept $C$, $D$, there exists the following proposition:

(1) $C \sqsubseteq D \Leftrightarrow C \sqcap \neg D$ is unsatisfiable;

(2) $C \doteq D$ (concept $C$ and $D$ are equivalent) $\Leftrightarrow$ both $(C \sqcap \neg D)$ and $(D \sqcap \neg C)$ are unsatisfiable;

(3) $C$ and $D$ are disjoint $\Leftrightarrow C \sqcap D$ is unsatisfiable.

### 16.6.2 *The dynamic description logic DDL*

Dynamic description logic DDL is formed through extending traditional description logic, while traditional description logic has many species. The dynamic description logic DDL studied here is based on description logic ALC (Schmidt-Schauß et al., 1991).

**Definition 1** The primitive symbols in DDL are:
concept names: $C_1, C_2, \ldots$;
role names: $R_1, R_2, \ldots$;
individual constant: $a, b, c, \ldots$;
individual variable: x, y, z, ...;
concept operator: $\neg$, $\sqcap$, $\sqcup$ and quantifier $\exists$, $\forall$;
formula operator: $\neg$, $\wedge$, $\rightarrow$ and quantifier $\forall$;
action names: $A_1, A_2, \ldots$;
action constructs: ;(sequence), $\cup$(choice), $^*$(iteration), ?(test);
action variable: $\alpha$, $\beta$, ...;
formula variable: $\varphi$, $\psi$, $\pi$, ...;
state variable: $u, v, w, \ldots$.

**Definition 2** Concepts in DDL are defined as follows:
Primitive concept P, top $\top$ and bottom $\bot$ are concepts;
If $C$ and $D$ are concepts, then $\neg C$, $C \sqcap D$, and $C \sqcup D$ are concepts;

If $C$ is concept and $R$ is role, then $\exists R.C$ and $\forall R.C$ are concepts;
If $C$ is concept and $\alpha$ is action, then $[\alpha]C$ is action too.

**Definition 3** Formulas in DDL are defined as follows, where C is concept, $R$ is role, a, b are individual constants, and x, y are individual variables:
(1) $C(a)$ and $R(a, b)$ are called assertion formulas;
(2) $C(x)$ and $R(x, y)$ are called general formulas;
(3) Both assertion formulas and general formulas are all formulas;
(4) If $\varphi$ and $\psi$ are formulas, then $\neg\varphi$, $\varphi\wedge\psi$, $\varphi\rightarrow\psi$, and $\forall x\varphi$ are all formulas;
(5) If $\varphi$ is formula, then $[\alpha]\varphi$ is also formula.

**Definition 4** A finite set of $\{a_1/x_1, \ldots, a_n/x_n\}$ is an instance substitution, where $a_1, \ldots, a_n$ are instance constants which are called substitution items, $x_1, \ldots, x_n$ are variables which are called substitution bases, $x_i \neq x_j$ for each pair $i, j$ in $\{1, \ldots, n\}$ such that $i \neq j$.

**Definition 5** Let $\varphi$ be a formula, let $x_1, \ldots, x_n$ be all the variables occurring in $\varphi$, and let $a_1, \ldots, a_n$ be instance constants. If $\varphi'$ is a substitution result of $\varphi$ with $\{a_1/x_1, \ldots, a_n/x_n\}$, then $\varphi'$ is called a instance formula of $\varphi$.

**Definition 6** A condition in DDL is an expression of the form: $\forall C$, $C(p)$, $R(p, q)$, $p=q$ or $p\neq q$, where $N_C$ is a set of individual constants, $N_X$ is a set of individual variables, $N_I$ is the union $N_C$ and $N_X$, p,q$\in N_I$, $C$ is concept of DDL, and R is role of DDL.

**Definition 7** An action description is of the form $A(x_1,\ldots,x_n) \equiv (P_A, E_A)$, where,
(1) $A$ is the action name;
(2) $x_1, \ldots, x_n$ are individual variables, which denote the objects on which the action operates;
(3) $P_A$ is the set of *pre-conditions*, which must be satisfied before the action is executed, i.e. $P_A = \{con \mid con \in condition\}$;
(4) $E_A$ is the set of *post-conditions*, which denotes the effects of the action; $E_A$ is a set of pair head/body, where head= $\{con \mid con \in condition\}$, body is a condition.
Remarks:
(1) Action defines the transition relation of state, i.e. an action $A$ transits a state $u$ to a state $v$, if action $A$ can produce state $v$ under state $u$. The transition relation

depends on whether states $u$, $v$ satisfy the *pre-conditions* and *post-conditions* of action $A$. The transition relation is denoted as $u\ T_A\ v$.

(2) Because some states that happened before action $A$ may influence *post-condition* of action $A$, there is some difference between *pre-conditions* and *post-conditions*. As to post-conditions *head/body*, if each condition of *head* can be satisfied in state $u$, then each condition of body can also be satisfied in state $v$.

**Definition 8** Let $A(x_1,...,x_n) \equiv (P_A, E_A)$ be a action description and let $A(a_1, ..., a_n)$ be the substitution of $A(x_1, ..., x_n)$ by $\{a_1/x_1, ..., a_n/x_n\}$. Then $A(a_1, ..., a_n)$ is called an action instance of $A(x_1, ..., x_n)$. $A(a_1, ..., a_n)$ is called atom action, $P_A(a_1, ..., a_n)$ is the precondition of $A(a_1, ..., a_n)$ and $E_A(a_1, ..., a_n)$ is the result set of $A(a_1, ..., a_n)$.

**Definition 9** Actions in DDL are defined as follows:
(1) Atomic action $A(a_1, ..., a_n)$ is action;
(2) If $\alpha$ and $\beta$ are actions, then $\alpha;\beta$, $\alpha\cup\beta$, and $\alpha*$ are all actions;
(3) If $\varphi$ is an assertion formula, then $\varphi?$ is action.

For detailed semantics of the dynamic description logic DDL, please consult the paper by Zhongzhi Shi et. al(Shi et al. 2005).

## 16.7 Inductive Logic

It is general for any deductive inference that the premises logically entail the conclusion, i.e., the truth of the premises guarantees the truth of the conclusion. However, such relationships do not hold for premises and conclusions of inductive inference. A conclusion of inductive inference may be out of the scope of the premises, and therefore it may not be truth even if the premises hold. Inductive logic is a family of logics for reasoning about probabilities.

The earliest idea of inductive logic can be traced back to ancient times. Logics studied in ancient China, ancient India and ancient Greece all touched upon the conception of induction. According to the record, in a lost writing named *Nomos*, some problems on induction and analogy were studied by the ancient Greece philosopher Democritus. After Democritus, cognitive methods based on induction were used by both Soocrates and Plato. A more detailed study on induction was carried out by Aristotle. Not only the perfect induction, but also the simple enumerative induction, as well as the induction as a scientific cognitive method, were all studied by Aristotle.

From the end of the 16th century to the early 18th century, modern science formed together with the establishment of European capitalist system and the development of production capability. New logic tools were demanded by the development of science, especially by the development of experimental science. Under these circumstances, classical inductive logic emerged. The founder of classical inductive logic is the British philosopher Francis Bacon, whose primary work on philosophy and logic is the book *New Organon*. Bacon divided induction into three stages. Firstly, collect empirical materials as much as possible. Both experiment and observation are approaches to collect empirical materials, and therefore are bases for the induction. Secondly, arrange and array these empirical materials. Bacon proposed the famous *three table method* for this phase, where the first table is about the presence of certain properties, the second table is about the absence of certain properties, and the third table is about the degrees of presence or absence. The last phase concentrates on the process of exclusions.

The British logician John Stuort Mill of 19th century is a famous researcher on classical inductive logic. He inherited and developed induction theories of Bacon, Herschel and Whewell, and in his masterpiece *A System of Logic* discoursed five methods for determining causal connections between appearances. These five methods are also called five canons of induction, including the method of agreement, the method of difference, the joint method of agreement and difference, the method of concomitant variation, and the method of residues. These five methods are refinement and normalization of the three table method of Bacon and the cause and effect decision of Herschel.

As while as classical inductive logic was developed forward in the 18th century, it was questioned by the British philosopher D. Hume as follows: were there any rational foundations for induction and how to defend the rationality of induction? Hume's answer was that it was impossible to defend the rationality of induction, the induction was not rational, and induction was just a mental instinct of human beings. Hume thought that all the inferences could be divided into two families. One family was inferences about thoughts and had the property of inevitability; the other family was inferences about experiential facts and had the property of probability. Hume thought that the order of induction was to deduce what would happen according to what had happened. It could not be defended with the former inference, since there were not logical inevitability between the past and the future. It could not be defended with the latter inference too, otherwise would result in a vicious circle.

In 1921, based on a combination of probability theory and inductive logic, the British famous economist J. M. Keynes built the first probabilistic logic system. It indicates the birth of modern inductive logic. After that, different inductive logic systems were proposed by logicians one after another. Modern inductive logic has the following properties. Firstly, the notion of probability was introduced into inductive logic. Probabilities of inductive inference were fully recognized by researchers; in order to quantify these probabilities, it was a natural approach to adopt notations of probability. Research works of modern inductive logic were almost based on probability and statistical theories. Secondly, induction was not treated as an activity of discovering and proving universal propositions (and rules or laws) any more, but treated as the activity of examining hypotheses. Thirdly, research works on inductive logic were greatly affected by methods of mathematical logic (i.e., modern deductive logic); methods of axiomatization and formalization were introduced into the research of inductive logic, and resulted in many types of formalized inductive logic systems.

Probabilistic inference refers that, when the premises are true, the conclusion is possible but not inevitable true. A distinguished feature of modern inductive logic is the fact that it systematizes and quantifies the probabilistic inferences. After the 1930s, as while as mathematical probability theory came to maturity, probabilistic inductive logic was born and developed. In probabilistic inductive logic, probability theory is used to study and represent probabilistic inference systematically. Some inductive logic theory based on non-mathematical probability theory was also proposed in bout 1970s, and was known as *non-Pascal probabilistic inductive logic*. However, compared with classical probabilistic inductive logic (i.e., Pascal probabilistic inductive logic), non-Pascal probabilistic inductive logic was still weak on the whole and need to be improved and developed.

Any theory of classical probabilistic logic satisfies the following three axioms of mathematical probability theory:

(1) Probability of any event or proposition is always greater than or equal to 0, i.e., $P(A) \geq 0$;

(2) Probability of any inevitable event or proposition is always equal to 1;

(3) For any mutually exclusive events or propositions $A$ and $B$, it is always $P(A \vee B) = P(A) + P(B)$.

For any event or proposition $A$, the probability $P(A)$ is called an *elementary probability*. Given elementary probabilities of a certain system, the logical function of a probabilistic axiom system is just to deduce other related probabilities. However, as regards these elementary probabilities, the probabilistic axiom system tells nothing except that the sum of all the elementary probabilities of a set of mutually exclusive and exhaustive events or propositions should be equal to 1. This case is similar to that of deductive logic. Deductive logic does not tell us how to get premises whose value are true, but only guarantee that if the premises are true then propositions deduced from them are also true. Therefore, it can be seen that probabilistic axiom system is only a branch of deductive logic or mathematics. Furthermore, just like the fact that it is the work of inductive logic to study how to get premises whose value are true, the problem that how to get elementary probabilities is also the work of inductive logic. Therefore, principles for deciding elementary probabilities belong to inductive principles. These principles and the probabilistic axiom system are put together to form an extended system, i.e., a probabilistic inductive logic system. According to the difference of principles for deciding elementary probabilities and the difference of interpretations on probability, different probabilistic inductive logic systems were resulted, which further resulted in different schools of probabilistic inductive logic. Up to now, primary schools of probabilistic inductive logic includes empiricism, logicism and subjectivism.

The Hume problem, i.e., the rationality problem of induction, is still a puzzling question for modern inductive logic. Importance of this problem is reflected in the following statement: if the inductive inference which is the foundation of experiential science is not rational, then the scientific activities of human beings will become unrational. Each denomination of modern inductive logic attempted to solve the Hume problem, but until now these is not any satisfying result. Besides the Hume problem, there are still many paradoxes in modern inductive logic, such as the Raven Paradox proposed by modern logician and philosopher N. Goodman, the Green-Blue Paradox by N. Goodman, and the Raffle Paradox by H. E. Kyburg. A common characteristic of these paradoxes is as follows: starting from principles which are generally accepted by people, some logical contradictions or some results which are contrary to common science will be deduced. An important mark for measure an inductive theory is to check that whether these paradoxes can be suitably solved.

In order to solve the Hume problem as well as some paradoxes, a family of idea named local inductive logic appeared in the 1960s and the 1970s. A feature of local inductive logic is that not all the non-deduced principles and knowledge are needed to defend; what should be defended are just some principles or knowledge which is questioned by scientists. Therefore, if the rationality of some frequently used inductive principle, such as the induction by simple enumeration, is not questioned by scientists, then philosophers don't have to worry about that inductive principle. It is clear that the Hume problem and other puzzling questions are rounded by local inductive logic. Although local inductive logic made considerable promotions for the development of modern inductive logic, its philosophical value was also questioned due to such an extensive localization. The subjectivism, i.e., the Bayes subjective probabilistic inductive logic adopted another approach between local inductive logic and total inductive logic, and was developed with a more and more strong momentum. The Bayes subjective probabilistic inductive logic is representing the development trend of modern inductive logic.

### 16.7.1 *Empirical probabilistic inductive logic*

Empirical probabilistic inductive logic was proposed by H. Reichenbach in 1930s and further developed by W. Salmon and other researchers [637]. In this logic, probability was defined as the limitation of relative frequency. In order to demonstrate the rationality of inductive inference and solve the Hume problem, Reichenbach constructed a probabilistic logic system in his book *The Theory of Probability* which was published in 1953. Firstly, by adding some notations and formulas into the predicate calculus, Reichenbach built an axiom system for probability calculus. One of these notations is $\ni_p$ for probability implication, where $p$ is a variable whose value is a rational number of the range [0, 1]. Following formula can be constructed with this notation to represent probability sentences:

$$(i)(x_i \in A \ni_p y_i \in B) \tag{16.1}$$

Where $(i)$ is a universal quantifier, $A$ and $B$ are two classes. Probability implication can be treated as a relation on classes; where $A$ is called the reference class, and $B$ is called property class. Let elements of the class $A$ and the class $B$ be organized as sequences, and let there be one-to-one correspondence between elements of $A$ and $B$, then the above probability sentence can also be represent as:

$$P(A, B) = p \tag{16.2}$$

There are five probability-related axioms in Reichenbach's probability calculus. Based on these five axioms and other axioms of predicate calculus, every result of mathematical probability theory can all be deduced.

Then, Reichenbach provided a frequency interpretation for probability. Let $F^n(A, B)$ be a relative frequency as follows:

$$F^n(A, B) = \frac{N^n(A \bullet B)}{N^n(A)} \tag{16.3}$$

where
$$N^n(A) =_{df} N^n_{i=1}(x_i \in A)$$
$$N^n(A \bullet B) =_{df} N^n_{i=1}(x_i \in A) \bullet (y_i \in B)$$

Considering the ordered pair $x_i y_i$, the relative frequency $F^n(A, B)$ is trending to the limit $P$ as while as $n \to \infty$, i.e.,

$$P(A, B) = Lim_{n \to \infty} F^n(A, B) \tag{16.4}$$

Reichenbach adopted the frequency interpretation of probability to deal with inductive inference. In fact, both probability calculus and probabilistic logic are deductive. Only the process of deciding elementary probability is inductive. With the frequency interpretation, each probability is a limitation of relative frequency and therefore is a limiting frequency. Reichenbach advocated positing limiting frequency according to inspecting relative frequency. I.e., by investigating the relative frequency $F^1(A, B), F^2(A, B), ..., F^n(A, B)$, it could be posited that the limiting frequency will trend to some $F^i(A, B)$ ($1 \le i \le n$) as while as $n \to \infty$. Such a postulate might be not right; if it happened, then one should continue the investigation and posit another $F^i(A, B)$ as the limiting frequency. With this approach, Reichenbach demonstrated the rationality of the simple enumeration method as follows: if the limiting frequency $Lim_{n \to \infty} F^n(A)$ exists, then it can be determined according to applying the simple enumeration method and amend older conclusions constantly as while as making new posit. But how do we know that whether the limiting frequency exists? Reichenbach thought that we can neither assert its existence nor assert its non-existence. If the limiting frequency exists, then it can be found out ultimately. However, if it does not exist, then not only the induction method but also any other methods will make mistakes. Therefore, compared with other method, induction method was thought by Reichenbach to be the simplest and best approach. This is the proposal proposed by Reichenbach to solve the Hume problem.

### 16.7.2 Logical Bayesian sect

The most influential theory of the logical Bayesian sect is the probabilistic logic theory proposed by R. Carnap. In this theory, Carnap divided the probability into probability 1 and probability 2, where probability 2 is a frequency interpretation, and probability 1 is a logical probability for representing the degree on how the evidence can corroborate the hypothesis. Carnap thought that the concept of logical probability is the base of every inductive inference. Consequently he thought that if some satisfying definition and theory can be found for logical probability, then an explicit and reasonable foundation can be provided for solving arguments on inductive inference ultimately. Carnap constructed a probabilistic logic system in a rigorous logical form. Given a language $L$, Carnap assumed that all the initial propositional function items of it were in the form $P_i(x_i)$, and all the elementary sentences of $L$ can be formed by substituting initial predicates and individual constants of $L$ into these function items. A state description was a conjunction expression in which each elementary sentence of $L$, or negation of this elementary sentence, occurs. Therefore every two state descriptions were inconsistent. Let there be an assignment of non-negative numbers to each state description, in such a way that the sum of these numbers is equal to 1; then these non-negative numbers are called measurements of these state descriptions. For any proposition $P$, the range of it was defined as the set of all state descriptions for states where $P$ holds; the proposition $P$ can also be represented as a conjunction of all of these state descriptions, and correspondingly, the sum of measurements of these state descriptions forms a measurement of $P$. Let $m(e)$ be the measurement of a proposition $e$. Then $m(e)$ was called the prior probability of $e$. Furthermore, let $c(h, e)$ be the degree of corroboration on proposition $e$ to proposition $h$, then it was

$$c(h,e) = \frac{m(h \wedge e)}{m(e)} \tag{16.5}$$

I.e., the degree of corroboration of $h$ on the basis of $e$ is defined as the quotient of dividing the prior probability of the conjunction of $h$ and $e$ by the prior probability of $e$. Here $c(h, e)$ was also called corroboration function or simply $c$-function. Now, a key point of Carnap's theory was how to assign non-integers to state descriptions. A simple approach was to assign the same measurement to every state description of a language $L$. However, this approach would result in $c(h, e)=m(e)$, i.e., the degree of corroboration of $h$ on the basis of $e$ is equal to the prior probability of $h$ always. It was obvious the result that Carnap did not want.

Therefore, Carnap introduced the concept *structural description*, which was defined as the conjunction of those state descriptions which can be translated into each other according to exchanging names of individual constants. Based on this new concept, one can firstly assign the same measurement to every structural description, and then share the measurement equally between state descriptions contained in each structural description. This approach avoided the difficulty of the former approach although it was far from perfect. At first Carnap believed that these was only one reasonable *c*-function, but he later found that some parameter $\lambda$ can be introduced, and that there is a *c*-function for each value of $\lambda$ ranging from 0 to $+\infty$; furthermore, a continuous set on corroboration functions can be reached according to different values of $\lambda$.

### 16.7.3 Subjective Bayesian sect

Both the frequency interpretation and the logical interpretation are objective measurements of probability. In fact, subjective beliefs and expectations are important factors for predicating the occurrence of random events, and these predications cannot be carried out without the involvement of human's mental factors. Therefore, it is natural for a subjective interpretation of probability. The subjective interpretation of probability is also called subjective probability, and is a measurement of subjective beliefs and expectations. As early as 1926, F. P. Ramsey had carried out some research works on the subjective interpretation which was related to inductive inference. Many researchers after Ramsey were affected by this works. For example, Carnap attempted to study probabilistic inductive logic from objective angels, but he found it was still unavoidable to deal with problems of subjective probability. In 1962, based on a combination of inductive logic and rational decision, Carnap studied the problem of subjective probability. Carnap introduced a *credence function* $Cr_X(h,T)$ to represent some person $X$'s actual degree of belief in some proposition $h$ at some time $T$. If $A$ is $X$'s total body of knowledge at the time $T$, and $X$'s degree of belief in $h$ depend merely on $A$, then $Cred_X(h, A)$ was called a *credibility function*, which represented the degree of belief that $X$ would have in $h$ in the case that $X$'s total body of knowledge is $A$. Carnap found out the following relation between credence function and credibility function:

$$Cr_X(h,T) = Cred_X(h, K(T)) \tag{16.6}$$

Where $K(T)$ is a conjunction of all the knowledge of $X$ before the time $T$. Based on these functions, Carnap reinterpreted the logical probability as rational credibility function, with an attempt to coordinate subjective factors with objective factors in an inductive logic. Research works on probability logics were further put forward by these works.

Researchers of subjective Bayesian sect think that the degree of belief can be determined freely by any agents. In another word, for the same even or proposition, different agents can choose different degrees of belief ranging from 0 to 1. A set of some agent's degrees of belief is consistent if and only if it obeys every axioms and rules of probability theory (e.g., the degree of belief in $P$ plus the degree of belief in the negation of $P$ should be 1). If a set of some person's degrees of belief is inconsistent, then this person might lose every betting. For some agent to win every betting, a necessary and sufficient condition is that every rule of probability calculation is satisfied by the set of degrees of belief. This result was also called by G. Levi as the *Dutch Book theorem*. In fact, not all the sets of degrees of belief are consistent. Therefore, what discussed by researchers of subjective Bayesian sect are the degrees of belief of rational and ideal persons, and are called *rational degrees of belief*.

With respect to a certain event or proposition, there are more than one set of degrees of belief which are rational. If there are two sets that both of them satisfy quantitative relations specified by elementary laws of probability theory, then it cannot be determined which one is more rational. It is obviously an unsatisfying result. Therefore, De Finetti introduced the concept of *sequence of exchangeable events*, and proposed a theorem on exchangeable events. According to De Finetti, if events of a sequence are admitted by agents to be exchangeable and these agents willing to learn by experience, then, even if they hold different degrees of belief in the occurrence of a same event, given a enough long part of this sequence as evidences, they will reach the same degree of belief in the occurrence of future events.

### 16.7.4 Conditional inductive logic

Conditional inductive logic was firstly proposed by the British philosopher C. D. Broad, and systematically studied and further developed by G. H. Von Wright. Fundamental ideal of conditional inductive logic is as follows. Firstly, for each conditional implication, a rigorous logic analysis is carried out for its first component, consequent, and the relation between first component and consequent. As a result, a rigorous logic system is constructed. Secondly, taken this logic as a tool, some conditional illuminations and processes are carried out for the method of agreement, the method of difference, and the joint method of agreement and difference which were proposed by John Stuort Mill. As a result, an inductive logic theory based on deductive conditional sentences is built up.

Mill's inductive method focuses on seeking the causal connection between appearances. However, in the language of daily life, there are many meaning for the word "cause". Furthermore, Mill's inductive method is lack of logical accuracy and formal tightness. Towards this problem, Wright and other researchers constructed conditional logic systems according to the following steps. Firstly, causal connections were described with the help of general conditional implications. Secondly, concepts such as the sufficient condition, the necessary condition, and the necessary and sufficient condition were formally defined. Thirdly, a series of theorems were proposed and proved for conditional relations or for the deduction of conditional relations. Based on this conditional logic system, Wright and other researchers employed the fundamental principles of conditional logic to deal with Mill's eliminative induction. They reduced every possibility of the cause into three kinds, i.e., the sufficient condition, the necessary condition, and the necessary and sufficient condition, and expressed some statements of causal connections as universal conditional sentences. As a result, the eliminative induction was translated to the problem of identifying the conditions for the existence of something. More precisely, given a phenomenon which was being studied, all the possible sufficient conditions (or necessary conditions, or necessary and sufficient conditions) for the existence of it were firstly listed in a table; then using some suitable method to rule out these conditions one by one until only one condition was left; finally, the remaining condition was just the sufficient condition (or necessary condition, or necessary and sufficient condition) for this phenomenon. Here the procedure of ruling out possible conditions was a deductive inference procedure.

Conditional inductive logic provides a relatively rigorous logic form and structure for Mill's eliminative induction. However, it was still a problem to be discussed that whether universal propositions of the form $(x)(Fx \supset Gx)$ were suitable for representing the order of nature and the law of causation. Towards this problem, any researchers advocated to introducing new connectives for the statement of cause and effect. Another problem was how to list the table before applying the eliminative induction, with an assumption that the condition which was looking for should be contained in the table. Towards this problem, Wright provided a fussy and complicated approach. In fact, this is a problem of experience, and should be left to concrete researchers. The last problem is that, even a table was listed by a researcher according to his experience and a finally result was obtained according to the use of exclusive method, this research was still not sure about the result absolutely.

### 16.7.5 *Inductive logic of non-pascal probability*

The concept of inductive logic of non-Pascal probability was firstly formally stated by L. J. Cohen in 1977, but research works on it can in fact be traced back to G. Shackle. Here the Pascal probability theory refers to classical probability theories which are characterized by a theorem $P(\neg H) = 1-P(H)$; this theorem is also called the law of negation or the law of complementation. Non-Pascal probabilistic inductive logic is characterized by the fact that this theorem does not hold in it.

In the book named *Expectation in Economics*, G. Shackle proposed the concept of non-distributed uncertainty and provided a subjectivist interpretation for it, and based on them set up those rules which were later called calculation rules of non-Pascal probability (Shackle, 1979). Let $h$ be any event or hypothesis and let $M>0$, then $P_I$ is a non-Pascal probability function which satisfies the following rules:

(1) $M \geq P_I(h) \geq 0$
(2) if $P_I(h)>0$, then $P_I(\neg A) = 0$   (the law of negation)
(3) $P_I(h_1 \wedge h_2) = \min\{ P_I(h_1), P_I(h_2) \}$   (the law of conjunction)
(4) $P_I(h_1 \vee h_2) = \max\{ P_I(h_1), P_I(h_2) \}$   (the law of disjunction)

Comparing these rules with calculation rules of Pascal probability, it is obvious that here the function $P_I$ dose not satisfy the law of complementation in Pascal probability theory.

Since non-Pascal probability does not satisfy the law of complementation, a hypothesis will never be negated thoroughly if it was ever supported with a degree above 0. Furthermore, if a hypothesis was ever supported with a high degree (such as 4/5) in an experiment $t_i$, then any negative experiment after $t_i$ will never reduce the supporting degree of this hypothesis. Such a result is obviously violative with practical situations of scientific test. To sum up, compared with Pascal probability theory, non-Pascal probability theory and the corresponding inductive logic are still underripe in both syntax and semantics. Many research works are needed for their improvement and development.

# Chapter 17

# Prospects

The 21st century will be the century of intelligence revolution and we are marching toward the entrance of the intellectual era along the information superhighway. Hi-Tech of regarding intelligence science and technology as core, taking life sciences as the leading factor, will raise a new revolution in the science and technology (i.e., intelligent technology revolution). Especially, intelligent technology, biotechnology are combined with nanotechnology, and the machine brain with biological characteristic are developed. It will be the breach of high technical revolution in 21st century. The biological machine brain with very small size, homogeneous with organism, able to be plant into the human brain and become man-machine homobium, will really bring a new era in which human and machine think together.

## 17.1 Intelligent Computers

Since J. W. Mauchly and J. P. Eckert from the University of Pennsylvania made the world's first electronic computer ENIAC in 1946, the development of computer has undergone four generations, i.e., four development stages:

The first generation was from 1946 to the late 1950s, whose main characteristics are: the host uses vacuum tube devices, and the main memory is composed of magnetic drum and magnetic core memory. They are mainly used for scientific computing, and the software is programmed with the machine programming language and symbol language. These systems are alone.

The second generation was from late 1950s to middle 1960s, and its main features include: the host uses semiconductor devices, the main memory is the magnetic core memory, the magnetic drum and disk are used as auxiliary memory, and the applications are expanded to data processing. Software began to use ALGOL (Advanced Language) programming, and operating systems began to appear, the computers began to be developed in series.

The third generation is from middle 1960s to early 1970s, and its main features are: the host and the main memory are composed of the integrated circuits; the auxiliary memory is hard disk, floppy disk or tape; the operating systems have became quite perfect; software engineering emerged, and its applications got expanded with the rapid development of the terminal equipments (including remote terminals).

The characteristics of the fourth-generation electronic computer include the following aspects. Host computer and main storage are adopted extensively with the large-scale and the very large scale integrated circuit. The structure of multi-processors has already showed its advantage. Disk, magnetic card and CD become the main secondary storage. The computer system has already developed toward networking, open, and distribution. With the development of the computer's hardware and software, all kinds of computer aided systems, e.g., aided design, aided production, aided decision, aided managing, aided medical treatment, and aided instruction and so on, give full play to the enormous economic benefits and social benefit. All these four generations of electronic computers are called Von Neumann architecture structure. This kind of architecture is composed by program controllers, memory, arithmetic unit and input and output equipment. It runs in serial way on the whole. This kind of computer mainly has the following problems.

(1) It can't handle the non-numeric problem, such as symbols, graphics, characters, images, sound, etc. To process these data, it requires the high processing functions, and must realize the functions, such as pattern match, association, with the hardware.

(2) Von Neumann structure adopts the method of sequential control, which effectively uses the least hardware function to reach a high speed.

(3) Because of needing a large scale of computing, the mainframe has a high ratio of performance/price, which generally uses the large capacity and high-speed computer to handle problems centralizedly. It is a general computer with the unitary architecture structure.

(4) The greatest problem of the present computer technology is that the cost of developing software has increased constantly.

According to the requirement of control system, multimedia, database, intelligence system and numerical calculation, the new generation computer system must have the knowledge information processing system that has extensive knowledge and has the ability to deduce. It must possess the following functions.

(1) It is easy to use even if without professional knowledge. Its man-machine interface is the natural language. It possesses human general knowledge, and exchange information with many kinds of mediums.

(2) It supports the function of judging, decision-making, deducing, and studying.

(3) It has the flexible structure suitable for the multiple operations. Besides for the numerical calculation, it should be suitable for various application fields.

(4) Easy programming is the way to solve the greatest obstacle existing in the present computer technology, and it is also the key to expand the applications, such as the import of nonprocedural language, the procedure automatically produced and corrected etc.

(5) The functions are needed in the reliability, for example, keeping secret, high-reliability, self-recovery, distributed process, improving the ration of performance/price.

Turing, one of the founders of the computing theory, defined the computer as the digital computer dealing with the discrete information. There are diametrically opposed views in whether the digital computer can imitate people's intelligence. In 1937, Church and Turing independently put forward the hypothesis that people's thinking ability is equivalent with the ability of recursive function. This unproved hypothesis was described by some artificial intelligence scholars later: if a problem is referred to the Turing machine, but it cannot be solved; then the problem cannot be solved by human thinking. This school, following the philosophical tradition, inherited the rationalism and reductionism, which emphasized the huge potential of computer imitating human's thinking. Some other scholars, such as philosopher D. Refos etc, determined that the digital computer based on Turing cannot imitate people's intelligence. They believed that the digital computer only deal with information formally, whereas human intelligent activities cannot all be formed or informationized, so human intelligence couldn't be regarded as the discrete, determined operation which was dominated by environment independent rules. This school did not deny that there was possibility that materials which are similar to brain can form the intelligent machine, but this generalized intelligent machine is different from the digital computer. Some scholars thought that any machine could not simulate intelligence, but more scholars believed that most of brain activities can be analyzed by symbols and computation. It is necessary to point out that the comprehension of computation is growing day by day. Some scholars consider the process which can be accomplished as computation. The gene can be regarded as switch, and the operation of a cell can be explained by computation, which is known as molecular computation. By this means, the generalized intelligent computer has the same category as the intelligent machine.

The different views on the intelligent computer also derive from the goals and starting points. One is from the view of scientific research, which puts emphasis on the understanding of mechanism of the human brain and requires the computer to act intellectually in the same way as human being. The other is from the view of project, which emphasizes that the computer is used to solve problems that need intelligence of human and ignores whether the human brain and computer work in the same way. From the view of projects, we care about the function of intelligence computer, rather than how to realize. In other words, the intelligent computer should posses the ability of perceiving, discerning, deducing, studying etc., and should have the ability to handle qualitative, uncertain knowledge. It can also communicate with human being in natural language, words and images, and has adaptability in practical application. It will take a long way to reach this goal.

The purpose of the development of the intelligent computer is to give full play to human and computer's own features to form a complementary and coordinated man-machine cooperation environment. The not very smart intelligent computer can make a clever person cleverer. In the harmonious environment of man-machine cooperation, people are mainly responsible for offering general knowledge involved in a wide range and be engaged in the creative work, and the machine as the assistant do other work that need a certain of intelligence. The intelligent machine is often remarkable clever in some respects, and very dull-witted in other respects, so designing a intelligent system for man-machine cooperation must reasonably confirm what people are responsible for, and what the machine are responsible for, and thus we can establish a very friendly man-machine conversation interface.

The scholars in various countries have done the unremitting efforts to the study of intelligent machine. They try to make computer have intelligence or show the intellectual behavior, taking cognitive psychology, neuro-physiology, human sociology and biological evolutionism as simulating basis.

(1) Symbol processing and knowledge processing. It is the mainstream of artificial intelligence to deal with problems of intelligence as symbol processing and knowledge processing. In 1975, Professor Newill and Simon proposed a hypothesis, named physical symbol system, in the speech of Turing Prize: the physical symbol system is a sufficient requirement with behavioral intelligence. This assumption puts the symbol processing in the key position of the development of intelligent machine. In sixty, the research of reasoning mechanism and problem solving technique made people realize that the ability of a intelligent system mainly rely on the knowledge contained in the system itself, instead of the reasoning mechanism, which is known as knowledge principle advocated by professor Feigenbaum. According to this principle, the key of building the intelligent machine system is to set up the knowledge base which includes a large number of general knowledge and special knowledge, and its technological difficulties lie in the knowledge acquisition automatically, knowledge maintenance and knowledge sharing ,etc. The foundation of this route is logic theory and cognitive science.

(2) Artificial neural network. Another source of building intelligent machine is the research results of neuron-physiology. In this way, lots of relatively simple processing units (i.e., artificial neuron) are used to build the neural network computer by complicated interconnection. This route focuses on large scale concurrent, representation and treatment of distribution, non-linear systematic behavior of dynamics, training and learning of system, and treatment of analog quantity, etc. Although the current proposed model on artificial neural network and various artificial neural network systems that have already developed are very different from the neural network structure of human brain, this new approach, which replaces logical reasoning with holistic statistics behavior and replaces algorithm with sample training and learning, is a threat to traditional rationalism and reductionism. The neural network computer has potentiality in respects of pattern recognition and low level perceiving simulation etc. However, it also has the limitations. It has a certain complementary relation with the traditional symbol treatment. The combination of these two can give play to one's own advantages.

(3) Hierarchical intelligent social model. The intricate human society is made up of a lot of people and the groups of the different levels. Similarly, the intellectual behavior can also be regarded as an interaction processes which belong to different levels and parallel operating. Lower the level, worse the intelligence, and the processing of the lowest level is not an intelligent behavior.

According to this thought, the key is to figure out how the combination of unintelligent activities generates the intelligent behavior, the secret of which lies in interrelationship. This is the so-called "intelligence society" model proposed by Professor Minsky. This school puts emphasis on the understanding of intelligent hierarchy and connection of every part in the system, treats thinking and intelligence mainly from the behavior of human society, and lays particular emphasis on the distributed artificial intelligence and the complicated huge systems in its realization.

(4) Intelligent system based on biological evolution. Human intelligence is produced through the extremely long biological evolution, which is known as the source of the intelligence. If the improvement of machine intelligence is considered as an evolution process, it is much faster than the generation of human intelligence. The key of biological evolution is the adaptive capacity in the dynamic environment. Based on this view, Professor Brookes proposes another way to develop intelligent machine: set up the intelligence system with perceiving and action ability in the real world, and improve its intellectual level from simplicity to complexity. This method emphasizes the self-adapting control, and advocates the intelligence system that does not need to be expressed and inferred.

Every route described above has its own theory background and application prospect. The function of brain is the result of cooperation of hundreds and thousands of subsystems with different special functions, so it is impossible for the essence of human intelligence to come down to several structured, succinct and beautiful basic principles, such as the wave function and three laws of kinematics. The intelligent machine can not be made according to a certain fixed mode. The study of the intelligent computer should adopt the comprehensive, integrated methods. Based on the several routes described above and new possible routes, the study should integrate complementary technologies, such as qualitative and quantitative, digital and analog, logic and statistics, electronics and non-electronics, etc., especially integrating of knowledge stored in machine and prior knowledge of human being, and gives play to the whole advantage of system and comprehensive advantage.

Japan thinks the computer industry is the key factor to the economic future of their country, and knowledge will become new wealth of the country. In April of 1979, Japan gathered 60 persons from company, university, users, and other fields, and established a committee to investigate the new generation of computer. The committee is charged by professor Motooka of Tokyo University. On

October 15, 1981, Japanese Information Processing Society made a speech named "The outlook of the fifth-generation computer" on the 23rd national conference. The international conference on fifth-generation computer was held by Motooka in Tokyo of Japan on Oct. 19-22, 1981. The concept map is constructed by the application system, model system (software) and machine system (hardware). Model system is mainly divided into question solving, reasoning function and functions of management of knowledge base. The interface between model system and machine system is the key language. The whole software system will be realized in the key language, the hardware system will carry out the key language directly.

### 1. Problem solving and reasoning system

Take logic language PROLOG as the key language, and develop question solving and deducing machine. The greatest ability of the fifth-generation computer is to carry out the logic reasoning 100 million to 1 billion per second (LIPS). Every logic reasoning operation needs 100 to 1000 steps by the current computer.

### 2. Knowledge base system

Take relational database and relational algebra as basis, research and develop the knowledge base machine, meet the requirement of knowledge expressed system and extensive knowledge base system, support the storage, retrieval, updating of large-scale knowledge data. Capacity of the knowledge base machine reaches 1,000 billion bytes to 100 billion, and can retrieve the result within several seconds.

### 3. Intelligent interface system

The intelligent interface system is able to carry on man-machine communication through natural language, sound, vision, figure, characters, etc., and information can be exchanged with people in its natural way. The treatment of natural language is the foundation of machine translation. The system will include 10000 basic vocabularies and 2000 rules of grammar, and the precision of syntactic analysis can reach 99%. Research and develop the specifical hardware processor and high-performance interface apparatus to carry out treatment of sound, figure, vision data effectively.

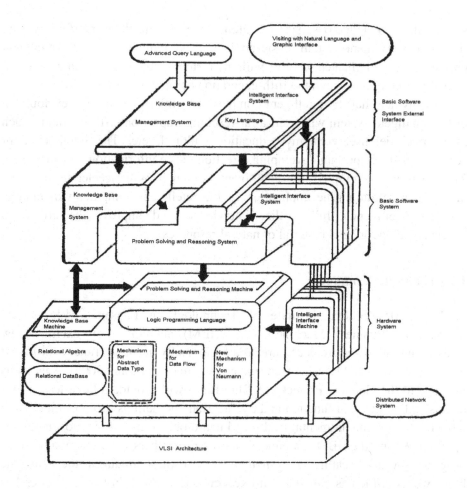

Fig. 17.1 Architecture of fifth-generation computer

Software and hardware system that have implemented the three functions mentioned above will form a common machine by combination. So, the architecture of the fifth-generation computer is shown in Fig. 17.1. This architecture is very flexible, since it not only offers the machine of common purpose, but also can form systems with special purpose that have various performance requirements. They can also form distributed processing system through network interconnection.

The Japanese planed to divide the research and development of the fifth-generation computer into five seminars, i.e., problem solving and reasoning system, the knowledge base system, intelligence man-machine interface system, support development system, basic application system. Because the intelligent problem is so complicated to solve with the former technology, Japan announced formally to stop to research the fifth-generation computer in 1992.

We convince that the intelligent computer and the research and development of the intelligent system will exert a far-reaching impact on different fields, such as national defense, economy, education, cultural, etc. The intelligence of computer is the important developing direction of the information industry in the 21st century. Developing the intelligent computer will accelerate the new industrial revolution. The application of the intelligent computer will enlarge people's intelligence, fully utilize knowledge, and improve the utilization efficiency of energy and material of natural resources.

## 17.2  Brain-like Computer

In July 2005, Federal Institute of Technology in Lausanne (EPFL) and International Business Machines Corp. (IBM) announced an exciting new research initiative - a project to create a biologically accurate, functional model of the brain using IBM's Blue Gene supercomputer (Markram, 2006). Analogous in scope to the Genome Project, the Blue Brain will provide a huge leap in our understanding of brain function and dysfunction and help us explore solutions to intractable problems in mental health and neurological disease. In November 18, 2009 on Wednesday IBM announced that its researchers have made significant progress toward creating a computer system that simulates the way the brain works, which is called brain-like computer. The brin-like computer has achieved a simulation with 1 billion neurons and 10 billion synapses using a supercomputer that has 147,456 processors. The advancement represents the first near real-time simulation of the brain that exceeds the scale of a cat's cerebral cortex, a structure within the brain that plays a key role in memory, attention and thought.

The Blue Brain Project is an attempt to reverse engineer the brain, to explore how it functions and to serve as a tool for neuroscientists and medical researchers. They intend to achieve insights into the basic nature of intelligence and consciousness using this tool, the Blue Brain Project is focused on creating a physiological simulation for biomedical applications.

A neuron's electrical properties are determined to a large extent by a variety of ion channels distributed in varying densities throughout the cell's membrane. To model the neocortical column, it is essential to understand the composition, density and distribution of the numerous cortical cell types. Each class of cells is present in specific layers of the column. The precise density of each cell type and the volume of the space it occupies provides essential information for cell positioning and constructing the foundation of the cortical circuit. Each neuron is connected to thousands of its neighbors at points where their dendrites or axons touch, known as synapses. In a column with 10,000 neurons, this translates into trillions of possible connections. The Blue Gene is used in this extremely computationally intensive calculation to fix the synapse locations.

On the basis of anatomical criteria, the cerebral cortex is divided into six layers ranging from the cortical surface to the gray matter to white matter border. The pattern of connections suggests different roles for these layers. For example, incoming connections typically contact layer IV, while layers II/III send outgoing connections to areas further down a processing stream. The simulations in this paper are based upon a model of layers II/III of the association cortex of the rat. It is an upscaled version of the model presented by Lundqvist et al. (Lundqvist, 2006).

In the neural network model each hypercolumn consists of 100 minicolumns. Each minicolumn contains 30 pyramidal cells that excite each other through short-range axons (Djurfeldt et al., 2008). Pyramidal cells project locally as well as to pyramidal cells in other minicolumns that belong to the same cell assembly and to regularspiking nonpyramidal (RSNP) cells in minicolumns belonging to other assemblies. The basket cell normalizes activity in the local hypercolumn. RSNP cells provide local inhibition of pyramidal cells. Each hypercolumn also contains a population of 100 inhibitory basket cells, which are excited by the pyramidal cells of that hypercolumn. The basket cells, in turn, inhibit the pyramidal cells of that hypercolumn, thereby providing a mechanism for normalization of activity. This enables the hypercolumn to operate like a winner-take-all module in which different patterns can compete. Each minicolumn also contains two inhibitory RSNP cells, which contact the local pyramidal cells. The abstract neural network model upon which the longrange connectivity of the present model is based suggests an additional way in which cell assemblies can compete. This competition has been realized through long-range axons from pyramidal cells to RSNP cells of minicolumns that belong to other cell assemblies. Since RSNP cells inhibit pyramidal cells within the local minicolumn, the activity of targeted assemblies will be suppressed. Such connections have not yet been identified anatomically. Connectivity is otherwise compatible with experimental data, to the extent that it is available. However, for simplicity, we have made the borders of minicolumns and hypercolumns sharp, in contrast to the local approximately Gaussian structure observed experimentally (Buzas et al., 2006).

## 17.3 Machine Brain

On the basis of understanding the human brain, the machine brain simulates and refers to all or some structure and functions of the human brain with the thought of evolving, and researches and develops the artificial system with human level intelligence. The machine brain should have characteristics of personalizing, ultra-high-speed, self-evolving, self-organizing, high parallelization etc. The computer can be used to simulate the decision-making process, and thus the artificial brain controller makes the robot cleverer. The machine brain makes its ability evolve constantly through studying. And the machine brain thinks and makes policy through the stimulus of perceiving the external environment, and makes the response to the external environment. The human brain is a highly complicated and exquisite intelligence system generated through the long-term evolution. Building the machine brain model with the intelligence similar to human needs the long-term hard work and multi-disciplinary research.

Since the forties of the 20th century, for the research on the brain model or artificial brain, researchers have made much exploration in many fields such as bionics, artificial intelligence, artificial neural network, pattern-recognition, supercomputer, etc. These researches have made many developments. Many models proposed are the simplified or local artificial brains, for example, the perceiving machine, Lenovo machine, cognition machine, consciousness machine, etc.

### 17.3.1 Cell -- Brain imitating machine

Cellar automation--CAM-Brain Machine (CBM) was a part of the artificial brain plan proposed by Evolutionary Systems Department of Kyoto Advanced Telecommunications Research (ATR) in Japan in 1993. Its goal was to develop a machine cat with the same IQ to a kitten within 8 years, including an artificial brain made up of 1 billion neurons. In the first stage, the research of the artificial brain was completed in April 1999, and carried on the formal show on November 9, 1999. In this show, the artificial brain of the machine cat has mainly adopted the artificial neural network technology, which includes about 37,700,000 artificial neurons. Although the number of artificial neurons in the artificial brain is much less than 100 billion neurons in a human brain, but its intelligence exceeds the insect (de Garis et al., 2000).

Cellar automation can be considered as a dynamic array constituted by several small units, among which every unit has the finite states. In the discrete sequences, every small unit, according to the identical rules, determines the new state by the states of its original state and the states of neighborhood units. At any moment, the pattern of the cellar automation is composed by the states of all units. The evolution from the initial pattern to the final pattern is processed by computer, and the final pattern is the result. In fact, every small unit of the cellar automation is a finite state automaton (FSA). Thus the cellar automation is the dynamic array of FSA, and the evolution process of the cellar automation is the process of parallel computing. The main function of the cellar automation is that it can simulate and handle the discrete courses and phenomenon by the local characteristics and simple consistent rules.

The cellar automation in the CAM-Brain Machine is constituted by 72 programmable array chip. Each chip includes a large number of transistors. Several transistors, as one unit, constitute a so-called cell to imitate the nerve cell and contact the dendritic and axon of this nerve cell (de Garis et al., 2000). In order to carry out some particular tasks, the neural network must have the abilities to learn, and it mainly achieves this purpose through imitating the biological evolution process of the natural brain. The cellar automation in the CAM-Brain Machine (i.e., the programmable array chip) has a characteristic different from a general chip, which can set up the internal circuit again and again, and thus high-efficiently change and filter the connecting relations among transistors. These connections relation is similar to the chromosome in the organism. When a certain connection is the best choice for the particular task, this chromosome information can be given hereditarily to the future generation. Through selecting generation by generation, the artificial brain will get the best configure automatically.

Cellar Automation in the CAM-Brain Machine is made up of 5 following subsystems:

(1) The cellar automation: the workspace adopts two same CoDi modules, and each module has 13824 cells;

(2) Genotype/phenotype memory: used as the chromosome or neural network;

(3) Evaluating fitness unit: used for evaluating the neural network;

(4) Genetic algorithm unit: used for running the genetic algorithm;

(5) Module-internal-relation memory: used for record the internal connection among 64640 pieces of CoDi module (de Garis et al., 2000).

### 17.3.2 Cognition machine model

In order to realize the fluent conversation between machine and people, the Media Laboratory of MIT in American proposed to construct a cognition machine, in which the esthesia, action, learning are imbed. Deb Roy proposed the Cross-channel Early Lexical Learning (CELL) model to understand the process that the infant learn the words in early days from many kinds of esthesia (Roy, 1999). Learning words need to search the structure of multiply input channels, so it is called cross-channel. CELL establishes a model of lexical items. A lexical item includes the specifications of the language units and the corresponding basic types of esthesia. CELL is the early stage of learning vocabularies.

### 17.3.3 Nano-based mahcine brain

In December 2001 by the U.S. National Science Foundation and the Ministry of Commerce came forward, the organization of government departments, research institutes, universities, and industry experts and academics gather in Washington specifically discuss "the convergence of technologies to enhance human capabilities" (Converging Technologies to Improve Human Performance) problem. Paper presented to the meeting and conclusions based on June 2002, the U.S. National Science Foundation and the U.S. Department of Commerce for over 468 co-sponsored the "Convergence Technical Report" (Roco and Bainbridge, 2002). The report mentions that cognitive science, biology, informatics and nano-technology for the rapid development in the current field, the four science and related technologies has been the formation of organic combination and integration of converging technologies (Converging Technologies), (English together nano-bio-info-cogno, referred to as NBIC). Cognitive areas, including cognitive science and cognitive neuroscience. Biological fields, including biotechnology, medical biotechnology and genetic engineering; the field of information, including information technology and advanced computing and communications; nanotechnology fields, including nanoscience and nanotechnology. Each of these disciplines a unique integration of research methods and technology will accelerate humanity's cognitive science and related disciplines, to promote and ultimately to promote social development.

One possible achievement of the NBIC covergence technology is constructing machine brain with high performance, high intelligence, small size and low consumption. Molecular nanotechnology operates on the molecular scale. It is especially associated with the concept of a molecular assembler producing a desired structure or device atom-by-atom.

## 17.4  Brain-Computer Interface

Brain-Computer Interface is the interface that connects the human brain or animal brain with the outside world. However, this connection is not in a normal and regular way, but in a special way to connect with the outside world, for example, stimulating the artificial cochlea, the external signal commanding mice to walk in the maze, the monkey taking bananas with the machine hand, and the brain wave controlling the computer. Someone thinks that the essence of the life is information. Since the essence of artificial brain and biological brain both are information and they have the same mechanism in the information processing, they should be able to exchange with the help of the interface. Information is uniform in essence, which will make a great development in computer techniques, artificial brain, combination of human brain and computer.

The scientists in MIT, Bell Laboratory and Institute of Nuroinformatics have successfully developed a microchip that can simulate the brain's nervous system. The microchip has been plant into the brain successfully, and utilizes the principle of bionics to repair the human nerve. It cooperates with brain and sends out the complicated orders to the electronic devices. The equipment has achieved the good performance in monitoring the activity of the brain. John France in Cambridge University thinks that, in the near future, people can put a microchip into the brain to increase memory, which makes the mankind have a spare brain.

The researchers in the American biocomputer field combine the tissue cell in brain and computer hardware to develop a new machine called the biology-electronic human or semi-robot. If the chip is identical with nerve endings, the chip can connect with the brain nervous system through the nerve fibre. The computer is able to improve people's brain function in this way.

T. Berger and J. Liaw in American University of Southern California proposed the neurocircuit model based on dynamic synapse in 1999 (Liaw et al., 1999), and developed the brain chip in 2003 that can replace hippocampi's brain. The experiment in brain chip successfully embedded in a little white mouse shows that the information processing in the circuit model and the living mouse's brain are identical. This project is a part of USA's Mind-Machine Merger plan. Wolpaw and his colleagues use a P300 event-related potential to develop brain-computer interface (Sellers et al., 2006). Lotte etc. adopt EEG to develop Brain-Computer Interfaces (Lotte et al., 2007).

## 17.5 Intelligent Robots

Based on the fact that "the computer culture" is rooted in the hearts of the people at the end of last century, the "robot culture" will have imponderable influence on the development of social productivity, the human life, work and thinking, as well as social development at the end of this century.

An intelligent robot is a remarkably useful combination of a manipulator, sensors and controls, which is capable of performing many complex tasks with seemingly human intelligence. The intelligent robot grows up from our mankind, studies our skill, and has common value standards with us, so it can be regarded as the offspring of our human thinking. The new generation robot being powerful with wider use is known as "common" robot. One of the famous authorities of the robot research field, Hans Moravec, predicts the situation of the robot in the future (Moravec, 1998). The first generation may appear in 2010. Its obvious characteristics are multifunction sentience, strong operational and mobility. The second generation will appear in 2020, with the outstanding advantage that it can learn the skill at work, and have learning ability of adaptability. The third generation of common robot will appear in 2030, with the ability of predicting. These robots can change the intention in time, if they predict that the worse result will appear. The fourth generation of common robot will appear in 2040, and this generation of robots will possess more complete deduction ability.

At present, the international robot community are strengthening the scientific research in common techniques of robot and aim to intelligence and diversification. The main research contents including the following 10 respects:

(1) Intelligence. With the robot system application environments from a structured environment to a unstructured environment and tasks from simple,

repetitive tasks to complex, uncertain, high risk, and even confrontational tasks, the perception of robot system capabilities, decision-making and control put forward higher requirements, the robot must have enough intelligence to cope with the complexity of the environment and objectives, the dynamic nature of uncertainty.

(2) The controlling technique of robot. The research focuses on the open, modular controlling system, of which the man-machine interface is much more friendly. The interface with language and graphic programming is under research. Standardization and networking of the controller of robot, and the network controller based on personal computer have already become the hot research directions. The technology of programming aims to improve effectiveness of online programming and focus on the practicality of off-line programming.

(3) Multi-sense systems. To further improve the intelligence and adaptability of the robot, the application of many kinds of sensors is the key resolution. The research emphasis lies in the feasible multi-sensors merge algorithms, especially the algorithms used in the situation of non-linear, non-steady, and non-normal distribution. Another research topic is the practical application of the sensing system.

(4) Biology-electro-mechanical mechatronics. The electro-mechanical system-based robotics integrate with biology, neuroscience, brain science etc. to develop biology - electromechanical robotic systems, both the use of organisms may be a signal controlled electromechanical system may also send control signals to the organism to control their body movements. Neural science, brain science and biology and robotics integration is likely to fundamentally change the concept of intelligent robots, fuzzy boundaries between biology and robotics.

(5) The remote control and monitor of robot, the technology of semi-autonomous and autonomous; the coordinated control between multi-robots and operator, the remote control system for large-scale through network, pre-reveal for remote control under delay condition.

(6) Virtual robot technology. Basing on multi-sensors, multimedia, virtual reality and sound-surround ambiance technique, these technologies implement virtual remote control operation of robot and human-computer interaction.

(7) Multi-agent technology. This is a new area of research for robot. The main research directions include the architecture of multi-agent, mutual communication, consultation mechanism, perception and learning, modeling and planning, and control of group behavior.

(8) Miniaturization. With MEMS technology, micro-sensors, micro-actuator, micro-controller, the development of small space work for miniaturization of robotic systems developed accordingly, such as the living body to complete testing, application, surgical robot systems, micro-nano operation of robots. The new driving method, structural design, perception and control of robotic systems will bring a whole new area.

(9) Pleasant-oriented. Robot system from the structure, perception, control, suitable to live together with others, able to work in people's living environment, safe, efficient and reliable service of human beings.

(10) Humanoid and bionic technology. This is a supreme realm of robot technical. Only some basic research has been carried on at present.

We can create a robot that is similar to human as far as possible, and then make it work in the human environment. The most important thing is to allow the robot to imitate the best possible shape and movements of humanity.

Robot World Cup (RoboCup) is a current noticeable match. It promotes the research and development of the robot. Someone predict that the football team composed of robots can defeat the professional football team in the 2050 World Cup.

## 17.6 Intelligent Internet

The Internet firstly appeared in 1960s, but it did not really cause the attention of public and grow popular until mid-1990s. In 1994, the number of world Internet users is only 13 million, while in September 30, 2009, the figure was more than 1733 million from Internet World Stats Website. During the several decades from the birth of the Internet to the present time, the explosive growth of technology is far more than any technological revolution at any time in human history. However, from the long-term development trends, the Internet is still in the initial stage of development, there is great potential for the Internet technology.

The basic characteristics of the Internet are its globalization. The hyperlinks can provide "any to any" links, which makes all the world's computers can be connected together to allow users to share the unlimited resources. However, today's Internet, after all, was designed specifically for people, and the page text, graphics, images and other media are available for people to read, and the network and the computers just play as simple intermediary tools. However, for users, due to the complex unlimited Internet resources, information overload is the biggest problem that how to effectively carry out a description, organization and management of a variety of information, data, knowledge and other resources to let the computers take full advantages of these resources to serve users. Therefore, we need to consider how to use computers to read, understand and deal with such a huge amount of resources and effectively extract information and knowledge for users and to provide users with a variety of convenient services.

Intelligent Web is another pattern of the next generation Internet, which is to effectively put Intelligence into the Web and let the computer programs with intelligence run in such dynamic and open Web environment and offer intelligent services to people. The president of W3C Berners-Lee presented a paper on semantic Web in 《 Scientific American 》 (Berners-Lee, 2001): Intelligent Internet is essentially a self-governing entity; it has automatic adjustment function; and the various sites in the network work together to ensure the effectiveness of application services. Agents are the intelligent people in the Internet, they are intelligent software entities, which are able to travel freely in the Intelligent Internet to provide users with a variety of intelligent services.

From the overall objective of Intelligent Web, it must solve the following crucial problems:

(1) The problem of semantic representation, i.e., how to effectively express and understand the various information and data in the Internet and turn them into "knowledge" possessed and then shared and processed by computers.

(2) The method that constructs the intelligent software identities and enable them to take different roles in the Intelligent Internet with intelligence, autonomy and adaptability and offer effective services to users.

(3) How to effectively manage the various resources in the Intelligent Internet and take reasonable allocation, sharing and utilization of them.

(4) As for the services provided in the Intelligent Internet, how to accurately describe them and effectively manage them so as to offer convenient service call.

(5) How to discover, extract and utilize the useful information from the Intelligent Internet so as to improve structure and utilizing efficiency of Intelligent Internet (Shi et al., 2003).

The author and his colleagues developed an Internet Intelligence Platform: Agent Grid Intelligence Platform (AGrIP). It combines the following characteristics: the simplicity of Web interface, powerful and transparent information retrieval capacity, server-based analytic system and the flexibility. AGrIP is composed with the bottom supporting platform MAGE (Multi-Agent

Environment), tool software layer and application layer. The tool software provides functions such as information retrieval, data mining, decision support and so on. First of all, the initial data are extracted from web pages, texts, and multimedia information with the Internet search tool GHunt, these data are changed into the useful information after the processing of data mining tool MSMiner, and then they are analyzed by the expert systems. Finally, the effective decision strategies are provided to the enterprises. The most crucial part is the MAGE integrating part, which effectively combines all the middleware tools into a whole system and make it a real Internet Intelligence Platform. Its system structure is showed in Figure 17.2 (Shi, 2006c).

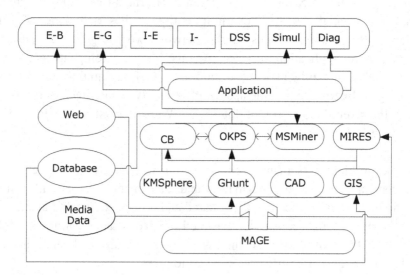

Fig. 17.2 Internet Intelligence Platform AGrIP

## 17.7 Complexity of the Brain

The human brain is the most complicated system in the known universe. It is formed by the huge quantity of neurons and synapses. The neurons and synapses both are highly complicated, highly multifarious and highly complete electronic-chemical apparatus. The beauty of thinking may just contain in the complexity of the brain. The research in neural science has revealed that a simple nervous may have the amazing complexity, which reflects that its function, evolution history, structure and encoding scheme will work on any future disciplines of the brain complexity.

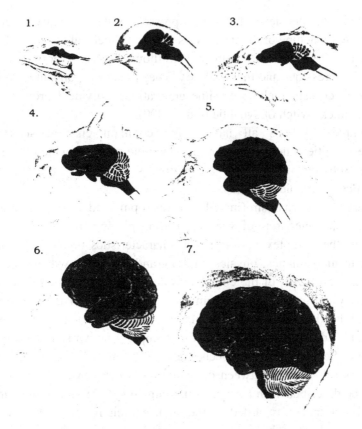

Fig. 17.3 Comparison on the size and shape of different vertebrate's brains

1. frog, 2. bird, 3. mouse, 4. cat, 5. monkey, 6. orangutan, 7. people

Choosing the L-amino acid as the construction package of the protein took place 3 billion years ago, whereas the division of race took place probably 100,000 years ago. It is very difficult to confirm, at the beginning stage of life, what happened when the information contained in one cubic micron changes from a physical system containing several bits to an original life system containing thousands of bits. Figure 17.3 shows the comparative results on the size and shape of different vertebrate's brains (the size relation between brains does not correspond to the true proportion). The change of the prefrontal cortex is particularly outstanding (Birbaumer, 1994).

Facing the survive pressure caused by acceleration evolving constantly, the strategies of the nervous system do not rely on the improvement of big biological molecule under the cell level, but it is expressed by the voluntary diversity and steady selection machine of the interaction among the cells above the cell level. It can be from 1/10 seconds to hundreds of millions of years to form dynamics of these neural expressions and their stability. They are correspondent to four pieces of time yardstick separately: germ-line generation, individual growth, learning process and quick switch of synaptic (Guo, 2000).

The complex systems all have some common characteristics. Behind changeable activities, there are a certain intangible order, in which the evolving, emergence, self-organization, self-adaptation, self-similarity are the common characteristics of complex systems.

The emergence mechanism (including catastrophic and creative emergence) is the common characteristics of various exciting phenomena, pattern and mode appearing in the complex systems. The characteristics and critical points of emergence in mathematics, physics, biology and sociology will be regarded as the important sign [210] of the complex system. The macrostructure emergence in complex system often derives from the self-organization mechanism, which has been validated in biology and sociology. Self-organization mechanism is also an important adjusting mechanism for complex network to adapt to the environment. Self-adaptation reflects the ability of self-control of complex systems. It is self-similar between complex system and every level subsystem, which can be described with fractal. In the human system, the complexity of the heart and brain can be regarded as the sign, especially the advanced function activities of the brain. The consciousness of the brain can be regarded as the whole dynamic functions of self-organizing neural systems. It is necessary to research on the dynamics foundations of colony emergence and consciousness.

# References

Aamodt, A. and Plaza, E. (1994). Case-based reasoning: foundational issues, methodological variations, and system approaches. *AI Communications* 7(1): 39-59.

Abbas, A. K., Andrew H. Lichtman, Jardan S. Pober (2003). Cellular and Molecular Immunology. W.B. Sarnders Company in the United Stated of American.

Ackley, D. H., G. E. Hinton, and T. J. Sejnowski (1985). A learning algorithm for boltzmann machines. *Cognitive Science*, Vol. 9, pp. 147-169.

Adrian, E. D. (1959). *The Mechanism of Nervous Action*. University of Pennsylvania Press, Philadelphia.

Agrawal, R, T. Imieliski, and A. Swami (1993). Mining association rules between sets of items in large database. In Proceedings of ACM SIGMOD International Conference on Management of Data (SIGMOD'93), 207-216, May.

Alonso, J. A., Borrego, J., Hidalgo, M. J., Martín, F. J. and Ruiz, J. L. (2007). A formally verified prover for the ALC description logic. In: LNCS, 4732. Springer, pp. 135-150.

Amari, Shun-ichi (1968). *A Geometrical Theory of Information* (in Japanese), Kyoritsu.

Amari, Shun-ichi (1985). *Differential Geometrical Methods in Statistics*. Springer Lecture Notes in Statistic, 28, Springer.

Amari, Shun-ichi (1994). Information geometry and manifolds of neural networks, in From Statistical Physics to Statistical Inference and Back, eds. P. Grassberger and J.-P. Nadal, Kluwer Academic Publishers, pp. 113-138.

Amari, Shun-ichi (1995). Information geometry of the EM and em algorithms for neural networks. *Neural Networks*, Vol. 8, No. 9, pp. 1379-1408.

Amari, Shun-ichi (1998). Future Perspective of 'Creating Brain' Program. ICONIP 1998: 7.

Amari, Shun-ichi (2000). Estimating functions of independent component analysis for temporally correlated signals. *Neural Computation* 12(9): 2083-2107.

Amari, Shun-ichi (2001). Information Geometry on Hierarchy of Probability Distributions, IEEE *Transactions on Information Theory*, Vol. 47, No. 5, pp. 1701-1711.

Amari, Shun-ichi (2002). Independent Component Analysis (ICA) and Method of Estimating Functions, IEICE *Trans. Fundamentals*, Vol. E85-A, No. 3, pp. 540-547.

Amari, Shun-ichi (2005). Population Coding, Bayesian Inference and Information Geometry. ISNN (1) 2005: 1-4.

Amari, Shun-ichi (2007). Integration of Stochastic Models by Minimizing *alpha*-Divergence. *Neural Computation*, 19(10): 2780-2796.

627

Amari, Shun-ichi (2008). Information Geometry and Its Applications: Convex Function and Dually Flat Manifold. Emerging Trends in Visual Computing (ETVC'08): 75-102, Paris.

Amari, Shun-ichi (2009). Measure of Correlation Orthogonal to Change in Firing Rate. *Neural Computation,* 21(4): 960-972.

Amari, S., K. Kurata and H. Nagaoka (1992). Information geometry of boltzmann machines, IEEE *Trans. on Neural Networks*, Vol. 3, No. 2, pp. 260-271.

Amari, S. and T. Ozeki (2001). Differential and Algebraic Geometry of Multilayer Perceptrons, IEICE Trans. Fundamentals, Vol. E84-A, No. 1, pp. 31-38.

Amari, S., Wu S. (1999). Improving support vector machine classifier by modifying kernel functions. *Neural Networks,* 12(1999): 783-789.

Amiez, C. and Petrides, M. (2007). Selective involvement of the mid-dorsolateral prefrontal cortex in the coding of the serial order of visual stimuli in working memory. Proceedings of the National Academy of Sciences USA, 104, 13786-13791.

Anastasio, T. J. (1991). A recurrent neural network model of velocity storage in the vestibulo-ocular reflex. Advances in Neural Information Processing Systems, Vol. 3, pp. 32-38, San Mateo, CA: Morgan Kaufmann.

Anastasio, T. J. (1993). Modeling vestibulo-ocular reflex dynamics: From classical analysis to neural networks. In F. Eeckman, ed. Neural Systems: Analysis and Modeling, pp. 407-430, Norwell, MA: Kluwer.

Anastasio, T. J. (1995).Vestibulo-ocular reflex: Performance and plasticity. In M.A. Arbib, ed. The Handbook of Brain Theory and Neural Networks, Cambridge, MA: MIT Press.

Anderson, J. A. (1972). A simple neural network generating an interactive memory. Mathematical Biosciences, Vol. 14, pp. 197-220.

Anderson, J. A., J. W. Silverstein, S. A. Ritz, and R. S. Jones (1977). Distinctive features, categorical perception, and probability learning: Some applications of a neural model. Psychological Review, Vol. 84, pp. 413-451.

Anderson, J. R. (1980). Cognitive Psychology. Freeman

Anderson, J. R. (1983). The Architecture of Cognition. Cambridge MA, Harvard University Press.

Anderson, J. R. (1993). The Adaptive Character of Thought, Hillsdale, NJ: Erlbaum.

Anderson, J. R. (1996). ACT: A simple theory of complex cognition. American Psychologist, 51, 355-365.

Anderson, J. R. (2007). How Can the Human Mind Occur in the Physical Universe? New York: Oxford University Press.

Anderson, J. R., Bothell, D., Byrne, M. D., Douglass, S., Lebiere, C., & Qin, Y. (2004). An integrated theory of the mind. Psychological Review 111, (4). 1036-1060.

Anderson, J. R., Fincham, J. M., Qin, Y., & Stocco, A. (2008). A Central circuit of the mind. Trends in Cognitive Science. 12(4), 136-143.

Anderson, J. R. & Lebiere, C. (1998). The atomic components of thought. Mahwah, NJ: Erlbaum.

Ashby, W. R. (1952). Design for a Brain. Wiley, New York.

Asperti, A, L. Padovani, C. Sacerdoti Coen, I. Schena (2001). HELM and the Semantic Math-Web. In Proc. of TPHOLS 2001, Springer-Verlag, Lecture Notes in Computer Science (LNCS) Series. http://helm.cs.unibo.it/bibliography.html.

Atkinson, R. C., & Juola, J. F. (1973). Factors influencing the speed and accuracy of word recognition. In S. Kornblum (Ed.), *Attention and Performance IV*, New York: Academic Press. pp. 583-612.

Atkinson, R. C., & Juola, J. F. (1974). Search and decision processes in recognition memory. In D. H. Krantz, R. C. Atkinson, R. D. Luce, & P. Suppes (Eds.), Contemporary developments in mathematical psychology: Vol. 1. Learning, memory and thinking. San Francisco: Freeman.

Atkinson, R. C., & Shiffrin, R. M. (1968). Human memory: A proposed system and its control processes. In K. W. Spence & J. T. Spence (Eds.), The psychology of learning and motivation: Advances in research and theory (Vol. 2). New York: Academic Press.

Ausubel, D. P., J. D. Novak, and H. Hanesian. (1978). Educational psychology: A cognitive view. 2nd edition. New York: Holt, Rinehart and Winston, Inc.

Baader, F., D. Calvanese, D. McGuinness, D. Nardi and P. Patel–Schneider (eds.) (2003). Description Logic Handbook: Theory, Implementation and Applications. Cambridge University Press.

Baddeley, A. D., Hitch, G. J. (1974). Working memory. In: Bower G A. The Psychology of Learning and Motivation [M]. New York: Academic Press, 47-89.

Baddeley, A. D. (2000). The episodic buffer: A new component of working memory? Trends in Cognitive Sciences, 4: 417-423.

Baddeley, A. D. (2001). Is working memory still working?. American Psychologist. 11: 851-864.

Baldi, P., S. Brunak (1998). Bioinformatics: the Machine Learning Approach. MIT Press.

Bandura, A. (1977). Social Learning Theory. New York: General Learning Press.

Bandura, A. (1986). Social Foundations of Thought and Action. Englewood Cliffs, NJ: Prentice-Hall.

Barlow, H. B. (1972). Single units and sensatioperceptual psychology? Perception, 1: 371-394.

Baars, Bernard (1988). *A cognitive theory of consciousness*, NY: Cambridge University Press.

Baars, Bernard (1997). In the Theater of Consciousness: The Workspace of the Mind, NY: Oxford University Press.

Barto, A. G. (1992). Reinforcement learning and adaptive critic methods. In Handbook of Intelligent Control, D. A. White and D. A. Sofge, eds., pp. 469-91, New York: Van Nostrand Reinhold.

Barto, A. G., R. S. Sutton, and C. W. Anderson (1983). Neuronlike adaptive elements that can solve difficult learning control problems. IEEE Transactions on Systems, Man, and Cybernetics, Vol. SMC-13, pp. 834-846.

Barto, A. G., S. J. Bradtke, and S. Singh (1995). Learning to act using real-time dynamic programming. Artificial Intelligence, Vol. 72, pp. 81-138.

Bashkirov, O. A., E. M. Braverman, and I. B. Muchnik (1964). Potential function algorithms for pattern recognition learning machines. Automation and Remote Control, Vol. 25, pp. 629-631.

Bell, A. J., and T. J. Sejnowski (1995). An information-maximization approach to blind separation and blind deconvolution. Neural Computation, Vol. 6, pp. 1129-1159.

Bern, S. (1998). Extracting Patterns and Relations from the World Wide Web. Proceedings of Web DB Workshop at EDBT'98, Valencia

Berners-Lee, T., Hendler, J., Lassila, O. (2001). The Semantic Web. Scientific American, May.

Bertsekas, D. P. (1995). Dynamic Programming and Optimal Control, Vol. I and Vol. II, Belmont, MA: Athenas Scientific.

Bertsekas, D. P. (1995). Nonlinear Programming, Belmont, MA: Athenas Scientific.

Bertsekas, D. P., and J.N. Tsitsiklis (1996). Neuro-Dynamic Programming, Belmont, MA: Athenas Scientific.

Biberman Y. (1994). A Context Similarity Measure. Machine Learning: ECML-94, Springer-Verlag, Berlin Heidelberg.

Birbaumer, N., Schmidt, R. F. (1996). Biologische Psychologie. Springer-Lehrbuch.

Blumer A, A. Ehrenfeucht, D. Haussler and A. Warmuth (1986). Classifying learnable geometric concepts with the Vapnik-Chervonenkis dimension. In Proceedings of 18th Annual ACM Symposium on Theory of Computation, Berkeley, CA.

Blumstein, S. E. (2004). Phonetic category structure and its influence on lexical processing. Proceedings of the Texas Linguistic Society, Cascadilla Press.

Blumstein, S. E. and Milberg, W. P. (2000). Language deficits in Broca's and Wernicke's aphasia: A singular impairment. In Y. Grodzinsky, L. Shapiro, and D. Swinney (Eds.). Language and the Brain: Representation and Processing. Academic Press.

Boahen, K. A. (1996). A retinomorphic vision system. IEEE Micro, Vol. 16, No. 5, pp. 30-39.

Boahen, K. A., and A. G. Andreou, (1992). A contrast sensitive silicon retina with reciprocal synapses. Advances in Neural Information Processing Systems, Vol. 4, pp. 764-772. San Mateo, CA: Morgan Kauftnann.

Boahen, K. A., P. O. Pouliqueen, A. G. Andreou, and R. E. Jenkins (1989). A Heterassociative memory using current-mode analog VLSI circuits. IEEE Transactions on Circuits and Systems, Vol. CAS-36, pp. 747-755.

Boring, E. G. (1950). *A history of experimental psychology* (2nd ed.). Englewood Cliffs, NJ: Prentice-Hall.

Braitenberg, V. (1967). Is the cerebella cortex a biological clock in the millisecond range? In The Cerebellum. Progress in Brain Research, C. A. Fox and R. S. Snider, eds., Vol. 25, pp. 334-346, Amsterdam: Elsevier.

Braitenberg, V. (1990). Reading the structure of brains. Network: Computation in Neural Systems, Vol. I, pp. 1-12.

Braitenberg, V. (1986). Two views of the cerebral cortex. In Brain Theory, G. Palm and A. Aertsen, eds., pp. 81-96. New York: Springer-Verlag.

Braitenberg, V. (1984). Vehicles: Experiments in Synthetic Psychology, Cambridge, MA: MIT Press.

Braitenberg, V. (1977). On the Texture of Brains, New York: Springer-Verlag.

Bredeche, N., Zhongzhi Shi, Zucker, J. (2003). Perceptual Learning and Abstraction in Machine Learning. IEEE ICCI 2003: 18-25.

Bregman , A. S. (1990). Auditory Scene Analysis. MIT Press.

Broadbent, D. (1958). Perception and Communication. London: Pergamon Press.

Brooks, R. A. (1991). Intelligence without reasoning. In Proceedings of IJCAI'91, Sydney, 569-595.

Brooks, R. A. (1991). Intelligent without representation. Artificial Intelligence, Vol. 47, 139-159.

Broomhead, D. S. and D. Lowe (1988). Multivariate functional interpolation and adaptive networks. *Complex Systems*, 2: 321-355.

Brown, A., Hinton, G. E. (2001). Products of Hidden Markov Models. In T. Jaakkola and T. Richardson eds., Proceedings of Artificial Intelligence and Statistics, Morgan Kaufmann, 3-11.

Brown, A., Hinton, G. E. (2001). Training Many Small Hidden Markov Models. To appear in Proceedings of the Workshop on Innovation in Speech Processing.

Brown, Ralf D. (1996). Example-Based Machine Translation in the Pangloss System. In *Proceedings of the 16th International Conference on Computational Linguistics* (COLING-96), pp. 169-174. Copenhagen, Denmark, August 5-9.

Brown, Ralf D. (2004). A Modified Burrows-Wheeler Transform for Highly-Scalable Example-Based Translation. in Machine Translation: From Real Users to Research, Proceedings of the 6th Conference of the Association for Machine Translation (AMTA-2004), Washington, D.C., USA, September/October 2004, pp. 27-36. Springer, LNAI3265, ISSN 0302-9743.

Bruner, J. S. (1957). Neural mechanisms in perception. Psychological Review, 64, 340-358

Bruner, J. S. (1964). The course of cognitive growth. *American Psychologist*, 19, 1-15.

Bruner, J. (1966). Toward a Theory of Instruction. Cambridge, MA: Harvard University Press.

Bruner, J. (1996). The Culture of Education, Cambridge, MA: Harvard University Press.

Bruner, J., & Haste, H. (Eds.). (1987). Making sense: The child's construction of the world. New York: Methuen.

Bryson, A. E., Jr., and Y. C. Ho (1969). Applied Optimal Control, Blaisdell. (Revised printing, 1975, Hemisphere Publishing, Washington, DC).

Burges, C. J. C. (1998). A tutorial on support vector machines for pattern recognition. Data Mining and Knowledge Discovery, 2(2): 121-167.

Burges, C. J. C. (1999). Geometry and invariances in kernel based methods, in Advance in Kernel Methods — Support Vector Learning, B. Scholkopf, C. Burge, and A. Smola, Eds., Cambridge, MA: MIT, Press, 89-116.

Burke, R. and Kass, A. (1996). Retrieving Stories for Case-Based Teaching. Case-Based Reasoning (Experiences, lessons, &Future Directions), AAAI/MIT Press, 93-110.

Burks, A. W. (1986). An architectural theory of functional consciousness. In (N. Rescher, ed) Current Issues in Teleology. University Press of America.

Burnet, F. M. (1978). Clonal selection and after. In: Bell G I, Perelson A S, Pimbley G H eds. Theoretical Immunology, New York: Marcel Dekker Inc., 63-85.

Buzas, P., K. Kovacs, A. S. Ferecsko, J. M. Budd, U. T. Eysel, and Z. F. Kisvarday, (2006). Model-Based Analysis of Excitatory Lateral Connections in the Visual Cortex. J. Comp. Neurol. 499, No. 6, 861–881.

Caprotti, Olga and Arjeh M. Cohen (1998). Draft of the OpenMath standard. The Open Math Society, http://www.nag.co.uk/projects/OpenMath/omstd/.

Carlisle, David, Patrick Ion, Robert Miner, and Nico Poppelier (2001). Mathematical Markup Language (MathML) version 2.0. W3c recommendation, World Wide Web Consortium. Available at http://www.w3.org/TR/MathML2.

Chalmers, D. J. (2000). What is a neural correlate of consciousness? In (T. Metzinger, ed) Neural Correlates of Consciousness: Empirical and Conceptual Issues. MIT Press.

Chen, L. (1982). Topological structure in visual perception. Science, 218, 699-700.

Chen, L. (2005). The topological approach to perceptual organization (invited lead paper). Visual Cognition, 12, 553-637.

Chickering D. and Heckerman D. (1996). Efficient approximations for the marginal likelihood of incomplete data given a Bayesian network. Technical Report MSR-TR-96-08, Microsoft Research, Redmond, WA.

Chomsky, N. (1957). Syntactic Structures. The Hague: Mouton.

Chomsky, N. (1966). Cartesian Linguistics: A Chapter in the History of Rationalistic Thought. New York/London: Harper and Row.

Chomsky, N. (1968). Language and Mind. New York: Harcourt, Brace and World.

Chomsky, N. (1977). Language and Responsibility. New York: Pantheon Books.

Chomsky, N. (1980). Rules and Representations. New York: Columbia University Press.

Chomsky, N. (1996). Language and evolution (letter). *New York Review of Books* (February 1).

Cho, S.-B. and G.-B. Song (2000). Evolving CAM-Brain to control a mobile robot. Int. Journal of Applied Mathematics and Computation (SCI), springer-verlag, 111(2-3): 147-162.

Churchland, P. (1995). The engine of reason, the seat of the soul: a philosophical journey into the brain. Cambridge, MA, MIT Press.

Churchland, P. S. and T. Sejnowski (1992). The computational brain. Cambridge, MA, MIT Press.

Cohen, M. A. (1992). "The construction of arbitrary stable dynamics in nonlinear neural networks," Neural Networks, Vol. 5, pp. 83-103.

Cohen, M. A., and S. Grossberg (1983). "Absolute stability of global pattern formation and parallel memory storage by competitive neural networks," IEEE Transactions on Systems, Man, and Cybernetics, Vol. SMC-13, pp. 815-826.

Collins, Allan M. & Quillian, M. Ross (1969). Retrieval Time from Semantic Memory, *Journal of Verbal Learning and Verbal Behavior,* 8: 240-247.

Collins and Loftus (1975). A spreading activation theory of semantic memory. Psychological Review, 82, 407-428.

Collins, J. J., Chow, C. C., Tmhoff, T. T. (1995). Stochastic resonance without tuning. Nature, 376: 236-238.

Colwell, Bob. Machine Intelligence meets neuroscience, Computer, 38(1), 2005, 12-15.

Cook, Vivian and Mark Newson (2000). Chomsky's Universal Grammar: An Introduction. Foreign Language Teaching and Research Press and Baickwell Publishers Ltd.

Cooper Greg F, and Herskovits E. (1992). A Bayesian Method for the Induction of Probabilistic Networks from Data. Machine Learning, (9): 309-347.

Cox, M. T., A. Ram (1999). Introspective multistrategy learning on the construction of learning strategies, Artificial Intelligence 112: 1-55.

Crick, F. (1984). Functions of the thalamic reticular complex: the searchlight hypothesis. Proc. Natl. Acad. Sci. USA, 81: 4586-4590.

Crick, F. (1994). The Astonishing Hypothesis. Scribner.

Crick, F. and Koch, C. (1992). The problem of consciousness. Scientific American, September, pp. 152-159

Crick, F., Koch, C. (1998). Consciousness and neuroscience. Cerebral Cortex, 8: 97-107.

Dai, H. P., Wright, B. A. (1995). Detecting signals of unexpected or uncertain durations. The Journal of the Acoustical Society of America, 98: 798-806.

Damasio, A. R., Eslinger, P., Damasio, H., Van Hoesen, G. W., & Cornell, S. Multimodal amnesic syndrome following bilateral temporal and basal forebrain damage. Archives of Neurology, 1985, 42: 252~259.

Darwin, C. J. (1989). Pattison H et al. Vowel quality changes produced by surrounding tone sequences. Journal of Experimental Psychology: Human Perception and Performance, 45: 333-342.

Dasarathy, B. V. (1991). Nearest Neighbor (NN) Norms: NN Pattern Classification. Techniques. IEEE Computer Society Press, Los Alamitos, CA.

Dasgupta, D, Attoh-Okine N. (1997). Immunity based systems: A survey. In: Proc IEEE International Conference on Systems, Man, and Cybernetics, Orlando, Florida, 369-374.

de Castro, L. N., Von Zuben, F. J. (1999). Artificial immune system; Part 1: basic theory and application. School of Electrical and Computer Engineering, State University of Campinas, Campinas-SR, Brazil: Technical Report RT-DCA 01.

de Castro, L. N., Von Zuben, F. J. (2000). Clonal selection algorithm with engineering applications. In: Proc GECCO'OO, Las Vegas, Nevada, USA, 36-37.

de Garis, Hugo, Michael Korkin, Felix Gers, Eiji Nawa, Michael Hough (2000). Building an Artificial Brain Using an FPGA Based CAM-Brain Machine. Applied Mathematics and Computation Journal, North Holland, 111(1-4): 163-192.

de Garis, Hugo, Michael Korkin (2002). THE CAM-BRAIN MACHINE (CBM) An FPGA Based Hardware Tool which Evolves a 1000 Neuron Net Circuit Module in Seconds and Updates a 75 Million Neuron Artificial Brain for Real Time Robot Control, Neurocomputing journal, Elsevier, 42: 35-68.

Deadwyler, S. A., Hampson, R. E. (1995). Ensemble activity and behavior: what's the code? Science, 270: 1316-1318.

Dehn, Milton J. (2008). Working Memory and Academic Learning: Assessment and Intervention, Wiley.

Denett, D. C. (1991). Consciousness Explained. Boston: Little Brown and Company.

Deerwester, S., Dumais, S. T., Furnas, G. W., Landauer, T. K., Harshman, R. (1990). Indexing by latent semantic analysis, Journal of the American Society for Information Science, 41.

Dempster, A. P., N. M. Laird, D. B. Rubin (1977). Maximum likelihood from incomplete data via the EM algorithm. J. Royal Statis. Soc., B39:1-22.

Dennett, D. C. (1991). The Consciousness Explain. Boston: Little Brown.

Denoeux, T. (2000). A neural network classifier based on Dempster-Shafer theory. IEEE Transactions on System, Man and Cybernetics A, 30(2): 131-150.

Deutsch, J. & Deutsch, D. (1963). Attention: Some theoretical considerations. Psychological Review, 70, 80-90.

D'haeseleer P, Forrest S, Helman P. (1996). An immunological approach to change detection algorithms: Analysis and implications. In: Proc IEEE Symposium on Security and Privacy, Las Alamitos, CA, USA, 110-119.

Djurfeldt, M., M. Lundqvist, C. Johansson, M. Rehn, O. Ekeberg, A. Lansner (2008). Brain-scale simulation of the neocortex on the IBM Blue Gene/L supercomputer. IBM J. RES. & DEV. VOL. 52 NO. 1/2: 31-41.

Domeshek, E., Kolodner, J. and Zimring, C. (1994). The Design of a Tool Kit for Case-Based Design Aids, In *Artificial Intelligence in Design*, Norwell, Ma., Kluwer.

Dreyfus, Hebert L. (1979). What Computers Can't Do, Harper & ROW, Publishers.

Duda, R. O., and P. E. Hart (1973). Pattern Classification and Scene Analysis, New York: Wiley.

Duifhuis, H., Willems, L. F. (1982) Measurement of pitch in speech: An implementation of Goldstein's theory of pitch perception. The Journal of the Acoustical Society of America, 71: 1568-1580.

Ebbinghaus, H. (1913). *Memory. A Contribution to Experimental Psychology*. New York: Teachers College, Columbia University.

Eccles, J. C. (1996). Brain and Conscious Experience. New York: Springer-Verlag.

Eliasmith, C. (1996). The third contender: a critical examination of the dynamicist theory of cognition. Philosophical Psychology, 9(4): 441-463.

Eliasmith, C. (1997). Computation and dynamical models of mind. Minds and Machines 7: 531-541.

Endoh, S., Toma, N., Yamada, K. (1998). Immune algorithm for n-TSP. In Proc IEEE International Conference on Systems, Man, and Cybernetics, San Diego, CA, USA, 3844-3849.

Engel, A. K., Konig, P., Kreiter, A. K., et al. (1991). Interhemispheric synchrozization of oscillatory neuronal responses in cat visual cortex. Science, 252: 1177-1179.

Engel, A. K., Konig, P., Kreiter, A. K., et al. (1992). Temporal coding in the visual cortex: new vistas on integration in the nervous system. Trends in Neuroscience, 15(6): 218-226.

Farber, I. B. & Churchland, P. S. (1995): 'Consciousness and the Neurosciences: Philosophical and Theoretical Issues'. In MS Gazzaniga (ed). The Cognitive Neurosciences (Cambridge, Massachusetts: MIT Press), 1295-1306.

Farmer, J. D., Packard, N. H., Perelson, A. S. (1986). The immune system, adaptation, and machine learning. Physica D, 22:187-204.

Faust, M. E., and Gernsbacher, M. A. (1996). Cerebral mechanisms for suppression of inappropriate information during sentence comprehension. Brain and Language, 53: 234-259.

Ferreira, F., Clifton, C. Jr. (1986). The independence of syntactic processing. Journal of Memory and language, 25: 348-368.

Ferster, D., Spruston, N. (1995). Cracking the neuronal code. Science, 270: 756-757.

Fodor, J. A. (1988). On modularity in syntactic processing. Journal of Psycholinguistic Research, 17: 125-168.

Forberg, James (1994). Quantum Consciousness and Your Immortality.

Fowler, N., S. Cross, C. Owens (1995). The ARPA-Rome Knowledge-Based Planning and Scheduling Initial. *IEEE Expert* 10(1), 4-9.

Fox, Susan (1996). Introspective multistrategy learning: Constructing a learning strategy under reasoning failure, Ph.D. Thesis, Technical Report No. GIT-CC-96-06, Georgia Institute of Technology, College of Computing, Atlanta, GA, ftp//ftp.cc.gatch.edu/pub/ai/ram/git-cc-96-06.html.

Franke, Andreas and Michael Kohlhase (2000). System description: MBase, an open mathematical knowledge base. In David McAllester, ed., Automated Deduction, CADE-17, No. 1831 in LNAI, pp. 455-459. Springer Verlag.

Fransén, E., A. Lansner (1998). A model of cortical associative memory based on a horizontal network of connected columns. Network: Comput Neural Syst., 9: 235-264.

Freek, W. (2003). Comparing Mathematical Provers. A. Asperti, B. Bchberger, J. H. Davenport (Eds.): MKM 2003, LNCS 2594, pp. 188-203.

Freeman, W. J. (1975). Mass Action in the Nervous System, New York: Academic Press.

Freeman, W. J. (1987). Simulation of chaotic EEG patterns with a dynamic model of the olfactory system, Biological Cybernetics, Vol. 56, pp. 139-150.

Freeman, W. J. (1988). Why neural networks don't yet fly: Inquiry into the neurodynamics of biological intelligence. IEEE International Conference on Neural Networks, Vol. II, pp. 1-7, San Diego, CA.

Freeman, W. J. (1991). The physiology of perception. Scientific American, Vol. 264 (2), pp. 78-85.

Freeman, W. J. (1992). Tutorial on neurobiology: From single neurons to brain chaos, International Journal of Bifurcation and Chaos in Applied Sciences and Engineering, Vol. 2, pp. 451-482.

Freeman, W. J. (1995). Societies of Brains. Hilisdale, NJ: Lawrence Eribaum.

Freeman, W. J. (2000). Neuraldynamics: An Exploration in Mesoscopic Brain Dynamics. London, UK: Springer-Verlag.

Freitag, D. (1998). Information extraction from HTML: application of a general machine learning approach. *AAAI-98.*

Freund, Y., Schapire R. E. (1997). A decision-theoretic generalization of on-line learning and an application to boosting. Journal of Computer and System Sciences, 55(1): 1119-139.

Fukai, T. (1994). A model of cortical memory processing based on columnar organization. Biol Cybern, 70: 427-434.

Gabbay, D. M. (1998). Fibring Logics, Oxford University Press.

Gernsbacher, M. A. (1990). Language comprehension as structure building. Hillsdale, NJ: Lawrence Erlbaum Associates, Inc.

Gers, Felix, Hugo de Garis, Michael Korkin (1997). CoDi-1Bit: A Simplified Cellular Automata Based Neuron Model, AE97, Artificial Evolution Conference, Nimes, France, Oct.

Gershon, D., B. W. Sobral, B. Horton (1997), Wickware P, Gavaghan H, Strobl M. Bioinformatics in a post-genomics age. Nature, 389: 417-422.

Gerstner, W., Kistler, W. M., Spiking (2002). Neuron Models Single Neurons, Populations, Plasticity. Cambridge University Press.

Gibson, J. J. (1966). The Senses Considered as Perceptual Systems. Boston: Houghton Mifflin.

Gibson, E. (1969). Principles of Perceptual Learning and Development. New York: Appleton.

Gibson, J. J. (1977). The theory of affordances. In R. Shaw & J. Bransford (eds.), Perceiving, Acting and Knowing. Hillsdale, NJ: Erlbaum.

Gibson, J. J. (1979). The Ecological Approach to Visual Perception. Boston: Houghton Mifflin.

Gilhooly, K. J., R. H. Logie, N. E. Wetherick, V. Wynn (1993) Working memory and strategies in syllogistic reasoning tasks. Memory and Cognition, 21: 115-124.

Girosi, F., M. Jones, and T. Poggio (1995). Regularization theory and neural networks architectures. Neural Computation, 7, 219-269.

Globus, G. G. (1992). Toward a noncomputational cognitive neuroscience. Journal of *Cognitive Neuroscience*, 4(4): 299-310.

Gödel, K. (1931). Über formal unentscheidbare Sätz der P. M. und verwandter Systeme I, Monathefte flir Math. und phvsik. 38, 173-198.

Gödel, K. (1958). ber eine bisher noch nicht benutzte Erweiterung des finiten standpunkten. Dialectica, 12, 280-287.

Godsmark, D., Brown J. (1999). A black board architecture for computational auditory scene analysis, Speech communication, 27: 353-366.

Goertzel, Ben. (1993). The Structure of Intelligence: A New Mathematical Model of Mind. Springer-Verlag January, Hardcover, ISBN: 3540940049.

Gold, E. M. (1967). Language identification in the limit. Information and Control, 10, 447-74.

Goldberg, D. E. (1989). Genetic Algorithms in Search, Optimization, and Machine Learning, Addison-Wesley.

Goleman, D. (1998). What makes a leader? Harvard Business Review, November-December.

Andrew S. Gordon and Jerry R. Hobbs (2004). Formalizations of Commonsense Psychology. AI Magazine, 25(4): Winter, 49-62.

Graf, P., & Masson, M. E. J. (Eds.) (1993). Implicit memory: New directions in cognition, development, and neuropsychology. Hillsdale, NJ: Erlbaum.

Graf, P., & Ryan, L. (1990). Transfer - appropriate processing for implicit and explicit memory. Journal of Experimental Psychology: Learning, Memory, and Cognition, 16, 978-992.

Graf, P., & Schacter, D. L. (1985). Implicit and explicit memory for new associations in normal and amnesic subjects. Journal of Experimental Psychology: Learning, Memory, and Cognition, 11, 501-518.

Granger, R. (2006). Engines of the Brain: The computational instruction set of human cognition. AI Magazine 27: 15-32.

Gray, C. M., König, P., Engel, A. K. and Singer, W. (1989). Oscillatory responses in cat visual cortex exhibit inter-columnar synchronization which reflects global stimulus properties. Nature, 338: 334-337.

Gray, C. M. and Singer, W. (1989). Stimulus-specific neuronal oscillations in orientation columns of cat visual cortex. Proceedings of the National Academy of Sciences of the United States of America, 86: 1698 – 1702.

Grossberg, S. (1967). Nonlinear difference.differential equations in prediction and learning theory. Proceedings of the National Academy of Sciences, USA, Vol. 58, pp. 1329-1334.

Grossberg, S. (1968). A prediction theory for some nonlinear functional-difference equations. Journal of Mathematical Analysis and Applications, Vol. 21, pp. 643-694, Vol. 22, pp. 490-522.

Grossberg, S. (1969). On learning and energy-entropy dependence in recurrent and nonrecurrent signed networks. Journal of Statistical Physics, vol. I, pp. 319-350.

Grossberg, S. (1969). A prediction theory for some nonlinear functional-difference equations, Journal of Mathematical Analysis and Applications, Vol. 22, pp. 490-522.

Grossberg, S. (1972). Neural expectation: Cerebellar and retinal analogs of cells fired by leamable or unlearned pattern classes. Kybernetik, Vol. 10, pp. 49-57.

Grossberg, S. (1976a). Adaptive pattern classification and universal recoding: II. Feedback, expectation, olfaction, illusions. Biological Cybernetics, Vol. 23, pp. 187-202.

Grossberg, S. (1976b). Adaptive pattern classification and universal recoding: 1. Parallel development and coding of neural detectors. Biological Cybernetics, Vol. 23, pp. 121-134.

Grossberg, S., (1977). Pattern formation by the global limits of a nonlinear competitive interaction in n dimensions. Mathematical Biology, Vol. 4, pp. 237-256.

Grossberg, S. (1978). Decision, patterns, and oscillations in the dynamics of competitive systems with application to Volterra-Lotka systems, J. Theoretical Biology, Vol. 73, pp. 101-130.

Grossberg, S. (1978). Competition, decision, and consensus. J. Mathematical Analysis and Applications, Vol. 66, pp. 470-493.

Grossberg, S. (1980). How does a brain build a cognitive code? Psychological Review, Vol. 87, pp. 1-51.

Grossberg, S. (1982). Studies of Mind and Brain, Boston: Reidel.

Grossberg, S. (1987). Competitive learning: from interactive activation to adaptive resonance. *Cognitive Science*, 11: 23-63.

Grossberg, S. (1988). Nonlinear neural networks: Principles, mechanisms, and architectures. Neural Networks, Vol. I, pp. 17-61.

Grossberg, S. (1988). Neural Networks and Natural Intelligence, Cambridge, MA: MIT Press.

Grossberg, S. (1988). Competitive learning: From interactive activation to adaptive resonance, in Neural Networks and Natural Intelligence, S. Grossberg, ed. Cambridge, MA: MIT Press.

Grossberg, S., (1990). Content-addressable memory storage by neural networks: A general model and global Liapunov method. In *Computational Neuroscience*, E. L. Schwartz, ed. pp. 56-65, Cambridge, MA: MIT Press.

Guilford, J. P. (1950). Creativity. *American Psychologist*, Vol. 5, pp. 444-454.

Guilford, J. P. (1967). *The Nature of Human Intelligence.* New York: McGraw-Hill.

Guilford, J. P. (1982). Cognitive psychology's ambiguities: Some suggested remedies. *Psychological Review*, 89, 48-59.

Guilford, J. P. & Hoepfner, R. (1971). *The Analysis of Intelligence.* New York: McGraw-Hill.

Guo, A. K. (1997). Emerging dynamic neuron assembly – new concept of brain temporal-spatial coding. ACTA BIOPHYSICA SINICA, 13: 695-702.

Guo, A. K. (2000). *Computing Neuroscience.* Shanghai: Shanghai Science and Technology Press.

Guo, Ai-ke, Yue-qin Peng, Ke Zhang, Wang Xi, (2009). Insect Behavior: Visual Cognition in Fruit Fly. *Chinese journal of Nature*, 31(2).

Guthrie, E. R. (1930). Conditioning as a principle of learning. Psychological Review, 37, 412-428.

Guthrie, E. R. (1935). The Psychology of Learning. New York: Harper.

Guthrie, E. R. (1938). The Psychology of Human Conflict. New York: Harper.

Guzman, A. (1968). Computer recognition of three-dimensional objects in a visual scene. Tech. Rep. MAC-TR-59, AI Laboratory, MIT.

Haken H. (1977). Synergetics, An Introduction. Nonequilibrium Phase-Transitions and Self-Organization in Physics. *Chemistry and Biology*, Springer.

Haken H. (1996). Principle of Brain Functioning: A Synergetic Approach to Brain Activity, Behavior, and Cognition. Springer.

Halpern, Diane F. (2002).*Thought & Knowledge.* Lawrence Erlbaum Associates.

Ham F. M., Kostanic I. (2001). *Principle of Neurocomputing for Science and Engineering.* McGraw-Hill Companies, Inc.

Hameroff S. (1998). Quantum computation in brain microtubules? The Penrose-Hameroff 'Orch OR' model of consciousness. Philosophical transactions of the Royal Society, Vol. 356, No. 1743.

Han, Jiawei, Micheline Kamber (2000). Data Mining: Concepts and Techniques. Morgan Kaufmann Publishers.

Hansel D, Sompolinsky H. (1997). Chaos and synchrony in a model of a hypercolumn in visual cortex. J Comp Neurosci, 4: 57-79.

Hansen, L. K., Salamon, P. (1990). Neural network ensembles. IEEE Trans Pattern Analysis and Machine Intelligence, 12(10), 993-1001.

Hawkins, Jeff, Sandra Blakeslee (2004). On Intelligence. Times Books, Henry Holt and Company, New York.

Haykin, S. (1994, 1998). Neural Networks: A Comprehensive Foundation. Macmillan/IEEE Press.

He, Kekang (2000). Creative Thought. http://www.iteonline.net/zhuanjiaxuzhe/hekk.files/hekekang.htm.

Hebb, D. O. (1949). The organization of behavior: A neuropsychological theory. New York: Wiley.

Heckerman, D., Meek, C., Cooper, G. (1997). A Bayesian Approach to Causal Discovery. MSR-TR-97-05, February.

Heckerman, D. (1997). Bayesian Networks for Data Mining, Data Mining and Knowledge Discovery, 1: 79-119.

Hieter, P., M. Boguski (1997). Functional genomics: its all how you read it. *Science*, 278(5338): 601-602.

Hinkle, D. and C. Tooney (1995). Applying Case-Based Reasoning to Manufacturing. *AI Magazine.* 65-73, Springer.

Hinton, G. E. (1989). Connectionist learning procedures, Artificial Intelligence, Vol. 40, pp. 185-234.

Hinton, G. E. (1989). Deterministic Boltzmann machine learning performs steepest descent in weight-space. Neural Computation, Vol. I, pp. 143-150.

Hinton, G. E., Sejnowski, T. J. (1983). Optimal Perceptual Inference. Proc. IEEE Soc. Conf. Comp. Vision & Pattern Recognition, Jun.

Hinton, G. E. and Sejnowski, T. J. (1986). Learning and relearning in Boltzmann machines. In Rumelhart, D. E. and McClelland, J. L., editors, Parallel Distributed Processing: Explorations in the Microstructure of Cognition. Volume 1: Foundations, MIT Press, Cambridge, MA.

Hinton, G. E., and T Sejnowski (eds.) (1999). Unsupervised Learning: Foundations of Neural Computation. June, MIT Press.

Hodgkin, A. L. (1965). The Conduction of the Nervous Impulse. Liverpool University Press, Liverpool, England.

Holland, J. H. (1975). Adaptation in Natural and Artificial Systems. University of Michigan Press.

Holland, J. H. (1985). Properties of the bucket brigade algorithm. In Proceedings of an International Conference on Genetic Algorithms and Their Applications. Pittsburg, PA.

Holland, J. H. (1998). Emergence-From Chaos to Order. Addison-Wesley Publishing Company.

Holland, J. H., K. J. Holyoak, R. E. Nisbett and P. R. Thagard (1986). Induction: processes of Inference, Learning, and Discovery. The MIT Press.

Hopfield, J. J. (1982). Neural networks and physical systems with emergent collective computational abilities. Proceedings of the National Academy of Sciences of the USA, 9(2554).

Hopfield, J. J. (1984). Neurons with graded response have collective computational properties like those of two-state neurons. Proceedings of the National Academy of Sciences of the USA, 81: 3088-3092.

Hopfield, J. J. (1995). Pattern recognition computation using action potential timing for stimulus representation.Nature, 376: 33-36.

Hopfield, J. J. and D. W. Tank (1985). Neural computation of decisions in optimization problems. Biol. Cybern, 52(14), 141-152.

Hornik K. M, Stinchcombe M, White H. (1989). Multilayer feed forward networks are universal approximators. Neural Networks, 2(2): 359-366.

Huber. D. E., Shiffrin, R. M., Lyie. K. B., Ruys, K. 1. (2001) Perception and performance in short - term word priming. Psychological Review, 108: 149-182.

Hull, C. L. (1943). Principles of Behaviour, New York: Appleton-Century-Crofts.

Hull, C. L. (1952). A Behaviour System, New Haven, Conn.: Yale University Press.

Intelligence Science Web site: http://www.intsci.ac.cn/.

Jackendoff, Ray (1987). *Consciousness and the Computational Mind*. Cambridge, Mass.: MIT Press.

Jackendoff, Ray (2007). *Language, Consciousness, Culture: Essays on Mental Structure (Jean Nicod Lectures)*. Cambridge, Mass.: MIT Press.

Jansen, B. H., Zouridakis, G., Brandt, M. E. (1993). A neurophysiologically-based mathematical model of flash visual evoked potentials. Biol Cybern, 68: 275-283.

Jansen, B. H., Rit, V. G. (1995) Electroencephalogram and visual evoked potential generation in a mathematical model of coupled cortical columns. Biol Cybern, 73: 357-366.

Jerne, N. K. (1973). The immune system. Scientific American, 229(1): 51-60.

Joachims, T., T. Mitchell, D. Freitag, and R. Armstrong (1995). Webwatcher: Machine learning and hypertext. In K. Morik and J. Herrmann, editors, GI Fachgruppentreffen Maschinelles Lernen. University of Dortmund, August.

Johnson, J. L., Padgett, M. L. (1999). PCNN models and applications. IEEE Trans on Neural Networks, 10(3): 480-498.

Johnson, Steven (2004). Mind Wide Open. Scribner, New York.

Jonides, J., Smith, E. E., Koeppe, R. A., Awh, E. Minoshima, S., & Mintun, M. A. (1993) Spatial working memory in humans as revealed by PET. Nature, 363, 623-625.

Judd, J. S. (1987). Learning in networks is hard. In: Proc the 1st IEEE International Conference on Neural Networks, San Diego, CA, 2: 685-692.

Kaelbling, L. P. (1993). *Learning in Embedded Systems*. MIT Press, Cambridge MA.

Kaelbling, L. P., Littman, M. L., and Moore, A. W. (1996). Reinforcement learning: A survey. *Journal of Artificial Intelligence Research*, 4.

Kaelbling, L. P. (1996). A special issue of machine learning on reinforcement learning. 22.

Kahneman, D. (1973). Attention and Effort. Englewood Cliffs, NJ: Prentice-Hall.

Kandel, E. R., Schwatz, J. H., Jessell, T. M. (1991). Principles of Neural Science 3rd Ed., Elsevier, NY. Amsterdam, London, Tokyo.

Karp, R. M., Rabin, M. O. (1987). Efficient randomized pattern-matching algorithms. IBM J. Res. Dev. 31(2): 249-260.

Kennedy, W. G., and Trafton, J. G. (2006). *Long-Term Learning in Soar and ACT-R*. Proceedings of the Seventh International Conference on Cognitive Modeling, pp. 162-168.

Kerlirzin, P., and F. Vallet (1993). Robustness in multilayer perceptrons. Neural Computation, Vol. 5, pp. 473-482.

Kinsbourne, M. (1988). Integrated field theroy of consciousness. In: Marcel AJ, Bisiach (eds.), Consciousness in Contemporary Science. Oxford: Clarendon Press.

Kintsch, W. (1988). The role of knowledge in discourse comprehension: a construction-integration model. Psychological Review, 95: 163-182.

Kirkpatrick, S. C. D. Gelatt, Jr., and M. P. Vecchi (1983). Optimization by simulated annealing. Science, Vol. 220, pp. 671-680.

Kirkpatrick, S. (1984). Optimization by simulated annealing: Quantitative Studies. Journal of Statistical Physics, Vol. 34, pp. 975-986.

Kirsh, D. (1991). Foundations of AI: the big issues. Artificial Intelligence, 47: 3-30.

Kitano, H. (1993). Challenges for massive parallelism. Proceedings of the Thirteenth International Conference on Artificial Intelligence, IJCAI-93, Chambery, Grance, Morgan Kaufmann, 81.

Kleene, S. C. (1957). Introduction to Metamathematics. Van Nostrand Reinhold.

Koffka, Kurt (1935). *Principles of Gestalt Psychology*. Lund Humphries, London.

Kohlhase, Michael (2000). OMDoc: An open markup format for mathematical documents. Seki Report SR-00-02, Fachbereich Informatik, Universit˜eat des Saarlandes, http://www.mathweb.org/omdoc

Kohonen, T. (1982). Self-organized formation of topologically correct feature maps. Biological Cybernetics, 43: 59-69.

Kohonen, T. (1984). *Self-organization and associative memory*. Springer Verlag.

Kohonen, T., Kashi, S. (2000). Self-Organization of a Massive Document Collection, IEEE Transactions On Neural Networks, 11(3).

Koller, D. (2001). Representation, Reasoning, Learning. Invited Talk, IJCAI'01, Seattle.

Kolodner, J. L. (1992). An introduction to case-based reasoning. *Artificial Intelligence Review* 6(1), 3-34.

Kolodner, J. L. (1993). Case-Based Reasoning. Morgan Kaufmann.

Kolodner, J. L. (1991). Improving Human Decision Making through Case-Based Decision Aiding, *AI Magazine*, 12(2): 52-68.

Konen, K. W., Maure, T., von der Malsburg C.(1994). A Fast dynamic link matching algorithm for invariant pattern recognition. Neural Networks, 7(6/7): 1019-1030.

Kostopoulos, P. & Petrides, M. (2003). The mid-ventrolateral prefrontal cortex: Insights into its role in memory retrieval. European Journal of Neuroscience, 17: 1489-1497.

Krech, David, Richard S. Crutchfield, Norman Livson et al. (1969). *Elements of Psychology*.

Krogh, A., Vedelsby, J. (1995). Neural network ensembles, cross validation. and active learning. In: Tesauro G, Touretzky D, Leen T eds. Advances in Neural Information Processing Systems 7, Cambridge, MA; MIT Press, 231-238.

Kunio, Yasue & Jibu Mari (1995). Quatum Brain Dynamics and Consciousness. John Benjamins.

Kurtzberg, J. M. (1987). Feature analysis for symbol recognition by elastic matching, in: int'l Business Machines J. of Research and Development 31: 91–9.

Laird, J. E. (2008). *Extending the Soar Cognitive Architecture.*In Proceedings of the First Conference on Artificial General Intelligence (AGI-08).

Laird, J., A. Newell, and P. Rosenbloom (1987). SOAR: An Architecture for General Intelligence. Artificial Intelligence, 33.

Langley, P. (1978). BACON. 1: A General Discovery System. In: Proceedings of the Second National Conference of the Canadian Society for Computational Studies of Intelligence, 173-80.

Langley, P. W. (1979). Descriptive Discovery Processes: Experiments in Baconian Science. Ph.D. dissertation, Carngie-Mellon University.

Langley, P. (2006). Cognitive architectures and general intelligent systems. *AI Magazine*, 27, 33-44.

Langley, P. and Michalski, R. S. (1986). Machine Learning and Discovery, Machine Learning, 1: 363-6.

Langley, P., Jones, R. (1988). A Computational Model of Scientific Insight. In: Sternberg, R. J. (ed.) The Nature of Creativity: Contemporary Psychological Perspectives. Cambridge University Press.

Langley, P., Laird, J. E., & Rogers, S. (2009). Cognitive architectures: Research issues and challenges. *Cognitive Systems Research, 10*, 141-160.

Langley, P., & Zytkow, J. M. (1989). Data-Driven Approaches to Empirical Discovery, Artificial Intelligence, 40, 1989: 283-312.

Langley, P. (2003). Heuristics for Scientific Discovery: the Legacy of Herbert Simon. In: Langley Website (2003, 6, 16)

Langley Website. http://wvvw.isle.org/langlev/discoverv.html (2002.4. 23).

Langton, C. (ed). (1987). Artificial Life. Vol I, MA:Addison-Wesley.

Leake D. B. (1994). Case-based reasoning. The Knowledge Engineering Review, 9(1): 61-64.

Leake, D. B., Plaza, E. (1997). Case-Based Reasoning Research and Development. LNAI No. 1266, Springer.

Lee, D. W., Sim, K. B. (1997). Artificial immune network based cooperative control in collective autonomous mobile robots. In: Proc 6th IEEE International Workshop on Robot and Human Communication, Sendai, Japan, 58-63.

Lehman, J. Fain, Lewis, R., and Rosenbloom, P. S., (2006). A Gentle Introduction to Soar: 2006 update.

Leech, G., Garside, R., Bryant, M. (1994). CLAWS: the tagging of the British national corpus. In Proc of 15th Int'l Conf on Cimputation Linguistics, Kyoto, Japan.

Lerbner, A. Ya., (1972). Fundamental of Cybernetics. Chapman and Hall.

Levelt, W. J. M. & Flores d' Arcais, G. B. (Eds.). (1978). Studies in the perception of language. New York: Wiley.

Levelt, W. J. M. (1989). Speaking: From intention to articulation. Cambridge, MA: The MIT Press.

Levelt, W. J. M. (Ed.) (1993). Lexical access in speech production. Cambridge: Blackwell.

Levelt, W. J. M. (1999a). Language. In G. Adelman, & B. H. Smith (Eds.), *Encyclopedia of Neuroscience* (2nd rev. and enlarged ed.) (pp. 1005-1008). Amsterdam: Elsevier Science.

Levelt, W. J. M. (1999b). Models of word production. *Trends in Cognitive Sciences, 3* (6), 223-232.

Levelt, W. J. M. (1999c). Producing spoken language: A blueprint of the speaker. In C. M. Brown, & P. Hagoort (Eds.), The neurocognition of Language (pp. 83-121). Oxford: Oxford University Press.

Levelt, W. J. M., Roelofs, A. P. A., & Meyer, A. S. (1999a). A theory of lexical access in speech production [target paper]. *Behavioral and Brain Sciences, 22* (1), 1-37.

Levelt, W. J. M., Roelofs, A. P. A., & Meyer, A. S. (1999b). Multiple perspectives on lexical access. Reply to commentaries. *Behavioral and Brain Sciences,* 22(1), 61-76.

Levelt, W. J. M., & Indefrey, P. (2001). The Speaking Mind/Brain: Where do spoken words come from. In A. Marantz, Y. Miyashita, & W. O'Neil (Eds.), *Image, Language, Brain* (pp. 77-94). Cambridge, MA: MIT Press.

Levelt, W. J. M. (2001). Relations between speech production and speech perception: Some behavioral and neurological observations. In E.Dupoux (Ed.), *Language, Brain and Cognitive Development: Essays in honor of Jacques Mehler* (pp. 241-256). Cambridge, MA: MIT Press.

Levelt, W. J. M. (2001a). Defining dyslexia. *Science,* 292(5520), 1300-1301.

Levelt, W. J. M. (2001b). Spoken word production: A theory of lexical access. PNAS. Proceedings of the National Academy of Sciences, 98(23), 13464-13471.

Li, Baodong, Zhongzhi Shi (1992). Case retrieval based on memory network. In Shi Zhongzhi (editor): Automated Reasoning, 275-285.

Li, Ming and Paul Vitanyi (1997). An Introduction to Kolmogorov Complexity and Its Applications. Springer Verlag.

Li, Su, Xianlin Xi, Hong Hu, Yunjiu Wang (2004). The synchronous oscillation in neural networks model of function column structure. China Science C, Life Science, 34(4): 385-394.

Li, Xiaoli, Jimin Liu, Zhongzhi Shi (2000). A Document Chassitie Based on Word Sementic Association. PRICAI'2000.

Liaw, J., T. Berger (1999). Dynamic Synapse: Harnessing the Computing Power of Synaptic Dynamics. Neurocomputing, 26-27: 199-206.

Lieberman, Henry, Hugo Liu, Push Singh, Barbara Barry (2004). Beating Common Sense into Interactive Applications. AI Magazine, 25(4): Winter, 63-76

Lin, Tsau Young (1999). Data Mining: Granular Computing Approach. In Proceedings of the Third Pacific-Asia Conference on Knowledge Discovery and Data Mining, April 26-28, Springer-Verlag, Lecture Notes in Artificial Intelligence series.

Lin, T. Y. (2003). Granular Computing: Structures, Representations, Applications and Future Directions. *In: the Proceedings of 9th International Conference, RSFDGrC 2003,* Chongqing, China, Lecture Notes on Artificial Intelligence LNAI 2639, Springer-Verlag, 16-24.

Linsker, R. (1986). From basic network principles to neural architecture (series). Proceedings of the National Academy of Sciences, USA, Vol. 83, pp. 7508-7512, 8390-8394, 8779-8783.

Linsker, R. (1987). Towards an organizing principle for perception: Hebbian synapses and the principle of optimal neural encoding. IBM Research Report RC12820, IBM Research, Yorktown Heights, NY.

Linsker, R. (1988). Towards an organizing principle for a layered perceptual network. in Neural Information Processing Systems, D.Z. Anderson, ed. pp. 485-494, New York: American Institute of Physics.

Linsker, R. (1988). Self-organization in a perceptual network. Computer, Vol. 21, pp. 105-117.

Linsker, R. (1989). An application of the principle of maximum information preservation to linear systems. Advances in Neural Information Processing Systems, Vol. I, pp. 186-194, San Mateo, CA: Morgan Kaufmann.

Linsker, R. (1989). How to generate ordered maps by maximizing the mutual information between input and output signals. Neural computation, Vol. I, pp. 402-411.

Linsker, R. (1990). Self-organization in a perceptual system: How network models and information theory may shed light on neural organization. Chapter 10 in Connectionist Modeling and Brain Function. The Developing Interface, S.J. Hanson and C.R. Olson, eds., pp. 351-392, Cambridge, MA: MIT Press.

Linsker, R. (1990). Perceptual neural organization: Some approaches based on network models and information theory. Annual Review of Neuroscience, Vol. 13, pp. 257-281.

Linsker, R. (1990). Designing a sensory processing system: What can be learned from principal components analysis? Proceedings of the International Joint Conference on Neural Networks, Vol. 2, pp. 291-297, Washington, DC.

Linsker, R. (1993). "Deriving receptive fields using an optimal encoding criterion," Advances in Neural Information Processing Systems, Vol. 5, pp. 953-960, San Mateo, CA: Morgan Kaufmann.

Livingstone, M., & Hubel, D. (1988). Segregation of form, color, movement and depth: anatomy, physiology, and perception. Science, 240: 740-749.

Logothetis, N. K. & Schell, J. D. (1989). Neuronal correlate of subjective visual perception. Science, 245: 761-763.

Lotte, F., M. Congedo, A. Lécuyer, F. Lamarche, B. Arnaldi (2007). *A Review of classification algorithms for EEG-based Brain-Computer Interfaces*, In: *Journal of Neural Engineering*, 2007, Vol. 4, p. R1-R13.

Luger, George E.(2005). *Artificial Intelligence*. Addison-Wesley.

Lundqvist, M., M. Rehn, M. Djurfeldt, and A. Lansner (2006). Attractor Dynamics in a Modular Network Model of Neocortex. Network: Computation in Neural Systems 17, No. 3, 253-276.

Machine Learning Department, 2008: http://www.cald.cs.cmu.edu/.

Mark, W., Simoudis, E., and Hinkle, D. (1996). Case-Based Expectations and Results. Case-Based Reasoning (Experiences, lessons, &Future Directions), AAAI/MIT Press, 269-294.

Markram, H. (2006). The blue brain project. *Nat Rev Neurosci.* 7, 153-160.

Markus, B.(1995). Binaural Modeling and auditory scene analysis. IEEE ASSP Workshop, 15-18.

Marr, D. (1982). Vision: a computational investigation into the human representation and processing of visual information. W. H. Freeman, San Francisco.

Matthews, Gerald, Zeidner, Moshe, Roberts, Richard D. (2004). *Emotional Intelligence : Science And Myth*. MIT Press.

Mayer, J., D. Wildgruber, A. Riecker, G. Dogil, H. Ackermann, W. Grodd (2002). Prosody Production and Perception: Converging Evidence from fMRI Studies. *Proceedings of Speech Prosody 2002*, Aix-en-Provence, France, April 11-13, 487-490.

Mayer, J., H. Ackermann, G. Dogil, M. Erb, W. Grodd (2003). Syllable Retrieval vs. Online Assembly: fMRI Examination of the Syllabary. Proceedings of the XVth International Congress of Phonetic Sciences (ICPhS), Barcelona, 2541-2544.

Mayeux R. and Kandel E. R. (1991). Disorders of Language: The Aphasias. In: Kandel E. R., Schwartz J. H. and Jessell T. M. (eds.). Principles of Neural Science, 3rd ed. Elsevier, pp 840-851.

McCarthy, John (1980). Circumscription---a form of non-monotonic reasoning. Artificial Intelligence, 13(1-2): 27-39.

McCarthy, John (1986). Applications of circumscription to formalizing commonsense knowledge. Artificial Intelligence, 28: 89-116.

McCarthy, John (2002). Actions and Other Events in Situation Calculus. KR 2002: 615-628.

McCarthy, John (2005). The Future of AI - A Manifesto. *AI Magazine*, 26(4): 39-.

McCarthy, John (2007). From here to human-level AI. Artif. Intell. 171(18): 1174-1182.

McCarthy, J., Minsky, M. L., Rochester, N., Shannon, C. E. (2006). A Proposal for the Dartmouth Summer Research Project on Artificial Intelligence. *The AI Magazine* **27** (Winter 2006): 12-14.

McClelland, J. L. and Rumelhart, D. E. (1988). Explorations in Parallel Distributed Processing: MIT Press.

McCulloch, W. S. and W. Pitts (1943). A logic calculus of the ideas immanent in nervous activity. Bulletin of Mathematical biophysics, Vol. 5, 115-133.

McCulloch, W. S. (1988). Embodiments of Mind. MIT Press, Cambridge, MA.

McDermort, K. B. Implicit memory. In: Kazdin, A. E. (Ed.) (2000). The encyclopedia of psychology. New York: American Psychological Association and Oxford University Press.

McDermott, K. B. (2002). Explicit and implicit memory. Encyclopedia of the human brain, Vol. 2. Pp. 773-781. V. S. Ramachandran (Ed.) Academic Press.

Mckoon, G., Ratcliff, R. (1998). Memory-based language processing: psycholinguistic Research in the 1990s. Annual Review of psychology, 49: 25-42.

Mead, C.A. (1990). Neuromorphic electronic systems. Proceedings of the Institute of Electrical and Electronics Engineers, Vol. 78, pp. 1629-1636.

Mead. C. A. (1989). Analog VLSI and Neural Systems, Reading, MA: Addison-Wesley.

Mead, C. A., and M.A. Mahowald (1988). "A silicon model of early visual processing," Neural Networks, Vol. 1, pp. 91-97.

Mead, C. A., X. Arreguit, and J. Lazzaro (1991). Analog VLSI model of binaural hearing. IEEE Transactions on Neural Networks, Vol. 2, pp. 232-236.

Medical dictionary Website: http://www.medterms.com/script/main/hp.asp.

Meersman, R. A., Zhongzhi Shi, Chen-Ho Kung (Eds.) (1990). Artificial Intelligence in Databases and Information Systems (DS-3). North-Holland Publishers.

Melis, E., J. Buedenbender, E. Andres, Adrian Frischauf, G. Goguadze, P. Libbrecht, M. Pollet, and C. Ullrich (2001). The ActiveMath learning environment. Artificial Intelligence and Education, 12(4), Winter.

Metropolis, N., A. Rosenbluth, M. Rosenbluth, A. Teller, and E. Teller (1953). Equations of state calculations by fast computing machines. Journal of Chemical Physics, Vol. 21, pp. 1087-1092.

Meyer, D. E. (1970). On the representation and retrieval of stored semantic information. Cognitive Psychology, 1, 242-300.

Meyer, D. E. (1971). Dual memory-search of related and unrelated semantic categories. Paper presented at the meeting of the Eastern Psychological Association, New York, April.

Meyers, J. L., E. J. O'Brien, J. E. Albrecht, R. A. Mason (1994). Maintaining global coherence during reading. Journal of Experimental Psychology, 20: 876-886.

Miller, G. A. (1956). The Magical Number Seven, Plus or Minus Two: Some Limits on Our Capacity for Processing Information. The Psychological Review, 1956, Vol. 63, pp. 81-97.

Minsky, M. (1975) A Framework for Representing Knowledge. The Psychology of Computer Vision, P. H. Winston (ed.), McGraw-Hill.

Minsky, M. (1986). *The Society of Mind*. New York, Simon & Schuster.

Minsky, M. (1989). Semantic Information Processing. Cambridge, MA.: MIT Press, Hall, R. P.

Minsky, M. (1991). Machinery of Consciousness. Proceedings, National Research Council of Canada, 75th Anniversary Symposium on Science in Society, June.

Minsky, M. (2006). *The Emotion Machine*. Simon & Schuster, New York.

Minsky, M. and Papert, S. (1969). *Perceptrons*. MIT Press.

Mitchell, T. (1997). Machine Learning. McGraw Hill

Miyake, A., P. Shan (1999). Models of working memory: mechanisms of active maintenance and executive control. New York: Cambridge University Press.

Mo, Hongwei (2003). Theory and Application of Artificial Immune System. Harbin Institute of Technology Press.

Mooney, R. J. (1997). Inductive logic programming for natural language processing. Inductive Logic Programming, 1314: 3-22.

Moravec, Hans (1998). Robot: mere machine to transcendent mind. Oxford University Press, November.

Mountcastle, V. B. (1957). Modality and topographic properties of single neurons of cat's somatic sensory cortex. J Neurophysiol, 20: 408-434.

Mountcastle, V. B. (1997). The columnar organization of the neocortex. Brain, 120: 701-722.

MoWGLI: Mathematics on the Web: Get it by Logics and Interfaces, http://www.mowgli.cs.unibo.it/html_yes_frames/home.html.

Nagel, Hans-Hellmut (2004). Steps toward a Cognitive Vision System. AI Magazine, 25(2): Summer, 31-50.

Nakano, H. and Blumstein, S. E. (2004). Deficits in thematic integration processes in Broca's and Wernicke's aphasia. *Brain and Language*, 88, 96-107.

Nason, S. and Laird, J. E. (2005). Soar-RL: Integrating Reinforcement Learning with Soar. Cognitive Systems Research, 6, 51-59.

Nathans, D., Smith, H. O. (1975). Restriction Endonucleases in the Analysis and Restructuring of DNA Molecules. Ann. Rev. Biochem. 44: 273-29.

Neal, R. M. (1995). Bayesian Learning for Neural Networks, Ph.D. Thesis, University of Toronto, Canada.

Neal, R. M. (1993). Bayesian learning via stochastic dynamics. Advances in Neural Information Processing Systems, Vol. 5, pp. 475-482, San Mateo, CA: Morgan Kaufmann.

Neal, R. M. (1992). Connectionist learning of belief networks. Artificial Intelligence, Vol. 56, pp. 71-113.

Neisser, Ulric. (1967). Cognitive Psychology. New York: Appleton-Century-Crofts.

Newell, Allen (1973). Productions systems: models of control structures. Pittsburgh, Pa: Carnegie Mellon University, Department of Computer Science.

Newell, Allen (1980) *Physical symbol systems*. Cognitive Science, 4: 135-183.

Newell, Allen (1981). Physical symbol systems. In Perspectives on cognitive science. Norman, D. A., ed. Hillsdale, N.J.: Lawrence Erlbaum Associates.

Newell, Allen (1990). *Unified Theories of Cognition*. Cambridge, Mass.: Harvard University Press.

Newell, Allen, John E. Laird, and Paul S. Rosenbloom (1987a). SOAR: An Architecture for General Intelligence. *Artificial Intelligence* 33(1): 1-64.

Newell, Allen, Paul S. Rosenbloom, and John E. Laird (1987b). Knowledge Level Learning In Soar. *AAAI 1987*: 499-504.

Newell, Allen, Paul S. Rosenbloom, and John E. Laird (eds.) (1993). The Soar papers: research on integrated intelligence. Cambridge, Mass. MIT Press.

Newell, Allen, and H. A. Simon (1956). The logic theory machine: A complex information processing system. *IRE Trans. Inf. Theory* IT-2: 61-79.

Newell, Allen, and H. A. Simon (1972). Human Problem Solving. Englewood Cliffs, N.J.: Prentice-Hall.

Newell, Allen, and H. A. Simon (1976a). Computer science as empirical inquiry: Symbols and search. Communications of the Association for Computing Machinery 19(3), 113-126. ACM Turing Award Lecture.

Newell, Allen, and H.A. Simon (1976b). Symbol manipulation. In *Encyclopedia of computer science*. A. Ralston and C.L. Meek (Eds.) New York: Petrocelli/Charter, 1384-1389.

Nilsson, N. (1965). Learning Machines. McGraw-Hill, New York.

Nicholls, J. G. et al. (2001). From Neuron to Brain, (4th ed) Sinauer Associates. Sunderland, MA.

Nicolis, G., Prigogine, I. (1987). Exploration of Complexity. New York: W. H. Freeman.

Norman, Donald A. 1981. Twelve issues for cognitive science. In Perspectives on cognitive science. Norman, D. A., ed. Hillsdale, N.J.: Lawrence Erlbaum Associates.

Norman, Donald A. 1981. "What is cognitive science?" In Perspectives on cognitive science. Norman, D. A., ed. Hillsdale, N.J.: Lawrence Erlbaum Associates.

Norman, D. A. (2002). Emotion and design: Attractive things work better. Interactions Magazine.

Olson, G.M. (1981). On language understanding process (in Chinese). *Shinli Kexue Tonxuin*, 3, 70-74.

Ornstein, R. E. (1977). The Psychology of Consciousness (2-ed.) New Work: Harcount Brace Jovaovich.

Pavlov, I. P. http://www.iemrams.spb.ru:8101/english/pavlov.htm.

Pawlak, Z. (1982). Rough Sets. International Journal of Computer and Information Sciences. 11: 341-356.

Pawlak, Z. (1992). Rough Sets: Theoretical Aspects of Reasoning About Data, Kluwer Academic Publishers.

Perelson, A. (1989). Immune network theory. Immunological Review, 110: 5-36.

Perkowitz, M. and Etzioni, O. (1995). Category translation: Learning to understand information on the Internet. *Proceedings of IJCAI-95*, Montreal, Morgan Kaufmann.

Perkowitz, M., Etzioni, O. (1998). Adaptive Web Sites: Automatically Synthesizing Web Pages. AAAI98.

Perry, V. H., Linden, R. (1982). Evidence for dendritic competition in the developing retina. Nature, 297: 683-685.

Petrides, M., Alivisatos, B., Meyer, E., & Evans, A. C. (1993). Functional activation of the human frontal cortex during the performance of verbal working memory tasks. *Proceedings of the National Academy of Sciences, U.S.A.*, 90, 878-882.

Petrides, M., & Pandya, D. N. (2004). The frontal cortex. In the Human Nervous System, G. Paxinos and J. K. Mai (Eds.), San Diego: Elsevier Academic Press, 2$^{nd}$ Edition, Ch. 25, pp. 950-972.

Piaget, J. (1963, 2001). *The psychology of intelligence.* New York: Routledge.

Piaget, J. (1970a). *Genetic epistemology.* New York: W.W. Norton & Company.

Piaget, J. (1970b). *Structuralism.* New York: Harper & Row.

Piaget, J. (1972). The Principles of Genetic Epistemology.

Piaget, J. (1972). Intellectual evolution from adolescence to adulthood. *Human Development, 15(1)*, 1-12.

Piaget, J. (1973). Memory and intelligence. New York: BasicBooks.

Piaget, J. (1974, 1980). Adaptation and intelligence: Organic selection and phenocopy. Chicago: University of Chicago Press.

Piaget, J. (1979). Le Structuralism.

Piaget, J. (1985). The Equilibration of Cognitive Structures: The Central Problem of Intellectual Development. Chicago: University of Chicago Press.

Piaget, J. (2001). *Studies in Reflecting Abstraction.* Hove, UK: Psychology Press.

Picard, R. W. (1997). Affective Computing. MIT Press, London, England.

Poggio, T. (1990). A theory of how the brain might work. Cold Spring Harbor Symposium on Quantitative Biology, Vol. 5, pp. 899-910.

Poggio, T., and D. Beymer (1996). Learning to see. *IEEE Spectrum*, Vol. 33, No. 5, pp. 60-69.

Poggio, T., and S. Edelman (1990). A network that learns to recognize three-dimensional objects. *Nature*, Vol. 343, pp. 263-266.

Poggio, T., Fahle, M., and Edelman, S. (1992). Fast perceptual learning in visual hyperacuity. Science, 256: 1018-1021.

Poggio, T. and F. Girosi (1989). A Theory of Networks for Approximation and Learning. Technical Report 1140, MIT AI Lab.

Poggio, T., and F. Girosi (1990). Networks for approximation and learning. Proceedings of the IEEE, Vol. 78, pp. 1481-1497.

Poggio, T., and F. Girosi (1990). Reguiarization algorithms for learning that are equivalent to multilayer networks. Science, Vol. 247, pp. 978-982.

Poggio, T., and C. Koch (1985). Ill-posed problems in early vision: From computational theory to analogue networks. Proceedings of the Royal Society of London, Series B, Vol. 226, pp. 303-323.

Poggio, T., V. Torre, and C. Koch (1985). Computational vision and regularization theory. *Nature*, Vol. 317, pp. 314-319.

Poldrack, R. A., Packard, M. G. (2003). Competition among multiple memory systems: converging evidence from animal and human brain studies. Neuropsychologia, 41(3): 241-4.

Popper, K. R. (1934, 1968). *The Logic of Scientific Discovery*. New York: Harper & Row.

Popper, K. R. (1968). Conjectures and Refutations.

Popper, K. R. (1972). *Objective Knowledge*: An Evolutionary Approach.

Posner, M. I. (1978). Chronometric explorations of mind. Hillsdale, NJ: Erlbuum.

Posner, M. I. (1994). Attention: the mechanism of consciousness. Proc. National Acad of Sciences, U.S.A., 91(16): 7398-7402.

Posner, M. I. (2003). Imaging a science of mind. Trends in Cognitive Sciences, 7: 10: 450-453.

Posner, M. I. (2004). The achievements of brain imaging: Past and present. To appear in N. Kanwisher & J. Duncan (Eds.), Attention and Performance XX, Oxford University Press (pp. 505-528).

Posner M. I. (ed) (2004). Cognitive Neuroscience of Attention. New York: Guilford.

Posner, M. I. & DiGirolamo (2000). Attention in cognitive neuroscience: an overview. In M. S. Gazzaniga (ed.) The New Cognitive Neurosciences Second Edition 621-632.

Powell, M. J. D. (1990). The Theory of Radial Basis Function Approximation. Cambridge University Numerical Analysis Report.

Powell, M. J. D. (1985). Radial basis functions for multivariate interpolation. In Algorithms for Approximation, eds. Mason, J. M. and Cox, M., 143-167.

Prigogine, Ilya, D. Kondepudi (1998). Modern Thermodynamics: From Heat Engines to Dissipative Structures. John Wiley & Sons, Chichester.

Prigogine, Ilya, G. Nicolis (1977). Self-Organization in Non-Equilibrium Systems: From Dissipative Structures to Order Through Fluctuations. Wiley & Sons, New York.

Quillian, M. Ross (1968). Semantic Memory, in Marvin Minsky (ed.) *Semantic Information Processing* (Cambridge, MA: MIT Press): 227-270.

Quillian, M. Ross (1969). The Teachable Language Comprehender: A Simulation Program and Theory of Language, *Communications of the Association for Computing Machinery*, 12(8): 459-476.

Quinlan, J. R. (1979). Discovering rules from large collections of examples: A case study. in Michie D. (editor). Expert Systems in the Micro Electronic Age, Edinburgh University Press.

Quinlan, J. R. (1983). Learning efficient classification procedures and their application to chess end-games. In R. S. Michalski, J. G. Carbonell and T. M. Mitchell (editors), Machine Learning: An Artificial Intelligence Approach, Tioga.

Quinlan, J. R. (1986). Induction of decision trees. Machine Learning, 1(1), 81.

Quinlan, J. R. (1986). The effect of noise on concept learning. In R. S. Michalski, J. G. Carbonell and T. M. Mitchell (editors), Machine Learning: An Artificial Intelligence Approach, Morgan Kaufmann.

Quinlan, J. R. (1987). Simplifying Decision Trees, Internat. Journal of Man-Machine Studies, Vol. 27, 221-234.

Quinlan, J. R. (1987). Generating production rules from decision trees. In Proceedings of IJCAI-87, Milan, Italy.

Quinlan, J. R. (1987). *Simplifying Decision Trees*, Internat. Journal of Man-Machine Studies, Vol. 27, 221-234.

Quinlan, J. R. (1988). An empirical comparison of genetic and decision-tree classifiers. In Proceedings of ICML-88, San Mateo, CA.

Quinlan, J. R. (1992). C4.5: Programs for Machine Learning. Morgan Kaufmann.

Quillian, M. R. (1968). *Semantic memory*. In M. Minsky, editor, Semantic Information Processing, pp. 216-270. The MIT Press.

Radford, Andrew (2000). Syntax: A Minimalist Introduction. Foreign Language Teaching and Research Press and Cambridge University Press.

Reiter, Raymond (2001). Knowledge in action: logical foundations for specifying and implementing dynamical systems. MIT Press, Cambridge, Mass.

Richmond, B. J., Optican, L. M, Podell, M. (1987). Temporal encoding of two-dimensional patterns by single units in primate inferior temporal cortex. J Neurophys, 57(1): 132-178.

Robertson, S. S., Cohen, A. H. and Mayer-Kess, R. G. (1993). Behavioural Chaos: Beyond the Metaphor. In SMITH, L. B. & THELEN, E. (Eds), *A dynamic systems approach to development: Applications* (Cambridge, MIT Press) pp. 120-150.

Robin, Nina & J. Holyoak (1995). Relational Complexity and the Functions of Prefrontal Cortex. In The Cognitive Neurosciences, VIII THOUGHT AND IMAGERY, M.S. Gazzaniga, ed. London: The MIT Press.

Riehle, A, Grun S, Diesmann M, et al. (1997). Spike synchronization and rate modulation differentially involved in motor cortical function. Science, 278: 1950-1953.

Roco, M. and Bainbridge, W. S. (eds.) (2002). Converging Technologies for Improving Human Performance: Nanotechnology, Biotechnology, Information Technology, and Cognitive Science National Science Foundation and Department of Commerce, Arlington, VA.

Rogers, C. R. (1951). Client-centered therapy: Its current practice, implications and theory. Boston: Houghton Mifflin.

Rosenblatt, F. (1958). The Perceptron: A probabilistic model for information storage and organization in the brain. Phychological Review, Vol 65, 386-408

Rosenblatt, F. (1962). Principles of Neurodynamics, Spartan Books.

Rosenbloom, P. S., Laird, J. E., and Newell, A. (Eds.) (1993). *The Soar Papers: Research on Integrated Intelligence*. Cambridge, MA: MIT Press.

Roy, Deb. (1999). Learning from Sights and Sounds: A Computational Model. Ph.D. Thesis, MIT Media Laboratory.

Rumelhart, D. E., and J. L. McClelland, eds., 1986. Parallel Distributed Processing: Explorations in the Microstructure of Cognition, Vol. I, Cambridge, MA: MIT Press.

Rumelhart, D. E., and D. Zipser (1985). Feature discovery by competitive learning. Cognitive Science, Vol. 9, pp. 75-112.

Rumelhart, D. E., G. E. Hinton, and R. J, Williams (1986). Learning representations of back-propagation errors. Nature (London), Vol. 323, pp. 533-536.

Rumelhart, D. E., G. E. Hinton, and R. J. Williams (1986). Learning internal representations by error propagation. In D. E. Rumelhart and J. L. McCleland, eds., Vol. I, Chapter 8, Cambridge, MA: MIT Press.

Russell, B. and A. Whitehead (1910-1913). Principia Mathematica. (3 volumes).

Samuel A. L. (1963). Some studies in machine learning using the game of checkers. In E. A. Feigenbaum and J. Feldman (editors), Computers and Thought, McGraw-Hill.

Sato, M., Y. Sato, L. C. Jain. (1997). Fuzzy Clustering Models and Applications. Springer-Verlag Company.

Saul, L. K., T. Jakkolla, and M. I. Jordan, (1996). Mean field theory for sigmoid belief networks. Journal of Artificial Intelligence Research, Vol. 4, pp. 61-76.

Saul, L. K., and M. I. Jordan (1996). Exploiting tractable substructures in intractable networks. Advances in Neural Information Processing Systems, Vol. 8, pp. 486-492, Cambridge, MA: MIT Press.

Saul, L. K., and M. I. Jordan (1995). Boltzmann chains and hidden Markov models. Advances in Neural Information Processing Systems, Vol. 7, pp. 435-442.

Schacter, D. L., McAndrews, M. P., & Moscovitch, M. (1988). Access to consciousness: Dissociations between implicit and explicit knowledge. In L. Weiskrantz (Ed.), Thought without language (pp. 242-278). New York: Oxford University Press.

Schaffer C. 1993. Overfitting Avoidance as Bias. In: ML Vol. 10, pp. 153-178.

Schank, R. C. (1972). Conceptual Dependency: {A} Theory of Natural Language Understanding, Cognitive Psychology, (3)4, 532-631.

Schank, R. C. and Abelson, R. P. (1977). Scripts, Plans, Goals and Understanding: an Inquiry into Human Knowledge Structures (Chap. 1-3), L. Erlbaum, Hillsdale, NJ.

Schank, R. C. (1982). Dynamic Memory: A Theory of Learning in Computers and People. New York: Cambridge University Press.

Schacter, D. L. (1987). Implicit memory: history and current status. Journal of Experimental Psychology: L. M, & C. 13(3): 501-518.

Schacter, D. L, McAndrews, M. P., Moscovitch M. (1988) Access to consciousness: dissociations between Imphcit knowledge in neuropsychological syndromes. In: Weiskantz L. (ed). Thought without Language. Oxford: Oxford University Press. 242-278.

Schank, R. C. (1975). Conceptual Information Processing. New York: Elsevier.

Schank, R. C. (1980). Language and Memory. Cognitive Science, Vol. 4, pp. 243-284.

Schank, R. C. (1982). Dynamic Memory: A Theory of Reminding and Learning in Computers and People. Cambridge University Press.

Schmidt-Schauß, M. and G. Smolka (1991). Attributive concept descriptions with complements. Journal of Artificial Intelligence, 48(1):1-26.Schnitzer, M. J., and M. Meister (2003). Multineuronal Firing Patterns in the Signal From Eye to Brain. Neuron, 37: 99-115.

Schreiber, Guus (2003). Knowledge Engineering and Management. MIT Press.

Schulze-Kremer, S. (1996). Molecular Bioinformatics: Algorithms and Applications. Walter de Gruyter. Berlin, New York.

Schuster, H. G, Wagner P. (1990). 1: A model for neuronal oscillations in the visual cortex. 2: Phase description of the feature dependent synchronization. Biol Cybern, 64: 77-85

Schwaighofer, A. and Volker Tresp (2001). The Bayesian committee support vector machine. In Proceedings of ICANN 2001.

Seidenberg, M. S. (1997) Language acquisition and Use: Learning and applying probabilistic constraints. Science, 275: 1599-1603.

Sejnowski, T. J. (1986). Open questions about computation in cerebral cortex. In: McClelland J. L., Rumelhart D. E., eds. Parallel distributed processing. Cambridge: MIT Press, 372-389.

Sejnowski, T. (1995). Time for a new neural code? Nature, 376: 21-22.

Sewell, W. and Shah, V. (1968). *Social class*, parental encouragement, and educational aspirations. American Journal of Sociology, 73: 559-572.

Sellers, E. W., D. J. Krusienski, D. J. McFarland, T. M. Vaughan, and J. R. Wolpaw, (2006). A P300 event-related potential brain-computer interface (BCI): The effects of matrix size and inter stimulus interval on performance. *Biological Psychology*, Vol. 73, Oct. 2006, pp. 242-252.

Shafer, G. (1976). A Mathematical Theory of Evidence. Princeton, NJ: Princeton University Press.

Shackle, G. L. S. (1979). *Expectation in E conomics*. Hyperion Pr.

Shannon, C. E. (1948). A mathematical theory of communication. *Bell System Technical Journal*, Vol. 27, pp. 379-423 and 623-656, July and October.

Shapiro, E.Y. (1981). Inductive inference of theories from facts. Research Report 192, Department of Computer Science, Yale University, New Haven, CT.

Shareef, N., Wang D. L., and Yagel R. (1999). Segmentation of medical images using LEGION. *IEEE Transactions on Medical Imaging*, Vol. 18, 74-91.

Shaw, R. D., Phuoc, T. V., Paul, A. O., Coulson, B. S. and Greenberg, H, B. 1986. Antigenic mapping of the surface proteins of rhesus rotavirus. Virology, 155: 434-451.

Shen, Kuo (1994). Chinese tone and intonation types of construction. Dialects.

Sherrington, C. S. (1906). The Integrative Action of the Nervous System, 1961 Ed. Yale University Press, New Haven, CT.

Shi, Jun, Zhongzhi Shi (2005). On Intelligence. Computer Science. 32(6): 109-111.

Shi, Zhiwei, Zhongzhi Shi, Xi Liu, Zhiping Shi. (2008). A Computational Model for Feature Binding. *Science Press, C-Life Sciences*, Vol. 51, No. 5, pp. 470-478.

Shi, Zhongzhi. (1984). Design and Implementation of FORMS. *Proceedings of International Conference on Computer and Applications*, Beijing.

Shi, Zhongzhi. (1987). Intelligent Scheduling Architecture in KSS. *The Second International Conference on Computers and Applications*, Beijing.

Shi, Zhongzhi. (1988a). On Knowledge Base System Architecture. *Proceedings of Knowledge-Based Systems and Models of Logical Reasoning*, Cairo.

Shi, Zhongzhi. (1988b). *Knowledge Engineering* (In Chinese). Tsinghua University Press.

Shi, Zhongzhi. (1989). Distributed Artificial Intelligence. *Proceedings on the Future of Research in AI*.

Shi, Zhongzhi. (1990a). Hierarchical model of mind. Invited Speaker. *Chinese Joint Conference on Artificial Intelligence*.

Shi, Zhongzhi. (1990b). Logic-object based knowledge model. *Chinese Journal of Computer*, No. 10.

Zhongzhi Shi. (1990c). Neural Computer. Proceedings of National Conference on Neural Network.

Shi, Zhongzhi. (1991). Distributed Artificial Intelligence, Future Directions in Artificial Intelligence, North-Holland.

Shi, Zhongzhi. (1992a). Hierarchical model of human mind. invited talk, *PRICAI-92*, Seoul.

Shi, Zhongzhi. (1992b). *Principles of Machine Learning*. International Academic Publishers.

Shi, Zhongzhi (Ed.) (1992c). *Automated Reasoning.* IFIP Transactions A-19, North-Holland.

Shi, Zhongzhi. (1993). *Neural Computing* (In Chinese). Electronic Industry Press.

Shi, Zhongzhi. (1994a). Artificial thought and intelligent systems, AI Summer School'94, 1994.

Shi, Zhongzhi (Ed.) (1994b). Proceedings of Pacific Rim International Conference on Artificial Intelligence, International Academic Publishers.

Shi, Zhongzhi. (2000). *Intelligent Agent and Application* (In Chinese). Science Press.

Shi, Zhongzhi. (2001a). *Knowledge Discovery* (In Chinese). Tsinghua University Press.

Shi, Zhongzhi. (2001b). *Advanced Computer Network* (In Chinese). Electronic Industry Press.

Shi, Zhongzhi. (2005a). Tolerance Rotation Based Granular Computing Model. Invited Speaker, IEEE ICGrC 2005.

Shi, Zhongzhi. (2005b). Autonomic Semantic Grid. Keynote speaker. IFIP AIAI2005, Sept., 7-9.

Shi, Zhongzhi. (2006a). *Intelligence Science* (In Chinese). Tsinghua University Press.

Shi, Zhongzhi. (1998, 2006b). *Advanced Artificial Intelligence* (In Chinese). Science Press.

Shi, Zhongzhi. (2006c). Agent Grid Intelligence Platform for Collaborative Working Environment. Keynote Speaker, SELMAS2006 (ICSE 2006), Shanghai, May 22-23.

Shi, Zhongzhi. (2006d). On Intelligence Science and Recent Progresses. Invited speech, ICCI2006, Beijing.

Shi, Zhongzhi. (2006e). Progress of artificial intelligence. ICAI2006, Beijing, 861-866.

Shi, Zhongzhi. (2007a). *Artificial Intelligence* (In Chinese). Defence Industry Press.

Shi, Zhongzhi. (2007b). DDL: Embracing Action Formalism into Description Logic. Invited Speaker, UNILOG'07, Xi'an, 20-22 Aug.

Shi, Zhongzhi. (2007c). Perspective on Intelligence Science. ISICA2007, Wuhan, 20-23 September.

Shi, Zhongzhi. (2008a). A Computational Model for Feature Binding. Invited speaker, 2008 UK-China Joint Workshop on From Nature to Computing and Back, Shanghai.

Shi, Zhongzhi. (2008b). *Cognitive Science* (In Chinese). University of Science and Technology of China Press.

Shi, Zhongzhi. (2008c). Nonstructured Information Retrieval based on Tolerance Granular Space Model. Keynote, IEEE International Conference on Granular Computing, Hangzhou China, Aug. 25-28.

Shi, Zhongzhi. (2009a). *Neural Networks* (In Chinese). High Education Press.

Shi, Zhongzhi. (2009b). On Intelligence Science. To be appeared in *International Journal on Advanced Intelligence.*

Shi, Zhongzhi. (2009c). Research on brain-like computer. LNAI5819, *Brain Informatics,* Springer.

Shi, Zhongzhi. (2009d). Semantic analysis and understanding of visual information. Invited Speaker, Workshop on Cognitive Computation for Visual Information, Beijing, 2009.

Shi, Zhongzhi. (2009e). *Advanced Artificial Intelligence.* World Scientific Publishing, Singapore.

Shi, Zhongzhi, Hu Cao, Yunfeng Li, Wenjie Wang, Tao Jiang (1998). A Building Tool for Multiagent Systems: AOSDE. IT & Knows, IFIP WCC '98.

Shi, Zhongzhi, Yuan Chen, Lejian Liao. (1996) Constraint reasoning system COPS. The Progress of Artificial Intelligence 1996, pp. 69-73.

Shi, Zhongzhi, Mingkai Dong, Haijun Zhang, Qiujian Sheng. (2002). Agent-based Grid Computing. Keynote Speech, *International Symposium on Distributed Computing and Applications to Business, Engineering and Science*, Wuxi, Dec. 16-20.

Shi, Zhongzhi, Mingkai Dong, Yuncheng Jiang, Haijun Zhang. (2005 A Logic Foundation for the Semantic Web. *Science in China, Series F Information Sciences*, 48(2): 161-178.

Shi, Zhongzhi, Boi Faltings, Mark Musen (Eds.) (2000). Proceedings of Conference on Intelligent Information Processing. Publishing House of Electronics Industry.

Shi, Zhongzhi and J. Han. (1990). Attribute Theory in Learning System, *Future Generation Computer Systems*, North Holland Publishers, No. 6.

Shi, Zhongzhi, Qing He, Ziyan Jia and Jiayou Li (2003). Intelligence Chinese Document Semantic Indexing System. International Journal of Information Technology and Decision Making, Vol. 2, No. 3: 407-424.

Shi, Zhongzhi, Hong Hu, Shiwei Ye. (1993). Neural Approximate Logic, *Chinese Journal of Electronics*, Vol. 2, No. 2.

Shi, Zhongzhi, He Huang, Jiewen Luo, Fen Lin, Haijun Zhang. (2006). Agent-based Grid Computing. Applied Mathematical Modeling, 30: 629-640.

Shi, Zhongzhi, Youping Huang, Qing He, Lida Xu, Shaohui Liu, Liangxi Qin, Ziyan Jia, Jiayou Li. (2007) MSMiner-A Developing Platform for OLAP. *Decision Support Systems*, 42(4): 2016-2028.

Shi, Zhongzhi, Qingyong Li, Zheng Zheng (2005). Visual Perceptual Learning. Invited speech, In Proc. IEEE International Conference on Neural Network & Brain, 75-80. Beijing, China.

Shi, Zhongzhi, Chunhuan Mo. (1995). Artificial Life (In Chinese). *Journal of Computer Research and Development*, Vol. 32, No. 12.

Shi, Zhongzhi, Jun Shi (2003). Perspectives on Cognitive Informatics, IEEE ICCI'03, 129-136.

Shi, Zhongzhi, Jun Shi, Jinhua Zheng (2004). Study on intelligence in artificial life. In: Xuyan Tu, Yixin Yin (Eds.): Artificial Life and Applications. Beijing University of Posts and Telecommunications Press, pp. 27-32.

Shi, Zhongzhi, Qijia Tian, Wenjie Wang, Tao Wang, (1996). Epistemic Reasoning About Knowledge and Belief Based on Dependence Relation. *Advanced Software Research*, Vol. 3, No. 2.

Shi, Zhongzhi, Qijia Tian, Yunfeng Li. (1999). RAO Logic for Multiagent Framework. *Journal of Computer Science and Technology*, 14(4): 393-400.

Shi, Zhongzhi, Tao Wang, Wenjie Wang, Qijia Tian, Meng Ye. (1995). A Flexible Architecture for Multi-Agent System, *PACES-95*.

Shi, Zhongzhi and J. Wu, H. Sun, J. Xu. (1990) OKBMS, An Object-Oriented Knowledge Base Management System. *International Conference on TAI*, Washington.

Shi, Zhongzhi and Zhihua Yu. (1990). *Cognitive Science and Computer*. Scientific Popularization Press.

Shi, Zhongzhi, Haijun Zhang, Mingkai Dong. (2003). MAGE: Multi-Agent Environment. *ICCNMC-03*, IEEE CS Press, pp. 181-188.

Shi, Zhongzhi, Jian Zhang, Liu Jimin. (1998). Neural Field Theory-A Framework of neural Information Processing. *Neural Network and Brain Proceedings*, 421-424.

Shi, Zhongzhi, Sulan Zhang (2005). Case-based Introspective Learning. IEEE ICCI'05

Shi, Zhongzhi, Zhikun Zhao, Hu Cao. (2002). A Planning Algorithm Based on Constraints Propagation. *International Conference on Intelligent Information Technology (ICIIT2002)*, Sep 22-25, Beijing, China, P410-416.

Shi, Zhongzhi and Zheng Zheng. (2007). Tolerance granular space model (In Chinese). In Miao Teqian etc. (Eds.) *Granular Computing: Past, Present and Future*. Science Press, 42-82.

Shi, Zhongzhi, Han Zhou Jun Wang (1997). Applying Case-Based Reasoning to Engine Oil Design. *AI in Engineering*, 11: 167-172.

Shieber, Stuart (Ed.) (2004). The Turing Test: Verbal Behavior as the Hallmark of Intelligence. The MIT Press.

Shivakumar, Vaithyanathan, Byron Dom (1998). Model-Based Hierarchical Clustering. PRICAI Workshop on Text and Web Mining.

Shouval, H. Z. (2007). Models of synaptic plasticity, Scholarpedia, 2(7), pp. 1605.

Simon, H. A. (1959). Theories of Decision-Making in Economics and Behavioral Science. American Economic Review, 49 (1), 253-283

Simon, H. A. (1979a). Information Processing Models of Cognition. Annual Review of Psychology, 30, 363-396.

Simon , H. A. (1979b). *Models* of Thought. New Haven, CT: Yale University Press.

Simon, H. A. (1986). Human cognition: information processing theory of thinking. Beijing, China: Science Press.

Simon, H. A. (1982). The Sciences of the Artificial. The MIT Press, 2ed.

Simon, H.A. (1983). Why should machines learn? In R. S. Michalski, J. G. Carbonell, and T. M. Mitchell (Eds.), Machine learning, an artificial intelligence approach (Chap. 2). Palo Alto, CA: Tioga Publishing.

Singer, W. (1994). Time as coding space in neocortical processing: a hypothesis. In: Buzsaki, G., Lllinas R, Singer, W. et al. (eds), Temporal Coding in the Brain. Berlin: Springer-Verlag, 51-79.

Skarda, C. A. and W. J. Freeman (1987). How brains make chaos in order to make sense of the world, *Behavioral* and Brain Sciences, 10: 161-195.

Skinner, B. F. (1954). The science of learning and the art of teaching. Harvard Educational Review, 24(2), 86-97.

Sloman, Aaron (2001). Varieties of Affect and the CogAff Architecture Schema. AISB2001, York.

Smale, S. (1997). Complexity Theory and Numerical Analysis. Acta Numerica, pp. 523-551.

Smith, E. E., Shoben, E. J., & Rips, L. J. (1974). Structure and process in semantic memory: A featural model for semantic decisions. *Psychological Review*, 81, 214-241.

Smith, D. J., Forrest S, Perelson A S. Immunological memory is associative. In: Dasgupta ed. Artificial Immune Systems and their Applications. Berlin: Springer, 1998. 105-112.

Sperling, G. (1960). The information available in brief visual presentations. Psychological Monographs: General and Applied, 74(11), 1-30.

Sperling, G. (1963). A model for visual memory tasks. Human Factors, 5, 19-31.

Sperling, G. (1967). Successive approximations to a model for short term memory. Acta Psychologica, 27, 285-292.

Sperry, R. W. (1966) Brain bisection and mechanisms of consciousness. In: Eccles JC (ed) Brain and Conscious Experience. New York: Springer-Verlag, 298-313.

Sperry, R. W. (1968). Hemisphere deconnection and unity in conscious awareness. Scientific American, 23, 723-733.

Sterling, P. (1990). Retina. in The Synoptic Organization of the Brain, G. M. Shepherd, ed., 3rd edition, pp. 170-213, New York: Oxford University Press.

Spohrer, J. and Engebart, D. (2004). Converging technologies for enhancing human performance: science and business perspectives. *Annals of the New York Academy of Sciences* 1013, pp. 50-82.

Sternberg, R. J. (1985). Beyond IQ: A triarchic theory of human intelligence. New York: Cambridge University Press.

Sternberg, R. J. (1988). The Triarchic Mind. New York: Viking.

Sternberg, R. J. (1999). A propulsion *model* of types of *creative contributions*. Review of General Psychology, 3, 83-100.

Sternberg, R. J. (2007). Wisdom, Intelligence, and Creativity Synthesized.

New York: Cambridge University Press.

Sternberg, R. J. (2003, 2009). *Cognitive Psychology (5th ed.)*. Belmont, CA: Wadsworth/Cengage.

Sternberg, R. J., Kaufman, J. C., & Pretz, J. E. (2002). The creativity conundrum: A propulsion model of creative contributions. Philadelphia, PA.

Sternberg, S. (1966). High-speed scanning in human memory. Science, 153, 652-654.

Sternberg, S. (1969). Memory-scanning: Mental processes revealed by reaction-time experiments. American Scientist, 57, 421-457.

Stewart, J., Varela, F.J. (1989). Exploring the meaning of connectivity in the immune network. *Immunol Rev,* **110**:37–61.

Sutton, R. S. (1984). *Temporal Credit Assignment in Reinforcement Learning*. PhD thesis, University of Massachusetts, Amherst, MA.

Sutton, R. S. (1988). Learning to predict by the method of temporal differences. *Machine Learning*, 3: 9-44.

Sutton, R. S. (1991). Planning by incremental dynamic programming. In Birnbaum, L. A. and Collins, G. C., editors, *Proceedings of the Eighth International Workshop on Machine Learning*, Morgan Kaufmann, San Mateo, CA. 353-357.

Sutton, R. S. (editor) (1992). *A Special Issue of Machine Learning on Reinforcement Learning*, Volume 8. *Machine Learning*. Also published as *Reinforcement Learnng*, Kluwer Academic Press, Boston, MA.

Sutton, R. S. (1996). Generalization in reinforcement learning: Successful examples using sparse coarse coding. In Touretzky D. S., Mozer M. C., and Hasselmo M. E., (editors), *Advances in Neural Information Processing Systems: Proceedings of the 1995 Conference*, Cambridge, MA. MIT Press, 1038-1044.

Sutton, R.S. and Barto, A. G. (1981). An adaptive network that constructs and uses an internal model of its world. *Cognition and Brain Theory*, 3: 217-246.

Sutton, R. S. and A. G. Barto (1998). Reinforcement Learning: An Introduction. MIT Press.

Takaaki, Koyatsu (1982). Memory Representation Traits and Structure. Modern Psychology, Vol. 4, Memory, in Japanese, University of Tokyo Press.

Tan, M. (1993). Multi-agent reinforcement learning: Independent vs. cooperative agents. In *Proceedings of the Tenth International Conference on Machine Learning*, Morgan Kaufmann, 330-337.

Tarsia, M. and E. Sanavio, (2003). Implicit and explicit memory biases in mixed anxiety-depression, Journal of affective disorders, 77(03), pp. 213-225.

Thelen, E. and L. B. Smith (1994). A dynamic systems approach to the development of cognition and action. Cambridge, MIT Press.

Tikhonov, A. N. (1963). Solution of incorrectly formulated problems and the regularization method. Soviet Math. Dokl., 4: 1035-1038

Timmis J, Neal M. (2001). A resource limited artificial immune system for data analysis. Knowledge Based Systems, 14(3-4): 121-130.

Timmis J., Knight T. (2001). Artificial immunes system: Using the immune system as inspiration for data mining. In: Abbass H. A., Sarker R. A., Newton C. S. eds. Data Mining: A Heuristic Approach. Hershey: Idea Publishing Group, 209-230.

Tolman, E. C. (1932). Purposive behavior in animals and men. New York: Century.

Tolman, E. C. (1938). The determinants of behavior at a choice point. Psychological Review, 45, 1-41.

Tolman, E. C., Ritchie, B.F., Kalish, D. (1992). Studies in spatial learning. I. Orientation and the short-cut. 1946. *Journal of experimental psychology. General* 121(4): 429–34, 1992.

Tonet, O., M. Marinelli, L. Citi, P. M. Rossini, L. Rossini, G. Megali, and P. Dario. (2008). Defining brain-machine interface applications by matching interface performance with device requirements. Journal of Neuroscience Methods, 167(1): 91–104.

Trabasso, T. & Bower, G. (1968). Attention in Learning. New York: Wiley.

Treisman, A. (1960). Contextual cues in selective listening. Quarterly Journal of Experimental Psychology, 12, 242-248.

Treisman, A. (1964). Selective attention in man. British Medical Bulletin, 20, 12-16.

Treisman, A. (1982). Perceptual grouping and attention in visual search for features and for objects. Journal of Experimental Psychology: Human Perception and Performance, 8, 194-214.

Treisman, A., & Gormican, S. (1988). Feature analysis in early vision: Evidence from search asymmetries. Psychological Review, 95, 15-48.

Treisman, A. (1996). The binding problem. Current Opinion in Neurobiology, 6, 171-178.

Treisman, A. & Gelede, G. (1980). A feature-integration theory of attention. Cognitive Psychology, 12: 97-136.

Trueswell, J. C., Tanenhaus, M. K., Garnsey, S. M. (1994). Semantic influences on parsing: Use of Thematic role information in syntactic disambiguation. Journal of Memory and Language, 33: 285-318.

Tulving, E. (1974). Cue dependent forgetting. American science, 62: 74-82.

Tulving, E, (1983). Elements of episodic memory. London, Oxford Clarendon Press.

Turing, A. M. (1950). Computing Machinery and Intelligence. Mind, 59, 433-460.

Valiant, L. G. (1984). A theory of the learnable. Communications of the ACM, 27(11), 1134-1142

van der Meulen, F. F, Meyer, A. S. & Levelt, W. J. M. (2001). Eye movements during the production of nouns and pronouns. Memory and Cognition, 29, 512-521.

van Essen D. C. (1985). Functional organization of primate visual cortex. In: Cerebral Cortex, Vol. 3, Ed. Peters A. and Jones EG. NewYoA: Plenum, 259-329.

van Gelder, T. and R. Port (1995). It's about time: An overview of the dynamical approach to cognition. Mind as motion: Explorations in the dynamics of cognition. R. Port and T. van Gelder. Cambridge, MA, MIT Press.

van Gerven, Marcel, Jason Farquhar, Rebecca Schaefer, Rutger Vlek, Jeroen Geuze, Anton Nijholt, Nick Ramsey, Pim Haselager, Louis Vuurpijl, Stan Gielen and Peter Desain, (2009). The brain–computer interface cycle. *J. Neural Eng.* 6(4).

Vapnik, V. N. and Chervonenkis, A. Ja. (1989). The necessary and sufficient conditions for for consistency of the method of empirical risk minimization. Yearbook of the Academy of Sciences of the USSR on Recognition, Classification, and Forecasting.

Vapnik, V. N. (1995). The Nature of Statistical Learning Theory. Springer-Verlag, New York.

Vapnik, V. N. (1998). Statistical Learning Theory. Wiley-Interscience Publication, John Wiley & Sons, Inc.

Vapnik, V, Golowich, S, Smola, A. (1997). Support Vector Method for Function Approximation, Regression Estimation, and Signal Processing, in Advances in Neural Information Processing Systems 9.

Vaseghi, S. V. (1995). State duration modeling in hidden Markov models. Signal Processing, 41: 31-41.

Venema, Yde, (2001). Temporal Logic. In Goble, Lou, ed., *The Blackwell Guide to Philosophical Logic*. Blackwell.

Voisin, J., Devijver, P. A. (1987). An application of the Multiedit-Condensing technique to the reference selection problem in a print recognition system. Pattern Recognition 5: 465-474.

von der Malsburg, C. (1983). How are nervous systems organized? In: Basar E., Haken H., Mandell A. J. eds. Synergetic of the Brain. Berlin: Springer,1983,238-249.

von der Malsburg C. (1985). Nervous structures with dynamical links. Ber Bunsenges Phys Chem, 89: 703-710.

von der Malsburg C. (1986). Am I Thinking Assemblies? In: Pelm G., Aertsen, A. eds. Brain Theory. Berlin: Springer-Verlag, 161-176.

von der Malsburg C., Schneider W.A neural cocktail-party processor. Biol Cybern, 1986, 54: 29-40.

Wainer, Howard (1997). Visual Revelations. Copernicus.

Wang, Xiaofeng, Liang Chang, Zhongzhi Shi (2010). A Dynamic Description Logic based System for Video Event Detection. *Frontiers of Electrical and Electronic Engineering in China, 2010*.

Wang, Yunjiu, Yufang Yang (eds) (2003). *Consciousness and the Brain*. People's Publishing House.

Wang, Yutian (Ed.) (1987). Introduction to Modern Logic Science. People's University of China Press.

Waterman, M. S., M. D. Perlwitz (1984). Line Geometries for Sequence Comparisons. Bull Math Biol, 46(4): 567-577.

Watson, John B. (1913). Psychology as the behaviorist views it. Psychological Review, 20, pp. 158-177. http://psychclassics.yorku.ca/Watson/views.htm.

Weng, Juyang (2001). Autonomous Mental Development by Robots and Animals, Science Issue of 26 Jan, 291 (5504): 599-600.

Werbos, P. J. (1974). Beyond regression: New tools for prediction and analysis in the behavioral sciences. Ph.D. Thesis, Harvard University, Cambridge, MA.

Werbos, P. J. (1989). Backpropagation and neurocontrol: A review and prospectus. International Joint Conference on Neural Networks, Vol. I, pp. 209-216, Washington, DC.

Wertheimer, M. (1923). Laws of organization in perceptual forms. First published as Untersuchungen zur Lehre von der Gestalt II, in Psycologische Forschung, 4, 301-350. Translation published in Ellis, W. (1938). A source book of Gestalt psychology (pp. 71-88). London: Routledge & Kegan Paul.

Wickelgren, W. A. (1965). Short-term memory for phonemically similar lists. *Amer. J. Psychol.*, 1965, 78, 567-574.

Widrow, B., (1962). Generalization and Information Storage in Networks of Adaline 'Neurons'. in Self-Organizing Systems 1962, M. C. Yovitz, G. T. Jacobi, and G. Goldstein, eds., Spartan Books, Washington, DC, 1962, pp. 435-461.

Wiener, Norbert (1948). Cybernetics, or control and communication in the animal and the machine. Cambridge, Massachusetts: The Technology Press; New York: John Wiley & Sons, Inc.

Wilson, D. (1972). Asymptotic Properties of Nearest Neighbor Rules using Edited Data. Institute of Electrical and Electronic Engineers Transactions on Systems, Man and Cybernetics 2: 408-421.

Winograd, Terry (1972). Understanding Natural Language. Academic Press.

Winograd, Terry (1983). Language as a Cognitive Process: *Syntax*, Addison-Wesley.

Winograd, Terry and Fernando Flores (1986). Understanding Computers and Cognition: A New Foundation for Design. Norwood, New Jersey: Ablex Publishing Corporation.

Woods, William A. (1970). Transition Network Grammars for Natural Language Analysis, *Comm. ACM*, 13, No. 10, October.

Woods, William A., James Schmolze (1992). The KL-ONE Family. *Computers & Mathematics with Applications*, Vol. 23, Nos. 1-5, pp 133-177.

Von Wright, G. H. (1984). *Logic and philosophy* in the *20th century.*Cornell University Press.

Xu, Lei (1995). Ying-Yang Machine: A Bayesian Kullback Scheme for Unified Learnings and New Results on Vector Quantization. The Proceeding of ICONIP'95, 977 – 988.

Yang, Jinchen, Yufang Yang (2004). The rhythm generation in speech production. Psychological Science. 1(4): 481-488.

Yanger, R. R., Fedrizzi, M. and Kacprzyk, J. (1994). Advances in the Dempster-Shafer Theory of Evidence. New York: Wiley.

Yao, Xin (1993). Evolutionary artificial neural networks. *International Journal of Neural Systems*, 4(3): 203-222.

Yao, Xin (1999). Evolving artificial neural networks. *Proceedings of the IEEE*, 87(9): 1423-1447, September.

Yao, Y. Y. (2005). Perspectives of Granular Computing. Proceedings of 2005 IEEE International Conference on Granular Computing, Vol. 1, pp. 85-90.

Zadeh, L. A. (1965). Fuzzy Sets. *Information and Control*, Vol. 8, 338-353.

Zadeh, A. (1979). Fuzzy sets and information granularity, In: M. M. Gupta, R. K. Ragade and R. R. Yager. eds., Advances in Fuzzy Set Theory and Applications, North-Holland, New York, pp. 2-18.

Zadeh, A. (1996). Fuzzy logic=computing with words. *IEEE Trans. On Fuzzy System*s, Vol. 4, pp. 103-111.

Zeigarnik, A. V. (2007). Bluma Zeigarnik: A Memoir. In *Gestalt Theory*, No 3, pp. 256-268.

Zhang, B., and Zhang, L. (1992). Theory and Application of Problem Solving. Elsevier Science Publishers, North-Holland.

Zhang, C. & Z. Zhou (2002). $Ca^{2+}$-independent but voltage-dependent secretion in mammalian dorsal root ganglion neurons. *Nature Neuroscience,* 5(5): 425-30.

Zhang, Jian (1996). Neural Field Computational Theory Based on manifold theory and its Applications in Financial Analysis. PhD Desertation, Beijing: Institute of Computing Technology, Chinese Academy of Sciences.

Zhang, Jian, Zhongzhi Shi (1995). An Adaptive Theoretical Foundation Toward Neural Information Processing NFT, Proceeding of ICONOP'95, 217-220.

Zhang, Jian, Zhongzhi Shi, Jimin Liu (1998). Topology Approximation Correction Approach — A Learning Mechanism of Neural Field Theory. Proceedings of International Conference on Neural Network and Brain, 421-424.

Zhang, Ling and Bo Zhang (1999). A Geometrical Representation of McCulloch-Pitts Neural Model and Its Application, IEEE Transactions on Neural Networks, 10(4): 925-929 July.

Zhang, W., Dietterich, T. G. (1995). A Reinforcement Learning Approach to Job-shop Scheduling. Proceedings of IJCAI95.

Zhang, W. (1996). Reinforcement Learning for Job-shop Scheduling. PhD thesis, Oregon State University. Tech Report CS-96-30-1.

Zhang, W. and Dietterich, T. G. (1995). A reinforcement learning approach to job-shop scheduling. In Proceedings of the Fourteenth International Joint Conference on Artificial Intelligence, 1114-1120.

Zhang, Ying, Ralf D. Brown, Robert E. Frederking, and Alon Lavie (2001). Pre-processing of Bilingual Corpora for Mandarin-English EBMT. In *Proceedings of the MT Summit VIII.* Santiago de Compostela, Spain, September.

Zhang, Ying, Zhongzhi Shi, Xiangtao You (1998). A Decision Trees Learning Algorithm Based On Bias Shift. Proc. Knowledge Discovery and Data Mining Workshop, PRICAI'98, Singapore, 71-81.

Zhou, Zhihua, Shifu Chen (2002). Neural network ensemble. *Journal of Computers*, 25(1): 1-8.